THE

DiMaggio
★ ★ ★ ★ ★ ★ ★ ★ ★ ★ ★ ★

A L B U M S

THE

ALBUMS

Selections from Public and
Private Collections
Celebrating the Baseball Career of
JOE DIMAGGIO

VOLUME 2
1942 · 1951

With an Introduction and Commentaries by
JOE DIMAGGIO

Compiled and Edited by
RICHARD WHITTINGHAM

G. P. PUTNAM'S SONS
New York

PUBLISHER'S NOTE

Some of the clippings and other material collected in these volumes were found or located in scrapbooks, private collections, and other sources, unaccompanied by the identity of the publisher, the author or other source of publication, so as to enable Weldon International Pty Limited to determine the identity of the holders of copyright (if any) in this material. Weldon International Pty Limited has made every effort, through independent research, to identify the sources of these items so that Weldon International Pty Limited could endeavor to obtain any copyright permissions that may be required in order to reproduce these items in these volumes. However, in some cases, this has proved impossible, due to the age of the material and the inability to identify, after a diligent search, the party or parties from whom copyright permission (if required) should be sought. Weldon International Pty Limited, and not Joe DiMaggio, is solely and exclusively responsible for the inclusion of these items in this work. Weldon International Pty Limited would be pleased to hear from any parties who can assist in identifying potential holders of copyright in this material so that necessary corrections can be made in future printings.

A Kevin Weldon Production

Designer Susan Kinealy
Production Manager Dianne Leddy
Endpapers Margo Snape

Published by
G.P. Putnam's Sons
Publishers Since 1838
200 Madison Avenue
New York, NY 10016

In association with
Weldon International Pty Limited
372 Eastern Valley Way,
Willoughby, NSW, Australia 2068

Library of Congress Cataloging-in-Publication Data

DiMaggio, Joe, date.
    The DiMaggio Albums: selections from public and
private collections celebrating the baseball career
of Joe DiMaggio / with an introduction and commentaries
by Joe DiMaggio.
        p.   cm.
    Includes index.
    ISBN 0-399-13487-5; ISBN 0-399-13501-4 (lim. ed.)
    1. DiMaggio, Joe, date. 2. Baseball players — United States —
Biography — Miscellanea. 3. DiMaggio, Joe, date — Collectibles.
I. Title.
CV865.D5A3   1989   /89–10528 CIP
796.357'092—dc20
[B]

Printed in the United States of America
1 2 3 4 5 6 7 8 9 10

Typeset in Australia by Savage Type Pty Ltd, Brisbane
Printed by R.R. Donnelley & Sons Company, Willard, Ohio

CONTENTS

VOLUME 2

1942 SEASON OF SURPRISES

Mortality: 409   Most Valuable Player award for 1941: 410   Signs contract: 413   Spring training; with Charlie Keller: 414   A 450-foot home run: 419   Hits .557 in 18 games: 423   All-Star game: 426   American League All-Stars *v* All-Service team: 428   Batting streak: 433   World Series: 434   Elected to 1942 All-Star Major League team: 446   With Dom and Vince DiMaggio: 447

1943 · 5 A DIFFERENT UNIFORM

A roommate to remember: 449   With Lefty Gomez and Buddy Hassett: 451   Joe DiMaggio joins the U.S. Army Air Force: 452   Plays for Santa Ana Air Base team: 454   Transferred to Hawaii: 457   Stomach disorder: 460   A memorable homer: 462   On furlough in New York: 464   In Atlantic City: 465   Released by army: 469

1946 · 7 COMING BACK

Hitters: 471   Batting technique: 478   Confronting fastballer Bob Feller: 481   With Ted Williams: 485   Pitchers: 486   Heel problems: 489   Spring training, 1947: 491   Batting .493 in 16 straight games: 495   All-Star game: 497   Joe DiMaggio day: 501   World Series: 504   Game-winning home run: 515   With Frank Shea: 516   Gionfriddo's famous catch: 519   DiMaggio crowned as most reliable outfielder: 526   Most Valuable Player award: 526

1948 A YEAR BETWEEN PENNANTS

Tough competition: 531   Signs contract: 532   With Connie Mack, Bill Dickey and Lefty O'Doul: 536   Yankees lose the first game of the season: 537   Babe Ruth presents the *Sporting News* trophy: 539   Three home runs in a double-header: 545   All-Star game: 546   Jimmy Cannon on DiMaggio: 555   *Time* cover story: 557   DiMaggio leads the American League: 562   Winter training: 563

1949 THE GREAT PENNANT RACE

Good to get back: 567   Signs contract: 568   Hospitalized with heel injury: 572   With Casey Stengel: 574   First workout: 578   Hits homer in his first game: 580   DiMaggio's bat beats Red Sox in three straight games: 583   All-Star game: 586   With Ted Williams: 592   The man behind the poker face: 596   Final game of American League championship: 599   A special Joe DiMaggio day at the Yankee Stadium: 603   Yankees win the pennant on the last day of the season: 606   World Series: 609   With Gene Woodling, Hank Bauer, Cliff Mapes, Johnny Lindell and Charlie Keller: 610

1950 ANOTHER PENNANT SEASON

Home run contest: 623   Voted Mr. Yankee: 626   Signs contract: 628   On the radio: 629   With Casey Stengel, Charlie Keller, Tommy Henrich, Ethel Barrymore, Julian Rosenthal, Toots Shor and W.C. Fields: 631   Spring training: 636   DiMaggio gets the 2,000th hit of his major league career: 639   Hitting spree continues: 641   Switch to first base: 643   Back to the outfield: 646   All-Star game: 651   With Rogers Hornsby: 657   First player to hit three homers in one game at Griffith Stadium: 662   Batting streak reaches 15 games: 665   World Series: 669   Game-winning homer: 676   With Toots Shor and Frank Sinatra: 685   In Korea, with Lefty O'Doul and General Douglas MacArthur: 690   In Japan: 691

1951 THE FINAL YEAR

Two teams: 695   Signs contract: 696   Spring training: 697   With Mickey Mantle: 698   Announces coming retirement: 699   Hitting streak: 701   All-Star game: 708   DiMaggio takes a rest: 710   Hits two homers against the White Sox: 716   DiMaggio ties with Babe Ruth in reaching his 10th World Series: 718   World Series: 719   The last World Series home run, at the Polo Grounds in New York: 726   The Final World Series hit — a double: 733   Breaks World Series records: 736   On tour in Japan: 739   The Clipper retires: 742   DiMaggio's records: 744   "Goodbye Joe": 746

AFTER THE GAME

On batting: 751   Elected to All-Time Yankee team: 752   DiMaggio as TV commentator: 753   With Casey Stengel: 754   Elected to the National Baseball Hall of Fame: 755   In Rome in 1955: 760   With Dom and Vince DiMaggio in 1956: 761   25th anniversary of DiMaggio's debut: 762   At Old-Timers game in 1962: 763   Receives Sultan of Swat Crown: 766   50th birthday party in San Francisco: 767   Joe and Dom DiMaggio coach youngsters: 770   The hit song "Mrs Robinson" by Paul Simon: 772   Becomes coach of Oakland Athletics: 774   With Ronald Reagan: 775   Retirement from coaching: 776   With Mickey Mantle, Yogi Berra, Whitey Ford and Casey Stengel: 780   Revisiting Yankee Stadium: 782   DiMaggio at 60: 783   With Willie Mays: 785   With Tommy Lasorda, Sandy Koufax, Ed Liberatore: 787   Still a Marquee Moniker: 788   The Yankee Clipper: 789

Acknowledgments 790

Index 792

PLATES

Facing pages listed

The first and only book published by Joe DiMaggio, *Lucky to be a Yankee*: 480   Joe DiMaggio slides in with a Yankee run in a 1946 game against the Detroit Tigers: 481   The Most Valuable Player award for 1947: 496 A book written about Joe DiMaggio: 497   Great modern center fielders — Duke Snider, Mickey Mantle, Joe DiMaggio, Willie Mays: 560   The DiMaggio rifle arm: 561   Baseball cards featuring Joe DiMaggio: 576   Joe DiMaggio's equipment bag, glove, hat and spikes: 577   Joe DiMaggio with Ted Williams: 640   A portrait of Joe DiMaggio painted by Victor Freudeman: 641   Joe DiMaggio on the cover of *Police Gazette* in August 1950: 656   Page one of the *Daily Mirror* of October 6, 1950, featuring Joe DiMaggio: 657   A painting by S. Rini of Vince, Dom and Joe DiMaggio: 704   Joe DiMaggio, painted by Doug West: 705   A painting by Mayo showing Joe DiMaggio as a batting coach: 720   Joe DiMaggio, after retirement, at a Yankees' spring training camp: 721   Joe DiMaggio in action at an Old-Timers game: 736   Joe DiMaggio with Barry Halper: 737   Joe DiMaggio, out of uniform, with bat in hand: 752   Joe DiMaggio, as he has appeared in advertisements: 753 Joe DiMaggio playing golf: 760   The locker where the classic number 5 hung; and a quiet moment in the locker room after an Old-Timers game: between pages 760 and 761   A smiling portrait: 761   Joe and Dom DiMaggio at an Old-Timers game: 768   Joe DiMaggio at the park in Clearwater, Florida, named in his honor: 769   Joe DiMaggio with Gene Autry: 784   Joe DiMaggio with the baseball signed by then U.S. President Ronald Reagan and Soviet leader Mikhail Gorbachev: 785

1942
SEASON OF SURPRISES

Joe DiMaggio batted .305 in 1942, the lowest in his first seven years with the Yankees.

MORTALITY

We beat out the Red Sox for the pennant again in 1942, just as we had the year before. It brought me to my sixth World Series in the seven years I had been with the Yankees. We were confident: we had won the other five, in fact none of them had even gone the entire seven games.

Now we faced the St. Louis Cardinals, who had a lot of fine players: Stan Musial, Marty Marion, Terry Moore, Enos Slaughter, and Mort Cooper had won 22 games for them. The Cards had edged out the Dodgers in a close race for the National League flag.

We were ahead 7–0 with two outs in the ninth inning of the first game, and it appeared that this might be the easiest Series of them all for us. But the Cards rallied for four runs. We still won that game, but the tide had truly turned.

After that they could do nothing wrong. They made almost impossible catches in the field. They got great pitching, especially from Johnny Beazely, a first-year man, and Ernie White, who shut out the Yankees in Game 3, the first time that had happened in a World Series in 16 years. They won four straight and we discovered that the Yankees in the World Series were indeed mortal.

Joe DiMaggio

1942

JOE DiMAGGIO STATISTICS

Games	154
At Bats	610
Hits	186
Doubles	21
Triples	13
Home Runs	21
Runs Scored	123
Runs Batted In	114
Bases on Balls	68
Strike Outs	36
Stolen Bases	4
Slugging Average	.498
Batting Average	.305

STANDINGS

	Won	Lost	Percentage	Games Behind
New York Yankees	103	51	.669	
Boston Red Sox	93	59	.612	9
St. Louis Browns	82	69	.543	19.5
Cleveland Indians	75	79	.487	28
Detroit Tigers	73	81	.474	30
Chicago White Sox	66	82	.446	34
Washington Senators	62	89	.411	39.5
Philadelphia A's	55	99	.357	48

Setting the Pace

By GRANTLAND RICE

Pen Sketch of Joe DiMaggio.

No greater effort than a breeze that blows
Across the field when some fly ball is struck.
A drifting phantom where the long smash goes,
That has no helping teammate known as luck.
No desperate stab—no wild one-handed catch,
Few ringing cheers that churn the summer air.
A shift—a turn—a movement none can match,
The ball drifts down—DiMaggio is there.

A swing—a slash—the ball is on its way,
But still no effort as the ball sails on.
The whipping ash still keeps the foe at bay,
A blur against the blue—and then the ball is gone.
Ty Cobb has ruled—and Ruth has sung his tune—
Tris Speaker was a melody in rime—
DiMaggio—you won't forget him soon—
Here is the master artist of our time.

DANIEL'S DOPE

By Dan Daniel

WASHINGTON, Jan. 19.—In selecting Joe DiMaggio, center fielder of the Yankees, as their Player of the Year, to be honored at their Feb. 1st dinner at the Commodore, the baseball writers of New York today backed up the committee which had designated Giuseppe as the American League's most valuable performer for 1941. And in nominating DiMaggio, the New York chapter doubtless also has reopened the old question as to his right to the No. 1 designation over Ted Williams, who hit .406 for the Red Sox.

It is interesting to note that in Ted's own bailiwick on the banks of the Charles, the baseball writers have picked DiMaggio over Williams for their chief award. Ditto in Philadelphia. It will be recollected that in the Associated Press annual poll, the result of which was announced during the Christmas holidays, DiMaggio was voted the No. 1 athlete of 1941. So much for the superior claims of the outfielder who set an incredible record by hitting in 56 consecutive games.

In achieving the Player of the Year plaque of the New York writers for the second time—he first got it in 1938—DiMaggio attained a distinction which has come to no other aspirant since the award was set up in 1931, with the nomination of .401 Bill Terry.

Until this year the New York chapter held to an unwritten law there be no repeaters. But when it came to considering the comparative baseball virtues of the candidates who stood out for the 1942 trophy, the baseball Boswells were convinced there was no alternative. They just could not pass up Giuseppe.

* * *

The DiMaggio-Williams situ-ation this year had a parallel in 1931, when Terry got the award over Babe Herman of the Dodgers. Babe had hit .393, with 35 home runs, in 1930, for the greatest season of his picturesque career. But the first baseman of the Giants had gone over .400, and Herman was just out of luck. He never did get the trophy.

* * *

DiMaggio in Regal
Company with Award.

In gaining the 12th annual Player of the Year designation of the New York chapter, DiMaggio once more finds himself in royal company. The 1932 plaque was presented to Lou Gehrig, and then came Herb Pennock and Carl Hubbell.

Pennock's 1932 performances were not the most brilliant in the major leagues. But the New York writers reserve the right to make their presentation merely as a gesture of friendship and recognition, if they so desire. In 1937 there were many superiors to Tony Lazzeri on performances, but the great second sacker was moving out of the picture and the scribes voted to shake his hand as he passed out of the Stadium.

The 1935 plaque was presented to Dizzy Dean, the first non-New York player to get the award. It was presented to Dizzy at a dinner which marked the local farewell of Will Rogers. The great Oklahoman delivered an extremely funny speech, in which he spurred Dizzy's demands for $25,000.

In 1936 Hank Greenberg won the Player of the Year prize, and then came Lazzeri, DiMaggio, Jimmy Foxx, Bucky Walters and Bobby Feller. Thus Giuseppe gets the prize again after honors to out-of-town heroes of three consecutive years.

The New York chapter's vote to break its unwritten law in favor of DiMag was unanimous.

* * *

With the selection of DiMaggio, the list of those whom the New York writers will honor at their 19th annual dinner is complete. Sergeant Hank Greenberg already had been announced as the recipient of an Extraordinary Service plaque, and to Mel Ott had been voted the Award of Merit for outstanding contributions to baseball over a long period of years.

Ted, Di Mag, Hugh Duffy Honored by Boston Scribes

By the Associated Press.

BOSTON, Jan. 28.—After waiting in modest silence for 47 years, Hugh Duffy, the peppery veteran who set baseball's all-time high batting mark of .438, will be publicly acclaimed when the Boston baseball writers award trophies to such modern sluggers as Champion Ted Williams of the Red Sox and Joe DiMaggio of the Yankees tonight while dining with 800 of their readers.

Williams, who expects to be inducted into the army within a few days, has been ordered to stay close to his Minneapolis draft board. As a result he has delegated Eddie Collins, his club's general manager, to accept the Jacob C. Morse Memorial, a trophy awarded annually to Boston's outstanding player, in his behalf. DiMaggio, however, has promised to be on hand to receive the Paul Shannon Memorial Trophy, which commemorates his astounding feat of hitting safely in 56 consecutive games for the current world champions.

Both awards, fixtures on the writers' banquet programs, are dedicated to old-time colleagues. Morse, one of the earliest of the baseball scribes, originated the present scoring system, and Shannon, another veteran, was president of the Baseball Writers Assn. of America when he died.

The writers' other regulation award, for Boston's outstanding rookie, has been voted to Dick Newsome, who pitched the Red Sox to 19 victories. Mere verbal praise, however, will not suffice for Duffy, for his press box admirers also have prepared a surprise for him.

DiMaggio Pay Offer Decided On; Season Openers Set Apr. 14

By KEN SMITH

After months of talk, baseball got down to cases yesterday; Joe DiMaggio's contract offer was completed and

Here's Jolting Joe DiMaggio and his pet bat. The great outfielder will soon receive his 1942 contract as President Ed Barrow stated yesterday that the Yankee documents would be placed in the mail this morning.

stuffed into an envelope, to be mailed the first thing this morning, and the 1942 major league opening day schedules were announced.

The Yankee Bomber's salary offer goes out together with all the other Yankee contracts. The American League's most valuable player probably will receive it sometime today or tomorrow by registered mail at his West Side apartment, provided he decides to delay his hop to Florida until it arrives.

Just what figure was decided upon has been kept a secret. Even Joe doesn't know, for he has had no preliminary consultation with Edward G. Barrow, Yankees' president as a starting point in negotiations. It is expected that Joe was offered the same salary he drew last year—$37,500. All baseball is curious about Joe's contract which may even contain a cut due to war conditions, or a raise.

DiMag Ends Holdout, Accepts $42,000

By Jack Smith

St. Petersburg, Fla., March 12.—Holdout Joe DiMaggio, hardest hitting and stubbornest of the Yanks, yielded to the purse and persuasion of big boss Ed Barrow here this evening and accepted the second-highest salary a Yank has ever received. Though figures were not made public, Barrow admitted he had come to a compromise above his last previous offer of $40,000, which automatically makes the Yanks' great slugger top man in the list of major league salaries. Joe apparently got pretty close to his reported demand for $42,500—probably $42,000.

Earlier, Barrow, who arrived here this afternoon, had told reporters he would not contact DiMag until tomorrow. However, he was so anxious to get his ace slugger into uniform, he changed his mind and phoned Joe this evening. Joe agreed to meet him and arrived at Barrow's hotel about nine o'clock.

CLOSE TO PLAYING WEIGHT

An hour later, DiMag stepped out of an elevator in the lobby, a broad grin on his face telling the story. "I can't say whether I got what I wanted or not," he explained. "However, I'm well satisfied and I'll be ready to play whenever Joe McCarthy says the word. I weigh about 195 pounds, which is as close to perfect playing weight as I'll ever get."

He looks remarkably well for a gent who hasn't exercised heavily all Winter. He's been here at a beachside apartment some 12 miles from town, lolling on the warm sands with his wife and infant son.

Joe's salary is still far from the $80,000 per season, which Babe Ruth received for two years but it moves him ahead of the late Lou Gehrig, who drew down $39,000 on one contract.

His long and angry duel with Barrow started when his first con-

How DiMag Salary Climbed

1942—	$42,000
1941—	35,000
1940—	32,000
1939—	27,000
1938—	25,000
1937—	15,000
1936—	8,000
Total	$184,000

Joe DiMaggio

tract arrived, calling for the same salary as he received last season—$37,500. This steamed DiMag plenty. By dint of his record breaking, 56-game hitting streak last season, he became the game's greatest gate attraction since Ruth and expected a fat raise.

NO BONUS CLAUSE

Barrow later raised the offer to $40,000 which Joe also turned down. Promises of a bonus still made no impression. He wanted the money cold. Barrow admitted they had again discussed a bonus clause in tonight's meeting but said the contract agreed to did not contain one.

Joe is in such fine condition, he may appear in tomorrow's game with the Reds as a pinch hitter. "I think he'll need a few days before he can play nine innings," Manager McCarthy said, "but I might use him tomorrow and against the Cards on Saturday and Sunday as a pinch hitter."

Although terms were reached tonight, DiMaggio did not actually sign his contract because no form was available. This detail will be taken care of tomorrow.

Barrow wasn't the only new arrival. Charley Keller, the long missing outfielder, checked in and donned a suit for his first drill. Hero of the "Mickey Owen" game in the World Series, the stumpy slugger looks a little overweight but not enough to indicate a slow start this year. McCarthy was glad to see him in harness, since some of the slugging burden will be dumped on his shoulders when the Army steps in and changes Tommy Henrich's uniform.

Taking a break at spring training in Florida are the two sluggingest Yankee outfielders of 1942, Charlie "King Kong" Keller (left) and Joe DiMaggio. That year Keller would hit 26 homers and drive in 108 runs and DiMaggio would slam 21 homers and account for 114 RBIs.

Slugger Says He'll Be OK To Play Within Few Days

Champs' Old Outfield to Face Dodgers in Camp Game Next Week

By DANIEL,
World-Telegram Staff Writer.

ST. PETERSBURG, Fla., March 13.—Joe DiMaggio looked at the calendar—Friday, the thirteenth—and grinned dubiously. But with a contract calling for $42,000 for the coming baseball season, the Yankee center fielder could afford to laugh at the ides of March, walk under ladders and thumb his nose at black cats. He had achieved the second highest salary yet paid to a New York ballplayer—second only to the all-time high of $80,000, set by the one and only Babe Ruth in 1930.

After an hour's conference with the freshly-arrived Edward G. Barrow, president of the Yankees, late last night, DiMaggio no longer was baseball's most distinguished holdout. He had won for himself an increase of $4,500 over his salary for last season. It will be recalled that in 1941, Giuseppe recorded the amazing feat of hitting successfully in 56 consecutive games. This gained for him the designation as the American League's most valuable player for the year over Ted Williams of the Red Sox, who had hit .406.

His financial troubles over—and settled altogether to his liking —DiMaggio rejoined the world champions, reclaimed his locker at Miller Huggins Field and took possession of a dozen new bats which just had come down from Louisville.

While a bad case of sunburn hampered Joe's first workout, he concurred with Joe McCarthy that five or six days would suffice to put him in condition to assume his old No. 4 spot in the New York batting order.

As Charley Keller, another beneficiary of a recent salary compromise, started training yesterday, the great outfield which carried the Bombers to their triumph over the Dodgers in the 1941 world series, after 101 victories in the American League, was scheduled to reappear in competition against the Brooklyn club here next Friday.

DiMaggio Compromise Made Without Fanfare.

Strange to say, the conference which effected the compromise with DiMaggio was even simpler and less pretentious than Lee's surrender at Appomattox Court House. In a hotel room in St. Petersburg, Joe and Barrow squared off at exactly 9 o'clock in the evening. Lucky for Giuseppe, Cousin Ed's first dinner here had agreed with him. An hour later DiMaggio came out smiling.

"We split our difference, but agreed not to tell anybody just how much the contract would call for," announced the mystery-loving president of the club.

"I got what I wanted," chuckled the outfielder. With $42,000 he would collect more than Lou Gehrig ever got out of a contract with the Yankees. The Iron Horse signed for no more than $39,000. That was in 1936. After the world series Jake Ruppert handed him a bonus of $2000.

Waiting down in the lobby while Joe and Ed had their final bout was Joe McCarthy. As he got the news the manager heaved a sigh of relief. The DiMaggio holdout had sustained a sense of uncertainty in the New York camp. Now Joe could get everybody straightened away toward another championship.

With DiMaggio in, McCarthy could concentrate on developing Gerald Priddy to fill Red Rolfe's place at third, and establish Buddy Hassett as the first base successor of Johnny Sturm, gone into the army.

After Barrow had conceded another $2000 to DiMaggio to bring the argument to a close, he gave the outfielder a lecture. Cousin Ed said that, especially in war time, any ball club tying itself down to paying a player $42,000 was entitled to a full season's work from that man.

"For heaven's sake, Joe, give us a full year's play this time," Barrow beseeched. "At the rates, we deserve it."

DiMaggio is going into his seventh year with the New York club without ever having played through a complete schedule or having had a full training season of work.

Joe came closest to playing out the schedule in 1940, when he appeared in 151 games. Only once has he been with the New York club in its opening contest. In 1932 he got off to a fine start, but suffered a knee injury which kept him out of 22 games.

DiMaggio faced the war season with a 3-A rating in the draft. He is not only married but has a 5-month-old son — Little Joe.

With Joe's acceptance of terms — the actual signing was scheduled for some time during the day, minus the news reels of the Ruth heyday — Red Rolfe was the only Yankee outside the fold. However, he is ill and apparently set to retire. Red Ruffing was the only other absentee, but he has made a satisfactory financial arrangement with Barrow. The record crop of holdouts of the world champions was gone.

DiMaggio Aims to Regain Batting Laurels This Year

Joe Doesn't Expect Ted Williams To Repeat Fast Pace of 1941

By DANIEL,
World-Telegram Staff Writer.

LAKELAND, Fla., March 17.—Opening up for the first time since he signed his $42,000 contract, Joe DiMaggio today announced his determination to recover the American League batting championship even from so formidable an antagonist as .406 Ted Williams. After having the world title two years in succession, the Yankee center fielder discovered that a .357 record had left him a cool 49 points behind the Boston buster.

Asked if Williams could be overhauled this year, DiMaggio replied, "Sure, why not? Any hitter, no matter how great, can be caught. Time, some other hitter and circumstances do the trick. In modern days only one .400 batter has repeated. Look in your book. My friend, Ty Cobb, .420 in 1911 and .410 in 1912.

"Look in your book some more. I had plenty of time to study those things while Mr. Barrow was considering my contract. Bill Terry won the National League championship in 1930 with .401, but the following season Chick Hafey's .349 beat him. Certainly this kid Williams can be caught.

"Don't misunderstand me about Ted. He is the greatest hitter I ever saw. Of course, I have been around only nine years—three with San Francisco and six with New York. But I have seen some pretty fair guys with that stick, and Williams tops them all.

"You never see Ted go for a bad ball. And you never have seen anybody like him with two strikes against him. But with all that, he can be caught."

Asked when he planned to reclaim his job in center field, DiMaggio indicated that he was in no hurry. In past years he rushed into play without having got into first-class condition, and the reaction, sometimes immediate, sometimes delayed, never was satisfactory.

"You see, I'm getting to be an old man," the 27-year-old most valuable player grinned. "I need more time to train. I'll go whenever McCarthy gives the word, but I'd rather take it slowly."

DiMaggio revealed that already his arm was giving him trouble.

"It's sore, but that's nothing unusual," he explained. "It has been that way in the spring for the last four or five years. But the arm's come along and I think I'll have a good year. Winning the batting, homer and runs-driven-in championships isn't impossible. Lou Gehrig did it and I'd like to do it, too."

DiMaggio already had announced his plan to put 10 per cent of his salary—and even more—into U.S. bonds.

Outfield Star Also Begins to Loosen Up Throwing Arm

Red Rolfe Rounding Into Form That May Crowd Priddy to Bench

By DANIEL,
World-Telegram Staff Writer.

MONTGOMERY, Ala., April 3.—Joe ($42,000) DiMaggio, who for a fortnight had advertised the loss of his batting eye, today announced its recovery. After having accomplished one puny single in 17 times at bat, and seen his average drop to an emaciated .213, Giuseppe crashed two gorgeous homers in the 9-to-1 victory at Savannah, and for the first time this spring looked like the ballplayer who last summer hit in 56 consecutive contests.

To say that overnight DiMaggio became a well-conditioned outfielder, all ready to open the American League season, would be stretching the truth well beyond the rubber limitations imposed by Mr. Henderson. But three days on the road have done more for Joe than a whole week at St. Petersburg. He is moving better in the field, and using his arm, too.

By the time the Bombers hook up with the Dodgers for seven games, beginning at Charlotte, N. C., on Monday, DiMaggio should be able to make the National Leaguers well aware of his presence. For the two contests thus far played with Brooklyn, Giuseppe shows only one hit in eight tries. He tripled the first time he faced a Dodger hurler.

Both of Joe's jackpot pokes in Savannah bore the old DiMaggio stamp. They were pulled hard and true. The first opened the fourth inning and located the left field bleachers, some 325 feet away.

The second homer, which scored Tom Henrich in front of Joe, went into the bleachers, arched out, and landed in the street beyond.

DiMaggio broke a tie with Gordon for the training season home-run championship of the Yankees. Joe now has four of the 11 credited to the club, with two for Trigger, and one each for Charley Keller, Gerry Priddy, Phil Rizzuto, Eddie Levy and Twink Selkirk.

An interesting Yankee development not found in the box scores concerns Red Rolfe, the rather spry convalescent. The veteran has been working out at third base before every game since the club hit the road, and looks as if he could step right in and take his old job. His batting has some spark, too.

There are no outward evidences that Rolfe has been fighting ulcerative colitis, and he appears to be holding the four pounds he brought to St. Petersburg. Joe McCarthy is not going to rush Rolfe, nor does Ruby Robert aspire to push Priddy right out of the picture.

A pocket watch is presented to Joe DiMaggio by Art Flynn of *The Sporting News* at the start of the 1942 season to commemorate his MVP season the year before. At DiMaggio's left is Yankee manager, Joe McCarthy.

Joe DiMaggio belts one of the 186 hits he accounted for in 1942.

Crossing the plate after hitting his first home run of the 1942 season, Joe DiMaggio is congratulated by teammate Tommy Henrich. It was a 450-foot blast off Bobo Newsom of the Washington Senators, who pitched against the Yankee Clipper back in the Pacific Coast League nearly a decade earlier.

Joe DiMaggio signs a ball for an admirer in 1942. It was the Clipper's last season before joining the U.S. Army Air Force, where he would spend the last three years of World War II.

It's Up to DiMag and Keller To Put Yanks Back in Stride

Pitching Tops on Tour of West, But Bombers Aren't Bombing!

By DANIEL,
World-Telegram Staff Writer.

ST. LOUIS, June 23.—Seven lengths to the good, with 92 games yet to be played, Joe McCarthy, manager of the recently harrassed Yankees, today hardly presented a subject for sympathy, even though his club had dropped six out of eight since quitting New York. Much as Marse Joe tried to laugh off that losing streak of five straight which Hank Borowy's shutout pitching had halted in Cleveland, the pilot had been shaken by the form reversal, and its possible implications.

As the Bombers awaited the opener of the series with the Browns under the lights tonight, with Spud Chandler and Johnny Niggeling the likely pitchers, Joe DiMaggio and Charley Keller were confronted with the necessity of snapping out of their season-long slumps with the bat.

On their hurling, the Yankees should have won every game on this trip. Despite their defeats, they had got no fewer than five route-going performances from Borowy, Red Ruffing, Jumbo Bonham, Chandler and Adonis Breuer, four of those in losing ventures. In these five consecutive setbacks, the opposition had scored only 13 runs on 32 hits.

But in those same five engagements, the New York attack had gathered just seven tallies on 23 blows, suffering a pair of shutouts. The socking had bogged down.

For weeks, Joe Gordon, Bill Dickey, Buddy Hassett and Tom Henrich had carried the attack. They had borne the brunt of the run-making with the first three batting far over their heads. It was inevitable that unless DiMaggio and Keller picked up their just and reasonable burdens, as two of the greatest hitters in the game, the day of reckoning could not be escaped. But Giuseppe was down to .253 and Charley was batting .242, and nobody was foolhardy enough to attempt to predict immediate resurgence.

DiMag Hitting Harder, But Still Luckless.

For DiMaggio it must be said that since he left the Stadium, he has been showing evidence of his old power. He has been hitting harder. But let it be confessed, he also has been pressing harder, and going after balls off his ear.

In Cleveland, Joe blasted quite a few long line drives which ordinarily would have gone for extra bases. But he seems to have used up this year's ration of luck in that 56-game batting streak last season. Those liners were caught.

In eight games on this trip, DiMaggio has been up 29 times for five hits—a .172 pace. Keller has done better. He has made six hits in 21 tries, for .286, and has gained five points. Charley watched two of the Cleveland games from the bench, but it did not take McCarthy long to come to the conclusion that Keller, even in a slump, was a more attractive bet than Tuck Stainback.

The Yankees took that slump like champions. They played their last four games without an error, and on this trip have accomplished no fewer than 12 double plays, to bring their total to 88.

The champions made a sorry showing in their Toledo exhibition last night, being defeated, 5–1, by the last place Mudhens, with Fred Samford, who has only two loop victories to his credit, outpitching Johnny Lindell. Hitting into four double plays didn't help the Yankees' cause.

Joe McCarthy used the game as a means of taking a good look at Red Rolfe, who played the complete contest at third base, with Frankie Crosetti resting.

OFFICIAL SCORE CARD 10c

·1942·

YANKEE STADIUM

YANKEES

AMERICAN LEAGUE BASEBALL CLUB OF NEW YORK

HARRY M. STEVENS, Inc., Publisher
OFFICES: 320 FIFTH AVE., N. Y.

Keystone Ace Has Hit .557 In His 18-Game Skein

Setting League Pace with .380; Hassett Continues Flashy Play

By DANIEL.

Past the quarter pole, eight lengths in front, and breezing, the Yankees today had adapted themselves to a change in field leadership which might well endure through the season.

Just one year ago they were organizing their drive out of third place under the impetus of Joe DiMaggio's dramatic batting streak, which was destined to last through 56 consecutive games. Now they were going into the June campaign with Giuseppe hitting a lack-lustre .253, and their new bellwether Joe Gordon, who had batted successfully in 18 straight contests.

Gordon emphasized his domination in the ranks of the Bombers, and DiMaggio sadly reflected his incredible decline, in the Sunday double-header in Philadelphia, attended by a suffocating 35,137 enthusiasts. In eight trips to the plate, Joe achieved one single. In his eight efforts, Gordon hit his sixth home run, a double and two singles, raised his league-leading average to .380, and his runs-driven-in total to 27.

It was in the wild first game, which the Bombers took by 11 to 7, that Gordon collected three of his blows. In the nightcap, which saw the Bombers stopped, 4 to 2, after they had run up a streak of eight straight, Trigger crashed that four-bagger off Luman Harris, sophomore knuckle ball pitcher who had gone the route only once before this season and who baffled the champions with four hits.

The highlights and shadows of striking contrast stood out at every angle in the Gordon and DiMaggio situations. On June 1, 1941, Giuseppe had hit in 16 consecutive games. He had registered 56 blows for .331 and had hit seven home runs. Ted Williams was pacing him in the averages, but a superior drama had begun to envelope the New York center fielder, whose streak and skills were to dim even Ted's .406 record. Today DiMaggio owned nine homers, but his old consistency had fled, and the experts wondered if it would return this season.

Joe DiMaggio is forced out at third in a 1942 game at Yankee Stadium.

DiMaggio Finds Batting Eye to Lead Yanks in 14-Hit Assault on Browns

Joe Blasts Triple And Two Singles

By DANIEL,
Staff Writer.

ST. LOUIS, June 24.—There was better news today from the Yankees' Western front. What with a sprouting winning streak of two, maintained with a 6 to 5 victory over the Browns under the lights, Joe DiMaggio's first three-hit performance since May 5, 42 games back, and a 14-blow accumulation which represented their most impressive attack since June 8, the Bombers appeared to have left their troubles behind. As the Red Sox had beaten the Tigers earlier in the day, the Yankee lead remained at seven lengths.

Most interesting of all the demonstrations as Joe McCarthy's pace-makers organized t h e i r strongest attack since they piled up 16 hits to beat the Indians in 11 innings 16 days ago was the marked improvement in the DiMaggio situation. Giuseppe got a 425-foot triple off the center field bleacher wall and two singles. His fifth-inning fly to center also was something that smacked of the DiMaggio of 1941. With his forty-seventh run driven in and his old zip and dash in the field, Joe hinted that at last he might be ready to take over from Joe Gordon the burden of leading the Bombers to another pennant.

Murphy and Rizzuto
Save Yankee Triumph.

Not that Gordon relaxed. On the contrary, he crashed two doubles and a single and was the same old vital factor he has been since the start of the season. It was noted that Trigger had discarded Charley Keller's 36-ounce bat for his own 34–34 and had moved up some five or six inches toward the plate.

In accumulating three blows DiMaggio achieved a trick he had performed on only four previous occasions this season. On May 5, against Johnny Rigney of the

Joe DiMaggio.   Joe Gordon.

White Sox, Joe got two homers and a triple and showed a .302 average. He has not touched the .300 level since. His other three-blow performances were clustered in April, one against Washington and two in games with the Athletics.

The Yankees fought for that game last night before 17,521 fans, the largest crowd of the Browns' season, as if it were a world series contest. They had lost six out of eight, with five in a row, before Hank Borowy's night-cap triumph in Cleveland on Sunday and they were challenged.

It was touch and go after the Browns had scored three runs in

Gordon Also Ends Slump at Plate

the eighth. In the ninth they had the tie on third base. But Grandma Murphy, who had rushed to the rescue of the tired Atley Donald in the previous round, induced George McQuinn to roll peaceably to the box and the Yankees had scored their forty-fourth victory.

To Donald went official credit for the victory, his fourth of the season. But it was Murphy's superb relief work that counted most.

A grand play by Phil Rizzuto also was a big help. With Elden Auker, running for Frank Hayes, on second, and two out in the ninth, Harlond Clift belted one down the fairway. The Flea scurried behind second. He could not save the hit, but he knocked the ball down and prevented the tieing tally from coming in. Murphy already had deflected the ball. The victory was scored at the expense of the veteran Al Hollingsworth, who was the ninth south-paw victim of the champions. That, too, marked progress. They had lost thrice to left-handers on this trip and to five of them altogether.

1 McKechnie, coach 30 Derringer, p.
2 Durocher, mgr.   31 Walters, p.
2 Marshall, o.f.   35 Frisch, coach
15 Melton, p.

UMPIRES
1 Ballanfant
2 Barlick

NATIONAL

3 Brown   16 Herman
     second base
5 Vaughan   8 Elliott
     third base
27 Reiser   8 Moore
     center field
10 McCormick
3 Mize   first base
4 Ott   9 Slaughter
     right field
11 Litwhiler
6 Medwick left field
10 Owen 5 Lombardi
15 W. Cooper catcher
1 Reese   7 Miller
     shortstop
13 M. Cooper
13 Passeau
33 Vander Meer
17 Wyatt   pitcher

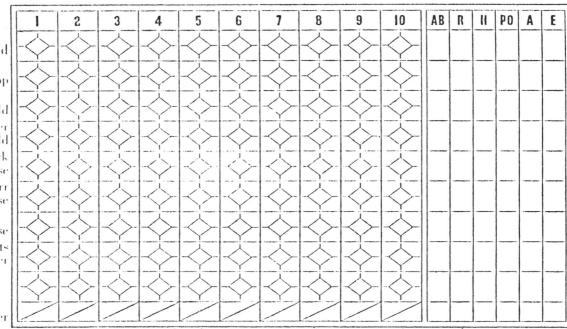

McCarthy, mgr.   21 Hughson, p.
15 Hudson, p.   28 Harris, coach
17 Bagby, p.   31 Fletcher, coach
19 Benton, p.   46 Smith, p.

UMPIRES
3 McGowan
4 Stewart

AMERICAN

7 D. DiMaggio
2 Spence   right field
5 Boudreau
10 Rizzuto shortstop
9 Williams
4 Johnson   left field
7 Henrich   center
5 J. DiMaggio   field
3 McQuinn   4 York
     first base
6 Gordon   1 Doerr
     second base
8 Keltner
     third base
8 Dickey   1 Tebbetts
12 Rosar   catcher
15 Ruffing
16 Newhouser
21 Chandler
20 Bonham   pitcher

TWO TWINKLE TILTS NET $193,000, FOR ARMY AND NAVY AID FUNDS

Inspiring Patriotic Spectacle at Cleveland Also Results in Sale of $62,094 in Victory Stamps; American League Stars Prove Superiority Over N. L. and Service Teams

By FREDERICK G. LIEB

BASEBALL and the metropolitan district of Cleveland did themselves proud in the great spectacle at Cleveland Stadium on the night of July 7, when the American League stars, winners of the annual All-Star game in New York the night before, climaxed the victory with a 5 to 0 shutout against Mickey Cochrane's service All-Stars, made up largely of famed big leaguers now in Uncle Sam's armed forces. But, for the great throng of 62,094 paid, and an additional 2,000 soldiers and sailors, the night remains engraved in their hearts and minds as a great display of tingling patriotism rather than a ball game. It was a fine exhibition of wartime team play, with the services co-operating with the National Game in putting over a spectacle such as one sees only once in a lifetime. Rumbling tanks, jumping jeeps, drilling Marines, music from the famous Great Lakes Naval Station's band, parading the colors of the Army, Navy and Coast Guard, and 65,000 awed persons filling one of the nation's great stadia, made an unforgettable spectacle. As though it were a contagion, one could feel the pa-·:· triotic fervor of the entire 65,000; it sent needles shooting down one's spine, started honest tears trickling down the cheeks, and made one murmur to one's self: "Thank God, I am an American!"

One had another eerie thrill during a two-minute total blackout, when one's neighbor disappeared into the inky darkness and only the grim outlines of the wings of the great stand were faintly visible on a moonless night. It made one feel alone with one's God.

Furthermore, the game, and its attending spectacle, proved conclusively the value of baseball as a wartime activity, also the loyalty of the fans of a great American city, a city cheated repeatedly out of baseball's highest honors by the fickle goddess of fate, to that game. Including the All-Star game played in New York on July 6, the two games drew a gate of $255,000, of which $62,094 went back to the Cleveland fans in War Stamp coupons. It was announced in New York the net receipts of the Polo Grounds game were around $94,000, and that the government would give out the actual receipts. The first $100,000 of the net receipts goes to the Clark Griffith Ball and Bat Fund.

Grand Show on a Grand Scale

Two hours before game time at Cleveland, the military show went on, and the finest of Uncle Sam's young men in white, khaki and olive drab did their stuff within the great double-decker on the shore of Lake Erie. A balmy summer evening, in sharp contrast to the wet session in New York the night before, completed the setting. Two former heavyweight champions, Lieut. Com. Gene Tunney of the Navy and Lieut. Jack Dempsey of the Coast Guard, vied with the baseball soldiers and sailors for attention.

Fort Custer, Mich., named after a man who typified the daring spirit of America at war, sent its mechanized units, tanks, jeeps, anti-tank and anti-air guns, also two of the big 28-ton General Grant tanks.

There was a much appreciated drill of a snappy platoon of Marines, while the Great Lakes, Ill., Naval Training Station band did its formations like a university band between the halves of a football classic. Eddie Peabody, crack banjo player and band leader, in his service uniform, led the band in a rendition at the home plate. However, the real thrill came with the parading of the colors, a military flag-raising and the playing of the national anthem, as the Navy and Coast Guard detachments formed a great white letter "V" with the home plate the apex of the triangle.

As for the game itself, the crack team of the American League, which had outpowered the National All-Stars the night before, simply was too strong for the baseball soldiers and sailors. Mickey Cochrane had a good ball club, a team many managers willingly would swap for their own, but when Chief Boatswain's Mate Bobby Feller, No. 1 pitcher of the majors before the war, was unable to stop McCarthy's sluggers, the cause of the Service team was doomed. Manager Mickey had planned to start Feller, let him go four or five innings, and then follow up with Johnny Rigney of the White Sox. The American leaguers put the wood to Rapid Robert so vigorously that they knocked Cochrane's plans all awry, and Mickey had to call in Rigney before a man was out in the second inning.

The White Sox star pitched five beautiful scoreless frames, and worked his way out of several holes. Mickey Harris of the Red Sox came all the way from the Canal Zone to pitch the seventh and was shot up for a double by Phil Rizzuto and triples by Ted Williams and George McQuinn. Johnny Grodzicki of the Cardinals retired the American League stars in order in the eighth.

McCarthy sent in the young Clevelander, Jim Bagby, Jr., for the first three innings, followed with Sid Hudson of the Senators for the next four, and wound up with Tex Hughson of the Red Sox. The three were combed for only six hits, yet the Service boys missed several good scoring opportunities.

Bob a Feller Who Needed a Friend

As in the All-Star game in New York, it was all over after the first inning. Cochrane's team had a great chance for a bunch of runs before Bagby found his control at the very outset, but Joe Grace of the Browns and Johnny Sturm of the Yanks blew the golden opportunity. A walk to Benny McCoy, a single to left by Don Padgett and another free gift to Cecil Travis, a star of the 1941 All-Star game in Detroit, filled the bases with one out. Then Grace was called out on strikes and Sturm grounded to Keltner.

The Cleveland fans then had two young idols to cheer to the rafters, their own Bobby Feller, as he trudged to the mound from which he had pitched so many brilliant successes, and Lou Boudreau, first man up for the American All-Stars, youthful manager of the Indians, and star of his league's victory the night before. Bobby retired Lou on a lift to Center Fielder Tiger Pat Mullin, but did little after that. Tommy Henrich singled and Ted Williams drew his first of three walks. Joe DiMaggio banged in Tommy with a single and sent Ted flying to third, from where he scored on Rudy York's long liner to Grace.

Ken Keltner opened the second for the McCarthy squad with a terrific triple to deep center, and came in on Buddy Rosar's single. That was all for Feller, and Rigney promptly retired the side. As Bagby attempted to bunt for a third strike, Frankie Pytlak picked Rosar off first base.

The Service Stars booted their second fine scoring opening in the seventh. After Hudson faced only nine men in the fourth, fifth and sixth innings, Sturm and Andres jolted the tall Senator with a pair of singles to open the seventh. The rally quickly perished, as Pytlak fanned and Brownie Johnny Lucadello, batting for Rigney, smacked into a double play.

The American leaguers broke out again in their half when Phil Rizzuto greeted Harris with a double, stole third and trotted home on Williams' long triple. Ted also waltzed in when McQuinn hit for three bags.

As for the service men—they lost, but their training had been for a bigger game! Their victory will come later.

RED, WHITE, BLUE HIGHLIGHTS

DESPITE the fact that the two teams had little chance to work together, the game was beautifully fielded, neither team making an error. "It was one of the cleanest defensive games I ever saw," said Joe McCarthy.

Feller's poor showing was later attributed in large measure to worries over the health of his father, who raised Bob, almost from infancy, to be a big leaguer. The elder Feller has been gravely ill for months, and shortly before the game the pitcher received a telegram from the family in Van Meter, Ia. What the telegram said, Bobby kept to himself, but the report was that the news was not good.

Ken Keltner left no doubt that he is the best third baseman in the American League, perhaps in both circuits. He played a bang-up game at third, hit a triple and a single, and belted out several terrific fouls that just missed being long hits. His third base opponent, Ernie Andres of the Louisville American Association Colonels, also played well, and though he was one of the few minor leaguers in the game, he was the only Service player to garner two hits.

Vincent Smith, young Pirate catcher, is Bobby Feller's buddie and battery-mate at the Norfolk, Va., Training Station and it was at Feller's request that Mickey Cochrane sent in Smith to catch the former Cleveland fireballer. When Bobby was lifted, Smith went right along with him.

Before Joe Grace was called out in the first, the count was three and nothing on him. Jim Bagby eventually worked it down to three and two, and then Joe looked foolish as he let the big one go by.

Joe McCarthy brought his entire winning team from New York, even Spud Chandler and Al Benton, his two winning pitchers of the Polo Grounds All-Star game. Joe kept Red Ruffing and Tiny Bonham under cover during both games. But, in the past, he has been criticized for using too many Yankees.

ONE COUNT IN WHICH N. L. EXCELLED

DESPITE the fact that the American League All-Stars won the game in New York and that the Service Stars were largely American leaguers, the National League had seven club presidents in Cleveland Stadium against three for the American League. Ford Frick, National League president, also made the trek to Cleveland, with his entire official family—Secretary Harvey Traband and Publicity Chief Bill Brandt. Horace Stoneham of the Giants brought along not only his daughter, but his manager, Mel Ott; his farm director, Bill Terry, and Secretary Eddie Brannick.

Before the All-Star game in New York, Joe Gordon and Bobby Doerr were keeping pace with Ted Williams' .348 for the batting leadership of the American League. Joe showed .347 and Bobby was right on his neck, with .346. Neither of the second sackers enhanced his batting reputation in the All-Star series, in which the illustrious second base pair finished "eight for 0," including four strikeouts. Following Gordon's futile swinging at the Polo Grounds, Doerr's four tries in Cleveland resulted in two pop fouls, a strikeout and an outfield fly.

Cleveland fans booed Joe DiMaggio every time he came up. Joe was morose as he dressed after the game. "I can't understand why the crowds should be on me," he said. "I do not know anything that I have done to deserve it."

When the fans discovered a white-clad figure in the press stand was Lieut. Jack Dempsey, former mighty Manassa Mauler, there was a steady parade of autograph-seekers to his perch. What's more, Jack belonged there; before he went into the Coast Guard he was sports editor of Liberty magazine.

Lieut. George Earnshaw, former big moose of Connie Mack's Athletics' crack pitching staff of 1929, '30 and '31, coached at third base for the Service team, and the old Sarge of World War I, Hank Gowdy, took care of the traffic at first base. Earnshaw is athletic officer at the large Naval Aviation Station at Jacksonville, Fla., and is a handsome chap in uniform. Gowdy, the only member of Cochrane's team not now in the service, was much touched at the opportunity to coach for Cochrane. "It was one of the proudest moments of my life, coaching out there," said Hank. "And what a thrill it would have been if we had won!"

Color guard from the Coast Guard, who took part in the military pageantry that preceded the game at Cleveland, July 7, between the American League All-Stars and the All-Service team.

Part of the crowd of 62.094 that turned out to witness the star-studded display in the Cleveland Municipal Stadium.

Commissioner Landis with Lieut. Cochrane, who managed All-Service team.

Lieut. Com. Gene Tunney seated with President Alva Bradley of the Cleveland Indians.

UNCLE SAM'S WAR-STARS STEP OUT AT GLEAM-GAME

The United States Marines were there doing their bit—marching in the brilliant pre-game ceremonies.

Jack Dempsey (right), now a lieutenant in the Coast Guard, with Com M. W. Rasmussen, chief of staff, 9th Naval District, U. S. Coast Guard

HISTORY MAKING CONTEST

SERVICE ALL-STARS

Player—Position.	AB.	R.	H.	TB.	O.	A.	E.
Mullin, center field	3	0	0	0	2	0	0
Chapman, center field	1	0	0	0	1	0	0
McCoy, second base	2	0	0	0	2	2	0
Mueller, second base	1	0	1	2	0	0	0
Padgett, left field	4	0	1	1	2	0	0
Travis, shortstop	3	0	1	2	0	2	0
Grace, right field	3	0	0	0	1	0	0
†Arnovich	1	0	0	0	0	0	0
Sturm, first base	2	0	1	1	6	0	0
Hajduk, first base	1	0	0	0	3	0	0
Andres, third base	4	0	2	2	2	3	0
V. Smith, catcher	1	0	0	0	0	0	0
Pytlak, catcher	2	0	0	0	5	1	0
Feller, pitcher	1	0	0	0	0	0	0
Rigney, pitcher	1	0	0	0	0	1	0
*Lucadello	1	0	0	0	0	0	0
Harris, pitcher	0	0	0	0	0	0	0
Grodzicki, pitcher	0	0	0	0	0	0	0
Totals	31	0	6	8	24	9	0

AMERICAN LEAGUE ALL-STARS

Player—Position.	AB.	R.	H.	TB.	O.	A.	E.
Boudreau, shortstop	2	0	0	0	0	1	0
Rizzuto, shortstop	2	1	1	2	1	4	0
Henrich, right field	1	1	1	1	0	0	0
Spence, right field	2	0	1	1	0	0	0
Williams, left field	1	2	1	3	2	0	0
J. DiMaggio, center field	4	0	1	1	2	0	0
York, first base	3	0	0	0	9	0	0
McQuinn, first base	1	0	1	3	5	0	0
Doerr, second base	4	0	0	0	1	4	0
Keltner, third base	4	1	2	4	3	3	0
Rosar, catcher	4	0	2	2	4	0	0
Bagby, pitcher	1	0	0	0	0	1	0
Hudson, pitcher	2	0	0	0	0	2	0
Hughson, pitcher	1	0	0	0	0	0	0
Totals	32	5	10	17	27	15	0

*Batted for Rigney in seventh.
†Batted for Grace in ninth.

Service All-Stars.. 0 0 0 0 0 0 0 0 0—0
American League.. 2 1 0 0 0 0 2 0 *—5

Runs batted in—J. DiMaggio, York, Rosar, Williams, McQuinn.

Two-base hits—Travis, Rizzuto, Mueller.

Three-base hits—Keltner, Williams, McQuinn.

Stolen base—Rizzuto.

Double plays—Pytlak and Sturm; Rizzuto, Doerr and York; Andres, McCoy and Sturm; Hudson, Rizzuto and McQuinn.

Pitching record—Feller 4 hits, 3 runs in 1 inning (pitched to two men in second); Rigney 3 hits, 0 runs in 5 innings; Harris 3 hits, 2 runs in 1 inning; Grodzicki 0 hits, 0 runs in 1 inning; Bagby 3 hits, 0 runs in 3 innings; Hudson 2 hits, 0 runs in 4 innings; Hughson 1 hit, 0 runs in 2 innings.

Bases on balls—Off Feller 1 (Williams), off Rigney 3 (Henrich, Williams 2), off Bagby 2 (McCoy, Travis), off Hudson 1 (Sturm).

Struck out—By Rigney 3 (Bagby, York, Doerr), by Grodzicki 1 (Hughson), by Bagby 2 (Grace, V. Smith), by Hudson 1 (Pytlak).

Earned runs—American League 5, Service All-Stars 0.

Left on bases—Service All-Stars 7, American League 7.

Winning pitcher—Bagby.

Losing pitcher—Feller.

Umpires—Stewart (A. L.) at plate; Ballanfant (N. L.) first base; McGowan (A. L.) second base; Barlick (N. L.) third base (for first 4½ innings); Barlick (N. L.) at plate; McGowan (A. L.) first base; Ballanfant (N. L.) second base; Stewart (A. L.) third base (last 4 innings).

Time—2:06.

Attendance—62,094.

First-Inning Assault on Cooper Gives A. L. Seventh All-Star Win

AMERICAN LEAGUE power, which so often has prevailed over the National League in World's Series and All-Star play, again carried the junior league's stars to victory in the tenth of the All-Star series, played at the Polo Grounds, New York, July 6, Joe McCarthy's All-Stars winning in a first-inning blitzkrieg, in which they scored all their runs on homers by Lou Boudreau and Rudy York, by a score of 3 to 1. The victory gave the American leaguers a lead of seven games to three over their battered National foes, the first time their margin has been greater than three games.

The attendance of 33,694 at the New York classic, a twilight affair, was disappointing, especially after the game, originally scheduled for Ebbets Field, Brooklyn, had been shifted to the Polo Grounds, because of the greater capacity of the Harlem ball orchard. However, there were many mitigating circumstances, all of which tended to hold down the crowd. There was a heavy afternoon rain in downtown New York, while a huge black cloud hovered over the Polo Grounds at 6 p.m., and for 40 minutes thereafter.

Then New York's baseball-loving mayor, Fiorella H. LaGuardia, chose this night for his second total blackout test, going into effect at 9.30, and lasting for 30 minutes. The game was completed just two minutes before the blackout. The gas shortage in the East and the fact that the admission price was doubled were other reasons given for 16,000 empty seats. However, that it was mostly the weather was evidenced from the fact that few people entered the stands after 5:45. Nevertheless, the game drew roughly $94,000, almost covering the $100,000 for the Ball and Bat Fund.

That strange perversity of fate, which so often has dragged down the National League in vital contests with its younger rival, took a hand in that first-inning attack. Morton Cooper of the Cardinals, the hottest National League pitcher until stopped by the Cubs, July 4, was Leo Durocher's starter. Prior to the Chicago defeat, Mort had a winning streak of nine straight; he had pitched six shutouts and had one stretch of 32 consecutive scoreless innings.

Delay May Have Hurt Career

Cooper and Spud Chandler, the American League starter, had both warmed up nearly an hour. Cooper perhaps chilled and stiffened; Chandler did not. Anyway, Lou Boudreau, who had hit only one American League home run this season, busted Cooper's second pitch into the upper right field stands for a homer. Henrich whanged an ordinary single to right, but it was slowed down by a pool of water, and before Mel Ott could come in for it, Tommy made second. Cooper then retired the two American League toughies, Ted Williams and Joe DiMaggio, bringing up Rudy York, slugging Tiger first baseman.

York, a righthanded batter, hits almost invariably to left field. In the American League batting practice, he drove ball after ball into the easy left field stands. Rudy took a swing at one of Cooper's fast ones and connected with the ball late. Mort's catching brother, Walker, later remarked: "I thought I already had that one in my glove." The result was something like a slice in golf. York sent the ball into the right field stands, near the foul lines, where the field measures only a little over 265 feet. On most any other big league field, the homer would have sliced foul. But it was a genuine four-bagger, Henrich scoring ahead of York, and there was the ball game.

After that stormy first frame, the American League hitters subsided and were pretty well handcuffed by Cooper, who pitched two more innings; Lefthander Johnny Vander Meer, who worked the middle three, and Claude Passeau and Bucky Walters, who wound up. The Americans put only one more runner on second, and he reached the midway on a muff by the Cardinal standby, Jimmy Brown, the only boot of the two nights. The four National League pitchers did not walk a man.

Top honors for the victorious American League must go to the two successful Harridge pitchers, Spud Chandler of the Yanks and Al Benton of the Tigers; Lou Boudreau, the boy manager of the Indians, and York. Taking advantage of the change in the 1942 rules, permitting a manager to work a pitcher five innings, McCarthy got by with two hurlers, his own Chandler, and the Tiger Benton. It was the eighth time in the ten games that the All-Star contest was started by a Yankee hurler; Lefty Gomez won the distinction five times, and Charley Ruffing started two others.

If there was a bit of luck in York getting his homer on a late swing, the National batting stars could do little with Chandler or Benton, getting to the pair for six scattered hits. In only the eighth, when Mickey Owen cracked a pinch home run, which incidentally was his first of the season, did the Nationals get two hits in one inning. Prior to that, Durocher's players had pushed only two runners to second base, one getting there on a passed ball. In justice to Chandler, it must be said that he had the same handicap as Cooper, warming up for a 6:30 game, which started at 7:22.

Boudreau Big Star of Game

Benton, who sat out the 1941 game as a member of last year's American All-Stars, justified his right to a second nomination for the squad. Though not listed as one of his league's foremost pitchers, he has the heart of a lion, and there is no tougher pitcher in either league for a four or five-inning shift. After he was touched up for a homer and single in the eighth, he came back strongly and retired the side in order in the ninth, as the outfield clock ticked away the minutes before the 9:30 blackout.

Most baseball men named Boudreau as the star of the tenth All-Star game. Free from his managerial worries for a night, the Illinois collegian played with the free and easy spirit of a kid on vacation. His early blast against Cooper proved to his side that the Cardinal righthander was no pitching demon, and unquestionably softened Mort for York's homer which followed. Lou also was brilliant on the defense and snuffed out the National leaguers whenever they threatened. Some have criticised Boudreau's shortstop play, saying he plays too close to second base, but this style made his two best plays possible. The lone Phil representative, Daniel Litwhiler, opened the sixth with a pinch single over Joe Gordon's head. Brown followed with what looked like another single, a drive a foot to the left of second base, but Boudreau nimbly picked it up, stepped on second for a force on Litwhiler, and doubled Brown at first.

In the seventh, the Nationals worked Enos Slaughter to second with two out, when the Cardinal outfielder singled and took second on Ernie Lombardi's walk. The Brooklyn delegation gave Pee Wee Reese a great cheer on his first time at bat. The popular Dodger did his best to make good, hitting a sharp liner to the left of second base. But the busy Boudreau lunged forward, speared the ball, and the threat was over.

For the Nationals, the best play was Ott's diving catch on Tommy Henrich, his rival right fielder. Mel skated in like a sea scooter, splashed water right and left as he dove, but he came up with the ball in his fist.

DiMaggio's Batting Streak Changes Boos to Cheers

With 10,893 paid in the opener with Cleveland, won by them for Swampy Donald by 4 to 0, the Yankees passed the 700,000 mark in attendance at the Stadium. . . . The exact figure was 700,-734. . . . Customer No. 700,000 was unidentified, but Ed Barrow toasted him just the same. . . . Frank Ciaffone, the World-Telegram most valuable high school player, from Lincoln of Brooklyn, who is to make the Western trip with the Bombers, reported to Joe McCarthy, got a Yankee uniform and worked out.

With DiMaggio on a batting streak the booing has stopped and cheers have taken its place. . . . The Yanks have taken the Tribe for seven out of 12. . . . In beating Chubby Dean the McCarthys made their score against lefties 11 to 8.

The visitors played very conservative ball. . . . Thrice, from the third through the seventh inning, Boudreau ordered a batter passed intentionally to fill the bases. . . . And every time the home guard got a run out of this situation. . . . In the third and fifth the intentional pass was given to DiMaggio, in the seventh to Gordon.

Keller really went to work in the fourth, when he got all three putouts. . . . Red Rolfe has been up 10 times without a hit. . . . Frankie Crosetti should be back soon. . . . Buddy Hassett had a field day with the bat, getting three straight singles off the southpaw Dean before he flied out twice.

Yankee double play No. 114 came in the second inning. . . . As Boudreau struck out Fleming was nabbed going to second, to retire the side. . . . The Yankees announced that on the Western trip opening in Cleveland next Tuesday they would play a night game in Kansas City on July 30. . . . Donald's shutout was No. 9 for the New York club, Bonham having turned the trick four times, Ruffing and Borowy twice each.

DiMag Bat A-Roaring

By TIM COHANE,
World-Telegram Staff Correspondent.

KANSAS CITY, July 30.—The surprising double setback of the Yankees by the White Sox, 6–5 in 11 innings, and 7–5, had in no wise today dimmed the luster of Joe DiMaggio's general batting resurgence. Once more the nation's juke boxes were cackling, "We want you on our side."

With a triple and a single in the daylight game, which began at 5:15, and a homer and triple in the nightcap, Joe had lifted his batting average to .302, the first time he has been on the right side of the .300 mark in many a moon, full or otherwise. That at least one of these wallops hadn't helped the Yanks to an even split with the Pale Hose was not Joe's fault. He tripled in the tenth inning of the opener but was left stranded.

DiMaggio's homer in the second game gave him the club leadership with 16 to Charley Keller's 15, and as the Yankees arrived here for a night exhibition game with their American Assn. cousins, Johnny Neun's Blues, the slugger was looking forward to a three-day weekend visit to Sportsman's Park, St. Louis, always a favored hunting ground of his.

DiMaggio began his explosive comeback fittingly on July 4, the day he instituted his recent 18-consecutive-game hitting streak. He's hit safely in all but two of the team's 26 games since and has a batting average of .392 over that period as a result of 40 safeties in 102 tries.

In the West, where the Yanks have six out of nine, DiMag has connected 14 out of 35 times for an even .400 gait. More significant than that, however, has been the growing power of his wallops. Of his eight hits in the three-game series at Comiskey Park three were triples and two homers. With six runs batted in against Jimmy Dykes' hurlers he had moved up to a second-place tie with Vernon Stephens, the Browns' shortstop. Each had 72.

Williams' Edge Pretty Big With Third of Season Left.

Last year Joe trailed Red Sox Teddy Williams in batting average and home runs, but topped that friendly rival in runs batted in, 125 to 120. DiMaggio admitted today that Ted's 95 runs batted in and his 21 homers to date presented formidable leads to overcome in approximately one-third of a season.

"But I'm in the groove now," he added, "and I'm going after him."

That twin killing by the Dykesmen was the second they have inflicted on the Yanks this season, both at Comiskey Park. In their other 15 double-headers the world's champions accomplished six sweeps and nine splits. So the White Sox have been their particular bargain-bill nuisances.

All told, the Yanks have played at a .618 clip in double-headers, or 101 percentage points below their pace of .691 in single games. With twilight-arclight double-headers facing them in St. Louis on Friday and Sunday, with a single game Saturday, they will have a chance to improve their twin-bill performance.

The Browns have been cooled off two straight by the Senators, yet they have won 14 out of their last 20. And in addition to the team battle the Missouri fans were looking forward to individual duels between DiMaggio and Laabs in home runs and DiMaggio and Stephens in runs batted in. These jousts might well decide who is to furnish Williams with his competition, if any, in those departments from here in.

1942

1942 ★ SPORTSMAN'S PARK

Souvenir Program
TWENTY-FIVE CENTS

WORLD SERIES

CARDINALS YANKEES

Comparative Fielding Averages

1942 CARDINALS
(Includes Games of Sept. 23)

Player and Position	G	PO	A	E	DP	Pct.
W. Cooper, c	114	505	59	17	7	.971
O'Dea, c	48	241	36	6	7	.979
Hopp, 1b	87	747	42	14	66	.983
Sanders, 1b	77	614	36	6	55	.991
Brown, 2b	81	214	221	13	52	.971
Crespi, 2b	82	174	186	12	41	.970
Marion, ss	145	290	451	32	84	.959
Kurowski, 3b	101	120	177	19	19	.949
Slaughter, of	149	282	15	4	2	.987
Musial, of	132	286	6	4	0	.986
Moore, of	125	274	9	5	0	.983
H. Walker, of	54	109	4	4	0	.966
Triplett, of	47	78	2	3	0	.964

1942 YANKEES
(Includes Games of Sept. 23)

Player and Position	G	PO	A	E	DP	Pct.
W. Dickey, c	79	324	45	8	6	.979
Rosar, c	57	247	25	1	7	.996
Hemsley, c	28	103	10	1	3	.991
Hassett, 1b	133	1120	115	10	130	.992
Gordon, 2b	146	347	446	29	120	.965
Rizzuto, ss	142	323	434	29	112	.963
Rolfe, 3b	58	56	127	7	16	.963
Crosetti, 3b	62	75	103	9	14	.973
Priddy, 3b	37	63	63	6	4	.943
Selkirk, of	19	36	0	0	0	1.000
Keller, of	151	317	10	5	1	.985
J. DiMaggio, of	153	304	10	8	3	.975
Cullenbine, of	79	171	13	8	2	.958

THIS IS BILLY SOUTHWORTH'S *first world series as manager but he played in two classics—1924 with the Giants and 1926 with the Cardinals. Incidentally, Billy was traded to the Cardinals on June 14, 1926, and registered a .320 batting average as the Red Birds dashed to their first pennant. Then "Billy the Kid" batted .345 against the '26 Yankees with 10 hits in 29 trips to the plate.*

Meet the Yankees

ROY J. CULLENBINE
Outfielder

Cullenbine is the outfielder obtained by the Yankees during the latter part of the season to take the place of Tommy Henrich, who entered the service, and he has more than filled the bill. Roy came to the major leagues with the Detroit Tigers in 1938 but was declared a free agent the following year and signed with Brooklyn. Later he served with the Browns, batting .317 in 1941. He was born Oct. 18, 1914 at Nashville, Tenn.

JOE DIMAGGIO
Outfielder

Here is one of the great players of all time. Little can be said about "DiMag" that isn't already known by a majority of baseball fans everywhere. Born Nov. 25, 1914, at Martinez, Cal., Joe has been with the Yankees since 1936. He came to the New Yorker after playing in the Coast League with San Francisco. He is most famous for his feat of hitting safely in 56 consecutive games, accomplished in 1941.

CHARLES E. KELLER
Outfielder

His powerful build has gained him the nickname "King-Kong," but no matter what you call him, Charlie is quite a ballplayer. Born Sept. 12, 1916, at Middletown, Md., he served two seasons with Newark beginning in 1937 and then moved to the Yankee Stadium. His freshman year he batted .334. Charlie hit three home runs in one game in 1940 and walloped 33 home runs during the entire 1941 season.

GEORGE SELKIRK
Outfielder

A Yankee veteran, Selkirk has been in organized baseball since 1927, joining the Bombers in 1934. Nicknamed "Twinkletoes," his ability as a defensive outfielder and consistent hitter is known to all. This is his sixth world series and he has also been in two All-Star games.

THE YANKEES *had won 10 World's Series games in succession before Whitlow Wyatt beat them, 3 to 2, in the second series game last year. Then they won the last 3 contests to make their record 11 triumphs in their last 14 series games. Chandler was the losing pitcher in that lone defeat. Yankee winning hurlers in the 1941 classic were Ruffing, Russo, Murphy and Bonham. Murphy's victory came in the relief role.*

· DiMaggio ·

1942

The Sporting News

THE BASE BALL PAPER OF THE WORLD

REG. U. S. PAT. OFF.

VOLUME 114, NUMBER 8   ST. LOUIS, OCTOBER 1, 1942   FIFTEEN CENTS

McCarthy Swinging to Make It 7 for 7 in World Series

Six Titles in as Many Classics, Joe's Unmatched Record as Yankee Pilot

Flag No. 7 in the Bag,

Bombers' Boss Seeks

Another Grand Slam

New York Teams, Under His Direction, Have Won 24 Out of 28 Games They've Played in Inter-League Sets

By FREDERICK G. LIEB

ONE HAS to dig deep in the record books to find anything to match Yankee Joe McCarthy's record of winning six pennants in the last seven years and seven in 12 seasons in New York. It was necessary to go beyond the start of the National League in 1876, to the National Association, the first organized professional league which operated from 1871 to 1875, inclusive, to discover anything to compare with McCarthy's record. The present National League was an off-shoot of that old circuit. Harry Wright, a center fielder who wore "side-boards," was the manager of the early Boston Red Stockings, who won the Association championships in 1872, '73, '74 and '75.

Wright's team, practically intact, was taken into the National League in 1876, when it lost to Albert G. Spalding's Chicago White Stockings. However, Harry's mustachioed Boston gladiators came through again in 1877 and 1878, when Ol' 'Arry, born in England and the son of a professional English cricketer, made it six flags in seven years. Of course, they played some seasons then that would be considered a joke in present-day major league ball. Wright's Boston club appeared in only 47 games in 1872, got up as high as 79 in 1875, when it won 71 and lost eight, but played only 48 in 1877, the second year of the National League.

Joe McCarthy, who had no cricketers in his family background when he first learned his baseball on the sandlots of Germantown, a Philadelphia suburban section, has matched all of Harry Wright's old pennants, flag for flag. And he did this over the 154-game distance, capturing four straight, as did Wright—in 1936, '37, '38 and '39. Then there was a one-year break, and Marse Joe won again in 1941 and '42. An earlier McCarthy pennant was won in 1932, Marse Joe's second year in New York.

However, when Wright won his league pennants, his teams were through for the year, except for some post-season barnstorming with his proud Boston champions. With McCarthy, winning a pennant has been only the forerunner of the more coveted honor, the world's championship. Including his first New York flag, in 1932, McCarthy has followed each of his league championships with the prized blue ribbon of professional ball.

And, now, despite the fact that the nation is in the midst of blood-letting global war, it is asking: "Joe did it before; can he do it again?" Can he follow that amazing six out of seven in the American League with the still more remarkable feat of six world's championships over a seven-year span?

Yanks Hold No Fears for Fighting Young Cards

A YOUNG, enthusiastic, rollicking Cardinal team, the youngest ever to win a major league championship, is the obstacle, and it may prove quite a hurdle before the first week of October is ended. A team which came from as far behind as the Redbirds, and trimmed the Dodgers five games out of six in two crucial late-season series, isn't likely to get stagefright and fold up merely because the opposing club has the magic words, "New York Yankees," on their uniforms.

They met those awe-inspiring Yanks in St. Petersburg last spring in a nine-game preview of the World's Series, and with no checks down, the New Yorkers weren't so fearsome. The Cards took the 1942 spring series, six games to three.

Game 1 September 30 at St. Louis

New York	Pos	AB	R	H	RBI	PO	A	E
Rizzuto	ss	4	0	0	0	2	2	0
Rolfe	3b	5	2	2	0	0	1	0
Cullenbine	rf	3	1	1	0	1	0	0
DiMaggio	cf	5	2	3	1	3	0	0
Keller	lf	4	0	0	0	4	0	0
Gordon	2b	5	0	0	0	2	1	0
Dickey	c	4	1	2	0	9	0	0
Hassett	1b	4	1	2	2	5	1	0
Ruffing	p	4	0	1	0	0	0	0
Chandler	p	0	0	0	0	1	0	0
Totals		38	7	11	3	27	5	0

Pitching	IP	H	R	ER	BB	SO
New York						
Ruffing (W)	8⅓	5	4	4	6	8
Chandler (SV)	⅔	2	0	0	0	0
St. Louis						
M. Cooper (L)	7⅓	10	5	3	3	7
Gumbert	⅔	0	0	0	0	0
Lanier	1	1	2	0	1	1

N.Y.	000	110	032			7	
St.L.	000	000	004			4	

St. Louis	Pos	AB	R	H	RBI	PO	A	E
Brown	2b	4	0	1	0	1	2	1
Moore	cf	4	0	2	1	1	0	0
Slaughter	rf	3	0	1	0	1	0	1
Musial	lf	4	0	0	0	1	0	0
W. Cooper	c	4	1	1	0	8	1	0
Hopp	1b	4	0	0	0	11	1	0
Kurowski	3b	3	0	0	0	1	0	0
b Sanders		0	1	0	0	0	0	0
Marion	ss	4	1	1	2	3	2	0
M. Cooper	p	2	0	0	0	0	1	0
Gumbert	p	0	0	0	0	0	0	0
a Walker		1	0	0	0	0	0	0
Lanier	p	0	0	0	0	0	1	2
c O'Dea		1	0	1	1	0	0	0
d Crespi		0	1	0	0	0	0	0
Totals		34	4	7	4	27	8	4

a Struck out for Gumbert in 8th.
b Walked for Kurowski in 9th.
c Singled for Lanier in 9th.
d Ran for O'Dea in 9th.

Doubles—Cullenbine, Hassett
Triple—Marion Sacrifice Hit—Cullenbine
Left on Bases—New York 9, St. Louis 9
Umpires—Magerkurth (N), Summers (A),
Barr (N), Hubbard (A)
Attendance—34,769 Time of Game—2.35

1st Inning
New York
1 Rizzuto grounded to short.
2 Rolfe struck out.
  Cullenbine walked.
  DiMaggio singled to deep short,
  Cullenbine stopping at second
3 Keller struck out.
St. Louis
1 Brown grounded to short.
  Moore walked.
  Slaughter walked.
2 Musial flied to right.
3 W. Cooper called out on strikes

2nd Inning
New York
1 Gordon grounded to second
  Dickey hit a bouncer off Brown's chest
  who threw wildly to first but W.
  Cooper backing up on the play trapped
2 Dickey between first and second,
  W. Cooper to Hopp to Marion
3 Hassett lined to second
St. Louis
1 Hopp popped to Rizzuto near the
  left field foul line
2 Kurowski struck out
3 Marion struck out

3rd Inning
New York
  Ruffing singled against the right
  field pavilion screen
  Rizzuto walked
1 Rolfe took a called third strike
2 Ruffing was picked off second,
  M. Cooper to Marion
3 Cullenbine rolled out to first
St. Louis
1 M. Cooper grounded to short.
  Brown walked
2 Moore flied to deep center
3 Slaughter struck out

4th Inning
New York
  DiMaggio singled to left
1 Keller popped to Marion near
  the mound.
2 Gordon popped to Hopp near the mound.
  Dickey walked
  Hassett doubled down the left field
  line, scoring DiMaggio with Dickey
  stopping at third
3 Ruffing grounded to short.
St. Louis
1 Musial flied to deep left.
2 W. Cooper flied to DiMaggio in
  left-center.
3 Hopp struck out.

5th Inning
New York
1 Rizzuto bunted out to first.
  Rolfe blooped a single to center.
  Cullenbine doubled off the right field
  wall, Rolfe stopping at third
2 DiMaggio bounced to Kurowski who tagged
  out Cullenbine but his throw to first
  was late and Rolfe scored.
3 Keller grounded to second
St. Louis
1 Kurowski struck out.
2 Marion grounded to second
3 M. Cooper grounded to third.

6th Inning
New York
1 Gordon struck out
  Dickey singled off the right
  field screen
2 Hassett struck out
3 Ruffing flied to deep center
St. Louis
1 Brown popped to Gordon, making an
  over-the-shoulder catch in
  right-center
2 Moore flied to deep left
  Slaughter walked
  Musial walked
3 W. Cooper popped to Gordon

7th Inning
New York
1 Rizzuto flied to left
2 Rolfe flied to deep right
3 Cullenbine grounded to first
St. Louis
1 Hopp flied to left
2 Kurowski struck out for the
  third time
3 Marion fouled to Hassett

8th Inning
New York
  DiMaggio singled to center
1 Keller called out on strikes
2 Gordon struck out
  Dickey singled to right, DiMaggio
  racing to third
  Hassett singled over Brown's glove,
  scoring DiMaggio with Dickey
  stopping at second
  Ruffing got to second on Slaughter's
  error as Dickey and Hassett scored
  For St. Louis—Gumbert now pitching
3 Rizzuto bounced back to the mound
St. Louis
1 Walker, batting for Gumbert,
  struck out
2 Brown popped to Rizzuto in short left
  Moore singled to right for St. Louis
  first hit in the game
3 Slaughter flied to deep center

9th Inning
New York
  For St. Louis—Lanier pitching
  Rolfe singled to right
  Cullenbine bunted and Lanier fielding
  the ball threw over Hopp's head,
  Rolfe scoring and Cullenbine going
  all the way to third (a sacrifice
  and an error)
1 DiMaggio grounded to the mound.
  Keller walked.
  Lanier failed to pick Keller off
  first and on the return throw
  Lanier lost the ball for an error,
  Cullenbine scoring as Keller held
  at first.
2 Gordon struck out for the third time.
3 Dickey grounded to first.
St. Louis
1 Musial fouled to Dickey.
  W. Cooper singled off Rolfe's glove.
2 Hopp flied to left.
  Sanders, batting for Kurowski, walked.
  Marion tripled to right, scoring
  W. Cooper and Sanders.
  O'Dea, batting for Lanier, singled to
  center, scoring Marion.
  Crespi ran for O'Dea.
  Brown singled to center, Crespi
  stopping at second.
  For New York—Chandler now pitching.
  Moore singled to left, scoring Crespi
  with Brown stopping at second
  Slaughter beat out a bouncer to
  short, loading the bases.
3 Musial grounded out, Hassett to
  Chandler

YANKEES SET BACK CARDINALS BY 7-4

Five Cardinal batters had walked in the first seven innings today, but there had been nothing even resembling a hit. And there were two out in the eighth when Terry Moore finally punched a clean single to right field only to see Slaughter, the next St. Louis batter, lift a high fly to DiMaggio in center to end that inning.

In the meantime, the crowd which had tossed $151,797 into the series pool that eventually will be shared with the USO, had sat in awed silence in the manner of nearly all hostile crowds whenever vaunted Yankee pressure and flawless precision play assert themselves.

Meets Difficulties Early

Cooper, the National League's twenty-two-game winner upon whom all St. Louis had looked to bring down those Yanks in the series opener, fared rather badly. He was in difficulties in the first and third innings when a single and a pass in each round put two Yanks on the base. He squirmed out of the first difficulty by fanning the renowned Charley Keller and turned back the American League threat in the third by whiffing Red Rolfe and retiring Roy Cullenbine on an easy infield grounder.

But those relentless Yanks never cease tracking down a foe and in the fourth Cooper finally had to give ground to the extent of a run. DiMaggio, who was to make three singles in this game, led off with a one-base blow to left.

Cooper, teamed up with his brother Walker Cooper as battery mate, retired Keller and Joe Gordon on infield pop flies, but Bill Dickey walked and Hassett must have sent an electrifying thrill through his native, distant Bronx, by lashing a double inside the left-field foul line to drive Dickey home.

To the popular Bronx Thrush, making his world series debut among a group of colleagues to whom this Fall classic is pretty old stuff, had gone the honor of driving in the first tally of the 1942 struggle.

Cullenbine Hits Double

In the fifth the Yanks widened their margin by another run when Rolfe, fanned the first two times by Cooper, singled sharply to center and swept around to third on a double by Cullenbine who, curiously, was the only other Yank making his world series bow.

DiMaggio here did not produce another hit, but he did succeed in pushing home the run. He slammed a hard grounder at Whitey Kurowski, Card third-sacker, who tagged out Cullenbine as the latter came down the baseline from second, but Rolfe in the meantime scooted home.

In the upper half of the eighth, with the Cards still hitless and runless, there came more agonizing moments for the crowd as the Yanks finished off Cooper and tallied three runs, with only the first one earned.

DiMaggio again opened with a single. There were cheers when Keller fanned for the second time and Gordon, destined to go hitless and whiff three times, also struck out. But the veteran Dickey, who has been catching all of Ruffing's world series efforts since 1932, singled to right and Hassett banged another hit into the same sector to drive in DiMaggio.

Even then matters still were not so bad, but Ruffing followed with a high drive toward right center. Slaughter gave chase and got under it, but dropped the ball for a two-base error while both Dickey and Hassett crossed the plate.

That was all for Cooper, and Harry Gumbert, one-time Giant right-hander, came on to face the Yanks. He finally put an end to the matter by retiring Phil Rizzuto on a grounder for the third out. However, the Cards were now trailing, 5 to 0.

Nor was this all. For at the start of the ninth the crowd, which up to now had had nothing to cheer about save Moore's lone single in the eighth, was to be plunged several fathoms deeper into its gloom, which hung like a heavy pall over the west bank of the old Mississippi.

Gumbert having stepped out for a pinch-hitter in the eighth, Southworth sent the left-handed Lanier to the mound, and Max immediately was greeted by a Rolfe single. Cullenbine then laid down what was to be a sacrifice bunt, but Lanier picked it up, fired wildly past first and, by the time the ball was retrieved, Rolfe was over the plate and Cullenbine on third.

Plainly flustered, Lanier walked Keller, and then came another harrowing play as Lanier tried to catch Keller napping off first, only to get caught napping himself. As First Baseman Johnny Hopp tossed the ball back to the mound Lanier let it get away from him, and while he was scuttling after it Cullenbine zoomed home from third.

Incredible as it may seem, the Yanks actually were showing the Cards a few tricks in the very methods by which the Redbirds had galloped off with their spectacular pennant.

Nor was there any indication of what was to follow when Stan Musial fouled to Dickey for the first Cardinal out in the ninth. There was a faint cheer, even mingled with a few groans, when Walker Cooper bounced a single off Rolfe's glove. With the game definitely lost, the crowd actually seemed disappointed over this, for it meant that Ruffing, doing a gallant job, was now deprived of a one-hitter.

Well, he still had a two-hitter, and it looked even more a two-hitter when Hopp flied to Keller in left for the second out. And then it came. The ball club, which had waited until mid-August to start wiping out an overwhelming Dodger lead in the National League's stirring pennant race finally woke up.

Ray Sanders, pinch-hitting for Kurowski, walked and Marion, lean, beanpole shortstop of the St. Louisans, sent a triple crashing down the right-field foul line. Gone definitely were Ruffing's dreams of a two-hitter, or even a shutout. Two runs were in.

Ken O'Dea, another ex-Giant, batting for Lanier, singled to center and Marion galloped home with the third run amid a deafening noise.

Jimmy Brown also singled to center, and with that Coach Art Fletcher, whose appearance from the Yankee dugout always comes like an executioner's signal to a faltering pitcher, waved old Ruffing out and Chandler came up from the bullpen.

Spud, a sixteen-game winner for the Yanks, but rarely used in relief roles, faced Moore and promptly got slapped for another single. That drove in Frank Crespi, who had been sent in to run for O'Dea.

Slaughter sought to make amends for his error and rammed a hard grounder at Rizzuto. The ball bounced off the mite shortstop's chest for another hit, the sixth of the inning, and the bases were full. A home run would now win the game and cap one of the most remarkable last-ditch rallies ever seen in world series play.

But Musial, who last week during the desperate pennant drive had hit a grand slam circuit blow in this same park against the Pirates, was unequal to the task of repeating that eye-filling performance. He slammed a hard grounder down the first-base line. Hassett fielded it, tossed the ball to Chandler, who dashed over to cover first, and the ball game was over.

Game 2 October 1 at St. Louis

New York	Pos	AB	R	H	RBI	PO	A	E
Rizzuto	ss	4	0	1	0	0	3	1
Rolfe	3b	4	0	1	0	0	2	0
Cullenbine	rf	4	1	1	0	2	0	0
DiMaggio	cf	4	1	1	1	7	0	0
Keller	lf	4	1	2	2	1	0	0
Gordon	2b	4	0	1	0	0	3	0
Dickey	c	4	0	2	0	5	0	0
a Stainback		0	0	0	0	0	0	0
Hassett	1b	4	0	1	0	9	0	1
Bonham	p	2	0	0	0	0	0	0
b Ruffing		1	0	0	0	0	0	0
Totals		35	3	10	3	24	8	2

a Ran for Dickey in 9th.
b Flied out for Bonham in 9th.

Doubles—W. Cooper, Gordon, Rolfe.
Slaughter. Triple—Kurowski Home
Run—Keller Stolen Bases—Cullenbine,
Rizzuto Sacrifice Hit—Moore
Double Play—Brown to Marion to Hopp
Left on Bases—New York 7, St. Louis 4
Umpires—Summers, Barr, Hubbard.
Magerkurth Attendance—34,255
Time of Game—1:57

N.Y.	000 000 030	3
St.L	200 000 11x	4

St. Louis	Pos	AB	R	H	RBI	PO	A	E
Brown	2b	3	1	0	0	0	3	0
Moore	cf	3	1	0	0	2	0	0
Slaughter	rf	4	1	1	0	2	1	0
Musial	lf	4	0	1	1	5	0	0
W. Cooper	c	4	0	1	2	4	0	0
Hopp	1b	3	1	2	0	11	0	0
Kurowski	3b	3	0	1	1	2	1	0
Marion	ss	3	0	0	0	1	4	0
Beazley	p	3	0	0	0	0	0	0
Totals		30	4	6	4	27	9	0

Pitching	IP	H	R	ER	BB	SO
New York						
Bonham (L)	8	6	4	4	1	3
St. Louis						
Beazley (W)	9	10	3	3	2	4

1st Inning
New York
  Rizzuto walked
1 Rolfe flied to center
    Rizzuto stole second
2 Cullenbine struck out
3 DiMaggio grounded to third
St. Louis
  Brown walked
  Moore safe when Bonham threw his bunt
    too late to second (a sacrifice and
    fielder's choice)
1 Slaughter flied to Keller in
  left-center.
2 Musial fouled to Hassett
  W. Cooper doubled to the right-center
    field wall, scoring Brown and Moore
3 Hopp flied to center

2nd Inning
New York
1 Keller flied to short center
  Gordon lined a double to left
2 Dickey grounded to first; Gordon
  advancing to third
3 Hassett rolled to second
St. Louis
1 Kurowski grounded to short
2 Marion fouled to Dickey
3 Beazley took a called third strike

3rd Inning
New York
1 Bonham grounded to first
2 Musial flied to deep left
  Rolfe doubled off the right field wall
3 Cullenbine flied to left
St. Louis
1 Brown flied to DiMaggio in
  left-center
2 Moore fouled to Dickey
3 Slaughter grounded to short

4th Inning
New York
1 DiMaggio fouled to Hopp
  Keller singled past Beazley's head.
2 Gordon lined to third, Kurowski's
  throw just missing the double play
  Dickey singled to right, Keller
  stopping at second on Slaughter's
  excellent throw
3 Hassett flied to deep right.
St. Louis
1 Musial grounded to Rizzuto racing in
  behind the mound
2 W. Cooper grounded to third.
  Hopp singled to right and continued
  to second when Hassett dropped
  Cullenbine's throw trying to get
  Hopp overrunning first.
3 Kurowski flied to DiMaggio in
  right-center.

5th Inning
New York
  Bonham walked
  Rizzuto singled to left, Bonham
  stopping at second
1,2 Rolfe hit into a double play, Brown
  to Marion to Hopp as Bonham went
  to third
3 Cullenbine flied to left
St. Louis
1 Marion flied to DiMaggio in left-center.
2 Beazley took a called third strike
3 Brown grounded to second

6th Inning
New York
1 DiMaggio grounded to Marion on a very
  slow roller at the mound
2 Keller flied to left
3 Gordon took a called third strike
St. Louis
1 Moore flied to center
2 Slaughter flied to right
3 Musial grounded to second

7th Inning
New York
1 Dickey popped to Hopp, halfway between
  home and first
2 Hassett flied to left
3 Bonham grounded to short
St. Louis
1 W. Cooper flied to center
  Hopp singled to right
  Kurowski lined a triple just inside the
    left field foul line, scoring Hopp
2 Marion grounded to third, Kurowski
  holding at third
3 Beazley struck out for the third
  consecutive time

8th Inning
New York
1 Rizzuto struck out
2 Rolfe grounded to second
  Cullenbine beat out a smash to second
    Cullenbine stole second
  DiMaggio singled to right, scoring
    Cullenbine
  Keller hit a two-run homer over the
    right field pavilion roof
3 Gordon struck out.
St. Louis
1 Brown grounded to second.
2 Moore flied to deep center, DiMaggio
  making a running catch
  Slaughter doubled into the right
    field corner, racing to third when
    Rizzuto fumbled Cullenbine's throw.
  Musial singled, scoring Slaughter.
3 W. Cooper flied to right.

9th Inning
New York
  Dickey singled to the left of second.
  Stainback ran for Dickey.
  Hassett singled to right, but Stainback
1 was out at third on Slaughter's great
    throw to Kurowski.
2 Ruffing, batting for Bonham, flied
  to right.
3 Rizzuto grounded to short.

Game 3 October 3 at New York

St. Louis	Pos	AB	R	H	RBI	PO	A	E
Brown	2b	4	1	1	1	1	2	0
Moore	cf	4	0	0	0	3	0	0
Slaughter	rf	4	0	1	1	3	0	0
Musial	lf	3	0	1	0	2	0	0
W. Cooper	c	4	0	0	0	8	0	1
Hopp	1b	4	0	0	0	8	0	0
Kurowski	3b	2	1	1	0	2	2	0
Marion	ss	3	0	1	0	0	1	0
White	p	2	0	0	0	0	0	0
Totals		30	2	5	2	27	5	1

Pitching	IP	H	R	ER	BB	SO
St. Louis						
White (W)	9	6	0	0	0	6
New York						
Chandler (L)	8	3	1	1	1	3
Breuer	*0	2	1	0	0	0
Turner	1	0	0	0	1	0

*Pitched to 3 batters in 9th.

New York	Pos	AB	R	H	RBI	PO	A	E
Rizzuto	ss	4	0	2	0	2	6	0
Hassett	1b	1	0	0	0	1	0	0
Crosetti	3b	3	0	0	0	1	1	0
Cullenbine	rf	4	0	1	0	0	0	0
DiMaggio	cf	4	0	2	0	2	0	0
Gordon	2b	4	0	0	0	3	3	0
Keller	lf	4	0	0	0	2	1	0
Dickey	c	3	0	1	0	5	1	0
Priddy	3b-1b	3	0	0	0	10	1	0
Chandler	p	2	0	0	0	1	2	0
a Ruffing		1	0	0	0	0	0	0
Breuer	p	0	0	0	0	0	0	1
Turner	p	0	0	0	0	0	0	0
Totals		33	0	6	0	27	15	1

a Struck out for Chandler in 8th.

St L.	0 0 1	0 0 0	0 0 1		2
N.Y.	0 0 0	0 0 0	0 0 0		0

Stolen Base—Rizzuto. Sacrifice Hit—White. Double Play—Keller to Dickey. Left on Bases—St. Louis 4, New York 6. Umpires—Barr, Hubbard, Magerkurth, Summers. Attendance—69,123. Time of Game—2:30.

1st Inning
St Louis
1 Brown grounded back to the mound
2 Moore struck out
3 Slaughter struck out.
New York
Rizzuto beat out a perfect bunt toward third
1 Hassett fouled to W. Cooper.
2 Cullenbine struck out
Rizzuto stole second and went to third on W. Cooper's throw over Marion's head into center
3 DiMaggio struck out.

2nd Inning
St Louis
For New York—Hassett was hurt while at bat in the first and was taken out. Priddy going to first with Crosetti coming in to play third
1 Musial grounded to short.
2 W. Cooper grounded to short.
3 Hopp grounded to short
New York
1 Gordon struck out.
2 Keller grounded to first.
Dickey singled to right-center
3 Priddy flied to Moore in left-center.

3rd Inning
St Louis
Kurowski walked
Marion beat out a bunt toward third
1 White sacrificed up both runners. Chandler to Gordon
2 Brown grounded to second, scoring Kurowski and Marion going to third
3 Moore took a called third strike
New York
1 Chandler lined to third
2 Rizzuto lined to third
3 Crosetti struck out.

4th Inning
St Louis
1 Slaughter grounded to first.
Musial singled to center
2 W. Cooper popped to Gordon in short center
3 Musial was caught trying to steal second, Dickey to Rizzuto.
New York
1 Cullenbine fouled to Hopp.
DiMaggio singled to left.
2 Gordon flied to deep left.
3 Keller flied to short right

5th Inning
St Louis
1 Hopp grounded to short.
2 Kurowski lined to short.
3 Marion grounded to third
New York
1 Dickey grounded to second.
2 Priddy fouled to Hopp
3 Chandler grounded to third.

6th Inning
St Louis
1 White grounded to short
2 Brown grounded to second.
3 Moore flied to center.
New York
1 Rizzuto fouled to W. Cooper.
2 Crosetti grounded to second. Cullenbine got a single on a Texas Leaguer to left-center
3 DiMaggio flied deep to Moore, making a running glove-handed catch in left-center.

7th Inning
St Louis
1 Slaughter fouled to Crosetti.
2 Musial grounded out. Priddy to Chandler
3 W. Cooper flied to left.
New York
1 Gordon flied to very deep left.
2 Keller flied to deep right
3 Dickey grounded to short.

8th Inning
St Louis
1 Hopp grounded to second. Kurowski singled past third
2 Marion forced Kurowski at second, Rizzuto to Gordon
3 White fouled to Dickey
New York
1 Priddy popped to second
2 Ruffing, batting for Chandler, struck out
Rizzuto singled over short
3 Crosetti grounded to third

9th Inning
St Louis
For New York—Breuer pitching.
Brown singled to right-center.
Moore bunted to Breuer who threw high to second, both runners safe.
Slaughter singled, scoring Brown as Moore went to third. Slaughter went to second on the throw to third.
For New York—Turner now pitching
Musial was intentionally passed, loading the bases.
1 W. Cooper flied to DiMaggio in short left-center, the runners holding.
2,3 Hopp flied to Keller in short left who fired to Dickey doubling up Moore trying to score.
New York
1 Cullenbine flied to short center.
DiMaggio singled to left.
2 Gordon fouled to Kurowski.
3 Keller flied to deep right.

Yankees Are Blanked in Series Play for First Time Since 1926

CROWD IS CLASSIC RECORD

Great Catches by Moore and Slaughter Aid Cards—Game Marked by Wrangling

By JOHN DREBINGER

This being a day and age wherein wonders never cease, it remained for the largest world series crowd on record to see diamond history made at the Yankee Stadium yesterday as the 1942 wartime classic came sweeping into New York.

The gathering, which totaled 69,123 and tossed $267,177 into the series till, saw Billy Southworth's doughty Cardinals, behind the brilliant hurling of their left-handed Ernie White, shackle Joe McCarthy's mighty Yankees and capture the pivotal third game, 2 to 0.

They filched one run in the third inning from Spud Chandler, crack right-hander who subsequently had to retire though he yielded only three singles in eight innings. They clipped Marvin Breuer for the other amid some tempestuous scenes in the ninth and, by means of these two tallies, the Cards not only moved ahead in the struggle, two games to one, but turned loose a flood of extraordinary statistical matter,

Achieved Last by Haines

It marked, among other things, the first time a Yankee team had been shut out in world series competition since away back on Oct. 5, 1926, when another Cardinal cast, the first to bring a pennant to St. Louis, blanked the American Leaguers, 4 to 0. Jess Haines pitched that one.

It also marked the first time since that 1926 classic that the Yanks had ever been turned back in two successive series games. Nor is it to be overlooked that not since Carl Hubbell of the Giants turned them back in the first game of 1936 have the Yanks ever so much as trailed in a world championship for a fleeting moment.

All this, therefore, was achieved by the Cards, 2-to-1 underdogs in the betting and nice little fellows who, conceded practically no chance whatever, wound up the afternoon by sending the proud McCarthy forces stumbling to their locker room stunned and bewildered.

Game 4 October 4 at New York

St. Louis	Pos	AB	R	H	RBI	PO	A	E
Brown	2b	6	0	2	0	1	5	0
Moore	cf	3	0	2	1	6	0	0
Slaughter	rf	4	1	0	0	1	0	0
Musial	lf	3	2	2	1	3	0	0
W. Cooper	c	5	1	2	1	2	0	0
Hopp	1b	3	2	1	0	7	0	0
Kurowski	3b	3	1	1	2	1	0	1
Marion	ss	4	1	0	1	6	4	0
M. Cooper	p	3	1	1	2	0	0	0
Gumbert	p	0	0	0	0	0	0	0
Pollet	p	0	0	0	0	0	0	0
a Sanders		1	0	0	0	0	0	0
Lanier	p	1	0	1	1	0	0	0
Totals		36	9	12	9	27	9	1

a Popped out for Pollet in 7th.
b Singled for Bonham in 9th.

Doubles—Moore, Musial, Priddy, Rolfe.
Home Run—Keller. Sacrifice Hits—Hopp,
Kurowski, Moore. Double Play—Marion to
Brown. Left on Bases—St. Louis 10, New
York 5. Umpires—Hubbard, Magerkurth,
Summers, Barr. Attendance—69,902.
Time of Game—2:28.

St. L	000	600	201						9
N.Y.	100	005	000						6

New York	Pos	AB	R	H	RBI	PO	A	E
Rizzuto	ss	5	1	3	0	4	2	0
Rolfe	3b	4	2	2	0	2	2	0
Cullenbine	rf	4	1	2	2	0	0	0
DiMaggio	cf	4	0	0	0	5	0	0
Keller	lf	4	1	1	3	4	0	0
Gordon	2b	4	0	0	0	3	2	0
Dickey	c	4	0	0	0	2	0	1
Priddy	1b	4	0	1	1	7	2	0
Borowy	p	1	0	0	0	0	1	0
Donald	p	2	0	0	0	0	0	0
Bonham	p	0	0	0	0	0	2	0
b Rosar		1	0	1	0	0	0	0
Totals		37	6	10	6	27	11	1

Pitching	IP	H	R	ER	BB	SO
St. Louis						
M. Cooper	5⅓	7	5	5	1	2
Gumbert	⅓	1	1	0	0	0
Pollet	⅓	0	0	0	0	0
Lanier (W)	3	2	0	0	0	0
New York						
Borowy	*3	6	6	6	3	1
Donald (L)	**3	3	2	2	2	1
Bonham	3	3	1	1	2	0

*Pitched to 6 batters in 4th.
**Pitched to 3 batters in 7th.

1st Inning
St. Louis
1 Brown grounded to short.
Moore doubled to left-center.
2 Slaughter tapped to the mound, Moore
holding second.
3 Musial flied to short center.
New York
1 Rizzuto grounded to second.
Rolfe doubled inside the left field line.
Cullenbine singled to left-center,
scoring Rolfe.
2 DiMaggio flied to Moore in short
left-center.
3 Keller flied to Musial in left-center.

2nd Inning
St. Louis
1 W. Cooper flied to DiMaggio in
right-center.
2 Hopp flied to DiMaggio in left-center.
3 Kurowski flied to short left.
New York
1 Gordon popped to short.
2 Dickey flied to Musial in short
left-center.
3 Priddy flied to center.

3rd Inning
St. Louis
1 Marion called out on strikes.
2 M. Cooper grounded to third.
Brown beat out a bouncer to third.
Moore walked.
3 Slaughter flied to short left.
New York
1 Borowy called out on strikes.
Rizzuto beat out a bunt to third.
Rolfe also beat out a bunt to third.
2,3 Cullenbine lined to Marion tossing
to Brown doubling Rizzuto off second.

4th Inning
St. Louis
Musial beat out a bunt to third.
W. Cooper singled, Musial going to third,
Cooper going to second on DiMaggio's
throw to third.
Hopp walked, loading the bases.
Kurowski singled to left, scoring Musial
and W. Cooper as Hopp raced to third.
Marion walked, loading the bases.
M. Cooper blooped a single to short right,
scoring Hopp and Kurowski with Marion
going to third.
For New York—Donald took the mound.
1 Brown flied to DiMaggio in short
right-center.
Moore singled to left, scoring Marion as
M. Cooper stopped at second.
2 Slaughter forced Moore, Priddy to
Rizzuto, M. Cooper going to third.
Musial doubled to right, scoring M. Cooper.
3 W. Cooper lined to second.
New York
1 DiMaggio flied to Moore in deep
left-center.
2 Keller struck out.
3 Gordon popped to Marion in short left.

5th Inning
St. Louis
1 Hopp popped to third.
2 Kurowski grounded to short.
3 Marion flied to left.
New York
1 Dickey flied to left.
2 Priddy flied to center.
3 Donald grounded to short.

6th Inning
St. Louis
1 M. Cooper struck out.
2 Brown grounded to third.
3 Moore flied to Keller, making a one-
handed catch at the bullpen gate.
New York
Rizzuto singled to left.
Rolfe walked.
Cullenbine singled to right, scoring
Rizzuto as Rolfe stopped at second.
1 DiMaggio popped to short.
Keller hit a three-run homer into the
lower right field stands.
For St. Louis—Gumbert pitching.
Gordon safe at first on Kurowski's
throwing error.
2 Dickey grounded to second, Gordon
advancing to second.
Priddy doubled to right-center,
scoring Gordon.
For St. Louis—Pollet came in to pitch.
3 Donald grounded to second.

7th Inning
St. Louis
Slaughter walked.
Musial walked, Slaughter running went
to third on Dickey's wild throw.
W. Cooper singled to center, scoring
Slaughter as Musial went to second.
For New York—Bonham took the mound.
Hopp sacrificed up both runners.
Priddy unassisted.
Kurowski intentionally walked,
loading the bases.
2 Marion flied to center, Musial scoring
and both runners advancing as DiMaggio's
throw to the plate was high.
3 Sanders, batting for Pollet, popped
to third.
New York
For St. Louis—Lanier pitching.
Rizzuto lined a single to left.
1 Rolfe forced Rizzuto at second.
Brown to Marion, the DP just missed.
2 Cullenbine flied to Moore in left-center.
3 DiMaggio grounded to short.

8th Inning
St. Louis
Brown singled to center.
1 Moore sacrificed, Bonham to Gordon.
2 Slaughter popped to short.
Musial was intentionally passed.
3 W. Cooper forced Musial, Gordon
to Rizzuto.
New York
1 Keller flied to Moore in right-center.
2 Gordon popped to Marion in short left.
3 Dickey popped to Kurowski near the mound.

9th Inning
St. Louis
Hopp singled to left-center.
1 Kurowski sacrificed Hopp to second,
Priddy to Gordon.
2 Marion grounded to short, Hopp
moving to third.
Lanier singled to right, scoring Hopp.
3 Brown forced Lanier at second,
Gordon to Rizzuto.
New York
1 Priddy grounded to short.
Rosar, batting for Bonham, singled over
short.
2 Rizzuto flied to right.
3 Rolfe grounded to second.

Game 5 October 5 at New York

St Louis	Pos	AB	R	H	RBI	PO	A	E
Brown	2b	3	0	2	0	3	4	2
Moore	cf	3	1	1	0	3	0	0
Slaughter	rf	4	1	2	1	2	0	0
Musial	lf	4	0	0	0	2	0	0
W Cooper	c	4	·	2	1	2	1	0
Hopp	1b	3	0	0	0	9	2	1
Kurowski	3b	4	1	1	2	1	1	0
Marion	ss	4	0	0	0	3	5	0
Beazley	p	4	0	1	0	2	0	1
Totals		33	4	9	4	27	13	4

Pitching	IP	H	R	ER	BB	SO
St Louis						
Beazley (W)	9	7	2	2	1	2
New York						
Ruffing (L)	9	9	4	4	1	3

St L	000	101	002		4				
N Y	100	100	000		2				

New York	Pos	AB	R	H	RBI	PO	A	E
Rizzuto	ss	4	1	2	1	7	1	0
Rolfe	3b	4	1	1	0	1	0	0
Cullenbine	rf	4	0	0	0	3	0	0
DiMaggio	cf	4	0	1	1	3	0	0
Keller	lf	4	0	1	0	1	0	0
Gordon	2b	4	0	1	0	3	3	0
Dickey	c	4	0	0	0	4	0	0
a Stainback		0	0	0	0	0	0	0
Priddy	1b	3	0	0	0	5	1	1
Ruffing	p	3	0	1	0	0	1	0
b Selkirk		1	0	0	0	0	0	0
Totals		35	2	7	2	27	6	1

a Ran for Dickey in 9th
b Grounded out for Ruffing in 9th

Home Runs—Kurowski, Rizzuto, Slaughter
Sacrifice Hits—Hopp, Moore
Double Plays—Gordon to Rizzuto to
Priddy, Hopp to Marion to Brown
Left on Bases—St Louis 5, New York 7
Umpires—Magerkurth, Summers, Barr,
Hubbard Attendance—69,052
Time of Game—1:58

1st Inning
St Louis
Brown walked
1 Moore struck out
2,3 Slaughter hit into a double play,
    Gordon to Rizzuto to Priddy,
New York
Rizzuto homered into the lower
    left-field stands
1 Rolfe grounded to second
2 Cullenbine grounded to first
3 DiMaggio flied to Moore in left-center

2nd Inning
St Louis
1 Musial popped to short
W Cooper singled through the middle
2 Hopp popped to Rizzuto on the
    left field grass
3 Kurowski popped to Gordon in
    short right-center
New York
1 Keller grounded to second
2 Gordon grounded to short
3 Dickey grounded to second

3rd Inning
St Louis
1 Marion fouled to Priddy, with a good
    glove-catch at the Cardinal dugout
2 Beazley called out on strikes, his
    fourth consecutive
Brown singled over second
3 Moore flied to right
New York
Priddy walked
1,2 Ruffing bunted into a double play on
    an attempted sacrifice, Hopp to
    Marion to Brown
3 Rizzuto flied to Moore in deep
    left-center

4th Inning
St Louis
Slaughter hit a home run deep into
    the lower right field stands
1 Musial flied to center
2 W Cooper grounded to first
3 Hopp grounded to second
New York
Rolfe beat out a bunt to first and
    continued to second on Beazley's
    wild throw
1 Cullenbine flied to Moore in deep
    right-center, Rolfe going to
    third after the catch
DiMaggio singled to left,
    scoring Rolfe
Keller singled to right, DiMaggio
    going to third
2 Gordon struck out, his 7th in the Series
3 Dickey forced Keller at second,
    Marion to Brown

5th Inning
St Louis
1 Kurowski flied to left
2 Marion flied to Cullenbine in short
    right-center
Beazley singled to right
3 Brown popped to third
New York
1 Priddy grounded to short
Ruffing beat out a slow roller to third
Rizzuto safe at first when Hopp threw
    his grounder into the dirt
Rolfe safe, loading the bases, on
    Brown's fumble
2 Cullenbine popped to Marion
    behind third
3 DiMaggio forced Rizzuto at third,
    Kurowski unassisted

6th Inning
St Louis
Moore singled to left
Slaughter singled to right-center,
    Moore advancing to third
1 Musial popped to Rizzuto in short
    left
2 W Cooper flied to right, Moore
    scoring after the catch, Priddy
    threw the relay wild and Slaughter
    went to third
3 Hopp flied to deep center
New York
1 Keller flied to deep left
2 Gordon grounded to third
3 Dickey flied to the wall in right

7th Inning
St Louis
1 Kurowski flied to DiMaggio
    in left-center
2 Marion popped to Rizzuto in
    short left
3 Beazley struck out
New York
1 Priddy grounded to short
2 Ruffing struck out
Rizzuto singled to left-center
3 Rolfe flied to Slaughter in front
    of the Cardinal bullpen

8th Inning
St Louis
Brown singled to left
1 Moore sacrificed Brown to second,
    Priddy to Gordon
2 Slaughter popped to short
3 Musial grounded to second
New York
1 Cullenbine grounded out, Hopp
    to Beazley
2 DiMaggio lined out to deep left
3 Keller grounded to first, Beazley
    making the putout unassisted

9th Inning
St Louis
W Cooper lined a single to
    right-center
1 Hopp sacrificed W Cooper to second,
    Ruffing to Gordon
Kurowski hit a two-run homer into the
    stands just inside the left field
    foul pole
2 Marion popped to Dickey, in front
    of the plate
3 Beazley popped to Rizzuto in short
    left-center
New York
Gordon singled to left
Dickey got safely to first when Brown
    fumbled his grounder, for his
    second error of the game
Stainback ran for Dickey
1 Gordon was picked off second,
    W Cooper to Marion
2 Priddy popped to Brown, racing
    in on the grass
3 Selkirk, pinch-hitting for Ruffing,
    grounded to second

Highlights

- The Cardinals won four straight games after losing the first, at that time only the second team to rally so successfully after dropping the opener (the other, the Red Sox of 1915).
- Red Ruffing of the Yanks set a new record when he earned his seventh Series win in Game 1.
- Stan Musial singled to drive in Enos Slaughter with the game-winning run in the ninth inning of Game 2.
- Ernie White hurled a six-hit shutout for the Cards in Game 3.
- The Cardinals scored six runs in the fourth inning of Game 4, and the Yanks scored five in the sixth.
- Whitey Kurowski hit a two-run homer in the ninth inning of Game 5 to break a 2–2 tie and give St. Louis the Series crown.

Best Efforts

Batting

Average	Phil Rizzuto	.381
Home Runs	King Kong Keller	2
Triples	Marty Marion	1
	Whitey Kurowski	1
Doubles	Red Rolfe	2
Hits	Phil Rizzuto	8
Runs	Red Rolfe	5
RBIs	Whitey Kurowski	5
	King Kong Keller	5

Pitching

Wins	Johnny Beazley	2-0
ERA	Ernie White	0.00
Strikeouts	Red Ruffing	11
Innings Pitched	Johnny Beazley	18

ST. LOUIS CARDINALS
NEW YORK YANKEES
1942

Reprinted, with permission, from *The World Series*, A Complete Pictorial History, by John Devaney and Burt Goldblatt (Rand McNally and Company, Chicago, © 1972).

To Be Young and Poor and Achin' To Be Rich

The Cardinals were the youngest team ever to play in a Series. The average age of the starters was 26; the oldest player, centerfielder Terry Moore, was not yet 30. In the other dugout the Yankees were their awesome selves: DiMaggio, Keller, Dickey, Gordon, Red Rolfe. When Red Ruffing shut out the young Cardinals for eight innings of the first game and was within a record four outs of the first Series no-hitter, ahead, 7-0, it seemed that the Yankees were on their way to their ninth successive world championship.

Then, in the ninth inning of that first game, the young Cardinals erupted, scoring four runs and showing a hunger to win and a lack of fear of the Yankees, but still losing, 7-4. Most of the Cardinals—Stan Musial, Country Slaughter, Walker and Mort Cooper, Marty Marion, Whitey Kurowski—had come from the dirt poor farms and the mill towns of the depression. By winning this Series some could win more money than the Cardinals had paid them for the entire season. Most were like Musial, who was a grocery-store clerk during the off-season in Donora, Pa., where he had grown up.

The Cardinals won four straight games to take the winners' purse. They won with their vaunted speed and unexpected power. "They might not be so hot at the plate," the Boston Braves' manager, Casey Stengel, had remarked, "but they sure got a lot of strength in their ankles." They showed strength at bat in the fourth game, whaling 12 hits to win, 9-6. And in the fifth and last game Country Slaughter and Whitey Kurowski clubbed home runs to give the Cardinals a 4-2 lead in the ninth.

The Yankees rallied in the last of the ninth, putting runners on first and second with no one out. Johnny Beazley, trying for his second Series victory, faced the next batter, Jerry Priddy. He threw. Catcher Walker Cooper grabbed the pitch

and threw to Marty Marion at second base, who tagged out Joe Gordon. That pick-off play broke the back of the rally. Beazley retired the next two hitters, and the young Cardinals were world champions in the biggest upset since the Braves surprised the A's in 1914.

Stan Musial:
"For me . . . the greatest Series . . . beating the Yankees four games in a row"

Stan Musial, now an executive with the Cardinals: *The thing was, we were a young team—most of us had played only two or three years in the big leagues and 1942 was my first full year. And the Yankees did have a hell of a ball club: DiMaggio, Ruffing, Rizzuto, Gordon, Keller, Dickey, all those great people. But I don't think we were nervous or awed by them or anything. In fact, that spring, we'd played them a city series in St. Petersburg and we'd beaten them in seven games. Then there was that first game. They were beating us pretty good and then we got four or five runs in the last of the ninth. We might have caught them, too, with that rally, I came up in the last of the ninth with the bases loaded and two out. A good long double might have tied the score. But I grounded out to first base. That rally really sparked us. After that Terry Moore made some great catches for us in centerfield. I was playing leftfield and that was the tough sun field at Yankee Stadium that time of the year. I could hardly see the ball. I lost one, it was hit by Di-Maggio, but Moore came over and made a great play to catch it. What also helped us, we had gone through a tough race with the Dodgers— we caught them late in September in a double-header at Brooklyn—and winning the pennant in a close race, I think, might have made us more aggressive—we might have been more up—than the Yankees were. For me it was the greatest Series I ever played in—being it was my first and then beating the Yankees four games in a row.*

Di Mag, Gordon, Bonham Placed on All-Star Team

By the United Press.

ST. LOUIS, Jan. 13.—The Yankees and the Red Sox each placed three players on the 1942 All-Star Major League Team selected by the Baseball Writers Assn. of America and announced today.

The team was picked for the Sporting News in a nationwide vote of the 260 members of the association.

Seven newcomers were elected to the team—an annual fixture since it was inaugurated in 1925 by the Sporting News—but the American League dominated the all-star group with six players, to five for the National League.

Joe DiMaggio in center field, Joe Gordon at second base and Pitcher Ernie Bonham were the Yankee nominees, while Ted Williams in left field, Johnny Pesky at shortstop and Pitcher Tex Hughson snared spots for the Red Sox. Rightfielder Enos Slaughter and Pitcher Mort Cooper represented the Cardinals.

Johnny Mize won the first-base slot for the Giants, Stan Hack garnered third base for the Cubs and Mickey Owen tabbed the catching post for the Dodgers.

Seven newcomers to the championship squad were Bonham, Cooper, Hughson, Owen, Slaughter, Mize and Pesky, largest proportion of new men since the team's inception. Additionally, Pesky and Hughson were playing their first full season in the big time.

The team, 1942 record and total votes:

Lf—Ted Williams, Red Sox, .356—219.
Cf—Joe DiMaggio, Yankees, .305—210.
Rf—Enos Slaughter, Cardinals, .318—138.
1b—Johnny Mize, Giants, .305—189.
2b—Joe Gordon, Yankees, .322—255.
Ss—Johnny Pesky, Red Sox, .331—87.
3b—Stan Hack, Cubs, .300—95.
C—Mickey Owen, Dodgers, .259—101.
P—Morton Cooper, Cardinals, 22 and 7 250.
P—Ernie Bonham, Yankees, 21 and 5 107.
P—Tex Hughson, Red Sox, 22 and 6 124.

In 1943, looking back on the previous year, the Baseball Writers Association of America selected DiMaggio as a member of the 1942 All-Star Major League Team.

Back in California before an exhibition game for charity, the major league DiMaggio brothers are seen in minor league uniforms. From left, Dom, Vince and Joe sign autographs for their youthful fans.

1943-45
A DIFFERENT
UNIFORM

Joe DiMaggio played some baseball during his military tour of duty, for the Santa Ana Air Base team in California, and the Seventh Army Air Force team in Honolulu, Hawaii. But stomach ulcers curtailed much of his activity on baseball fields in those days.

A ROOMMATE TO REMEMBER

For several seasons before I joined the U.S. Army in 1943, I roomed with Lefty Gomez, a good friend, and one of the finest pitchers in the game until his arm went bad in the early 1940s. When I was with the Yankees, before doing war service, Lefty always provided just the right touch of comic relief we all needed. El Goofy was the nickname that was tagged on him, but he was anything but goofy. He was just very funny.

When Gomez's arm began to fail him, it became more and more necessary to relieve him in the late innings. Joe McCarthy, our manager then, usually called on Johnny Murphy, one of the best relief pitchers around, and he saved an awful lot of games for Gomez. At spring training in his last year with the Yankees, a sportswriter asked Lefty how his arm was and how many games he thought he would win that season.

"Why ask me?" Lefty said. "Go ask Murphy how he feels. If *his* arm is in shape, I should win 15 or 20."

Lefty was a terrific pitcher. He won 189 games for the Yankees and lost only 101. He won six World Series games, and never lost one, and earned for himself a plaque in the Hall of Fame.

Joe DiMaggio

By Joe Williams

Next to Ruth Di Mag Was Yanks' Best Buy

Not counting Babe Ruth—who came from another world, anyway—Joe DiMaggio, headed for the armed forces, was the best buy the Yankees ever made. All he cost was $25,000 in cash.

Maybe you never heard the full details before.

He was a product of the San Francisco sandlots and gravitated naturally to the professional ball club of that city. The Seals they are called.

He started as a shortstop, played three games at that position before Charley Graham, the club owner, demanded he be shifted to the outfield. . . . "That guy will kill what few customers we've got," fumed Graham. DiMaggio's throws from short were high, wide and lethal.

This was in '32. He had good seasons in '33 and '34, and the majors began to look him over. But it turned out he had hurt his knee in '34, wrenched it getting out of a taxicab and couldn't play over long stretches. This scared prospective purchasers off . . . all except the Yankees.

The Yankees have a scout on the West Coast named Bill Essick. It's his business to flush young talent for the Yankee farms of which George Weiss is the director.

Surgeon Was Optimistic About Joe's Knee.

Essick got Weiss on the phone: "I don't know whether this kid's knee will come back sound or not, but this much I can guarantee you: If it does you'll have something more than a good ball player . . . you'll have a great one."

At Weiss' suggestion Essick took DiMaggio to a noted surgeon and bone specialist in Los Angeles. The surgeon was optimistic. He said he thought the knee would stand up.

This was the beginning of the deal, a deal from which practically every club in the two majors shied away. The Giants, for instance, under Bill Terry, wanted no part of him. Simply weren't interested.

"What can we get him for?" asked Weiss.

"Well, Graham knows he can't get much money for a ball player with a bad knee, so he's more interested in making a deal for players. Anything to round out a winning team for the home fans."

Weiss was up to his ears in all types of job-lot players—as he always was in those days—so he listed five mediocrities named Cecil Q Bananas and said: "Tell Graham we'll give him these guys and $25,000." The deal was closed.

But it had a catch: If DiMaggio's knee didn't stand up the Yankees were to get their $25,000 back. All they'd lose were the castoff players for whom they had no use . . . and in the end one of these didn't report.

DiMaggio Would Have Brought $150,000 in 1935.

That was all right with Graham. He'd keep DiMaggio through the '35 season, and if by September of that year the Yankees didn't want him he'd return the dough. No, that isn't correct, because the Yankees didn't put up any dough until they decided they were sold on the player.

DiMaggio blossomed to full flower that season. He hit .398 and led the Coast League in everything, including home runs. By mid-July all the major league club owners who had given up on him the year before were frothing at the mouth. Graham wasn't any too pleased, either. He could have got $150,000 for him like breaking sticks.

There is no getting away from the solid contributions DiMaggio made to the Yankees, either. Immediately he was what the boys call the difference. The Yankees had finished second three straight

George Weiss.   Joe DiMaggio.   Joe Gould.

times before DiMaggio joined them. They won the very first year with him in the lineup, which was '36, and repeated successively the following three years. He was the main reason why a chronic second-place club became a consistent pennant winner. He was with the club seven years and played in six world series.

Considering these facts, we were not surprised at Joe McCarthy's petulance when he learned he was losing DiMaggio to the service. "Whatever he does is his affair. I have nothing to say," said McCarthy, a wartime commentary which will scarcely outlive Lincoln's Gettysburg address.

Joe Wasn't Exactly Popular Around Here.

For all his greatness DiMaggio wasn't altogether popular around here. This was probably due to his repeated holdouts and the manner in which he went about them. He listened to persons who had nothing to do with baseball, and the advice he received was not always the wisest. At one time he was supposed to be under the influence of Joe Gould, a Broadway fight manager who had ostentatiously attached himself to the ball player. Anyway, the business relations between DiMaggio and the Yankee front office were somewhat on the strained side. The addicts seemed to resent this for some reason and were begrudging in their acclaim.

The most DiMaggio ever got was $42,500—obviously a compromise following a controversy. This was as close as he ever came to Ruth's fabulous $80,000. He was nowhere near the turnstile draw that Babe was . . . and, of course, who was? There was only one season in which he left a definite imprint on the commercial side, and that was in '41 when he hit safely in 56 consecutive games, or before Pitchers Smith and Bagby stopped him at night in Cleveland. There appeared to be as much national interest in that streak as there ever had been in one of the Slambino's home-run streaks. It was the first time the addicts dropped their reserve and gave out all the way for the Walloping Wop.

Personally we always found DiMaggio a fine, upstanding, likeable fellow, and we wish him luck. We're happy, too, to note he's won another holdout victory . . . this time with his gorgeous wife.

Rickey Rates DiMag' All-time Top

DiMag All-Time Greatest, Says Cronin

By the United Press.

HONOLULU, Jan. 21.—Manager Joe Cronin of the Boston Red Sox, who is here as a special representative of the Red Cross, said today that the service will do "a great deal" for Ted Williams and the rest of the American League "if they keep Joe DiMaggio for four years after the war."

"Joe may or may not go into the army," Cronin said, "I don't know but I do believe he is the greatest all-around ball player of all time. From a Red Sox standpoint, I hope they keep him in at least four years after the war is over."

As for Williams, the Red Sox's power-hitting outfielder, Cronin classed him as a "great hitter who needs a kick in the pants because of his doggone moods."

Los Angeles, Feb. 24 (A. P.).—The greatest all-around player in baseball, said Branch Rickey yesterday, is Joe DiMaggio

That's high praise, coming as it does to an American Leaguer from an eminent National League man.

The new president of the Brooklyn club nominated DiMaggio as the most versatile of them all.

Branch really warmed up to his subject as he asked questions and answered them himself. "Who can outthrow Joe?" he queried. "Who can outfield him? Who outhit him, consistently and for distance? Why, nobody I ever saw. Some players excelled DiMaggio in some departments of the game. None, within my recollection, and it goes back quite a while, was better in all departments.

"In my lifetime I never saw a ball player superior to him, and that goes for Ty Cobb and all the other great ones.

"On any one day, against the same pitching, with the same ball, in the same park and under identical conditions, DiMaggio would outperform the best in my memory."

Rickey cited DiMaggio's all-time major league average of .341, the fact he collected 206 hits his first complete season (1936) with the Yankees, his 1937 season in which he led the American League in home runs, 46, in runs scored, 151, in total bases, and in total putouts by outfielders, 413. "And he led his league in 1939 and 1940 in batting with .381 and .352," Rickey pointed out.

Only in base stealing, said Rickey, is DiMaggio inferior to some of the stars of yesterday, "and even in a sprint he could outrun most of them. He is faster than most people give him credit for being. Under conditions that prevailed thirty years ago Joe would be an outstanding base stealer, if he had to."

Maybe this flattery, coming from the astute Branch Rickey, will take the place of the $43,500 the New York Yankees were paying Joe. Uncle Sam's Army paycheck is about $42,900 a year less.

In the visitors' clubhouse at Fenway Park in Boston, Joe DiMaggio congratulates teammate and roommate, Lefty Gomez (center), on the birth that morning of the pitcher's son. Looking on is fellow Yankee, Buddy Hassett.

Joe DiMaggio is sworn in, as he joins the U.S. Army Air Force in February 1943.

DIMAGGIO STARS IN GAME

Army-Navy All-Stars Win, 5–2, From Hollywood With Rally

HOLLYWOOD, April 11 (AP)—An Army-Navy all-star team, headed by such former big leaguers as Joe DiMaggio, Red Ruffing and Harry Danning, uncorked a three-run, ninth-inning rally to win an exhibition baseball game today from Hollywood of the Coast League, 5—2.

DiMaggio, Yankee center fielder until his recent enlistment in the Army air forces, struck two doubles and a single in five chances. His hit with the bases full and two out in the ninth drove in two runs.

The score by innings.

```
                              R.H.E.
All-Stars ................. 1 0 0  0 0 0  1 0 3–5 12 0
Hollywood ............... 0 0 0  0 1 1  0 0 0–2  4 1
```
   Batteries—Ruffing, Papke, Brysch and Danning. Dapper. Lloyd; Root, Joiner, Thomas and Frost, Hill.

Private Joseph Paul DiMaggio.

The classic swing, this time for the Santa Ana Air Base team in April 1943.

DIMAGGIO STILL HITTING

Bats .333 in Five Games, Though Army Limits Baseball

SANTA ANA, Calif., April 16 (AP)—Private Joe DiMaggio's Spring training has been somewhat different this year and not much time is devoted to baseball at the Santa Ana Army air base, where he is stationed, but the Yankee Clipper hasn't lost his batting eye.

In five games Joe has made six hits for eighteen times at bat, an average of .333. He went hitless in his first game, March 26, against the Fullerton Junior College nine, and Pete Mallory, pitcher for the Los Angeles club of the Pacific Coast League, blanked him this week.

On the other side of the ledger and when the going was toughest Joe smacked three hits in five tries, the last a game-winning blow in the ninth with two out that gave an all-star service team a 5–2 triumph over the Hollywood Coast League team.

DiMag got one for three when the University of Southern California beat his team, 18 to 10, the first time, and two out of four when the Trojans won again, 9 to 0.

DIMAGGIO REGAINS PENNY

Joe Recovers Indian Head Put in Trolley Box by Mistake

SAN FRANCISCO, Sept. 30 (AP)—On leave from the Army, Joe DiMaggio swung aboard a street car and dropped five pennies in the coin box.

"Wow," the former Yankee outfielder groaned as the coins trickled out of reach. "There goes my home-run penny—a 1905 Indian head. Get it out."

Conductorette Mary Griffin explained the coin box was locked and she was helpless to recover the copper. However, Municipal Railway officials, to whom appeal was taken, emerged today from a mountain of pennies—three days later—with Joe's lucky piece.

Di Mag, Ruffing Fail to Make Army All-Stars

By the Associated Press.

WASHINGTON, Nov. 13.—The Army Times, weekly newspaper published for servicemen, came out today with an army all-star team of former major leaguers—and missing was the name of Joe Di Maggio, former Yankee outfielder and the American League's most valuable player of 1942.

Also absent was the name of Red Ruffing, Yankee pitching great, now wearing khaki.

Noting that some well-known ball players were not on it, the paper said it was because their names were not submitted or their records were incomplete.

Making up the squad were:

Pitchers: Sid Hudson (Senators), Hugh Mulcahy (Phillies), Tommy Hughes (Phillies), Johnny Beazley (Cards) and Bob Carpenter (Giants).

Catchers: George (Birdie) Tebbets (Tigers) and Ken Silvestri (Yankees).

Infielders: 1b George Archie (Browns), 2b Lou Stringer (Cubs), ss Cecil Travis (Senators), 3b Don Kalloway (White Sox), utility Roy Bell (Tigers) and Nathan Blair (Athletics).

Outfielders: Peter Reiser (Dodgers), Carvel Rowell (Braves), Andrew Gilbert (Red Sox), Al Robergs (Braves) and Pat Mullins (Tigers).

Joe DiMaggio clouts a home run for the Santa Ana Air Force Base team in a 1943 exhibition game against the Pacific Coast League's Los Angeles Angels.

Joe DiMaggio

DiMag to Head Pacific Tour?

*Army Team of Former
Major Stars Reported to
Be Preparing for Trip*

By JOHN B. OLD
LOS ANGELES, Calif.

Rumors along the Pacific slope insist a team of former major league stars. who now are in the Army. is being formed to tour the Central Pacific. In fact, two teams may be going over, as it is reported that the McClellan Field team, composed largely of former major and Double A players, was instructed to prepare for overseas duty.

Sgt. Joe DiMaggio of the Army Air Forces is expected to head the major league all-stars. He left the Santa Ana (Calif.) Army Air Base last week under orders and he is said to be headed for the South Pacific. At this writing, however, Joe was believed to be in San Francisco, awaiting orders. Santa Ana Army officials had no comment to make. other than to admit "DiMaggio is not at the base."

DiMaggio's transfer orders came from high officials in Washington, it was learned on good authority.

Among the better-known players on the McClellan Field team were Dario Lodigiani of the White Sox, Walter Judnich of the Browns. Mike McCormick of the Reds and Gerry Priddy of the Senators.

A couple of major leaguers serving in the military during World War II: Joe DiMaggio, and Brooklyn Dodger shortstop, Peewee Reese, sign baseballs for the brass in Hawaii.

Some photographs of Joe DiMaggio wearing uniforms strikingly different from the Yankee pin stripes: on board ship in the Pacific and disembarking in Hawaii.

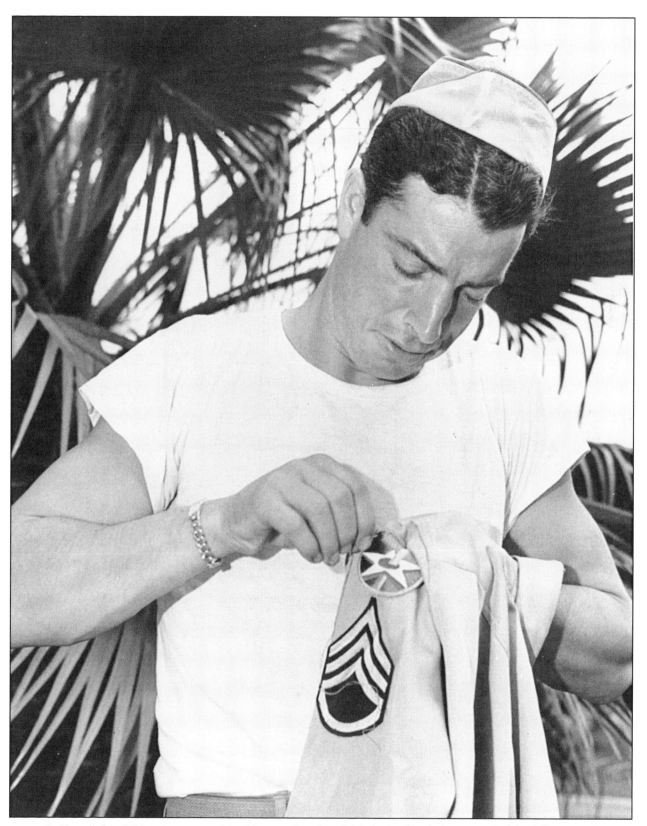

In Hawaii, Joe DiMaggio sews on his stripes and regimental insignia after being promoted to staff sergeant.

DiMaggio Leads Hawaii League

HONOLULU, July 27.—The headline read: "DiMaggio leads batters in Hawaii League."

Yes, it's joltin Joe himself. The former New York Yankee, now a sergeant playing centerfield for the 7th AAF, led the Hawaii League at the end of the third round with an average of .441 for 34 times at bat.

Joe DiMaggio to Stay in Army

HEADQUARTERS, SEVENTH ARMY AIR FORCE, Aug. 17 (AP)—Mainland reports that Joe DiMaggio, former baseball star, soon would be discharged from the Army were scotched today by a Seventh AAF spokesman. Sergeant DiMaggio has been out of the outfit's baseball line-up for three weeks with a stomach ailment which required hospitalization, but Lieut. Tom Winsett, team manager, expects the former Yankee ace back "in the near future." Gerry Priddy, former infielder with the Senators and Yankees, has been returned to the Long Beach, Calif., AAF base because of hay fever.

Di Mag Now in Hospital, Back At Duty Soon

By the United Press.

HONOLULU, Aug. 17.—Former Yankee home-run specialist Joe DiMaggio is under observation in a hospital for a stomach disorder but is expected to return to duty shortly, officials of the Seventh Army Air Forces revealed today.

It was emphasized that DiMaggio had not applied for a medical discharge from the army, spiking reports he might be mustered out in time to rejoin the Yankees in a last-ditch bid for the American League pennant.

In the Central Pacific loop DiMaggio leads in homers with five, despite the fact that he has played in only 11 of 30 games. He hit a home run recently which has become legendary, going 475 feet on the fly.

DiMaggio is leading the Hawaii League in batting with a mark of .411 and is in the first 10 in the Central Pacific League.

His old teammate with the Yankees, Joe Gordon, also is with the AAF squad and, like DiMaggio, is sidelined at present with a recurrence of an old leg injury.

Other ex-major league players now on the islands include Johnny Mize of the Giants, Walter Masterson of the Senators, Harold (Peewee) Reese of the Dodgers, Al Brancato of the Athletics, Barney McCoskey of the Tigers and Charley Ruffing, former Yankee pitching star.

Joe DiMaggio, with the Seventh Army Air Force team, poses with an unidentified ballplayer who caught for the Navy in an inter-service All-Star game in Hawaii.

It's not in records but 'twas a memorable homer

I Remember DiMaggio

By Sam Elkin

BACK ON MAY 23, 1948, Joe Di-Maggio hit two homers off Bob-by Feller and one off Reliever Bob Muncrief in successive times at bat at Municipal Stadium in Cleveland. Later, in talking to reporters, Joe remarked that this was the best day he had ever had in baseball.

Now I know how much, even to-day, Joe must cherish the memory of those three home runs in one game.* But there was a homer Joe hit one night, and not in a major or minor league park, either, which he probably doesn't remember, but which I saw, and haven't forgotten, and won't forget — ever. Joe may not remember that particular hom-er, for it is not in the record books, but I'm sure he'll remember Con-vention Hall in Atlantic City, late in 1944.

In the late fall and winter of that year I was stationed at Atlantic City along with a good many other G.I's, including a staff sergeant named Joe DiMaggio. I saw Joe for the first time, one cold November day, on the enormous floor of Con-vention Hall.

Convention Hall had been com-pletely taken over by the Army and its main floor was laid out for many different sports. There was a full-sized softball field, three basketball courts, about 18 ping-pong tables, several badminton courts, a reg-ular-distance archery range and two full-sized tennis courts. We had mass exercise at least twice a week and the first time I showed up for it Joe DiMaggio walked out in front of us.

*DiMaggio also hit three homers in a game two other times, June 13, 1937, and Sept. 10, 1950, but not in successive times at bat.

In appearance he was unassuming — even a bit shy. His voice was low but forceful. And he sent us through our drills quickly and eas-ily. After the exercise everybody crowded around him until it began to look and sound like a press con-ference. He didn't have to answer questions, but he did. And he didn't have to sign autographs, but he did that too, although I could see that he didn't like doing it while in a G.I. uniform.

I saw Joe DiMaggio off and on after that. Often at night I would go back to Convention Hall to work — we had our offices in one section of the building — and along about seven or eight I'd go out on the balcony overlooking the main floor of the hall. And there would be Joe DiMaggio playing softball with one team or another that had come to play without the required number of men.

One night I got into one of the games and DiMaggio was on my side. Against us was one of the fastest softball pitchers I had ever seen. As you probably know, soft-ball is quite different from baseball. The playing infield is smaller, the bases are closer, the ball is larger than a baseball and the pitcher is many feet nearer to the batter. When you get a real softball pitcher against you, I don't see how any-body manages to hit him.

Joe DiMaggio didn't see how that night, either. Twice he went to bat — and twice he struck out. He was swinging way behind the pitch. None of us was doing any better, but it was obvious that the pitcher was bearing down partic-ularly when DiMaggio got up to bat. With the rest of us he played cat and mouse, tossing up slow

curves, fast curves, let-up pitches. But when DiMaggio got up, he con-centrated on zooming that ball through there, three pitches and all strikes. When Joe struck out the second time, I looked at the pitcher and saw one of those irritating little smiles curl his lips.

I didn't like that pitcher from then on. He was medium height, but stocky and solid. He was ob-viously a professional softball pitch-er, and when he struck DiMaggio out the second time, I could almost hear him saying: "Boy, if I only had you in my league!"

I'm sure Joe wasn't aware of this, because each time he missed the third strike he'd come back to the bench, smiling and shaking his head and shrugging his shoulders, as if to say: "That kid's really got it out there."

But I was well aware of it. For me the game had become a battle, real and significant, and I kept wishing that Joe would really tag one the next time he got to bat. I just wanted to see the pitcher's face when that happened.

In our half of the seventh I led off and walked into a slow curve. The umpire waved me on to first base and there I stayed while the next two men struck out. Then Joe DiMaggio walked up to the plate and I started to yell to the pitcher, trying to unnerve him.

As far as the pitcher was con-cerned, I could have been out in left field or up in the balcony. He never even looked at me. He just went through his full underhand motion and shot that ball past Di-Maggio twice — two strikes. And Joe didn't move a muscle. He kept his eyes on the pitcher, his bat back and ready, his feet spread apart. It looked as though he was studying the pitcher — just standing there, watching and studying the pitcher.

I roared my lungs out as the pitcher wound up for the third pitch and laid the ball in. Joe came around with his bat and the ball shot foul down the first-base line.

"That's it! . . . Now you got him, Joe!" I yelled. "The big one! . . . Get the big one, Joe! . . . You can do it! . . . This guy's only a bum!" The pitcher just gave me a quick look, shook his head once, and faced Joe again. DiMaggio was standing in the box, as before, watching, waiting.

The pitcher's face was tight and set as he stepped on the mound. His right arm went up, then down and around, and I didn't see the ball go in — but, brother, I saw it go out! Joe caught it full, as he had caught many a pitch before at Yankee Stadium, and the ball rocketed away from his bat, straight up into the balcony in left field.

I just stood there on first base and laughed and yelled until a voice behind me said: "You moving, or do I have to climb over you?" I looked around and laughed up at Joe. I jogged around the bases, touched home plate, turned around, and shook Joe's hand as he crossed the plate. For one quick moment I felt as though I were in a Yankee uniform, shaking Joe DiMaggio's hand in Yankee Stadium.

"The greatest homer I ever saw you hit, Joe," I said as we walked back to the bench. He smiled, and

I glanced out at the mound and saw the pitcher, nervously bouncing a new ball in his glove, his chin on his chest, his eyes on the ground.

Well, a lot of years have gone by since then and I don't suppose Joe DiMaggio remembers that 'home run of his. But I do. I haven't forgotten it — and I'll never forget it. In fact, it takes on a legendary luster for me as the years go by, and no matter what ball park I'm in, no matter who is hitting a ball in the stands, the one home run I inevitably bring up in comparison is the one Joe DiMaggio hit into the balcony of Convention Hall in Atlantic City on a November night in 1944.

By Joe Williams

Why Blame Star Athletes For U.S. Errors?

The Case of Joe Di Maggio.

Almost any day now I think you will be reading that Joe Di Maggio has been discharged from the army and, of course, right away there will be speculation as to whether he will return to the Yankees, on which team he was the top salaried man. This can't miss turning out to be another Snead incident. It so happens I've known Di Maggio from the first day he reported to the big leagues, and in a very personal way, too.

Tom Laird wrote me about him. At that time Mr. Laird was the Scripps-Howard sports editor of our San Francisco paper. "A great young ballplayer is coming up. Take him in hand and show him around," he wrote. Mr. Laird, in the kindness of his soul, meant well, but it was like saying take Dempsey around and show him how to fight. At any rate a close association developed; the first week Di Maggio was in camp he ate most of his meals with me. (It wasn't long, of course, before he grew weary of waiting for me to finish my fifth Martini.)

Now Di Maggio is another fellow, another Snead, who should never have been accepted by the army; certainly not in accordance with army physical standards, for Di Maggio has always been what we called a "stomach case." Right away the optimists say ulcers, and the pessimists studiedly say incipient cancer. But the fact is everybody in baseball knew Di Maggio had this ailment, serious or not. It was definitely chronic.

Where were the doctors when they inducted him? Twice now Di Maggio has been shipped back from a far away base in the Pacific because of stomach uproars. It doesn't make sense there is going to be a third time. There must be something more important out there than the fact that Di Maggio burps excessively. A closing point: Di Maggio joined up early. He said to me: "I'm not going to have them booing me." Now wouldn't it be ironic if and when he comes back they started to boo him all over again? Don't do it. Let's assume the army and the navy know what they are doing.

DiMag Back in New York as GI Joe

S-SGT. JOE DI MAGGIO, now on furlough, enjoys a luncheon at Toots Shor's restaurant in New York. From left, Art Flynn of THE SPORTING NEWS, Toots Shor, DiMaggio, Dan Daniel of the New York World-Telegram and Capt. Dick Sarno of the Signal Corps, Astoria, L. I.

Ex-Yank Star on Furlough, Scoffs at Reports He'll Receive Discharge

By DAN DANIEL
NEW YORK, N. Y.

Staff Sergeant Joseph Paul DiMaggio, Jr., Army Air Corps, again is in circulation here, and will continue to be for at least two more weeks. He came here on a 21-day furlough, on his way to the Rehabilitation Center at Atlantic City, N. J.

Joe is headed for the spot where the Yankees will do their training again, and still may be there when the Bombers arrive. But, take it from Joe, he is not getting out of the Army, just yet.

DiMaggio said he had been discharged from treatment as a stomach ulcer case, and soon would be re-assigned in the Air Corps. He had six weeks of hospitalization in Hawaii, and three more in California.

The Army medicos have told Joe that so long as he sticks to his diet he will not suffer a recurrence.

On this mush diet, DiMaggio could do little soldiering. He could, of course, continue in special service. And that's what he appears to be in for, after a term at Atlantic City, N. J.

Appeared Peaked, Thin

DiMaggio said he weighed 210 when he went into the Army, and was now down to 187. He looked thin, even peaked, and the writer doubts if he could have tipped the beam at 180.

This past season, Joe was stricken with a recurrence of the ulcer he had four years ago, and was able to play in only 35 games, in which he hit .401. He saw the big Army-Navy series in Hawaii, and came away with an admiration for the managerial abilities of Bill Dickey, and the skills of Phil Rizzuto at second or third, and Joe Gordon around short.

DiMaggio's first question, as he sat down to luncheon, was: "How did the Yanks lose four straight to the Browns in that final series?" The experts offered no enlightenment.

DI MAGGIO HEADED FOR ATLANTIC CITY

But Joe Is Going to Army's Rehabilitation Center, Not Yank Camp, He Says Here

By JOHN DREBINGER

Looking slim and trim, although he admitted illness rather than hard physical exercise had him down to his old time playing weight of 187, Joe DiMaggio, who once bludgeoned the Yankees to six pennants in seven years, renewed acquaintances with New York baseball scribes at Toots Shor's yesterday and revealed that, so far as he knew, his next point of destination would be Atlantic City.

However, before either the Yanks or their followers take too optimistic a view on the matter let it be hastily explained that Jolting Joe's presence at the resort where the Yanks themselves most likely will arrive later for their 1945 training still promises to be nothing more than coincidental.

DiMaggio's stay at Atlantic City will be in the rehabilitation center where he is to continue with the reconditioning program that was mapped out for him following the siege of illness that laid him low in Honolulu last summer.

Recurrence of Ailment

Stricken with a recurrence of stomach ulcers from which he first suffered some four years, DiMaggio said he spent six weeks in a hospital in Honolulu, and three more in a hospital on the Coast, but believed he was now through with hospitalization.

So far as any immediate return to baseball was concerned, the former Yankee star said he knew absolutely nothing about that. He said he had heard nothing of any plans to give him a medical discharge from the Army, adding that he certainly had no intention of asking for one.

In excellent spirits, Jolting Joe, who quit the Yanks after the 1942 world series to enlist in the Army Air Forces in which he now holds the rank of staff sergeant, said he enjoyed the special work he had been doing very much. He regretted having been forced out of the service "world series" in the South Pacific in which Bill Dickey's Navy team vanquished the Army

in six straight games. Joe, who was to have played for the Army, was taken ill the day before the series started but saw most of the games.

Hails Work of Dickey

"Dickey did a great job of managing," said Joe, "and it was a great series, as well it might be, considering there were enough Yankees in it to have made a team by themselves."

In addition to Dickey, some of the other former McCarthymen were Joe Gordon, converted into a shortstop; Phil Rizzuto, now a third baseman, and Catcher Ken Sears. Prior to his illness, Di-Maggio said he played in about thirty-five games last summer and hit .401.

Louis, Di Maggio Due to Referee Service Bouts

Staff Sgt. Joe Louis and Sgt. Joe Di Maggio will be guest referees at the boxing bouts tonight for trainees at the United States Maritime Service station at Sheepshead Bay. Lt. Cmdr. Benny Leonard and Ensign Bob Olin will stage the bouts.

Honolulu Recommended by Joe DiMaggio As Post-War Training Camp for Yankees

By The Associated Press.

ATLANTIC CITY, N. J., Dec. 30 —Joltin' Joe DiMaggio, who gave up baseball for an Army Air Forces uniform two years ago, today answered cryptically fans who asked if he'd be back in center field for the New York Yankees next spring.

What Staff Sergeant Joe said was: "When's the war going to end?"

At the Atlantic City AAF Redistribution Station No. 1 to which he returned recently after six months in Hawaii with the Seventh Air Force, DiMaggio said the Honolulu ball park appealed to him as a possible post-war spring training camp for the Yankees.

He said he had heard the Chicago Cubs were interested in the site, and he thought the idea was practical if the Cubs could accom-

pany another big-league team to the same area.

"They've got an average size ball park, nice accommodations, good weather and—most of all—baseball fans who would really support such a trial," DiMaggio said.

DiMaggio, who was assigned to Special Services in Hawaii said he had played ball, done radio work, visited convalescent hospitals and answered "a lot of questions like who I thought was a better hitter, Ted Williams or me. I said Williams, of course."

He said he'd run into several other former Yankee ball players in Hawaii, among them Phil Rizzuto, Bill Dickey and Joe Gordon.

DiMaggio said the winning of the American League pennant by the St. Louis Browns had been a surprise to him. He had felt the Yankees were going to top the league, and if not the Yanks, then the Detroit Tigers.

"But they (the Browns) deserved to win," he said. "They were up there so long."

Of the post-war, Joltin' Joe had this to say: "It will take a lot of overtime for me to regain my coordination . . . but, of course, I've got my heart set on coming back. I miss the game."

Joe DiMaggio served in the US Army Air Force from 1943 through 1945, and also played baseball to entertain the troops during that time. In 1944, playing for the Seventh Army Air Force team, he batted .401 over a 90-game stretch, before stomach ulcers sidelined him.

DiMaggio Will Not Rejoin Yankees for Duration -- Even If Discharged

By DAN DANIEL

ATLANTIC CITY, N. J.

Sgt. Joe DiMaggio, on duty as physical training instructor in the AAF Redistribution Station here, sniffed the soft spring air on the Boardwalk and sighed.

About a mile and a half away, at Bader Field, Hershel Martin, Bud Metheny and Tucker Stainback, organized by Joe McCarthy as the first Bomber outfield of the year, were trying their level best to give a wartime imitation of DiMaggio, Charlie Keller and Tommy Henrich.

"Am I going to show up at the Yankee workouts?" Joe repeated the question and shrugged his shoulders. "How many of the 1945 Yankees do you suppose I know? Swampy Donald, Hank Borowy, Frankie Crosetti, Jumbo Bonham. Oh, I'll drop around. But I am not going to work out with the boys. I am busy here every day except Sunday. Then I go home to New York.

"Would I like to be back with McCarthy? Well, what do you think? I'd give anything to be able to take the field with the Yanks in the American League race. But if I were discharged tomorrow, I would not return to the club. I would not play ball with the war still on.

"You say the fans would not hoot a man with a medical discharge. Well, I would not take the chance. I never will forget the going over some of the boys in the Stadium gave me before I went into the service.

"I'd like to meet Larry MacPhail. He should be very interesting." DiMaggio chuckled. "Ed Barrow was a little tough on me. Didn't he pay me? Sure. But not enough.

"Barrow followed a system. He always handled my contract last. I suppose he figured he could shame me into signing. Well, every man to his own system, but MacPhail should be interesting."

DiMaggio hasn't played ball in more than a year. Would it take him long to get his eye on the leather again?

"Oh, about a month would be enough time to get ready," he laughed. "Just finish the war and you'll see how fast I can work.

"Meanwhile, has McCarthy a serious chance to win the pennant? Will he have enough pitching? What about Borowy and Bonham?"

Strange, but DiMaggio was repeating the very questions which had stumped McCarthy on his arrival.

"The manpower situation is far from settled and it is impossible for any manager to discuss his roster or outlook," Marse Joe said.

Harridge Sees AL Players Back as Stars After War

By the United Press.

CHICAGO, Sept. 7.—With most of baseball's brightest stars in uniform and the end of the war in sight, one of the sports world's biggest questions is whether such players can return to their peacetime diamond roles.

Bob Feller's right arm, the impetus for baseball's fastest pitch, and Joe DiMaggio's powerful wrists, the source of the Yankee Clipper's batting fame, have performed unfamiliar tasks in answering the country's needs. What war chores have done to such ball players is a constant question.

President William Harridge of the American League is confident that practically all of the junior loop's players currently on duty will doff service uniforms and resume their prewar stardom when hostilities cease.

After a check of ages, American League headquarters reported that with the possible exception of Hank Greenberg, 33, Detroit Tigers; Cecil Travis, 31, Washington; Bill Dickey, 37, New York Yankees, and Luke Appling, 35, Chicago White Sox, the American League's servicemen will shift back to an active player list with all men having many good playing days left.

There is one outstanding absentee at present, Phil Marchildon, the Athletics' 17-game winner, who is reported missing in action.

Report Based On Comeback Records.

The American League's report was based on baseball's comeback records of the first world war, the excellent physical condition of our fighting men, and today's marks of the two big leaguers who have made great comebacks already.

In 1918, there were such cases as Sgt. Hank Gowdy of the American expeditionary force who returned from active combat to major league prominence with the Red Sox, and Red Faber, who donned his baseball uniform after the war to pitch winning ball for the White Sox.

In the excellent-condition department are players such as Feller, the Cleveland Indians' durable fire-baller who has reported that he is in good shape, has been playing some ball while handling his petty officer duties and is "ready to go right back in."

At Great Lakes, Ill., Virgil (Fire) Trucks, the former Tiger pitcher, has just finished a 10–0 season with the bluejackets.

"I'm in the best shape of my life," Trucks said.

The same holds true of DiMaggio, who has been playing in a servicemen's league in Honolulu, setting batting records and hitting record-length home runs.

Then there is the thriving example of the former serviceman who has returned to stick—Myril Hoag, the erstwhile Yankee outfielder. He went from the White Sox to the Army Air Corps. About a year ago, Hoag received a medical discharge because of reoccuring dizziness due to an old baseball head injury. He rejoined the Sox, gave in-and-out performances, and then went to Cleveland where he now is hitting .300.

The $50,000 freshman beauty also came back. Dick Wakefield, after going through the gruelling program of the navy preflight training, left the Iowa preflight school when navy pilot needs were cut and resumed his slugging role with the Tigers.

DIMAGGIO SHORT ON POINTS

Medical Release From Air Forces Up to War Department

ST. PETERSBURG, Fla., Aug. 21 (AP)—Because he is a national figure, orders for the discharge of S/Sgt. Joe DiMaggio from the Army Air Forces will have to come directly from the War Department at Washington, it was announced today by an Army Air Corps spokesman.

DiMaggio, Yankee outfielder, is not eligible for a discharge on points as he has only 35, but can receive a medical discharge. He was transferred recently to the Don Ce-Sar convalescent hospital here for treatment of a stomach disorder.

DiMaggio expressed doubt he would play ball for the Yankees this season, but said he might "get out in time to join the team on its Pacific tour after the regular season."

DIMAGGIO, YANKEES RELEASED BY ARMY

Slugging Outfielder is Not Expected to Rejoin Club Until Next Spring

ST. PETERSBURG, Fla., Sept. 14 (AP)—Staff Sgt. Joe DiMaggio, former outfield star for the Yankees, returned to civilian life today.

Stomach ulcers for which he was hospitalized several weeks after tours of duty in the Pacific theatre and on the Pacific Coast and at Atlantic City brought about the outfielder's release from the Army Air Forces Don Ce-Sar convalescent hospital.

DiMaggio is expected to leave within the next day or two for New York to confer with Yankee officials before going to his home in San Francisco for the winter.

Although he could not be reached immediately for comment, he had indicated earlier he would not join his club until next season, and he would need several weeks to get into playing condition.

The slugging baseballer set an all-time record by hitting in fifty-six consecutive games for the Yanks in 1941 and has a seven year batting average of .339. He entered the Army after the 1942 season.

President Larry MacPhail of the Yankees said yesterday he had spoken with Joe DiMaggio over the long-distance phone on Tuesday but that no part of the conversation dealt with Joe's possible return to the club this season. Whether the hard-hitting, smooth fielding outfielder will rejoin the Yankees is a matter of conjecture so far as the New York front office is concerned.

DiMaggio is expected here shortly and after a conference with MacPhail more definite news of his plans will be forthcoming.

DiMaggio at Stadium

NEW YORK, N. Y.—Joe DiMaggio, Army Air Forces dischargee as of September 14, saw his first major game, as a spectator, on Sunday, September 16, in the Yankee Stadium. He attended the doubleheader between the Yankees and the Browns, and what he saw made him believe that he would be able to get his place back in the New York outfield in 1946. DiMaggio was accompanied by his former wife and 4-year-old son.

The returned sergeant had a talk with Col. Larry MacPhail and said he was willing to get into a Yankee uniform for the rest of the season. However, Larry advised against this, even though a DiMaggio Day on September 30 would mean plenty at the gate.

DiMaggio said he was going to San Francisco to look into his restaurant venture and see the income tax people. He will make his home in New York.

In the Sunday nightcap, Spud Chandler worked for the Yankees as a civilian. He got his discharge at Fort Bragg, N. C., September 14. And he won his game.

1946-47
COMING BACK

At the start of spring training in 1946, Joe DiMaggio wields a bat for the Yankees, something he had not done since the 1942 World Series, having spent the intervening three years in the U.S. Army Air Force. The exhibition game is at Sarasota, Florida, against the Boston Red Sox, and the catcher is Frank Pytlak.

HITTERS

The three best hitters I played against had to be Jimmie Foxx, Hank Greenberg, and Ted Williams. They all could hit the long ball, and Williams was the last player to hit above .400 (.406 in 1941).

Foxx took the American League batting crown in 1938, a year I thought I had a good crack at it. He hit 50 home runs that year as well, and he came close to breaking Babe Ruth's record back in 1932 when he hit 58. Greenberg hit 58, too, in 1938. Both Foxx and Greenberg were right-handed hitters, and when Foxx retired only Babe Ruth had hit more home runs than he had (714 to 534).

Ted Williams, however, was the best natural hitter I've ever seen. And he had the best eye I ever saw. He rarely bit at a bad pitch; it had to be in the strike zone for him to swing. The one hit I remember him best for was the home run he hit to win the 1941 All-Star game at Briggs Stadium in Detroit. With two outs in the ninth, I was on first and we had another runner on base too, but we were losing 5–4. Williams came up and hit the ball against the right field roof and we won 7–5.

Joe DiMaggio

1946

JOE DiMAGGIO STATISTICS

Games	132
At Bats	503
Hits	146
Doubles	20
Triples	8
Home Runs	25
Runs Scored	81
Runs Batted In	95
Bases on Balls	59
Strike Outs	24
Stolen Bases	1
Slugging Average	.511
Batting Average	.290

STANDINGS

	Won	Lost	Percentage	Games Behind
Boston Red Sox	104	50	.675	
Detroit Tigers	92	62	.597	12
New York Yankees	87	67	.565	17
Washington Senators	76	78	.494	28
Chicago White Sox	74	80	.481	30
Cleveland Indians	68	86	.442	36
St. Louis Browns	66	88	.429	38
Philadelphia A's	49	105	.318	55

1947

JOE DiMAGGIO STATISTICS

Games	141
At Bats	534
Hits	168
Doubles	31
Triples	10
Home Runs	20
Runs Scored	97
Runs Batted In	97
Bases on Balls	64
Strike Outs	32
Stolen Bases	3
Slugging Average	.522
Batting Average	.315

STANDINGS

	Won	Lost	Percentage	Games Behind
New York Yankees	97	57	.630	
Detroit Tigers	85	69	.552	12
Boston Red Sox	83	71	.539	14
Cleveland Indians	80	74	.519	17
Philadelphia A's	78	76	.506	19
Chicago White Sox	70	84	.455	27
Washington Senators	64	90	.416	33
St. Louis Browns	59	95	.383	38

They did not shoot at Joe DiMaggio during World War II, but he was not so lucky when he returned to the Yankee pin stripes in 1946, taking a stinger here.

Graham's Corner

By Frank Graham
Of the New York Journal-American

*Hughson and Trucks
Are Toughest for Joe.*

*He's Lucky Against
Feller and Newhouser.*

DI MAGGIO AND THE PITCHERS

NEW YORK, N. Y.

Joe DiMaggio

Joe DiMaggio was talking about pitchers. They're all tough to hit, he said. Only some are tougher than others.

"Who, for instance?"

"Well, Tex Hughson," he said. "He has given me a lot of trouble ever since he's been in the league. Looks like he never has an off day against me. Even when I'm going good, he gets me out."

"Who else?"

"Virgil Trucks."

"What does he do to you?"

"On and off, he murders me. Sometimes I do all right against him. But just when I think I've got him where I want him, he has me on the hook again."

"What has he got that bothers you so much?"

"It isn't so much what he's got . . . although he's got plenty. It's the way he mixes it up. He is a very patient pitcher, although you might not think so from watching him because he works fast. But he keeps trying stuff on you. He'll give you a fast ball, a curve ball, a slider or a change of pace ball. He'll work around you until he gets you just right and when he does, you're through for the afternoon. He pitches a lot like Mel Harder used to. Harder always was tough for me. Very tough.

"Against Feller, I'm just plain lucky," he said. "It's funny at that, isn't it? Nobody has a right to hit him the way I do. And there's no way to account for it. Even when nobody else on our club is hitting him, I hit him."

"Any other good pitcher have as much trouble with you as Feller does?"

"Yes," he said. "Hal Newhouser. I'm lucky against him, too. I think he's disgusted with me. He should be. He has pitched perfectly to me—and I've got base hits on pitches I had no license to hit. Now it looks to me as if he figures it's no use trying to pitch to me, with my luck, so he just tries to throw his fast ball by me, right through the middle. I just love it when they do that," he said.

"How about the young pitchers?"

"Listen," he said. "There are two young fellows in our league that I think are going to have a great season: Houtteman of Detroit and Lemon of Cleveland. They have more stuff and more pitching sense than any other young fellows I've seen come up in a long while."

* * *

Never Takes His Eyes Off the Pitchers

There are almost as many theories about hitting as there are good hitters. One hitter will tell you the most important factor is the stance. Another, keen eyesight. Still another, the stroke.

"What's your notion, Joe?"

He shrugged.

"I've never tried to tell anybody how to hit," he said. "I don't know whether you can teach somebody to hit or not. I mean, what works for me might not work for somebody else. I just concentrate on the pitcher. I never take my eyes off him. That's the reason you never see me move around at the plate.

"I try to keep the ball in sight as much as I can from the time I go up there. Some pitchers make it hard for you to do that. They hide it on you, the way they hold it or the way they twist their bodies just before they pitch. But I always have a pretty good idea where it is all the time and when they are going to let it go.

"That's why I take a short step and don't raise my left foot any further than necessary. I try just to slide it out. And I hit into the pitcher. If you pull away from the plate, you're likely to take your eye off the ball."

"Do you guess with the pitcher?"

"Sometimes," he said. "It's not a good thing to do all the time. At least, I don't think so. Because, don't forget, he may be guessing with you—and you may guess wrong. I usually look for a fast ball—and hit a curve. I mean, if you're looking for a fast ball and he throws you a curve, you have time to hit it because it isn't as fast as a fast ball. But if you look for a curve and he throws you a fast ball, it may hit you on the head."

"Ever been hit on the head?"

He tapped his knuckles against the table.

"Not yet," he said. "Not by a pitcher. Pitchers have hit me on the arm, the leg, the shoulders and the back, but not on the head. The only one to hit me on the head was an infielder, last summer. I was caught between the bases and every time I ran toward this fellow, he threw the ball at my head, making me duck and throwing me off my stride. The last time, he hit me right on the forehead. That stopped me. Then he picked up the ball and tagged me. The next day he said to me:

"'Joe, I didn't mean to hit you. On the level.'

"'Maybe not,' I said, 'but I got to say that it seems like the best way to catch a fellow when you're running up and down.'"

* * *

Batting Practice—and Slumps

Hitters also vary in their estimates of the value of batting practice. None of them ever avoid it because they all like to step up and belt the ball, but some of them think it doesn't mean too much

"How about it, Joe?"

"I think it's important," he said. "And I think it should be taken seriously, although I know some fellows, right on our own ball club, who just clown through it. I've tried to tell them where they're wrong, but they don't pay any attention to me.

"I do the same thing in batting practice that I do in a game. I concentrate on the pitcher and hit into him, and I'm trying just as hard as I am when I'm trying for a base hit."

"What causes a slump?"

A shrug.

"You are doing something you shouldn't be doing," he said. "Sometimes you don't know what it is and you ask the other fellows on the club to watch you and tell you what you are doing wrong. Everybody tells you something different and you get so confused you are worse off than before. Sometimes you know what you are doing, but can't get yourself out of it.

"In my case, it generally looks as though somebody had shortened the distance between the plate and the box and the pitcher is right on top of me. The result is that when I swing, my bat is back here when it should be out there and I am not able to get it out in time to meet the ball."

"What do you do then?"

"I worry," he said. "My stroke is off and I just can't seem to get it back. Then one day it comes back and my worries are over."

More Stars, More Fans, More Everything

Superlatives mark the post-war baseball season which opens on Tuesday with tumult and shouting.

By ARTHUR DALEY

THE last warm-up pitch has been delivered and the catcher has made the time-honored throw to second base. The umpire takes a quick step toward the plate and flicks away the last few grains of dust from the rubber with his trusty whiskbroom. Then he adjusts his mask over his weather-beaten features and calmly says, "Play ball!"

That scene will be enacted in eight major league baseball parks on Tuesday as the long-awaited first post-war season moves off with gigantic stride. When the first batter steps up to the plate, he will be greeted by roars of anticipation from the stands, echoing off Coogan's Bluff behind the Polo Grounds in New York and rolling out over the prairies from Sportsman's Park in St. Louis.

Roars of anticipation? They will be all of that. For so many they will represent dreams come true—dreams in the clinging mud of foxholes, on the bomb-scarred decks of warships, in shot-riddled planes, in heat, cold, misery and peril. Dreams of baseball were dreams of sanity. To the dreamers the game was a symbol of the things-that-were, of the things-yet-to-be.

* * *

TO returning veterans the opening of the season dwarfs any previous start of a diamond campaign because it means that all of them have the inherent right of any civilian to sit sunning themselves in the stands, to munch peanuts contentedly, to root unashamedly for the home team and to bellow, "Kill the umpire!"

To the even larger group of stay-at-homes, who gave the major leagues their largest total attendance a year ago, the new season means only one thing. No longer will their long-suffering gaze have to be turned on the reasonable facsimiles of baseball players they have been watching for the past few seasons.

For the professionals are back. They bring with them all those skills that have been missing for so long. The fielders are sure-fingered and rifle-armed. The hitters rattle the distant fences with their lusty drives, the pitchers have control and speed and a baffling assortment of curves. The players all have that almost indefinable know-how to set them apart from the ersatz brand that was with us in wartime.

* * *

MOST sports writers have one incurable weakness. In the excitement of the moment, they frequently talk in superlatives. This is the greatest or that is the greatest. And every one of them—including the few jaundiced operatives who hold that a kick in the pants always is to be preferred to a pat on the back—agrees that the new baseball season will be the greatest in history. There are no ifs, ands or maybes. This will be the greatest. Period.

Even the devious mind of a Russian diplomat would have trouble in marshaling arguments against that statement. Since money talks and there is nothing quite so impressive as statistics, it is prophesied that attendance figures will surpass all previous records and that large chunks of folding money will accumulate in the various club treasuries. That statement will prove itself later on. Slightly more difficult to test statistically since it entails a matter of judgment, is the unanimous expectation that the caliber of play will be the finest ever.

In professional sport the box office is generally accepted as the criterion of success or failure. So let us take a look at the speed with which the turnstiles have already begun to spin.

In Florida during spring training teams played to overflow crowds all over the Grapefruit League and money poured into the till in unprecedented streams. Never was interest in the game higher. Up north the fans hungrily gobbled up every morsel of news about their heroes. Their continuing hunger has been reflected in an unprecedented advance sale of tickets. Most teams reported weeks ago that the rush for opening-day tickets indicated record crowds for the opening games and there are heavy bookings for Sunday, holiday and night games.

* * *

NO organization can come within shouting distance of the New York Yankees, who once had the quaint notion that a thousand-dollar advance sale represented a monumental amount of wealth. That was before Larry MacPhail entered the picture. The rambunctious redhead doesn't enter anything quietly. Every stride he takes is accompanied by a fanfare of trumpets and shouting from the housetops. Last season was his first year as president and guiding genius of the Bronx Bombers. The very moment the war ended he leaped forward gleefully and gave the box office a shot of ephedrine. He practically ripped the staid Yankee Stadium apart in rearranging his box seats. He tore out the innards of the House that Ruth Built and created his exclusive Stadium Club, two swank taverns under the stands where thirsty holders of season tickets can quaff a stray beaker.

THE SUPERMEN RETURN

Hank Greenberg,
Detroit Tigers.

Johnny Mize,
New York Giants.

Pete Reiser,
Brooklyn Dodgers.

Stan Musial,
St. Louis Cardinals.

Bobby Feller,
Cleveland Indians.

Joe Di Maggio,
New York Yankees.

Dick Wakefield,
Detroit Tigers.

Peewee Reese,
Brooklyn Dodgers.

Ted Williams,
Boston Red Sox.

Joe DiMaggio slides safely into third in an exhibition game against the Brooklyn Dodgers before the 1946 season. The Dodger third baseman is Cookie Lavagetto and the umpire is Charlie Berry.

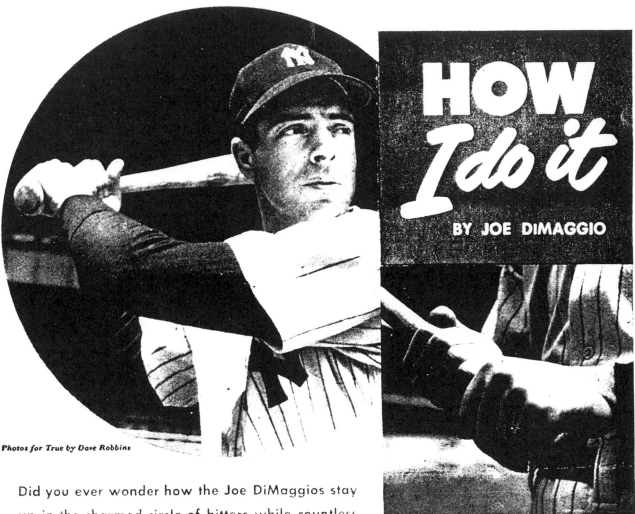

Photos for True by Dave Robbins

HOW I do it
BY JOE DIMAGGIO

DiMaggio uses a plain grip at the extreme end of the bat, his fingers flat against the handle.

Did you ever wonder how the Joe DiMaggios stay up in the charmed circle of hitters while countless stumblebums fail to bat the size of their hats? The DiMag gives you the answer in words and pictures

In short, the first requirement for good hitting is keen vision. If you can't see it, you can't hit it. The pitcher shoots the ball to the plate at a speed of almost 100 miles per hour. He can make it curve, slide, glide or hop. The batter has two-fifths of a second to decide whether it is a good one or a bad one, whether to take it or let it go by, and—if he decides to swing—to get the bat around and connect.

All this requires good stereoscopic vision: perception of depth and an ability to judge position in space. Even the air cadet with 20-20 vision in each eye is unable to land his plane if he can't sense its depth in relation to the ground. And the automobile driver who can't judge correctly the distance of his right front fender from other objects on his right lacks depth perception.

Of course, the good hitter must also have quick reflexes, good timing, judgment, confidence and strength of arms, wrists and shoulders. That means a good hitter is born, not made. Yet, whatever may be his natural attributes, there are two elements of hitting over which the batter can have full control: the type of bat he uses and how he swings it.

In 1946, a United States Army timing device clocked Bob Feller's fast ball at 146 feet per second over the regulation pitching distance of 60 feet 6 inches—a speed of 99.5 miles per hour. Believe me, a ball traveling that fast can at times look as small and as active as a Mexican jumping bean. Actually it is not quite three inches in diameter and weighs about five ounces.

Against that the batter waves a wooden club—usually ash—no more than 42 inches long, two and three-quarters inches thick at its fattest part and weighing a little more than two pounds. Within these limits there are long bats and short ones, heavy ones and light ones, thin- and thick-handled bats. In spring training, I always use a heavy bat; then switch to a lighter one for the season. It's a matter of proper balance. Perhaps as good a rule as any is to choose the heaviest bat that can be swung without difficulty.

When it comes to the swing, the first consideration is the stance. There are three of them: the even stance, in which both feet are the same distance from the inside line of the batter's box; the closed stance, in which the left foot is closer to the inside line, and the open stance, in which the

right foot is closer to the inside line. The main thing is that the stance must be comfortable. If the hitter feels awkward or tied up, it will affect his timing, his stride and his swing.

Some hitters stand far back in the batter's box, others closer to the forward line. The box, by the way, is six feet long and four feet wide, the shorter side toward the pitcher and the inside line being four inches from the plate.

Most players grip the bat with the two hands close together, although Ty Cobb and Honus Wagner, two of the greatest hitters the game ever knew, held their hands a few inches apart as they addressed the plate, sliding them together as they swung. And almost all batters use a plain grip, the fingers of each hand flat against the handle. An exception was Ernie Lombardi, who used an interlocking grip, the little finger of his right hand laced between the forefinger and second finger of his left. Frank Frisch came out of Fordham University batting cross-handed, but he dropped that style after a year in the majors.

Usually, long-ball hitters hold the bat at the extreme end,

enclosing the knob in the palm of the bottom hand. My grip is at the end, with just the knob showing. Choke hitters grip the club at least four inches from the end. But whatever the grip and the stance, the hitter must put the fat part of the bat over the heart of the plate.

He stands up at the plate with his weight on his right foot (we're illustrating with a right-hander), spikes gripping the ground firmly, knees slightly relaxed to give them flexibility, bat held in comfortable position off the right shoulder. And the less preliminary bat-waving he does, the less chance there is that he will be out of position when the ball is delivered.

The swing itself must be level—the bat traveling in a plane parallel to the ground. Unless it's level, the hitter can't get all his power into his swing. The woodchopper who swings down on the ball merely beats it into the dirt for easily handled grounders, often double-play balls. The uppercutter raises easy flies. Jimmy Dykes, then managing the White Sox, once cracked to a pinch-hitter who lofted a high pop foul to the catcher: "That's an excellent imita-

In picture No. 1, DiMag has already cocked his wrists and taken his short stride, shifting his weight to his left leg. Note the close left elbow, level bat and rising right foot as he pivots. His right hand appears to loosen its grip as ball meets bat (No. 5). Shot No. 7 reveals force of momentum as he whips into follow-through.

tion of a man hitting a ball out of a well."

Keeping the left elbow (right-handed batters) close to the body helps to guide the bat in a level plane. A batter may lower the plane to hit a ball breaking down or raise it to meet a rising ball, but he must keep the swing level.

He begins his swing by cocking his wrists and moving the bat back slightly, then swinging it around his body with the strength of his arms, wrists, and shoulders behind it. As he cocks his wrists, he steps toward the pitcher with his left foot and shifts his weight to his left leg, which becomes the axis around which his swing turns. The leg is straight, the knee firm.

He must not hurry his swing. The bat must gather speed so that the maximum power is applied as it meets the ball. This means that the batter does not uncock his wrists until almost the instant he connects. The left wrist, for a right-handed batter, guides the bat, and both wrists throw on the power.

Once he hits the ball, the batter must follow through, swinging the bat on until its heavy end has made a big

"U" around his shoulders. Remember, the arms *and* the wrists *and* the shoulders give the power. Hurrying the swing and uncocking the wrists too soon cuts off the wrist power. Letting the swing die or failing to follow through cuts off the shoulder power.

The stride is one of the most important parts of the swing, for it not only governs the follow-through but rules the transfer of the weight from the right foot to the left foot at the instant the ball is hit. The stride must be exactly right for the batter's individual style and build.

Overstriding is one of the worst batting flaws and one of the most difficult to correct. A batter who overstrides not only can't pivot for a follow-through but also is thrown off balance as he tries to connect.

The first and only book written by Joe DiMaggio, *Lucky to Be a Yankee*, published in 1946.

Joe DiMaggio slides safely in with a Yankee run in a 1946 game against the Detroit Tigers. The lunging catcher is Paul Richards, looking on is Yankee second baseman Joe Gordon, and the umpire is Bill Summers.

The classic confrontation: fastballer Bob Feller of the Cleveland Indians and the slugging Joe DiMaggio face each other at Yankee Stadium in 1946.

The view Joe DiMaggio had every game-day from his post deep in center field at Yankee Stadium. The lights were not installed until after World War II. The first night game for DiMaggio and the Yankees here was May 28, 1946.

PRICE TEN CENTS

FENWAY PARK

HOST TO THE

ALL-STARS

OF THE

1946 GAME

Joe DiMaggio was selected for the 1946 American League All-Star team but did not participate in the game, because of a torn cartilage in his left knee and a sprained left ankle, sustained on a slide into second base in a July 7 game against the Philadelphia A's.

Joe DiMaggio strolls with good friend and famed restaurateur, Toots Shor, down 51st Street in New York outside Shor's legendary eatery, one of the most famous celebrity hangouts of the day.

The pre-eminent hitters of their time, Ted Williams of the Boston Red Sox, and Joe DiMaggio of the Yankees. During his career, DiMaggio led the league in batting twice and took the home run crown two other years; his best single-season efforts were a .381 average in 1939 and 46 home runs in 1937. Williams led the American League in hitting six times and tagged the most home runs four times. His most productive years were 1941, with a .406 average, and 1949, when he hit 43 homers. Both players missed the 1943, 1944, and 1945 seasons, serving in the U.S. armed forces in World War II.

PITCHERS

One of the most fearsome pitchers I've ever seen broke into the major leagues the same year as I did. He was Bob Feller of the Cleveland Indians, and he was only seventeen years old at the time. He was known, of course, for his blazing fastball, but he was also wild, which struck a lot of fear in more than a few batters. As the years went on, he developed more and more pitching finesse, especially a curve — a quick, darting pitch that was very hard to follow.

The Yankees did better against Feller than any other team in the league, but we did not necessarily do it with our bats. Our manager, Joe McCarthy, had a strategy. He knew no team was going to score many runs off Feller, so he contrived to always have one of our best pitchers well rested and available to go against him. When we beat Feller, it was ordinarily by a score of something like 1–0 or 2–1.

The pitcher I had the toughest time batting against was a right-hander with the Cleveland Indians, but it was not Bob Feller. It was Mel Harder. He had a good sinker, which he could fool you with. I learned a lot about the various pitchers I faced over the years, but I guess I never really figured out Harder, because I never had much success against him.

Joe DiMaggio

Joe DiMaggio appears on the very first edition of *Sport* Magazine, in September 1946.

A *SPORTRAIT* of Joe DiMaggio by Baseball's Great Personalities

"Joe DiMaggio is one of the great outfielders of all time. My only regret is that he is not in the National League."
—BRANCH RICKEY, President, Brooklyn Dodgers

"The greatest break I ever got as a pitcher was that Joe DiMaggio was on my side."
—VERNON (Lefty) GOMEZ, Former Pitcher, N.Y. Yankees

"Joe DiMaggio keeps alive the Murderer's Row reputation of the Yankees."   —BABE RUTH, Home Run King

"I have had the pleasure of managing a lot of great ball players and Joe DiMaggio is one of the greatest."
—JOE McCARTHY, Manager, N.Y. Yankees

"After pitching to Joe for six years I have found out that he is not the only one that is 'lucky', the Yankees are 'lucky' to have Joe. He is a ball player's ball player."
—BOB FELLER, Pitcher, Cleveland Indians

"In my opinion Joe does everything pertaining to baseball in the right way. His character has been outstanding and a great inspiration to American youth."
—CONNIE MACK, American Baseball Club of Philadelphia

"I want to congratulate Rudolph Field for publishing the autobiography of Joe DiMaggio because in my opinion he is as good a ball player as ever put on a spiked shoe."
—JOE CRONIN, Manager, Boston Red Sox

DiMag in Opener? Docs Won't Say

By the United Press.

BALTIMORE, March 10.—Doctors at Johns Hopkins refused today to predict how soon Joe Di Maggio would be able to play baseball after a skin graft which will be performed "as soon as possible" on the Yankee outfielder's heel.

Stating that the heel has improved considerably since Di Maggio was admitted to the hospital more than a week ago, the physicians said the graft would be done as soon as the incision from a previous operation heals sufficiently. Yankee officials, meanwhile, feared that the slugging star would not be ready for the opening game with Washington on April 14.

NEW SHOE IS DESIGNED AS AID TO DIMAGGIO

BALTIMORE, March 12 (AP)—Whether Joe DiMaggio will be in centerfield when the Yankees and the Senators touch off the baseball season at Washington April 14 depended largely today on a piece of skin the size of a special delivery stamp and a new cutaway shoe for his left foot.

"I hope I'll make it," said the Yankee slugger. "But I've got no idea how long I'll be here. We'll be able to tell a lot more when the bandages come off Sunday."

Joe is recuperating from a skin-graft operation performed at Johns Hopkins Hospital yesterday to close an open wound inside his left heel. Dr. Edward M. Hanrahan, plastic surgeon, transferred the patch of epidermis from the back of Joe's right thigh.

The special baseball shoe for Joe's left foot—size 8½—is being designed by Dr. George E. Bennett, Hopkins orthopedic specialist. Part of the heel will be cut away, with a narrow band at the ankle to keep the shoe on.

Joe said he didn't think it would be necessary to adopt a new batting stance to favor the foot. Removing the skin from his thigh won't keep him from sliding.

DiMag's Heel Operation Called Success

By the Associated Press.

BALTIMORE, March 17.—A skin-grafting operation on Joe DiMaggio's left heel was tabbed "successful" at Johns Hopkins  Hospital today but doctors still declined to speculate on exactly when the Yankee center fielder will be able to start training.

Joe DiMaggio.

Dr. Edward M. Hanrahan, Hopkins plastic surgeon who performed the operation last Tuesday, took off the bandages yesterday and found the wound healing satisfactorily.

The hospital announced that DiMaggio "could be expected to rejoin the team soon."

A piece of skin the size of a special delivery stamp was transferred from the back of Joe's right thigh to the inside of his left heel. A raw wound had been left there by removal of a bone spur that developed after he bruised the foot rounding second last May.

Joe still has hopes of being in the lineup when the Yanks open the season against the Senators at Washington April 14.

Harris Resigned To Start Season Without DiMaggio

ST. PETERSBURG, March 20.—Marius Russo, veteran left-hander, today told Bucky Harris that he was ready to pitch. ... Russo will work against the Reds in Tampa tomorrow unless there is a second straight washout today and the Yankee pilot is forced to rearrange his hurling schedule. ... An all-day rain cancelled a second shot at the Tigers, in Lakeland.

Bucky Harris has resigned himself to starting the season without DiMaggio, who has missed four of his eight openers since he came to the New York club in 1936. ... They call Billy Johnson the forgotten man around here ... Golden boy Bobby Brown appears to have the third base job sewed up, even though he has not been hitting.

It appears likely that the hearing of Larry MacPhail's charges against Branch Rickey and Leo Durocher in Sarasota on Monday will be open to the press. ... The late Judge Landis held only one open hearing, and that was his last one, which resulted in affirmation of his decision forcing Bill Cox to sell control of the Phillies.

JOE DIMAGGIO TESTS FOOT

May Quit Hospital Tomorrow— Melton Recovering Fast

BALTIMORE, March 24 (AP)—Joe DiMaggio, New York Yankee centerfielder, who has been recuperating from a skin graft at the Johns Hopkins Hospital, tried his weight on the ailing left foot for the first time today, and physicians said he probably will be discharged Wednesday.

Dr. Edward M. Hanrahan, Hopkins plastic surgeon who performed the graft in an effort to heal the wound left by removal of a bone spur from the heel, said the ballplayer would be returned to the care of Dr. Mal Stevens, club physician, who will make the final decision on when he will be fit for action.

Hopkins attaches ended that Rube Melton, Brooklyn Dodger pitcher, is recovering rapidly from surgical removal of a bone chip from his elbow and will be discharged from the hospital in about two days.

DIMAGGIO EN ROUTE TO REJOIN YANKEES

Joe Limps Out of Baltimore Hospital Resigned to Missing Opening Contest Again

BALTIMORE, March 26 (AP)—Joe DiMaggio limped out of Johns Hopkins Hospital today with a big bandage still on his left heel and only slight hope that he would be in center field for the Yankees' opening American League game next month.

Joe checked out of the hospital and in less than an hour was on a train for St. Petersburg, Fla., to rejoin the Yankees at their spring training camp.

He walked under his own power, but limped. A padded bandage protected the wound on the inside of his left heel where doctors fifteen days ago had transplanted a piece of skin the size of a special delivery stamp. He wore a loose, low cut shoe.

Dr. Edward M. Hanrahan, plastic surgeon, and Dr. George Bennett, orthopedic specialist, declined to predict when DiMaggio would be able to get into training. Nor would they be pinned down on whether Joe's foot would be in playing condition when the Yanks launch their baseball campaign against the Senators in Washington April 14.

Joe was resigned to missing the curtain raiser in Washington. It will be nothing new for him. In eight previous years with the Bronx Bombers he played on opening day only twice.

The hospital did say that the wound on his heel had made fine progress toward recovery since he came here from Puerto Rico on Feb. 28. At that time Joe had a raw, open cut left by removal a month earlier of a bone spur resulting from a bruise suffered rounding second in a game at Philadelphia last May.

When Dr. Hanrahan applied a new dressing today he turned DiMaggio over to the care of Dr. Mal Stevens, Yankee club physician. Dr. Stevens will determine when Joe can play ball.

Yanks Run Extra Camp For DiMag

By DANIEL,
Staff Writer.

ST. PETERSBURG, March 28.—Joe DiMaggio is here. But for all the good he is likely to do the

Joe DiMaggio.

Yankees in the next month, aside from the morale value of his presence, he might as well be in Kamchatka.

Giuseppe is not going to be anywhere near ready for the American League opening in Washington on April 14.

He very likely will not be able to start serious training much before a fortnight.

"How long will it take me to get in shape once I am able to do some running? Frankly, at the age of 32, I can't say," DiMaggio admitted.

"I used to be able to get ready in two weeks. But I just got out of a hospital bed after having been in it for a month. Back in January, I had that first siege after the operation on my heel. Now I am a little discouraged, and, quite bewildered."

When told of Bucky Harris' plan to keep him here after the Yankees break camp a week from today, and assign three pitchers, a catcher and Frankie Crosetti to the exclusive DiMaggio setup at Miller Huggins Field, Joe said, "I am glad to hear that. It sounds like a very good scheme.

"I came here to get some sun and build myself up before tackling hard work. Dr. Edward Hanrahan, who did the pinch-grafting job on me at Johns Hopkins, said there was nothing else the hospital could do.

Weighs 190 Pounds And Looks Pale.

"If a grafting operation of that sort is 60 per cent effective, it is regarded as a success. Mine is 80 per cent good.

"There is still some seepage through a small hole in the new skin. In a few days that should heal, and the crust should harden. Meanwhile I dare not

Joe DiMaggio, Yankee slugger, leaving Johns Hopkins Hospital in Baltimore yesterday to return to the club's camp at St. Petersburg, Fla.
Associated Press Wirephoto

step down on my heel, and I need this cane to navigate."

"Remember what a fine tan I had in Puerto Rico?" DiMaggio said to Tommy Henrich. "Just look at this pale-face now. I weigh 190 pounds, I should weigh around 200 and that is one of the things I am going to work for down here.

"Incidentally, does the club actually want me? I got no word from anybody in authority. I just got on a train and went."

DiMag in Practice Proves Tonic To All Yankees

Special to the World-Telegram.

ST. PETERSBURG, Fla., April 4.—Joe DiMaggio today had his second batting practice of the training season, and saw the world from a brighter angle. . . . His first session, at Al Lang Field, with all of his teammates looking on, proved a tonic for the club. . . . Joe could not run. . . . Nor could he put a baseball shoe on his left foot. . . . But he hit well. . . . He belted one out of the park foul by inches and walloped three line drives off the pitching of Spud Chandler, Allie Reynolds and Al Lyons. Giuseppe, who is going to be left behind here with seven other players, Dr. Mal Stevens and trainer Gus Mauch, when the Yankees leave here this evening for Atlanta, never was more eager to get started. . . . Snuffy Stirnweiss, with a stiff left knee, will linger here for a few days and rejoin the Yankees in Brooklyn next Friday.

Bucky Harris says Johnny Lindell's new stance permits him to drive the ball harder and be more mobile on the high inside pitch, which had been bothering the outfielder. . . . Mel Queen, one of those to be left here, is very much on trial.

DiMaggio Expects to Be Back In Yankee Lineup Before May 1

By DANIEL,
Staff Writer.

ATLANTA, April 5.—New York's revamped bidders for the American League pennant, with Bobby Brown at third base and Yogi Berra in right field, made their annual appearance in Atlanta today but their big drawing card was not with them. They had left Joe DiMaggio to continue his workouts under a hot sun at St. Petersburg, Fla.

Predicting that Giuseppe would be ready to do some running by April 15, when he is scheduled to rejoin the Bombers in New York, and would be able to reclaim his center field berth by May 1, Bucky Harris landed here with a bright Easter outlook on his chief problem.

"The way Joe shapes up to me, he is not likely to miss as many as 20 games," the Yankee manager said. "He will be a few days getting over those blisters on his hands. By then his heel should be healed, and he should be able to take a firm stance and do some hitting. The next stage will be running, and before you know it, you will be seeing DiMaggio in the box scores again."

Harris, of course, was just guessing, and wishing. Nobody knows when Joe will be running, nobody knows when he will be playing again. And until he does return to the lineup, the Yankees won't be the real Bombers any more than the Tigers look like the true Bengals without Hank Greenberg.

One thing in this DiMaggio situation is ultra-important. He is more eager to play baseball than at any time since he came to the Yankees from San Francisco in 1936.

"This is my most critical year," said Joe as he bade the Bombers goodbye. "I've got to get going. I've got to make good, otherwise, where will I be? Where will I stand when it comes time to sign a contract for 1948? If it's up to me, you will see me in there before May 1."

Brown Somewhat Backward, Harris Admits.

Harris was forced to admit Golden Boy Brown had not yet come up to expectations.

It is an open secret that the New York camp is divided as regards the comparative merits of the young medical student, who got a $30,000 bonus from Col. MacPhail, and Billy Johnson, who played so important a role in the pennant and world series triumphs of 1943.

Brown, who hit .341 with Newark last season-end, would be rated a success if he could maintain a .285 pace with the Bombers, but he has not been vivid either around the bag or at the plate.

However, Johnson has not exactly been a ball of fire, himself, on attack. Whoever gets hot from now on will get the opening day call. "I will admit Brown has not come along as well as I had hoped," Harris said. "But I still am confident that he has the stuff. He may break out here, he may get going in Brooklyn. In the meantime, I have to reiterate that Johnson hasn't shown me too much.

"As for the belief among some of the writers that Brown can't make plays on slow hit balls, and has missed some sharply rapped hits toward the bag, my own opinion does not support these complaints."

Harris got enthusiastic when the conversation shifted to Phil Rizzuto, who is far superior to the shortstop he was at this time in 1946. Phil still weighs only 150, and could stand another eight or nine pounds.

Yanks Are Futile Without DiMag

By DANIEL.

Doubtless the most worried baseball player in the major leagues today is Joseph Paul DiMaggio Jr. of the Yankees.

Giuseppe sat on the bench in the Stadium while the Bombers were celebrating Bucky Harris' debut as their manager by taking a 6-to-1 trouncing from the Athletics, undisputed candidates for the American League cellar.

Joe saw his associates achieve no heights of emotional play. He took in their eighth-inning escape from a shutout by Phil Marchildon through the titanic expedient of a long fly ball.

Then DiMaggio went home and said to himself, "Gee, whizz, what a job lies before me! They need a leader on the field about as badly as I need a big year. I've got to come back soon, and in prewar form, too, or there will be trouble by the Harlem, and sobbing in the Bronx."

Of course, one game, even though it be the highlighted opener of a reconstructed Yankee team under a new leader, means little. The badly beaten of today may be the overwhelmingly victorious of the morrow.

But the fact remains the task which lies before DiMaggio, if this New York outfit is to finish as high as second, is a somewhat complicated one.

No less exacting than the job confronting Joe is the one which lies before Harris.

He knows all about MacPhail's outspoken criticism of the 1945 and 1946 Bombers as lacking life, pepper, alertness.

Bucky has gone into the pennant race without making any special appeal for fire and daring. He got neither in his first game. He may get them from now on. But if he doesn't, Harris will make Spartacus sound like Suzie in her first school declamation.

Henrich on Bench Seems Bad Business.

It was odd to see the Yankees starting their drive with Tommy Henrich on the bench. But for a bad wrist, he would have opened in center field, in place of Johnny Lindell, who not only failed to get a hit, but struck out twice against Marchildon's well-controlled fork ball. Phil never had anything like that pitch before the war.

It is part of Harris' overall job to get Tommy off the bench and into action. Somehow, somewhere.

Another player who will be in there soon, against right-handed hurling, is Bobby Brown, at third base. Billy Johnson's two strikeouts hardly raised him in the opinion of his manager, who quite frankly believes the younger though less experienced Brown to be the better man for the job.

In short, with DiMaggio, Henrich and Brown out, with Yogi Berra still a bit frightened by the enormity of the task that has been thrown on his shoulders, and the entire setup a bit jittery in the face of the fans' expectations of the new Stadium regime, the Yankees still are in a state of flux.

The one Bomber who held his head high through the sour inaugural was Phil Rizzuto, with his two hits and a lively tempo in the field. But even he perpetrated an error that gave the Athletics two runs.

The biggest disappointment of the drab afternoon was Spud Chandler, 20-game winner last season, but yesterday knocked out in the seventh inning by the terrific Athletics, led by that redoubtable youngster and ball of fire, Eddie Joost.

A reflective Joe DiMaggio in the Yankee dugout.

Yanks, with DiMag Back, All Set to Take On Red Sox

By LESTER BROMBERG.

The Red Sox are coming, by appointment, but it surely will be a surprise to Dom DiMaggio to find Brother Joe a reasonable facsimile of his peerless self, instead of a dugout-haunting convalescent.

In fact, New York's DiMag, who punctuated his first 1947 game yesterday at Philadelphia with a soaring three-run homer, says: "Barring injuries, I'll be in there the rest of the season."

The surprisingly early return of the center field bellwether is only one of several developments which give the Yankees, home from a brief road trip, a new outlook for the American League race.

Winning and losing at Washington, and sweeping a Sunday double-header with the Athletics, 6–2 and 3–2 (10 innings) is hardly prima facie evidence that the mere entrance of Bucky Harris' men at the Stadium will make the 1946 champions cringe in speechless terror. Boston plays the Yanks tomorrow, Wednesday and Thursday.

Yet there must be respectful consideration for Don Johnson, tall young right-handed fastballer who, in his first major league start, with few runs to work on, defeated Connie Mack's rebellious serfs in overtime in the second Sunday game. Neither would it be intelligent to ignore Spud Chandler's improvement. Driven out by the same A's in New York in the opener, the 37-year-old standby kept them tolerably well in hand in yesterday's first game. In spite of a painful left ankle suffered in the fourth, too. A sharp earth-skimmer from Mickey Guerra's bat did it. No after-effects, however, Trainer Ed Froelich affirms.

The assay of assets includes the gathering crispness of Bobby Brown's hitting. The fleet young man still needs plenty of grooming at third, but, in his last nine times at bat, he got four hits. Anybody who had seen Larry (Yogi) Berra at camp took it for granted he would come out of his inaugural jitters. His four-for-five against the Senators last Friday got him rolling. With eight out of 25, he is behind only Brown and—would you believe it?—George McQuinn.

The refugee from Shibe Park mocked the 33,446 there yesterday with three for four in the first game. He's the handsomest handler of the first-to-second-to-first double-play since Bill Terry. Still, the sudden embarrassment of riches that has descended on Harris means that McQuinn is not sure of a job. Tommy Henrich does an acceptable job at first, and his shrewd timely hitting renders it imperative to have him in there as often as possible. Right wrist still bothering him, he nevertheless rapped a double into deep left to chase Phil Rizzuto home from first in the 10th with the winning run in the chill dusk.

The pitching picture benefited, naturally, from Allie Reynolds' shutout of Washington. Harris expects to use him Wednesday, after opening the Red Sox series with Bill Bevens, who won from the A's in the Stadium.

Wind Robbed DiMag Of Second Homer.

DiMag, who turned over center field to Henrich in the second game, grinned: "I'd have connected for another homer in the seventh, if it hadn't been for the wind. It blew the ball just to the left

Joe DiMaggio.   **Tom Henrich.**

of the foul line." The one that counted came on a 3–1 pitch by Jess Flores. The ball sailed a mere 375 feet.

"I'm still not sure of my pins," admitted Joe. He was really leg-shy. In the fourth he clutched at Mickey Guerra's hit after a slow approach, and a run scored from second. In the eighth he collided with bulky Berra. Nobody hurt, though. This was opening day in the field for DiMag, weeks before anybody expected to see him. Wait till the old co-ordination comes back.

DiMaggio's Current Batting Pace Outstrips Record Streak of 1941

By DANIEL,
Staff Writer.

DETROIT, June 4.—Hotter by far than he was at a similar stage of his record batting streak of 56 consecutive contests in 1941, Joe DiMaggio today showed a .493 gait for a skein of 16 straight games, as against .377 for a similar number six years ago.

With four successive blows, one of them a double, against Detroit's redoubtable Hal Newhouser in a 3 to 0, five-hit shutout triumph for Frank Shea which left the Yankees only two lengths behind the Tigers, Giuseppe seized the leadership of the American League with .368. He had delivered 49 hits in 133 efforts and never looked more resplendent, never more dramatic in an early surge. Joe's present streak includes 33 hits in 67 times at bat. In those 16 contests, he had accounted for 21 runs and slugged four of his six homers.

With three straight hits, two of them homers, in Sunday's victory in Cleveland and four off Newhouser, Giuseppe had seven in a row when he was stopped by the right-handed Hal White in the ninth inning.

DiMaggio's success against Newhouser, punctuated with a .428 record last season, this year has scaled the .727 heights. Giuseppe has faced the southpaw 11 times and has registered eight hits, four of them doubles. Joe also has belted in four runs against Hurricane Hal. If Walter O. Briggs Sr., thinks he owns Newhouser he is mistaken. DiMaggio can show the papers.

What lies behind the DiMaggio drive? Did it start in resentment over having been fined $100 for failure to pose for a Signal Corps news reel?

"Resentment my eye," Joe laughed as he faced today's double-header with the Bengals. "My heel mended, my timing came back, and I began to find pitchers I could hit," he explained.

**Shea Scores Second
Shutout Against Hal.**

Shea, who has won six in a row since his debut defeat by Ted Hughson, 1 to 0, has scored two shutouts against Newhouser. The first was a 5-0 four-hitter, under the Stadium lights on May 21. Then, as was the case yesterday, Hal was not around at the finish.

For Newhouser, who has lost six and won five, there are many poignant evidences that this is not a merry year. Here it is June 4 and he has yet to land his first success of the season against the Yankees. He has faced them thrice and has come no closer to victory than a 2 to 2 six-inning tie with Spud Chandler.

Time was when Hal beat the Yankees seven straight. In 1946, he won four out of six from them. His career record against New York now is only one game over .500— 19 won and 18 lost.

Shea's latest triumph, in which the Tigers failed to advance a runner to third and got only three as far as second base, stressed the vitality of Bucky Harris' freshman pitching. Of the 22 games which stand to the credit of the Bombers, 11 have been turned in by rookies. Yearling hurlers have lost only thrice.

In eight starts, Shea has achieved six complete games. Yesterday the Bengals thought they had the Connecticut curver on the run in the second inning, which produced a single by Pat Mullin and George Kell's double. But thereafter the league leaders got to Frankie for only three separated blows, by Hal Wagner, Dick Wakefield and Kell, who beat out a desperation bunt in the seventh.

Only once did he need extraordinary support. And he got it, in the sixth, when Wakefield doubled with two gone, and Tommy Henrich made an amazing running one-handed stab on Mullin's potential triple.

There is little doubt that Shea is headed for the All-Star game. Joe Page once achieved that distinction as a freshman, only to finish the season with Newark. But the like of that isn't going to hit Frankie.

Joltin' Joe & Big John

The great Joseph Paul (Joe) DiMaggio, a man who had not been looking his best, was at last coming up to snuff. For the first time in seven seasons, his name topped all American League batsmen—with a .361 average. Last week in St. Louis, Joe banged two homers in two days.

Joe had started the 1947 season with a sore heel and a special bat. When the heel got better, so did his hitting. The bat, one ounce lighter than the one he used last year, got bruised and discolored. Joe nursed it tenderly. He heated the bat and then melted powdered rosin into it, to keep it from splintering. The bat broke last week in Detroit, but the New York Yankees were ready to buy him a hundred more just like it. For the Yankees, who were breathing hot on the necks of the league-leading Detroit Tigers, it was like the old days—when bleacherites chanted a song called *Joltin' Joe DiMaggio*.

Said smiling Joe DiMaggio, at 32 an old hand at ups & downs: "Rogers Hornsby once said he'd rather be lucky than good. . . . Luck is the big thing."

DiMaggio's comeback had taken some of the headlines away from another New Yorker with a talented swing: balloon-faced Big John Mize of the Giants, who was leading both leagues in home runs. Big John was one reason why the amazing Giants were battling for first place in the National League, after finishing last in 1946. Unlike DiMaggio, who tries to out-guess the pitcher, Mize's theory is that "a guy does a lot better if he goes up there not thinking about anything." Last week Big John spat some tobacco juice into the dirt and, without thinking of a thing, banged Homer No. 15 into the stands, with the bases loaded.

Lighter Bat Key To DiMaggio's Hitting Surge

By the Associated Press.

CHICAGO, June 11.—The Yankees' Joe DiMaggio is back in his prewar hitting groove mainly because he is using a 26-ounce bat instead of a 42-ounce club.

"When I was swinging a 42-ounce bat," says DiMaggio, "you hardly ever saw anything but fast balls and curves. You got so you could gauge those pitchers and time your swing with the heavy bat to meet 'em just right. But today you're looking at knucklers, sinkers, sliders and what-not. Every pitcher has four or five different deliveries.

"You have to wait longer to see what the ball is going to do—and that means a lighter bat is better 'cause you can wave it around at the last second."

DiMag and Ted In Nip-and-Tuck All-Star Battle

Joe DiMaggio and Ted Williams keep alternating in the lead in the popular balloting for the All-Star game. . . . The latest figures show Ted on top with 74,854, Joe second, with 72,387, and Enos Slaughter leading the National Leaguers with 71,517. . . . DiMaggio's total is especially interesting because no newspaper in this area is involved in the canvass.

Ted Lyons, chief of the visiting White Sox, today took a crack at the condition of left field in the Stadium. . . . He said that as a result of the rodeo there were cowtracks in that terraine. . . . Mel Queen, who saved his job with the Yankees with six innings of shutout pitching against the Giants, is due for an early start against one of the Western teams here. . . . It had been expected that with the expiration of Queen's year of freedom from inclusion in the 25-player limit, as a returned serviceman, he would be sent to Kansas City. . . . But Tommy Byrne got the demotion in Mel's place.

Four Yankees show better than 30 runs batted in apiece, and Tommy Henrich has 29. . . . The four are Joe DiMaggio, 36; Charley Keller, 36; Bill Johnson, 34; George McQuinn, 31. . . . McQuinn has hit safely in nine straight games and again is a contender for the league lead. . . . He has been shut out only nine times in 51 contests with the Yanks. . . . The Bombers have had no fewer than 33 route-going performances from their pitching staff. . . . Frank Shea Day will be celebrated in the Stadium on Sunday. . . . There will be only one game that afternoon. . . . The double-header with Detroit will be played Saturday.

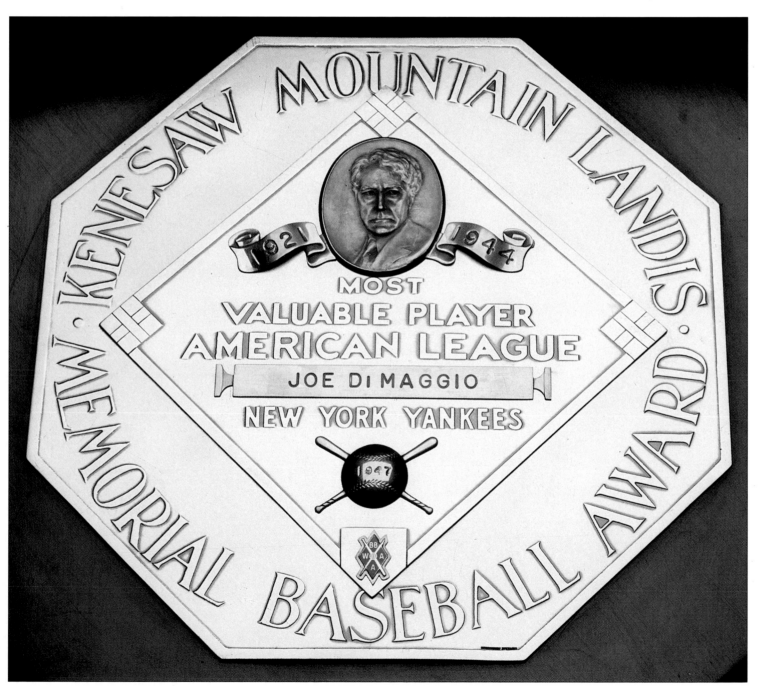

The Most Valuable Player award, earned by Joe DiMaggio in 1947. He won MVP plaques for 1939 and 1941 as well.

THE THRILLING STORY OF

JOE DiMAGGIO

100 PICTURES ● ONE DOZEN TITLES

JOE'S LIFE STORY ● BIG LEAGUE TIPS
"DiMAG" THE MAN ● "DiMAG" THE BALL PLAYER

Best always,
Joe DiMaggio

One of many books written about The Yankee Clipper during the 1940s and 1950s.

ALL STAR SOUVENIR PROGRAM 25¢

WRIGLEY FIELD · CHICAGO 1947

AMERICAN LEAGUE

GEORGE McQUINN
New York

CHARLIE KELLER
New York

JOE DI MAGGIO
New York

JOE PAGE
New York

LUKE APPLING
Chicago

BOB FELLER
Cleveland

JIM HEGAN
Cleveland

JOE GORDON
Cleveland

LOU BOUDREAU
Cleveland

Sain's Wild Throw Big All-Star Break

These A. L. Stars Started From Here ∴ and Came Out on Top in Classic

MANAGER JOE CRONIN and the starting line-up of his victorious American League forces. Left } to right, Cronin, Hal Newhouser, Buddy Rosar, } Joe Gordon, George McQuinn, Lou Boudreau, Joe } DiMaggio, Ted Williams, Buddy Lewis and George } Kell.

Score Reflects Thin A. L. Edge in Skill in Drama-Packed Scrap Before 41,123

N. L. Entered Game With Edge in Extra-Base Punch; Players' Pension Fund Enriched $105,314 by Classic

By DAN DANIEL

CHICAGO, Ill.

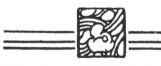

Stan Spence

American League supremacy in the All-Star Game asserted itself for the tenth time in 14 contests, 2 to 1, at Wrigley Field, July 8, before 41,123 onlookers who paid $105,314.90 into the players' pension fund, which from now on will be the sole beneficiary of this enterprise.

The American League won again. But this was no fiasco like the 12 to 0 overthrow of the National League side at Fenway Park, Boston, in 1946. It was the toughest, tightest, most dramatic, closest of all the inter-league scraps since the All-Star meeting was inaugurated at Comiskey Park in 1933.

There had been a previous one-run margin, the National League's 4 to 3 triumph at Braves Field in Boston in 1936. But this was 2 to 1, the issue in doubt right up to the last out, the margin the smallest possible.

And the score told the story quite accurately. The margin between the contending forces, the edge in skill, in high ability, was no greater than the final result indicated.

All-Star Figures

Score — American League, 2; National League, 1.

Standing of series—American League, 10; National League, 4.

Attendance—41,123.

Where played—Wrigley Field, Chicago.

Net receipts—$105,314.90.

Winning pitcher—Frank Shea, New York.

Losing pitcher — Johnny Sain, Boston.

Last year's result—American League, 12; National League, 0.

Actually, a wild throw by John Sain, No. 3 pitcher for the Nationals, was the big break. It was a well-played, well-pitched struggle in the All-Star tradition, worthy of All-Star designation, a credit to the two sides, a powerful impetus to baseball interest. And productive of better than $100,000 for the pension kitty.

Insofar as the unbiased onlooker was concerned, it was the greatest of all the 14 All-Star contests. There was no shutout, the margin of victory could have been no smaller. And there were heroes in greater profusion than we ever saw in some of the high-run contests of the past.

Power in National Lineup

To be sure, defeat was a tremendous disappointment for the National League. With so impressive an array of power hitters, the National had felt certain that it would turn the tables on its rival.

Rarely, if ever before, had the National League gone into the battle with so decided an edge in extra-base punch, once the sole prerogative of the American League.

This power broke out just once. With two out in the fourth inning, and Rookie Frank Shea of the Yankees pitching, Johnny Mize, who had hit 24 homers for the Giants, lofted a ball into the right field bleachers. This was no mere fly ball. It was a well-hit, well-directed, honest-to-goodness homer, the ninth hit by a National leaguer in All-Star competition. This put the old circuit in front.

However, in the sixth inning, the American League tied. Luke Appling, pinch-hitter, opened with a single to left off Cat Brecheen. Luke dashed to third on Ted Williams' hit to right. When Joe DiMaggio jammed into a double play, the battle became deadlocked.

The Americans won in the seventh, with Sain working for the Nationals and not looking too impressive.

Bobby Doerr, up for the first time as Joe Gordon's replacement, singled to left. He stole second. Doerr took quite a lead, and Sain wheeled and heaved the ball with erring aim. The leather struck the base runner, got away from Pee Wee Reese, and made it possible for Doerr to dash to third.

That was the big break of the game. Perhaps Doerr would have scored anyway on Stan Spence's hit with two out. But, it was a damaging break, just the same.

Sain put on full steam to fan Buddy Rosar. But Spence was a tougher customer. He was sent in to hit for Shea and quickly Sain got two strikes and no balls on the Washington outfielder.

Sain Warned About Spence

Before going to the mound, Sain had been warned, "If you face Spence, throw no high fast one." When Spence appeared at the plate, Eddie Dyer once again warned him, "Throw no high fast one."

Yet, with two strikes and no balls—a high fast one. Spence belted it into right-center, the tie was broken, the All-Star Game had been won.

The American League made eight hits, none for more than two bases. Joe Gordon and Ted Williams got wasted doubles. No error appeared in the American column.

The National League got five hits, with Mize's homer the only one for extra bases. In fact, after Mize had scored, the National League did not advance more than one runner as far as third. Willard Marshall got to the far turn in the eighth, when he walked and dashed on after Mize's single, following Phil Cavarretta's strikeout.

With runners on first and third and two gone, with the issue in the balance, Enos Slaughter faced Joe Page, who had replaced Walter Masterson when Mize came up.

Here came the fielding play of the game, the adroit manuever which broke the back of the attack of the representatives of the Frick circuit.

Slaughter cracked a sharp bounder to the right of second base. Doerr could not get it. But Lou Boudreau did. He saved the ball game.

Blackie "As Good As Feller"

The biggest thrill of the battle was contributed by a player on the losing side—Ewell Blackwell, Cincinnati ace who had pitched a no-hitter against Boston, an immediately following two-hitter against Brooklyn, five shutouts, and 14 victories. Blackwell came into the All-Star game with 12 straight victories.

He turned out to be everything the National League had said he was—and more.

Boudreau exuberated, "Right now he is as good as Bobby Feller." Bucky Harris became downright ecstatic: "Deadly speed, deadly curve, buggy-whip arm, deadly sidearm sinker, deadly sidearm curve. Deadly all over. And withal, calm and collected."

Blackwell worked the first three heats. He faced ten men. Joe DiMaggio cracked him for a single off a sharp curve opening the second. Joe went to second on a passed ball, to third on a wild pitch. Then Blackwell got Boudreau on strikes, George McQuinn flied to short left, Joe Gordon whiffed. George Kell and Ted Williams had gone out on strikes in the first inning.

No less effective, if not quite so dramatic, was Hal Newhouser, who also pitched a one-hit shutout in the first three innings. The American League's southpaw ace retired eight men in a row and then was nicked for a hit by Bert Haas, batting for Blackwell. Hurricane Hal let out another notch and got Harry Walker on strikes.

The Official Box Score

NATIONAL LEAGUE	AB.	R.	H.	O.	A.	E.
H. Walker (Phil.), cf	2	0	0	1	0	0
Pafko (Chicago), cf	2	0	1	2	0	0
F. Walker (Bk.), rf	2	0	0	2	0	0
Marshall (N. Y.), rf	1	0	0	3	0	0
Cooper (N. Y.), c	3	0	0	6	0	0
Edwards (Bk.), c	0	0	0	2	0	0
xCavarretta (Chi.), 1b	1	0	0	1	0	0
Mize (N. Y.), 1b	3	1	2	8	0	0
yMasi (Boston), c	0	0	0	0	0	0
Slaughter (St. L.), lf	4	0	0	0	0	0
Gustine (Pitts.), 3b	2	0	0	0	2	0
Kur'ski (St. L.), 3b	2	0	0	0	1	0
Marion (St. L.), ss	2	0	1	0	1	0
Reese (Brook.), ss	1	0	0	0	2	0
Verban (Phila.), 2b	2	0	0	0	0	0
Stanky (Brook.), 2b	2	0	0	2	2	0
Blackwell (Cin.), p	0	0	0	0	0	0
*Haas (Cincin.),	1	0	1	0	0	0
Brecheen (St. L.), p	1	0	0	0	1	0
Sain (Boston), p	0	0	0	0	0	1
§Musial (St. L.),	1	0	0	0	0	0
Spahn (Boston), p	0	0	0	0	0	0
zRowe (Phila.)	1	0	0	0	0	0
Totals	32	1	5	27	9	1

*Batted for Blackwell in third.
†Batted for Lewis in sixth.
‡Batted for Shea in seventh.
§Batted for Sain in seventh.
xBatted for Edwards in eighth.
yRan for Mize in eighth.
zBatted for Spahn in ninth.

AMERICAN LEAGUE	AB.	R.	H.	O.	A.	E.
Kell (Detroit), 3b	4	0	0	0	0	0
Johnson (N. Y.), 3b	0	0	0	0	0	0
Lewis (Wash.), rf	2	0	0	2	0	0
†Appling (Chi.)	1	1	1	0	0	0
Henrich (N. Y.), rf	1	0	0	3	0	0
Williams (Bos.), lf	4	0	2	3	0	0
DiMaggio (N. Y.), cf	3	0	1	1	0	0
Boudreau (Clev.), ss	4	0	1	4	4	0
McQuinn (N. Y.), 1b	4	0	0	9	1	0
Gordon (Clev.) 2b	2	0	1	0	4	0
Doerr (Boston), 2b	2	1	1	0	2	0
Rosar (Phila.), c	4	0	0	0	0	0
Newhouser (Det.), p	1	0	0	0	0	0
Shea (N. Y.), p	1	0	1	0	0	0
‡Spence (Wash.)	1	0	1	0	0	0
Masterson (Wash.), p	0	0	0	0	0	0
Page (N. Y.), p	0	0	0	0	0	0
Totals	34	2	8	27	11	0

American League	0	0	0	0	0	1	1	0	0—2
National League	0	0	0	1	0	0	0	0	0—1

Runs batted in—Mize, Spence. Two-base hits—Williams, Gordon. Home run—Mize. Stolen base—Doerr. Double play—Reese, Stanky and Mize. Bases on balls—Off Shea 2 (Slaughter, Mize), off Spahn 1 (DiMaggio), off Masterson 1 (Marshall), off Page 1 (Reese). Struck out—By Blackwell 4 (Kell, Williams, Boudreau, Gordon), by Newhouser 2 (Cooper, H. Walker), by Brecheen 2 (McQuinn, Kell), by Shea 3 (Marshall, Kurowski), by Sain 1 (Rosar), by Masterson 2 (Reese, Cavarretta), by Spahn 1 (Henrich). Pitching Summary—Off Blackwell 1 hit, 0 runs in 3 innings; off Brecheen 5 hits, 1 run in 3 innings; off Sain 2 hits, 1 run in 1 inning; off Spahn 0 hits, 0 runs in 2 innings; off Newhouser 1 hit, 0 runs in 3 innings; off Shea 3 hits, 1 run in 3 innings; off Masterson 0 hits, 0 runs in 1 2-3 innings; off Page 1 hit, 0 runs in 1 1-3 innings. Wild pitch—Blackwell. Passed ball—Cooper. Left on bases—National 8, American 6. Earned runs—American 2, National 1. Winning pitcher—Shea. Losing pitcher—Sain. Umpires—Conlan (N. L.) at plate; Boyer (A. L.) first base; Henline (N. L.) second base; Passarella (A. L.) third base (first 4½ innings); Passarella (A. L.) at plate; Conlan (N. L.) third base; Boyer (A. L.) second base; Henline (N. L.) first base (last 4½ innings). Time of game—2:19. Attendance—41,123. Net Receipts—$105,314.90. Scorers—Tommy Holmes, Brooklyn Eagle; John Carmichael, Chicago Daily News; Irving Vaughan, Chicago Tribune.

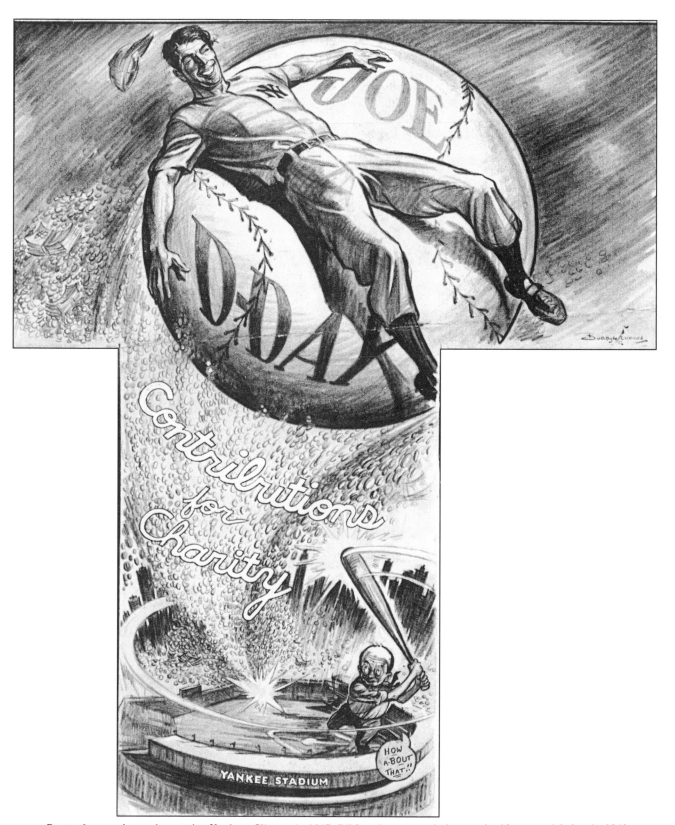

Poster from a day to honor the Yankee Clipper in 1947. DiMaggio was again honored with a special day in 1949.

SPORT

SEPTEMBER 25¢

ASEBALL · FOOTBALL · BOXING · SWIMMING · TENNIS · GOLF

DOM AND JOE DiMAGGIO

Hey DiMag! THE GREAT STORY OF TWO BROTHERS
BY TOM MEANY

I REMEMBER ★ IF YOU WERE
ROCKNE ★ JACKIE ROBINSON
BY GRANTLAND RICE ★ (SEE PAGE 40)

Homerless Series? Could Happen

By JOE KING

Beg pardon. Just came in and don't want to be a nuisance. But what this world series seems to need is a gent named Johnny Mize. Or Walker Cooper. Or Willard Marshall. Or Bob Thomson. In brief, a home run hitter, or to be briefer, a Giant. This is just the amazed conclusion of one who has ducked his head all season every time a Giant swung a bat.

But it does look like a homerless series. Think it couldn't happen?

Peewee Reese Jackie Robinson.

But it is a possibility. The Dodgers, for instance, actually went through a series without clocking one, in 1920, the year Elmer Smith hit the grand slam off Burleigh Grimes.

In fact, Brooklyn holds the all-time homerless title of world series history. In three tries, in modern times as they say, Brooklyn whacked only two. Hi Myers hit one off Babe Ruth in 1916. He socked it over the left field once in Boston and no one got any kind of run off the Babe for the ensuing 28 innings he pitched in world series games.

Nor did any Dodger put a ball out of the park in the 1941 series until Pete Reiser stung one over the scoreboard in Ebbets Field in the fifth inning of the fourth game that year, to give the Dodgers "victory" until that ball got away from Mickey Owen in the ninth.

Of course, the Yankees are another case of goods. Or another can of peas for the pitchers. Traditionally, that is, But the Yankees hit only two in 1941. Tommy Henrich and Joe Gordon lost the ball. No one else. No old-time Bomber show.

Coming up to 1947, and the chance for a homerless world series, let us look at the record. The Dodgers hit so few homers those blows seem to be strictly accidental. And the Yankees will play without their top man, Charlie Keller.

Brooklyn hit only 83 homers. You might say nine major leaguers, gathered at random, could do that by swinging the bat through 154 games. There are enough fat pitches thrown to do that almost blindfolded. All you have to do to concede that is to look at the leading Dodger homerists, Pee Wee Reese and Jackie Robinson, tied at 12, and neither bearing the faintest resemblance to a slugger. Dixie Walker slowed down to nine, and the wall must have taken something out of Reiser, who made only five.

The Yankees, with 115, don't look much better without Keller. Joe DiMaggio connected for 20, but we all know Joe will hit straightaway, and not give himself up trying to pull impossible pitches. That drops us down to Tommy Henrich, who figures to be the deadliest homer threat against that Dodger staff. But he hit only 16 this season. After that comes that magnificent relic, George McQuinn, with 13. After that, it's casual.

So it could be a homerless series. Even though the last such negation was in 1918, when the Cubs and Red Sox fought it out with hammerlocks.

And there could be a 1-0 game. What odds would you take against that? Be very careful. The last 1-0 game in world series history was in 1923, when Art Nehf knocked off Sad Sam Jones in the Stadium by that count.

And before you bet on a homer-

Tommy Henrich. Joe DiMaggio.

less series, reflect that Allie Reynolds and Ralph Branca, the top winners for each side, each allowed the handsome total of 23 homers for the season.

But as an old Giant man, those homer figures are depressing. Why, the Giants have four men, Mize, Cooper, Marshall and Thomson, who hit a total of 150, more than either series team. And the Giant club hit more, 221, than both series outfits combined.

Yes, we know where the Giants finished. But beg pardon, just came in.

Final Standings in Majors

NATIONAL LEAGUE.

	W.	L.	Pct.	G.B.
Brooklyn	94	60	.610	—
St. Louis	89	65	.578	5
Boston	86	68	.558	8
New York	81	73	.526	13
Cincinnati	73	81	.474	21
Chicago	69	85	.448	25
Philadelphia	62	92	.403	32
Pittsburgh	62	92	.403	32

Yesterday's Results.
Boston 3, Brooklyn 2.
Pittsburgh 7, Cincinnati 0.
Chicago 3, St. Louis 0.
New York 4, Philadelphia 1 (1st game).
Philadelphia 3, New York 1 (2nd game).

AMERICAN LEAGUE.

	W.	L.	Pct.	G.B.
New York	97	57	.630	—
Detroit	85	69	.552	12
Boston	83	71	.539	14
Cleveland	80	74	.519	17
Philadelphia	78	76	.506	19
Chicago	70	84	.455	27
Washington	64	90	.416	33
St. Louis	59	95	.383	38

Yesterday's Results.
New York 5, Philadelphia 2.
Washington 5, Boston 1.
Chicago 5, St. Louis 2.
Detroit 1, Cleveland 0.

And This Was '46 Finish

NATIONAL LEAGUE.

	W.	L.	Pct.	G.B.
St. Louis	*98	58	.628	—
Brooklyn	*96	60	.615	2
Chicago	82	71	.536	14½
Boston	81	72	.529	15½
Philadelphia	69	85	.448	28
Cincinnati	67	87	.435	30
Pittsburgh	63	91	.409	34
New York	61	93	.396	36

*Includes two playoff games.

AMERICAN LEAGUE.

	W.	L.	Pct.	G.B.
Boston	104	50	.675	—
Detroit	92	62	.597	12
New York	87	67	.565	17
Washington	76	78	.494	28
Chicago	74	80	.481	30
Cleveland	68	86	.442	36
St. Louis	66	88	.429	38
Philadelphia	49	105	.318	55

BASEBALL · BASEBALL

The Sporting News

THE BASE BALL PAPER OF THE WORLD
REG. U. S. PAT. OFF.

Section One — In Two Sections

VOLUME 124, NUMBER 8   ST. LOUIS, OCTOBER 1, 1947   ★ ★ ★   PRICE: TWENTY CENTS

YANKS PIT POWER AGAINST DODGER SPEED

Relief Aces Viewed as Big Factors

Championship Series Likely to Wind Up as Struggle of Reserve Strength

By STAN BAUMGARTNER
NEW YORK, N. Y.

Only a fellow with bats in his belfry would go out on the limb and predict the outcome of a World's Series in which the rival pilots did their last bits of managing for the Philadelphia Phillies.

That is the situation that pre-

Frank Shea

sents itself to anyone who would dare prognosticate the result of the 1947 classic. Bucky Harris, leader of the American League champions, the New York Yankees, piloted the Blue Jays in 1943 and Burt Shotton, manager of the Dodgers, was at the helm of the old Phils from 1928 to 1933.

Harris was in last place when relieved by Fred Fitzsimmons in 1943 and Shotton reached the first division (fourth place) in only one year—1932. All of which proves exactly nothing in view of what happened this season. For both have done tremendous 1947 jobs in the face of difficulties.

But the spectre of the old Phillies is only one of several unusual angles of the 1947 Series, the forty-fourth fall classic, in which the American League has won 26 previous engagements and the National League 17. It also is the second meeting between this year's opponents. The Yankees defeated the Dodgers four games to one in 1941. The Yanks have won 14 pennants and ten world's titles. Brooklyn has won four pennants since the World's Series was inaugurated, but never a world championship.

* * *

Neither Strong in Pitching

The present Series looks like a tossup. Neither manager has an outstanding pitching staff. Bucky Harris will depend on Frank Shea, Allie Reynolds, Bobo Newsom and Floyd Bevens—all right-

handers. Shotton will put his chips on Ralph Branca, Hal Gregg, Vic Lombardi, Joe Hatten and Harry Taylor (if his arm is okay). Hatten and Lombardi are lefthanders.

Each has superlative relief pitchers. The Yankees have the incomparable Joe Page, a southpaw; the Dodgers have Hugh Casey and Hank Behrman, both righthanders. And it is upon these men that the result of the Series may hang.

Pitching is 80 per cent of the Series and in this case there is no assurance that any one of the starting hurlers on either club will be able to finish what he begins. This means relief pitching and plenty of it.

It is a gag around the Yankees that they will win because Joe Page will win four and lose three. In Brooklyn the Dodgers say that Hugh Casey will win two, and so will Hank Behrman.

OFFICIAL PROGRAM. FIFTY CENTS

1947
WORLD SERIES

Dodgers
Yankees

2 Crosetti, coach   17 Raschi, p.   29 Lollar, c.
3 Clark, o.f.   18 Gumpert, p.   31 Corriden, coach
6 Brown, i.f.   19 Drews, p.   33 Schulte, coach
7 Dressen, coach   25 Wensloff, p.   36 Phillips, i.f.
12 Keller, o.f.   26 D. Johnson, p.   37 Harris, mgr.
14 Frey, i.f.

UMPIRES

American League   National League
William McGowan   Ralph Pinelli
Ed Rommel   Larry Goetz
Alternate—   Alternate—
   Jim Boyer   George Magerkurt

NEW YORK

1 Stirnweiss — second base
15 Henrich — right field
27 Lindell — left field
5 DiMaggio — center field
9 McQuinn — first base
21 Johnson, W. — third base
8 Robinson
32 Houk
35 Berra — catcher
10 Rizzuto — shortstop
22 Reynolds
34 Newsom
20 Shea
21 Chandler
16 Bevens
11 Page — pitchers

	1	2	3	4	5	6	7	8	9	10	AB	R	H	PO	A	E

Earned runs................ Two-base hits................ Three-base hits................ Home Runs................
Passed balls................ Wild pitches................ Bases on balls................ Bases on hit by pitcher................
Struck out................ Left on bases................ Double Plays................ Time................

MEET THE

PHIL RIZZUTO

JOE DIMAGGIO

Little Phil Rizzuto, a half-pint among Yankee bombers, was a product of New York's sandlots, captured by Paul Krichell in a Stadium tryout class. A minor league sensation, Phil moved into the big show in 1941 and immediately found himself in a World Series that Fall against the Dodgers. The Scooter is a double-play specialist—made five in one game in 1942, led the league's short-stops in that department in 1941 and '42. Served in the Navy (Pacific) three years, 1943 through 1945; thus this is his third World Series in four active years.

If, year in and year out, there is a more valuable player than Joltin' Joe DiMaggio, don't try to prove it to Yankee fans who have been following the fortunes of the Bronx Bombers since his arrival in 1936. Pennants followed immediately—1936, '37, '38, '39, '41 and '42, before Joe moved into the Army. Named the American League's Most Valuable Player in '39 and '41, the Yankee Clipper lists among his more outstanding accomplishments a 56-game hitting streak ('41); seven appearances in the annual All-Star games, a season's batting average of .381 ('39), 206 hits his first year in the majors, and more than 100 RBIs eight consecutive seasons. Joe is a ball player they'll remember long after incidents in this World Series are forgotten.

TOMMY HENRICH

GEORGE STIRNWEISS

"Old Reliable" and "The Clutch" are nicknames they've put on Tommy Henrich and Yankee fans know how richly he deserves them. Prolonging rallies or climaxing them is Tommy's forte. Town of Massillon, O., famous for its football, is proud of its No. 1 baseball son. Henrich is one of the game's most versatile stars— an excellent first baseman as well as one of the most capable out-fielders in the game. He even tried some left-handed shortstopping in the Coast Guard but, as Henrich tells it, "I was my own boss then—I was the manager." Off-field highlight—membership in Ohio's state championship Barber Shop quartet.

George (Snuffy) Stirnweiss is one of the game's most active men. As soon as the season is concluded, he takes up college basketball and football coaching duties. Then he is dean of a baseball school in Florida. Stirnweiss is another product of New York, having played on championship Fordham Prep teams (baseball and foot-ball) before moving to University of North Carolina for additional headlines. Stole 73 bases for Newark in 1942 and led the American League with 55 in 1944. Was the A.L.'s No. 1 hitter in 1945 and also was tops in hits, runs, total bases, triples, slugging percent-age and stolen bases the same season.

The Rookie of the Year in his only pre-war season, 1943, Billy Johnson batted .280 and drove in 94 runs. He returned to the Yankees after the '46 season was well under way and so he has the distinction of playing in the World Series and the All-Star game his only two full seasons. A native of Montclair, N. J., "The Bull," so dubbed because of his rugged build and strength, hit a cool .300 in the 1943 World Series triumph over St. Louis, including a double and triple among his half-dozen safeties.

At last George McQuinn plays for the Yankees in a World Series— something he dreamed about when he was in their farm system while the late Lou Gehrig held forth at the getaway station. Drafted out of the organization by the St. Louis Browns in 1938, McQuinn batted safely in 34 consecutive games that season and became recognized as one of the game's classiest first basemen. He finally made the World Series with the Browns of '44 and batted .438 in the classic. Traded to the Athletics, he was unconditionally released by Connie Mack and phoned Bucky Harris to ask him if the Yankees could use a first baseman. McQuinn's comeback is one of the most dramatic stories of the year.

BILLY JOHNSON

GEORGE McQUINN

Game 1 September 30 at New York

Brooklyn	Pos	AB	R	H	RBI	PO	A	E
Stanky	2b	4	0	1	0	0	4	0
J. Robinson	1b	2	1	0	0	8	1	0
Reiser	cf-lf	4	1	1	0	3	0	0
Walker	rf	4	0	2	1	1	0	0
Hermanski	lf	2	0	0	0	2	0	0
b Furillo	cf	1	0	1	1	2	0	0
Edwards	c	4	0	0	0	8	0	0
Jorgensen	3b	2	0	0	0	0	1	0
c Lavagetto	3b	2	0	0	0	1	0	0
Reese	ss	4	1	1	0	0	2	0
Branca	p	2	0	0	0	0	0	0
Behrman	p	0	0	0	0	0	1	0
d Miksis		1	0	0	0	0	0	0
Casey	p	0	0	0	0	0	0	0
Totals		32	3	6	2	24	9	0

a Walked for Shea in 5th.
b Singled for Hermanski in 6th.
c Popped out for Jorgensen in 7th.
d Struck out for Behrman in 7th.

Double—Lindell. Stolen Bases—Reese, Robinson. Double Play—Johnson to McQuinn. Hit by Pitcher—Johnson (by Branca). Wild Pitch—Page. Balk—Shea. Left on Bases—Brooklyn 5, New York 3. Umpires—McGowan (A), Pinelli (N), Rommel (A), Goetz (N), Magerkurth (N), Boyer (A). Attendance—73,365 (**A new Series record**). Time of Game—2:20.

Bkn.	1 0 0	0 0 1	1 0 0					3
N.Y.	0 0 0	0 5 0	0 0 x					5

New York	Pos	AB	R	H	RBI	PO	A	E
Stirnweiss	2b	4	0	0	0	3	1	0
Henrich	rf	4	0	1	2	3	0	0
Berra	c	4	0	0	0	5	0	0
DiMaggio	cf	4	1	1	0	2	0	0
McQuinn	1b	3	1	0	0	7	2	0
Johnson	3b	2	1	0	0	1	2	0
Lindell	lf	3	0	1	2	3	0	0
Rizzuto	ss	2	1	1	0	1	3	0
Shea	p	1	0	0	0	1	2	0
a Brown		0	1	0	1	0	0	0
Page	p	1	0	0	0	1	2	0
Totals		28	5	4	5	27	12	0

Pitching	IP	H	R	ER	BB	SO
Brooklyn						
Branca (L)	*4	2	5	5	3	5
Behrman	2	1	0	0	0	0
Casey	2	1	0	0	0	1
New York						
Shea (W)	5	2	1	1	2	3
Page (SV)	4	4	2	2	1	2

*Pitched to 6 batters in 5th.

1st Inning
Brooklyn
1 Stanky flied to left.
  Robinson walked.
    Robinson stole second.
  Reiser hit back to the box and Robinson
2   was trapped on a run-down between
    second and third, Shea to Rizzuto.
    Reiser got to second on the play.
  Walker singled to left, scoring Reiser.
3 Hermanski fanned.
New York
1 Stirnweiss grounded to second.
2 Henrich fanned.
3 Berra flied to center.

2nd Inning
Brooklyn
1 Edwards flied to deep center.
2 Jorgensen fanned.
3 Reese grounded to short.
New York
1 DiMaggio grounded to short.
2 McQuinn grounded to third.
3 Johnson grounded to second.

3rd Inning
Brooklyn
1 Branca grounded out, McQuinn to Shea.
2 Stanky rolled to Johnson.
  Robinson walked.
    Robinson went to second on Shea's
    balk.
3 Reiser flied to right.
New York
1 Lindell struck out.
2 Rizzuto flied to left.
3 Shea fanned.

4th Inning
Brooklyn
  Walker singled past first.
1,2 Hermanski lined to Johnson who threw
    to McQuinn to double up Walker.
3 Edwards flied to center.
New York
1 Stirnweiss took a called third strike.
2 Henrich flied to center.
3 Berra fanned.

5th Inning
Brooklyn
1 Jorgensen flied to left.
2 Reese grounded back to the mound.
3 Branca fanned.
New York
  DiMaggio was the first Yankee base-
  runner on a single to deep short.
  McQuinn walked.
  Johnson was hit by a pitch, loading
  the bases.
  Lindell doubled to left, scoring
  DiMaggio and McQuinn with Johnson
  stopping at third.

5th Inning (continued)
  Rizzuto walked to again fill the bases.
  Brown, pinch-hitting for Shea, got two
  balls when Branca was removed;
  For Brooklyn—Behrman pitching to Brown.
  Brown walked, forcing in Johnson.
1 Stirnweiss forced Lindell at the
  plate, Robinson to Edwards.
  Henrich singled to left, scoring
  Rizzuto and Brown.
2 Berra flied to right.
3 DiMaggio flied to left.

6th Inning
Brooklyn
  For New York—Page pitching.
  Stanky singled through the box.
1 Robinson forced Stanky at second,
  Rizzuto to Stirnweiss.
  Reiser singled to first when McQuinn
  missed the tag.
2 Walker flied to right.
  Furillo, pinch-hitting for Hermanski,
  singled to center, scoring Robinson
  with Reiser moving to third.
3 Edwards forced Furillo at second,
  Rizzuto to Stirnweiss.
New York
  For Brooklyn—Furillo in center with
  Reiser moving to left.
1 McQuinn fouled to Edwards.
2 Johnson flied to left.
3 Lindell grounded out, Behrman to
  Robinson.

7th Inning
Brooklyn
1 Lavagetto, batting for Jorgensen, popped
  to second.
  Reese singled to right.
2 Miksis, pinch-hitting for Behrman,
  fanned as Reese stole second.
    Reese scored from second on a wild-
    pitch by Page.
3 Stanky grounded out to the pitcher.
New York
  For Brooklyn—Lavagetto at third, Casey
  pitching.
  Rizzuto singled to left.
1 Page grounded to second.
2 Stirnweiss grounded to short, moving
  Rizzuto to third.
3 Henrich grounded to second.

8th Inning
Brooklyn
1 Robinson flied to left.
2 Reiser grounded out, McQuinn to Page.
3 Walker grounded to short.
New York
1 Berra flied to center.
2 DiMaggio flied to center.
3 McQuinn struck out.

9th Inning
Brooklyn
  Furillo walked.
1 Edwards flied to right.
2 Lavagetto fanned.
3 Reese bounced back to the mound.

Joe DiMaggio beats a pick-off throw by diving back to first in the 1947 World Series. The Dodgers' first baseman is former second baseman and future Hall of Famer, Jackie Robinson.

Game 2 October 1 at New York

Bkn.	0 0 1	1 0 0	0 0 1	3
N.Y.	1 0 1	1 2 1	4 0 x	10

Brooklyn	Pos	AB	R	H	RBI	PO	A	E
Stanky	2b	4	0	1	0	3	2	1
J. Robinson	1b	4	0	2	1	5	0	0
Reiser	cf	4	0	1	0	4	0	1
Walker	rf	4	1	1	1	1	0	0
Hermanski	lf	3	1	0	0	3	0	0
Edwards	c	4	0	1	0	5	1	0
Reese	ss	3	1	2	0	0	0	0
Jorgensen	3b	4	0	1	1	3	5	0
Lombardi	p	2	0	0	0	0	0	0
Gregg	p	0	0	0	0	0	2	0
a Vaughan		1	0	0	0	0	0	0
Behrman	p	0	0	0	0	0	0	0
Barney	p	0	0	0	0	0	0	0
b Gionfriddo		1	0	0	0	0	0	0
Totals		34	3	9	3	24	10	2

New York	Pos	AB	R	H	RBI	PO	A	E
Stirnweiss	2b	4	2	3	1	1	2	0
Henrich	rf	4	1	2	1	3	0	0
Lindell	lf	4	1	2	2	2	0	0
DiMaggio	cf	4	0	1	0	4	0	0
McQuinn	1b	5	1	2	1	6	1	0
Johnson	3b	5	2	2	0	1	2	0
Rizzuto	ss	5	0	1	1	3	4	0
Berra	c	3	1	0	0	6	1	1
Reynolds	p	4	2	2	1	1	0	0
Totals		38	10	15	7	27	10	1

Pitching	IP	H	R	ER	BB	SO
Brooklyn						
Lombardi (L)	*4	9	5	5	1	3
Gregg	2	2	1	1	1	2
Behrman	⅓	3	4	4	1	0
Barney	1⅔	1	0	0	1	0
New York						
Reynolds (W)	9	9	3	3	2	6

*Pitched to 2 batters in 5th.

a Flied out for Gregg in 7th.
b Grounded into force out for Barney in 9th.

Doubles—Lindell, Rizzuto, Robinson. Triples—Johnson, Lindell, Stirnweiss. Home Runs—Henrich, Walker. Stolen Base—Reese. Sacrifice Hit—Henrich. Double Plays—Jorgensen to Stanky to Robinson, Stirnweiss to Rizzuto to McQuinn. Wild Pitches—Barney, Behrman. Left on Bases—Brooklyn 6, New York 9. Umpires—Pinelli, Rommel, Goetz, McGowan, Boyer, Magerkurth. Attendance—69,865. Time of Game—2:36.

1st Inning
Brooklyn
1 Stanky fanned.
2 Robinson fanned.
3 Reiser flied to left.
New York
Stirnweiss singled to right.
Henrich singled to center, Stirnweiss going to third.
1,2 Lindell grounded into a double play, scoring Stirnweiss, Jorgensen to Stanky to Robinson.
DiMaggio singled off Reese's glove.
3 McQuinn struck out.

2nd Inning
Brooklyn
1 Walker lined to center.
2 Hermanski fouled to Johnson.
3 Edwards fanned.
New York
1 Johnson flied to right.
2 Rizzuto grounded to third on a bunt.
3 Berra grounded to second.

3rd Inning
Brooklyn
Reese walked.
1 Jorgensen flied to right.
2 Lombardi flied to center.
Reese stole second.
Stanky singled through the box, Reese going to third.
Robinson singled to left, scoring Reese and Stanky going to second.
3 Reiser struck out.
New York
1 Reynolds grounded to third.
Stirnweiss tripled to right-center.
2 Henrich fouled to Jorgensen.
Lindell tripled to center, scoring Stirnweiss.
DiMaggio got an intentional pass.
3 McQuinn fanned.

4th Inning
Brooklyn
Walker homered into the lower right field stands (on the first pitch).
1 Hermanski grounded out, McQuinn to Reynolds.
2 Edwards popped to first.
Reese singled to right.
3 Reese caught stealing, Berra to Rizzuto.
New York
Johnson tripled to center.
Rizzuto's short fly to left dropped in for a double, scoring Johnson.
1 Berra flied to center, Rizzuto moving to third after the catch.
On Reynolds' hit to Jorgensen, Rizzuto
2 was trapped in a run-down between third and home, out Edwards to Jorgensen. Reynolds took second on the play.
3 Stirnweiss fanned.

5th Inning
Brooklyn
1 Jorgensen fanned.
2 Lombardi grounded to short.
3 Stanky grounded to short.
New York
Henrich homered into the right-center field bleachers.
Lindell bounced a ground-rule double into the lower left field stands.
For Brooklyn—Gregg pitching with a 1-0 count to DiMaggio.
1 DiMaggio grounded to third, Lindell holding second.
McQuinn singled to center, Lindell scoring.
Johnson safe at first when Stanky dropped Gregg's throw to force McQuinn
2 Rizzuto flied to deep center
3 Berra fanned.

6th Inning
Brooklyn
1 Robinson flied to center.
Reiser singled to left.
2,3 Walker hit into a double play, Stirnweiss to Rizzuto to McQuinn.
New York
Reynolds singled to left.
Stirnweiss walked.
1 Henrich sacrificed, Gregg to Stanky, advancing both runners.
2 Lindell flied to left, Reynolds scoring after the catch.
3 DiMaggio took a called third strike.

7th Inning
Brooklyn
1 Hermanski called out on strikes
Edwards singled to right.
2 Reese flied to right.
Jorgensen got to first on a single in front of the plate with Edwards going to third on Berra's wild throw.
3 Vaughan, pinch-hitting for Gregg, flied to center.
New York
For Brooklyn—Behrman pitching.
McQuinn singled to right.
McQuinn to second on a wild pitch.
Johnson singled to center, scoring McQuinn and going all the way to third as Reiser lost the ball.
1 Rizzuto popped to second
Berra intentionally walked.
Reynolds singled on a squeeze bunt, scoring Johnson and moving Berra to third.
For Brooklyn—Barney pitching.
Stirnweiss singled to first, scoring Berra.
2 Henrich flied to center, Reynolds to third after the catch
Reynolds scored on a wild pitch, and Stirnweiss to second.
Lindell walked.
3 DiMaggio forced Stirnweiss at third, Jorgensen unassisted.

8th Inning
Brooklyn
1 Stanky grounded to third.
Robinson doubled to left.
2 Reiser flied to right.
3 Walker rolled to short.
New York
1 McQuinn flied to left.
2 Johnson flied to center.
3 Rizzuto flied to left.

9th Inning
Brooklyn
Hermanski walked.
1 Edwards flied to left.
Reese singled past short, Hermanski moving to third.
2 Jorgensen forced Reese at second, scoring Hermanski, Stirnweiss to Rizzuto.
3 Gionfriddo, pinch-hitting for Barney, forced Jorgensen at second, Johnson to Stirnweiss.

Joe DiMaggio

by Red Smith
from *The Red Smith Reader*, Random House, New York, 1982

1947

After the Yankees chewed up the Dodgers in the second game of the World Series, Joe DiMaggio relaxed in the home club's gleaming tile boudoir and deposed at length in defense of Pete Reiser, the Brooklyn center fielder, who had narrowly escaped being smitten upon the isthmus rhombencephali that day by sundry fly balls.

The moving, mottled background of faces and shirt collars and orchids, Joe said, made a fly almost invisible until it had cleared the top deck. The tricky, slanting shadows of an October afternoon created a problem involving calculus, metaphysics, and social hygiene when it came to judging a line drive. The roar of the crowd disguised the crack of bat against ball. And so on.

Our Mr. Robert Cooke, listening respectfully as one should to the greatest living authority on the subject, nevertheless stared curiously at DiMaggio. He was thinking that not only Reiser but also J. DiMaggio had played that same center field on that same afternoon, and there were no knots on Joe's slick coiffure.

"How about you, Joe?" Bob asked. "Do those same factors handicap you out there?"

DiMaggio permitted himself one of his shy, toothy smiles.

"Don't start worrying about the old boy after all these years," he said.

He didn't say "the old master." That's a phrase for others to use. But it would be difficult to define more aptly than Joe did the difference between this unmitigated pro and all the others, good, bad, and ordinary, who also play in major-league outfields.

There is a line that has been quoted so often the name of its originator has been lost. But whoever said it first was merely reacting impulsively to a particular play and not trying to coin a mot when he ejaculated: "The sonofagun! Ten years I've been watching him, and he hasn't had a hard chance yet!"

It may be that Joe is not, ranked on his defensive skill alone, the finest center fielder of his time. Possibly Terry Moore was his equal playing the hitter, getting the jump on the ball, judging a fly, covering ground, and squeezing the ball once he touched it.

Joe himself has declared that his kid brother, Dominic, is a better fielder than he. Which always recalls the occasion when the Red Sox were playing the Yanks and Dom fled across the county line to grab a drive by Joe that no one but a DiMaggio could have reached. And the late Sid Mercer, shading his thoughtful eyes under a hard straw hat, remarked to the press box at large: "Joe should sue his old man on that one."

Joe hasn't been the greatest hitter that baseball has known, either. He'll not match Ty Cobb's lifetime average, he'll never threaten Babe Ruth's home-run record, nor will he ever grip the imagination of the crowds as the Babe did. Or even as Babe Herman did. That explains why the contract that he signed the other day calls for an estimated $65,000 instead of the $80,000 that Ruth got. If he were not such a matchless craftsman he might be a more spectacular player. And so, perhaps, more colorful. And so more highly rewarded.

But you don't rate a great ballplayer according to his separate, special talents. You must rank him off the sum total of his component parts, and on this basis there has not been, during Joe's big-league existence, a rival close to him. None other in his time has combined such savvy and fielding and hitting and throwing—Tom Laird, who was writing sports in San Francisco when Joe was growing up, always insisted that a sore arm "ruined" DiMaggio's throwing in his first season with the Yankees—and such temperament and such base running.

Because he does so many other things so well and makes no specialty of stealing, DiMaggio rarely has received full credit for his work on the bases. But travel with a second-division club in the league for a few seasons and count the times when DiMaggio, representing the tying or winning run, whips you by coming home on the unforeseen gamble and either beats the play or knocks the catcher into the dugout.

Ask American League catchers about him, or National Leaguers like Ernie Lombardi. Big Lom will remember who it was who ran home from first base in the last game of the 1939 World Series while Ernie lay threshing in the dust behind the plate and Bucky Walters stood bemused on the mound.

These are the reasons why DiMaggio, excelled by Ted Williams in all offensive statistics and reputedly Ted's inferior in crowd appeal and financial standing, still won the writers' accolade as the American League's most valuable in 1947.

It wasn't the first time Williams earned this award with his bat and lost it with his disposition. As a matter of fact, if all other factors were equal save only the question of character, Joe never would lose out to any player. The guy who came out of San Francisco as a shy lone wolf, suspicious of Easterners and of Eastern writers, today is the top guy in any sports gathering in any town. The real champ.

Game 3 October 2 at Brooklyn

N Y	0 0 2	2 2 1	1 0 0		8
Bkn.	0 6 1	2 0 0	0 0 x		9

New York	Pos	AB	R	H	RBI	PO	A	E
Stirnweiss	2b	5	0	2	1	2	3	0
Henrich	rf	4	0	1	1	0	0	0
Lindell	lf	4	1	2	1	0	0	0
DiMaggio	cf	4	1	2	3	3	0	0
McQuinn	1b	4	0	0	0	8	1	0
Johnson	3b	4	1	1	0	2	1	0
Rizzuto	ss	5	0	1	0	5	2	0
Lollar	c	3	2	2	1	2	1	0
e Berra	c	2	1	1	1	2	0	0
Newsom	p	0	0	0	0	0	1	0
Raschi	p	0	0	0	0	0	0	0
b Clark		0	1	0	0	0	0	0
Drews	p	0	0	0	0	0	2	0
c Phillips		1	0	0	0	0	0	0
Chandler	p	0	0	0	0	0	0	0
d Brown		1	1	1	0	0	0	0
Page	p	1	0	0	0	0	0	0
Totals		38	8	13	8	24	11	0

a Doubled for Reiser in 2nd.
b Walked for Raschi in 3rd.
c Flied out for Drews in 4th.
d Doubled for Chandler in 6th.
e Homered for Lollar in 7th.

Brooklyn	Pos	AB	R	H	RBI	PO	A	E
Stanky	2b	4	2	1	2	4	5	0
J. Robinson	1b	4	1	2	0	10	1	0
Reiser	cf	0	0	0	0	0	0	0
a Furillo	cf	3	1	2	2	0	0	1
Walker	rf	5	0	2	1	1	0	0
Hermanski	lf	3	2	1	1	4	0	0
Edwards	c	4	1	1	1	5	0	0
Reese	ss	3	1	1	1	1	3	0
Jorgensen	3b	4	0	2	1	1	3	0
Hatten	p	2	1	1	0	0	0	0
Branca	p	1	0	0	0	0	0	0
Casey	p	1	0	0	0	1	1	0
Totals		34	9	13	9	27	13	1

Pitching	IP	H	R	ER	BB	SO
New York						
Newsom (L)	$1\frac{2}{3}$	5	5	5	2	0
Raschi	$\frac{1}{3}$	2	1	1	0	0
Drews	1	1	1	1	0	0
Chandler	2	2	2	2	3	1
Page	3	3	0	0	1	3
Brooklyn						
Hatten	$4\frac{1}{3}$	8	6	6	3	3
Branca	2	4	2	2	2	1
Casey (W)	$2\frac{2}{3}$	1	0	0	1	1

Doubles—Brown, Edwards, Furillo, Henrich, Jorgensen, Lollar, Stanky. Home Runs—Berra, DiMaggio. Stolen Bases—Robinson, Walker. Sacrifice Hit—Robinson. Double Plays—Reese to Stanky to Robinson, Stanky to Robinson. Passed Ball—Lollar. Hit by Pitch—Hermanski (by Drews). Wild Pitches—Drews, Page. Left on Bases—New York 9, Brooklyn 9. Umpires—Rommel, Goetz, McGowan, Pinelli, Magerkurth, Boyer. Attendance—33,098. Time of Game—3:05.

1st Inning
New York
Stirnweiss singled to right.
1,2 Henrich grounded into a double play Reese to Stanky to Robinson
3 Lindell grounded to third.
Brooklyn
1 Stanky grounded back to the mound
Robinson singled to center
Robinson stole second on Lollar's low
2 throw but was out as he overran the bag, Stirnweiss to Rizzuto
Reiser walked.
3 Reiser got caught stealing, Lollar to Rizzuto.

2nd Inning
New York
1 DiMaggio popped to short.
2 McQuinn called out on strikes
Johnson singled to right.
3 Rizzuto grounded to third.
Brooklyn
1 Walker grounded to short
Hermanski walked.
Edwards doubled, Hermanski scoring.
Reese singled to center, scoring Edwards.
2 Jorgensen flied to center
Hatten singled to left, Reese at second
Reese went to third and Hatten to second on Lollar's passed ball
Stanky doubled to right, scoring Reese and Hatten.
For New York—Raschi pitching
Robinson singled, moving Stanky to third.
Furillo, pinch-hitting for Reiser, doubled off the scoreboard, scoring Stanky and Robinson.
3 Walker grounded to short.

3rd Inning
New York
For Brooklyn—Furillo playing center
Lollar singled to center.
Clark, batting for Raschi, walked
1 Stirnweiss took a called third strike.
2 Henrich flied to left.
Lindell singled to center, Lollar scoring and Clark stopping at second
DiMaggio singled, scoring Clark
3 McQuinn fanned.
Brooklyn
For New York—Drews pitching
Hermanski hit by a pitch.
Hermanski to second on a wild pitch.
1 Edwards grounded to Drews, Hermanski to third.
2 Reese also grounded to Drews.
Jorgensen singled, Hermanski scoring.
3 Hatten forced Jorgenson at second, Rizzuto to Stirnweiss.

4th Inning
New York
Johnson walked.
1 Rizzuto flied to left.
Lollar doubled to right, Johnson scoring.
2 Phillips, pinch-hitting for Drews, flied to left.
Stirnweiss singled to center to score Lollar and took second as Furillo threw past Edwards for an error
3 Henrich grounded to second.
Brooklyn
For New York—Chandler pitching.
Stanky walked.
1 Robinson sacrificed Stanky to second, McQuinn to Stirnweiss.
Furillo walked.
Walker singled to center, Stanky scoring with Furillo going to third
Hermanski singled to center, scoring Furillo with Walker stopping at second.
2 Edwards fanned.
Reese walked, loading the bases
3 Jorgensen grounded easily to first.

5th Inning
New York
Lindell walked.
DiMaggio hit a two-run homer into the upper left field deck
1 McQuinn grounded to third
For Brooklyn—Branca pitching.
2 Johnson fanned.
Rizzuto singled past first
3 Lollar forced Rizzuto at second, Reese to Stanky.
Brooklyn
1 Branca lined to third
2 Stanky popped to short
3 Robinson popped to short.

6th Inning
New York
Brown, pinch-hitting for Chandler, doubled to right.
1 Stirnweiss grounded to short, Brown moving over to third.
Henrich doubled off Stanky's glove to score Brown
2 Lindell fouled to Jorgensen.
DiMaggio walked.
McQuinn walked to load the bases.
3 Johnson popped to second.
Brooklyn
For New York—Page is the fifth pitcher.
Furillo singled to right.
1 Walker forced Furillo in an attempted sacrifice, Johnson to Rizzuto.
2 Hermanski popped to third.
Walker stole second.
Edwards walked.
3 Reese called out on strikes.

7th Inning
New York
1 Rizzuto flied to left.
Berra, pinch-hitting for Lollar, homered into the scoreboard.
For Brooklyn—Casey pitching.
2 Page grounded to short.
3 Stirnweiss took a called third strike.
Brooklyn
For New York—Berra stayed in to catch.
Jorgensen doubled to right.
1 Casey fanned.
2 Stanky popped to first.
3 Robinson flied to center.

8th Inning
New York
Henrich walked.
Lindell singled to center, Henrich stopping at second.
1,2 DiMaggio grounded into a double play, Stanky tagging Lindell and throwing to first getting DiMaggio. Henrich to third on the double killing.
3 McQuinn grounded to first.
Brooklyn
1 Furillo grounded to short.
Walker singled to left.
Walker to second on a wild pitch.
2 Hermanski took a called third strike.
3 Edwards flied to center.

9th Inning
New York
1 Johnson grounded out, Robinson to Casey who covered first.
2 Rizzuto flied to right
3 Berra grounded out off Casey's glove to Stanky who threw to Robinson

DiMag Extols Casey's Great Relief Job

By JOE KING,
Staff Writer.

EBBETS FIELD, Oct. 3.—Wild Bill Halloran dropped in on the Yankees before today's game, and Chuck Dressen said, "I wish we had that guy pitching for us." The remark typified the sentiments of all hands in this series. Everybody is looking for a pitcher.

The Yankees talked about Joe Page and Hugh Casey with great respect. The performance of these two great relief pitchers yesterday was the highlight of the series to the players.

Joe Di Maggio explained his fatal double play grounder off Casey. "The trouble was he was getting that curve ball over the plate every time. The hitter didn't have any hope he would miss, and he had no leeway to let one go. The hitter had to be ready to go for anything, and any time a pitcher has you that way, you have very little chance. He doesn't have to come in with the fast ball, which is the hitter's best chance."

The Yankees, incidentally, have the greatest respect for the Dodgers, and have had from the start of the series. They have not at any time knocked down any Dodger. There are enough good pros among the Yankees who know no team can be taken lightly.

Tommy Henrich spoke admiringly of that six-run Brooklyn inning yesterday. "I have been in on quite a few of those big innings as a Yankee, and there is no bigger thrill. A club that gets hot like that is awful hard to stop. Sometimes it doesn't matter what pitcher comes in against them. Even a star will be batted down just like a fair-to-middling pitcher. I often wonder why a team in a hot inning doesn't go on for 10 or 12 runs. When you are in it there is a feeling nothing can stop you."

In the third game of the 1947 World Series, Joe DiMaggio crosses home plate after whacking a two-run homer. Despite the blast, the Yankees lost to the Brooklyn Dodgers, 9–8. Greeting the Clipper is Johnny Lindell (27), who scored on the home run. Also in the picture are Yankee first baseman George McQuinn (9), Brooklyn catcher Bruce Edwards, and umpire Ed Rommel.

Game 4 October 3 at Brooklyn

New York	Pos	AB	R	H	RBI	PO	A	E
Stirnweiss	2b	4	1	2	0	2	1	0
Henrich	rf	5	0	1	0	2	0	0
Berra	c	4	0	0	0	6	1	1
DiMaggio	cf	2	0	0	1	2	0	0
McQuinn	1b	4	0	1	0	7	0	0
Johnson	3b	4	1	1	0	3	2	0
Lindell	lf	3	0	2	1	3	0	0
Rizzuto	ss	4	0	1	0	1	2	0
Bevens	p	3	0	0	0	0	1	0
Totals		33	2	8	2	*26	7	1

* Two out when winning run was scored.
a Walked for Gregg in 7th.
b Ran for Furillo in 9th.
c Walked for Casey in 9th.
d Ran for Reiser in 9th.
e Doubled for Stanky in 9th.

Doubles—Lavagetto, Lindell.
Triple—Johnson. Stolen Bases—Gionfriddo,
Reese, Rizzuto. Sacrifice Hits—Bevens,
Stanky. Double Plays—Reese to Stanky to
Robinson, Gregg to Reese to Robinson,
Casey to Edwards to Robinson.
Wild Pitch—Bevens. Left on Bases—
New York 9, Brooklyn 8. Umpires—Goetz,
McGowan, Pinelli, Rommel, Boyer, Mager-
kurth. Attendance—
33,443.
Time of Game—2:20.

1st Inning
New York
Stirnweiss singled to left.
Henrich singled through the box with
Stirnweiss stopping at second.
Berra safe at first on his hit to
Robinson who tried to start a DP but
Reese dropped the ball to load the
bases.
DiMaggio walked, forcing in Stirnweiss.
For Brooklyn—Gregg pitching.
1 McQuinn popped to short.
2,3 Johnson hit into a double play,
Reese to Stanky to Robinson.
Brooklyn
Stanky walked
1 Reese grounded to second, with Stanky
going to second.
2 Robinson grounded to third, Stanky holding
Walker walked.
3 Hermanski fouled to Johnson.

2nd Inning
New York
1 Lindell grounded to short.
Rizzuto singled to left.
Rizzuto stole second.
2 Bevens flied to center.
3 Stirnweiss struck out.
Brooklyn
1 Edwards fanned.
2 Furillo grounded to Rizzuto.
Jorgensen walked.
3 Gregg struck out.

3rd Inning
New York
1 Henrich struck out.
2 Berra grounded to first.
DiMaggio walked.
McQuinn singled in front of the plate
and went all the way to second on
Edward's wild throw but DiMaggio was
3 out trying to score on the error.
Walker to Edwards.
Brooklyn
Stanky walked.
1 Reese flied to left.
Stanky went to second on a wild
pitch.
2 Robinson fouled deep to Lindell.
3 Walker popped to third.

4th Inning
New York
Johnson tripled to center.
Lindell doubled to right to score
Johnson.
1,2 Rizzuto grounded to first with Lindell
going to third.
2 Bevens grounded to short.
3 Stirnweiss called out on strikes.
Brooklyn
1 Hermanski flied to center.
2 Edwards took a called third strike.
3 Furillo fouled to Berra.

5th Inning
New York
1 Henrich grounded to short.
2 Berra grounded to second.
3 DiMaggio popped to second.

	N.Y.	1 0 0	1 0 0	0 0 0	2
	Bkn.	0 0 0	0 1 0	0 0 2	3

Brooklyn	Pos	AB	R	H	RBI	PO	A	E
Stanky	2b	1	0	0	0	2	3	0
e Lavagetto		1	0	1	2	0	0	0
Reese	ss	4	0	0	1	3	5	1
J. Robinson	1b	4	0	0	0	11	1	0
Walker	rf	2	0	0	0	0	1	0
Hermanski	lf	4	0	0	0	2	0	0
Edwards	c	4	0	0	0	7	1	1
Furillo	cf	3	0	0	0	2	0	0
b Gionfriddo		0	1	0	0	0	0	0
Jorgensen	3b	2	1	0	0	0	1	1
Taylor	p	0	0	0	0	0	0	0
Gregg	p	1	0	0	0	0	1	0
a Vaughan		0	0	0	0	0	0	0
Behrman	p	0	0	0	0	0	1	0
Casey	p	0	0	0	0	0	0	0
c Reiser		0	1	0	0	0	0	0
d Miksis		0	1	0	0	0	0	0
Totals		26	3	1	3	27	15	3

Pitching	IP	H	R	ER	BB	SO
New York						
Bevens (L)	9	1	3	3	10	5
Brooklyn						
Taylor	**0	2	1	0	1	0
Gregg	7	4	1	1	3	5
Behrman	1⅓	2	0	0	0	0
Casey (W)	⅔	0	0	0	0	0

**Pitched to four batters in 1st.

5th Inning (continued)
Brooklyn
Jorgensen walked.
Gregg walked.
1 Stanky sacrificed up both runners, Berra
to Stirnweiss.
2 Reese safe on a fielder's choice as
Rizzuto got Gregg at third with
Jorgensen scoring on the play
Reese stole second and continued on
to third on Berra's wild throw.
3 Robinson fanned.

6th Inning
New York
1 McQuinn called out on strikes
2 Johnson flied to left.
3 Rizzuto flied to center.
Brooklyn
Walker walked.
1 Hermanski popped to second.
2 Edwards fanned.
3 Furillo flied to right.

7th Inning
New York
1 Bevens fanned.
Stirnweiss walked.
2,3 Henrich grounded into a double play.
Gregg to Reese to Robinson.
Brooklyn
1 Jorgensen lined to center
Vaughan, pinch-hitting for Gregg, walked.
2 Stanky popped to short.
3 Reese grounded to first.

8th Inning
New York
For Brooklyn—Behrman pitching.
1 Berra grounded to second.
DiMaggio safe at first on Jorgensen's
fumble
2 McQuinn flied to left.
3 Johnson grounded to third.
Brooklyn
1 Robinson grounded to third.
2 Walker grounded back to the mound.
3 Hermanski flied to right.

9th Inning
New York
Lindell singled past third.
1 Rizzuto forced Lindell at second,
Behrman to Reese.
Bevens sacrificed and was safe at first
when Edwards' throw to get Rizzuto
was not in time.
Stirnweiss singled to center, loading
the bases.
For Brooklyn—Casey now pitching.
2,3 Henrich grounded into a double play
on the first pitch, Casey to Edwards
to Robinson.
Brooklyn
1 Edwards flied to very deep center.
Furillo walked.
2 Jorgensen fouled to McQuinn.
Gionfriddo ran for Furillo.
Reiser was batting for Casey, while
Gionfriddo stole second.
Reiser intentionally walked.
Miksis ran for Reiser.
Lavagetto, pinch-hitting for Stanky,
doubled off the right field wall to
score Gionfriddo and Miksis with the
winning runs. **The first and only hit
allowed by Bevens.**

Game 5 October 4 at Brooklyn

New York	Pos	AB	R	H	RBI	PO	A	E
Stirnweiss	2b	3	0	0	0	3	4	0
Henrich	rf	4	0	2	0	1	0	0
Lindell	lf	2	0	0	0	3	0	0
DiMaggio	cf	4	1	1	1	3	0	0
McQuinn	1b	4	0	0	0	7	0	0
Johnson	3b	3	0	0	0	2	1	0
A. Robinson	c	3	1	0	0	7	0	0
Rizzuto	ss	2	0	0	0	1	1	0
Shea	p	4	0	2	1	0	1	0
Totals		29	2	5	2	27	7	0

a Walked for Hatten in 6th.
b Doubled for Behrman in 7th.
c Walked for Stanky in 7th.
d Ran for Reiser in 7th.
e Ran for Edwards in 9th.
f Fanned for Casey in 9th.

Doubles—Henrich, Shea, Vaughan.
Home Run—DiMaggio. Sacrifice
Hit—Furillo. Double Plays—Reese to
Stanky to J. Robinson, Reese to Miksis to
J. Robinson. Passed Balls—Edwards 2.
Hit by Pitcher—Lindell (by Casey).
Wild Pitch—Barney. Left on Bases—New
York 11, Brooklyn 8. Umpires—McGowen,
Pinelli, Rommel, Goetz, Magerkurth,
Boyer. Attendance—34,379.
Time of Game—2:46.

1st Inning
New York
Stirnweiss walked.
Henrich doubled to right-center,
Stirnweiss stopping at third.
Lindell walked, loading the bases.
1 DiMaggio struck out.
2 McQuinn forced Stirnweiss at the plate.
Barney to Edwards.
3 Johnson fanned.
Brooklyn
1 Stanky grounded to second.
2 Reese fouled to Johnson.
3 J. Robinson grounded to third.

2nd Inning
New York
1 A. Robinson flied to center.
Rizzuto walked.
Rizzuto went to second on a
wild pitch.
2 Rizzuto out trying to steal third.
Edwards to Jorgensen.
3 Shea lined to third.
Brooklyn
1 Walker lined to second.
2 Hermanski flied to left.
3 Edwards struck out.

3rd Inning
New York
1 Stirnweiss lined to center.
Henrich walked.
Lindell walked.
2,3 DiMaggio grounded into a double play.
Reese to Stanky to J. Robinson.
Brooklyn
1 Furillo popped to second.
2 Jorgensen struck out.
3 Barney grounded to second.

4th Inning
New York
1 McQuinn flied to left.
2 Johnson struck out.
A. Robinson walked.
Rizzuto walked.
Shea singled to left, scoring A. Robinson
with Rizzuto stopping at second.
Stirnweiss walked, loading the bases.
3 Henrich grounded to second.
Brooklyn
1 Stanky flied to center.
Reese walked.
2 J. Robinson popped to first.
3 Walker grounded to second.

5th Inning
New York
1 Lindell grounded to short.
DiMaggio homered into the left field
stands.
2 McQuinn popped to second.
Johnson walked.
For Brooklyn—Hatten pitching.
3 A. Robinson popped to third.
Brooklyn
Hermanski singled to right.
1 Edwards lined to left.
2 Furillo popped to second.
3 Jorgensen fanned.

	N.Y.	0 0 0	1 1 0	0 0 0	2
	Bkn.	0 0 0	0 0 1	0 0 0	1

Brooklyn	Pos	AB	R	H	RBI	PO	A	E
Stanky	2b	3	0	0	0	2	2	0
c Reiser		0	0	0	0	0	0	0
d Miksis	2b	0	0	0	0	1	1	1
Reese	ss	2	0	0	0	2	3	0
J. Robinson	1b	4	0	1	1	5	0	0
Walker	rf	4	0	0	0	1	0	0
Hermanski	lf	4	0	1	0	2	0	0
Edwards	c	3	0	1	0	9	2	0
e Lombardi		0	0	0	0	0	0	0
Furillo	cf	3	0	0	0	2	0	0
Jorgensen	3b	4	0	0	0	3	0	0
Barney	p	1	0	0	0	0	1	0
Hatten	p	0	0	0	0	0	0	0
a Gionfriddo		0	1	0	0	0	0	0
Behrman	p	0	0	0	0	0	1	0
b Vaughan		1	0	1	0	0	0	0
Casey	p	0	0	0	0	1	0	0
f Lavagetto		1	0	0	0	0	0	0
Totals		30	1	4	1	27	10	1

Pitching	IP	H	R	ER	BB	SO
New York						
Shea (W)	9	4	1	1	5	7
Brooklyn						
Barney (L)	4⅓	3	2	2	9	3
Hatten	1⅓	0	0	0	1	1
Behrman	1	1	0	0	1	2
Casey	2	1	0	0	0	1

6th Inning
New York
1 Rizzuto popped to short.
2 Shea fanned.
3 Stirnweiss fouled to Edwards.
Brooklyn
Gionfriddo pinch-hitting for Hatten,
walked.
1 Stanky fanned.
Reese walked.
J. Robinson singled to center, scoring
Gionfriddo with Reese going to
third. Robinson to second on
DiMaggio's throw to third.
2 Walker fouled to Johnson.
3 Hermanski flied to center.

7th Inning
New York
For Brooklyn—Behrman pitching.
Henrich singled to center.
1 Lindell fanned.
DiMaggio walked.
2 McQuinn struck out but Edwards let the
ball go through him to advance
Henrich and DiMaggio (a passed ball).
3 Johnson grounded back to the mound.
Brooklyn
Edwards walked.
1 Furillo flied to center.
2 Jorgensen flied to left.
Vaughan, pinch-hitting for Behrman,
doubled to right, sending Edwards
to third.
Reiser, batting for Stanky, got an
intentional walk.
Miksis ran for Reiser.
3 Reese took a called third strike.

8th Inning
New York
For Brooklyn—Casey pitching and Miksis
playing second.
1 A. Robinson popped to short.
2 Rizzuto lined to left.
Shea doubled to left.
Shea to third on a passed ball.
3 Stirnweiss fanned.
Brooklyn
1 J. Robinson fanned.
2 Walker grounded to short.
3 Hermanski grounded to second.

9th Inning
New York
Henrich safe at first on Miksis' error.
Lindell hit by a pitched ball.
1,2 DiMaggio grounded into a double play,
Reese to Miksis to J. Robinson with
Henrich to third.
3 Henrich out trying to score on a
passed ball, Edwards to Casey.
Brooklyn
Edwards singled to left.
Lombardi ran for Edwards.
1 Furillo sacrificed Lombardi to second,
Shea to Stirnweiss.
2 Jorgensen flied to right.
3 Lavagetto, pinch-hitting for Casey,
fanned.

LAVAGETTO FAILS TO REPEAT AS HERO

'Didn't Have It in Me,' He Says About Strike-Out in Ninth by Shea of the Yanks

SEES NO ONUS ON FURILLO

Shotton of Dodgers Writes Off His Inability to Advance Edwards With Bunt

By ROSCOE McGOWEN

Cookie Lavagetto's return to the clubhouse after yesterday's bitter loss to the Yankees was vastly different from his triumphal entrance the day before.

In common with nearly all the Dodgers, the Oakland, Calif., veteran had his head down and his expression was quite unhappy.

"Where was that bolt of lightning today, Cookie?" one writer asked him, thereby bringing the first grin to Cookie's face.

"I didn't have it in me, I guess," he replied. "That three-and-one pitch from Shea was the big one," he went on, "but I fouled it."

It would be superfluous to point out that had Lavagetto connected for a hit for the second straight day as a ninth-inning pinch hitter he would have owned Borough Hall and half of Brooklyn today.

Brooks Still Confident

But neither Cookie nor any of his mates were "down" about the defeat in the fifth game.

"We'll beat that Reynolds tomorrow," growled Fireman Hugh Casey. "You can bet your life on that."

"I'd like to know where they got all that stuff about the Yankees slaughtering us in a world series," said Eddie Stanky.

"I don't see any slaughter going on. They can boast about a little power, but what about the rest of it? In base running, for instance, they're not even close to us."

Manager Barney Shotton wasn't inclined to put any blame on Carl Furillo for failing to achieve a sacrifice in the seventh inning, which Bruce Edwards had opened with a walk.

"You can't be sure what would have happened after that," said Shotton. "Vaughan might not have got the same pitch to hit."

Failure to Bunt Fatal

But several of the Dodgers had their minds on that bunt, including Carl himself. They felt that had Edwards been on second base with only one out they at least would have tied the score. "We'd be out there playing right now, at least," was Stanky's comment.

Perhaps the biggest "out" Spec Shea got was Dixie Walker in the Dodgers' scoring sixth. Peewee Reese was on third base and a reasonably long fly ball by Walker would have turned the trick. But there were many "might-have-beens" in a game as close as that one.

If Rex Barney, the tall youngster who turned in such a remarkable performance for three innings, considering his wildness, had been able to make the same pitch to Joe DiMaggio he had made twice before—to get DiMag on strikes and to ground into a double play—the story would have had a different ending.

DiMaggio Hit High Pitch

"I threw him a low fast ball when I struck him out and the same thing when he hit into the double play," said Rex. "But the one he hit into the stands was up here"—and he gestured to indicate a pitch about letter high.

"You know," added Barney, somewhat wistfully, "that's my first start since July 4."

Clyde Sukeforth, when asked what he had been saying to Barney when he made a trip to the mound in the third inning, said:

"I just told him to stop aiming the ball, because that's why he wasn't getting it over."

The scene in Doc Wendler's "radio room" was much the same as on the previous day—but it didn't have the same happy ending.

Little Al Gionfriddo, whose theft of second base, according to Shotton, was the key play of the winning frame, was perched on a rubbing table listening to the final description by Mel Allen.

Homer That Never Came

He watched a scribe putting down the plays in his scorebook and, leaning forward, said softly: "Go on—put down a home run for Cookie. He's gonna get it."

But when he heard that Cookie had fouled the three-and-one swing, the hopefulness in his black eyes dimmed a bit—and faded completely when Cookie had swung in vain for the final out.

Other players who had been listening filed out slowly, headed for their lockers or the showers, and nobody had much to say. Losing ball teams don't like to talk too much about it immediately after a defeat. They'll say plenty the following week or the following year.

Shotton retained his smile, although it wasn't the wide, ear-threatening one he wore while hugging Lavagetto the previous afternoon.

Asked about his pitching plans for the Stadium today, Barney made this rather cryptic reply: "I just made a wild guess. It's probably Lombardi—but I don't think so."

Asked what one was supposed to do with a statement like that Shotton merely grinned and said nothing.

However, Coach Dressen of the Yankees, who is supposed to know all about the Dodgers, was quoted as saying:

"Who's Shotton trying to fool with that Lombardi? It'll be Branca tomorrow!"

So perhaps Shotton had better take up his pitching plans with Dressen before today's game in order to pick the right pitcher.

34,379 Pay $165,921 At Fifth Series Game

Standing of the Clubs
By The Associated Press.

	W	L	Pct.
New York (A)	3	2	600
Brooklyn (N)	2	3	400

Fifth Game Statistics

Paid attendance—34,379.
Receipts (net)—$165,921.50.
Commissioner's share—$24,888.20.
Leagues' share—$36,258.27.
Clubs' share—$35,258.27.

Five-Game Totals

Paid attendance—244,150.
Receipts (net)—$1,133,911.33.
Commissioner's share—$170,086.67.
Leagues' share—$117,537.40.
Clubs' share—$117,537.40.
*Players' share—$493,674.83.
*Players participate in receipts of first four games only.

Jubilation in the locker room after Game 5 of the 1947 World Series is shared by Joe DiMaggio and Frank Shea, who holds the ball he pitched for the last out in the Yankees' 2–1 victory over the Dodgers. DiMaggio contributed the game-winning home run.

Game 6 October 5 at New York

Bkn.	2 0 2	0 0 4	0 0 0					8
N.Y.	0 0 4	1 0 0	0 0 1					6

Brooklyn	Pos	AB	R	H	RBI	PO	A	E
Stanky	2b	5	2	2	0	4	2	0
Reese	ss	4	2	3	2	2	1	0
J. Robinson	1b	5	1	2	1	7	1	0
Walker	rf	5	0	1	1	3	0	0
Hermanski	lf	1	0	0	0	0	0	0
b Miksis	lf	1	0	0	0	0	0	0
Gionfriddo	lf	2	0	0	0	1	0	0
Edwards	c	4	1	1	0	5	0	0
Furillo	cf	4	1	2	0	4	1	0
Jorgensen	3b	2	0	0	0	1	1	1
c Lavagetto	3b	2	0	0	1	1	0	0
Lombardi	p	1	0	0	0	0	0	0
Branca	p	1	0	0	0	0	1	0
d Bragan		1	0	1	1	0	0	0
e Bankhead		0	1	0	0	0	0	0
Hatten	p	1	0	0	0	0	0	0
Casey	p	0	0	0	0	0	1	0
Totals		39	8	12	6	27	9	1

a Singled for Phillips in 3rd.
b Popped out for Hermanski in 5th.
c Flied out for Jorgensen in 6th.
d Doubled for Branca in 6th.
e Ran for Bragan in 6th.
f Lined out for Newsom in 6th.
g Singled for Raschi in 7th.
h Hit into force out for Wensloff in 9th.

Doubles—Bragan, Furillo, Lollar, Reese, J. Robinson, Walker.
Double Play—Rizzuto to Phillips.
Passed Ball—Lollar. Wild Pitch—Lombardi.
Left on Bases—Brooklyn 6, New York 13.
Umpires—Pinelli, Rommel, Goetz, McGowan, Boyer, Magerkurth. Attendance—74,065.
(A new Series record). Time of Game—3:19.

New York	Pos	AB	R	H	RBI	PO	A	E
Stirnweiss	2b	5	0	0	1	1	6	0
Henrich	rf-lf	5	1	2	0	1	0	0
Lindell	lf	2	1	2	1	0	0	0
Berra	rf	3	0	2	1	1	0	0
DiMaggio	cf	5	1	1	0	5	0	0
Johnson	3b	5	1	2	1	1	5	0
Phillips	1b	1	0	0	0	4	0	0
a Brown		1	0	1	1	0	0	0
McQuinn	1b	1	0	0	0	6	0	1
Rizzuto	ss	4	0	1	0	6	1	0
Lollar	c	1	1	1	0	1	0	0
A. Robinson	c	4	1	2	0	2	0	1
Reynolds	p	0	0	0	0	0	0	0
Drews	p	2	0	0	0	0	1	0
Page	p	0	0	0	0	0	0	0
Newsom	p	0	0	0	0	0	0	0
f Clark		1	0	0	0	0	0	0
Raschi	p	0	0	0	0	0	0	0
g Houk		1	0	1	0	0	0	0
Wensloff	p	0	0	0	0	0	1	0
h Frey		1	0	0	1	0	0	0
Totals		42	6	15	6	27	14	2

Pitching	IP	H	R	ER	BB	SO
Brooklyn						
Lombardi	2⅓	5	4	4	0	2
Branca (W)	2⅓	6	1	1	0	2
Hatten	*3	3	1	1	4	0
Casey (sv)	1	1	0	0	0	0
New York						
Reynolds	2⅓	6	4	3	1	0
Drews	2	1	0	0	1	0
Page (L)	1	4	4	4	0	1
Newsom	⅓	1	0	0	0	0
Raschi	1	0	0	0	0	1
Wensloff	2	0	0	0	0	0

*Pitched to two batters in 9th.

1st Inning
Brooklyn
Stanky singled to left.
Reese singled to center with Stanky stopping at second.
J. Robinson singled to left when Lindell lost the ball in the sun to load the bases.
1,2 Walker hit into a double play, Rizzuto to Phillips. Stanky scored and Reese went to third on the double play.
Reese scored on Lollar's passed ball.
Hermanski walked.
3 Edwards grounded to third.
New York
1 Stirnweiss flied to right.
2 Henrich popped to second.
Lindell singled to left.
3 DiMaggio grounded to second.

2nd Inning
Brooklyn
1 Furillo flied to center.
2 Jorgensen grounded to second.
3 Lombardi flied to center.
New York
1 Johnson fanned.
2 Phillips grounded to first.
3 Rizzuto grounded to short.

3rd Inning
Brooklyn
1 Stanky flied to center.
Reese doubled over third.
J. Robinson got a ground-rule double to left, scoring Reese.
Walker doubled to right, J. Robinson scoring.
For New York—Drews pitching.
2 Hermanski grounded to second, moving Walker to third.
3 Edwards flied to center.
New York
Lollar doubled to left.
1 Drews fanned.
Lollar went to third on a wild pitch.
Stirnweiss was safe at first on Jorgensen's fumble, Lollar scoring.
Henrich singled to center, however
2 Stirnweiss was out trying for third, Furillo to Jorgensen.
Lindell singled to center to score Henrich.
DiMaggio singled through third, Lindell stopping at second.
For Brooklyn—Branca pitching.
Johnson on a single to right scored Lindell and moved DiMaggio to third.
Brown, pinch-hitting for Phillips, singled to left, scoring DiMaggio and moving Johnson to third.
3 Rizzuto lined to second.

4th Inning
Brooklyn
For New York—McQuinn at first, A. Robinson catching, Berra in right as Henrich moves to left.
Furillo singled behind second.
1 Jorgensen forced Furillo at second, Stirnweiss to Rizzuto.
2 Branca forced Jorgensen at second, Drews to Rizzuto.
3 Stanky forced Branca at second, Stirnweiss to Rizzuto.
New York
A. Robinson singled to center.
1 Drews called out on strikes.
2 Stirnweiss took a called third strike.
Henrich singled to center with A. Robinson stopping at second.
Berra singled over first to score A. Robinson and moving Henrich to third.
3 DiMaggio forced Berra at second, Jorgensen to Stanky.

5th Inning
Brooklyn
Reese walked.
1 J. Robinson forced Reese at second, Johnson to Stirnweiss.
For New York—Page relieved Drews with a 2-1 count on Walker.
2 Walker went down swinging.
3 Miksis, batting for Hermanski, popped to short.
New York
For Brooklyn—Miksis playing left.
1 Johnson grounded back to the pitcher.
2 McQuinn popped to second.
Rizzuto singled to left.
3 A. Robinson grounded to second.

6th Inning
Brooklyn
Edwards singled to right.
Furillo doubled to left, moving Edwards to third.
1 Lavagetto, pinch-hitting for Jorgensen, flied to right, Edwards scoring after the catch.
Bragan, batting for Branca, doubled to left, Furillo scoring.
Bankhead ran for Bragan.
Stanky singled to right, Bankhead going to third. Stanky went on to second when A. Robinson lost Berra's throw to the plate.
For New York—Newsom pitching.
Reese singled to left, scoring Bankhead and Stanky.
2 J. Robinson lined to left.
3 Walker fouled to Johnson.

6th Inning (continued)
New York
For Brooklyn—Hatten pitching, Lavagetto at third and Gionfriddo going to left.
1 Clark pinch-hitting for Newsom, lined to short.
Stirnweiss walked.
2 Henrich fouled to Edwards.
Berra singled to left with Stirnweiss stopping at second.
3 DiMaggio flied to left where Gionfriddo made the catch of the Series, a glove-handed catch at the 415 foot mark just in front of the bullpen.

7th Inning
Brooklyn
For New York—Raschi pitching.
1 Gionfriddo grounded to third.
2 Edwards fanned.
3 Furillo rolled to second.
New York
1 Johnson flied to right.
McQuinn walked.
Rizzuto walked.
2 A. Robinson flied to center.
Houk, pinch-hitting for Raschi, singled past the box to load the bases.
3 Stirnweiss flied to center.

8th Inning
Brooklyn
For New York—Wensloff pitching.
1 Lavagetto grounded to third.
2 Hatten rolled to the box.
3 Stanky grounded to third.
New York
1 Henrich lined to right.
2 Berra flied to center.
3 DiMaggio grounded to third.

9th Inning
Brooklyn
1 Reese grounded to second.
2 J. Robinson popped to short.
Walker safe at first on McQuinn's fumble.
3 Gionfriddo flied to center
New York
Johnson singled to left.
McQuinn walked.
For Brooklyn—Casey pitching.
1 Rizzuto flied to center.
A. Robinson singled to left, loading the bases.
2 Frey, pinch-hitting for Wensloff, forced A. Robinson at second, J. Robinson to Reese. Johnson scored on the force out, with McQuinn going to third.
3 Stirnweiss grounded back to the mound.

The hit, a towering drive to left in the sixth inning of Game 6 of the 1947 World Series, travels 415 feet. But to Joe DiMaggio's surprise and chagrin, at the Yankee Stadium wall was a Dodger named Al Gionfriddo.

The famous catch by reserve outfielder Al Gionfriddo of the Dodgers, which robbed Joe DiMaggio of a potentially game-winning, three-run homer in Game 6 of the 1947 World Series. The Yanks lost that game 8–6, but came back the next day to win the Series 4 games to 3.

DiMAG: I WUZ ROBBED

Says he had kick coming after Gionfriddo catch

By FILIP BONDY

You've seen it on every baseball highlight film that ever filled air time during a rain delay. Or maybe you were lucky enough to be at Yankee Stadium on Oct. 5, 1947.

There is Brooklyn Dodger outfielder Al Gionfriddo catching Joe DiMaggio's towering fly over his shoulder in Death Valley, 415 feet away from home plate. There is DiMaggio kicking the dirt near second base in — can you believe it? —disgust. The moment continues to stand as DiMaggio's one public concession to human emotion.

"The reason I let my feelings show then was that I'd never had a Series where I'd been lucky," DiMaggio recalled yesterday, prior to Old-timers Day and Salute to Joe DiMaggio ceremonies at the Stadium. "Against St. Louis (in 1942) Enos Slaughter and Terry Moore made some great catches against me.

"That catch by Gionfriddo was the straw that broke the camel's back," DiMaggio said.

GIONFRIDDO'S catch, which came in the sixth inning of Game 6 in the Series, was set up in dramatic fashion. The Yankees led the Series, 3-2, but the Dodgers were winning the game, 8-5. There were two men on base and two out, with reliever Joe Hatten pitching.

When DiMaggio came to the plate, Brooklyn manager Burt Shotton called time and replaced leftfielder Eddie Miksis with the little-used Gionfriddo.

"Miksis was having trouble picking up the ball in left, so he brought Gionfriddo in and on the very next play I hit the ball out there," DiMaggio said.

DiMAGGIO DROVE the ball hard to left, in the deep Stadium recesses that had claimed so many of his potential home runs. Gionfriddo caught up with the ball, then tumbled over the short wall and into the bullpen. He held on. The Dodgers went on to win the game, 8-6, and the Yankees were forced to go seven games before winning the Series.

"It's a good thing I didn't kick the bag at second, because I would have busted my foot," DiMaggio said.

For Gionfriddo, the play was the highlight — and the fielding finale — of a spotty four-year career. He did not play in Game 7, and retired after the season.

"I thought I just made another catch at the time," said Gionfriddo, who was present at yesterday's Old-timers Day and received some nostalgic boos from the crowd. "My hat fell off, and Carl Furillo picked it up and handed it to me. That was that.

"I didn't even think about keeping the ball at the time," Gionfriddo said. "I came up in the next inning, and fouled the same ball off Allie Reynolds and into the stands. It was gone.

"By the time Joe went out to the outfield, his anger was over. He didn't say anything to me afterwards. There was another game to play."

Team Makes DiMag Victim With Pictures

By JOE KING.

YANKEE STADIUM, Oct. 6.— The Yankees had fun with Joe DiMaggio before today's game. One of the photo services had made about a hundred prints of Gionfriddo's catch, and distributed samples to the Yankees as well as the Dodgers. Johnny Schulte, the coach, jokingly proffered his copy to DiMag and asked for an autograph. Half a dozen Yankees got on to the stunt, and DiMag had to push kidding teammates aside time after time. Finally he said: "I guess you fellows don't know that I know he caught that ball."

Charlie Keller took hitting practice for the first time since he withdrew in June. Not to get ready for action today, but to "get the feel of it again." Charlie must wear a brace six weeks more, and then he will go in training.

Ralph Kiner is a deep student of DiMaggio's hitting style from behind the batting cage every time the big boy takes his practice cuts.

Bucky Harris was serious and intent on the bench and did not smile and joke as much as usual. He was asked whether Tommy Henrich would do well in left. "Tommy is a top ball player wherever he is and can handle that very rough sun in left field."

Phil Rizzuto and Harry Lavagetto ribbed each other on the Italian angle, and if you look over yesterday's box score you will appreciate that there was indeed an Italian angle.

The freak autograph of the series was given by Allie Reynolds who was approached by a fan with an arm in a cast and a request to sign said coating.

Game 7 October 6 at New York

Brooklyn	Pos	AB	R	H	RBI	PO	A	E
Stanky	2b	4	0	1	0	3	1	0
Reese	ss	3	0	0	0	0	1	0
J. Robinson	1b	4	0	0	0	3	2	0
Walker	rf	3	0	0	0	3	0	0
Hermanski	lf	2	1	1	0	2	0	0
b Miksis	lf	2	0	1	0	2	0	0
Edwards	c	4	1	2	1	5	0	0
Furillo	cf	3	0	1	0	4	0	0
Jorgensen	3b	2	0	1	1	0	1	0
d Lavagetto	3b	1	0	0	0	0	0	0
Gregg	p	2	0	0	0	1	0	0
Behrman	p	0	0	0	0	1	0	0
Hatten	p	0	0	0	0	0	0	0
Barney	p	0	0	0	0	0	0	0
e Hodges		1	0	0	0	0	0	0
Casey	p	0	0	0	0	0	0	0
Totals		31	2	7	2	24	5	0

a Doubled for Bevens in 4th.
b Grounded out for Hermanski in 6th.
c Singled for Berra in 6th.
d Popped out for Jorgenson in 7th.
e Struck out for Barney in 7th.

Doubles—Brown, Jorgensen. Triples—Hermanski, Johnson. Stolen Base—Rizzuto. Sacrifice Hit—McQuinn. Double Play—Rizzuto to Stirnweiss to McQuinn. Left on Bases—Brooklyn 4, New York 9. Umpires—Rommel, Goetz, McGowan, Pinelli, Magerkurth, Boyer. Attendance—71,548. Time of Game—2:19.

Bkn.	020 000 000	2
N.Y.	010 201 10x	5

New York	Pos	AB	R	H	RBI	PO	A	E
Stirnweiss	2b	2	0	0	0	5	4	0
Henrich	lf	5	0	1	1	2	0	0
Berra	rf	3	0	0	0	1	0	0
c Clark	rf	1	0	1	1	2	0	0
DiMaggio	cf	3	0	0	0	3	0	0
McQuinn	1b	2	1	0	0	7	0	0
Johnson	3b	3	2	1	0	1	1	0
A. Robinson	c	3	0	0	1	4	2	0
Rizzuto	ss	4	2	3	1	2	2	0
Shea	p	0	0	0	0	0	0	0
Bevens	p	1	0	0	0	0	0	0
a Brown		1	0	1	1	0	0	0
Page	p	2	0	0	0	0	0	0
Totals		30	5	7	5	27	9	0

Pitching	IP	H	R	ER	BB	SO
Brooklyn						
Gregg (L)	3⅔	3	3	3	4	3
Behrman	1⅔	2	1	1	3	1
Hatten	⅓	1	0	0	0	1
Barney	⅓	0	0	0	0	0
Casey	2	1	1	1	0	0
New York						
Shea	1⅓	4	2	2	1	0
Bevens	2⅔	2	0	0	1	2
Page (W)	5	1	0	0	0	1

1st Inning
Brooklyn
Stanky singled to right-center.
1 Stanky was caught stealing, A. Robinson to Stirnweiss.
Reese walked.
2 J. Robinson lined to right.
3 Reese caught stealing, A. Robinson to Rizzuto.
New York
1 Stirnweiss flied to right.
2 Henrich flied to left.
3 Berra grounded out, J. Robinson to Gregg.

2nd Inning
Brooklyn
1 Walker fouled to McQuinn.
Hermanski tripled to right.
Edwards singled to left, Hermanski scoring.
Furillo singled to center with Edwards stopping at second.
For New York—Bevens pitching.
Jorgensen doubled to right, Edwards scoring with Furillo stopping at third.
2 Gregg to first on a fielder s choice. Rizzuto took his hit and threw Furillo out at the plate.
3 Stanky popped to short.
New York
1 DiMaggio flied to center
McQuinn walked.
2 Johnson popped to second.
A. Robinson walked.
Rizzuto singled to left, McQuinn scoring with A. Robinson stopping at second.
3 Bevens fanned.

3rd Inning
Brooklyn
1 Reese fanned.
2 J. Robinson fanned.
Walker walked.
3 Hermanski lined to third.
New York
Stirnweiss walked.
1 Henrich flied to right.
2 Berra flied to center.
3 DiMaggio flied to left.

4th Inning
Brooklyn
Edwards singled to left.
1 Furillo popped to second.
2 Jorgensen popped to second.
3 Gregg grounded to second.
New York
1 McQuinn fanned.
Johnson walked.
2 A. Robinson fanned.
Rizzuto singled to left with Johnson stopping at second.
Brown, pinch-hitting for Bevens, doubled to left to score Johnson and sending Rizzuto to third.
For Brooklyn—Behrman pitching.
Stirnweiss walked, loading the bases.
Henrich singled to right, Rizzuto scoring with the bases still loaded.
3 Berra grounded out, J. Robinson to Behrman.

5th Inning
Brooklyn
For New York—Page pitching.
1 Stanky grounded to second.
2 Reese flied to right.
3 J. Robinson lined to left.
New York
DiMaggio walked
1 McQuinn sacrificed DiMaggio to second, Jorgensen to Stanky (covering first).
2 Johnson grounded to second, moving DiMaggio to second.
3 A. Robinson flied to right.

6th Inning
Brooklyn
1 Walker lined to center
2 Miksis, pinch-hitting for Hermanski, grounded to third.
3 Edwards flied to center.
New York
For Brooklyn—Miksis in left.
Rizzuto beat out a bunt.
Rizzuto stole second.
1 Page fanned.
Stirnweiss walked.
For Brooklyn—Behrman pitching.
2 Henrich fanned.
Clark, pinch-hitting for Berra, singled to center to score Rizzuto.
For Brooklyn—Barney pitching.
3 DiMaggio flied to center

7th Inning
Brooklyn
For New York—Clark in right.
1 Furillo fouled to McQuinn.
2 Lavagetto, pinch-hitting for Jorgensen, popped to second.
3 Hodges, batting for Barney, fanned.
New York
For Brooklyn—Lavagetto stays in at third with Casey pitching.
1 McQuinn grounded to short.
Johnson tripled to left.
2 A. Robinson flied to left, Johnson scoring after the catch.
3 Rizzuto popped to second.

8th Inning
Brooklyn
1 Stanky flied to right.
2 Reese lined to right.
3 J. Robinson flied to center.
New York
1 Page grounded to first.
2 Strinweiss flied to center
3 Henrich flied to left.

9th Inning
Brooklyn
1 Walker grounded to second.
Miksis singled to center.
2,3 Edwards grounded into a double play, Rizzuto to Stirnweiss to McQuinn.

NEW YORK, TUESDAY, OCTOBER 7, 1947.

YANKS WIN SERIES, PAGE TAKING FINAL FROM DODGERS, 5-2

Relief Pitcher Hero as 11th Title Goes to American Leaguers Before 71,548

RECEIPTS HIT $2,137,549

Total Attendance Also Sets Record at 389,763—M'Phail Resigns Club Presidency

By JOHN DREBINGER

The Yankees had a trump card after all, and as a consequence the Bronx Bombers are back once more in a long-familiar role as baseball champions of the universe.

They brought the 1947 world series to a close at the Stadium yesterday in almost perfunctory fashion as they downed the Dodgers in the seventh and deciding game by a score of 5 to 2.

And the ace in the deck who nailed down the final trick before a gathering of 71,548 was the fellow whom Bucky Harris had toasted all summer with the quaint line: "Gentlemen, Joe Page."

The 30-year-old southpaw from Cherry Valley, Pa., in another of his inimitable relief jobs, stepped into the breach immediately after the Yanks had grabbed a 3-2 lead in the fourth inning on hits by Phil Rizzuto, Bobby Brown and the old reliable Tommy Henrich, and he never allowed Burt Shotton's Flock to come up for air again in the first $2,000,000 world series ever played.

A Startling Resignation

Thus to the Yanks, most successful baseball organization in all history, came another world's title, the eleventh since it bagged the first, in 1923, and the first under the aegis of Larry MacPhail who, curiously, chose this dramatic moment to announce his retirement as president of the club.

The fiery redhead made the announcement at the very moment his players came thundering into their dressing room to celebrate the final triumph. It startled everyone but in no way interrupted the celebration that started with congratulations being showered upon the popular Manager Harris, who, after twenty-three long years, is once more riding a world champion.

The late Miller Huggins brought them their first championships in 1923, 1927 and 1928. Then Joe McCarthy, most successful of all, skippered the series winners in 1932, '36, '37, '38, '39, '41 and '43.

American Leaguers also were rejoicing, for this marked the twenty-seventh victory for the junior loop against sixteen for the National.

It was the second time that the Yanks had toppled the Dodgers, who have failed to win the world championship in four tries. They bowed to the Red Sox in 1916, the Indians in 1920 and the Yanks in 1941.

Came Closer This Time

The only consolation the Dodgers had last night was the fact that this time they had come closer to their goal than any of their predecessors. They had waged a great fight, carrying the struggle to the seven-game limit through some of the most thrilling battles ever seen on the diamond.

But when it came down to the final test with all the blue chips in the middle, they simply didn't have it, and the fellow who convinced them of that was the one they were toasting in the Yankee clubhouse, Joe Page.

Only the previous afternoon Page had taken a heavy battering from the Bums from Flatbush for a victory that kept their series hopes alive for another twenty-four hours. But yesterday the southpaw simply smothered the Brooklyn boys in this final "struggle of the bullpens."

In an amazing come-back, Page faced only fifteen batters in his five innings on the mound. Not until one had been retired in the ninth could a Dodger get on base. He was Eddie Miksis, who singled. A moment later Bruce Edwards banged into a double play and the classic was over.

Even the fact that the Yanks began the day with another curious strategic move could not alter the result. They started Frank Shea, although he had only a single day's rest, and the move provided about the only thrill of the afternoon. For the Brooks belted the Naugatuck Nugget—winner of two games—out in the second inning, in which they scored both their runs.

Each club ended the day with seven hits, but there the similarity ended. For this day, at least, and when it counted most, the Yanks were as superior to their rivals as they had been in the first two games in the Stadium.

But those intervening battles in Brooklyn, along with the one in the Stadium on Sunday, had easily made this one of the most thrilling struggles ever seen, and one whose outstanding events will long be remembered.

Fans swarm onto the field in front of the Yankee dugout to congratulate the 1947 world champions on clinching the Series, defeating the Brooklyn Dodgers, 5–2. The group of three players at the left are (top to bottom) winning pitcher Joe Page (bareheaded); pitcher, Bobo Newsom; and catcher, Aaron Robinson; in the center is second baseman, George Stirnweiss, and at the right is Joe DiMaggio.

SERIES HEARD IN MOSCOW

Russians Alarmed by Tumult as Baseball News Comes In

MOSCOW, Oct. 6 (UP)—"These Americans!" mused the policeman in the street outside American House—residence of non-commissioned officers, enlisted men and embassy clerks in Moscow.

He had reason to shake his head. There was a terrific amount of noise coming from inside. A sergeant just going to work noticed the puzzled policeman.

"It's not a fight," the sergeant revealed. "The boys are just listening to the world series baseball game—plus some transatlantic static."

The games are being heard distinctly in Moscow this year from the armed forces network station at Frankfurt.

Highlights

- The Yankees, appearing in their fifteenth World Series, won their eleventh world championship.
- This was the first World Series to be televised.
- Jackie Robinson, the first black to play major league baseball, became the first black to participate in a World Series.
- The eight runs scored by Billy Johnson of the Yankees tied the record for a seven-game Series. His three triples set another mark.
- Johnny Lindell's batting average of .500 tied the record for a seven-game Series.
- The Dodgers twice tied a Series record when they hit three doubles in one inning: Game 3, the second: Bruce Edwards, Eddie Stanky, and Carl Furillo; and Game 6, the third: PeeWee Reese, Jackie Robinson, and Dixie Walker.
- The attendance for Game 1 at Yankee Stadium—73,365—set a new Series standard.
- Losing 1-0, the Yankees erupted for five runs in the fifth of Game 1, with Johnny Lindell and Tommy Henrich each driving in two runs. The Yanks got only four hits all day, but still won.
- Yogi Berra hit the first pinch-hit home run in Series history in the seventh inning of Game 3.
- The Dodgers scored six runs in the second inning of Game 3, with Eddie Stanky and Carl Furillo driving in two apiece.

- Yankee hurler Bill Bevens had a no-hitter with two outs in the bottom of the ninth of Game 4 when pinch-hitter Cookie Lavagetto spoiled it with a double. Two runs scored on Lavagetto's hit, enough to win the game for the Dodgers as well.
- An RBI by Yankee pitcher Spec Shea and a home run from Joe DiMaggio provided the winning margin in Game 5. Shea went the distance, allowing the Dodgers only four hits.
- The 38 players who appeared for the Yankees and the Dodgers in Game 6 still stands as the most ever in a nine-inning game. The 21 used by the Yanks also set a mark for the most by one ballclub.
- A new Series attendance record was set at Game 6—74,065—played at Yankee Stadium.
- Reserve outfielder Al Gionfriddo saved Game 6 for the Dodgers by making a spectacular catch when he reached over the railing at the 415-foot mark to steal what would have been a three-run homer from Joe DiMaggio.

Best Efforts

Batting

Average	Johnny Lindell	.500
Home Runs	Joe DiMaggio	2
Triples	Billy Johnson	3
Doubles	Johnny Lindell	3
Hits	Tommy Henrich	10
Runs	Billy Johnson	8
RBIs	Johnny Lindell	7

Pitching

Wins	Spec Shea	2-0
	Hugh Casey	2-0
ERA	Hugh Casey	0.87
Strikeouts	Spec Shea	10
	Hal Gregg	10
Innings Pitched	Spec Shea	15⅓

NEW YORK YANKEES 1947
BROOKLYN DODGERS

Reprinted, with permission, from
The World Series, A Complete
Pictorial History, by John Devaney
and Burt Goldblatt (Rand McNally
and Company, Chicago, © 1972).

For Cookie, Bill, and Al,
It Was Here Today and Gone Tomorrow

The three names that are remembered from this 1947 Series were names dropped from big league box scores by 1948. All three were by then toiling in the minor leagues. Not forgotten, though, were the Series heroics of Cookie Lavagetto, Floyd (Bill) Bevens, and Al Gionfriddo, three unexpected and unlikely heroes.

Two other names in the 1947 box scores were rookies who would go on to the Hall of Fame. One was Brooklyn infielder Jackie Robinson, the first black major-leaguer. The other was New York's stumpy outfielder-catcher, Yogi Berra, who played rightfield in this Series, the first of a record 14 for Yogi.

Lavagetto and Bevens combined to make the fourth game, played at Ebbets Field, one of the most memorable of all time. For 8⅔ innings Bevens, 31, and a journeyman pitcher, had not yielded a hit, the closest anyone had ever come to pitching a no-hitter in the Series. He had walked nine, however, costing him a run, but the Yanks led, 2-1. There were two out in the bottom of the ninth, Carl Furillo on first base after a walk.

Dodger manager Burt Shotton sent in the speedy little Gionfriddo, a utility infielder-outfielder, to run for Furillo. Gionfriddo surprised everyone by stealing second. Yankee manager Bucky Harris then violated conventional baseball wisdom by purposely walking pinch-hitter Pete Reiser, putting the winning run on base. Eddie Miksis ran for Reiser.

Lavagetto, 34, and a part-time third baseman, batted for Eddie Stanky. He leaned into an outside pitch and smashed it on a line toward the rightfield wall. The ball hit high on the wall and bounded away from Tommy Henrich. Gionfriddo and Miksis raced home with the tying and winning runs, the Dodgers winning 3-2. Bevens trudged off the field a one-hit loser.

Two days later the biggest crowd in Series history up to then, 74,065, squeezed into Yankee Stadium to see the sixth game. With the Dodgers ahead, 8-5, in the sixth, Joe DiMaggio came to bat with two men on and two out. He hit a soaring drive toward the bullpen in leftfield. Gionfriddo raced to the bullpen railing, stuck out his glove, and snared the drive that would have tied the score. The Dodgers won the game, 8-6, but lost their fourth Series the next day, stopped by the fireballing reliefer Joe Page.

Cookie Lavagetto:
". . . that's all there was to it . . ."

Cookie Lavagetto, the former Dodger third baseman and big league manager, was interviewed at an Oldtimers' Day in New York. *People have asked me for years about that hit off Bevens,* he said. *To me it was like any other game. It was my last year with the club. The previous spring they had offered me a minor league managing job but I had turned it down because I thought I could play another season in the big leagues. I was used mostly as a pinch-hitter that year and I did all right as a pinch-hitter. I think I hit over .250 [.261]. So when I went up there to pinch-hit against Bevens, it was something I had been used to doing all year. The pitch was right out there and I got hold of it good. I ran down to first base and turned and saw the two runs scoring and that's all there was to it.*

DiMag Happy Here, Denies Urging Trade

By DANIEL.

Preparing for a visit to his family in San Franciso, Jo DiMaggio today expressed mystification over reports concerning his relations with the Yankees which recently had gained circulation. These had Giuseppe seeking a change of scene, with hints that he wanted to join his brother, Dominic, on the Red Sox and to get back under the management of Joe McCarthy.

"Such yarns are founded on thin air," DiMaggio said. "Here is where I belong. I like it in the Stadium, I like the New York club. I like to work for Bucky Harris. He's OK with me."

DiMaggio might have added that he particularly admired the new picture in the offices of the new president and the new general manager of the New York club.

Joe was not precisely enamoured of Col. Larry MacPhail, and this feeling existed even before Larry plastered a $100 fine on him for "failure to co-operate with the front office in the matter of publicity." The player had refused to take part in an Army movie advertising new types of uniforms.

DiMaggio did not have quite the year he expected. But he did bat .315, with 20 homers, 167 hits and 96 runs driven in. He appeared in 139 games. Only one other outfielder, Tommy Henrich, played in more, 140.

DiMaggio is waiting for a summons from the reorganized front office to talk about his contract. He got $42,500 this year, and appears likely to receive $50,000.

World Series Shares Below Expectations.

According to an announcement by Commissioner Albert B. Chandler today, each Yankee entitled to a full share of the world series gravy will receive $5800, while each regular Dodger will collect $4000.

These figures were highly disappointing to the players, as they had expected the winning share to come to $6700 and the losing split $4700.

Despite the fact that the players' pool achieved the all-time high of $493,674.82, the Yankees did not come near the $6544 which each Tiger collected in 1935, nor did the Superbas match the $4829 which each got on the losing end in 1941.

The commissioner explained this with the statement that, up to 1946, money received for the radio rights went into the general pool. This time the $175,000 which Chandler got for the broadcasting privileges, and the $65,000 he got for the television rights, went into the players' pension fund.

The commissioner has disapproved the allotment of a full share to Leo Durocher, which the Dodgers voted before the series.

Daniel's Dope
DiMag Again Headed For Johns Hopkins
By Dan Daniel

Baseball news these days is largely clinical. Our local ball club mouthpieces are taken up with reports on impending operations, temperatures and other purely physiological matters. For example, the latest communique from Red Patterson, holler guy for the Yankees.

It seems that Joe Di Maggio, who hates to let a winter pass without tangling with the surgeons, again is headed for Johns Hopkins in Baltimore, and a possible cutting job on his throwing arm, the right.

Di Maggio will enter Hopkins on Sunday and the following morning will get a going-over by Dr. George Bennett.

Giuseppe hurt his flipper years ago. In his first season with the Bombers, in 1936, as a matter of fact. Since then the arm has been hot and cold by turns. In the last month of the 1947 campaign, he injured it quite severely.

The story was kept covered up by Bucky Harris and Eddie Froelich because they feared its discovery by the Brooklyn spy system. Once the classic had ended, Joe revealed that he could not have made two good throws in any one afternoon.

Last year at this time Di Maggio was getting ready for that ill-fated operation for the removal of a spur from his heel.

The calcium was chiseled out but the heel failed to heal, and Joe had quite a time of it.

DiMag Fields .997

The Joe DiMaggio-over-Ted Williams most valuable player controversy in the American League, which favored the Boston star when the batting averages were issued early in the week, today took a Giuseppe turn with publication of the fielding records.

The official defense data crowned DiMaggio as the most reliable outfielder. He made only one error in 319 chances, for .997. In 139 contests, Joe put together 316 outs, but he had only two assists. They took no liberties with his arm, even after he had injured it early in September. This weakness is said to have been eliminated by recent removal of a small bone which had impacted on a nerve.

Williams appeared in 156 games, with .347 outs, 10 assists and 9 errors, for a .975 rating.

Joe DiMaggio Named Most Valuable American League Player for Third Time

YANKEE STAR LEADS WILLIAMS BY POINT

DiMaggio Selected for Player Award With Score of 202 by Baseball Writers

BOUDREAU IS RATED THIRD

Page Is Fourth, Just Back of Indians' Manager, Despite Seven First-Place Votes

By JOHN DREBINGER

By the slender margin of a single point, Joe DiMaggio, star centerfielder of the Yankees has been named the American League's most valuable player for 1947, it was announced yesterday by the Baseball Writers Association of America.

In being voted the Kenesaw Mountain Landis Memorial award, Jolting Joe received 202 points in the poll of the scribes' twenty-four-man committee as against 201 for Ted Williams, Red Sox star slugger and winner of the prize last year.

Third ranking also was gained by only a single point with Lou Boudreau, manager-shortstop of the Indians, scoring 168 points to 167 for Joe Page, the tireless left-hander who did an amazing relief job for the Yankees last summer. Fifth place went to George Kell, Tiger third sacker, who scored 132.

First Honored in 1939

It marked the third time that DiMaggio had finished on top, the Yankee clipper having first captured the award in 1939 and again in 1941. And for Williams it was the third time Boston's temperamental "problem child" had failed to win the prize despite a distinguished personal record.

In 1941 Williams hit .406, yet bowed to DiMaggio who that year had set his spectacular fifty-six-game hitting streak. In 1942 Williams again won the batting crown with .356 but trailed behind Joe Gordon, then with the Yanks, for the MVP award.

The past season again saw Williams lead individual batting as well as top the field in homers and runs batted in. But the scribes apparently estimated DiMaggio the more valuable team worker.

Jolting Joe polled eight first place ballots as against only three for Williams who drew most of his points from ten second place ratings. As in the National League vote, points were distributed on a basis of 14 for first place, 9 for second, 8 for third and so on down to one for tenth.

McQuinn Rated Sixth

Curiously Page, whom his manager, Bucky Harris, openly named as the year's most important factor in the Yanks' pennant victory, had the second highest first place votes to DiMaggio, the lefty appearing No. 1 on seven ballots.

George McQuinn, the veteran Mack cast-off, whose astonishing comeback at first base also played a strong role in the Yankee victory, received three first-place votes which helped him finish sixth with 77 points. In all, eighteen of the twenty-four writers named a Yankee for the No. 1 spot. Eddie Joost of the Athletics got two of the remaining first ballot votes, while Boudreau got the other.

The Bombers, in fact, did exceptionally well, placing eight men among the thirty-four who received points. Tommy Henrich, Frank Shea, Yogi Berra and Allie Reynolds are bunched between 33 and 18 points, while a little further down the line Bill Johnson appears with 9.

That it was a tough year for old favorites was indicated when Hal Newhouser, winner in 1944 and 1945, this year had to be satisfied with honorable mention, for which no points are awarded. But Joe Gordon, who as a Yank had won in 1942, still was able to make a presentable showing as an Indian. He placed seventh with 59 points, one more than Cleveland's Bob Feller received.

AGAIN THE 'MOST VALUABLE PLAYER'

Joe DiMaggio, his right arm in a cast following a recent operation, turns southpaw as he takes his turn at Thanksgiving dinner plate.
Associated Press

The complete point score follows:

DiMaggio, Yankees, 202; Williams, Red Sox, 201; Boudreau, Indians, 168; Page, Yankees, 167; Kell, Tigers, 132; McQuinn, Yankees, 77; Gordon, Indians, 59; Feller, Indians, 58; Marchildon, Athletics, 47; Appling, White Sox, 43; Joost, Athletics, 35; McCosky, Athletics, 35; Henrich, Yankees, 33; Shea, Yankees, 23; Berra, Yankees, 18; Reynolds, Yankees, 18; Dillinger, Browns, 13; Pesky, Red Sox, 11; Fain, Athletics, 9; W. Johnson, Yankees, 9; Spence, Senators, 9; Hutchinson, Tigers, 8; Wynn, Senators, 7; Doerr, Red Sox, 6; Rosar, Athletics, 6; Christman, Browns, 4; McCahan, Athletics, 4; Mitchell, Indians, 4; Cullenbine, Tigers, 3; Dobson, Red Sox, 3; Heath, Browns, 1; Lopat, White Sox, 1; Stephens, Browns, 1; Wright, White Sox, 1.

Honorable Mention—Red Sox: D. DiMaggio, Murrell Jones. White Sox: Finney, Haynes, Tresh. Tigers: Newhouser, Evers, Overmire. Yankees: Rizzuto, Newsom, Keller, Stirnweiss, Lindell. Athletics: Valo, Suder, Majeski, Fowler. Browns: Lehner, Judnich. Senators: Vernon, Yost.

The Most Valuable Player plaque for 1947 is awarded to Joe DiMaggio by Joe King, Chairman of the New York Chapter of the Baseball Writers' Association. Looking on are baseball commissioner, A. B. "Happy" Chandler (left), and New York governor, Thomas E. Dewey (right).

Racks Up Third Most Valuable Citation

YANKEE CLIPPER JOE DI MAGGIO, SPARKPLUG OF BOMBER CHAMPIONS

DIMAGGIO, THE UNRUFFLED

Portrait of a ballplayer who just keeps hitting 'em

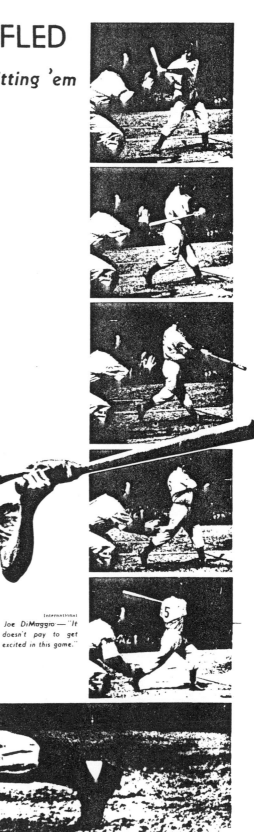

International

Joe DiMaggio — "It doesn't pay to get excited in this game."

# 1948
A YEAR BETWEEN PENNANTS

Joe DiMaggio signs his Yankee contract for 1948. Having won the American League MVP award the year before, DiMaggio earns a new contract, reportedly for $70,000, the highest salary paid to a player since Babe Ruth collected $80,000 in 1931. Seated with the Yankee Clipper is Dan Topping, one of the club owners, and looking on are Yankee general manager, George Weiss (left), and DiMaggio's manager, Bucky Harris.

TOUGH COMPETITION

One of the finest teams we faced in my years with the Yankees was the Boston Red Sox just before and shortly after World War II. My brother Dom played center field for them. Ted Williams was in his prime. They had Jimmie Foxx before the war, and plenty of other good ballplayers over those years like Bobby Doerr and Vern Stephens and pitchers like Tex Hughson, Mel Parnell, and Ellis Kinder.

We usually beat them out of the American League pennant, but not always. They took it in 1946. We played quite a few exciting games at Yankee Stadium and Fenway Park over the years, and the match-up almost always drew large and very vocal crowds in both ballparks.

I remember one game especially. It was at the end of the 1948 season and we were playing up in Boston. There was a very close pennant race that year between the Yankees, the Red Sox, and the Cleveland Indians. I was suffering badly from the bone spur in my heel but was still in the lineup. I got four singles that day, and each time I really hobbled down to first base. After the fourth hit, Bucky Harris put in a pinch runner and as I limped off the field the Boston fans, who knew I was hurting and probably should not have been playing at all, gave me an ovation, despite what I had been doing to their team that day. That was something I'll always remember. As it turned out, we both lost the pennant to the Indians that year.

Joe DiMaggio

1948 JOE DiMAGGIO STATISTICS

Games	153
At Bats	594
Hits	190
Doubles	26
Triples	11
Home Runs	39*
Runs Scored	110
Runs Batted In	155*
Bases on Balls	67
Strike Outs	30
Stolen Bases	1
Slugging Average	.598
Batting Average	.320

* Led the American League

STANDINGS

	Won	Lost	Percentage	Games Behind
Cleveland Indians**	97	58	.626	
Boston Red Sox	96	59	.619	1
New York Yankees	94	60	.610	2.5
Philadelphia A's	84	70	.545	12.5
Detroit Tigers	78	76	.506	18.5
St. Louis Browns	59	94	.386	37
Washington Senators	56	97	.366	40
Chicago White Sox	51	101	.336	44.5

**Defeated Boston Red Sox in a 1-game playoff

DiMaggio Signs 1948 Contract With Yankees for Salary Placed at $70,000

BOMBERS' ACE GETS SUBSTANTIAL BOOST

DiMaggio Signed to Contract Reported Second Highest in Yankees' History

DUROCHER LAUDS SHOTTON

Dodger Manager Says He Will 'Be Himself' in Direction of Club This Season

By JOHN DREBINGER

Beating the city's latest snow flurry by a matter of a few hours, winter baseball broke out on two fronts in the metropolitan area yesterday.

In the offices of the world champion Yankees, Joe DiMaggio bobbed up all smiles to announce he had just signed his 1948 contract with the Bombers. Although terms were not revealed it was generally accepted Jolting Joe, the American League's most valuable player in 1947, will receive approximately $70,000, thereby making him the second highest paid performer in Yankee history. Only Babe Ruth, with $80,000, ever received more from the Bombers.

No sooner had this breathless event been duly recorded by a battery of scribes and news photographers than all hands galloped off for the Montague Street offices of the Dodgers in Brooklyn where Branch Rickey and his reinstated manager, Leo Durocher, held court.

Close to Williams' Figure

With the ink scarcely dried on his newly signed contract, DiMaggio emerged from General Manager George M. Weiss' office all smiles. Both parties apparently had agreed not to divulge the exact amount and Joe parried all inquiries with the reply that he was "very happy." Weiss admitted the figure was "pretty close" to the $75,000 the Red Sox paid Ted Williams last summer.

Besides Ruth the only others ever to have topped that figure are Bob Feller, who was reputed to have received $85,000 last season, while Hank Greenberg drew $80,000 in his one year with the Pirates.

"I found Mr. Weiss the most pleasant man I've ever dealt with," said DiMaggio, adding that actually they came to terms Monday night at a conference which Dan Topping, club president, also attended. His previous high with the club, he said, was $43,750, which, exclusive of his three years in military service, is the salary he has been receiving ever since 1942.

"Mr. Weiss and I," said Joe, "had only one other meeting prior to last night. That was last week and at that time we barely touched on salary. We talked mostly of my physical condition."

Declares Himself Fit

On the latter item DiMaggio declared himself as fit as ever he has been during an off season. He scales an even 200 and he has completely recovered from the elbow operation he underwent at Johns Hopkins on Nov. 17. All that remains from that are two parallel scars, all healed.

"The arm feels great and I could throw right now," said DiMag, who today plans to head for Miami for a three weeks' vacation before returning for the New York baseball writers' dinner. He seemed to feel he deserved it after his long struggle to elevate himself into baseball's top-salaried bracket.

As the rookie of the year in 1936 he drew $7,500 and in the succeeding years this was boosted to $15,000, $25,000, $27,500, $32,000, $37,500 and finally $43,750, which he received in 1942, his last pre-war campaign, and in the past two seasons.

Sports of the Times

By ARTHUR DALEY

DiMaggio Comes into His Own

JOSEPH PAUL DIMAGGIO has finally solved the problem of the high cost of living. No longer does he have to go along on a hand-to-mouth basis, struggling to keep the wolf off the doorstep at a paltry $43,750 a year. The Jolter now is in the chips at a handsome $70,000 or so per season. More power to him, though; it couldn't happen to a nicer guy—or greater ball player.

It's ironic, perhaps, that the Yankee Clipper will receive his richest financial reward after a campaign which cannot compare statistically with others he has had. However, mere figures don't always tell the story. If they were the only true guide, Ted Williams would have been voted the Most Valuable Player in the American League last year because the Red Sox star led the circuit in practically every department except most stolen sweatshirts.

Boston writers have been seething and growing more and more indignant because DiMag was given the nod over their hero. It must be admitted here that they have a certain amount of justification for their howls. But the feeling in this corner is that Jolting Joe did a comparatively better job. Williams merely lived up to expectations, even though they could be termed Great Expectations.

However, the Yankee Clipper was at the crossroads of his career. He'd had a miserable, discouraging campaign in 1946, his initial postwar season. For the first time in his life he'd fallen below .300. Was DiMag washed up? Was he finished as a super-star? No one knew, Joe least of all. Then by way of adding to his mental torment he underwent a last-minute operation on his heel just before spring training.

Key Yankee

DiMaggio appears phlegmatic. But that's merely a surface indication. Down below he's as high-strung and sensitive as the true artist he is. He worried. Impatience gnawed at his vitals. He was fully aware of the truth in what Bucky Harris had been saying from the very first day in Puerto Rico. The Yankee manager answered all queries as to his pennant chances with the stock reply, "It all depends on the Big Fellow. If he has a good season, we're in." He didn't have to identify the Big Fellow. Everyone knew—including DiMag.

The season opened and the Yankees floundered. They desperately needed a Take-Charge guy. They didn't have him. In mid-May the impatient Joe walked over to Harris. "I'm ready, Bucky," he announced simply. He wasn't, though. When the impetuous Larry MacPhail issued the opinion that the Jolter had returned to action too soon, DiMaggio popped off.

"Who does MacPhail think he is?" he stormed to this reporter as we stood near the batting cage one day. And then he let go a blast which certainly wouldn't have looked good in print at that time. But now that the Roaring Redhead has departed, it's safe enough to mention the fact. DiMag was too hurt and angry to care much then, but if his friends won't protect him in times of emotional strain, no one will.

By June the Yankee Clipper was hitting in the vicinity of .360 and carrying the entire team on his broad shoulders. Oddly enough, he began to press, which is unusual for him. Batters ordinarily press only in a slump, but Joe was forcing in the middle of a hitting streak, so anxious was he to make his comeback a glorious success. So his batting began to tail off. He still wound up with a mark of .315, a fancy enough figure for anyone but a DiMaggio.

In one respect, though, Joe was very lucky. Furthermore, he admitted it quite frankly. "I was very lucky at the start of the season," he once confided. "We had so much rain then that the outfields were soft and cushiony, perfect for my bad heel. If the fields had been hard and sun-baked, I doubt that I could have stood up under the strain. As it was, I could continue to keep going, injured heel and all, while frequent postponements gave me extra and welcome rests."

Grand Larceny

He wasn't always lucky, however. In the world series, for instance, Carl Furillo robbed him of a triple off the bleacher wall and Al Gionfriddo committed grand larceny on the "home run" shot into the bullpen in the sixth game. That Gionfriddo theft left the Jolter dazed and shaken for a week. He walked around unseeingly, unbelievingly, with thoughts in a whirl and emotions jumbled.

It's always amazing how much the element of luck enters into hitting. As a rule, the law of averages will take care of the good batters over the course of a season while the bad ones always seem to operate with the "luck of a .230 hitter." They never get the breaks. The good ones make them.

Take the time DiMaggio was embarked on his magnificent record string of hitting safely in fifty-six consecutive games. There were practically few flukes in that streak. Once he topped a ball for a mighty accidental and providential hit. On another occasion he dribbled one at Luke Appling. But the ball struck a pebble and caromed off the forehead of the White Sox shortstop. Unquestionably it was a safety, but the official scorer hesitated. "Darn you, DiMaggio," he moaned, "I'll give you a hit this time, but everything has to be clean from now on." On his next trip to the plate the Jolter crashed out a majestic homer.

Joe had one scary game against the Browns when Eldon Auker kept him hitless until the ninth and DiMag was the fourth batter. But the Clipper got his chance and made good. On another occasion Johnny Babich of the Athletics refused to give him a good pitch, walking him repeatedly. Finally Joe McCarthy signaled permission to swing at the "cripple" and the Jolter almost cut the pitcher's legs from under him with a screaming single through the box. The streak ended in a night game in Cleveland when Ken Keltner made two impossible catches of liners which were ticketed for doubles. Joe's luck had run out on him at long last.

And now DiMaggio is up near Babe Ruth's brackets as a salaried serf. To repeat, it couldn't happen to a nicer guy—or greater ball player.

Daniel's Dope

Joe Joins Baseball's Opulent, at Last

By Dan Daniel

Boasting a new one-year contract for $60,000, Joseph Paul DiMaggio, center fielder of the Yankees, today finally had joined the ranks of the real potentates of major league financial history.

In 10 years with the Bombers—he was cut for two in the Army—DiMaggio has collected $343,250 in salary, $39,090.78 in world series prizes, and $1000 in third place pickups. All this comes to a neat $383,250.78. With his sixty grand for 1948, Giuseppe will move very close to the half million mark.

However, what with income taxes, expenses while he was in service, the settlement he made on his divorced wife and losses incurred in his ill-fated restaurant venture in San Francisco, DiMaggio is not one of our opulent ball players. That's why he is jubilant over his new contract.

When Joe came to the New York club in 1936, in one of the greatest deals put over by a major league organization, Ed Barrow signed him for $7500. And not without a scrap. In fact, DiMaggio says that for years he had to fight Cousin Ed every inch of the way, and his recollections of Barrow are not what you would call amicable.

The Yankees got Joe with an investment of only $30,000. The original deal called for $25,000 and five players. One of these, Dr. Eddie Farrell, refused to go. Barrow had to turn over another $5000.

Within 30 days after the deal had been consummated, the Red Sox offered $60,000 for DiMaggio. They could have had him for the price paid by Barrow. But Joe's knee injury had scared Boston and other clubs off the bargain. But for that hurt, DiMaggio's tag would have read $100,000.

* * *

DiMaggio's freshman season with the Yankees having proved spectacular—he hit .323, slugged 29 homers and drove in 125 runs—our hero made a holler for $25,000 in 1937. He had to settle for $15,000. However, he hit the $25,000 mark in 1938. In 1939, Joe's salary was $27,500. He jumped to $32,000 in 1940, $37,500 in 1941, and then $43,750 for the next three years. His new contract represents a neat jump of $16,250. Not bad. That $60,000 contract is the best yet won by a .315 hitter.

* * *

Joe Only 33, May Be Top Man Yet.

DiMaggio is only 33. If he takes care of himself, and doesn't run into any more hard luck, he should have four or five big years left. The way things are going in the Stadium, Joe may yet turn out to be another Babe Ruth in the all-time big league financial ratings.

The Babe hit the $80,000 jackpot in salary in 1930 and 1931, and in addition got 10 per cent of the exhibition net. That lagniappe is not for Joe or any other big league star. Ruth was the only player who could win that sort of arrangement.

DiMaggio already is the second best paid Yankee. He became that when he got his $43,750 contract, passing Lou Gehrig's $41,000. Can you imagine what Gehrig could command today? Or what he would have received but for being forced to play second fiddle to Ruth?

VIEWS OF SPORT

By Red Smith

Copyright, 1948, New York Herald Tribune Inc.

One Guy Stood Out

ST. PETERSBURG, Fla., March 10.—There was at least an hour and a half to go before the ball game but already a fairish crowd had forsaken the shuffleboard hells and horseshoe sinkholes of St. Pete and gathered in the stands of Al Lang Field. The batting cage was up for the Cardinals' hitting practice and most of the Yankees were dressed and on their bench, identifying the rookies as they came to bat and talking about Howie Pollet, who was working easily on the mound.

A group of perhaps half a dozen Yankees came out from under the stands on the Cardinals' side and walked across behind the plate toward their bench. There was a spontaneous burst of applause and, looking up, you saw why. Joe DiMaggio was in the group.

It is hard to say why he stood out. He was hatless, but so were some of the others. He didn't strut or swagger or walk ahead of the rest. He just strolled across, seeming at home and looking big league, and the crowd, which had been silent and a little bored, picked him out and automatically started clapping.

Nobody had any doubt about whom they were applauding. Cuddles Marshall, the pitcher, was walking with DiMaggio - - and somebody on the New York bench yelled, "listen to the cheers for Marshall." Cuddles grinned, a little self-consciously. He kept on walking as Joe stopped behind the cage to shake hands with Eddie Dyer, the Cardinals' manager.

Red Smith

A Great Catch

THEN he came on alone. He hadn't acknowledged the welcome. hadn't actually seemed aware of it, although he must have known it was meant for him. He was just at ease, that's all. When some one in the stands shouted, "Hiya, Joe," he looked up and flashed his toothy, lazy grin. He stopped just short of the bench among a cluster of newspaper men.

A man in the stands came down to the screen and called, "Mr. DiMaggio, will you look up this way?" Joe looked up into the muzzle of a movie camera and waited until the camera stopped whirring, meanwhile taking a small, casual part in a small, casual conversation with the reporters.

One of the group said, "Joe, I saw Gionfriddo's name in a news story from the Dodgers' camp, where he got beaned, and it made me think of something. How late in the game was it when he made that catch off you in the World Series?"

"The sixth inning," Joe said.

"And the Yankees were three runs behind at the time?"

"That's right, 8 to 5, no, 9 to 6, I think."

"So, where should Gionfriddo have been playing with you coming up?"

Joe was grinning broadly.

"That's right," he said.

"It has taken me," the reporter said, "five months to think of that."

And a Bad Play

JOE kept grinning.

It was obvious he had realized from the start what the man was getting at. With the Yankees three runs behind late in the ball game, two runners on base and two out, where should a left fielder play DiMaggio? With the seat of his pants pinned to the wall, of course, because it was a cinch that the Yankees' power guy wouldn't be bunting.

So there never should have been a great catch by Gionfriddo. He should have been standing there all the time, waiting for the ball. Yet because he ran a country mile and twisted himself all out of shape and still contrived to get the ball, we've all been raving about the play ever since, never pausing to consider the situation and discover that it was a bad play.

There was a somewhat similar catch by Ernie Orsatti in the World Series of 1934 and the crowd was still gasping when the Cardinals got into their clubhouse. Frank Frisch, the St. Louis manager, then ordered the doors locked and the visitors excluded for five minutes, which time he devoted to chewing the innards out of Orsatti for being out of position and making a difficult play out of an easy one.

All this was recalled while the newspaper man was saying in disgust, "five months it's taken me to see that Gionfriddo play straight."

But DiMaggio, still grinning, said of Gionfriddo.

"He was right. He made it right."

Man With the Right Answers

JOE went on talking idly and easily among friends. Later on, when the Yankees were playing the Cardinals, he came up as a pinch-batter in the seventh inning. The Yanks had made one hit off Al Brazle and Jim Hearn but were leading, 2 to 0. This time DiMaggio acknowledged the applause by touching the bill of his cap. He hit a long, hard drive to left which was caught. The crowd applauded again as he went off the field.

"Can you imagine him a few years ago standing there chatting with the press?" a fellow asked. "A few years ago he would have ducked because he wouldn't have known what to say."

A few years ago DiMaggio was one of a fairly big group at a table in Toots Shor. People kept stopping by for a word or so, and always it was Lefty Gomez who replied, tossing off a quip, having exactly the right answer for everybody. Joe sat and listened and scarcely opened his mouth.

"I'd give anything," he said envying Gomez's self-assurance, "if I could do that."

He does that all the time now, and never gives it a thought.

The crown becomes the champ.

Joe DiMaggio and some baseball friends: Connie Mack (top); Bill Dickey (left); and Lefty O'Doul (right).

Yankees Lose Stadium Inaugural to Red Sox

44,619 SEE BOSTON HALT BOMBERS, 4-0

Williams Blasts Three Hits, One a Homer, and Red Sox Record First Triumph

HARRIS YIELDS 5 BLOWS

Sharp Defense Helps Him to Gain Shut-Out—Shea, Loser, Relieved After Fifth

By JOHN DREBINGER

Joe McCarthy returned to the Stadium yesterday in a rather unfamiliar role at a Yankee inaugural, but Marse Joe still doesn't seem to have lost his winning touch.

He wore a Red Sox uniform and he no longer had a Joe DiMaggio in his corner. But he did have a fellow named Ted Williams and that more than sufficed.

For Boston's Splendid Splinter exploded three hits, one a homer, and by these means so demoralized Bucky Harris' Bombers that the world champions never came out of their stupor. Mickey Harris, the left-hander, shut them out on five hits; their own mound ace, Frank Shea, vacated the scene after five rounds, and to the Bosox went this season's opener on the New York scene by a score of 4 to 0.

It was, therefore, a rather disappointing inaugural for the majority in a gathering of 44,619 that included Governor Dewey, who officially launched the Bombers' homecoming by tossing out the first ball. It was a swell pitch, too, landing squarely in Catcher Gus Niarhos' mitt. If the Yanks made any mistakes after that it perhaps could have been that they didn't allow the Governor to keep right on pitching.

Old Law of Averages

However, it cannot be denied the law of averages in the young season was working heavily in favor of the Sox and their new member,

THE BASEBALL SEASON GETTING UNDER WAY AT THE STADIUM

Dom DiMaggio out at second on Pesky's grounder in the sixth inning. The play went from Souchock to Rizzuto.

McCarthy, who for years ruled the roost in New York. Tagged as powerful pennant contenders, the Sox had blown their first three games and that sort of thing could not go on forever. Now, with this first victory in the initial joust with their formidable foes, they stand as good as the world champions. Each has won only one game in four played, a situation that might indicate the world is truly upside down.

No sooner had the impressive inaugural ceremonies been disposed of than one could feel the Bosox taking charge, with Williams and Southpaw Harris primed for the killing. In fact, Williams, rarely at his best at the Stadium, not only carried the Boston banner yesterday but clearly overshadowed his arch rival, Joe DiMaggio, as well.

Jolting Joe had the tide running against him all day. Twice he hit the ball hard only to see it caught. Once he singled but to no purpose.

In the third he fumbled a Williams single to let in the first Boston run and in the fifth experienced his most disappointing moment when, with the bases full, he lifted an infield pop-up for the third out.

Stormy in the Third

Making his first appearance of the season, Shea, the Bombers' 1947 freshman star, ran into his first squall in the third when he walked Harris. He also walked Dom DiMaggio and while pitching to the Little Professor there also came the season's first rhubarb when Shea, in an attempt to trap Harris off first, threw past Steve Souchock, the Yankee first sacker for the day.

The ball, however, caromed off the stand and Steve recovered it in time to throw for a put-out at second only to have the umpires rule out the play. This mystified everybody until it was explained that Umpire Bill McGowan behind the plate had called time.

After Dom DiMaggio walked to put two on with none out, Shea retired Johnny Pesky on a short fly. But Williams, who already had punched a single through the Yanks' "right side" defense in the first, now singled sharply to center. It was such a hard hit ball that had Joe DiMaggio fielded it cleanly, Harris could never have advanced beyond third. But the Yankee Clipper momentarily bobbled the ball and the Sox had their first run.

In the fourth they picked up another on singles by Bobby Doerr and Birdie Tebbetts and in the fifth picked up two more. Williams produced the first one with a rifle shot into the right field stand, the ball just eluding Tommy Henrich's great leap.

A Boot by Johnson

Then Stan Spence doubled, moved to third when Bill Johnson booted Vern Stephens' sharp grounder and counted on Doerr's long fly to DiMaggio in center. That was more than ample.

With Shea passing out for a pinch hitter in the same round Joe Page and Red Embree divided the final four innings of pitching for the Bombers and blanked the Sox. But the day's damage had been done beyond repair.

The Bombers missed their best chance to score in the fourth, when DiMaggio singled and two passes filled the bases with only one out. But Phil Rizzuto slapped into a double play.

Two passes and Henrich's second single of the day filled the bases again for the Yanks in the fifth, but DiMaggio, popping to Pesky, ended this threat.

After that only one Yank got on base. Johnny Lindell, who, with Souchock was presenting the Yank's right-handed attack against a left-hander, doubled with one down in the eighth and DiMaggio followed with a vicious drive toward left. But Pesky froze to the ball and the Yanks remained congealed for the rest of the misty afternoon.

The pre-game ceremonies were carried off with customary Stadium neatness and dispatch. There was the traditional parade to the centerfield flagpole, led by Capt. Sutherland and his Seventh Regiment Band, an institution older than the Stadium itself, for they were here when the arena was opened in 1923 and they have been at every opening since.

There were other reminders, too, of that eventful afternoon a quarter of a century ago. Most prominent of all, Babe Ruth, whose thoughts, as he sat behind the Yankee dugout, doubtless went back to that first Stadium game ever played, when the Bambino, almost single-handed, turned back another Red Sox team, 4 to 1, with a three-run homer.

Arrived at the flagpole, the paraders stood at attention while Miss Lucy Monroe sang "The Star-Spangled Banner" and Old Glory was hauled aloft. Following this came another flag raising as the Yanks unfurled their eleventh world series pennant.

Will Harridge, president of the American League, presided over this detail, assisted by Managers Harris and McCarthy. It was Bucky's first as a Yankee skipper, but it was old stuff to Marse Joe, who in bygone years had directed seven of those world titles to the Stadium.

Series Emblems Awarded

Back at home plate, Mel Allen, the Stadium's ace broadcaster, took over as master of ceremonies while Commissioner A. B. Chandler, smiling good naturedly at the customary round of boos that seems invariably to mark his New York receptions, distributed the individual World Series emblems—rings and watches—to the Yankee players.

Mightiest ovation of all came when Joe DiMaggio received the Kenesaw Mountain Landis plaque as the American League's most valuable player for 1947. Joe King, chairman of the New York chapter of the Baseball Writers Association, made this presentation.

Following this, Allen stepped aside as the M. C. to receive the Sporting News Trophy as the American League's outstanding broadcaster for 1947.

There being, by now, no more gifts to bestow upon anybody, the Red Sox stepped in to take perhaps the most important prize of the day. That, of course, being the ball game itself.

The box score:

BOSTON (A.)	ab.	r.	h.	po.	a.	e.
D. DiM'gio, cf	2	0	0	8	0	0
Pesky, 3b	5	0	0	3	1	0
Williams, lf	5	1	3	3	0	0
Spence, 1b	3	1	1	8	0	0
Stephens, ss	5	0	0	0	3	0
Doerr, 2b	5	1	2	1	1	0
Mele, rf	4	0	0	3	0	0
Tebbetts, c	3	0	1	1	0	0
Harris, p	3	1	0	0	0	0
Total	35	4	7	27	5	0

NEW YORK (A.)	ab.	r.	h.	po.	a.	e.
Stirnw's, 2b	4	0	0	1	2	0
Henrich, rf	4	0	2	3	0	0
Lindell, lf	2	0	1	1	0	0
J. DiM'gio, cf	4	0	1	7	0	1
Souchock, 1b	4	0	0	5	1	0
Johnson, 3b	3	0	0	2	0	1
Rizzuto, ss	4	0	1	3	3	0
Niarhos, c	3	0	0	5	0	0
Shea, p	1	0	0	0	1	0
aBrown	1	0	0	0	0	0
Page, p	0	0	0	0	0	0
bLollar	1	0	0	0	0	0
Embree, p	0	0	0	0	0	0
Total	31	0	5	27	7	2

aFouled out for Shea in fifth.
bFlied out for Page in seventh.

Boston .... 0 0 1 1 2 0 0 0 0—4
New York .... 0 0 0 0 0 0 0 0 0—0

Runs batted in—Tebbetts, Williams, Doerr. Two-base hits—Spence, Lindell. Home run—Williams. Double play—Stephens, Doerr and Spence. Left on bases—Boston 11. New York 8. Bases on balls—Off Shea 3, Harris 4, Page 3, Embree 1. Struck out—By Shea 2, Harris 1, Page 2, Embree 1. Hits—Off Shea 6 in 5 innings, Page 1 in 2, Embree 0 in 2. Losing pitcher—Shea. Umpires—McGowan, Hubbard and McKinley. Time of game—2:15. Attendance—44,619 paid.

The Sporting News Trophy for Meritorious Service to American Youth is presented to Joe DiMaggio by the great Babe Ruth. The Sultan of Swat, Ruth, ailing of cancer at the time, died later that year.

DiMaggio... Everybody's Ball Player
The Human Side of a Great Hitting Machine

SCALPEL! SCISSORS! NEEDLE! THREAD! GLUE!

THEY PRACTICALLY HAD TO SEW THE MAN TOGETHER FOR EACH WORLD SERIES GAME!

AMERICAN LEAGUE 1948

WITH DIMAGGIO AT HIS PEAK—THAT CAN BE THE DIFFERENCE!

LAST YEAR'S DI MAGGIO HIT .315 WITH MORE THINGS WRONG WITH HIM THAN THE ONE HOSS SHAY!!

PULLED MUSCLE IN RT. SHOULDER

TORN NECK MUSCLE

TWO BONE CHIPS IN ELBOW

PULLED MUSCLE IN LEFT SHOULDER

TORN LEG MUSCLES

LAME BACK

TRICK KNEE

WHAT WILL HE DO THIS YEAR WITHOUT AN ACHE OR A WORRY IN THE WORLD?

MUSCULAR STRAIN IN INSTEP

UNHEALED 3 INCH SCAR UNDER HEEL FROM BONE SPUR OPERATIONS

Joe's Arm Sound

WASHINGTON, D. C. — Joe DiMaggio. gave fair warning to American League base-runners that his arm is again sound in the opening game of the season here, April 19. when he made his most sensational throw of the spring against the Senators. From an off-balance position in the first inning. DiMaggio, who underwent an operation on his arm last winter, almost nipped Al Kozar at the plate after grabbing Mickey Vernon's fly. Even the Yankees were dazzled.

Quiet Star a Big Favorite of Fans, Writers, Players

Press Box Portrait of Yankee Clipper Sketched by Daniel, Chronicler of Career Since Rookie Days

By DAN DANIEL

NEW YORK, N. Y.

Among the many ceremonies listed for opening day in Yankee Stadium was the presentation of the 1947 Most Valuable Player award of the American League, the Landis Memorial plaque, to Joseph Paul DiMaggio, center fielder of the Bombers.

For Giuseppe, this was in the nature of old stuff, and yet, more thrilling an experience than ever. He had achieved the most valuable citation for 1939. but that was when he was only 25, in his fourth season with New York.

In 1941, DiMaggio won the accolade a second time. Now he had it again, at the age of 34, after three years of Army service had hit him at the peak of his remarkable career. To gain the grand

acknowledgment at this time was summa cum laude, with palms and laurels.

Not a very great deal actually has been written about this brightest member of the DiMaggio constellation. In fact, not a great deal really has been written about any of our baseball heroes with the exception of George Herman Ruth.

The tendency in baseball writing is toward recognition of the evidences in arithmetic. There is powerful worship of the almighty batting average, the spectacular home run total, the runs driven in figure. the won and lost and earned run figures in the pitching histories.

About the men behind the arithmetic-

al evidences, comparatively little has been done.

It seems to me that this is a weakness -- understandable and inevitable though it may be, but a weakness just the same—of our system of baseball writing.

There is a trend toward the creation of pictures of automata. The baseball star is made out to be a puppet. But he has his sensations and his feelings, he has his ills and his hopes and fears, he has his stomach aches and his nights of walking the baby, he has his scraps with the Missus or his courting misunderstandings with the Miss.

A diamond hero fans thrice in a row, and your man in the stands says, "Chumley looks like a bum today." What he doesn't know is that Chumley's father died at three in the morning.

This is an effort to give you a picture of the Joe DiMaggio we of the New York press box know. The Joe DiMaggio I have been close to since 1936, in the clubhouse, on the field before games, in the railroad car.

My introduction to Joe, my first experiences with him, make an interesting and significant story.

Joe's closest friend among the baseball writers in San Francisco was Tom Laird, now a real estate tycoon in Sacramento.

* * *

"Just See My Friend Dan"

Laird said to Joe, "You are going to St. Petersburg, Fla., to join the Yankees. Don't make any mistakes. Don't do what Myril Hoag did, for example.

"Myril walked into the Yankee camp and found Dan Daniel waiting for him. Dan said, 'Suppose we sit down over here and talk things over.'

"Hoag replied, 'I want to go out and play golf. How about six o'clock?' To which Dan replied, 'By six o'clock, Mr. Hoag, my interest in you will have vanished.' Hoag did not play golf.

"Now, you go to Dan and whatever he suggests, you do. He is a close friend of mine, and you will find that he will be a good friend of yours."

Joe called on me as soon as he arrived in St. Petersburg and my first word of advice was: "Don't be suspicious of the writers. Don't be too talkative, but don't crawl into a shell and stay there. As I size you up, you have a level noggin and a sense of humor. Those are the two main essentials in relations with the press. Just be yourself."

It took about three days to note that in DiMaggio the Yankees had one of the greatest players in their history.

The sports editor of the New York World-Telegram—Joe Williams, at that time—telegraphed. "Get DiMaggio to do his life story."

I put the matter to Giuseppe and he said he would be delighted to collaborate with me. We sat around for a few hours and he told me how he had

Truth of DiMag Knee: His Leg Went to Sleep

Highly Publicized Injury To Limb Was Crumpling After Jitney Ride

got into baseball, how he had yearned for a place in the Yankee outfield.

No sooner had the World-Telegram advertised the DiMaggio yarn than our opposition got after Joe. One organization offered him $3,000 to do the story exclusively for it.

DiMaggio said to me, "I can get this dough from the other paper. What do you want me to do?"

I replied, "Joe, the series is in type, I can offer you no compensation. But we have advertised the Life Story of Joe DiMaggio.

"Now, you have signed no release. If you choose to sell the story to our opposition, we have no hold on you. It's up to you. Sign the release to the World-Telegram, or sign up with the other paper."

DiMaggio's contract with the Yankees called for $7,500 for the season, and $3,000 was a lot of dough to Joe.

He said, "Make out the release and I will sign it. You got there first, and you are entitled to the story."

That gives you a pretty fair picture of Joseph Paul DiMaggio. I do not know of any other ball player within my experience who would have done what Joe did that morning in St. Petersburg. Not one other.

DiMaggio made an excellent impression right from the start of his Yankee career.

There was nothing phony about him. Often, when you put the vacuum on a new player, he will give you a song and dance which smacks of the movie gal. She was a soda jerk or a waitress in a beanery, but will tell you how she was sent to a convent by her wealthy mama. Actually, Mom was running a cheap boarding house in Houston, Tex., when sis ran off to go to work.

Ball players sometimes will give you pictures of early lives in sequestered homes. But Joe said, "I am the luckiest guy in the world. But for the grace of God, I would be driving a truck or working in a fruit market, in San Francisco. I never did go for that fishing life which my dad and my brother Tom took up for a living, and which they still follow.

"We are poor people, tickled to death that our parents came over to a country in which opportunity is so rich that Joe DiMaggio is in the outfield of the Yankees, and getting $7,500 a season for being there."

Joe got off to a bad start with the

DiMag, With $65,000 Pact, 'Going All-Out This Season'

NEW YORK, N. Y. — Very important in the brighter psychology, keener determination and generally pleasant outlook of Joe DiMaggio is his new contract, for $65,000.

Said Joe when the Yankees opened their drive in Washington on April 19. "I am going all-out this season."

He got two hits in the opening victory, 12 to 4. He made a throw reminiscent of his early days with the Yankees, and he made a first to third dash on a medium single, which showed there was nothing wrong with his speed.

New York club. Early in the training season at St. Petersburg in March, 1936, he suffered a severe burn on a foot and had to miss 16 games of the championship season.

* * *

Joe's Sugar-Coated Knee

The inside story of that burn never has been written before. Doc Painter, then the trainer of the Yankees, came in for a lot of castigation which was unjust. DiMaggio came to the Yankees with a bad knee. But for that injury, he never would have landed in New York. He would have been sold to the Red Sox for $100,000, the kind of money Ed Barrow was told he no longer could spend for a player after the $103,000 purchase of Lyn Lary and Jimmy Reese from Oakland had proved unsuccessful.

At St. Petersburg, DiMaggio showed no evidence of the old knee ailment, but he did pick up a bad ankle.

Painter put the hoof under the diathermia machine. How was Doc to know that DiMaggio's blood chemistry ran a little high in sugar?

Painter gave DiMaggio no more time with the diathermia hipper-dipper than he had given any other player. Doc did not put the DiMag hoof into the oven and go off about other matters and forget the big dish.

DiMaggio's foot burned just like a cake with too much sugar frosting would have burned if left in the oven. Painter got merry hallelujah for what was supposed to be an error in judgment. But it wasn't his fault. And Joe said so.

Stories about DiMaggio's San Francisco days, from 1932 through 1935, have had Joe getting hurt in competition. As a matter of fact, that famous knee injury was suffered off the field.

"I played a Sunday double-header in the Seals' Stadium, and then had to dash for my sister's home for dinner," Giuseppe told me.

"I did not get the kind of dough which would permit the use of cabs. I got a seat in a jitney bus. It became crowded to suffocation and my legs were jammed in a cramped position. The circulation of blood in my legs became impeded and they got completely numb.

"When I hopped off the jitney, my leg crumpled under me. My knee was gone. I went to my sister's and had to remain there overnight. I could not walk. That was in 1934. I played only 101 games that season. I was told my major league hopes would have to be forgotten. But I decided not to take that verdict. I gave it a fight, and here I am."

* * *

A $100,000 Markdown

Because of that ride on a jitney, Joe DiMaggio turned out to be the greatest bargain in the history of a club which has made many a highly fortunate purchase.

When word got around that Giuseppe's knee was gone, the major league ivory hunters who had been tailing him lost interest. The price tag was changed from $125,000 to $100,000. Then to $75,000.

Finally, Charley Graham of the Seals got panicky, and sold Joe to the Yankees for $25,000 in cash, and five players. One of these, Doc Farrell, now a successful dentist in New Jersey, refused to report and Ed Barrow had to give Graham another $5,000.

Before making the deal, Barrow ordered Bill Essick, Coast representative of the Yankees, to take DiMaggio to a prominent surgeon in Los Angeles. This specialist said, "There is nothing wrong with the knee that a little time will not cure."

No sooner had the Yankees purchased Joe than Eddie Collins of the Red Sox offered them a profit of $40,000.

Baseball is in the blood of Joe's family. Dominic is with the Red Sox. Vince played for the Reds, Pirates, Phillies, Braves and Giants. Tom, the fisherman, also played a little ball.

Dominic is a great ball player in his own right. But older brother Giuseppe is his idol.

Joseph Paul DiMaggio is a quiet guy. Many folks think he is high hat. He isn't. He's merely diffident, to the point of being scared of crowds. Joe likes a certain amount of attention. But he does not luxuriate in adulation. Being made a fuss over by a lot of people definitely is not his dish.

Joe is a good-looking fellow. He has a pleasant face, a direct look, he is formed like a greyhound. Six feet, one and a half inches tall, 200 pounds.

* * *

Voice in Picking Reynolds

Joe is a keen student. The management knows this. When Joe Gordon was traded to Cleveland, Larry MacPhail and Bucky Harris decided to take Red Embree. Then they put it up to Joe. He said "Reynolds." Reynolds it was. Allie won 19 games for the Bombers, and beat the Dodgers in the World's Series, in addition.

DiMaggio is the kind of hombre who would appeal to women. But his history in that direction is not flamboyant. He has had one marital adventure. It turned sour. There was a divorce.

Out of this union DiMag got Little Joe. He brings the boy to the Stadium clubhouse. He would like him to be a ball player. The son embarrasses the father by exclaiming, "My dad is the greatest ball player in the whole world."

DiMaggio's relations with the public always have been perfect. He never has had a quarrel with the press. He is the writers' ball player, the manager's delight, the ball players' ball player, the umpires' ball player. And the idol of the fans.

DiMaggio's closest friend on the club is Joe Page.

DiMaggio Gains 13 Pounds in 13 Years With Yankees

NEW YORK, N. Y.—Though 13 years older than when he first joined the Yankees, Joe DiMaggio weighs only 13 more pounds, one for each year, as he starts another season with the Bombers. Joe reveals he weighed 187 when he came up and now tips the scales at 200. "I never seem to fatten up, no matter what sort of diet I follow," says Joe.

DiMaggio also declares he never felt in better shape, but is keeping his fingers crossed, for he missed half of his opening dates in ten active seasons with the Yankees. "I've always had a sore arm, a Charley horse or some ailment for a week or so during training. This time I've been set all spring," he reveals.

Joe's Row With MacPhail Only Yank Office Run-In

NEW YORK, N. Y. — In 1947, when Col. Larry MacPhail, the ebullient, the effervescent and the unaccountable, was running the Yankees, Joe DiMaggio had his one and only run-in with the front office.

MacPhail ordered Joe to pose for an Army movie in which new uniforms were played up.

Joe felt that he should not appear in the movie. He didn't.

MacPhail fined him $100. The money later was returned. Joe gave it to the Damon Runyon cancer fund.

JOE DIMAGGIO

Joe DiMaggio

NEW YORK, N. Y.

America's most talked-about ball player when the Yankees came out of the West was Joe DiMaggio. Most talked about because of stirring achievement with the bat, and continued brilliant performance in the field.

Hats off to a man who is one of the greatest all-around center fielders the game has developed.

Hats off to a grand athlete and fine personality, who has not permitted his achievements to have anything to do with the size of his chapeau.

Hats off to Giuseppe because:

(1)—On May 23, before 78,431 persons in the Cleveland Stadium, he hit three home runs in successive appearances at the plate, after an introductory single, two of the four-baggers off Bob Feller, the third against Bob Muncrief, who relieved Feller, to drive in all of his team's runs in a 6 to 5 victory over Rapid Robert.

(2)—On May 20, in Chicago, he hit two homers, a triple, a double and a single, to drive in six runs in a 13 to 2 victory.

(3)—In four days, he hit six homers.

(4)—In seven contests on the first western trip of the Yankees, through the record double-header in Cleveland, he drove in 16 runs and hit at a .407 clip, lifting him over .300 for the first time this year.

Those three homers in dramatic succession in Cleveland marked Joe's second such performance of his career.

The repeat production was especially notable as his first came in 1937. To turn a trick like that after an interval of 11 seasons, three lost from baseball in the Army, was a monumental achievement. But then, Joseph Paul DiMaggio is a monumental ball player. DAN DANIEL.

DiMaggio scores in a cloud of dust in the first inning of a game against the Washington Senators at Yankee Stadium in late May 1948. The throw from Washington outfielder, Gil Coan, got away from catcher, Jake Early, and the Yanks won 5-4.

Joe DiMaggio connects for an extra base hit in a 1948 game against the Indians at Cleveland. DiMaggio collected 190 hits that year and batted .320.

DiMaggio Smashes 3 Homers as Yankees Beat Browns

BOMBERS TRIUMPH AT ST. LOUIS, 4-2, 6-2

Double Victory Sends Yanks Into Second Place Ahead of Faltering Athletics

RASCHI WINS 8TH IN ROW

Goes Route for the First Time Since June 6 — Nightcap Annexed by Embree

By JOHN DREBINGER
Special to THE NEW YORK TIMES.

ST. LOUIS, June 20—Joe Di-Maggio exploded three home runs today and while one may have been more or less ornamental, there was no questioning the importance the other two played in the day's events.

The first one came late in the opener of the afternoon's twin bill. It cleared the left field bleachers with the bases empty and as the Yanks toppled the Browns, 4 to 2, the shot merely made it a little easier for Vic Raschi to record his eighth mound victory of the campaign and eighth in a row against a single defeat.

But in the afterpiece the Yankee clipper really tossed his weight around. With Red Embree locked in a two-all deadlock with Bryan Stephens, the great DiMag opened the eighth inning with another resounding shot that cleared the wall back of the left field bleachers. And in the ninth, with two colleagues on the basepaths, he smashed his third of the day into the same stand.

Keep Pace With Indians

That, to the dismay of 10,845 Brownie sympathizers, gave the Bombers the battle, 6 to 2, for a sweep of the twin bill. It catapulted the world champions into second place over the Athletics and enabled them to maintain their three-and-a-half-length distance behind the Indians with whom they are about to clash in a four-game series.

The three clouts boosted DiMaggio's seasonal total to fourteen and marked the second time this year that he has smacked that many in one day, although his trio on May 23 all fell in the opener of a twin-bill with the Indians.

Until DiMaggio cut loose in the nightcap the Bombers were having a time of it. Doubles by Tommy Henrich and George Stirnweiss had given them a run in the third and in the sixth George McQuinn doubled home another. But the persistent Browns also counted a run in each of these innings.

Frank Biscan was the victim of DiMaggio's final ninth inning wallop which came after Phil Rizzuto had singled and Johnny Lindell had walked. That gave Embree his fifth triumph of the year against a lone defeat.

Weathering a ninth inning squall, Raschi came through neatly enough to bag the opener. Opposed at the outset by Fred Sanford, the Bombers sent their big righthander off to a two-run lead in the first, which Rizzuto, at the top of the batting order again, opened with a pass. Henrich got a single and a double off the right field screen by Lindell fetched home one. The other tallied while DiMaggio was being tossed out at first. For the next four rounds Sanford held the champions in check but they came up with a gift tally in the sixth in which DiMaggio seemed to bear a charmed life. He lifted a high fly over short which Ed Pellagrini at the very last moment lost in a hazy sun.

Score One in Seventh

That gave Jolting Joe a single. Then Yogi Berra grounded to Gerry Priddy, who thought he had tagged DiMaggio on the way to second before tossing the ball to first for a twin killing. But Umpire Charlie Berry ruled Priddy had missed the tag and that put Joe on second. A moment later he was over the plate when McQuinn singled to left.

Two innings later, the Jolter greeted Relief Hurler Al Widmar with a resounding smash that sailed clear over the left field bleachers just inside the foul line.

In the meantime, Raschi was holding the Brownies well in hand until they finally broke through for a tally in the seventh on singles by Roy Partee and Chuck Stevens and a fly to right by Pinch Hitter Joe Schultz.

In the ninth came another Brownie flurry as Les Moss, Stevens and Bob Dillinger cut loose with a trio of singles. Raschi, however, had enough left to finish on his own power and thus turned in his first complete game since June 6, when he blanked these same Browns with a three-hitter.

Since then Raschi had been taken out after two starts, but in each instance the loss was charged to somebody else, so that Vic's unbeaten string of eight, longest currently running in the majors, is still intact.

Box Scores of Yankees' Games

FIRST GAME

NEW YORK (A.)	ab.	r.	h.	po.	a.	e.
Rizzuto, ss.	4	1	0	3	4	0
Henrich, rf.	4	1	1	1	0	0
Lindell, lf	4	0	1	2	0	0
DiMaggio, cf.	4	2	3	6	0	1
Berra, c	4	0	1	4	0	0
Niarhos, c	0	0	0	1	0	0
McQuinn, 1b	4	0	1	7	1	0
Johnson, 3b.	4	0	1	1	2	0
Stirn'ss, 2b.	1	0	0	1	4	0
Raschi, p	3	0	1	1	0	0
Total	31	4	8	27	11	1

ST. LOUIS (A.)	ab.	r.	h.	po.	a.	e.
Dillinger, 3b	5	0	1	1	1	0
Zarilla, rf.	4	0	1	2	0	0
Priddy, 2b.	3	0	0	4	4	0
Platt, lf	4	0	2	2	0	1
Lehner, cf.	3	0	0	2	1	0
Partee, c	3	0	1	3	0	0
aFannin	1	0	0	0	0	0
Moss, c	1	1	1	1	1	0
Pella'ni ss.	2	0	0	1	2	0
bBinks	1	1	0	0	0	0
Dente, ss	1	0	0	1	1	0
Stevens, 1b.	4	0	2	10	3	0
cSchultz	1	0	0	0	0	0
Widmar, p	0	0	0	1	1	0
dAnderson	1	0	1	0	0	0
Total	35	2	9	27	14	1

aRan for Partee in seventh.
bHit into force play for Pellagrini in seventh.
cFlied out for Sanford in seventh.
dSingled for Widmar in ninth.

New York .... 2 0 0 0 0 1 0 1 0—4
St. Louis .... 0 0 0 0 0 0 1 0 1—2

Runs batted in—Lindell, DiMaggio 2, McQuinn, Schultz, Anderson. Two-base hits—Lindell, Johnson, Raschi. Home run—DiMaggio. Sacrifices—Rachi 2, Stirnweiss. Double plays—Dillinger, Priddy and Stevens; Stirnweiss, Rizzuto and McQuinn. Left on bases—New York 7, St. Louis 8. Bases on balls—Off Sanford 3, Widmar 1, Raschi 2. Struck out—By Sanford 1, Raschi 4. Hits—Off Sanford 7 in 7

innings, Widmar 1 in 2. Losing pitcher—Sanford. Umpires—Hurley, Berry and Jones. Time of game—2:00.

SECOND GAME

NEW YORK (A.)	ab.	r.	h.	po.	a.	e.
Rizzuto, ss.	5	1	1	3	10	0
Henrich, rf.	4	0	2	1	0	0
Lindell, lf.	3	2	0	1	0	0
DiMaggio, cf.	5	2	2	1	0	0
Berra, c	4	0	1	2	2	1
Lollar, c	1	0	0	3	0	0
McQuinn, 1b.	4	0	2	14	1	0
Johnson, 3b.	4	0	1	1	0	0
Stirnweiss, 2b	4	1	1	4	5	0
Embree, p	4	0	0	0	0	0
Total	38	6	10	27	18	1

ST. LOUIS (A.)	ab.	r.	h.	po.	a.	e.
Dillinger, 3b.	4	0	0	0	1	
Zarilla, rf.	4	1	2	6	0	0
Priddy, 2b.	3	0	0	6	2	0
Platt, lf	3	0	1	5	0	0
Lehner, cf.	3	0	2	2	0	0
Moss, c	3	0	2	0	0	
Dente, ss	2	0	0	1	5	1
Stevens, 1b.	2	1	1	5	0	0
Stephens, p	2	0	0	0	0	0
aSchultz	1	0	0	0	0	0
Biscan, p	0	0	0	0	1	0
Total	27	2	6	27	8	2

aGrounded out for Stephens in eighth.

New York .... 0 0 1 0 0 1 0 1 3—6
St. Louis .... 0 0 1 0 0 1 0 0 0—2

Runs batted in—Henrich, Dillinger, McQuinn, Platt, DiMaggio 3. Two-base hits—Stirnweiss, Henrich, Stevens, McQuinn, Zarilla. Home runs—DiMaggio 2. Stolen base—Zarilla. Sacrifices—Moss, McQuinn, Henrich. Double plays—Stirnweiss, Rizzuto and McQuinn 2, Rizzuto, Stirnweiss and McQuinn. Left on bases—New York 10, St. Louis 4. Bases on balls—Off Embree 5, Stephens 3, Biscan 1. Struck out—By Embree 2, Biscan 1. Hits—Off Stephens 7 in 8 innings, Biscan 3 in 1. Wild pitch—Biscan. Losing pitcher—Stephens. Umpires—Berry, Jones and Hurley. Time of game—1:56. Attendance—10,845 (paid).

1948

ALL STAR GAME

SPORTSMAN'S PARK

SAINT LOUIS

TUESDAY, JULY 13
1948

Souvenir

OFFICIAL SCORE BOOK

Joe DiMaggio was named to the 1948 American League All-Star but did not start in the game because of a painful heel and swollen knees. He did pinch hit, however, and drove in a run with a sacrifice fly.

American All-Stars

WALTER EVERS

JOE DIMAGGIO

PAT MULLIN

National All-Stars

RALPH KINER

STANLEY MUSIAL

RICHIE ASHBURN

N. L. Guilty of Dumb Ball in Losing No. 11 of 15 All-Star Tilts

Pafko Takes Nap and Vernon Steals Third; Schmitz, With Two-Day Rest, Makes Sucker Pitch

By STAN BAUMGARTNER

ST. LOUIS, Mo.

It's an old adage "that big oaks from little acorns grow" and the 5 to 2 defeat of the National League by the Americans in the All-Star Game at St. Louis, July 13, was a most potent example.

The National League went into that game with its finest opportunity in years. The Americans were without the services of Joe DiMaggio and Ted Williams, two of their greatest stars and greatest hitters.

The National League had an All-Star lineup of lefthanded hitters and the American League did not have a lefthanded hurler to oppose them except Relief Pitcher Joe Page. Hal Newhouser, who was selected by Bucky Harris, was in uniform and acted as a pinch-runner, but was unable to throw a ball.

So the senior loop, with everything in its favor, sustained what amounted to its greatest defeat . . . and why it did so is as clear as crystal . . . it was the little things that upset its apple cart.

In the first inning, for example, they had jittery Walt Masterson on the ropes. The big fellow pitched two inside strikes to Stan Musial and then gave him a 2-0 pitch over the middle that resulted in a home run with Richie Ashburn on base to give the National leaguers a 2 to 0 lead.

Johnny Mize followed with a single to center and Enos Slaughter walked. The stage was set for a killing . . . a big four or five-run inning. Masterson was wild . . . he might have walked a dozen, but Andy Pafko swung at two bad inside balls and sent an easy roller to Ken Keltner on the bag forcing Mize. There was still a chance with Walker Cooper at bat, but the big fellow hit the same kind of a low inside pitch on his handle for an easy forceout of Pafko at second.

"Flubbed Big Opportunity There"

A veteran baseball man sitting in the press box remarked, "The Nationals flubbed their big opportunity there. Now they are a cinch to get licked."

Hoot Evers came along in the second inning to smash a home run into the left field stands and give the American leaguers their first tally. A home run is a part of baseball. Branca could not be censured for the slam by Hoot.

But in the next inning Branca and Pafko combined to give the Americans their second run without the aid of a

Evers Second First-Year Player to Homer in Bow

ST. LOUIS, Mo.—Hoot Evers, a native St. Louisan who now makes his off-season home in nearby Collinsville, Ill., became the second player in All-Star Game history to hit a home run in his first time at bat.

The Tiger outfielder drove the second pitch served to him by Ralph Branca of the Dodgers into the left field stands in the second inning for the American leaguers' first run in their triumph.

Max West became the first player to achieve the feat in 1940, when the mid-summer classic was also staged in St. Louis. West, then with the Braves, socked a three-run homer in the first inning of the 1940 game, won by the National League, 4 to 0.

hit. One of the first rules in the baseball book is to get the ball over the plate. George Stallings, late manager of the Boston Braves, said bases on balls would send him to his grave—and they did. Bases on balls sent the National leaguers to theirs.

Branca walked Mickey Vernon and Pat Mullin. Then came the little play unnoticed by many—that changed the tide. Branca fanned Tommy Henrich. On the pitch Vernon started for third. An experienced third baseman would have rushed back to the bag as he saw Henrich swing and miss the third strike, but Pafko is not an experienced third sacker. He is playing the spot for the first time this year—so he did not go back and Vernon and Mullin executed a double steal.

So, what should have been a double play was a double theft. And with men on second and third, and one out, instead of only a runner on second and two out, Lou Boudreau sent a fly to right—that scored Vernon with the tying run.

Schmitz Needs Four Days' Rest

What happened in the fourth inning should never have happened to Johnny Schmitz. Charlie Grimm or some one with the Cubs should have told Leo Durocher that Schmitz can't pitch with two days' rest. Warren Brown, veteran Chicago scribe, said that everyone in the Windy City knows that unless Schmitz has four days' rest he can't throw hard enough to get Aunt Kate out.

Schmitz got Hoot Evers with a fly to short. Ken Keltner then walloped him for a single to left and when George McQuinn, a southpaw hitter, smacked Johnny's fast ball for a line drive hit to center one of the National leaguers moaned, "Better get him out of there."

But Schmitz walked Tebbetts to load the bases to concentrate on Vic Raschi. Raschi never won any honors as a hitter. But like every righthanded batter who faces a lefthanded pitcher he can hit a high curve that breaks over the plate and in to his bat. Raschi smashed one high curve like a bullet into the third base stands—foul. But even that failed to teach Schmitz a lesson. He served up another—and the ball game was over. Raschi hit the pitch like a bullet into left field and two runs crossed the plate.

The line drive off the bat of Joe DiMaggio, which enabled Tebbetts to score from third a moment later, was extra baggage.

The National League had two more opportunities to score after the first frame but muffed them. With one out in the third Stan Musial singled to center. Johnny Mize then hit to Joe Gordon. Instead of sliding hard and fast into second base to break up the double play, Stan slid half heartedly and did not even reach the bag. The result was that when Boudreau muffed Gordon's throw, Musial was still two feet from the bag and could not stretch out and tag it before Boudreau picked up the ball. Enos Slaughter followed with a hit that would have loaded the bases with one out. But another chance to score was gone.

Ashburn Looks at a Third Strike

In the sixth the Nationals loaded the sacks with two out against Vic Raschi on singles by Bob Elliott, Phil Masi and a walk to Eddie Waitkus who batted for Johnny Sain. This brought Richie Ashburn to the plate. The sensational youngster of the Phillies had made two previous hits. But with the count 2 and 1, he took a third strike.

It is one of the cardinal rules in baseball that with men on bases, the man at bat keeps swinging at anything that might be called a strike.

Shotton Makes First Pitch of Game

THE HONOR of throwing out the first ball for the fifteenth annual All-Star Game was awarded to Burt Shotton, who lost the chance to pilot the National League entry on the return of Leo Durocher, suspended in 1947. Left to right, Fray Nano, famed editor of the Mexican sports daily, La Afición; Commissioner A. B. Chandler, Shotton, J. G. Taylor Spink, publisher of THE SPORTING NEWS, and Clarence Rowland, president of the Pacific Coast League.

This curve ball broke directly across the plate, but Ashburn, because of his inexperience, was caught flatfooted.

The National League has lost several All-Star games in the past on home runs by Babe Ruth, Lou Boudreau, Rudy York, Bobby Doerr and Ted Williams, but it never went down to defeat because a pitcher hit a single over third base.

It was the little things that wrecked the Nationals. Just as pennant races turn on one poor pitch, the failure to back up a wild throw and world championships such as the Cardinals' victory over the Yankees in 1942 turned on the failure of such fine throwers as King Kong Keller to prevent St. Louis from taking extra bases.

Ford Frick, president of the National League took cognizance of this—without pointing a finger at anyone—when he said that the players selected by the fans should not be forced to start the game . . . that it should be enough if they appeared in the lineup.

Summing it all up, it was an ordinary game, won by an ordinary team which defeated another ordinary club. There were no particularly tense moments, no great plays, no thrilling pitching feat to compare with Carl Hubbell's when he fanned five American leaguers in succession. Johnny Sain approached Hubbell's accomplishment when he struck out Vern Stephens, Bobby Doerr and Hoot Evers in succession in the fifth inning with a wide sweeping

curve that made even the fans gasp, but by that time the game was in the American League's bag.

The finest fielding play of the day was Stan Musial's splendid pick-up and throw of Ken Keltner's drive along the left field line. From the click of the bat it was labeled a two-bagger, but Musial hurried in, made a quick peg and perfect throw to keep Keltner at first base. It meant nothing, however, as it was later in this frame that Raschi put over the winning sock.

The weather started out boiling hot, then a thunderstorm rolled around the park, but it did not hit it. Finally rain fell just as the National leaguers' final hopes were dampened in the ninth inning.

Game in Detail

St. Looie Blues for National League

First Inning

NATIONAL—Ashburn beat out a bounder to Gordon and then stole second. Schoendienst grounded to McQuinn, Ashburn moving to third. Musial hit on top of the right field stands at the 360 mark, scoring behind Ashburn. Mize went to second on a wild pitch. Slaughter walked. Pafko grounded to Keltner, who stepped on third, forcing Mize. Cooper bounced to Keltner, who threw to Gordon, forcing Pafko. Two runs, three hits, no errors.

AMERICAN—Mullin struck out. Henrich also fanned. Boudreau bounced to Reese. No runs, no hits, no errors.

Second Inning

NATIONAL—Reese struck out. Keltner threw out Branca. Henrich took Ashburn's short fly. No runs, no hits, no errors.

AMERICAN—Gordon flied to Musial. Evers lined into the left field bleachers. Keltner walked. McQuinn lifted to Ashburn. Rosar flied to Slaughter. One run, one hit, no errors.

Third Inning

NATIONAL — McQuinn took Schoendienst's foul fly. Musial got a broken-bat single to center. Mize forced Musial, Gordon to Boudreau. Slaughter beat out a slow roller down the third base line. Pafko forced Slaughter, Gordon to Boudreau. No runs, two hits, no errors.

AMERICAN—Vernon batted for Masterson and walked. Mullin also walked. Vernon and Mullin worked the double steal as Henrich fanned. Boudreau flied to Slaughter, Vernon scoring after the catch. Reese threw out Gordon. One run, no hits, no errors.

Fourth Inning

NATIONAL—Raschi pitching and Tebbetts catching. Cooper grounded to Keltner. Reese hit a hard smash to Keltner, who threw him out. Gustine batted for Branca and struck out, Tebbetts dropping the third strike, but throwing him out at first. No runs, no hits, no errors.

AMERICAN—Schmitz pitching. Reese went into left field for Evers' high fly. Keltner singled over third. McQuinn singled to center, Keltner stopping at second. Tebbetts walked, filling the bases. Raschi singled to left, scoring Keltner and McQuinn, Tebbetts going to third. Sain relieved Schmitz on the mound for the Nationals. DiMaggio batted for Mullin and lined to Musial, Tebbetts scoring after the catch. Henrich popped to Reese. Three runs, three hits, no errors.

Fifth Inning

NATIONAL—Zarilla went to right field, Doerr to second and Stephens to short for the Americans. Ashburn singled to center. Schoendienst hoisted to Zarilla. Musial struck out. Mize grounded to Doerr. No runs, one hit, no errors.

AMERICAN—Masi catching, Elliott at third and Kerr at short for the Nationals. Stephens was called out on strikes. Doerr struck out. Evers was the third strikeout victim of the inning. No runs, no hits, no errors.

Sixth Inning

NATIONAL — Slaughter tapped to Raschi. Elliott singled to left. Masi singled to center, Elliott stopping at second. Keltner threw out Kerr, Elliott going to third and Masi to second. Waitkus batted for Sain and walked, filling the bases. Ashburn was called out on strikes. No runs, two hits, no errors.

AMERICAN—Holmes went to right and Blackwell to the mound for the Nationals. Keltner lined to Holmes. McQuinn

dropped a Texas leaguer in left. McQuinn stole second. Tebbetts was called out on strikes. Williams batted for Raschi and walked. Newhouser ran for Williams. Zarilla forced Newhouser, Schoendienst to Kerr. No runs, one hit, no errors.

Seventh Inning

NATIONAL — Coleman pitching. Schoendienst rolled to Doerr. Musial walked. Mize fanned. Holmes tapped to Coleman. No runs, no hits, no errors.

AMERICAN—Kiner in left, Musial in center and Rigney at second for the Nationals. Henrich walked. Stephens singled between third and short, Henrich stopping at second. Doerr, attempting to sacrifice, popped to Mize. Rigney came in between the mound and plate for Evers' infield fly. Keltner lined to Kiner. No runs, one hit, no errors.

Eighth Inning

NATIONAL—Elliott lined to Zarilla. McQuinn took Masi's foul fly. Kerr was called out on strikes. No runs, no hits, no errors.

AMERICAN—McQuinn rolled to Mize. Tebbetts walked. Coleman sacrificed, Mize to Rigney. Zarilla flied to Musial. No runs, no hits, no errors.

Ninth Inning

NATIONAL — Thomson batted for Blackwell and struck out. Kiner bounced to Keltner. Rigney walked. Musial rolled to Doerr. No runs, no hits, no errors.

National League.	AB.	R.	H.	PO.	A.	E.
Ashburn (Phillies), cf	4	1	2	1	0	0
Kiner (Pirates), lf	1	0	0	1	0	0
Schoendienst (Cards), 2b	4	0	0	1	0	0
Rigney (Giants), 2b	0	0	0	2	0	0
Musial (Cards), lf-cf	4	1	2	3	0	0
Mize (Giants), 1b	4	0	1	4	1	0
Slaughter (Cards), rf	2	0	1	2	0	0
Holmes (Braves), rf	1	0	0	1	0	0
Pafko (Cubs), 3b	2	0	0	0	0	0
Elliott (Braves), 3b	2	0	1	0	4	0
Cooper (Giants), c	2	0	0	3	0	0
Masi (Braves), c	2	0	1	4	0	0
Reese (Dodgers), ss	2	0	0	2	2	0
Kerr (Giants), ss	2	0	0	1	0	0
Branca (Dodgers), p	1	0	0	0	0	0
†Gustine (Pirates)	1	0	0	0	0	0
Schmitz (Cubs), p	0	0	0	0	0	0
Sain (Braves), p	0	0	0	0	0	0
§Waitkus (Cubs)	0	0	0	0	0	0
Blackwell (Reds), p	0	0	0	0	0	0
zThomson (Giants)	1	0	0	0	0	0
Totals	35	2	8	24	4	0

American League.	AB.	R.	H.	PO.	A.	E.
Mullin (Tigers), rf	1	0	0	0	0	0
‡DiMaggio (Yankees)	1	0	0	0	0	0
Zarilla (Browns), rf	2	0	0	2	0	0
Henrich (Yankees), lf	3	0	0	1	0	0
Boudreau (Indians), ss	2	0	0	2	0	0
Stephens (Red Sox), ss	2	0	1	0	0	0
Gordon (Indians), 2b	2	0	0	1	2	0
Doerr (Red Sox), 2b	2	0	0	0	3	0
Evers (Tigers), cf	4	1	1	0	0	0
Keltner (Indians), 3b	3	1	1	1	6	0
McQuinn (Yankees), 1b	4	1	2	14	0	0
Rosar (Athletics), c	1	0	0	1	0	0
Tebbetts (Red Sox), c	1	1	0	5	1	0
Masterson (Senators), p	0	0	0	0	0	0
*Vernon (Senators)	0	1	0	0	0	0
Raschi (Yankees), p	1	0	1	0	1	0
xWilliams (Red Sox)	0	0	0	0	0	0
yNewhouser (Tigers)	0	0	0	0	0	0
Coleman (Athletics), p	0	0	0	0	1	0
Totals	29	5	6	27	14	0

*Walked for Masterson in third.
†Struck out for Branca in fourth.
‡Flied out for Mullin in fourth, scoring Tebbetts from third.
§Walked for Sain in sixth.
xWalked for Raschi in sixth.
yRan for Williams in sixth.
zStruck out for Blackwell in ninth.

National League	2	0	0	0	0	0	0	0	0—2
American League	0	1	1	3	0	0	0	0	0—5

Runs batted in—Musial 2, Evers, Boudreau, Raschi 2, DiMaggio. Home runs—Musial, Evers. Stolen bases—Ashburn, Vernon, Mullin, McQuinn. Sacrifice—Coleman. Bases on balls—Off Masterson 1 (Slaughter), off Branca 3 (Keltner, Vernon, Mullin), off Schmitz 1 (Tebbetts), off Raschi 1 (Waitkus), off Blackwell 3 (Williams, Henrich, Tebbetts), off Coleman 2 (Musial, Rigney). Struck out—By Branca 3 (Mullin, Henrich 2), by Masterson 1 (Reese), by Raschi 3 (Gustine, Musial, Ashburn), by Sain 3 (Stephens, Doerr, Evers), by Blackwell 1 (Tebbetts), by Coleman 3 (Mize, Kerr, Thomson). Pitching summary—Off Masterson 5 hits, 2 runs in 3 innings; off Branca 1 hit, 2 runs in 3 innings; off Schmitz 3 hits, 3 runs in 1-3 inning; off Sain 0 hits, 0 runs in 1 2-3 innings; off Raschi 3 hits, 0 runs in 3 innings; off Blackwell 2 hits, 0 runs in 3 innings; off Coleman 0 hits, 0 runs in 3 innings. Wild pitch—Masterson 1. Left on bases—National 10, American 8. Earned runs—American 5, National 2. Winning pitcher—Raschi. Losing pitcher—Schmitz. Umpires—Berry (A. L.), plate; Stewart (N. L.), first base; Paparella (A. L.), second base; Reardon (N. L.), third base, first 4½ innings; Reardon (N. L.), plate; Paparella (A. L.), first base; Stewart (N. L.), second base; Berry (A. L.), third base, last four innings. Time of game—2:27. Attendance—34,009. Net receipts after taxes—$93,447.07. Scorers—Ed Burns, Chicago Tribune; Sid C. Keener, St. Louis Star-Times; Robert L. Burnes, St. Louis Globe-Democrat.

A welcoming committee awaits Joe DiMaggio as he crosses the plate after clubbing a bases-loaded home run to give the Yankees a 6–5 victory over the Cleveland Indians in 1948. Offering congratulations are Yogi Berra (8), Charlie Keller (12), and George Stirnweiss (1). The Cleveland catcher is Jim Hegan and the umpire is Art Passarella.

SPORT

SEPTEMBER
25¢

BEBALL · FOOTBALL · GOLF · TENNIS · BOXING ·

BOSTON

NY

WHO'S THE
GREATEST:
TED OR DiMAG?

Who is the world's GREATEST BALLPLAYER?

All over the country the argument rages. You can't be indifferent. Whose side are you on?

IN THIS most flourishing of all major-league base-ball seasons, the hottest controversy is: Who's the Number One individual star in the game? Most experts agree that the choice lies between one of two American League heroes—Joe DiMaggio and Ted Williams. A lot of people, of course, have other candidates. Stanley Musial of the St. Louis Cardinals, for one. Johnny Mize of the Giants, Ralph Kiner of the Pirates, Lou Boudreau of the Indians, are others who command wide support. But whenever you poll the press box, or shoot a question at the ordinary fan, the names that come back on top are Joseph Paul DiMaggio of the New York Yankees, and Theodore Samuel Williams of the Boston Red Sox. So SPORT has designed this feature to give you a chance to get right into the middle of the argument. On the following pages, you will find exclusive Magic-Eye camera sequences showing each man's batting form, plus a pair of articles discussing the play of each; along with capsule records of each star's past performances. Then turn to the big contest that lets *you* have *your* say!

International

is it DiMAGGIO ➤

He was named Most Valuable Player in the American League in 1939, 1941, and 1947. His hitting streak of 56 consecutive games in 1941 set a new major-league record. He led his league in batting in 1939 and 1940, and was tops in home runs in 1937 with 46, and in runs scored with 151. He boasts a lifetime batting average of .332 in nine years in big-league ball, and has rapped out a grand total of 264 home runs. He tied an American League record for outfielders last year when he committed only one error in 141 games for a neat .997 percentage.

is it WILLIAMS ⬇

International SPORTrait

Acme SPORTrait

He was voted the American League's Most Valuable Player in 1946. He became the first major-leaguer in over a decade to hit above .400 when he led all batters in 1941 with a lusty .406. He won his league's batting crown in 1941, 1942, and 1947, and won home-run honors in each of those years. His lifetime batting average, after six years in big-league ball, is a sporty .352, and his RBI total has reached 752. He has hit an even .500 in five All-Star games, and he personally conducted the American League to victory in 1941 with a crushing homer in the last of the ninth.

or is it ➤ ?

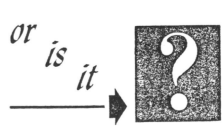

SPORT

Jimmy Cannon Says:

Joe DiMaggio No Doubt Is Best Of His Generation

The ball player is not a man of mysterious and previous skills but a manual laborer of show business. Any knowledge of the sport is worthless if the body is not sound. They are acrobats without music but the tumblers and the lifters and the tramboline workers are obscure, poorly paid and open the bill in vaudeville. The ball player is well publicized; gets a full season's work as long as he is active; is revered by many children; admire din most saloons.

There are a lot of them who use peculiarities of character, to compensate for flaws of grace and style as the acrobats dress up as bull fighters, mandarins and sometimes as clowns. Others counterfeit personalities which they believe will appeal to the people who support the game. Their comedy is low, much like that used in grind bulresque houses, only sanitary and strictly pantomime.

Some inferior players use violence. So do some managers. They cut the opposition with their spikes, swagger and brag, start arguments, annoy umpires, lecture reporters on their ability to steal the other team's signs, crouch into round-shouldered postures at the plate to get walks and deliver foul-mouthed harangues from the top step of the dugout.

It is not unusual for the able player to invent other methods than the act of baseball to perpetuate importance. It is unintentional in most instances but discouraged if the journalists use it for features on rainy days. Some, who have the right to be identified as great, are remembered as much for what they did in street clothes as baseball suits.

People recall Dizzy Dean as a quarrelsome humorist who spoke a back country argot. Rogers Hornsby demanded attention with a fierce loyalty to the insulting truth. They discuss Ted Williams' rages as aften as they do his batting average.

But Joe DiMaggio's reputation is not located in such myths. The tricks of the thespians of baseball do not interest him. There are no legends connected with him except those- explained in the box score. There is no doubt that he is the best of his generation. His achievements are unassisted by the fables which help the fame of others.

There are many who complain he lacks showmanship. But this is an athlete of authentic greatness. DiMaggio's feats are measured by action, not by anecdotes denoting wit or flamboyance of character. DiMaggio is not a humble man but aggressiveness is not one of his traits. The four home runs he hit in three games were probably the most important he ever struck. They were made in the first league games he has played this year. But on the telephone he was casual and had a tendency to minimize what he had done.

The long distance operator told me Boston was ready after the call had been in for an hour.

"What's doing?" DiMaggio asked and wanted to know about some of our mutual acquaintances.

"What have you been doing?" I said with a clumsy slyness.

"I took in a picture," DiMaggio replied. "I'm in bed. I'm a little tired."

"You really broke out," I said.

"A couple of balls dropped in for me," DiMaggio said.

"The stories I read said they were well hit," I explained.

"I like this park," DiMaggio said because the left field fence in Boston is short.

"How does the heel feel?" I asked.

"It's a little swollen," DiMaggio said. "But pretty good."

"You sound like a new guy," I said.

"I got lucky and got hold of a couple," DiMaggio said. "It peps you up."

* * *

There were occasions this year when DiMaggio must have felt he was through. He was sick with doubt and irritable. The heel was full of pain. On pay day when he picked up his check he was ashamed of himself. Seldom does any athlete feel he is fleecing an employer when there is a contract to guarantee him a salary.

The inactivity changed him. It made him a recluse. The telephone was shut off in his apartment. He ducked intimates. He sat home and watched the telephone and played jazz records endlessly. At the Stadium, he gave me the impression he felt himself an intruder.

* * *

They allowed him to sit on the bench without putting on a uniform. But he was miserable and figured he bothered the umpires. The water fountain is at the far end of the Yankee bench. DiMaggio went back to the clubhouse when he was thirsty.

"I didn't want the umpires to think I was showing off," he explained, "walking up and down the bench."

* * *

The Yanks were winning without him. But they needed him and they wanted him in there. Billy Johnson, the third baseman, watched DiMaggio, who is normally a man of slouching grace, walk with a stiff slowness out of the trainer's room.

"That guy," Johnson said, "what he did for this club last season . . . playing in the shape he was in. I don't want to see him play until he's ready. If he don't play a game this season he earned his money last season."

It's the way I feel, too. But it is typical of him and a true indication of what he is when he said a couple of balls had dropped in for him in Fenway Park. DiMaggio doesn't have to make it better. You don't have to when you're the best.

Joe DiMaggio receives the warmest of greetings after hitting a grand slam home run in a mid-September game in 1948 against the then league-leading Boston Red Sox. The blast helped the Yanks to an 11–6 victory. Welcoming the Clipper are pitcher, Frank Shea (20), Gus Niarhos (center), and Tommy Henrich. Not joining the celebration is Boston catcher, Birdie Tebbetts.

TIME

THE WEEKLY NEWSMAGAZINE

Alfred Eisenstaedt—Pix

THE YANKEES' JOE DIMAGGIO
With runs on the bases, his bat spells bingo.
(Sport)

$6.50 A YEAR   (REG. U. S. PAT. OFF.)   VOL. LII NO. 14

Joe DiMaggio makes the cover of *Time* magazine for the second time in his career.

SPORT

The Big Guy

(See Cover)

The center-fielder of the New York Yankees had the worst charley horse he could remember. He wore a thick bandage over his left thigh (to support the strained muscles) and a second bandage around his middle to hold up the first one. Said Joseph Paul DiMaggio, more in simple fact than in complaint: "I feel like a mummy."

On any ordinary day such aches & pains would have put Center-fielder DiMaggio out of the line-up. But no day last week was an ordinary one in the American League. The Yankees were fighting for survival in the hottest pennant race in history, and they needed DiMag.

The visiting Boston Red Sox treated him with proper respect, crippled or not. Twice he came to bat with runners on base, and a buzz of excitement rippled through Yankee Stadium and down the pitcher's back. Twice he banged in a run. The third time, the crowd let go an angry bellow: the Sox, trying to protect a slim lead, sent him to first base on a pass instead of letting him swing at the ball. Joe scored the run that put the Yankees out in front, anyway.

That night, with the scores all in, the Yankees, the Red Sox and the Cleveland Indians found themselves knotted in a triple tie for the American League lead (*see chart*)—a state of affairs so unprecedented that league officials had to powwow hurriedly to consider what should be done if a season happened to end that way.*

Jeez! Jeez! Across the U.S. last week, the seesaw race had baseball fans quivering. Cleveland motorists had to wait for their gasoline until absent-minded attendants finished listening to another play on their radios; business in downtown movie houses slumped 25%. In Boston, scalpers asked and got as much as $30 for a pair of tickets. One New Yorker, his nose buried in the box scores, tripped over a fire hydrant and banged his head hard enough to need stitches.

The ballplayers felt the tension too. In the Yankee dressing room, they kept nervously assuring each other that they didn't have pennant jitters. (The strain registered on steady Joe DiMaggio: he was up to a pack of Chesterfields a day.) Cleveland's Indians had lost only three games since Sept. 8; all anybody had to do to make them jump was strike a match.

* Their decision in case it happens this year: a playoff game between Cleveland and Boston on Oct. 4, with the winner to take on the Yankees Oct. 5. The World Series begins Oct. 6.

HOME-RUN HITTER DIMAGGIO & RECEPTION COMMITTEE AT THE PLATE
For an old pro, a reverent roar.

When high-strung Lou Boudreau, the Indians' manager and shortstop, juggled his line-up last week and lost a game, there were public mutterings that maybe Club President Bill Veeck should have fired him last year, after all. One afternoon Boudreau sat listening to a broadcast of a Boston Red Sox game. He raked his hair with his fingers and exclaimed, "Jeez! Jeez!" every time the Sox scored. The Sox, under square-jawed Manager Joe McCarthy, seemed a shade less panicky. They had power to burn—what they prayed for was pitchers able to last nine innings. This week, with only five games to go, Cleveland edged one big game ahead of both the Yankees and the Red Sox.

Sirens in Boston. The National League race, too, had been a thriller for most of the summer, but by contrast it was winding up as quietly as a Quaker meeting. For a fortnight it had been clear (to all but bitter-enders) that Billy Southworth's Boston Braves were too far ahead to be caught. This week the Braves clinched it —their first pennant since 1914. Boston's Acting Mayor Tom Hannon called for the blowing of sirens all over town.

In both leagues, 1948 had been a season in which the quantity of excitement outweighed the quality of play. The home-run mark was never threatened; American League pitchers set a new record for bases on balls (5,045), and one outfielder allowed himself to be hit on the head by a fly ball he was supposed to catch. Baseball was still showing the interfering effects of World War II: not enough good young recruits had come up through the minor leagues to replace fading oldtimers.

In a year like 1948, a handful of indispensable "old pros" stand out like Gullivers among the Lilliputians. Each of the top teams in the American League race has one.

For the Red Sox it is tall, willowy Left-fielder Ted Williams, 29. He has a batting average of .368, the league's best, despite the variety of defensive shifts against him. And Cleveland would scarcely be out front without the 31-year-old Boudreau. His ankles are bad, and he is notoriously slow on the base paths, but his ability to anticipate plays makes him the best shortstop in baseball this year. In addition, he runs his team and hits .354.

With the New York Yankees, it is Joe DiMaggio. He had only missed one game all season, and he was leading the big parade in baseball's most spectacular departments: home runs (39) and runs batted in (153).

No Pushups. At 33, Joe DiMaggio has black hair, beginning to be flecked with grey. Tall (6 ft. 2 in.) and solid (198 lbs.) in the smart double-breasted suits he

wears off the playing field, he might be mistaken for a man with an office in midtown Manhattan. The tipoff that he is an athlete is his walk. It has a flowing, catlike quality, without waste motion.

Unlike his perennial Red Sox rival, Ted Williams, who does pushups every morning to strengthen his wrists and forearm muscles, DiMag frowns on off-the-field exercise, likes to loll in bed until 10 a.m. or later. He is also fond of his food: "I don't diet. I believe in three square meals a day and I'm not ashamed to say I'm nuts about spaghetti."

Part of Joe's notions about his daily regimen come from a talk he once had with Ty Cobb, after DiMaggio's first year with the Yankees. Cobb told him that a good outfielder was crazy to spend 15 minutes a day shagging fly balls once he got in shape: "Don't spend your hitting energy chasing flies. Grab a few and then sit down in a cool, shady spot." DiMag has been conserving his energy ever since. He even seems to conserve it on the playing field.

One of the sights of baseball is watching DiMaggio take a practiced look at a ball heading his way, turn, and without a backward look glide to the spot where the ball is coming down, swing around casually and let the ball fall into his glove. Like all champions, he makes it look too easy. "It's just getting the jump on the ball."

No Difference. The fans, however, don't think of DiMag as a fielder. They come to see him knock one out of the park. Whether at Yankee Stadium or on the road, a reverent roar greets him as he strides to the plate. Joe tells himself that the pitchers should be more worried than he is, and they usually are. He is a cool, relaxed figure, his bat held high and motionless, as he waits for the ball to zip in from the pitcher's box, 60 ft. away, at something like 91 m.p.h.

Unlike Babe Ruth, who used to stand with feet close together and fanny toward the pitcher, DiMaggio takes an abnormally wide stance (with feet 36 in. apart) squarely in the center of the batter's box. He waits until the very last moment before swinging. His system: "I look for his fast ball. Then if he comes in with a curve, I still have time to swing."

Joe, a right-handed hitter, prefers batting against left-handed pitchers. Reason: like many right-handers, he thinks he sees the ball sooner and follows it better from a southpaw delivery. But whether the pitcher is right- or left-handed seems to make no practical difference. He hits

Right-hander Bob Feller and Left-hander Hal Newhouser as if he owned them. Last fortnight he became the eighth man in baseball history to hit 300 home runs.✻

Like all ballplayers, DiMag has his hitting slumps. What causes them? Says Joe: "Oh, pressing too hard, hot weather —almost anything. I don't like to talk about slumps." Around the league he is known as a "loner" who shuns locker-room monkeyshines. After a ball game, Joe will sit quietly on the bench in front of his locker, slowly consuming a bottle of beer. "I go back over the ball game," he says. When asked if it helps, he replies, "Not much."

"A Little Extra on Big Days." DiMaggio does not hit the ball as hard as the mighty Ruth did, nor as often as Ted Williams does. But as a clutch hitter he is terrific. With men on bases and the chips down, his bat spells bingo.

This useful faculty resulted in one of the season's most dramatic moments. At Boston's Fenway Park three weeks ago the score was tied, 6-6, in the tenth. The bases were loaded, and two were out as Joe stepped to the plate. In the pressbox a sportwriter sympathized with the Red Sox pitcher: "I'd rather be anybody in the world than Earl Caldwell right now. I'd rather be Henry Wallace."

Caldwell pitched, Joe swung, and a tremendous drive hit the net by the left field roof—foul by inches. Thinking about it after the game, Joe said, "My God! You don't hit two balls that hard in one day." But he did, and this time it was fair.

Boston's center-fielder, who happens to be Joe's younger brother Dominic, whirled and started running. Then he stopped. The ball, one of the longest home runs ever hit in Fenway Park, went to the right of the flagpole high above the 379-ft. distance marker. It scored four runs and kept the Yankees in the pennant race. Says Joe: "Maybe you give it a little extra on big days. But you don't feel it. You must do it unconsciously. It's inside you and it does something to you. But you don't know it's there." Joe DiMaggio candidly accepts the fact that he is good.

So do the fans. There is a "Joe DiMaggio Fan Club of Pittsburgh," which rides special buses to Cleveland (Joe's nearest stopping point to Pittsburgh) to cheer him on. When the Yankees play in Phila-

---

✻ The other seven: Babe Ruth, Lou Gehrig, Hank Greenberg, Jimmy Foxx, Chuck Klein, Mel Ott and Rogers Hornsby.

delphia, another fan club lets go with "D-i-M-a-g-g-i-o" locomotives—like undergraduates at a football game. Does he like it? "Sure," says Joe. "A guy's got to like it. But it makes you feel embarrassed if you have a bad day."

He accepts as part of the job the autograph seekers who accost him in hotel lobbies and restaurants. He doesn't mind the kids so much, he says—it's the adults: "They always wait till you are about to put the steak in your mouth."

For his part, Joe looks with awe on Broadway footlights and the people who work behind them. In Manhattan, he lives in a 54th Street apartment hotel, not far from the theatrical swirl, and he sees as many plays as he can (some recent favorites: *High Button Shoes, Show Boat, Annie Get Your Gun*).

He never acquired the ballplayer's habit of chewing tobacco (he likes pistachio nuts) nor the ballplayer's trait for pinching a penny. As a result, he has hung on to only about a fifth of the $500,000 he has earned from baseball. (This year he will make about $67,000.) He owns a few blue chip stocks, a small annuity, and until recently a part interest with two of his brothers in DiMaggio's Famous Restaurant, a seafood place on San Francisco's Fisherman's Wharf.

"Baseball, What Is That?" San Francisco, where Joe grew up, is still the city he knows best. He comes from an old-fashioned Italian family, poor to begin with, but proud of each other and extremely close-knit. His parents, who had come from Isola delle Femmine, an islet off the coast of Sicily, had a ground-floor flat on Taylor Street, on the slope of Russian Hill. Joe was the eighth of nine children.

Papa DiMaggio, who ran a fishing boat from the wharf at the foot of Taylor Street, believed that his five sons should be fishermen too. All the boys—Tom, Michael, Vince, Joe and Dominic—worked on the boat at one time or another, but most of the time they preferred to play baseball. "Baseball, what is that?" Papa DiMaggio used to shout. "A bum's game! A no good game! Whoever makes a living at baseball?"

One of his objections to baseball was that it wore out shoes too fast. But when Joe's older brother Vince (who later played with National League teams) was hired as a professional ballplayer for the San Francisco Seals, Papa's objections melted. Joe was peeping through a knothole one afternoon, watching brother Vince play, when a Seals' scout, Spike Hennessey, clapped him on the back. How would he like to come inside for a tryout? Joe could think of nothing he wanted more. Five years later, little brother Dom

was given his chance too, on the strength of being a DiMaggio.

Within the DiMaggio family circle, relative batting averages are a cause of pride, but bear no relationship to the affection the members feel for each other. Bespectacled Dom is the family pet. "Oh, you ought to see him run the bases," his sister Marie says. "He's like a little rabbit." The entire family, including Joe, has been extremely pleased by the couplet that Red Sox fans have been chanting this year to the tune of *Maryland, My Maryland:*

*He's better than his brother Joe—
Dom-in-ic Di-Mag-gi-o!*

When the boys send money home (Joe has bought his parents a new house, Mike a new fishing boat), Papa shows no favoritism. Says he of Joe: "Justa one of my boys."

Ruppert's Rookie. In the early '30s, nonetheless, it didn't take long for Joe, the pea-green rookie, to outshine Vince and the other Seals. In his first full season (1933) he smashed the Pacific Coast League record by hitting safely in 61 consecutive games. He struck up a friendship with the team's first baseman, a fancy dresser and wisecracker, aped his dress and manners. From the Seals' trainer, an oldtime featherweight boxer, he soaked up fancy words. For a while, his stock reply to anyone asking him where he had been was: "Oh, I've been nonchalantly meandering down the pike."

In 1935, he helped win the Seals the coast league pennant with a .398 batting average and was voted the league's most valuable player. To get Joe on the Yankee string, the late Colonel Jake Ruppert paid out $25,000 (plus five other players). When Joe reported to the Yankee training camp at St. Petersburg two seasons later, he had been given the biggest buildup ever given a rookie.

Reporters inspected him as if he were a prize bull at a cattle show. He answered their questions. No, he'd never been east of the Rockies before . . . He didn't think Florida was as pretty as he'd heard it was . . . He didn't know whether he could hit big league pitching, but he was glad to try.

He hit 29 home runs that season, played in the All-Star game, and the World Series.

Matter of Dates. After that season, everything DiMaggio did seemed to make headlines. His wedding to Dorothy Arnold Olson in 1939 (later ended in divorce) was easily the biggest public wedding ever seen in San Francisco. Fans climbed trees and stood on rooftops to catch a glimpse of the couple leaving the church. Joe made more news as baseball's balkiest holdout. Then, too, he seemed to suffer more than his share of injuries; fans were forever reading accounts of sore arms and pulled ligaments.

Joe made what he now considers the grave error of bickering with the Yankees over salary matters. After a long holdout siege, he missed the first twelve days of the 1938 season. He was booed all over the circuit, and the booing in Yankee Stadium was loudest & longest.

"It got so I couldn't sleep at night," says DiMaggio. "I'd wake up with boos ringing in my ears. I'd get up, light a cigarette and walk the floor sometimes till dawn." Nevertheless, he bore down and had a big year: 32 homers, 140 runs batted in, a batting average of .324.

In 1943, with the U.S. at war, DiMaggio made up his mind to join up. He was 28 and married, and his draft board had classified him in 3-A. He went in voluntarily, became Private J. DiMaggio, U.S. Army Air Forces. In the Air Forces, he put in three years' service in the physical training program for flight cadets. He rose to staff sergeant. Joe had one hitch in Hawaii during 1944; otherwise he was not overseas. He had a chance to play in a couple of exhibition games, entertaining troops, but that was all the baseball he had in those three years.

When he returned to the Yankees in 1946, there was no more of the old booing. After his long layoff, he had one poor season, then struck his stride last year and edged out Ted Williams for the American League's "Most Valuable Player" award (his third). Gruffed Williams: "It took the big guy to beat me, didn't it?"

Without the big guy and another old reliable, Tommy Henrich, who leads the American League in doubles, triples, and runs scored, the 1948 Yankees would not be much of a ball club. They were certainly not in the same class with the great Yankee teams of the '20s (Ruth and Gehrig) nor the teams of the '30s (Gehrig, Dickey, Lazzeri, Rolfe). Yet even with DiMaggio hobbling last week, they had been able to keep the American League race so close that the race might not be over till the last day of the season.

Lou Boudreau's Cleveland Indians had one substantial advantage: in the final days of the race, they would not have to play either the Red Sox or the Yankees. The Sox and Yanks, playing two of their last five games against each other, might knock each other out of the title. Baseball weisenheimers were cracking that nobody was going to win the pennant—two teams were going to lose it.

The DiMaggio boys were doubly involved in all that. When Joe telephoned his mother in San Francisco the other day, she told him of Dominic's plans to be married. Dom, she said, would get married on Oct. 7—unless the Red Sox won the pennant and had to play in the World Series, in which case it would be Oct. 17. "Mama," said Joe, "I'll see that Dom is free to get married on the seventh."

The greatest center fielders of modern times: with Joe DiMaggio are, from left, Duke Snider of the Brooklyn Dodgers, Mickey Mantle of the Yankees, and Willie Mays of the New York Giants and subsequently of the San Francisco Giants.

JOE DI MAGGIO

The rifle arm was another trademark of Joe DiMaggio, whom legendary sportswriter Grantland Rice once described as "the most complete ballplayer I have ever watched".

By Joe Williams

DiMaggio Becomes Big Town's Top Sports Figure

It was a football gala, the W-T's annual salute to the prep and high school stars of the metropolitan district and there were a number of glamorous grid figures present, but the center of attention was a ballplayer. And quite naturally. Name? J. DiMaggio.

It should never surprise any one to discover that DiMaggio stands out in any sort of gathering, sports, social or otherwise, because with the passing years he has become the most popular and best-liked young man in our town.

Broadway Jack Doyle, the odds maker, used to tell me about Turkey Mike Donlin who played with the early Giants under McGraw. "You should have known him," Doyle would say. "Strictly a class guy." In Doyle's language there was no higher praise. To be a class guy was to be everything a great athlete and a sportsman could be.

The compliment fits DiMaggio snugly and attractively. He's affable, gracious, mannerly and generous. And no artist ever approached his profession with more respect or greater dignity. To DiMaggio baseball is not just a game, just a way to make a fast buck, it's an important calling that demands the best a man can give. This goes a long way in explaining his pre-eminence.

I've watched many a young ballplayer come along in my time, moving through the awkward freshman stage on up to varsity acclaim but nothing in this category has given me more personal satisfaction than DiMaggio's progress. Our association started the very first day he joined the Yankees in St. Petersburg. A mutual friend, Tom Laird, noted San Francisco sports editor, had told him to get in touch with me.

Joe Gave Yanks Their '47 Flag.

*   *   *

This was in the spring of '36. And although he had just completed his best season in baseball, this with the 'Frisco Seals, hitting .398, driving in 154 runs and belting out 34 homers, he was shy as a schoolgirl, practically apologetic. I readily took Laird's word for the youngster's exceptional talents but I wondered what would happen to him if he ever found the going rough. He seemed much too pleasant ever to be a fighter or a leader.

But I was studying DiMaggio the boy. DiMaggio the man developed into something else. Did he have in him the stuff that makes fighters? He gave you the answer to that the last two seasons when he limped through a whole schedule on one good leg. As a day-in-and-day-out ordeal baseball has known no grittier performance.

He lacked the drive and the force and the compelling personality to be a leader, a take-charge guy? That was the question, wasn't it? Let's go back to the '47 season when the Yankees, torn by dissension due to front office interference and in a rebellious mood, nevertheless joined ranks and marched forward to win the pennant.

Bucky Harris got the credit for that one and his contributions were important because he's a gifted con man and knows how to treat mental fever blisters. But it was the Yankee Clipper, as the baseball writers refer to DiMaggio, who was the active Here's-How leader. The old hands responded to his drive and the younger ones, adoring him anyway, began to play over their heads.

That season ended and another World Series triumph packed away, Harris, a graceful winner, gave the larger credit to the work of a relief pitcher. "A toast to Joe Page," he'd repeatedly say. In the same breath he could have added "and to DiMaggio as well." For it was the Clipper who straightened out Page so that he worked in 56 games and won 14.

*   *   *

First, the Babe; Second, the Clipper.

DiMaggio has been around so long he's taken for granted by Yankee fans and there's a tendency to disremember how tremendously he has influenced the fortunes of the ball club. Next to the immortal Ruth . . . and if baseball ever produced an immortal it was the old Slambino . . . DiMaggio stands next as the Yankees' all-time great.

Gehrig, Dickey, Gomez, Henrich, Gordon? Men of rare skills, I grant you, but just the same you must place the Clipper after Ruth. The figures show he belongs. When Ruth stepped out Gehrig's bat was not heavy enough to carry the Yankees. They had finished second three straight times, '33 through '35, when DiMaggio came up. Immediately they recaptured their winning ways.

The temptation to add "and how!" is irresistible. They went on to win four straight pennants with their new center fielder. Incidentally, for a player that must be some sort of record in itself. To carry the Ruth-DiMaggio analogy further: the Yankees have won a total of 15 pennants. There was only one of these that Ruth or DiMaggio didn't have a hand in and the war had something to do with that. It didn't take much to win in '43, you know.

I am frequently asked what in my judgment was the best deal the Yankees ever made. The one for DiMaggio, of course. They got him for $25,000 and five frozen spectators who were left over from the preceding Army-Notre Dame game. It was the most spectacular swindle since Peter Minuit's deal with Jim Thorpe's ancestors.

Joe DiMaggio, Williams Set Pace For Sluggers in American League

Yankee Outfielder First in Runs Batted In, Total Bases and Homers—Ted Topped Loop With Percentage of .615

The rivalry for honors in the American League between the Yankees and the Boston Red Sox which went right down to the season's play-off ending, carried over into the chain of record performances achieved by the junior circuit through the 1948 campaign. A compilation of the marks yesterday revealed the American League accounted for no fewer than forty-three record performances in major league and American League marks shattered or tied.

In the establishment of major league standards Joe McCarthy's squad led his old Yankee horde by a count of six to four. The key man in this record display was the irrepressible Bobby Doerr, who accounted for three major league marks.

Doerr established a new major league mark of 414 chances at second base without an error, had the most consecutive errorless games at second base, 73, and shattered the old major league mark behind George Stirnweiss of the Yankees for highest fielding percentage at second base, with .9925. Stirnweiss came up with a high percentage of .9930.

On team play the Red Sox collected 823 bases on balls for a new major league record and gained further heights with a mark for most runs by a club in a single inning, 14. The McCarthy squad likewise was the most futile in nailing base-runners bent on theft, finishing the season with but 17, a major league low.

For hitting more than 100 home runs through the campaign the Yankees established a major record for achieving the feat for the twenty-fifth year. The Yanks also grabbed a record for fewest assists by one club in a season, 1,493.

Joe DiMaggio added the runs-batted-in honors to his American League home-run and total-base laurels in the best year the Yankee ace enjoyed since coming out of the Army. After two seasons of sub-par production, DiMaggio clouted in 155 runs through 1948, far ahead of Vern Stephens, who hammered in 137 for the Red Sox. Only twice since he came up in 1936 has DiMaggio failed to hammer in 100 or more runs through a season. In 1946 he accounted for 95, and the following year Joe had 97.

The slugging title went to Ted Williams with a percentage of .615, 17 points higher than DiMaggio's. Tommy Henrich was third in the list of sluggers with .554. In the RBI department Williams was third in the list of ten players who accounted for 100 or more. The Red Sox clouter drove in 127 runs, three more than Joe Gordon of the Indians, who was fourth.

Williams picked up thirty-six less walks than in 1947, but still led the American League pedestrians with a total of 126.

Notable among the record performances was the explosion of Pat Seerey in celebration of his shift from the Indians to the Chicago White Sox. The rotund outfielder, who played in 95 games, minimized the dubious distinction of leading the league with 102 strike-outs, tying the major league mark for home runs in a game, with four, a performance which enabled him also to equal the major league record for most extra bases on long hits in a game, 12, and most total bases in a game, 16.

American League Slugging Percentages

INDIVIDUAL RECORDS
20 OR MORE RUNS BATTED IN

	G.	BB.	RBI.	SO.	GI. DP.	SLG. PC.
DiMaggio, New York	153	67	155	30	20	.598
Stephens, Boston	155	77	137	56	25	.471
Williams, Boston	137	126	127	41	10	.615
Gordon, Cleveland	144	77	124	68	16	.507
Majeski, Philadelphia	148	48	120	43	19	.454
Keltner, Cleveland	153	89	119	52	23	.522
Doerr, Boston	140	83	111	49	13	.505
Boudreau, Cleveland	152	98	106	9	15	.534
Evers, Detroit	139	51	103	31	16	.454
Henrich, New York	146	76	100	42	14	.554
Berra, New York	125	25	98	24	9	.488
Fain, Philadelphia	145	113	88	37	17	.396
DiMaggio, Boston	155	101	87	58	11	.401
Robinson, Cleveland	134	36	83	42	13	.408
Platt, St Louis	123	39	82	51	14	.410
Mullin, Detroit	138	77	80	57	5	.504
Priddy, St. Louis	151	86	79	71	15	.443
Zarilla, St. Louis	144	48	74	48	8	.482
Seerey, Cleve.-Chicago	105	90	70	102	10	.419
Chapman, Philadelphia	123	55	70	50	18	.413
Stewart, N. Y.-Wash.	124	49	69	27	4	.438
Tebbetts, Boston	128	62	68	32	22	.381
Wertz, Detroit	119	48	67	70	5	.396
Doby, Cleveland	121	54	66	77	8	.490
Goodman, Boston	127	74	66	44	18	.387
Johnson, New York	127	41	64	30	22	.446
Spence, Boston	114	82	61	33	7	.391
Wright, Chicago	134	39	61	18	13	.365
Hegan, Cleveland	144	48	61	74	10	.407
Coan, Washington	138	41	60	78	5	.333
Suder, Philadelphia	148	60	60	60	10	.345
Vico, Detroit	144	39	58	39	23	.392
Kozar, Washington	150	60	54	52	18	.326
Michaels, Chicago	145	69	56	42	11	.329
Mitchell, Cleveland	141	45	56	17	9	.431
Lindell, New York	88	35	55	56	8	.511
Joost, Philadelphia	135	119	55	87	4	.395
Pesky, Boston	143	99	55	32	10	.365
Lupien, Chicago	154	74	54	38	3	.316
Wakefield, Detroit	110	70	53	55	6	.472
Lipon, Detroit	121	68	52	22	9	.397
Rizzuto, New York	128	60	50	24	6	.328
Yost, Washington	145	82	50	51	15	.367
Brown, New York	113	48	48	16	7	.405
Vernon, Washington	150	54	48	45	17	.332
Appling, Chicago	139	94	47	35	17	.354
Lehner, St. Louis	103	39	46	19	9	.363
Moss, St. Louis	107	39	46	50	16	.424
Valo, Philadelphia	113	81	46	13	11	.394
McCosky, Philadelphia	135	68	46	22	10	.386
Keller, New York	83	41	44	25	7	.417
Kell, Detroit	92	33	44	15	10	.402
Dillinger, St. Louis	153	65	44	34	18	.415
Mayo, Detroit	106	30	42	19	12	.324
Philley, Chicago	37	50	42	33	11	.387
Rosar, Philadelphia	100	39	41	12	3	.338
McQuinn, New York	94	40	41	38	5	.421
Kokos(zka), St. Louis	81	28	40	32	1	.426
Christman, Washington	120	25	40	19	14	.318
Robinson, Chicago	98	46	39	30	8	.380
Arft, St. Louis	99	45	38	43	7	.363
Clark, Cleveland	91	23	38	13	12	.443
Kolloway, Chicago	129	18	38	18	10	.369
Hodgin, Chicago	124	21	34	11	9	.338
Swift, Detroit	123	51	33	29	9	.284
Stirnweiss, New York	141	86	32	62	13	.336
Moses, Boston	78	21	29	19	1	.365
McBride, Washington	92	28	29	15	11	.325
Judnich, Cleveland	79	56	29	23	5	.372
Evans, Washington	93	38	28	20	10	.338
Early, Washington	97	36	28	33	1	.276
White, Philadelphia	86	19	28	16	6	.328
Pellagrini, St. Louis	105	34	27	40	5	.307
Weigel, Chicago	66	13	26	18	5	.313
Stevens, St. Louis	85	41	26	26	3	.340
Lund, St. Louis	63	10	25	17	1	.398
Mele, Boston	66	13	25	21	5	.344
Outlaw, Detroit	74	31	25	15	8	.343
Batts, Boston	46	15	24	9	4	.441
Guerra, Philadelphia	53	18	23	13	6	.289
Coleman, St. L.-Phila.	85	33	23	22	13	.318
Wooten, Washington	88	24	23	21	4	.322
Robertson, Washington	71	24	22	26	2	.369
Dente, St. Louis	98	22	22	8	5	.326
Scheib, Philadelphia	52	8	21	17	3	.490
Lemon, Cleveland	52	8	21	23	0	.487
Gillenwater, Wash.	77	39	21	36	9	.367
Hitchcock, Boston	49	7	20	9	4	.379

CLUB RECORDS

	BB.	HBP.	SO.	RBI.	GI. BP.
Boston	823	32	552	854	145
New York	623	23	478	886	134
Cleveland	616	24	575	802	148
Philadelphia	726	22	523	685	137
Detroit	671	27	504	661	134
St. Louis	578	19	372	623	131
Washington	568	20	372	538	124
Chicago	595	12	528	532	119
Total	5,230	179	4,304	5,501	1,058

'I Read and Try to Go to Sleep, But Toss and Turn'

DiMag in Winter Training for Owl Ball

Yankee Star Battles Sleepless Nights While Recovering From Heel Surgery

Inactivity During Convalescence Makes Joe Jittery; Considers European Trip After Holiday Visit to Folks

By WILL WEDGE
NEW YORK, N. Y.

Is winter training for night ball the game's newest twist—and will it seem as much fun in May as in December? We ruminated recently on this subject while strolling in the Fancy Fifties, hard by Park Avenue and the row of Christmas trees down the middle of that glittering thoroughfare, after a visit with a renowned burner of the midnight mazdas.

Attendants at the winter baseball meetings may have felt a professional pride in the long hours they had to keep, talking deals in those smoke-filled rooms in Minneapolis and Chicago, yet a New York champ, Joe DiMaggio, can outpoint any of 'em in the Stay-Up-Late League.

This is not from choice, but because DiMag has developed insomnia while convalescing from the latest of his series of heel operations. Thus he has indirectly been getting an advance tune-up for the programs under the arcs at the Stadium, and around the circuit, in which he will be participating next spring and summer.

Many an affliction can be turned to advantage by those with the right courageous resources. Thus it may be with DiMaggio, we concluded after visiting the renowned night-owl in his chambers on the smart East Side. Likely he'll hit more homers after dark in 1949 than the half dozen he got under the lights the past season, after all the late staying-up he has been doing this winter.

* * *

He Arises at 2 P. M.

It was 2 o'clock the other afternoon when we buzzed the buzzer of Joe's fifth floor suite at the fashionable Hotel Elysee, on East Fifty-fourth street. There was a slight delay, then the cheery sound of crutches on the parquet floor, and the door was opened by a tousle-haired, unshaven but affable invalid, struggling to get into his dressing gown while manipulating the wooden props under his arm.

"Hullo," said the Yankee slugger. "You're just in time to join me in some coffee. Or would you rather have tea? Got some nice Orange Pekoe, but I'm better making coffee. I'm just getting up, as you can see. Looks like a nice morning. Wish I could get out. What time is it, anyway?"

Joe was told that it was a little after two in the afternoon.

"Well, that's all right," he said. "That's early for me. Couldn't fall asleep until 5 o'clock last night, or rather this morning."

He looked thin, but it might have been because he had on only silk pajamas under his tartan plaid dressing gown, and the crutches added to his elongated appearance.

* * *

Down to 188 Pounds

"I might be a bit down at that," said Joe, dropping into a huge red damask chair beside his teakwood coffee table, and taking the lid off a Copenhagen china sugar bowl. "I weighed 196 when I left the hospital, in Baltimore, more than three weeks ago. Now I'm down to 188.

"But that's because I've been indoors so much. I'm nervous and restless. Too much loafing around, reading and smoking.

"Look at this place: two bedrooms and a sitting room and kitchenette. There's a total of four beds and a couch here, yet with all my facilities for rest, I'll be darned if I can ever fall asleep before dawn. I turn and

Yankee Clipper Slowest on Club Getting Dressed

NEW YORK, N. Y.—Although one of the fastest men who ever chased a fly ball, Joe DiMaggio is chronically pokey in his personal habits, being the slowest Yankee player in the memory of the oldest scribe in getting dressed after a game.

His faculty for relaxing when there is no need to hurry may have helped last season when the Bronxites' center fielder led the American League in homers, with 39, and led the majors in runs batted in, with 155.

After many of the night games at the Stadium last summer, DiMaggio would still be loafing around the clubhouse at 2:30 in the morning, when everybody else but the night watchman had departed. For one thing, Joe is basically a bit shy, and reserves the privilege of having plenty of time to himself. He likes to commune with his thoughts, and take his own time about getting ready to go out and face the demands of his admirers and autograph seekers.

toss, and read, and toss some more."

There could be no doubt about the reading, we could readily observe. Never had we been in a ball player's quarters so crammed with books and periodicals. They even overflowed on top of the big new television cabinet.

"How'd you like 'The Naked and The Dead?'" said Joe. "Mighty fine war book, and it helped to keep me up till 5 this morning."

The phone rang, and Joe reached for his crutches and swung himself into one of his bedrooms and, stretching out on his stomach on one of the twin beds, he talked for quite a while.

"Just somebody who heard the cast was off my foot and called to ask when I'd be going out and about again," he explained.

Finishing his coffee, Joe put the cup and saucer and sugar bowl on a walnut knee-hole desk, and shifted his long legs onto the coffee table. His feet were bare, and in heel-less slippers.

Takes Stand

JOE DI MAGGIO canes his way into the World-Telegram all-scholastic grid dinner in New York.

"I'll shed the crutches soon, use a cane for about a week, and then I'll be fine and ready. Every winter for three years now I've had to go to the repair pits. It's been making my life a dedication to baseball and its consequences a full-time job right around the calendar," he sighed.

"But it's paid you well," Joe was reminded.

* * *

Talks About Little Joe

"I suppose you could say that," said the Yankee Clipper, casting an affectionate eye around his sumptuous suite. . . . "Well, what can I do to entertain you? Would you rather see the scar of my latest operation or look at this new picture of my son Joe. He's 7, and attends the Walt Whitman Progressive School, on East 78th. He's getting to be a dandy kid. When he's up here visiting he gets better results twiddling with the dials of the tele-

vision than I do.

"But let's see what luck I have," and Big Joe got up and turned on the machinery.

He was rewarded by the faint image of a lady flitting onto the screen. She was sitting at a sewing machine, demonstrating how to sew seams. . . . Joe sighed, and snapped the thing off.

"I guess it would be more fun for you if I showed you my heel," he said. "But wait a minute till I go into the kitchenette and brew some more coffee."

Coming back with another cup, Joe elevated his right leg and loosened the bandage over his heel.

"Don't you think it looks pretty good?"

There was a four-inch incision on the inside of the right heel that had grown together again in healthy fashion.

"See how straight the cut is," said Joe admiringly. "Like it had been done with a ruler guiding the knife. That Dr. George Bennett of Johns Hopkins knows his stuff. Had me on the table 40 minutes, and sewed me up with ten stitches. I never did see the bone spur he chopped off.

* * *

Thirty Stitches in Heel

"There must have been 30 stitches on my heel which was operated on here in New York, January 7, 1947," continued DiMaggio. "That's what you get when you have feet that sprout silly bone spurs. But they tell me I won't be bothered any more by this sort of thing.

"My other heel, the left one, isn't completely closed yet, in spite of all the grafting I had done on it. But it's formed protective callouses and doesn't bother me. What a pair of dogs. I must pound too hard when I run.

"This last operation has resulted fine, but it's made me fidgety, sitting around waiting to get on my feet again. I've tried to be very patient. But being indoors since my carving of November 15 has thrown my habits all out of whack.

"I sit around and smoke and listen to the radio and read. No exercise. That's what's been tough. As a result, my appetite is no good now. I'm irregular about ordering my meals sent up. Often I'm content just heating up a can of soup for myself in the kitchenette, and making coffee.

"I'm a kinda loner, as you know, though, of course, there are guys often dropping in to talk. We punch the bag and listen to the radio, and when they go I read, and try to fall asleep, but I just turn and toss till 5 a. m., or later.

"Maybe it's the coffee," it was suggested, for by now Joe was on his third cup, and he had been joined by another visitor, Jimmy Ceres, an old personal friend. Also, a camera man had appeared delivering some huge cabinet photos of the interesting invalid, a couple of which Joe duly autographed and returned to the photographer.

* * *

Not Even a Glass of Beer

"Coffee?" said Joe. "Coffee doesn't hurt me. There are a lot worse drinks, and you know I don't bother with the other sort, except beer, and it's been a long time since I had a beer."

"Don't you ever get downstairs to the Monkey Bar, or into the Weylin?"

"Not on crutches," said DiMag. "I've become practically a recluse—a homebody, though I've a date tonight I must keep—practically my first airing in ages —to make an appearance at a scholastic banquet. I'll try a walking stick for the occasion, rather than crutches, if I can manage.

"Why you poor old shut-in," said the commiserating visitor. "You really have had a thin time lately. Doesn't your neighbor, Tallulah Bankhead, give you the friendly hullo now and then?"

"Tallulah of Noel Coward's 'Private Lives,' at the Plymouth? Alas, no," said Joe. "Tallulah tells me she has no interest in me whatever unless I get traded to Horace Stoneham's club. She's the greatest Giant fan in town."

"Oh, so no wonder you've taken to coffee: imitating Eddie Brannick of the Giants," we said. "It isn't surprising you can't sleep. . . . Or can it be you're worrying about something — worrying for fear they might trade your pal, Joe Page. Is that what keeps you awake till 5 o'clock in the morning?"

Page Down to 202

DiMaggio laughed. "I wouldn't want to see Page leave our team, that's sure," said DiMag. "I'd hate to have to bat against him, when he's right. Funny thing, but he called me up long distance just the other night to ask about my heel. Told me he was down to 202, after tramping around hunting.

"If we'd had a little more pitching help last season, we would have won. For instance, if we'd had Bill Bevens for even just a few games, that might have done it. I don't think the Yankees need much tinkering to be a factor again, and we were good enough last year to be a pennant possibility until the second last game of the season.

"Those stories about the Yankees lately have puzzled me. I mean the reports that they're ready to trade everyone but Tommy Henrich and me. Everyone! Why, that's ridiculous. For instance, how could they afford to trade a guy like Phil Rizzuto—unless they could get Lou Boudreau in exchange. In my book, no shortstop except Lou is better than Phil, and you can imagine how easy it would be to pry Lou off the Indians.

"Phil will be back, I bet, as good as ever for us. He was with me at Johns Hopkins, where he was told that he did not need an elbow operation. That took a great weight off Phil's mind and after a winter's rest he'll be himself again.

* * *

Cy Young for Indians?

"The Indians make interesting reading, the way they sign on coaches. Steve O'Neill, I see, is their latest. Maybe Cy Young will be added before they go to camp. Anything can happen under Veeck. He likes a bench top-heavy with age and brains, with youth and antics and whoopla all over the rest of the premises."

"Then you rather like the Indians?" we asked. "Do you figure they will repeat?"

"Not necessarily, by any means," said DiMaggio firmly. "I still like the Red Sox. And you can bet I also like our club. We came mighty close for Bucky Harris last year. We'll try to put out the same effort for Casey Stengel. Casey knows the ropes, and the front office has faith in him. We'll be up there again, and once more it will be a three-team race—the same three—and maybe we'll have the luck this time."

The phone had been ringing, and Joe got up to answer it.

"Now they want me to go down to Miami, around the first of the year, for an appearance at a Children's Cardiac Clinic," he explained. "It's a good cause, and I'll have to consider it. But first I want to get out to San Francisco for a Christmas visit with my parents.

"After that I am thinking of treating myself to a little vacation to Europe. Four or five weeks in France and Italy, as a freshener before heading for St. Petersburg and another spring of Florida training. I feel that by the end of February my system will be in tune again, and my sleeping schedule back to normal, and I'll be ready for another good season.

"If my heel aggravations are really behind me for good, I'll do some good stepping and good sticking. Do you realize this right heel of mine bothered me nearly all of last year? I felt wonderful during training, but the regular season wasn't more than a week old before the heel started hurting me, and it kept getting progressively more of a nuisance, though I plugged right along, saying very little about it.

"After what I went through with that heel, and the operation it necessitated in November, I think I rate a little European jaunt to celebrate my recovery. Only, wish I would have time enough to work it in before training. I don't want to miss a single day of the drill. I'll need lots of fresh air and sunshine to re-establish the right

Joe Joins in Grid Banquet

CONVALESCING from the latest operation to remove a spur on his right heel, Joe DiMaggio appeared at the New York World-Telegram's all-scholastic football banquet. DiMag is shown with Dr. Mal Stevens (left), former Yankee team physician, who is now associated with the Sister Kenny Foundation, and Chick Meehan, former N. Y. U. grid coach.

balance in my physical system. An ocean voyage might be fine preliminary medicine."

"Where would you head for—Paris?" we asked.

"Probably—and the south of France, and on to Rome. You see I have a sort of Roman invitation," and Joe pointed to his desk where stood a lupine statue of silver, of the familiar Romulus and Remus allegorical theme.

"From one wolf to another, eh, Joe?"

"Now is that nice to say to a guy on crutches who has been behaving himself," said the slugger.

"Rome! A place I always wanted to see. But there's one thing that makes it uncertain I could ever get up my nerve to go there. How would I feel, and how would the Italians react when they discovered I can only speak about a half dozen words of their lingo?"

DiMag's Best Yule Present —Being Able to Run Again

NEW YORK, N. Y.—"For the first December in a long, long time, I'll actually be able to run, if running is necessary. I mean hard running—within two weeks. That's the best Christmas present I've had in years."

Thus spoke Joe DiMaggio, Yankee outfielder, on throwing away his crutches and leaving his invalid's cane with the Salvation Army, December 15, following recovery from an operation to remove a spur on his right heel.

1949
THE GREAT PENNANT
RACE

Joe DiMaggio checks on his bothersome and severely painful right heel. Despite the injury, DiMaggio had missed only one game in 1948, but felt the full effects of it in 1949.

GOOD TO GET BACK

We were not expected to win the American League flag in 1949. The year before, we had landed in third place behind the Indians and the Red Sox, and we were now under a new manager, Casey Stengel. I was doomed to miss the first 65 games of that season and we were beset with injuries to a lot of other players as well — Yogi Berra, Charlie Keller, Phil Rizzuto, and Hank Bauer among the most noteworthy.

They had operated to remove a bone spur from my right heel in November of 1948. In spring training down at St. Petersburg, Florida, in 1949, however, I found I could not run on it, the pain was too great. The doctors said the spur was gone but the heel was in a "hot condition" as a result of calcium deposits and damaged tissue. So it was back to treatment at Johns Hopkins hospital in Baltimore.

It was not until late June before I got back in the lineup at the start of a three-game series against the Red Sox at Fenway Park. I got a single in my first at bat and four home runs during that series. And thanks to the likes of Tommy Henrich, Yogi Berra, Phil Rizzuto, Vic Raschi, and Fireman Jo Page, we surprised the Yankee critics by going on to win the pennant.

Joe DiMaggio

1949

JOE DiMAGGIO STATISTICS

Games	76
At Bats	272
Hits	94
Doubles	14
Triples	6
Home Runs	14
Runs Scored	58
Runs Batted In	67
Bases on Balls	55
Strike Outs	18
Stolen Bases	0
Slugging Average	.596
Batting Average	.346

STANDINGS

	Won	Lost	Percentage	Games Behind
New York Yankees	97	57	.630	
Boston Red Sox	96	58	.623	1
Cleveland Indians	89	65	.578	8
Detroit Tigers	87	67	.565	10
Philadelphia A's	81	73	.526	16
Chicago White Sox	63	91	.409	34
St. Louis Browns	53	101	.344	44
Washington Senators	50	104	.325	47

DiMaggio Reported All-Time Top-Salaried Player With $90,000 Contract

THE YANKEE CLIPPER SIGNING HIS 1949 CONTRACT

Joe DiMaggio as he came to terms at the club's offices here yesterday. Looking on are Dan Topping (left), one of the owners, and George Weiss, general manager.

The New York Times

CLIPPER ACCEPTS TERMS FOR A YEAR

Figures of DiMaggio Pact Not Revealed but Yanks Admit He Got Big Increase

DREW $70,000 FOR 1948

New Stipend Believed Above Ruth's $80,000 Peak—Star Leaves on Mexican Trip

By JOHN DREBINGER

All further speculation on whether Joe DiMaggio would be in uniform when the Yankees open their spring training operations March 1 came to an end yesterday when the famed Clipper came to terms with his employers for the 1949 season.

Announcement of this came after an hour's conference at the club's Fifth Avenue offices between the star center fielder and Dan Topping, president of the Yanks, and General Manager George Weiss. It failed to disclose the actual salary figures. There was no further reference to this item of curiosity beyond the terse statement that it provided an increase.

To this DiMaggio added that it was "the best of the eleven contracts I have signed to date with the Yankees." Topping also produced a broad smile of satisfaction the while a battery of press and newsreel photographers made it look as though the baseball writers were putting on an encore to their show of the previous night at the Waldorf-Astoria.

Most logical of various estimates was that the Clipper settled for a flat salary of about $90,000. That could be about correct, for it was understood DiMaggio had been asking $100,000, an amount the Yankees were willing enough to pay if a bonus arrangement based on attendance figures produced that amount. When DiMag steadfastly declined to accept a bonus contract such as he received last year, the $90,000 figure was accepted as a compromise.

Off for Mexican Resort

Immediately after the signing, the Clipper, who declared himself in fine physical trim except for being a few pounds underweight, packed his grips for a two weeks' vacation trip and last night was winging by plane toward Acapulco, Mexico. He said he would be back Feb. 21 to spend a few more days in New York before heading for the St. Petersburg training camp.

Thus, the 34-year-old son of an Italian immigrant fisherman, who used to sell newspapers for a dollar and a half a day on the streets of San Francisco, becomes the highest salaried ball player in Yankee history and perhaps in all baseball, although this distinction cannot become official until the club sees fit to disclose the actual figures.

For in the days when Babe Ruth was soaring to his $80,000-per-annum peak in 1930 and 1931 Col. Jacob Ruppert, then owner of the Bombers, made it a point to let in the public on the exact amount. Also, it is a certainty the late Bambino still holds the all-time high for "take home money," as the players call it, for there were no staggering income tax slashes in those days. In addition, the Babe also drew a 10 per cent net from all exhibition game receipts.

The present Yankee regime, however, has always declined to reveal contract figures at the time of signing, and it was not until yesterday that admission was made that DiMaggio had received approximately $70,000 for 1948.

Started at $7,500

At that, should the $90,000 be correct, the Clipper by next fall could bring his all-time earnings to about $475,000 as a Yankee, which isn't bad considering he started as a $7,500 rookie in 1936 and then "lost" three years in the Army, when his pay dropped to "sixty-a-month" as a corporal.

According to Arthur E. Patterson, the club's publicity director, the Yanks' No. 1 Bomber has received about $345,750 in salary, plus $40,809.20 in world series revenues, making a grand total of $386,559.20. Of his world series checks, seven were for actual series participation, the top figure being $6,471.10, which Joe drew as a winning Yank in the last all-New York series in 1937. Last year he drew a third-place share of $778.88.

Although he received regular boosts following his 1936 debut, DiMaggio's salary rises hit a snag with the war, which left him with a $43,750 contract for 1942. Under baseball law he had to accept this same figure when he returned in 1946, and when he encountered difficulty in regaining his earlier form in his first post-war season he settled for a similar amount in 1947.

Drove a Hard Bargain

Because of his magnificent comeback last year, plus the fact that he always felt the Yanks had treated him rather shabbily in pre-war years, it is generally felt the Clipper this time drove a sharp bargain.

Before leaving for Mexico, DiMaggio said that he had recovered completely from the operation performed on his right heel last November and that, barring mishaps, he expected to enjoy a good season.

"I never bother with any special exercises in winter," said Joe, "because I just naturally don't put on weight. In fact, I usually lose a little and am a few pounds off now which I'd like to put back before reporting."

He said he scales at present about 193. His average weight through the last playing season was around 196.

DiMaggio's Salary Record

Following is a list of the estimated salaries and world series checks which Joe DiMaggio has received as a Yankee since 1936:

	Estimated Salary.	World Series Checks.
1936	$7,500	$6,430.55
1937	15,000	6,471.10
1938	25,000	5,782.76
1939	27,500	5,614.26
1940	32,000	546.59
1941	37,500	5,943.31
1942	43,750	3,018.77
1943-44-45	(Served in Army)	
1946	43,750	392.95
1947	43,750	5,830.03
1948	70,000	778.88
Total	$345,750	$40,809.20

Grand total, $386,559.20.

DiMag Worth 100 G's a Year

By John C. Hoffman

Condensed from the Chicago Sun-Times

To those of us who like to worry about other people's money, it may be something of a surprise that the New York Yankees' Joe DiMaggio will demand $125,000 for 1949 and it's a certainty that he will be the first player in major league history to get at least $100,-000.

DiMaggio is known to have confided in close friends that he will demand $125,000 as meat and potato money for his presence next season and he won't be kidding. And it is only logical to suppose that the Messrs. Del Webb, Dan Topping and George Weiss, not to mention Manager Casey Stengel, will want him around. They have only to recall where the Yankees might have been in 1948 but for the great Guiseppe.

And why shouldn't DiMaggio be paid $100,000?

The first reaction by many who have heard of this fantastic figure was to say, "Babe Ruth didn't get that much." But the late Bambino's $80,000 salary was $80,000 and reckoned in monetary values of today it would be $160,000.

DiMaggio's $100,000 won't be "take-home" pay. When Uncle Sam gets through digging, it will be considerably less than that and even with what is left the great Guiseppe

won't be able to buy anywhere near the things Ruth bought when he was spraying dollars around.

DiMaggio's best days are behind him. But his argument won't be so much what he will expect to produce as what he already has contributed to the Yankees. And he won't be concerned with any comparisons between himself and Boston's Ted Williams.

In the final stages of the bitter American League pennant race last season, almost anybody who saw DiMaggio and Williams day in and day out will tell you that Guiseppe was a champion and Williams was just another guy who wore his uniform bloomers almost down to his ankles.

Playing with a painful charley horse on one leg and a spur on the other, DiMaggio was scarcely able to run out his numerous base hits, but there wasn't a day when you wouldn't have preferred to have him on your side rather than Williams. And Guiseppe was still that way when he made four hits the last day of the season after everybody else had given up on the Yankees.

All right, go ahead and look at the averages and you will see that Williams outhit DiMaggio for the season. But you won't see there that indefinable something DiMaggio had and Williams didn't have when the chips were down during the final weeks of the struggle.

In the final analysis, Bucky Harris, after he had been fired by the Yankees, observed, "I may be able to forget I ever managed the Yankees, but I'll never forget how that DiMaggio played ball for me when I needed him."

●

He's a Write Guy, Too

WE DON'T know how much mail a reigning movie queen receives daily, but it can't be much higher than the fan tribute to Joe DiMaggio. He draws about 200 messages a day in the season, and hit far above that during his recent spell in the hospital in Baltimore for another heel operation.

Joe doesn't talk about his fan mail. The breakdown on DiMaggio's mail comes from Jackie Farrell, a well-known former newspaperman hereabouts, who is now in the Yankee promotion department, and who screens the fan output to DiMag.

The highest fan response Farrell ever saw previously was on a day soon after Joe's feat of hitting three homers against the Indians, two off Feller. The count hit 308 that day.

Not every communication is adulatory. Fans blame Joe for everything bad, and praise him for everything good.

An average of two or three writers per day try to put the touch on Joe.

The best of all, according to Farrell, came last year after a DiMag homer against Cleveland had been nullified by rain. The fan wrote while he was standing at a hot-dog stand, sticking around and rooting that Joe's homer wouldn't be washed out, his wallet was lifted. He explained his wife thought he was working every day, but in reality he went to the races and was lucky enough to show sufficient profit to support the frau. The fan had twenty-five dollars in his wallet, and while he didn't expect DiMag to make good on all of it, he would appreciate twenty dollars, which was to be mailed to him at a saloon in Lodi, N. J., this latter so that his wife would not get wise to him.

Farrell shunts most mail to secretaries for routine replies, but he has a standing order from Joe to deliver to him personally any mail from shut-ins, particularly from kids. DiMag, of course, is a sucker for kids.

Most amusing communications are those from organizations running dinners for various sorts. At least a dozen times in the season one of these groups will request Joe's presence, holding out the promise he will not have to eat the grub of the day, but any special dish he may desire.—*Joe King in the San Francisco Chronicle.*

●

Lefty's Legs Okay!

LEFTY GOMEZ hasn't run out of good ones. When a writer was leaving the room to get food for the scribes at a recent Canadian-American League meeting in Rome, N. Y., the great pitcher, now connected with a sporting goods firm, grabbed him by the arm and stopped him.

"Wait a minute," ordered El Goofo, "let me go. My arm went dead . . . not my legs!"—*Al De Santis in the Schenectady (N. Y.) Union-Star.*

Joe DiMaggio to Miss Yankee Opener

HEEL SENDS STAR TO HOSPITAL AGAIN

New Treatment Prescribed for DiMaggio at Johns Hopkins in Effort to Stop Pain

OUT FOR INDEFINITE TIME

Yankees' Keyman to Miss His Eighth Opening Game—Bauer, Woodling to Play Center

By JAMES P. DAWSON
Special to The New York Times.

FORT WORTH, Tex., April 12 —The Yankees will launch their quest of the 1949 American League pennant one week from today without the aid of Joe DiMaggio. Wallopin' Joie is in for another siege at Johns Hopkins Hospital, Baltimore.

The $100,000 keyman of Yankee fortunes left the club today because of aggravated pain in his right heel, the heel that has been causing him trouble since the training campaign opened March 1 last at St. Petersburg, Fla.

When DiMaggio will return to the club is unknown. He faces hospital treatment of a different nature than any he has undergone before for an indefinite period.

Indeed, it is becoming a matter of speculation among his playing mates and the correspondents following the club on the exhibition tour which leads to the Stadium in the Bronx for the April 19 opener whether DiMaggio ever will play again.

Shortened Other Careers

It is a pretty solid conviction with those close to the situation that DiMaggio never again will be the DiMaggio of old. Along with his years of service, dating back to 1936, the slugging outfielder is handicapped with a podiatric condition, which has shortened the careers of more than one baseball star, among them Rogers Hornsby.

Despite a restricted training schedule and the use of corrective measures which included whirlpool bath treatment, heat treatment, the use of sponge rubber heels as cushions and, finally, the

removal of the spikes from the heel of his right playing shoe, all calculated to work a cure and at the same time permit DiMaggio to train lightly, the player's heel now is so painful as to preclude possibility of his running on it at all.

The latest corrective measure came only last night when, at Dallas, DiMaggio had a leather support nailed to his street shoe, between the ball of the foot and the heel, sort of an arch-support arrangement, on the outside of the shoe. This was to relieve the pain DiMaggio experiences even while walking.

DiMaggio was booked out of here today on an American Airlines flight at 1:45 P. M. A room had been reserved for him at Johns Hopkins.

Limps Off the Field

The decision to subject DiMaggio to his second hospital visit within six weeks was made last night in Dallas. DiMaggio limped off the field at Beaumont last Saturday after playing seven innings. He reported that night his right heel was bothering him as much as at any other time since training started.

Joe had undergone an operation last November for the removal of a bone spur in the right heel. The operation was performed by Dr. George Bennett at Johns Hopkins and was declared successful. However, following the first day of practice, DiMaggio complained of a recurrence of pain in the heel and he was flown to Baltimore. Dr. Bennett diagnosed the condition as a "thickening" in the heel which should disappear with ordinary precautions.

Manager Casey Stengel ordered DiMaggio to work only as and how he deemed wise. For the remainder of the training schedule DiMaggio followed this routine. Dr. Bennett visited St. Petersburg, examined DiMaggio and, with Dr. Sidney Gaynor, club physician, agreed a light work schedule by DiMaggio would produce no ill effects. Treatments were prescribed and, at the same time, changes were made in the playing shoes DiMaggio used, calculated to keep weight off the heel as much as possible.

Affects His Hitting

Nevertheless, DiMaggio has not experienced the cure that was anticipated. His playing was restricted to pinch hitting as the Yankee exhibition schedule got under way. On March 30 he started his first game. He has played in seven since. The running to base and after balls hit to the outfield has kept the pain in his heel alive in a more or less excruiating degree, and, of course, his playing

and hitting were affected. In 31 times at bat DiMaggio has collected seven hits for a batting average of .226. He has played 43 innings in center field.

The limit was reached when DiMaggio limped off the field after seven innings at Beaumont. He complained, but agreed to try another game. He limped off the field Sunday at Greenville, Tex., in even greater pain.

At Dallas yesterday Co-Owner Del Webb of the Yankees and Manager Stengel quietly called Dr. Bennett in Baltimore and General Manager George Weiss in New York. Dr. Bennett recommended examination by Dr. P. M. Girard, an orthopedic specialist of Dallas.

Dr. Girard ordered X-rays taken and gave DiMaggio a general examination which took about four hours. The examination revealed a "hot" condition, which was said not to be in evidence when DiMaggio was examined on his hurried flight to Baltimore or subsequently on his return to St. Petersburg, Fla.

DiMaggio's left heel, on which he was operated in 1947, was found to be perfectly all right save for surface scars. Dr. Jules Gordon performed this operation in January, 1947, when a spur was removed.

Dr. Girard recommended hospitalization for new treatment, which will take the form of injections and X-ray treatment. Club officials were vague about the proposed injections, although it was said novocaine will be one of the ingredients.

It was announced that Dr. Girard expressed the belief that under the new treatment the complaint will run its course and DiMaggio will be cured. How long the treatments will require was not specified. How long DiMaggio will be lost to the club likewise was unknown.

In the room at the Worth Hotel here, when writers were summoned for the announcement, DiMaggio said he could not forecast the length of time he will be away from the ball club. He was a solemn, grim-visaged DiMaggio, as he has been throughout the training season.

Reaches Baseball Heights

It was plain he was worried about a condition which, in the case of a 34-year-old ball player, who has been active through eleven seasons, not including three years in the Army, may very well affect his future. Particularly regrettable is it in DiMaggio's case at a time when he has touched the heights in baseball with a contract reported to provide a $100,000 salary for this year.

"All I know is that I am going to miss the opening of a season again," said DiMaggio, a tone of resignation emphasizing the depressed feeling he manifested. "This just didn't come on me now. It has been bothering me all the time. But, it got worse in Beaumont and in Greenville. I certainly hope this new treatment works a cure. I want to get out there and play again, but quick. However, I'll be in the hands of the doctors now. When they say it's all right for me to return, I'll be back."

Manager Stengel expressed his regret at the condition in which DiMaggio finds himself and made no attempt to minimize DiMaggio's importance to the Yankees. The current situation makes the eighth time in his eleven active baseball years that DiMaggio will miss a season's opening through injury, illness, accident or salary dispute.

Stengel's immediate plan is to use Hank Bauer and Gene Woodling as alternate center-field replacements for DiMaggio, he said. He added that he intended to keep Tommy Henrich in right field, pointing out he did not think the Yankees could afford to lose DiMaggio and Henrich from their picket line at the same time. This last was a reference to the possibility of Henrich's being shifted to first base. The manager reiterated his intention of experimenting with Billy Johnson at first, at least until the Brooklyn Dodgers exhibition series, starting Friday.

JOE KEPT ON ACTIVE LIST

Yanks Stress DiMaggio's Wish to Play as Soon as Possible

"There's no sense in thinking, at the present time, of putting Joe DiMaggio on either the disability or the retirement list," said General Manager George M. Weiss of the Yankees last night. "It's embarrassing even to discuss such possibilities when everything is problematical. I know that Joe is anxious to play and we're anxious to have him do so."

While DiMaggio may not be available for awhile, Weiss is hopeful that the Yankee keyman's heel will respond to treatment and that he will be back with the team.

"Until we know definitely whether DiMaggio will be able to play or not, why even discuss the point?" said Weiss.

If the Yankees were to place DiMaggio on the disability list, he immediately would become ineligible to play for sixty days.

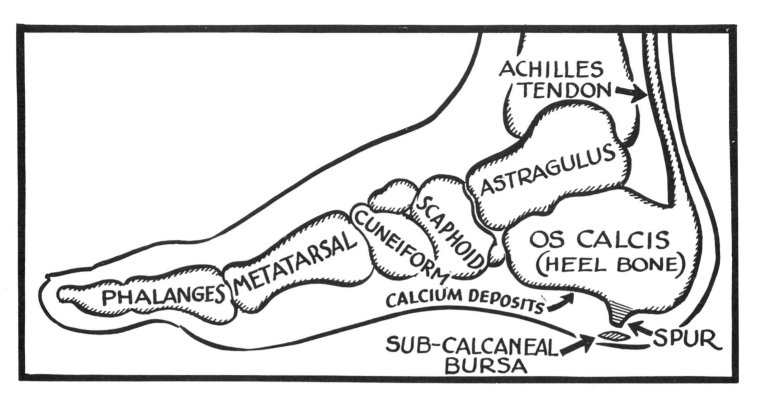

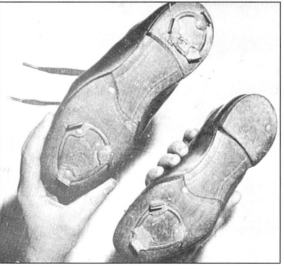

Some insights into the heel problems plaguing Joe DiMaggio in 1949. Above is a diagram showing a bone spur which needed removal. On the left, he leaves hospital after treatment for calcium deposits in the right heel, and on the right are the baseball shoes he wore when playing against the Red Sox in 1949: one heel had no spikes, and was built up with sponge rubber to ease pressure on the injury.

Joe DiMaggio greets the new Yankee manager, Casey Stengel, in 1949.

Yank Hopes Totter on DiMaggio's Heel

Jolter Returns to Hopkins for Further Treatments, Forced to Quit After Testing His Leg in Southwest

By DAN DANIEL

NEW YORK, N. Y.

Just when Joe DiMaggio will be able to start earning his $100,000 with the Yankees, nobody knows. He has returned to Johns Hopkins Hospital in Baltimore, and while the doctors are optimistic, there is no definite dope on which to base a prediction concerning Giuseppe's unveiling in 1949 American League competition. Not only is there no information on Joe's debut, but his entire baseball setup is shrouded in doubt.

Dr. George E. Bennett of Baltimore and Dr. P. M. Girard of Dallas have assured DiMaggio that the spur which the Hopkins surgeon removed from Joe's right heel last November is not growing back.

Dr. Girard said he had found the heel in "hot condition," recommended novocaine injections and X-ray treatment, got Dr. Bennett to concur on that course and sent Joe flying to Baltimore out of Fort Worth on April 12.

Dr. Girard said the trouble would run its course, and clear up. And DiMaggio was quite eager to accept that prediction.

"Please deny that I have any intention of retiring," said Joe as he flew northward.

The Yankees, of course, pay Joe his hundred grand even if he fails to play a single game. That is, unless they give him an unconditional release. And there is absolutely no chance of that with DiMaggio out temporarily.

Casey Stengel, however, was confronted with the necessity of revamping the outfield of a club which had dropped from third rating to some indeterminate location, pending more definite information about Joe and his heel.

Henrich to Stay in Outfield

Casey begged for time to think out his problems. He no longer was thinking of shifting Tommy Henrich from right field to first base, where he had placed Billy Johnson.

"You cannot take Henrich out of any outfield which is minus its ace," Casey explained.

"I wish I could be sure about Charlie Keller. He has encouraged me lately, but he still is a question mark. I think he will make it.

"Well, suppose we have Keller and Lindell in left, Hank Bauer and Gene Woodling in center, and Henrich in right. Would that be a weak combination? Certainly not. Maybe Bauer will be able to carry the load without help."

DiMaggio left the club after having played 43 innings in eight games and having come up 12 times as a pinch-hitter. His batting rating was .226, on

Belted .226, Seven Safeties in 31 Spring Appearances

When Joe DiMaggio left the Yankees in the South to go to Baltimore for re-examination and treatment of his injured heel, he had a batting average of .226 for the spring exhibition season.

Joe had played 43 innings in seven games and before that had made pinch-hitting appearances in a dozen. His over-all record was seven hits in 31 tries, with four walks. As a pinch-hitter, Giuseppe had contributed three blows and three passes.

seven hits in 31 efforts.

Joe ran into real trouble on April 9, in Beaumont, when he ran from first to third on a double, and had to slide. The next day, when the Bombers lost a 4 to 3 decision to the Class B Big State League club in Greenville, Tex., Joe scored from second on a single and had to do his hardest running of the spring. That did it.

After DiMaggio had been examined, Johns Hopkins spokesmen said he had "immature calcium deposits" in the tissue adjacent to his heel bone.

DiMaggio was to remain in Baltimore until these calcifications were dissolved. How long? Nobody could say.

The other question marks of the Bombers, when the training season got under way, were Pitchers Joe Page and Frank Shea. Page's situation became all the more involved when he injured his arm fanning Ted Williams on March

Interest Matches Bambino's Famous '25 Stomachache

Pointing to a Baltimore surgeon's disfavor to the wide publicity given Joe DiMaggio's aching heel, Frank Graham, sports columnist of the New York Journal-American, observed:

"Not since Babe Ruth had his famous stomach ache on the way north in the spring of 1925 and was taken off a train on a stretcher at Asheville, N. C., and from there shipped to New York and bedded down in a hospital, has there been such tremendous interest in the physical condition of the Yankees.

"This, although it distresses the doctor, is one of the finest tributes ever paid DiMaggio in the course of his distinguished career. It is another reminder of the fact that, as Stanley Harris said so truly:

"'Since DiMaggio has been with the Yankees he has been the Yankees.'

"The viewpoint of the doctor, looking on DiMaggio only as a patient, is understood by the reporters. Unfortunately, the doctor cannot grasp the viewpoint of the reporters which, like his own, is professional. In a sense, Joe is their patient, too. Whatever they think of him . . . and there isn't a reporter with the Yanks to whom Joe isn't a hero . . . he is making the news that they must write."

14. However, the lefthander has come along impressively, and at this time is Casey's No. 1 reliever.

Weight No Longer Worrying Shea

Shea, on the other hand, has done next to nothing and will have to be discarded as a possible aid to the early drive. Last September, Spec fell on his shoulder trying to elude being hit by a ball pitched by Earl Caldwell, then with the Red Sox. A muscle in his neck became involved and he could not pitch. This trouble returned early in March, and it wasn't until April 5 that Spec was unveiled in a camp clambake. He hurled for two innings and looked terrible.

Shea has been working hard, and excess weight, which ruined him in 1948, no longer is his bugbear. But that arm is not coming along.

Despite Shea's failure to make it, Casey's pitching looks formidable. In fact, it could turn out to be about as good a staff as any in the league.

It is on his hurling that Stengel is banking so enthusiastically. He will carry ten pitchers, which means releasing one. That hurler may be Wally Hood. Paul Hinrichs has been sent to Kansas City, to whom he belongs.

The Yankee infield is unsettled. First base continues to plague Casey. He started the training season with four candidates, and Henrich in the offing.

Babe Young was the first eliminated, with an unconditional release, and then Joe Collins was sent to Kansas City.

This left Dick Kryhoski, lefthanded hitter, and Jack Phillips, a righthander, for the home stretch battle. They seemed to be doing well. In fact, Stengel talked of a shift.

However, Phillips and Kryhoski suddenly stopped hitting, and Casey made a surprise announcement the day the Bombers quit St. Petersburg.

"I am turning Billy Johnson into a first baseman," said the pilot.

This was received by the press with lifted eyebrows and doubt as to the ultimate success of the experiment.

Johnson had his initial try at first in Beaumont, April 9. He handled 11 chances with ease, but none of them was difficult. He was using a new mitt, purchased just that morning.

Bobby Brown has been given the third base job, to do what he can with it.

"I believe that he can hit lefthanders," said Casey when he left Brown in sole possession by shifting Johnson.

◼ ——————————— ◼

Press 'Driving Me Batty,' DiMag Says at Hospital

BALTIMORE, Md.—Annoyance at reporters has been added to Joe DiMaggio's heel irritation.

Stopped by newsman and photographers as he hobbled through the Johns Hopkins Hospital lobby on crutches, April 14, the Yankee outfielder was asked if he had anything to tell the press.

"You're damned right I want to tell them something," snapped Joe. "Don't you think you've gone far enough? You guys are driving me batty. Can't you leave me alone? This affects me mentally, too, you know."

DiMaggio was driven away to a hotel, which he declined to name, where he will stay while taking treatments at the hospital, which are expected to continue for ten days. Previously, he had been in the hospital for two days for examination and treatment.

The outfielder's trouble was diagnosed as "immature calcium deposits in tissues adjacent to his heelbone."

◼▬▬▬▬▬▬▬▬▬▬▬▬▬◼

How Long Will It Hang?

DIMAGGIO LOCKER IN YANKEE STADIUM

ALL★STAR GAMES

DiMag homers in Yankee Stadium

1939   **AL 3 · NL 1**

YANKEES

JOE DIMAGGIO · Centerfielder

JOE DI MAGGIO

Among the baseball cards most sought after by collectors are those of Joe DiMaggio.

Joe DiMaggio's equipment bag, glove, hat, and spikes.

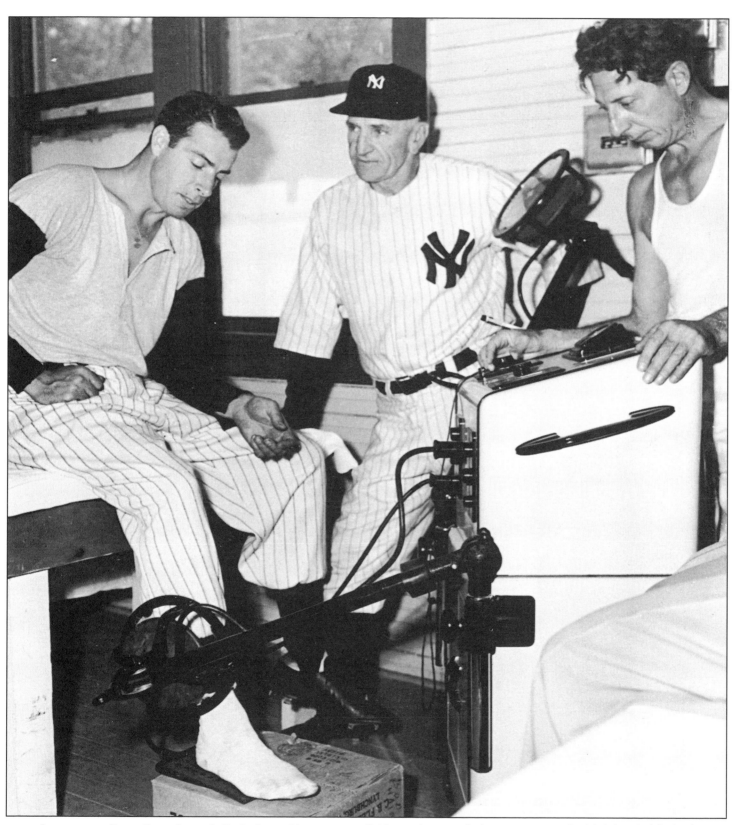

As manager, Casey Stengel, worriedly looks on, his star center fielder undergoes diathermy treatment for his injured right heel.

Joe DiMaggio Reconciled to Long, Drawn Out Comeback Process

Associated Press Photo

JUST A WORKOUT, but it's enough to stimulate Yankee hopes that the one and only Joe DiMaggio will be back in his old center field spot in the not-too-distant future. The Clipper (left) hauls down a fly ball in pre-game practice before last night's Stadium game with the St. Louis Browns as teammates Hank Bauer (25) and Cliff Mapes watch. DiMag took part in batting practice, too.

By MILTON GROSS

Easy does it for Joe Di-Maggio, who said today that his "comeback" will be a day-to-day proposition as he attempts to learn just how much his right heel will take.

In this, DiMaggio is being seconded by Dr. Sid Gaynor, Yankee club physician, who says, "We've no plans for Joe because we must wait to see each day just what working the day before will do to the heel.

"Joe can take his batting in practice and do some easy running in the outfield, but everything will be dependent upon what happened the day before."

Thus the Yankees and DiMaggio, who finally returned to uniform last night as a prelude to the Yanks' 10-3 victory over the Browns before 37,376 Stadium fans, can do no more than work, wait and hope.

Manager Casey Stengel possibly is most optimistic of all. He plans on having DiMaggio available for some pinch-hitting when the Yanks take to the road Memorial Day. DiMag and Dr.

Gaynor though, say they're unable to say that Joe will accompany the team on the trip.

Casey Has Hopes

It is Stengel's feeling that if Joe is able to accompany the Yankees on their next trip, "I'll be able to go out to the park for perhaps a half hour early each morning and get in some uninterrupted batting practice.

Undoubtedly, DiMag would like that—if he goes west. He exhibited such eagerness to swing last night that he found himself with blisters on the palms and fingers of both hands.

It was as if this were the start of spring training, which, in fact, it was for Joe. He hit as early as 4:30 and again, after having his hands taped, during regular batting practice for the benefit of a battery of photographers who covered his coming out party like the World Series.

The net effect is that today—possibly also tomorrow—Joe will do no hitting at all so that callouses can form. His heel, which is protected by a foam rubber cushion and insole arch support which takes the pressure off the sore point, still hurts. It likely will continue to, but the question is how much. Joe isn't

wearing spikes, but has a built-up heel on both shoes.

DiMag took some work in the outfield, but it was nothing more than a token gesture. He jogged as little as possible and threw not at all. Then he returned to the dugout to watch his teammates dismember the Browns.

For the second successive game the Yankees came up with surprisingly strong pitching from an unexpected source. On Saturday Fred Sanford picked up for Frank Shea and hurled one-hit ball for 6 2-3 innings. Last night Ed Lopat's control was awry as the Browns collected three runs and three hits off him in 1 2-3 innings and Allie Reynolds, making his first relief appearance of the year, supplied the stopper.

Reynolds limited the Browns to two hits to gain his fourth victory. He has lost one. Behind him and Lopat the Yanks battered starter Ned Garver and reliefer Bill Kennedy for 13 hits, including Tommy Henrich's first inning three-run homer. Tommy's eighth homer of the year was one of those mammoth blows which bounced off the facade of the upper right field deck.

Jimmy Cannon Says . . .

There was a blue serge suit hanging in Joe DiMaggio's locker in the Yankee clubhouse at the Stadium before the ball game last night.

"It's good to have some clothes hanging alongside of me," said Joe Page, the lefthanded pitcher who dresses next to DiMaggio.

DiMaggio, who was wearing a baseball uniform for the first time since April 11, was back in the humid room where Gus Mauch, the trainer, works. Mauch was bandaging DiMaggio's mercurocrome stained hands.

"What happened?" a reporter asked.

"They're blistered from hitting," DiMaggio said. "You can't lead a banker's life like I have and not get these."

"We use alum and alcohol in the spring to toughen them up," Mauch explained.

"Blisters make your hands feel like balloons," DiMaggio said.

There is a neuro-muscular stimulator in the Yankee clubhouse. Frank Shea, the pitcher, was being tapped with a coil of glass tubes shaped like a pitchfork. They lit up as they touched the pitcher's arm.

"Machines," DiMaggio said. "They got to prove those machines to me. I've tried every kind of machine and nothing helps."

*   *   *

The clubhouse boy handed him a container of pale coffee.

"I had plenty of good cuts out there tonight," DiMaggio said.

"How is the heel?" a guy asked.

DiMaggio kicked his right foot. The playing shoes he wears are 9 double E, a size larger than normal. There are no cleats on the heels, and they are lined with a special padding.

"It feels good," DiMaggio said. "But I'll have to wait until tomorrow."

"What about the pain?" the guy wanted to know.

"There's no real pain," he said. "I don't want to be pessimistic. But I'll wait until tomorrow to see how it is."

*   *   *

They talked about hitting and DiMaggio explained what it was like to go up and take in batting practice after a despair-nagged holiday.

"It's not the fastness," DiMaggio said. "I always need twenty, thirty pitches to get an idea where the ball's going. Every pitch looks good when it leaves the pitcher's hand at first. You have to adjust your eyes to the strike zone. It doesn't take an awful amount of time. I don't intend to do much. You try to go too fast the first day all the time. At least I do. Once you get the uniform on—boff. You don't pull up. You never know when to pull up."

*   *   *

They wanted to know how long it would be before he could play.

"If the heel was a 100 per cent perfect," DiMaggio said, "around ten days. But it's not 100 per cent. I don't want to be pessimistic . . . but that's the way it is."

He examined his hands which were criss-crossed with band-aids.

"I don't know how these hands of mine got so tender," Di Maggio said. "I had such wonderful callouses . . . About an eighth of an inch thick. You'd never think they'd get so tender so soon."

One of them said it was unusual for an athlete to lose weight when he was idle.

"Laying idle always takes weight off me," said DiMaggio, who has lost seven pounds. "This thing has me going. I have to exercise to put on weight."

The photographers made pictures. He returned to the clubhouse.

The workmen wheeled the batting cage away. DiMaggio came out and sauntered toward the outfield. There were more people. They stood up and applauded as he went to center field. Tommy Byrne, the pitcher, hit fungos to him. They were easy catches. But one was hit to his right. He labored after it, lame and struggling, and caught it in his glove. The people shouted. He did this a while, limping when he had to run. When he was done shagging them he ambled toward the dugout but the applause reached him and he trotted to the bench.

"I didn't think I could do that much," he said.

"How does the heel feel?" a guy asked.

"All right," DiMaggio said. "I don't want to be pessimistic. But I'll see how it is tomorrow."

Dr. Sidney Gaynor, the Yankee physician, was in the clubhouse when DiMaggio came in.

"It's a day-to-day thing," the physician said when you asked him how DiMaggio shaped up after the workout.

DiMaggio's 2-Run Homer Helps Yanks Win

JOE IN FIRST START AS BOMBERS SCORE

Red Sox Are Set Back by 5-4, Yankees' DiMaggio Hitting Home Run and a Single

CLIPPER CATCHES 6 FLIES

Bauer Smashes 4-Bagger With 2 Mates Aboard—Page Saves Reynolds in the Ninth

By LOUIS EFFRAT
Special to THE NEW YORK TIMES.

BOSTON, June 28—Joe DiMaggio became a Yankee in good standing tonight. Too long was the wait for his official return and there were probably times during the sixty-five games he missed because of an ailing right heel that all concerned wondered if the Clipper ever would make it. But make it he did for the first time this season tonight—and how!

Before the season's biggest turnout and the largest after-dark attendance in Fenway Park history, 36,228 fans, DiMaggio started to earn the $90,000 or $100,000 he is being paid. Like the DiMaggio of old, he made the enemy cringe, as he carried his team to a thrilling 5-4 victory over the red-hot Red Sox.

Carried is the word, too. For Joltin' Joe, directly and indirectly, had his hand in the scoring of all the New York runs. In his first time at bat, DiMaggio opened the second inning with a solid single to left center. The next two Yankees were fanned by Southpaw Maurice McDermott, so that if Joe had not hit, the visitors would have been retired.

Drives Into the Screen

Given this life by DiMaggio, the Bombers remained alive and, after Johnny Lindell walked, Hank Bauer hit his third homer of the campaign, giving the New Yorkers a 3-0 bulge. Nor did DiMaggio stop there. In the third, with Phil Rizzuto aboard via a single, Di-Maggio came through with his first homer, a dynamic clout into the screen above the high left-field wall and it was 5—0.

Idle so long, in need of batting practice and facing a brilliant, 20-year-old lefthander with a fair strikeout record, the Yankee Clipper was hitting 1.000 after his first two trips to the plate. In two other attempts, Joe grounded to the pitcher and walked, but he had provided the big punches that enabled his team to stave off Boston's strong closing bid.

This was a good game for the Yankees to capture. The Red Sox, with a 4-game winning streak and 10-out-of-11, had to be stopped by the league leaders. Casey Stengel entrusted Allie Reynolds with the pitching chores and, though he needed the help of Lefty Joe Page in the ninth, Reynolds notched his eighth triumph of the season against a single setback—thanks, principally to Joe DiMaggio.

Wears Special Shoe

Wearing a special shoe on his right foot—no spikes under the heel—DiMaggio patrolled center field flawlessly. He captured six flies and fielded three ground singles that came his way with his old-time grace. In the eighth, when Joe walked, Yogi Berra grounded to Bobby Doerr. DiMaggio was an easy force-out at second, but his take-out slide prevented Vern Stephens from completing a double play. In short, it was a tremendous night for the returning hero.

DiMaggio, with an assist from Bauer, supplied Reynolds with a big lead, which, at the finish proved barely sufficient. The Red Sox, who outhit the Yankees, 11—8, retrieved two runs in the fourth when, with the bases loaded and one out, Reynolds passed Al Zarilla, forcing one over, and the other tallied after a fly to left by Matt Batts.

Doerr hit his sixth homer of the season in the eighth and in the ninth a triple by Batts and a pinch single by Birdie Tebbets brought Page to the rescue.

Dom DiMaggio sacrificed, placing the tying run—Lou Stringer ran for Tebbetts—at second. Johnny Pesky then smashed a sizzler off Page's foot. However, the carom went to Jerry Coleman, who threw out Pesky, Stringer advancing to third.

This brought up Ted Williams, who earlier had achieved two scratchy singles. A hit here would have deadlocked the issue, a homer would have given it to Joe Mc-Carthy's men. Williams swung hard and drove the ball nearly 400 feet to deep center, but DiMaggio—Joe—made the catch look easy, the Yankees were home free and McDermott was charged with his first defeat.

Rizzuto and Pesky collided while the Scooter was making a double play in the first. It appeared that Rizzuto was hurt but after a couples of minutes he arose and continued in the game.

If the Red Sox had a park large enough to accommodate all the fans who wanted to see this contest, about 100,000 would have been on hand.

The box score:

NEW YORK (A.)	ab.	r.	h.	po.	a.	e.	BOSTON (A.)	ab.	r.	h.	po.	a.	e.
Coleman, 2b	5	0	1	2	2	0	D.DMgio, cf	4	0	0	4	0	0
Rizzuto, ss	4	1	1	4	2	0	Pesky, 3b	5	0	2	1	0	0
Henrich, 1b	4	0	0	7	2	0	Williams, lf	5	1	2	2	0	0
J.D'Mgio, cf	3	2	2	6	0	0	Stephens, ss	4	0	1	2	4	0
Berra, c	4	0	0	4	1	0	Doerr, 2b	3	2	1	4	1	0
Johnson, 3b	3	0	0	0	1	0	G'dman, 1b	4	0	2	4	1	0
Lindell, lf	3	1	0	4	0	0	Zarilla, rf	3	0	1	1	0	0
Wordling, lf	0	0	0	0	0	0	Batts, c	3	1	1	3	0	0
Bauer, rf	4	1	3	0	0	0	M'D'mott, p	3	0	0	2	0	0
Reynolds, p	4	0	1	0	0	0	aTebbets	1	0	1	0	0	0
Page, p	0	0	0	0	0	0	bStringer	0	0	0	0	0	0
Total	34	5	8	27	8	0	Total	35	4	11	27	8	0

aSingled for McDermott in ninth.
bRan for Tebbets in ninth.

New York . . . . .0 3 2 0 0 0 0 0 0—5
Boston . . . . 0 0 0 2 0 0 0 1 1—4

Runs batted in—Bauer 3, J. DiMaggio 2, Zarilla, Batts, Doerr, Tebbetts.

Three-base hit—Batts. Home runs—Bauer, J. DiMaggio, Doerr. Sacrifice—D. DiMaggio. Double plays—Rizzuto and Henrich; Berra and Coleman. Left on bases—New York 5, Boston 8. Bases on balls—Off Reynolds 3, McDermott 3. Struck out—By Reynolds 3, McDermott 9. Hits—Off Reynolds 11 in 8 innings (none out in 9th), Page 0 in 1. Winner—Reynolds (8—1). Loser—McDermott (2—1). Umpires—Summers, Stevens, Grieve and Honochick. Time of game—2:28. Attendance—36,228.

THE YANKEE CLIPPER IN ACTION AT BOSTON'S FENWAY PARK

Joe DiMaggio scores the first run in the same inning on Hank Bauer's homer.

Associated Press Wirephotos

Major League Baseball

Batting Averages

Wednesday, June 29, 1949

National League

LAST NIGHT'S RESULTS

New York 2, Boston 1.
Brooklyn 5, Philadelphia 3.
Cincinnati at Pittsburgh, rain.
St. Louis 5, Chicago 0.

STANDING OF THE CLUBS

	Brooklyn	St. Louis	Philadel.	Boston	New York	Cincinnati	Pitts'gh	Chicago	Won	Lost	Perc'tage	Games Behind
Bklyn.	—	5	3	5	9	7	8		40	25	.615	—
St. L.	6	—	5	7	3	6	5		39	26	.600	1
Phila.	4	7	—	2	3	5	8	8	37	31	.544	4½
Bost.	5	2	7	—	3	6	6	7	36	31	.537	5
N. Y.	3	4	6	4	—	5	5	5	32	32	.500	7½
Cinc.	2	2	6	5	3	—	4	5	27	36	.429	12
Pitts.	3	3	2	6	3		—	3	25	39	.391	14½
Chic.	2	3	2	5	5	5	3	—	25	41	.379	15½
Lost..	25	26	31	31	32	36	39	41	—	—	—	

American League

LAST NIGHT'S RESULTS

New York 5, Boston 4.
Philadelphia 6, Washington 1.
Cleveland 4, Detroit 2.
St. Louis 7, Chicago 6
(12 innings).

STANDING OF THE CLUBS

	New York	Philadel.	Cleveland	Boston	Detroit	Wash'gtn	Chicago	St. Louis	Won	Lost	Perc'tage	Games Behind
N. Y.	—	4	5	6	5	6	5	9	42	24	.636	—
Phila.	4	—	7	2	5	7	9	4	38	29	.567	4½
Cleve.	6	4	—	7	3	5	4	5	34	28	.548	6
Bost.	2	5	2	—	7	3	9	7	35	29	.547	6
Det.	6	6	3	4	—	7	5	5	36	30	.545	6
Wash.	2	2	6	3	3	—	4	10	30	34	.469	11
Chic.	2	3	4	2	6		—	7	27	41	.397	16
St. L.	2	5	1	5	4	1	1	—	19	46	.292	22½
Lost..	24	29	28	29	30	34	41	46	—	—	—	

YANKEES

DiMaggio	3	2	.667	Mapes	132	33	.250
Silvera	27	11	.407	Johnson	135	33	.244
Niarhos	14	5	.357	Reynolds	34	8	.235
Brown	136	44	.324	Stirnweiss	70	15	.214
Phillips	85	27	.318	Keller	19	4	.211
Page	16	5	.313	Lindell	110	23	.209
Kryhoski	138	43	.312	Byrne	33	6	.182
Henrich	223	66	.296	Shea	11	2	.182
Bauer	100	29	.290	Raschi	43	7	.163
Woodling	163	47	.288	Lopat	32	5	.156
Berra	224	63	.281	Sanford	15	2	.133
Rizzuto	259	71	.274	Marshall	4	0	.000

Team Batting—2247 6 12 .272.

GIANTS

Lafata	30	10	.333	Mize	214	51	.238
Webb	9	3	.333	Milne	26	6	.231
Thomson	274	87	.318	Jansen	42	9	.214
Gordon	246	78	.317	Hartung	35	7	.200
Marshall	203	62	.305	Hausmann	27	5	.185
Lockman	250	72	.288	Kennedy	38	6	.158
R Mueller	110	30	.273	Koslo	19	2	.105
Rigney	117	31	.265	Jones	33	3	.091
Lohrke	152	40	.263	Galan	16	1	.063
Haas	23	6	.261	Behrman	4	0	.000
D. Mueller	40	10	.250	Hansen	4	0	.000
Westrum	37	9	.243	Higbe	4	0	.000
Kerr	133	32	.241				

Team batting—2268. 592. .261.

DODGERS

Brown	27	10	.370	Cox	151	36	.238
Robinson	263	96	.365	Jorgensen	51	12	.235
Reese	269	87	.324	Newcombe	28	6	.214
Hodges	253	82	.324	Whitman	30	6	.200
Rackley	63	20	.317	Martin	10	2	.200
Minner	10	3	.300	Miksis	57	10	.175
Snider	264	77	.292	Banta	18	3	.167
Hermanski	110	32	.291	Barney	21	3	.143
Furillo	248	72	.290	Hatten	30	4	.133
Campanella	189	53	.280	Roe	29	3	.104
McCormick	81	21	.259	Branca	33	2	.061
Edwards	54	13	.241	Palica	6	0	.000

Team batting—2,346. 646. .275.

In his first appearance of 1949, in late June, Joe DiMaggio drives a single to left field in a game against the Boston Red Sox. The Boston catcher is Birdie Tebbetts.

1949

Yanks Breathe Defiance With DiMaggio Back in Lineup

Joe's Delayed-Action Bombs Exploding

Marks His Return With Home Runs

Clipper's Blasts Beat Bosox Three Games in Row in Fenway Park

By DAN DANIEL

BOSTON, Mass.

A two-run homer to beat the Red Sox in his 1949 American League debut, 5 to 4, on the night of June 28.

Two home runs, one of them with two runners ahead of him, to humble the local contenders the following afternoon, 9 to 7, after they had taken a 7 to 1 lead in four innings.

Another homer, with two on, June 30, for the margin in the Yanks' 6 to 3 victory and giving Joe nine runs batted in during the three games here.

That is how Joseph Paul DiMaggio broke into the pennant doings after having missed the first 65 games.

As he sat in the clubhouse after the second game here, DiMaggio was asked by a Boston writer, "Could you have come back sooner?"

Joe laughed, "Young man, I am no Jake. Remember that. I came back two weeks ahead of my schedule. Now that I am back, I hope I don't have to return to the dugout with a new flare-up in that right heel."

"Just Go Up and Swing"

"You say you had only eight workouts, then you rip our boys to pieces," said another Boston Boswell. "How do you do it?"

Joe replied, "Just go up and swing, and manage to hit the ball. There is, of course, no skill involved."

Does the heel still hurt? Yes, a little now and then. A lot sometimes. Joe limps perceptibly. But he believes he is back to stay. Perhaps he will have to take an occasional day off, or leave when the score permits. But, "I feel

Crashing the Pennant Party

JOE DIMAGGIO ... stepping out for smashing comeback.

fine. I think I am going to make it."

DiMaggio looked good enough in the field. But not superlative. He had a little trouble with a double by Bobby Doerr in the second game. But, everything considered, he has been doing a great job.

"I don't have that drive in the legs which I need out there to make quick starts," Joe explained. "I certainly was glad that the first game wasn't tied up in the ninth and sent into overtime, because I would have been forced to quit. The legs would not have carried me into the tenth.

"New shoes? Yes. I ordered them in New York on June 28. They will be lighter than my present shoes. Rubber cushioned, with spikes on the right heel.

"But the way I am going, I will not change shoes. Ball players are superstitious."

Casey Stengel watched Joe those three days with something more than delight.

As the manager exulted over the big show Joe put on in the second game, a Boston writer asked, "Where would the Yankees be if Joe had been able to start the season with them, and had played those 65 games he missed?"

"I don't like to speculate about such things," replied Casey. "I am more interested in what Joe's return means from now on."

"Don't you believe the Yankees would be ten games out in front if you had had Joe all the way," the writer persisted.

"Well, what interests me is this—how are the other contenders going to take Joe's return?" said Stengel. "They won't like it too much, will they?

"Babe Ruth alone could match Joe's flair for drama, for putting on a show and responding to an occasion. And

not even Ruth would have put on the kind of demonstration DiMaggio staged here. Eight workouts, and then socko. Four homers. The answer is this—the man is a pro."

The room quickly filled with Boston writers. DiMaggio explained that his two homers of the second game, against Ellis Kinder and Earl Johnson, had been hit off curve balls.

Ten feet away, Casey was on a new tack. "Rizzuto is the greatest shortstop I ever have seen. Miracles every day. The guy belongs on top for the All-Star Game."

Joe laughed. "Casey isn't kidding. That Rizzuto is terrific. And a strong boost to Joe Page for his great relief pitching today, and on all other occasions."

DiMaggio's spectacular pennant debut served notice on the rest of the American League that the Yankees were very much in the pennant fight. They were up there minus Joe; they are going to be so much tougher with DiMaggio in action.

Previously, there had been another important Yankee development.

On the night of June 23, when the lineup of the Yankees was announced for the opener of a series with Detroit, the Stadium crier shouted: "Tommy Henrich, first base."

This shift of the American League's standout right fielder to the position in which he had played the last 46 games of the 1948 season had been predicted by many, but I had not expected it just yet.

In fact, only the day before, Casey Stengel had said, "I believe we need a shakeup very badly. Sure, we are four games in front. But I think we are about to slip.

"I may send Billy Johnson to first base during the series with Detroit. I

Still Limps, But Believes He Can Stay

Only Ruth Could Match His Flair for the Dramatic, Declares Stengel

may use him at second.

Casey Changes His Mind

"Henrich at first base? I don't want to make that change. Tommy is the greatest right fielder in the game. No, not Henrich at first, unless an emergency develops."

Yet, the next evening, Casey shifted Henrich to first base, and Thomas celebrated with his fifteenth homer and two singles and drove in five runs in support of Tommy Byrne's one-hit shutout over the Bengals, 12 to 0.

"What happened over night?" Casey repeated the query and laughed. "I told you yesterday that I would not shift Henrich. Well, I got here today with a hunch."

I told Stengel that I had suspected all along he would make his big fight with Henrich in the infield. I wrote that back in March and again in April, and I was convinced there would be a change even when Dick Kryhoski and Jack Phillips were giving the bag a .330 average between them.

Yanks Sweep Double-Header With Red Sox

63,876 SEE BOMBERS TRIUMPH BY 3-2, 6-4

Raschi Wins 13th With Aid of a Force-Out at Plate in 9th on Apparent Boston Hit

RED SOX DROP 8TH IN ROW

Joe DiMaggio Paces Yanks in Afterpiece With 5th Homer and Clever Base Running

By JAMES P. DAWSON

In swirling dust kicked up by an embryo twister, the Yankees wrote a new page in baseball history yesterday as they grabbed the first game of a double-header with the Red Sox, 3 to 2.

Then they won the afterpiece, 6 to 4, to make it a perfect day for 63,876 onlookers. After this game, featured by Joe DiMaggio's power hitting, fleetness on the bases and headwork before darkness forced a halt at the end of seven and one-half innings, the Bostonians left the field grumbling over their eighth straight defeat in the first Yankee sweep of a twin bill this season.

In the unparalleled ninth inning of the opener, a legitimate single was converted into a prosaic force-out at the plate which averted what would have been the tying run for the Sox. That helped Vic Raschi ride above the dust storm and eccentricities of Yogi Berra to bag his thirteenth triumph.

Entering the ninth, the New Yorkers led by a run despite homers by Dom DiMaggio and Vern Stephens. The professor exploded his on Raschi's second pitch, but Walt Masterson's lead was short-lived. Jerry Coleman doubled in the tying run in the third inning and Joe DiMaggio streaked home with another in the fourth as a double-play was being executed.

Stephens Connects in Fifth

Stephens' four-master arrived in the fifth to square accounts. In the Yankee half, though, Cliff Mapes opened with a double and sent the Yanks to the front again by crossing the plate as Birdie Tebbetts dropped Masterson's flip on Coleman's bunt.

That marker was Raschi's edge in the 'ninth as Joe McCarthy called on Earl Johnson and Ellis Kinder in desperate strategic moves. After zipping over a called third strike on Dom DiMaggio, Raschi yielded a single to Johnny Pesky. Ted Williams singled for his third hit. When Stephens drew a pass, the bases were jammed with one out and over the field hung wind-tossed dust which almost obliterated a view of Joe DiMaggio in center and caused a brief pause.

When play was resumed, Al Zarilla shot what should have been a single to right. With the crack of the bat, Pesky was off for the plate, but in the dusty darkness he thought Mapes might make a shoe-string catch of a line smash and headed back for third to tag up.

When he realized the ball had dropped safely, Pesky thundered for the plate again, but Mapes made a perfect throw to Yogi Berra anchored at home. The ball arrived just a stride ahead of the runner.

Doerr's Fly Ends Game

Following this Mapes pulled down Bobby Doerr's wind-blown fly near the grandstand.

In the second game, Joe DiMaggio's fifth homer tied the score at 4-all in the fifth after Fred Sanford had been shelled to cover. Billy Johnson's single with the bases loaded in the seventh drove in the two deciding runs against Mel Parnell as Clarence Marshall triumphed in relief.

A single by Johnson also paved the way for a run in the second inning. In the third, after Hank Bauer's successful bunt, DiMaggio singled, chasing Bauer to third, and galloped to second on the throw to head off Bauer. A wild pitch let Bauer score and sent DiMaggio rounding third on high to befuddle Matt Batts into a throw that went into left field, permitting DiMaggio to tally.

In the Boston fourth Stephen's double, Zarilla's single, a pass to Doerr and Parnell's double resulted in three runs and a 3-3 tie. Pesky's triple broke the tie in the fifth, but when DiMaggio hit into

the lower left-field stand in the Yankee half the score was knotted again.

In the seventh Phil Rizzuto singled, DiMaggio walked with one out, a wild pitch advanced the runners and made an intentional pass to Johnny Lindell advisable. When Johnson shot his single between Parnell's legs Rizzuto and DiMaggio galloped home.

Rain Causes 48-Minute Delay

It took a rainstorm early in the afterpiece to drive that old Haverstraw first baseman, Jim Farley, out of the park, after the nerve-tingling opener. The rain caused a 48-minute intermission, but most of the crowd remained.

In addition to blowing down the Sox, the modified sirocco which sprang up suddenly as the opener neared its denouement blew down the center-field bleacher screen. The umpires ruled that any ball hit into the flapping curtain would be a ground-rule double, but for the second game the screen was removed.

Joe DiMaggio's No. 5 was the 308th home run of his big league career, lifting him even with Johnny Mize's record for active players.

Yankee home attendance soared to 1,005,343 for thirty-five home games. Last year the Yanks passed the million mark in game No. 33.

Juvenile admirers running on the field to get Joe DiMaggio's signature provided brief interruptions to the two games. DiMaggio obliged on each approach while the crowd cheered.

In the opener, Berra erred, missing Tebbetts' easy foul pop in the fifth, messed up Billy Hitchcock's following pinch pop in front of the plate until Raschi finally speared the ball himself, and caused apprehension in the eighth overtaking a missed third strike on pinch hitter Matt Batts as Doerr thundered over the plate with what would have been the tying run. However, the kid from the hill in St. Louis had the presence of mind just to stand on the plate for that curious force play in the ninth.

Doerr had a ten-game hitting streak broken in the nightcap.

Pending examination, Tommy Henrich had the day off. Dr. Sidney Gaynor will decide today when the Massillon macer should return to action.

Jack Phillips suffered a strained muscle in the left shoulder following his base sliding in Washington and is lost to the Yanks indefinitely.

1949

1949

ALL-STAR GAME

AMERICAN LEAGUE

	1	2	3	4	5	6	7	8	9	10		AB	R	H	PO	A	E

1 Joost, Philadelphia, IF
4 J. Gordon, Cleveland, IF
5 J. DiMaggio, New York, OF
5 Stephens, Boston, IF
6 Dillinger, St. Louis, IF
7 D. DiMaggio, Boston, OF
7 Michaels, Chicago, IF

8 Berra, New York, C
8 Tebbets, Boston, C
9 Williams, Boston, OF
10 Goodman, Boston, IF
10 Hegan, Cleveland, C
15 Henrich, New York, OF

17 Parnell, Boston, P
17 Raschi, New York, P
19 Brissie, Philadelphia, P
20 Wertz, Detroit, OF
21 Kell, Detroit, IF
21 Lemon, Cleveland, P

22 Kellner, Philadelphia, P
22 Reynolds, New York, P
22 Trucks, Detroit, P
25 E. Robinson, Washington, IF
34 Mitchell, Cleveland, OF
37 Doby, Cleveland, OF

Manager: 5 Boudreau, Cleveland
Coaches: 41 McKechnie, Cleveland; 42 Ruel, Cleveland
Trainer: Max (Lefty) Weisman, Cleveland
Batting Practice Pitchers: 43 Harder, Cleveland; 20 Zoldak, Cleveland
Batting Practice Catcher: 44 Susce, Cleveland

Umpires: Cal Hubbard, American League
William Summers, American League
William Grieve, American League alternate
Albert J. Barlick, National League
Arthur Gore, National League
Lee E. Ballanfant, National League alternate

AMERICAN LEAGUE ALL-STAR ROSTER

Player	Club	Birth Date	Birth Place	Height	Weight	Bats	Throws
CATCHERS							
Lawrence Berra	New York	5-12-25	St. Louis, Mo.	5'8"	180	L	R
James Hegan	Cleveland	8-3-20	Lynn, Mass.	6'2"	195	R	R
George Tebbets	Boston	11-10-14	Nashua, N. H.	5'11"	185	R	R
PITCHERS							
Leland Brissie	Philadelphia	6-5-24	Anderson, S. C.	6'4"	215	L	L
Alex Kellner	Philadelphia	8-26-24	Tucson, Ariz.	6'	198	R	L
Robert Lemon	Cleveland	9-22-20	San Bernardino, Cal.	6'	185	L	R
Melvin Parnell	Boston	6-13-22	New Orleans, La.	6'	180	L	L
Victor Raschi	New York	3-28-19	W. Springfield, Mass.	6'1"	185	R	R
Allie Reynolds	New York	2-10-18	Bethany, Okla.	6'	195	R	R
Virgil Trucks	Detroit	4-26-19	Birmingham, Ala.	6'	192	R	R
INFIELDERS							
Robert Dillinger	St. Louis	9-17-18	Glendale, Calif.	5'11½"	167	R	R
William Goodman	Boston	3-22-26	Concord, N. C.	5'11"	162	L	R
Joseph Gordon	Cleveland	2-18-15	Los Angeles, Calif.	5'11"	180	R	R
Edwin Joost	Philadelphia	6-5-16	San Francisco, Calif.	6'	175	R	R
George Kell	Detroit	8-23-22	Swifton, Ark.	5'9"	175	R	R
Casimer Michaels	Chicago	3-4-26	Detroit, Mich.	5'10"	175	R	R
Wm. E. Robinson	Washington	12-15-20	Paris, Texas	6'2½"	205	L	R
Vernon Stephens	Boston	10-23-20	McAllister, N. M.	5'10"	180	R	R
OUTFIELDERS							
Dominic DiMaggio	Boston	2-12-18	San Francisco, Calif.	5'9"	160	R	R
Joseph DiMaggio	New York	11-25-14	Martinez, Calif.	6'2"	195	R	R
Lawrence Doby	Cleveland	12-13-24	Camden, S. C.	6'½"	182	L	R
Thomas Henrich	New York	2-20-16	Massillon, Ohio	6'	180	L	L
Dale Mitchell	Cleveland	8-23-21	Colony, Okla.	6'1"	195	L	L
Victor Wertz	Detroit	2-9-25	York, Pa.	6'	186	L	R
Theodore Williams	Boston	10-30-18	San Diego, Calif.	6'3"	190	L	R

Ted's Catch Highlight of All-Star Slugfest

Turned Bases-Full Triple for Nationals Into Big Out

Game Most Loosely-Played of Mid-Summer Series; Goat Role to Southworth for Starting With Spahn

By DAN DANIEL

NEW YORK, N. Y.

Insofar as the 32,577 onlookers, who paid $79,-225 into the players' pension fund, were concerned, the sixteenth All-Star Game was a tense and dramatic affair.

Insofar as the experts in the press box were concerned, the American League's 11 to 7 victory was achieved in a loose and somewhat drab contest. In fact, those who had seen all of the inter-league meetings since 1933 were of the opinion that the Battle of Flatbush was the least thrilling and certainly the loosest played of the entire sequence.

There was some good pitching and a lot of bad pitching. There was some spectacular hitting. But the American League, which in the past had made it a habit to overpower its old rival, could not muster a home run. Stan Musial and Ralph Kiner each slugged a two-run circuit blow for the Nationals.

Vic Raschi

The American League had an errorless demonstration to its credit until, with two out in the ninth, Dale Mitchell booted Andy Pafko's single.

The National League piled up five errors, setting an All-Star record. Eddie Kazak and Pee Wee Reese committed misplays in the first inning which helped the Americans to four runs with two out. Willard Marshall, Andy Seminick and Roy Campanella also contributed errors for the losers and sent the fiesta into the sloppy side.

The error by Kazak came after long deliberation by Official Scorers Roscoe McGowen. Milt Gross and Lew Niss.

The first call on this play on a grounder by George Kell was an error for Johnny Mize for a muff. The later call recognized the misplay as a low throw by Kazak. Mize had the ball and the out and dropped the leather and the error should have remained his.

Musial Standout for N. L.

The hero would have been Musial with a homer, two singles and a walk if the Nationals had won. As it was, Stan's achievements were buried under the wreckage of National League hopes in a contest which saw that or-

All-Star Game in 1950
Back Where It Started

NEW YORK, N. Y.—The 1950 All-Star Game will be played at Comiskey Park in Chicago. It was in this arena that the inter-league contest was born in 1933. More than 47,000 fans packed the park to see Babe Ruth lead the American League to a 4 to 2 victory with a homer. The Phillies, the only club which has not been host to the affair, are expected to be awarded the game in 1951.

ganization drop its twelfth decision and its fourth in a row in the mid-season interlude.

The heroes of the American League victory were Joe DiMaggio, Ted Williams and Vic Raschi.

Giuseppe drove in three runs with a single and double and his hits came at critical times. Joe's single in the first inning, with George Kell on second and two out, drove in the first tally and touched off the four-run outburst. DiMaggio's sixth-inning double

WARREN SPAHN of the Braves delivering the first pitch of the sixteenth annual All-Star Game to Dom DiMaggio of the Red Sox. The catcher is Andy Seminick of the Phillies and the umpire Al Barlick of the National League.

gave his league a two-run cushion against the pair of tallies put over by the National in its half of that frame.

Williams came up four times. Twice he was walked. Twice he failed to hit. His heroic role was achieved in the field with the bases loaded and nobody out in the second inning and Virgil Trucks coming in to relieve a harassed Mel Parnell. Don New-

Sparklers on Parade ∴ Before the Fireworks Started

GREATEST OF THE GAME'S present-day stars who performed in the sixteenth annual All-Star Game of the majors at Brooklyn, July 12, were introduced on the eve of the classic to the crowd at the round robin game between the Bombers, Giants and Dodgers played for charity at Yankee Stadium on the night of July 11. Left to right, Enos Slaughter, Sid Gordon, Johnny Mize, Walker Cooper, Bob Thomson, Andy Seminick, Vern Bickford, Ewell Blackwell, George Munger, Warren Spahn, Muddy Ruel, Bill McKechnie, Bucky Walters, the announcer, Bill Corum, ace sports columnist of the New York Journal-American; Burt Shotton, Preacher Roe, Don Newcombe, Vic Raschi, Ralph Branca, Allie Reynolds, Yogi B e r r a, Roy Campanella, Birdie Tebbetts, Gil Hodges, Jackie Robinson, Ralph Kiner, Pee Wee Reese, Joe DiMaggio and Stan Musial.

combe, the big Brooklyn righthander, crashed one for the left field stands. The ball fell short of the target, but appeared to be labeled a triple. Somehow, Theodore grabbed that ball. It was as spectacular and as vital a catch as has been made in the All-Star competition. The Nationals got only one run out of that drive, and then Pee Wee Reese, a flop all day, jammed into a double play.

Had that ball got away from Williams I am convinced the National League, with three runs in and a runner on third and nobody out, would have won the game.

Trucks got official credit for the victory, but Raschi did the best pitching.

After the Yankee righthander's ninth-inning collapse against Washington the previous Saturday, it had been expected that Lou Boudreau would pass him up and work his own Bob Lemon. But the manager of the Indians by-passed Lemon and let Raschi pitch the last three innings against a desperate National League side. Vic blanked the old league with one hit, Andy Pafko's ninth-inning single.

In calling on Newcombe after Starter Warren Spahn had been boffed around, Billy Southworth appeared to tab the Negro rookie of the Superbas the top righthander of the National League. It was Newcombe who was charged with the defeat, but there were worse pitchers than Don on the National side.

Neither manager covered himself with glory in his opening selection. I certainly would have named neither Mel Parnell nor Warren Spahn for the first volleys.

In fact, I am inclined to name my old friend Southworth the goat of the game for his choice of Spahn. With six righthanded hitters on the American League starting club, the experts felt that a righthander should and would open for the National League. But Southworth crossed up the press box with Spahn and Billy paid the penalty.

How the runs were made, all 18 of them, you will discover in the play-by-play story of the game.

How the hits were made—all 25 of them—you also will learn from the blow-by-blow yarn. There, too, you will get the sad details of the six errors and the five showers which turned the muggy afternoon into a trial. There was one time-out for rain—14 minutes in the sixth inning.

The American League used four hurlers—Parnell, Trucks, Lou Brissie and Raschi.

The National League used seven pitchers, passing up only Ralph Branca. Those who served were Spahn, Newcombe, Red Munger, Vern Bickford, Howie Pollet, Ewell Blackwell and Preacher Roe.

Blackie Baffles Sluggers

Blackwell's chore was brief and artistic. He went only one inning, faced only three men, fanning Vernon Stephens and Joe Gordon.

The star catch on the National League side was made by Andy Pafko when he robbed Vic Wertz in the seventh.

The game was notable in that it marked the first appearance of Negro players. Jackie Robinson, Roy Campanella and Don Newcombe, all of the Dodgers, and Larry Doby of the Indians were the Negro pioneers in All-Star play.

That five-error bag of the Nationals set a record. That six-run first inning ditto. There were other matters in which the book was concerned.

But there have been many All-Star games among players who looked less tired and more dramatic.

Game 'All Wet' From Start--and Not From Rain

By STAN BAUMGARTNER
BROOKLYN, N. Y.

Stan Musial

The best way to describe the sixteenth annual All-Star Game at Ebbets Field, July 12, was that it was "all wet" from start to finish. And it wasn't just the rain.

The American League won as usual, 11 to 7; a couple of good numbers if you play them right. The American League did, the National League didn't. It was the American leaguers' twelfth win in 16 games.

As more than one sports writer remarked after the game: "All they needed was a keg of beer at third base," and then it would have been a regular married men vs. single men at a picnic. It always rains at picnics—and they had that, too.

It was played under atrocious conditions and it was an atrocious game, no matter whom you wanted to win. The

Musial, Kiner Belt Homers for Losing Side

(CONTINUED FROM PAGE 7)
National League played as if it had a double case of jitters in the first inning and then broke the record for errors in the classic, which had been set at four by the American leaguers at Cincinnati in 1938.

Warren Spahn had nothing and he wasn't helped by his mates in that horrible (for the National leaguers) first inning.

Newcombe Tagged With Loss

The irony of the game was that the fellow who pitched the best ball for the National leaguers was Don Newcombe, the loser. He and the senior leaguers were the victims of the luckiest hit ever made in an All-Star Game. The National was leading, 5 to 4, in the fourth inning after an uphill fight, with George Kell, who singled, and Ted Williams, who walked, on base when Eddie Joost came to bat with two down.

Newcombe had Joost swinging with his left foot in the dugout, but Eddie managed to reach an outside pitch with the end of his bat. The ball squirted off like a miscued billiard ball, did a dance toward Gil Hodges at first base and then at the last moment—just as if it had eyes—ran away from Hodges, caromed off his fist and dribbled into right field, scoring both men and putting the American leaguers in front.

The National leaguers seemed to lose heart at this—as if to say, "Oh, what's the use? We can't win no matter what we do." And they lost.

Stan Musial and Joe DiMaggio were the standouts as it should be. The Cardinal star looked like an All-Star. So did the Yankee Clipper. Both lived up to everything a hero-worshipper would expect. Musial had a home run and two singles and DiMaggio a double and a single.

Newcombe, George Munger, Ewell Blackwell and Preacher Roe did the best pitching for the Nationals; Lou Brissie and Vic Raschi for the Americans. The American League looked like the best club and it won.

There was one noticeable variation to the game. The long distance hitting was done by the National, not the American. The junior league won on singles and pitching, the senior league lost with home runs and not too good pitching.

The number of runs and errors established new records for the All-Star series.

How they played baseball at all in such weather—under such conditions—was the real $64 question. And how can you blame or praise anyone when the ball was so wet? It should have had handles.

It Happened In Brooklyn!

American League.	AB.	R.	H.	O.	A.	E.
D. DiMag'o (R. Sox), rf-cf	5	2	2	2	0	0
Raschi (Yankees), p	1	0	0	0	1	0
Kell (Tigers), 3b	3	2	2	0	1	0
§Dillinger (Browns), 3b	1	2	1	0	2	0
Williams (Red Sox), lf	2	1	0	1	0	0
Mitchell (Indians), lf	1	0	1	1	0	1
J. DiMag'o (Yankees), cf	4	1	2	0	0	0
xDoby (Indians), rf-cf	1	0	0	2	0	0
Joost (Athletics), ss	2	1	1	2	2	0
Stephens (Red Sox) ss	2	0	0	2	0	0
E. Rob'son (Senators), 1b	5	1	1	8	0	0
Goodman (Red Sox), 1b	0	0	0	1	1	0
Michaels (White Sox), 2b	2	0	0	1	3	0
J. Gordon (Indians), 2b	2	1	1	3	2	0
Tebbetts (Red Sox), c	2	0	2	2	2	0
Berra (Yankees), c	3	0	0	2	1	0
Parnell (Red Sox), p	1	0	0	0	1	0
Trucks (Tigers), p	1	0	0	0	0	0
Brissie (Athletics), p	1	0	0	0	0	0
zWertz (Tigers), rf	2	0	0	0	0	0
Totals	41	11	13	27	14	1

National League	AB.	R.	H.	O.	A.	E.
Reese (Dodgers), ss	5	0	0	3	3	1
J. Rob'son (Dodgers), 2b	4	3	1	1	1	0
Musial (Cards), cf-rf	4	1	3	2	0	0
Kiner (Pirates), lf	5	1	1	3	0	0
Mize (Giants), 1b	2	0	1	1	0	0
*Hodges (Dodgers), 1b	3	1	1	8	2	0
Marshall (Giants), rf	1	1	0	1	0	1
Bickford (Braves), p	0	0	0	0	0	0
yThomson (Giants)	1	0	0	0	0	0
Pollet (Cards), p	0	0	0	1	0	0
Blackwell (Reds), p	0	0	0	0	0	0
Roe (Dodgers), p	0	0	0	0	0	0
aSlaughter (Cards)	1	0	0	0	0	0
Kazak (Cards), 3b	2	0	2	0	0	1
S. Gordon (Giants), 3b	2	0	1	0	4	0
Seminick (Phillies), c	1	0	0	3	0	1
Campanella (Dodgers), c	2	0	0	2	0	1
Spahn (Braves), p	0	0	0	0	0	0
Newcombe (Dodgers), p	1	0	0	0	0	0
†Schoendienst (Cards)	1	0	1	0	0	0
Munger (Cards), p	0	0	0	0	0	0
‡Pafko (Cubs), cf	2	0	1	2	0	0
Totals	37	7	12	27	10	5

*Ran for Mize in third.
†Singled for Newcombe in fourth.
‡Struck out for Munger in fifth.
§Ran for Kell in sixth.
xRan for J. DiMaggio in sixth.
yFlied out for Bickford in sixth.
zFlied out for Brissie in seventh.
a Flied out for Blackwell in eighth.

American League	4	0	0	2	0	2	3	0	0—11
National League	2	1	2	0	0	2	0	0	0—7

Runs batted in—J. DiMaggio 3, E. Robinson, Tebbetts, Musial 2, Newcombe, Kazak, Joost 2, Kiner 2, D DiMaggio, Dillinger, Mitchell. (Joost scored on Reese's error in first). (J. Robinson scored when Kiner hit into double play in third). Two-base hits—J. Robinson, Tebbetts, S. Gordon, D. DiMaggio, J. DiMaggio, J. Gordon, Mitchell. Home runs—Musial, Kiner. Stolen base—Kell. Double plays—Michaels, Joost and E. Robinson; Joost, Michaels and E. Robinson; J. Robinson, Reese and Hodges. Bases on balls—Off Spahn 2 (Joost, Williams), off Parnell 1 (Marshall), off Trucks 2, (J. Robinson, Marshall), off Newcombe 1 (Williams), off Munger 1 (Michaels), off Bickford 1 (Kell), off Brissie 2 (Campanella, Reese), off Raschi 3, (S. Gordon, Pafko, Musial). Struck out—By Spahn 3 (D. DiMaggio, Williams, Parnell), by Parnell 1 (Mize), by Brissie 1 (Pafko), by Raschi 1 (Campanella), by Blackwell 2 (Stephens, J. Gordon). Pitching record—Spahn 4 hits, 4 runs in 1 1-3 innings; Newcombe 3 hits, 2 runs in 2 2-3 innings; Muncrief 0 hits, 0 runs in 1 inning; Bickford 2 hits, 2 runs in 1 inning; Pollet 4 hits, 3 runs in 1 inning; Blackwell 0 hits, 0 runs in 1 inning; Roe 0 hits, 0 runs in 1 inning; Parnell 3 hits, 3 runs in 1 inning (none out in second); Trucks 3 hits, 2 runs in 2 innings; Brissie 5 hits, 2 runs in 3 innings; Raschi 1 hit, 0 runs in 3 innings. Hit by pitcher—by Parnell 1 (Seminick). Left on bases—National League 12, American League 8. Earned runs—American League 7, National League 7. Winning pitcher—Trucks. Losing pitcher—Newcombe. Umpires—Barlick (N. L.) at plate; Hubbard (A. L.) first base; Gore (N. L.) second base; Summers (A. L.) third base; Ballanfant (N. L.) right field; Grieve (A. L.) left field (for first 4 1-2 innings); Summers (A. L.) at plate; Gore (N. L.) first base; Hubbard (A. L.) second base; Ballanfant (N. L.) third base; Grieve (A. L.) left field (for the last 4 1-2 innings). Time of game—3:04. Attendance—32,577.

Sad Story for N. L.

First Inning

AMERICAN—D. DiMaggio struck out. Kell was safe on Kazak's low throw. Williams struck out as Kell stole second. J. DiMaggio singled to left, scoring Kell. Joost walked. E. Robinson singled to right, scoring J. DiMaggio and sending Joost to third. Reese bobbled Michaels' bounder, Joost scoring on the error and E. Robinson going to second. Tebbetts singled to left, scoring E. Robinson, and Michaels raced to third when the bag was left unprotected. Parnell fanned. FOUR RUNS, THREE HITS, TWO ERRORS.

NATIONAL — Parnell threw out Reese. J. Robinson doubled to left. Musial homered over the right field screen, scoring J. Robinson ahead of him. Kiner fouled to Tebbetts. Mize fanned. TWO RUNS, TWO HITS.

Second Inning

AMERICAN—D. DiMaggio fouled to Mize. Kell singled to center. Williams walked. Spahn was replaced by Newcombe. J. DiMaggio flied to Kiner. Joost popped to J. Robinson. NO RUNS, ONE HIT.

NATIONAL—Marshall walked. Ka-zak singled to left. Seminick was hit by a pitched ball. Parnell was replaced by Trucks. Newcombe lined to Williams, scoring Marshall from third. Reese grounded into a double play, Michaels to Joost to E. Robinson. ONE RUN, ONE HIT.

Third Inning

AMERICAN—E. Robinson flied to Marshall. Michaels flied to Kiner. After Seminick dropped his foul, Tebbetts lined a double to center and took third when Marshall fumbled the ball. Trucks flied to Kiner. NO RUNS, ONE HIT, TWO ERRORS.

NATIONAL—J. Robinson walked. Musial singled to left, sending J. Robinson to third. Kiner grounded into a double play, Joost to Michaels to E. Robinson, J. Robinson scoring. Mize singled to right. Marshall walked. Hodges ran for Mize. Kazak singled to left, scoring Hodges. Seminick grounded to Kell. TWO RUNS, THREE HITS.

Fourth Inning

AMERICAN—Hodges went to first base, S. Gordon to third, and Campanella went in to catch for Nationals. D. DiMaggio grounded out to S. Gordon. Kell singled to left. Williams walked. S. Gordon threw out J. DiMaggio. Joost singled off Hodges' bare hand, Kell and Williams scoring. E. Robinson flied to

First of Race to Play in All-Star Game

THIS YEAR'S ALL-STAR GAME marked the first time in history that a Negro player performed in the classic. Four Negroes were chosen and all appeared in the game. They are, left to right, Roy Campanella, Larry Doby, Don Newcombe and Jackie Robinson.

Musial. TWO RUNS, TWO HITS.

NATIONAL—Brissie went in to pitch and Berra to catch for the Americans. Schoendienst, batting for Newcombe, singled to center. Reese grounded to Michaels, who tossed to Joost, forcing Schoendienst. J. Robinson flied to D. DiMaggio. Musial beat out an infield hit to E. Robinson. Kiner flied to D. DiMaggio in right. NO RUNS, TWO HITS.

Fifth Inning

AMERICAN—Munger went in to pitch for the Nationals. Michaels walked. Berra forced Michaels, Hodges to Reese. Brissie hit into a double play, J. Robinson to Reese to Hodges. NO RUNS, NO HITS.

NATIONAL—J. Gordon went to second base and Stephens to shortstop for Americans. Hodges bounced to J. Gordon. Marshall grounded out to J. Gordon. S. Gordon doubled off the wall in left-center. Campanella was intentionally passed. Pafko batted for Munger and fanned. NO RUNS, ONE HIT.

Sixth Inning

AMERICAN—Pafko replaced Marshall and went to center field, Musial moving to right, and Bickford went in to pitch for the Nationals. D. DiMaggio doubled down the left field line. Kell walked. Williams flied to Pafko in right-center, D. DiMaggio taking third after the catch. Dillinger ran for Kell. J. DiMaggio doubled to left-center, scoring D. DiMaggio and Dillinger. J. DiMaggio took third when Kiner's throw eluded Campanella. Doby ran for J. DiMaggio. Stephens grounded to S. Gordon. E. Robinson grounded to Hodges. TWO RUNS, TWO HITS, ONE ERROR.

NATIONAL — Dillinger went to third base, Mitchell to left field, Doby to right and D. DiMaggio switched to center for the Americans. Reese walked. J. Robinson forced Reese at second, Dillinger to J. Gordon. Play was interrupted for ten minutes by rain. Musial tapped in front of the plate and was thrown out by Berra. Kiner homered into the lower left field stands, scoring behind J. Robinson. Hodges beat out infield hit to third. Thomson batted for Bickford and flied to Mitchell. TWO RUNS, TWO HITS.

Seventh Inning

AMERICAN — Pollet went in to pitch for the Nationals. J. Gordon doubled to right. Berra went out, Reese to Hodges. Wertz batted for Brissie and flied to Pafko, who made a diving catch. D. DiMaggio singled to left, scoring J. Gordon, and went to second on the throw-in. Dillinger singled to left, scoring D. DiMaggio. Mitchell doubled to left, scoring Dillinger. Doby grounded to Hodges, who threw to Pollet for the putout. THREE RUNS, FOUR HITS.

NATIONAL—Raschi went in to pitch, Wertz replaced D. DiMaggio for Americans, going to right field, and Doby switched to center. S. Gordon walked. Campanella popped to Stephens. Pafko walked. Reese popped to Stephens. Raschi threw out J. Robinson. NO RUNS, NO HITS.

Eighth Inning

AMERICAN — Blackwell went in to pitch for Nationals. Stephens struck out. E. Robinson popped to Reese. J. Gordon fanned. NO RUNS, NO HITS.

NATIONAL—Goodman went to first base for Americans. Musial walked. Kiner lined to Doby. J. Gordon trapped Hodges' pop fly, but Hodges beat throw to first; E. Robinson then threw to Stephens in time to force Musial at second. Slaughter, batting for Blackwell, flied to Doby. NO RUNS, NO HITS.

Ninth Inning

AMERICAN—Roe went in to pitch for Nationals. Berra flied to Musial. Wertz grounded to Reese. Raschi rolled out to S. Gordon. NO RUNS, NO HITS.

NATIONAL—S. Gordon rolled to Dillinger. Campanella struck out. Pafko singled to left and went to second when Mitchell let the ball get through him. Reese popped to J. Gordon. NO RUNS, ONE HIT, ONE ERROR.

Joe DiMaggio and Ted Williams posed together at just about every All-Star game in the 1940s, except for their years in military service. This time it was before the All-Star classic of 1949. As it turned out later that day, they were the heroes in the American League's victory — DiMaggio drove in three runs with a double and a single, and Williams saved a slew of runs with a great catch to rob the National League of an extra base hit with the bases loaded.

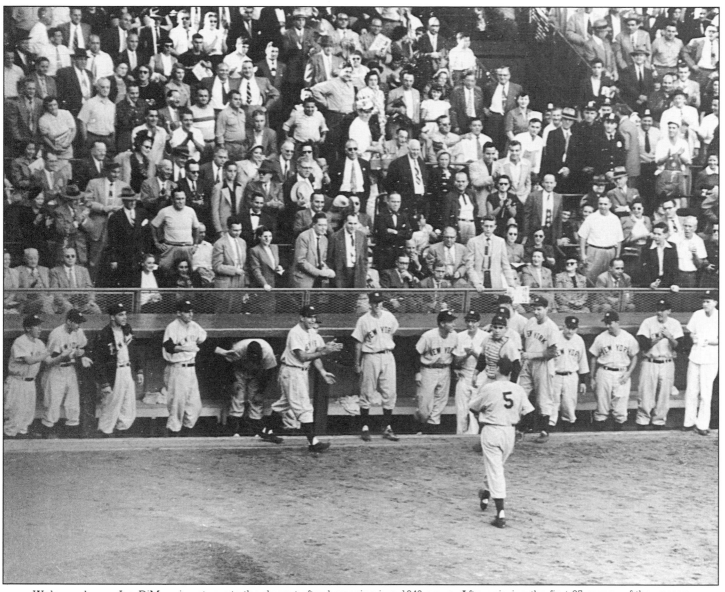

Welcome home. Joe DiMaggio returns to the dugout after homering in a 1949 game. After missing the first 65 games of the season, the Yankee Clipper returned to the lineup to hit at a clip of .346.

A smiling Joe DiMaggio once again graces the cover of *Life* magazine.

YANKEE CLIPPER SCORES ON HIS GRAND-SLAM CLOUT

BOMBERS DEFEAT MACKMEN, 13-4, 5-2

Yankees Club 16 Blows, 5 by Johnson, as Raschi Gains 18th Triumph in Opener

DIMAGGIO IS FORCED OUT

Retires With Leg Cramps in Second Game but Quickly Recovers—Byrne Scores

By JOHN DREBINGER
Special to THE NEW YORK TIMES

PHILADELPHIA, Sept. 5—The Yankees, with re-enforcements pouring in from all sides, wound up their six-city tour on a triumphant note today as they shot down the Athletics in both ends of the holiday twin bill before a gathering of 32,844.

They bagged the opener, 13 to 4, with Joe DiMaggio blasting five runs across the plate, four on a grand slam homer. Hank Bauer and Bill Johnson also connected for circuit blows to pave an easy trail for Vic Raschi as the big right-hander posted his eighteenth victory of the campaign.

Then, though the great DiMag had to retire after only an inning and a half in the nightcap, Casey Stengel's Bombers rolled right on to win this one for Tommy Byrne, 5 to 2. DiMaggio, after just missing another homer by a few feet in the top half of the second, was seized with an attack of cramps in both legs. He recovered quickly after retiring to the Yankee dressing room, however.

The twin triumph enabled the Yanks to match the day's exploits of the still frantically pursuing Red Sox and Indians, and as they chugged back to New York tonight their margin over the Bosox was still a game and a half while the important "lost" column revealed an even more impressive four-game advantage over the Boston entry, which moves into the Stadium Wednesday night.

Hold Losing Side Edge

This is the same edge on the losing side the Bombers held over the Bosox when they left New York on Aug. 21, although at that time the Yankee lead was two and a half lengths. The Indians today were also held safely at bay, four and a half lengths away.

The nightcap, called on account of darkness at the close of seven innings, witnessed a typical Byrne performance, the dazzling southpaw as usual playing both sides of the board. In six innings he walked eight, yet allowed only two hits.

However, when the Mackmen, still three runs behind, clipped him for two singles in the last of the seventh, Stengel decided to take no further chances. He called on Joe Page and the southpaw relief ace quickly snuffed out the threat.

As for the Yanks, they virtually clinched it in the fourth when they ripped into Joe Coleman for six singles. That accounted for four tallies, two riding in when Sam Chapman let Jerry Coleman's single to center skid between his legs.

The opener was what one might call a tense pitching duel between Raschi and Lou Brissie for just two rounds. Then the Mack southpaw, with one out in the third, saw Raschi single, Phil Rizzuto outgallop a bunt for a hit and Bobby Brown walk to fill the bases.

Brissie Fans Bauer

Brissie here fanned Bauer but scarcely had the cheers subsided before DiMaggio cut loose with a tremendous drive that soared clear over the left pavilion roof for his thirteenth homer and first grand slammer of the year.

On the heels of that one Johnson hit his No. 8 and that was the ball game, although actually it dragged on for nearly three hours. Continuing their assault on Carl Scheib and Charlie Harris, the Bombers amassed a total of sixteen blows, with Johnson contributing five. Buffalo Bill, who covered first base in both games, had opened with a strike-out. But in the wake of his homer came three singles and a double.

In the sixth Bauer outgalloped a homer inside the park for his No. 10 and with that shot the Yanks' home-run total reached 100. It marked the twenty-sixth time the Bombers have hit the century figure, improving on their own major league record.

Behind this barrage Raschi had no difficulty annexing his eighteenth victory. Even so, the heat sort of got him near the end and Ralph Buxton hurled the eighth and ninth.

Casey and Shea Report

The newly acquired Hugh Casey and the recalled Frank Shea reported to Stengel and said they were ready to toss their weight into the flag race—which in each case looked to be considerable.

Hughie insisted he was never trimmer, since on his Wisconsin fishing trip he ate but little and caught only one fish.

Although they have only four road games to play, the Yanks already have cracked the American League road attendance of 1,762,399, set by the Indians last year. Their new mark rose today to 1,802,717. They also are almost certain to surpass the all-time major league high of 1,863,542 established by the Dodgers in 1947.

Heading for New York tonight, the Bombers concluded their six-city tour with a record of eight victories against six defeats. . . . And now for an open date tomorrow and then the vital clash with the Red Sox that opens at the Stadium Wednesday night. . . . Incidentally, twenty-one of the Bombers' remaining twenty-five games are to be played at home. The Bosox have only nine of their twenty at Fenway Park.

DiMAG — THE MAN BEHIND THE POKER FACE
By JACK SHER

Possessed of a magnificent athletic talent that has enabled him to become the highest salaried player in the history of baseball, Joe DiMaggio is, nevertheless, an incurably lonely man. Here is the complete, intimate account of the paradox in the life of the famous Yankee Clipper and how it came to be

THERE is a certain moment—a moment which seems to stretch into a terrible and bitter eternity—in the life of every champion worthy of the name, every great athlete. It is that painful moment when he realizes that he is no longer able to do, wholly and completely, the things that have set him apart and above all other competitors.

Such a moment has come to every variety of athlete in American sport, the savage and the gentle, the clownish and the serious. And this loss of greatness seldom happens gracefully.

The battered Dempsey's moment came between rounds in the first Tunney fight, and later that night the scowl became a twisted grin as he said, "I forgot to duck."

And the beloved Babe Ruth must have known the terror of the moment when he hung up his Yankee uniform in 1934 and moved on to the Braves.

Dizzy Dean felt it, sickeningly, while pitching his last World Series game for the Cubs, winging them in there with nothing but savvy and a prayer.

The large, quiet Lou Gehrig knew the nightmare of the moment in Spring training in 1939 when his big body refused to obey him and he fell down like a helpless child.

It is less throat-catching when the moment arrives swiftly and dramatically, the way it usually does in the ring. In most other sports, the moment is dragged out. This year, such a moment stretched into half a painful Summer of sorrowful moments, of doubts and fears interspersed with blinding flashes of hope that were almost equally hard to bear for a great performer, the most beautiful ballplayer of our era, Joseph Paul DiMaggio.

To Joe DiMaggio, to the perfectionist spirit in him that had always demanded such flawless performances, this has been a year of deep distress and melancholy, followed only after a long, bitter period of uncertainty by the feeling of well-being Joe gets from crashing out those mighty base-hits, from gloving those spectacular catches. When he's not playing baseball, the roof seems to have fallen in. To him, it is more than the personal loss of physical power or fame or money—it is the loss of no longer being able to *give*, to give the utmost to a cause bigger than himself. Joe's cause is baseball.

While Joe was out of uniform and his baseball future was enshrouded in a dark cloud, he suffered torture. A storybook hero might have taken this misfortune with squared shoulders and a defiant grin, but the way Di-Mag behaved during the unhappy days of inaction was much more real and human than most of what you'll find in fiction. On the sidelines, he was lost and lonely. His face was pale, he was losing weight, he was seldom seen in public places.

The ballplayer lives in a small hotel in New York's East Fifties. Few people visited him while he was not playing because he did not want visitors. He is not the sort of man who can feed on the glory of past accomplishments. He is a modest man. He always has been. He has always felt that he was just as good as the last ball game he played.

In a sense, the self-driving, selfless DiMaggio was responsible for his long siege of inactivity. In the manner of all champions, he didn't know when to quit. During those last gruelling days of the 1948 season, he drove himself through game after game on crippled legs, pain shooting through his heels, trying in herculean, gallant fashion to bring the Yankees another pennant. He finished the season in agony.

As Arthur Daley of the New York *Times* wrote, "Every game was a torture and a torment of such severity that he confided to intimates he couldn't possibly force his rebellious flesh to withstand such a purgatory again. Often, during the Winter, he'd wake up in a cold sweat just from dreaming of it."

And yet, in the Spring he was out jogging on the heel again. He would try to run and it made you wince to watch him. It gives you a small idea of how much he really is devoted to his cause, baseball.

Why the Yankees front office didn't bench him late last year is still a mystery to many who value men more than pennants. Or why they allowed him to attempt to get into shape so fast this year is not very understandable. Sure, $100,000 is a lot of loot to lose, but DiMag is a one-in-a-million ballplayer, the kind it isn't sane to risk for the sake of one season's success or even a husky chunk of money.

Horace Stoneham offered DiMaggio the use of his ranch, if Joe would go away for a rest or a post-operative convalescence. Even Larry MacPhail, who has never been very friendly with the Clipper, made the same sort of gesture. Joe couldn't accept the offers, although it would undoubtedly have done him a tremendous amount of good to remove himself from territory where baseball is being played.

Early last Spring, tense with worry about the way his heel had bothered him in training, Joe became abrupt and ill-tempered to a Baltimore newspaperman who was badgering him for a story. The aftermath of this action made him feel wretched. It plagued him so much that he felt compelled to call in a group of New York scribes and explain his behavior. His shy apology was in the "gentleman" tradition of great Yankees of the past.

And like another quiet, immortal man of the Yankees, Lou Gehrig, the fans have showed their affection and respect for Big Joe more during his hour of trial than they ever did when he was playing. Letters poured into the Stadium every day, expressing regret, hope, telling DiMaggio they had not forgotten him, begging him to take care of himself, recalling great hits he has slammed out and im-

possible catches made in the days when, in his own words, he was lucky to be a playing Yankee.

If, as some fear, DiMaggio's greatest days are behind him, the baseball historians of the distant future may not consider the end of his career as having been tragically cut off. He has done too much. In 10 years of major-league play, he has compiled a record that is complete and overpowering and permanently shining. When most other ballplayers of the post-depression decade have been relegated to mere footnotes in the book of baseball, Joe DiMaggio will loom large and chapter-like.

He is one of the three great Yankees —Ruth, Gehrig, DiMaggio. He has uprooted Tris Speaker as the greatest center-fielder of all time. He's a cinch for Cooperstown. In the "first team" nines of now and tomorrow there will always be a place for Jolting Joe.

Perhaps the lovers of the game will debate, down through the years, the right of the Clipper to push the renowned old Gray Eagle, Speaker, out of the center-field spot he held for so long on the mythical all-time squad. But the simple fact that the argument will rage is proof enough of the genius of the man. Not so many years ago it would have been considered heresy to imply that anybody could ever displace the great Spoke.

THE writer who 10, 20, or 50 years from now will be digging for details on the life of the Yankee Clipper, will find a surprising lack of personal, anecdotal material from the time he was at his height. Predecessors of DiMaggio's stature, Ruth, Cobb, Diz Dean, were easy to glamorize. Their deeds and quirks were put down with regularity in the more permanent print of magazines and books. DiMag has seemed to belong exclusively to the sports pages.

The fanatic baseball fan, the guy who turns to the box scores first, has found the career of DiMaggio to be fascinating, colorful, and dramatic. Outsiders know little about him. In the Babe's heyday, any housewife, poet, or school girl could reel off interesting information about him. It is doubtful if the average person could tell you how many homers Joe hit in any year, the name of his ex-wife, or his hometown.

Even the sportswriters, who devoted so much copy to Joe's brilliant performances, had in the beginning little of the hero worship for the quiet San Franciscan that they lavished on lesser athletes of the thirties. One of the favorite fillers in any DiMaggio story was a paragraph pointing out that the fans "wouldn't lay it on the line just to see Joe, the way they once crowded the Stadium for the sake of the Bambino alone." It was stated as a fact, but it was actually opinion. Not until DiMag was out of action for so long did baseball people realize what a whopping drawing card he was.

The present tremendous popularity of the Jolter was not built by the phrase-makers. It came about slowly. It piled up by reason of the day-to-day work of this incomparable ballplayer. Now, in the year 1949, features are being turned out regularly about him. Stories are lovingly embellished with incidents, and memories come flooding in of a greatness that was so often just taken for granted.

After you eliminate Ruth, Cobb, and Wagner, where will you find a ballplayer of DiMaggio's calibre? And Cobb couldn't hit the long ball with the regularity of the Bronx Bomber. Ruth couldn't run or throw on a par with Joe. Honus could do just about everything DiMag can, but he was no symphony of gracefulness about it, the way Joe has always been.

Old Tyrus was a great fielder, and don't let anyone ever tell you he wasn't, but he used to just about break his neck making catches that Joe would grab while loping easily. Ask Hank Greenberg about DiMaggio and he will tell you the only way he could hit safely was "to hit 'em where Joe wasn't," which was in left or right field. Perhaps the greatest catch of all time was one Joe made on a long drive from Hank's bat one day in the Stadium. This towering clout sailed over 450 feet into the outfield. It was one of the longest balls ever hit inside a park. Well, Joe grabbed it on the run, over his shoulder, and when the ball hit his glove the lumbering Hankus had almost reached third!

Unquestionably, DiMaggio deserves to be called the greatest team player of all time. The reason is solid. In 10 years, he led the Yanks to seven pennants, four of them in a row! And with the Jolter in the line-up, the Bronxites won six of their last seven World Series. Ruth had hitters like Meusel and Gehrig behind him in making the Yankees invincible. Cobb and Wagner, as great as they were, could not hold up weak teams alone. Year after year it has been the play of DiMaggio that has kept the fire in the stove for the Yankees.

With the exception of one year (1941), when Joe hit safely in 56 games to establish a major-league record, he has never been glorified to the degree of other diamond greats. That year, the radios across the country blared out a song called "Jolting Joe DiMaggio" and, for a time, his name was on everyone's lips. But his praise was puny compared to what the Bam got when he poled those 60 homers in one season.

The point is, you *can* compare the Clipper to the Bambino, which is a ridiculous thing to attempt to do with almost any other ballplayer. Babe's most electrifying season was the Summer of the "60." He hit .356. And Joe's big 56-straight-games record was done to the tune of a .357 average, and he lifted 30 out of the parks.

Always harassed by injuries—with three of what undoubtedly would have been brilliant years chopped out by the war—the record the Jolter has chalked up makes even these fair and qualifying remarks seem unnecessary. His lifetime batting average to date is .330. His fielding average is .977. He led the league in homers in 1937 with 46 and again in 1948 with 39. He has never hit under 20 four-masters in any season, and was the American League batting champion in 1939 and '40, voted the Most Valuable Player in 1939, 1941, and 1947.

Think back—can you remember an All-Star team that has not included Joe DiMaggio? He missed it only once in 10 years, in 1946, when his personal life was pitiful and he had been out of major-league play for three seasons. In 1941 and 1948, he led the league in runs-batted-in. He was way out in front in total bases in 1937, 1941, and '48. He not only holds the major-league record for hitting safely in consecutive games, but he got at least one hit in 61 straight games for the San Francisco Seals in 1933, when he was only 18 years old! He also tied major and American League records for the most extra bases on long hits in an inning, 6, and total bases, in an inning, 8—both marks made during the fifth inning in a game against the Chicago White Sox on June 24, 1936.

DIMAG has few peers as a World Series performer. The following are all World Series records: Most hits in one inning (co-holder); most putouts in one series, 20, in five games; most putouts in one inning, three in the ninth inning of a game in 1936 and he did it again in the 1937 series; only player to compete in four World Series in his first four years as a major-leaguer.

In seven World Series, Joe made only one error, and that in his first one. All this has been accompanied by a healthy .290 batting average.

As impressive as DiMaggio's honors are, they are not nearly so awe-inspiring as the all-time records of Cobb, Ruth, and Wagner. And yet, as a writer who has personally interviewed, researched, and profiled these immortals, it seems to me that Joe is as great as any one of them. No ballplayer can be completely judged by

what is to be found in the record books. The time in which he played, the length of his career, his effect on the game, must also be considered.

And also the man, in and out of uniform.

As a player, it is not enough to say that Joe DiMaggio is the greatest center-fielder of all time. The way you had to see Ruth hit a homer to realize how kingly he was in this department, you have to see Joe in action to appreciate him fully. Everything he does shows such superb skill, is so breath-takingly graceful. The way he swings, runs, catches, and throws is more than just good baseball. It is art—with a capital A. From Cap Anson to now, there has never been a ballplayer who possessed such perfect physical co-ordination, who has been so wonderful to watch. This quality of Joe's must be taken into consideration in evaluating him, because baseball is, after all, a sport for spectators and the *way* something is done matters a great deal.

YANKS WIN, 5-4, GO INTO FINAL DAY EVEN WITH RED SOX

Before the Game at the Stadium

HOME RUN DECIDES

Lindell's Clout in the 8th Sets Back Boston Before 69,551 in Stadium

YANKS ONCE TRAIL BY 4-0

Page Pitches Brilliantly in Relief After Wobbly Start— DiMaggio Doubles, Singles

By JOHN DREBINGER

And so, it develops, those battered Bombers with their countless aches and bruises, weren't ready to be rolled into a boneyard after all.

At least, on this, the final day of the American League championship season, they are still standing, and what is more, they are standing as well as their formidable rivals, the hale and hearty Bosox.

For, with Johnny Lindell exploding an eighth-inning homer to break a four-all tie, Casey Stengel's Yankees brought down Joe McCarthy's Red Sox in the penultimate encounter of the campaign in the stadium yesterday by a score of 5 to 4, and with that the raging pennant race once more goes into a deadlock.

Both the Yanks and Bosox stand tied this morning at 96 victories against 57 defeats and everything now hangs on the slender thread of a single game which these two keen foes will play this afternoon. Vic Raschi, the Bombers' 20-game winner, will oppose Ellis Kinder, Boston's 23-game hurler.

Joe DiMaggio leans over for a kiss from his mother as his brother, Dom, of the Red Sox, and his son, Joe Jr., watch. Hidden behind Mrs. DiMaggio is another brother, Tom.

Soul-Stirring Spectacle

It was a soul-stirring spectacle those Bombers put on display yesterday to electrify a gathering of 69,551 and bring to an almost story-book climax baseball's long awaited Joe DiMaggio day.

In an amazing hour-long ceremony before the game, close to $50,000 in gifts had been showered upon Joltin Joe, and the Clipper, in response to this overwhelming tribute, forgot all about his con-

valescence and played the full nine innings.

He played them well, too, despite the fact that he still is far from having recovered from the siege of virus infection which laid him low three weeks ago.

He paced the first Yankee tally home in the fourth inning with a double, and then contributed a single in a rousing fifth-inning rally in which the Bombers scored twice to route McCarthy's redoubtable

25-game winner, Mel Parnell, and plunge the battle into a deadlock.

But in the end it was that most extraordinary relief specialist, perhaps of all time, Joe Page, and the unsung Johnny Lindell who were the heroes of this epic struggle that now enables the Yanks to carry the flag fight right down to the final day.

Winning Run Scored by the Yankees Over the Red Sox

Johnny Lindell coming in on his homer in the last half of the eighth inning. He is being congratulated by the bat boy as Birdie Tebbetts, the Boston catcher, looks on disconsolately. *The New York Times*

HEROES OF VICTORY MOBBED BY MATES

Page, Mound Ace, and Lindell, Who Hit Ball Into Stands, Acclaimed by Yankees

STENGEL SELECTS RASCHI

Vic to Pitch Pay-Off Contest Today—McCarthy Nominates Kinder for the Red Sox

Orderly, rational and matter-of-fact, as if they had just won by 10—0 rather than by 5—4, the Yankees filed into their dressing room immediately after Phil Rizzuto threw out Dom DiMaggio for the game-ending play yesterday. Billy Johnson strode calmly through the door, followed by a smiling Yogi Berra and a grinning Tommy Henrich.

One by one the Yankees walked into the seclusion of their quarters. Anxious interviewers had agreed to allow the Bombers the luxury of five minutes of privacy, but when the door was opened to permit a player to enter, hilarious voices, studded with "yippees," could be heard and a quick peek revealed that Lefty Joe Page was being mobbed by his mates.

Along about this time Johnny Lindell made his way into the room and was mobbed. Then came Joe DiMaggio, tired but obviously happy. Manager Casey Stengel, Bobby Brown, Frank Crosetti, Jim Turner, Bill Dickey, Cliff Mapes—all the victors—also moved in gentlemanly fashion.

"This is it," said Stengel, a few minutes later. He was, of course, referring to today's pay-off game. "We've got a chance," he added with a twinkle in his eye. "It will be Vic Raschi, with Allie Reynolds and Joe Page ready, if necessary."

Of Page's excellent relief chore, the pilot was chockfull of praise. "He was wonderful," Casey said, acknowledging that the southpaw ace had pitched his longest game of the season. "Before I sent him in, I asked Joe 'how far can you go?' and he answered 'a long way.' So I said 'get going' and he did."

Joe DiMaggio Acknowledging the Gifts of the Fans

The Yankee Clipper with the two automobiles he received from his admirers. One of the cars was given to his mother

Page, accepting congratulations. revealed that he was not loose at the outset, but that he pitched his way clear of the sluggishness and felt strong at the finish. "Right now," he said, "I feel I could work again tomorrow, but I hope that isn't necessary."

Lindell, hero of this "must" victory, disclosed that he had walloped a fast ball into the stands. Reminded that he is not supposed to be able to hit right-handers, Lindell retorted, "I was a long time overdue."

DiMaggio said he "felt cramps in my shin bones for the last two hours." Of his double to right, DiMaggio explained that he didn't aim to hit to right. "That's all the strength I had," he said.

Over in the Red Sox quarters, the silence was pronounced, as expected. "Just like a world series," said Manager Joe McCarthy, admitting the scribes. "Well, it can't be a tie," he concluded, but before he did he named Ellis Kinder as today's starter for Boston.

Catcher Birdie Tebbetts, who called for Joe Dobson to throw a high, fast ball to Lindell, said, "I'd call it again, too. It's the one we got him out with the other day."

Mrs. Rosalie DiMaggio, mother of Joe and Dom, said she did not root for either of her famous sons. "Impartial" was the word relayed from Tom, another DiMaggio son.

Fans Everywhere Join New York in Honoring Guy Named Joe

"Thank Lord for Making Me a Yankee,' Says Jolter

69,551 Fans Cheer DiMag on His Big Day; Mother and Little Son on Hand

By DAN DANIEL
Of the New York World-Telegram
NEW YORK, N. Y.

Joe DiMaggio, blinking back the tears, stood at home plate in huge Yankee Stadium, October 1, as the roaring cheers of 69,551 fans beat on his ears.

It was Joe DiMaggio Day and the Yankee Clipper was engulfed in an avalanche of gifts and a wave of affection which rolled in from bleachers to boxes.

"I'd like to thank the Good Lord for making me a Yankee," said baseball's great slugger into the microphone.

But his first thought was of the fans in the bleachers who have caught his home run balls with glee and watched the graceful figure make hundreds of leaping catches.

"I'd like to apologize to the people in the bleachers," he said, "for having my back turned to them."

Joe, who never chokes up when the chips are down in the ninth inning, admitted:

"This is one of the few times I have choked up. Many years ago Lefty O'Doul said. 'Joe, don't let the big town scare you, New York is the most generous town in the world.'

"This day proves that New York is the friendliest town in the world. I have played for three managers and all taught me something. If we don't win, I will say to McCarthy (Joe McCarthy, Red Sox manager), 'If we did not win. I'm glad you did.'

"The Red Sox are a grand team and a grand bunch of guys, and that does not include the guy out in center field (his brother Dominic) who spends so much time annoying me."

Brother Dom walked to Joe's side as Joe said he wanted to thank Manager Casey Stengel and the other Yankees — "the gamest, fightingest bunch of guys who ever lived."

The Yankee Clipper's little son, Joe, Jr , was there. So was Mother DiMaggio, who was sure of having one son in the World's Series, no matter what happened. Giuseppe kissed her as she stood proudly at home plate.

There was a tribute from Mayor

Even Yanks' Pup Mascot Goes on the Hospital List

NEW YORK, N. Y.—Among the gifts showered on Joe DiMaggio on his day, October 1, was a baby cocker spaniel, which was promptly adopted as the team mascot. The pup lost no time in proving that he was a member of the injury and illness-ridden Yankee troupe. He proceeded to develop a cold, with noisy sniffles, which sent DiMag on the run for a vet.

William O'Dwyer, who said to Giuseppe:

"How well we all knew that you would not accept any of the money donated by the fans, and would give it to the Heart and Cancer funds.

"You came here from San Francisco. After today you will never leave New York."

This writer, speaking for the baseball writers, said:

"Joe came to St. Petersburg (Florida training camp) wearing a size 7¼ hat, and he still wears the same size. The player's player, the manager's player, the fans' player, the player of the writers who have been with him and the Yankees for many years."

Baseball had seen some amazing days for diamond heroes, but this one was in a class by itself.

Among the gifts were a car for Joe, one for his mother, a speedboat from New Haven fans, several television sets, a bike for little Joe, portraits, a cocker spaniel, all sorts of electric equipment, golf bags and sticks, plaques, rifles, loving cups, a ship's clock, 300 quarts of ice cream, a big Wisconsin cheese, traveling b a g s, money clips, a mattress and box spring and cases of oranges from California.

A Bleacher on Wheels

NEW YORK, N. Y.—A nine-car train on the New York, New Haven and Hartford railroad, October 1, was virtually converted into a bleacher on wheels. It was the "Joe DiMaggio Special" from New Haven, Conn., to Grand Central Terminal. The 700 passengers, who purchased train tickets and admission to Yankee Stadium for $4.25, came especially to honor the Yankee Clipper.

Gifts Include Auto for Him, One for Mom and About Everything a Store Sells

There also was a four-year college scholarship for any boy Joe would select.

Medals, fishing tackle, a thermos jug, 500 shirts, a key chain, electric blankets, phonograph records, a statuette from the Boy Scouts—well, the list was just without end.

None could estimate the total amount of money, from piggy-bank pennies to $500 wads, which Joe has routed into the coffers of the N. Y. Heart Assn. and Damon Runyon Cancer Fund.

This writer also presented THE SPORTING NEWS plaque to Joe, in the absence of Publisher J. G. Taylor Spink.

Of the messages, two were standouts:

"The guy with a heart of gold named Joe," penned Pat Trevisone, and from Art Lipton:

"The pride of New York City, a wallopin' one-man show;
That's why we're here, that's why we cheer
Joltin' Joe . . . DiMaggio."

Ethel Merman sang. "Take Me Out to the Ball Game," and later the national anthem.

Mel Allen did a remarkable job as master of ceremonies. From start to finish, it was a tremendous and memorable occasion, a striking tribute to a great player and a fine personality.

Joe McCarthy got a tremendous hand from the 69,551 when he came out to the plate and congratulated DiMaggio, who had made his Yankee debut in 1936 under Marse Joe's leadership.

It was a great day, the weather was ideal, and the climax was a real thriller for the customers—a Yankee victory.

Gifts Presented to DiMag

Cadillac automobile, fans of the city of New York; Dodge automobile for his mother, fans of Hoboken, N. J.; Cris-Craft boat, fans of New Haven, Conn.; Baro Thermo calendar watch, fans from Longines Wittenaur Watch Co.; Waltham watch, chain, knife, Knickerbocker Social Club, Westerly, R. I.; wallet with religious gifts, Helen Amen; gold cuff links, Helen Marshall; gold belt buckle, tie pin, cuff links, Crane Social Club, Newark, N. J.; 14-karat gold cuff links and tie pin fashioned from Joe's bat, fans of Swank Jewelry Co.; art work suitable for framing, Charles Flanders, artist; Ray E. Dodge 51-inch loving cup trophy, employes of Dodge, Inc.; television set, employes of A. B. Dumont Co.; television set, employes of Admiral T. V. Corp.; deer rifle, employes of Marlin Firearms Co.; bronze plaque, Grantwood (N. J.) Italian-American Club; $100 fedora hat, MacLachlan Hats, Norwalk, Conn.; golf bag, Delores (Vic) Surmonte Berra-DiMaggio Fan Clubs; electric blanket and radio, General Electric; Thermos water jug set, Billy Pedace, Norwich, Conn.; 14-karat gold key chain, autograph in links, Jacques Kreisler Jewelry Co.; silver loving cup, John F. Prince Post, V. F. W.; 25 volumes of Joe DiMaggio records for Yankee Juniors, Capital Records; set of Lionel trains for Joe, Jr., Lionel Corporation; driving and sun glasses for Yankee Juniors, W. S. Wilson Corporation; Christmas candy baseball and bat, Independence (Kan.) Chamber of Commerce; 500 Joe DiMaggio shirts in Joe's name to Yankee Juniors, Allison Mfg. Co. and Saks-34th Street; ship's clock, General Electric; oil painting of Joe DiMaggio, Phillip Patchen, Mamaroneck, N. Y.

Carpeting of his living room, Amsterdam (N. Y.) Rugmakers (Yankee farm club); Westinghouse roaster, Westinghouse Electric Co.; 14-karat gold money clip with open house privileges at Hotels Concourse Plaza and Martinique, from the hotels; four-year college scholarship for a boy of Joe's selection, Il Progresso Newspaper; medal of honor, Il Progresso; 300 quarts of ice cream for any institution designated by Joe, Cardani Ice Cream Co.; statuette, neckerchief and clip, Boy Scouts of America; Air Foam mattress and box spring, Englander Company; cheese, from Fond du Lac (Wis.) farm club; 14-karat gold watch with diamond numerals, Italian Welfare Association, Elizabeth, N. J.; case of shoestring potatoes, Grand Forks (N. D.) farm club; case of Ventura County oranges, sack of walnuts, case of lemonade and case frozen lima beans, from Ventura (Calif.) Chamber of Commerce; hand-painted tie, Christine Wells, Chatham, N. J.; polished wood paperweight, Twin Falls (Ida.) farm club; leather wallet, Joplin (Mo.) farm club; metal elephant for "good luck," Mrs. Lee Taylor, Hoboken, N. J.; Sterling silver rosary beads for Joe, Jr., St. Joachim's Holy Name Society, Trenton, N. J.; portrait, Frank Paladino, Brooklyn, N. Y.; THE SPORTING NEWS plaque, THE SPORTING NEWS; dozen golf balls, ash tray and Thermo Tote bag, Newark (O.) baseball club; Columbia bicycle for Joe, Jr., fishing tackle, luggage, Newark (N. J.) committee; a cocker spaniel, American Spaniel Club; plaque, Columbia Civic Club, Newark, N. J.; traveling bag, Mr. Spivicha; certificate of recognition, Italian Historical Society of America; traveling alarm clock, Lux Clock Co. admirers, Waterbury, Conn.; Sterling silver money clip, Lorraine Coville; hand-painted ties for Joe and Joe, Jr., Adele G.; two trophies engraved by children, Mending Heart Foundation, Miami, Fla.; taxi service for 300 fans from Newark—"This ride is on Joe D.," Brown & White Cab Co., Newark, N. J.

DAN DANIEL of the N. Y. World-Telegram and correspondent for THE SPORTING NEWS, presenting THE SPORTING NEWS plaque on The Clipper's day, October 1.

JOE ACKNOWLEDGES GIFTS TO CROWD

FAMILY REUNION—Joe kisses his mother during ceremonies at Yankee Stadium. Joe, Jr., stands with his famed dad, while Dom, brother of the Yankee star, is at left. Among the gifts was an automobile for Joe's mother, who made the trip from San Francisco to attend ceremonies honoring the Jolter.

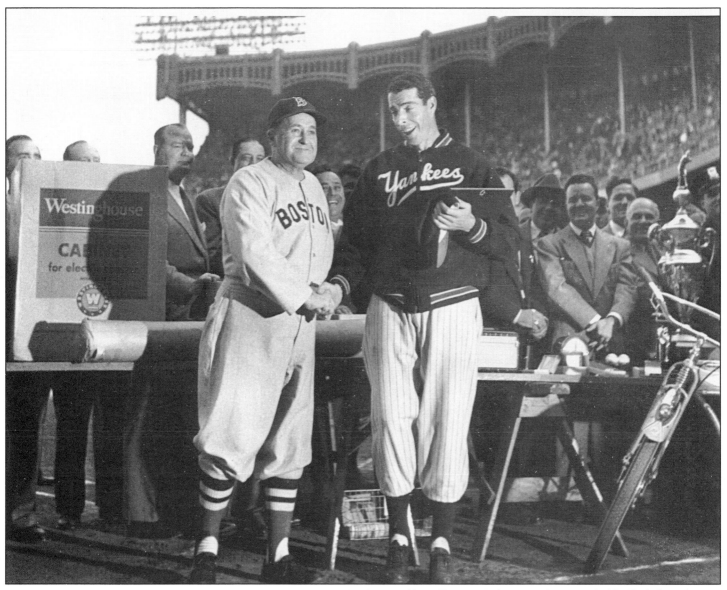

Joe DiMaggio Day is held at Yankee Stadium in 1949, thanks to his legion of fans. Congratulations are also extended by Joe's former manager, Joe McCarthy, who was then piloting the rival Red Sox.

Yanks, Dodgers Win on Last Day

by WILLIAM J. BRIORDY

NEW YORK, Oct. 3, 1949—IT WILL BE THE NEW YORK YANKEES AGAINST THE BROOKLYN DODGERS IN the 1949 edition of the world series starting Wednesday at Yankee Stadium.

In pulse-quickening finishes to the keenest major league races in forty-one years, the battered Yanks staved off a last-inning rally to beat the Boston Red Sox, 5 to 3, to win the American League pennant before 68,055 Yankee Stadium onlookers, while the Dodgers collared the National League flag by halting the Phillies, 9 to 7, in ten innings at Philadelphia's Shibe Park yesterday.

When the Yanks and Dodgers come to grips Wednesday, it will mark the third world series meeting of the interborough rivals and the second in three years. The Yanks won both previous series—in 1941 and 1947. The triumph was the sixteenth in the American League for the Yanks. Starting with 1890, the Dodgers have annexed the National League championship eight times. The Yanks' margin over the Dodgers in 1941 was 4 to 1 and in 1947 it was 4 to 3.

The Yanks and Red Sox were in a flat-footed tie when the teams took the field at the Stadium yesterday. The Dodgers entered the final day with a one-game lead over the St. Louis Cardinals, who snapped out of a four-game losing streak to beat the Chicago Cubs, 13 to 5.

The Cards pulled out of their tailspin too late to catch the Brooks. The Yanks and Dodgers annexed their respective league titles by one game and, interestingly enough, the winners and runners-up in each circuit finished with identical records, 97 and 57 for the champions and 96 and 58 for the second-place clubs.

Stouthearted hurling by their big right-hander, Vic Raschi, enabled the gallant Yanks to defeat Joe McCarthy's Red Sox. It was a bitter pill, too, for the sixty-two-year-old McCarthy, who saw his pennant hopes smashed in the same stadium where he led the Bombers to eight American League pennants and seven world championships. Moreover, it was the second straight season the Bosox were beaten out in the last stage of

the campaign. Last year the Red Sox lost in a play-off with Cleveland.

Raschi held Boston in check for eight innings behind a one-run lead which a triple by Phil Rizzuto had given him in the first inning. The Bomber hurler, up to the ninth, had the Bosox blanked on two hits in a tense mound battle with Ellis Kinder, who was trying for his twenty-fourth decision of the year.

In the last of the eighth the Yanks put on the rally that won the flag. With Kinder going out for a pinch hitter, the desperate Mc-Carthy nominated Mel Parnell, his 25-game winning southpaw, to hold the Bombers until his own power hitters could have one last fling at Raschi.

Old Reliable Tommy Heinrich greeted Parnell with a home run into the right-field stands. Yogi Berra singled and Tex Hughson was called on to relieve Parnell. Joe DiMaggio hit into a double play but the Yanks proceeded to fill the bases. Then Jerry Coleman, rookie second baseman, cleared them with a pop fly two-bagger to short right field. That four-run outbreak carried the day, though the aroused Bosox lashed back for three runs in the ninth.

The first two Red Sox runs in the ninth came in on Bobby Doerr's triple over the head of Joe DiMaggio, running on shaky legs. The Clipper then called time and dramatically took himself out of the game. Joltin' Joe, a sick man these past three weeks, received a great ovation as he walked off the field.

Dusk was settling over Shibe Park as the Dodgers put over their rousing tenth-inning rally to down the Phillies. Jack Banta, young relief pitcher, handcuffed the dangerous Philadelphia hitters for four innings after the Brooks had dissipated a 5-0 bulge.

Peewee Reese, who in five previous visits to the plate hadn't hit the ball out of the infield, dropped a single into left to open the top half of the tenth. Then the Dodgers proceeded to rush their two tallies across like real champions. Reese moved to second on Eddie Miksis' sacrifice and big Duke Snider sent the Dodger captain home when he rapped a sizzler through the legs of Pitcher Ken Heintzelman, nemesis of the Brooks all season.

With 36,765 fans cheering them on, the Brooks sewed it up. After Jackie Robinson had been purposely passed, Luis Olmo smashed a single past Willie Jones into left field to drive across Snider, who had taken second on the throw to the plate as Reese counted.

The jubilant Dodgers mobbed Banta at the end of the game. It was the tenth victory of the season for the big right-hander, who had come into the game after Don Newcombe and Rex Barney had been driven to the showers, but none of his successes was as important as this one.

In the Yankee clubhouse, 1949. It was a painful year for DiMaggio because of his wounded heel, but ultimately a memorable one in which he went to his eighth World Series in eleven years with the Yankees.

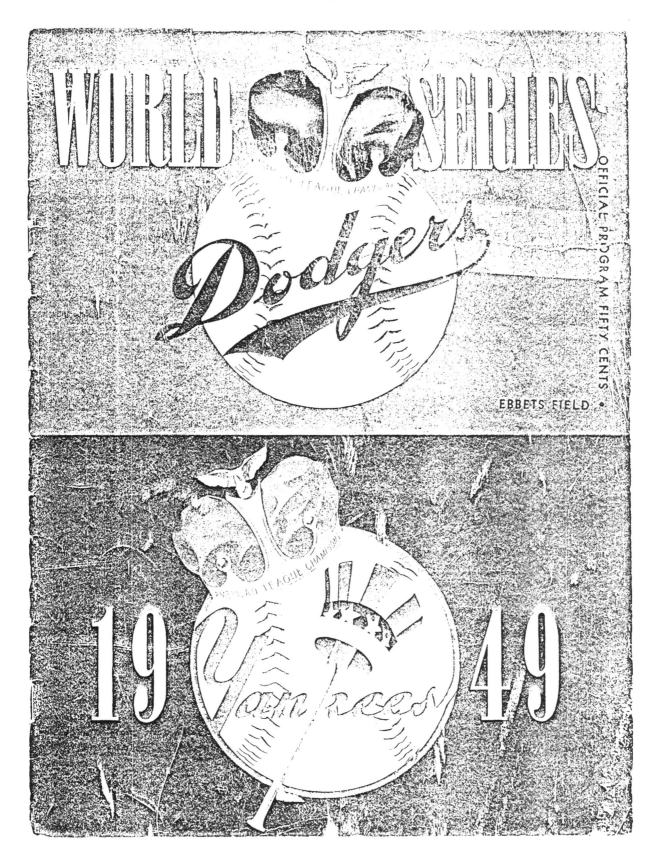

The Yankees were six deep in slugging outfielders in 1949. Here they pose at the World Series, no doubt with the intention of intimidating the Brooklyn Dodgers' pitching staff. From the left: Gene Woodling, Hank Bauer, Cliff Mapes, Johnny Lindell, Joe DiMaggio, and Charlie Keller.

MEET THE

PHIL RIZZUTO

TOMMY HENRICH

LARRY BERRA

A half pint among bombing behemoths, **Phil Rizzuto** is the biggest little man in Little Old New York this World Series week. This is the Scooter's fourth series in six years of Yankee campaigning. Took three-year time-out for Navy duty but '46 and '48 only active seasons which failed to produce the October pot o' gold for the popular Phil. A native New Yorker, a product of local sandlots, Rizzuto was signed after one of Paul Krichell's tryout classes at Yankee Stadium back in 1936. He's a double-play specialist, a tough man in a pinch and one of the game's best bunters.

★

Greatest baseball story of the year was the comeback of **Joe DiMaggio.** Sidelined by a bone spur in his right heel and harnessed to the bench during the first sixty-five Yankee games, Joe the Jolter blazed back into action with a never-to-be-forgotten flurry of four-base blows as the Yankees swept a 3-game June series with the Boston Red Sox. Then he settled down to become the Yankees' most productive run-maker over the final half of the race as the Bronx Bombers staved off one challenge after another to carry on to their sixteenth A.L. championship. For DiMaggio this is World Series No. 8—1936, 1937, 1938, 1939, 1941, 1942, 1947 and 1949. He has played in ten All-Star games. In 1941 he hit safely in fifty-six straight games—one of the top records of the game. DiMaggio will go down in baseball history rated with the all-time greats—Cobb, Ruth, Gehrig et al.

★

The "Old Reliable" tag hung on **Tommy Henrich** by Mel Allen, the Voice of the Yankees, was never more richly deserved than during the 1949 season. When Joe DiMaggio was unable to take his accustomed role as larruping leader of the Yankees over the first half of the season, it was the Massillon Mauler who took charge. And, despite a string of injuries which would have caused a less courageous player to hang up his spikes and call it a season, Tommy was in there at the finish, too. One of the game's most versatile players, Henrich is as expert at first base as he is in right field. Says he'd like to try shortstop (lefthanded) some time. Versatile off the field, too, with hobbies running from hunting to singing tenor on a state championship Barber Shop quartet.

★

It was said by many, and not without foundation, that **Joe Page** won the world championship for the Yankees in 1947. He was that good. He gave one of the most remarkable relief pitching performances of all time when he appeared in 56 games during the season and four out of seven in the World Series. That was a performance they said would never be topped. No? Study the 1949 season record of handsome Joe—and watch him if Casey Stengel beckons him toward the mound this week. Page had a checkered career before '47. In 1944 he was picked for the A.L. All-Star game, yet finished the season in Newark. He was a so-so performer as a starting pitcher until sent to the bullpen in '47. He has been haunting the headlines ever since.

★

The magazine editors of the nation discovered **Yogi Berra** this season. At one time he had five feature writers trailing him from town to town. For their troubles they all got good yarns. There isn't a more colorful character study than Yankee Yogi. A product of St. Louis sandlots, Berra was discovered by ex-coach Johnny Schulte. Yogi moved up the baseball ladder without delay. Jumped from Norfolk to Newark and was in a Yankee uniform his second season in pro ball. Caught in the World Series of '47, moved to the outfield in '48 but was reinstated to the mask-and-mitt brigade again in 1949. To Bill Dickey, one of the game's greatest receivers, must go a large share of the credit for Berra's excellent catching job this season.

★

One of the Yankees' greatest World Series performers was just a spectator last time the Bronx Bombers were in the October Classic. Many counted **Charley Keller** out of baseball when he suffered a severe back injury in mid-season of '47 but the Maryland Mauler refused to stay out. He was a batting practice pitcher for his Yankees before that season was concluded, struggled through a trying campaign in '48 and chipped in more than a few timely blows in '49. And there's nothing more he would like to do than top it all off with a blazing World Series. He has had 'em before, hitting .438 in 1939 against the Reds and .389 in 1941 against the Dodgers in compiling a .306 average in four October series. In nineteen games he is credited with having driven in eighteen World Series runs. That's just about par for the course.

JOE DiMAGGIO

JOE PAGE

CHARLIE KELLER

Game 1 October 5 at New York

Bkn.	000	000	000			0
N.Y.	000	000	001			1

Brooklyn	Pos	AB	R	H	RBI	PO	A	E
Reese	ss	4	0	1	0	2	2	0
Jorgensen	3b	3	0	1	0	0	2	0
Snider	cf	4	0	0	0	3	0	0
Robinson	2b	4	0	0	0	4	0	0
Hermanski	lf	3	0	0	0	0	0	0
Furillo	rf	3	0	0	0	0	0	0
Hodges	1b	2	0	0	0	4	0	0
Campanella	c	2	0	0	0	11	0	0
Newcombe	p	3	0	0	0	0	0	0
Totals		28	0	2	0	*24	4	0

New York	Pos	AB	R	H	RBI	PO	A	E
Rizzuto	ss	4	0	0	0	1	2	0
Henrich	1b	4	1	1	1	9	0	0
Berra	c	3	0	0	0	9	0	0
DiMaggio	cf	3	0	0	0	1	0	0
Lindell	lf	3	0	1	0	0	0	0
Johnson	3b	3	0	0	0	2	3	0
Mapes	rf	3	0	0	0	4	0	0
Coleman	2b	3	0	1	0	1	2	1
Reynolds	p	3	0	2	0	0	1	0
Totals		29	1	5	1	27	8	1

* None out when winning run scored.

Pitching	IP	H	R	ER	BB	SO
Brooklyn						
Newcombe (L)	8	5	1	1	0	11
New York						
Reynolds (W)	9	2	0	0	4	9

Doubles—Coleman, Jorgensen, Reynolds.
Home Run—Henrich. Stolen Base—Reese.
Sacrifice Hit—Hodges. Double
Play—Reynolds to Coleman to Henrich.
Left on Bases—Brooklyn 6, New York 4.
Umpires—Hubbard (A), Reardon (N),
Passarella (A), Jorda (N), Hurley (A),
Barr (N). Attendance—66,224.
Time of Game—2:24.

1st Inning
Brooklyn
1 Reese grounded to first.
 Jorgensen doubled to left-center
 over Lindell's head.
2 Snider struck out.
3 Robinson flied to right.
New York
1 Rizzuto fouled to Hodges on an
 attempted bunt.
2 Henrich grounded to short.
3 Berra popped to short.

2nd Inning
Brooklyn
 Hermanski walked.
 Furillo walked.
1.2 Hodges grounded into a double play.
 Reynolds to Coleman to Henrich as
 Hermanski went to third.
3 Campanella flied to right.
New York
1 DiMaggio struck out.
 Lindell singled to left.
2 Johnson struck out.
3 Mapes struck out.

3rd Inning
Brooklyn
1 Newcombe grounded to short.
2 Reese bunted out to third.
3 Jorgensen grounded to second.
New York
1 Coleman called out on strikes.
 Reynolds doubled to left.
2 Rizzuto popped to second.
3 Henrich popped to short.

4th Inning
Brooklyn
1 Snider fouled to Johnson.
2 Robinson grounded to third.
3 Hermanski flied to right.
New York
1 Berra grounded to short.
2 DiMaggio popped to second.
3 Lindell flied to center.

5th Inning
Brooklyn
 Furillo safe at first when his
 grounder got through Coleman
 for an error.
1 Hodges sacrificed Furillo to
 second, Johnson to Henrich.
 Campanella walked.
2 Newcombe struck out as Berra
 held his foul tip.
3 Reese forced Furillo at third,
 Johnson unassisted.
New York
1 Johnson struck out.
2 Mapes struck out.
3 Coleman struck out.

6th Inning
Brooklyn
 Jorgensen walked.
1 Snider struck out.
2 Robinson flied to center.
3 Hermanski struck out.
New York
 Reynolds singled to left.
1 Rizzuto forced Reynolds at second,
 Jorgensen to Robinson.
2 Henrich flied to center.
3 Berra struck out.

7th Inning
Brooklyn
1 Furillo popped to first.
2 Hodges called out on strikes.
3 Campanella called out on strikes.
New York
1 DiMaggio popped to second.
2 Lindell called out on strikes.
3 Johnson grounded to third.

8th Inning
Brooklyn
1 Newcombe called out on strikes.
 Reese singled through the middle.
 Reese stole second.
2 Jorgensen struck out.
3 Snider struck out, for the third
 time in the game.
New York
1 Mapes struck out for the third time.
 Coleman doubled down the right
 field line.
2 Reynolds called out on strikes.
3 Rizzuto flied to center.

9th Inning
Brooklyn
1 Robinson grounded to short.
2 Hermanski popped to short.
3 Furillo flied to right.
New York
 Henrich, on a 2-0 count, hit a
 game-winning home run into the
 lower right field stands.

Game 2 October 6 at New York

Brooklyn	Pos	AB	R	H	RBI	PO	A	E
Reese	ss	4	0	0	0	1	3	1
Jorgensen	3b	4	0	1	0	1	4	0
Snider	cf	4	0	1	0	3	1	0
Robinson	2b	3	1	1	0	3	1	0
Hermanski	rf	3	0	1	0	2	0	0
d Furillo		1	0	0	0	0	0	0
McCormick	rf	0	0	0	0	1	0	0
Rackley	lf	2	0	0	0	0	0	0
Olmo	lf	2	0	1	0	2	0	0
Hodges	1b	3	0	1	1	9	1	0
Campanella	c	2	0	1	0	4	0	0
Roe	p	3	0	0	0	1	1	1
Totals		31	1	7	1	27	11	2

Pitching	IP	H	R	ER	BB	SO
Brooklyn						
Roe (W)	9	6	0	0	0	3
New York						
Raschi (L)	8	6	1	1	1	4
Page	1	1	0	0	0	0

1st Inning
Brooklyn
1 Reese flied to left.
2 Jorgensen grounded to first.
3 Snider grounded to short.
New York
   Rizzuto singled down the left field line.
1 Henrich flied to left.
2 Bauer fouled to Robinson
3 DiMaggio flied to center.

2nd Inning
Brooklyn
   Robinson doubled to left
1 Hermanski fouled to Coleman deep behind first, Robinson moving to third after the catch
2 Rackley grounded to third, Robinson holding at third
   Hodges singled to left, scoring Robinson and went to second on Lindell's fumble
   Campanella intentionally walked
3 Roe struck out
New York
1 Lindell flied to right
2 Johnson flied to center
3 Coleman flied to center

3rd Inning
Brooklyn
1 Reese grounded to short
2 Jorgensen fouled to Silvera
3 Snider grounded to second
New York
1 Silvera popped to third
2 Raschi grounded to short. Rizzuto safe when Reese fumbled his grounder
   Rizzuto stole second
3 Henrich grounded to short.

4th Inning
Brooklyn
1 Robinson struck out
   Hermanski tripled to center when his liner wildly bounced past DiMaggio
2 Rackley hit into a fielder's choice, Coleman to Silvera getting Hermanski trying to score
3 Hodges flied to right.
New York
   Bauer singled to center but was out
1 trying for a double, Snider to Reese
   For Brooklyn—Olmo replaced Rackley in left.
2 DiMaggio struck out
3 Lindell hit back to Roe

5th Inning
Brooklyn
   Campanella singled to left, trying for second on Lindell's bobble but was
1 out, Lindell to Coleman.
2 Roe called out on strikes
3 Reese grounded to third.
New York
1 Johnson fouled to Campanella.
   Coleman doubled to left.
2 Silvera grounded to short, Coleman going to third.
3 Raschi grounded to third.

Bkn	010 000 000	1
N Y	000 000 000	0

New York	Pos	AB	R	H	RBI	PO	A	E
Rizzuto	ss	3	0	1	0	0	6	0
Henrich	1b	4	0	0	0	11	0	0
Bauer	rf	4	0	1	0	1	0	0
DiMaggio	cf	4	0	1	0	1	0	0
Lindell	lf	4	0	0	0	2	1	1
Johnson	3b	4	0	1	0	0	2	0
Coleman	2b	4	0	1	0	6	3	0
Silvera	c	2	0	0	0	6	0	0
a Mize		1	0	1	0	0	0	0
b Stirnweiss		0	0	0	0	0	0	0
Niarhos	c	1	0	0	0	0	0	0
Raschi	p	2	0	0	0	0	0	0
c Brown		1	0	0	0	0	0	0
Page	p	0	0	0	0	0	0	0
Totals		33	0	6	0	27	13	1

a Singled for Silvera in 8th
b Ran for Mize in 8th
c Struck out for Raschi in 8th
d Popped out for Hermanski in 9th

Doubles—Coleman, Jorgensen, Robinson
Triple—Hermanski Stolen Bases—Johnson,
Rizzuto. Sacrifice Hits—Rizzuto,
Robinson. Double Play—Rizzuto to
Coleman to Henrich. Left on
Bases—Brooklyn 5, New York 7
Umpires—Reardon, Passarella, Jorda
Hubbard, Hurley, Barr. Attendance—70,053
Time of Game—2:30

6th Inning
Brooklyn
   Jorgensen doubled to left
1 Snider flied to center
2 Robinson grounded to short, Jorgensen going to third
3 Hermanski grounded to first
New York
1 Rizzuto grounded to first
2 Henrich grounded out. Hodges to Roe
3 Bauer grounded to third

7th Inning
Brooklyn
   Olmo singled to right
1,2 Hodges hit into a double play, Rizzuto to Coleman to Henrich
3 Campanella flied to left
New York
1 DiMaggio grounded to third
2 Lindell flied to left
   Johnson singled to left.
   Johnson stole second
3 Coleman grounded to second

8th Inning
Brooklyn
1 Roe struck out for the third time
2 Reese grounded to short
3 Jorgensen lined to second
New York
   Mize, pinch-hitting for Silvera singled to center
   Stirnweiss ran for Mize
   Brown, pinch-hitting for Raschi took a called third strike
   Rizzuto safe at first as Roe dropped his bunt sacrifice for an error
2 Henrich flied to left
3 Bauer forced Rizzuto at second, Jorgensen to Robinson

9th Inning
Brooklyn
   For New York—Page pitching and Niarhos catching
   Snider singled to left
1 Robinson sacrificed Snider to second, Henrich to Coleman
2 Furillo, pinch-hitting for Hermanski, popped to second
3 Olmo bounced to short
New York
   For Brooklyn—McCormick playing right. DiMaggio beat out a roller to third
1 Lindell struck out.
2 Johnson popped to second
3 Coleman flied to right.

Game 3 October 7 at Brooklyn

New York	Pos	AB	R	H	RBI	PO	A	E
Rizzuto	ss	4	0	0	1	0	0	0
Henrich	1b	3	0	0	0	10	0	0
Berra	c	3	1	0	0	7	2	0
DiMaggio	cf	4	0	0	0	4	0	0
Brown	3b	4	1	1	0	0	2	0
Woodling	lf	3	1	1	0	2	0	0
Mapes	rf	2	1	0	0	2	0	0
a Mize		1	0	1	2	0	0	0
b Bauer	rf	0	0	0	0	0	0	0
Coleman	2b	4	0	1	1	2	4	0
Byrne	p	1	0	1	0	0	0	0
Page	p	3	0	0	0	0	1	0
Totals		32	4	5	4	27	9	0

a Singled for Mapes in 9th.
b Ran for Mize in 9th.
c Struck out for Banta in 9th.

Double—Woodling. Home Runs—Campanella, Olmo, Reese. Double Play—Berra to Coleman. Hit by Pitcher—Reese (by Byrne). Left on Bases—New York 5, Brooklyn 6. Umpires—Passarella, Jorda, Hubbard, Reardon, Barr, Hurley.
Attendance—32,788. Time of Game—2:30.

1st Inning
New York
1 Rizzuto grounded to third
2 Berra grounded to first
3 Berra struck out.
Brooklyn
   Reese was hit by a pitched ball.
1,2 Miksis fouled to Berra who threw to Coleman doubling Reese trying to advance after the catch.
3 Furillo flied to left.

2nd Inning
New York
1 DiMaggio struck out.
2 Brown popped to second
3 Woodling fouled to Miksis
Brooklyn
1 Robinson popped to second
2 Hodges fouled to Berra
3 Olmo grounded to third

3rd Inning
New York
   Mapes walked (the first walk in the Series given up by Dodger pitchers).
1 Coleman called out on strikes. Byrne singled to center, Mapes going to third.
2 Rizzuto flied to right, Mapes scoring after the catch. Henrich walked.
3 Berra popped to second
Brooklyn
1 Snider flied to left.
2 Campanella grounded to third.
3 Branca struck out and was thrown out Berra to Henrich when Berra dropped the third strike.

4th Inning
New York
1 DiMaggio struck out
2 Brown fouled to Miksis Woodling doubled off the right field scoreboard
3 Mapes rolled out, Robinson to Branca.
Brooklyn
   Reese hit a home-run into the lower left-center field stands
1 Miksis flied to center Furillo singled to left. Robinson walked Hodges walked, loading the bases. For New York—Page pitching.
2 Olmo fouled to Henrich.
3 Snider grounded to second.

5th Inning
New York
1 Coleman flied to center.
2 Page struck out.
3 Rizzuto grounded to short
Brooklyn
1 Campanella grounded to second.
2 Branca took a called third strike.
3 Reese bounced back to the mound.

N.Y.	001 000 003	4
Bkn.	000 100 002	3

Brooklyn	Pos	AB	R	H	RBI	PO	A	E
Reese	ss	2	1	1	1	1	2	0
Miksis	3b	4	0	1	0	3	1	0
Furillo	rf	4	0	1	0	2	0	0
Robinson	2b	2	0	0	0	2	3	0
Hodges	1b	3	0	0	0	8	0	0
Olmo	lf	4	1	1	1	0	0	0
Snider	cf	4	0	0	0	8	0	0
Campanella	c	4	1	1	1	7	0	0
Branca	p	3	0	0	1	0	1	0
Banta	p	0	0	0	0	0	0	0
c Edwards		1	0	0	0	0	0	0
Totals		31	3	5	3	27	6	0

Pitching	IP	H	R	ER	BB	SO
New York						
Byrne	3⅓	2	1	1	2	1
Page (W)	5⅓	3	2	2	4	4
Brooklyn						
Branca (L)	8⅓	4	4	4	4	6
Banta	⅔	1	0	0	0	1

6th Inning
New York
1 Henrich flied to right.
2 Berra grounded to first.
3 DiMaggio popped to first.
Brooklyn
1 Miksis flied to right.
2 Furillo grounded to second. Robinson walked.
3 Hodges flied to center.

7th Inning
New York
1 Brown grounded to second.
2 Woodling flied to center.
3 Mapes flied to center.
Brooklyn
1 Olmo fouled to Berra
2 Snider grounded to first
3 Campanella flied to left.

8th Inning
New York
1 Coleman called out on strikes
2 Page grounded to short.
3 Rizzuto popped to short.
Brooklyn
1 Branca took a called third strike. Reese walked. Miksis singled to left, Reese stopping at second.
2 Furillo flied to right.
3 Robinson flied to center.

9th Inning
New York
1 Henrich grounded to second. Berra walked
2 DiMaggio fouled to Miksis. Brown singled to right, Berra stopping at second. Woodling walked, loading the bases. Mize, pinch-hitting for Mapes, singled against the right field fence, scoring Berra and Brown with Woodling going to third. For Brooklyn—Banta replaced Branca on the mound. Bauer ran for Mize. Coleman singled to center, scoring Woodling with Bauer going to third.
3 Page struck out.
Brooklyn
   For New York—Bauer playing right.
1 Hodges grounded to second. Olmo hit a home run into the lower left field stands.
2 Snider struck out. Campanella hit a home run into the left field stands.
3 Edwards, pinch-hitting for Banta, was called out on strikes.

With the score tied at 1–1 in the top of the ninth in Game 3 of the 1949 World Series against the Brooklyn Dodgers, DiMaggio lets this pitch go by. Moments later he fouled out, but the Yankees went on to score three runs, then hold off the rallying Dodgers, and win the game, 4–3.

YANKS TOP DODGERS WITH 3-RUN 9TH, 4-3

Ebbets Field seems to inspire the Yanks to some amazing ninth-inning stunts. It was back in 1941 that they snatched victory from defeat there when Mickey Owen let a third strike slip away from him.

This time Bobby Brown rifled a single into right field and Berra sped around to third. That appeared to rattle Branca. He walked Woodling, filling the bases, and Coach Clyde Bukeforth bustled out of the dugout to head a council of war around the big right-hander. Just off home plate stood Cliff Mapes, next scheduled hitter.

Whatever it was that the board of strategy told Branca with regard to Mapes all went for naught. For at that point Professor Stengel, the Yanks' managerial wizard, chose to make his master stroke.

Mapes Withdraws for Mize

He withdrew Mapes and called on the massive Mize, the big first sacker Leo Durocher had thought long through as a player to bring about the surprise deal which sent the "Big Cat" from the Giants to the Yankees on Aug. 22. To be sure, Mize has not played much for the Bombers, for after a week of action in which his heavy bludgeon helped win a couple of games, he injured his right shoulder and has not been able to field his position since.

But Big Jawn still can swing a bat with damaging effect, especially when the target happens to be Brooklyn's right-field barrier. With scarcely an effort and with the count one strike and two balls, Mize stroked a fast pitch, belt high, and sent it for a ride.

It didn't have quite enough carry to clear the wall, but the ball did strike the wire screening. Though Carl Furillo recovered quickly enough to hold Lumbering John to a single, both Berra and Brown scored and Woodling pulled up at third.

Stepping out to allow Hank Bauer to run for him, Mize received a thunderous ovation from the American Leaguers and doubtless, too, drew many a hearty cheer from National Leaguers with whom the good-natured Georgian had been an idol throughout his career. Just what Durocher's thoughts may have been as he watched it all from a box seat alongside the Brooklyn dugout may be conjectured. Certain it is they were doubled in spades by those of the Dodgers.

Banta Greeted With Single

Anyway, the Yanks were ahead, 2 to 1, and Banta, another right-hander, replaced the crestfallen Branca. But Banta didn't catch up with that elusive third out at once either, for Young Coleman greeted him with a sharp single to center and Woodling counted the third run of the inning.

Before it was all over that tally was to become the most important one of the day, because of the jarring home runs which Ohno and Campanella touched off in the ninth before Page nailed down the Flock for keeps.

Incidentally, those two homers, along with the one Reese had hit earlier, gave the Dodgers as many circuit blows as they had driven in all their previous world series appearances. Hy Myer hit one in 1916, Pete Reiser the next in 1941 and Dixie Walker the last previous in 1947.

There was another world series mark tied when Rizzuto, usually in one brilliant fielding play after another for the Yanks, went through this game at short without a single chance. That equaled the record set by Dave Bancroft with the Phillies in 1915 and matched by Joe Boley of the Athletics in 1920 and Reese with the Dodgers two years ago.

Mize, World Series Hero at Long Last.

SLUGGER IDOLIZED BY JUBILANT MATES

Mize Shares Glory of Victory In the Third Contest With Joe Page and Coleman

STENGEL NEVER WORRIED

Knew Big Jawn Would Get Hit or Walk—DiMaggio 'Down' Over Failure to Connect

By JAMES P. DAWSON

"Tickled? I'll say I'm tickled. Say, it's one of the happiest moments of my life."

Johnny Mize was talking above the din in the Yankee clubhouse at Ebbets Field. He at long last was a world series hero after a sparkling career that had stamped him one of baseball's leading sluggers. He was talking about the two-run single he cracked in the ninth inning, pinch-hitting for Cliff Mapes.

"I like to hit where you can see those fences all around," he said, his big, red face lit up in a wide grin. "At the Polo Grounds you have that big gap in center where the clubhouse is. It does something to you. Here, you see nothing but fence. Your target is unbroken and, when you swing, something generally happens. I'm glad it happened today—the way it did."

Big Jawn had come through to glory. For the second straight time at bat in his first world series, he had come through with a pinch-hit and this second one, a single off the screen at the top of the concrete wall in right field with the bases loaded, sent home two runs, broke a 1–1 tie and moved into scoring position the run that was propelled home by the youthful Jerry Coleman. This tally eventually proved to be the winner.

Started Career In 1930

This strange sensation, the role of series hero, came to Mize in the twilight of a career that extends back to the time in 1930 when he signed up with Greensboro in the Piedmont League for his first fling at organized ball. It had eluded the clubber through six years with the Gas House Gang of the St. Louis Cardinals and through four years, and part of a fifth that he spent with the Giants before being sold down the river last Aug. 25.

But the emotional reaction was accentuated because of the delay, and Big Jawn good-naturedly became the center of a dressing-room mob scene, sharing the spotlight with Coleman and the indefatigable Joe Page, the three individuals most responsible for bringing the Yanks the 4–3 triumph that put them 1-up on the Dodgers again.

"I hit a fast ball just about belt-high. Or maybe a little bit lower," said Mize. "You know, though, for a fraction of a second I didn't know whether I'd get the chance to hit. His (Branca's) first pitch was in close and in the split second you get to think about it I was planning to let it hit me and get on. That would have forced in a run. But it was too close to my right elbow. That's my sore shoulder side.

Coleman Is Lionized

"I looked at a strike because it wasn't my kind of pitch. I was going to make him give me a good one or walk me. Either way it was all right. But he gave me one with the count one and two, and it was the one I was waiting for. They tell me it would have been a home run in the Stadium, bouncing off the screen out there as high as it did. Maybe so. But it got us a couple of runs, and that's what counts."

The 25-year-old Coleman was elated over the single with which he greeted Jack Banta to drive in Gene Woodling with what proved to be the winning run. The trim youngster from California, in his first world series in his first major league year, because he was such a good stand-in when George Stirnweiss fell ill at the beginning of the season, was rushed through an exciting ordeal by photographers and interviewers when the Yanks finally got into the clubhouse and started celebrating.

Mr. Stengel Wise-Cracks

Manager Casey Stengel was in wise-cracking form. "We had 'em all the way," he smiled, with a wink. "Say, that big guy (Mize) came through, didn't he? What a shot. Sure I'm happy that they gave little Rizzuto a vacation today, tickled that Coleman came through, satisfied again with that man Page. And I'll throw Ed Lopat at them tomorrow.

"No, I never gave thought to taking Mize out if they changed pitchers. He's a pro. He hits right-handers or lefties. He's proved that often. And besides, I had a two-way shot. He could get a base on balls or a hit. He got the hit. We got the game. I wasn't too worried about Page, either. We were three runs ahead when they started hitting those homers. We were still in front when Page finished them."

Tommy Byrne was more disillusioned than distracted at being "lifted" in his first world series start before surviving four innings. "Reese hit a high fast one for his homer," said the Yankee lefty. "I didn't think he got too much of the ball. Then I turned around and saw it going into the seats. I couldn't get my curve over the plate and that didn't help me any, either. But we won, and that's the big thing."

Joe DiMaggio was "down". With only a scratch hit to show in three games, he was snapping replies to questions. "Don't ask me about pitchers, we've said too much about pitchers already," he shouted. "Let's talk about hits, when I'm going to get some hits."

His admirers are beginning to wonder about the same thing.

Game 4 October 8 at Brooklyn

New York	Pos	AB	R	H	RBI	PO	A	E
Rizzuto	ss	4	0	2	0	1	4	0
Henrich	1b	4	1	3	0	10	0	0
Berra	c	5	1	1	0	10	1	0
DiMaggio	cf	3	1	0	0	1	0	0
B. Brown	3b	3	1	2	3	0	3	0
Woodling	lf	3	1	0	0	2	0	0
Mapes	rf	2	1	1	2	1	0	0
a Bauer		2	0	0	0	2	0	0
Coleman	2b	4	0	0	0	0	0	0
Lopat	p	3	0	1	1	0	1	0
Reynolds	p	1	0	0	0	0	0	0
Totals		34	6	10	6	27	9	0

Pitching	IP	H	R	ER	BB	SO
New York						
Lopat (W)	5⅓	9	4	4	1	4
Reynolds (SV)	3⅔	0	0	0	0	5
Brooklyn						
Newcombe (L)	3⅓	5	3	3	3	0
Hatten	1⅓	3	3	3	2	0
Erskine	1	1	0	0	0	0
Banta	3	1	0	0	1	1

N Y	000	330	000			6
Bkn	000	004	000			4

Brooklyn	Pos	AB	R	H	RBI	PO	A	E
Reese	ss	4	1	2	0	0	2	0
Miksis	3b	2	0	0	0	0	2	1
c Cox	3b	2	0	1	0	1	0	0
Snider	cf	4	0	0	0	4	0	0
Robinson	2b	3	1	1	1	2	3	0
Hodges	1b	4	1	1	0	8	1	0
Olmo	lf	4	1	1	1	2	1	0
Campanella	c	4	0	1	1	5	2	0
Hermanski	rf	4	0	2	1	4	0	0
Newcombe	p	1	0	0	0	1	1	0
Hatten	p	0	0	0	0	0	0	0
b T. Brown		1	0	0	0	0	0	0
Erskine	p	0	0	0	0	0	0	0
d Jorgensen		1	0	0	0	0	0	0
Banta	p	0	0	0	0	0	0	0
e Whitman		1	0	0	0	0	0	0
Totals		35	4	9	4	27	12	1

a Flied out for Mapes in 5th.
b Flied out for Hatten in 5th.
c Singled for Miksis in 6th
d Struck out for Erskine in 6th
e Struck out for Banta in 9th

Doubles—B. Brown, Lopat, Mapes, Reese
Triple—B. Brown Double Plays—Miksis
to Campanella to Robinson, Rizzuto to
Henrich. Left on Bases—New York 7,
Brooklyn 5 Umpires—Jorda, Hubbard
Reardon, Passarella, Hurley, Barr
Attendance—33,934 Time of Game—2:42

1st Inning
New York
Rizzuto singled to center
Henrich singled to right, Rizzuto
racing to third
1,2 Berra grounded to Miksis, and Rizzuto
caught in a rundown was declared out
running out of the base line to
elude Campanella's tag. Campanella
threw to Robinson to double up
Henrich who had rounded second
DiMaggio walked
B. Brown walked, loading the bases
3 Woodling flied to center
Brooklyn
Reese doubled off the left-center
field wall
1 Miksis tapped out, Berra to Henrich
Reese holding second
2 Snider grounded to third, Reese
still holding second
3 Robinson grounded to short

2nd Inning
New York
1 Mapes grounded back to the mound
2 Coleman fouled to Campanella
3 Lopat flied to center
Brooklyn
1 Hodges flied to left
2 Olmo flied to left
3 Campanella bounced to the pitcher

3rd Inning
New York
1 Rizzuto grounded to third
2 Henrich grounded out, Hodges to Newcombe
3 Berra flied to right
Brooklyn
1 Hermanski struck out
2 Newcombe struck out
3 Reese popped to first

4th Inning
New York
1 DiMaggio flied to center
B. Brown doubled off the wall in
left-center
Woodling walked
Mapes doubled down the left field
line, scoring B. Brown and Woodling
2 Coleman flied to left
Lopat doubled off the wall in
left-center, scoring Mapes
For Brooklyn—Hatten replaced Newcombe
on the mound
Rizzuto singled to left, but Lopat
3 was out trying to score, Olmo to
Campanella

4th Inning (continued)
Brooklyn
1 Miksis was called out on strikes
2 Snider flied to right
Robinson walked
3 Hodges struck out

5th Inning
New York
Henrich walked
Berra singled to right, Henrich
stopping at second, but when
Hermanski's throw was muffed by
Miksis, both runners advanced
a base
DiMaggio intentionally walked, loading
the bases
B. Brown tripled clearing the bases
1 Woodling flied to center
2 Bauer, batting for Mapes, lined to
right
3 Coleman grounded to short
Brooklyn
For New York—Bauer playing right
1 Olmo fouled to Berra
2 Campanella grounded to short,
Hermanski singled to right
3 T. Brown, pinch-hitting for Hatten,
flied to right

6th Inning
New York
For Brooklyn—Erskine pitching
1 Lopat popped to first
2 Rizzuto flied to left
Henrich hit a long single off the
right field wall
3 Berra popped to second
Brooklyn
Reese singled to center
Cox, batting for Miksis, beat out a
roller to third, Reese stopping at
second
1,2 Snider hit into a double play,
Rizzuto to Henrich, Reese going
to third
Robinson singled to left, scoring Reese
Hodges singled to center, Robinson
going to third
Olmo singled to center, scoring
Robinson with Hodges going to third
Campanella singled to left, scoring
Hodges as Olmo stopped at second
Hermanski singled to right, Olmo
scoring as Campanella raced to third
For New York—Reynolds replaced Lopat
on the mound
3 Jorgensen, pinch-hitting for Erskine,
took a called third strike

7th Inning
New York
For Brooklyn—Cox playing third with
Banta the new pitcher
1 DiMaggio grounded to second
2 B. Brown grounded to second
3 Woodling grounded to second
Brooklyn
1 Reese lined to right
2 Cox flied to center
3 Snider struck out

8th Inning
New York
1 Bauer grounded to short
2 Coleman flied to right
3 Reynolds fouled to Campanella
Brooklyn
1 Robinson grounded to third
2 Hodges grounded to short
3 Olmo called out on strikes

9th Inning
New York
Rizzuto walked
Henrich singled to right, Rizzuto
going to third
1 Rizzuto was picked off third,
Campanella to Cox
2 Berra flied to right
3 DiMaggio struck out
Brooklyn
1 Campanella grounded to third
2 Hermanski struck out
3 Whitman, pinch-hitting for Banta,
struck out

Game 5 October 9 at Brooklyn

N.Y.	203 113 000	10
Bkn.	001 001 400	6

New York	Pos	AB	R	H	RBI	PO	A	E
Rizzuto	ss	3	2	0	0	3	3	0
Henrich	1b	4	2	1	0	8	0	0
Berra	c	5	0	0	1	11	0	0
DiMaggio	cf	4	1	1	2	2	0	0
B. Brown	3b	4	2	3	2	0	1	0
Woodling	lf	4	2	3	0	3	0	0
Mapes	rf	3	1	0	0	1	0	1
Coleman	2b	5	0	2	3	1	0	0
Raschi	p	3	0	1	1	0	0	0
Page	p	1	0	0	0	0	1	0
Totals		36	10	11	9	27	5	1

Pitching	IP	H	R	ER	BB	SO
New York						
Raschi (W)	6⅔	9	6	6	4	7
Page (SV)	2⅓	2	0	0	1	4
Brooklyn						
Barney (L)	2⅔	3	5	5	6	2
Banta	2⅓	3	2	2	0	2
Erskine	⅔	2	3	3	1	0
Hatten	⅓	1	0	0	0	0
Palica	2	1	0	0	1	1
Minner	1	1	0	0	0	0

Brooklyn	Pos	AB	R	H	RBI	PO	A	E
Reese	ss	5	0	2	1	1	0	0
Jorgensen	3b	3	1	0	0	0	0	0
e Miksis		1	0	1	0	0	0	0
Snider	cf	5	2	2	0	5	0	0
Robinson	2b	4	0	1	1	1	2	1
Hermanski	rf	3	1	1	1	1	0	0
Hodges	1b	5	1	2	3	9	1	0
Rackley	lf	3	0	0	0	2	0	0
c Olmo	lf	1	0	0	0	2	0	0
Campanella	c	3	1	1	0	5	1	0
Barney	p	0	0	0	0	1	1	1
Banta	p	1	0	0	0	0	1	0
a T. Brown		1	0	0	0	0	0	0
Erskine	p	0	0	0	0	0	0	0
Hatten	p	0	0	0	0	0	0	0
b Cox		1	0	0	0	0	0	0
Palica	p	0	0	0	0	0	1	0
d Edwards		1	0	1	0	0	0	0
Minner	p	0	0	0	0	0	1	0
Totals		37	6	11	6	27	7	2

a Struck out for Banta in 5th.
b Struck out for Hatten in 6th.
c Struck out for Rackley in 7th.
d Singled for Palica in 8th.
e Doubled for Jorgensen in 9th.

Doubles—Campanella, Coleman, Miskis, Snider, Woodling 2. Triple—B. Brown. Home Runs—DiMaggio, Hodges. Sacrifice Hits—Mapes, Rizzuto. Double Play—Page to Rizzuto to Henrich. Left on Bases—New York 9, Brooklyn 9. Umpires—Hubbard, Reardon, Passarella, Jorda, Barr, Hurley. Attendance—33,711. Time of Game—3:04.

1st Inning
New York
Rizzuto walked.
Henrich walked.
Rizzuto went to third and Henrich to second on Barney's wild pick off attempt, the ball sailing over Reese's head into center field.
1 Berra struck out.
2 DiMaggio flied to deep center, Rizzuto scoring and Henrich going to third after the catch.
B. Brown singled through the box, scoring Henrich.
Woodling walked.
3 Mapes called out on strikes.
Brooklyn
1 Reese grounded to short.
2 Jorgensen grounded to third.
3 Snider struck out.

2nd Inning
New York
1 Coleman popped to short.
Raschi walked.
2 Rizzuto sacrificed Raschi to second, Hodges unassisted.
3 Henrich grounded out, Hodges to Barney.
Brooklyn
1 Robinson lined to second.
2 Hermanski flied to right.
3 Hodges grounded to short.

3rd Inning
New York
1 Berra bounced back to the pitcher.
2 DiMaggio lined to center.
B. Brown walked.
Woodling singled to center, B. Brown advancing to third.
Mapes walked, loading the bases.
Coleman singled to left, scoring B. Brown and Woodling with Mapes stopping at second.
For Brooklyn—Banta came in to pitch.
Raschi singled to center, Mapes scoring and Coleman stopping at second.
3 Rizzuto flied to center.
Brooklyn
1 Rackley struck out.
Campanella doubled to left.
2 Banta grounded to first, Campanella advancing to third.
Reese singled to right, scoring Campanella.
3 Jorgensen popped to short.

4th Inning
New York
1 Henrich grounded to second.
2 Berra lined to first.
DiMaggio hit a home run into the lower left field stands.
3 B. Brown struck out.
Brooklyn
1 Snider struck out.
Robinson singled to center.
2 Hermanski flied to left.
Hodges singled off the right field wall, Robinson going to third.
3 Rackley struck out.

5th Inning
New York
Woodling hit a double off the scoreboard in right.
1 Mapes sacrificed Woodling to third, Banta to Hodges.
2 Coleman grounded to first, scoring Woodling.
3 Raschi took a called third strike.
Brooklyn
1 Campanella lined to short.
2 T. Brown, pinch-hitting for Banta, struck out.
Reese singled to left.
3 Jorgensen grounded to first.

6th Inning
New York
For Brooklyn—Erskine pitching.
Rizzuto walked.
Henrich singled to left, Rizzuto going to third.
1 Berra flied to deep left, Rizzuto scoring after the catch.
2 DiMaggio popped to second.
B. Brown tripled off the right field wall, scoring Henrich and also scored on Robinson's wild relay to the plate.
For Brooklyn—Hatten came in to pitch.
Woodling doubled off the left-center field wall.
3 Mapes flied to left.
Brooklyn
Snider doubled off the left-center field wall.
Robinson walked.
Hermanski singled to right, scoring Snider as Robinson stopped at second, but Robinson went to third on Mapes' fumble.
1 Hodges struck out.
2 Rackley bounced to first, Robinson holding and Hermanski going to second.
Campanella walked, loading the bases.
3 Cox, pinch-hitting for Hatten, struck out.

7th Inning
New York
For Brooklyn—Palica now pitching.
1 Coleman grounded to second.
2 Raschi grounded back to the mound.
3 Rizzuto struck out.
Brooklyn
1 Reese lined to left.
Jorgensen walked.
Snider singled to center, Jorgensen moving to third.
2 Robinson flied to left, Jorgensen scoring after the catch.
Hermanski walked.
Hodges hit a three-run homer into the lower left field stands.
For New York—Page came in to pitch.
3 Olmo, pinch-hitting for Rackley, struck out.

8th Inning
New York
For Brooklyn—Olmo playing left.
1 Henrich lined to Snider, making a fantastic diving catch.
2 Berra flied to center.
DiMaggio walked.
B. Brown singled to left, DiMaggio stopping at second.
3 Woodling flied to left.
Brooklyn
1 Campanella popped to first.
Edwards, batting for Palica, singled to left.
2,3 Reese hit into a double play, Page to Rizzuto to Henrich.

9th Inning
New York
For Brooklyn—Minner pitching.
1 Mapes flied to left.
Coleman doubled off the right-center field scoreboard.
2 Page grounded to the mound.
3 Rizzuto lined to right.
Brooklyn
Miksis, batting for Jorgensen, doubled down the left field line.
1 Snider struck out.
2 Robinson struck out.
Hermanski walked.
3 Hodges struck out.

'WON LIKE CHAMPS' IS STENGEL PRAISE

Pilot Gives All Credit to His 'Fighting Gang' for Triumph In Series

'THEY WON IT; I DIDN'T'

But Says 'Biggest Thrill' of All Came After the League Pennant Victory

By JAMES P. DAWSON

Casey Stengel was so happy in the Yankee clubhouse yesterday after his team had' routed the Dodgers by 10 to 6 to win the World Series in five games that he congratulated Commissioner A. B. Chandler for "doing a great job."

The Yankee skipper didn't mention whether the commissioner pitched air-tight ball, hit a couple of home runs or plucked a homer out of the air before it fell into the seats. But the incident indicates the tremendous, delirious joy for the K. C. veteran, in the first flush of his paramount triumph which had been so long denied him as a manager.

No adjectives can describe the scene in the clubhouse of the victors, although a number of them have been through these World Series triumphs before. They went in for extremes. Yells, whistles, shouts, shrieks split the air in ear-shattering crescendo. Punches were like slaps—delivered good-naturedly, but resoundingly. Among the celebrants the miracle was that none was hurt.

The contrast? It was supplied by Charley Keller. Off in a corner he sat, munching a sandwich while still and movie cameramen and writers flitted hither and yon, grabbing this one and that one, and well-wishers added to the general pandemonium by trampling players and working persons under foot to present their congratulations.

Maryland Mauler Silent

Off in a corner, like little Jack Horner, only he wasn't eating a pumpkin pie. The rugged veteran of five of these orgies now, survivor of the baseball campaigns as a Yankee from 'way back in 1939, he who used to be leading the parade to victory with his war club, just sat there, munching, unnoticed.

Oh, he was happy over the victory. He had contributed to the triumph up to his physical best. Although a lame back handicapped him, he had helped toward the American League pennant. But he took no actual part in this series

triumph and he was letting the youth of the club have its day in the sun.

Just a few feet away from Keller photographers and writers were swarming around Joe DiMaggio, Cliff Mapes, Vic Raschi, Lefty Joe Page, Gene Woodling, Jerry Coleman, Tommy Henrich, as they quaffed beer or soft drinks or lunched on snacks. DiMaggio was smiling for the first time since the series began. Everybody was smiling. The rushing tide of confusion swept along, but it brushed by Keller, never touched him. And he smiled when one who had seen him come up as a raw rookie and go out like the fighting man he is, clasped his hand and congratulated him on his contribution, however small.

Not the Biggest Thrill

Stengel was beside himself with joy. But he had no exclusive rights on this emotion. Everybody was the same. The Yankee skipper, whose pennant hopes had been dashed as a manager with Brooklyn and Boston, had taken an injury-riddled ball club and piloted it to baseball's heights in his first year back with the majors after going down to the minors, tagged a failure. His felicitations for his club knew no exceptions.

"The biggest thrill of my life? No. I wouldn't say it was," Stengel exclaimed, shouting hoarsely to make himself heard above the din. "I'd say the big thrill came when we got in there. If we hadn't won the pennant we wouldn't be here. Winning the pennant took some doing, after all we'd been through.

"I'll say this. This is the greatest ball club a man could manage. Certainly the best I've ever known. We have been one happy family from the time spring training started. There has never been a sour note in the clubhouse, on the dugout bench or on the field. A really great bunch of fellows and I am indebted to them for the way they came through for me. They won it. Not me.

"I won't say nothing happened through the season. But the only things that interrupted our happy family life came from out there on the field, injuries and accidents and sickness as the boys gave it all they had. A real good gang. Take my word for it. And, I'm thankful, too, to Mr. Topping and Mr. Webb and Mr. Weiss for giving me this kind of a ball club. I don't know of another club that could come through like them

Sorry It Was Brooklyn

"If I said the series went the way I expected I'd sound like I was popping off. It went the way I expected only in that we won. We won from a pretty good ball club, too. And, we won like real champions. I'm only sorry it had to be Brooklyn. I spent most of my playing days here. The fans here have always been wonderful to me, giving their support all the time. I hope they are glad we won.

"I had Sandford warming up in the fourth, not because I was worried, but because I wanted to be ready. I was figuring on him as my pitcher for tomorrow if need

be. Then I was coming in with Byrne and Reynolds, again. You have to think of those things, you know. Our clubs were about on a par. They had a tough time winning their pennant. So did we. In the end, I guess it just amounts to the fact we lasted five days longer than they did."

The conquering skipper went across the room to shake the hand of the smiling DiMaggio, and thank him for getting back into action when he should have been in a sickbed.

DiMaggio was happy over his home run into the left-field stands in the fourth inning. The master's stroke lifted some of the gloom that has hung over the Clipper because he never got to slugging through the series. His 8-year-old son, Joe Jr., was at his right shoulder.

"Daddy, I lost one of your balls," said Joe, Jr., explaining he had mislaid one of the autographed balls Wallopin' Joe was saving for friends.

"That's all right, son," smiled daddy, "we can afford to lose one today. I lost one myself." DiMaggio is going to California without delay.

33,711 Pay $167,165 To Watch Fifth Game

By The Associated Press.

Final Standing of Clubs

	W.	L.	Pc.
New York (A.)	4	1	.800
Brooklyn (N.)	1	4	.200

Fifth-Game Statistics

Attendance—33,711.

Receipts— (net)—$167,185.45.

Commissioner's share — $25,074.81.

Clubs' and Leagues' share—$142,090.64.

Five-Game Totals

Attendance—236,710.

*Receipts (net)—$1,129,627.88.

Commissioner's share — $169,444.17.

Clubs' and Leagues' share—$469,327.96.

†Players' share—$490,355.75.

*Does not include radio and television fee.
†Players share in first four games only.

Highlights

- The Yankees earned their twelfth world crown.
- Casey Stengel managed the Yankees to the first of what would prove to be seven world titles.
- The two triples hit by Yank Bobby Brown tied the Series mark for a five-game Series.
- Allie Reynolds pitched a two-hit shutout for the Yankees in Game 1, and struck out nine Dodgers in the process.
- Tommy Henrich hit a home run in the bottom of the ninth to destroy Don Newcombe's shutout and win Game 1 for the Yankees.
- Preacher Roe allowed the Yankees only six hits in his shutout for the Dodgers in Game 2.
- Gil Hodges singled to send Jackie Robinson across with the game-winning run of Game 2.
- A pinch-hit double by Johnny Mize in the ninth inning of Game 3 drove in two runs, and a single by Jerry Coleman added another to give the Yanks a one-run victory.
- The Dodgers scored their three runs in Game 3 on solo homers by PeeWee Reese, Luis Olmo, and Roy Campanella.
- Bobby Brown tripled with the bases loaded in the fifth inning of Game 4 to provide the Yanks with their winning margin.
- The Yankees tied a Series record when they hit three doubles in one inning, the fourth of Game 4 (Bobby Brown, Cliff Mapes, Eddie Lopat).

Best Efforts

Batting

Average	Bobby Brown	.500
Home Runs	(six players)	1
Triples	Bobby Brown	2
Doubles	Jerry Coleman	3
	Gene Woodling	3
Hits	Bobby Brown	6
	PeeWee Reese	6
Runs	Tommy Henrich	4
	Bobby Brown	4
RBIs	Bobby Brown	5

Pitching

Wins	(five players)	1
ERA	Allie Reynolds	0.00
	Preacher Roe	0.00
Strikeouts	Allie Reynolds	14
Innings Pitched	Vic Raschi	14⅔

NEW YORK YANKEES
BROOKLYN DODGERS

1949

Reprinted, with permission, from
The World Series, A Complete
Pictorial History, by John Devaney
and Burt Goldblatt (Rand McNally
and Company, Chicago, © 1972).

A Wink from Casey
and an Answer from Yogi

In the first game of another Subway Series, the Dodgers' big Don Newcombe and the Yankees' Allie Reynolds pitched shutout ball for 8½ innings. In the bottom of the ninth the Yankees' Old Reliable, Tommy Henrich, drove a Newcombe fastball into the rightfield seats for a 1-0 victory. It was the first World Series victory as a manager for the Yankees' new leader, Casey Stengel.

After the game a reporter reminded Stengel about the last Series game that was won 1-0 by a homer. That game was in the 1923 Series, and the man who hit the homer for the Giants against the Yanks was Casey Stengel. But Casey's homer, a reporter pointed out, wasn't as dramatic as Henrich's, because it was hit in the seventh and not in the bottom of the ninth. "You're right," Casey growled with a wink. "You see, I'm a nervous fellow and I couldn't wait that long."

The second game was another 1-0 duel, this time won by the Dodgers behind Preacher Roe, the run scoring on a double by Jackie Robinson and a single by Gil Hodges. The Yankees won another close one, 4-3, in the third game, when Johnny Mize, a veteran slugger, came up in the ninth with the bases loaded and drove in two runs. It was the second pinch hit in two tries during this Series for Mize, who would become famous during the next few years for his Series pinch hits.

The Yankees won the next two games to win the Series, four games to one, the first of five straight championships for the Casey Stengel-model Yankees. The fifth game was the first Series game to be played under lights, which were turned on in the late innings.

During the Series the fleet Dodgers stole several bases when Yogi Berra threw poorly to second base. Yogi shrugged off the criticism he heard. "If you got them all out stealing," he said, "the game wouldn't be interesting."

Jackie Robinson:
"When I came up, he threw peas"

I never hit well in most of the Series I played in, said Jackie Robinson, later an East Coast business executive. *I don't know why except in a short Series, the pitching will tend to be good and good pitching will always stop hitting. Like Allie Reynolds. You never saw a guy pitch better against me. When I came up, he threw peas. The Yankees were a great ball club who beat you by taking advantage of every situation. If somebody made a mistake, you were just dead. And they never seemed to make a mistake in important situations. I don't think their personnel was any better than ours, but they were excellent in crisis situations. They were an opportunistic team. They made the breaks go their way. And they had confidence. It wasn't that we were nervous or afraid. But they would come out and you could sense they thought they could beat you.*

1950
ANOTHER PENNANT
SEASON

Joltin' Joe DiMaggio was 35 years old in 1950, coming off several years of serious heel problems. He still had the best slugging average in the American League — .585 — and whacked 32 homers while driving in 122 runs.

HOME RUN CONTEST

After we defeated the Philadelphia Phillies in the 1950 World Series, I went on a tour of the Far East. The Korean War was under way and the purpose was to entertain the troops over there. With me was my good friend, Lefty O'Doul, manager then of the San Francisco Seals.

On the way, we stopped in Japan to visit some of the servicemen in hospitals there. The country was crazy about baseball, and so it was arranged for me to take part in a 10-day home run contest with Makoto Kuzuru, who was known as Japan's "Babe Ruth".

I had not brought my own supply of bats, and the one they provided for me over there felt like an Italian sausage. It was shorter, lighter, and made of a softer wood than the Louisville Sluggers I normally used. For three days I was outslugged by Kuzuru, but on the fourth day I got my hands on a Slugger that had been left over there on O'Doul's trip the year before. Because of the artful work of the bat makers in Louisville, Kentucky, I managed to win the home run derby over the next seven days.

Joe DiMaggio

1950

JOE DiMAGGIO STATISTICS

Games	139
At Bats	525
Hits	158
Doubles	33
Triples	10
Home Runs	32
Runs Scored	114
Runs Batted In	122
Bases on Balls	80
Strike Outs	33
Stolen Bases	0
Slugging Average	.585*
Batting Average	.301

* Led the American
  League

STANDINGS

	Won	Lost	Percentage	Games Behind
New York Yankees	98	56	.636	
Detroit Tigers	95	59	.617	3
Boston Red Sox	94	60	.610	4
Cleveland Indians	92	62	.597	6
Washington Senators	67	87	.435	31
Chicago White Sox	60	94	.390	38
St. Louis Browns	58	96	.377	40
Philadelphia A's	51	102	.338	46

Jolting Joe Feels 'Big Year' in His Muscles

Exercise and Mom's Cooking Build Up Clipper's Weight and Vigor

—Photo by Frank Rino of the New York Journal-American

THERE'S NOTHING GLOOMY about the facial expressions of Joe DiMaggio, who expects his 1950 season with the Yankees to be a big one. Looking forward to a contract calling for last year's salary of $100,000 the Yankee Clipper expects to play in all spring exhibitions, the full 154-game schedule and the World's Series. He's back at 200 pounds—just 15 pounds short of his best playing weight.

— By HUGH BRADLEY of the New York Journal-American

NEW YORK, N. Y.

Joe DiMaggio said he guessed a 35-year-old player shouldn't anticipate the future as eagerly as a rookie. Then he grinned and proceeded to do so anyhow.

"Maybe it's the reaction from the past season, when I had the roughest time of my life," he went on. "All I know is that something tells me this year that's coming up could be a big one."

The few months that have elapsed since the end of the World's Series provide the basis for the Clipper's optimism. In October he was worn to a frazzle, mentally and physically. Today he has regained the weight he lost during his late-season siege of virus pneumonia and is brimming with all kinds of health.

Regular hours have helped as much as regular meals. With the strain of the red-hot pennant campaign over, he has been able to relax.

"Proper exercise and the establishment of a routine of living have done a lot for me," he said. "Out in California, where I've been most of the time since the Series, I've been playing golf and going hunting.

"The exercise—and some days I walk 20 miles—has been a good test of my muscles. And it makes me hungry so that I get back home and eat plenty of Mom's cooking, which helps me pick up weight. Last year when I was under a mounting tension so much of the time because I had to be on the bench and couldn't help the fellows, I guess I kind of neglected my eating."

DiMaggio flew back to San Francisco after his brief visit here. He doesn't plan to return until the season opens. That is, not unless the big brass of the Yankees summons him to a salary conference.

"Definitely I haven't discussed contract terms for 1950," he said. "How much do I expect to ask? It would be premature to discuss that now. When the bosses get around to the subject they'll be in touch with me."

Told that he ought to be a cinch to receive the same top 100-G salary with which he was rewarded last season, he responded with his best poker face. But it may not have been entirely accidental that his next remarks dealt with the future.

"My legs feel better than they have for years," he said. "Not a sign of pain in my heels where those bone spurs were removed. The way I am picking up weight I should be able to start the season at 215 pounds, which is just a little heavier than I was in 1937 when I had one of my best years.

"All that means I'm expecting to be in the full 154 games as well as in the exhibitions and the World's Series. Of course, you never can tell precisely what's going to happen, but definitely that's the way I'm anticipating things."

The anticipation also extends to more than one campaign. He really feels good.

"I know that you've got to take each season as it comes along," the Clipper said. "Maybe it would be tempting fate to go popping off. Nevertheless the way I feel now I can't see any reason why there should not be three or four more good years ahead of me."

* * *

Aiming for 10 World's Series

Naturally they're to be with the Yankees. Having been in eight World's Series with the club already, he has a notion that he may stick around with the same outfit until he's tied or cracked Babe Ruth's record of ten.

"I guess the more things you do, the more you want to do," he said.

"Getting back to the club, though, I wouldn't be surprised if 1950 turned out to be another Series year. I know the Red Sox and Indians will be rough, and that the Tigers have improved, but—well, if a fellow doesn't expect to finish first, what's the sense of him being a Yankee?"

Yanks to Start Contract Round-Up With DiMaggio Holding Spotlight

Club Will Mail 31 Documents Next Week for Pennant Winners—Clipper Is Expected to Remain at $100,000 Mark

By JAMES P. DAWSON

Contract time has arrived for the Yankees, and with it comes the annual outbreak of speculation over cuts and raises, conditional and straight documents.

Arthur Patterson, who manages somehow to keep Yankee doings before the public, released the contract tidings yesterday. Following a telephone conversation with General Manager George Weiss, who was in Phoenix, Ariz., Patterson announced contracts will be sent to the Yankee squad next Monday or Tuesday. He added thirty-one documents will go into the mails, far ahead of the deadline.

Under baseball law these contracts must be mailed not later than Jan. 31 or the individual player automatically becomes a free agent. Unless a player has accepted terms in advance he is not permitted to engage in spring training.

Interest in the Clipper

Chief interest centers about the contract which will be offered the game's highest-salaried player Joe DiMaggio. Although it has never been officially announced, it has never been denied that DiMaggio signed for $100,000 last year.

Handicapped by an ankle injury which retarded his spring training and sent him home while the club was playing exhibitions in Texas, DiMaggio was lost to the club for half the season. The Clipper got into seventy-six games, returning when the pennant race was keenest and aided no little in bringing Casey Stengel the distinction of winning an American League flag in his first year.

That DiMaggio will be offered a reduced salary is doubted. That Wallopin' Joe will ask for an increase, likewise, is extremely doubtful, all things considered. Nor is it likely the best box-office attraction the Yanks have had since the days of Babe Ruth will be asked to sign a conditional contract.

Patterson did relay the news from Mr. Weiss that reports of DiMaggio's health have been gratifying. DiMaggio expressed complete satisfaction with his condition on a visit here several weeks ago and appeared in perfect shape. Details of the slugger's contract likely will be worked out at a conference with Weiss before the Yankee squad heads for St. Petersburg on Feb. 27.

Henrich May Sign Here

A number of the players living near by also are expected to be called into conference at headquarters. These include Tommy Henrich, who seems destined for first base; Phil Rizzuto, Gene Woodling and George Stirnweiss, all of whom live in near-by New Jersey towns. The "fireman" of the relief pitching staff, Lefty Joe Page, is another who may arrange contract terms at the home office. Page is expected to come here within a fortnight for a medical check-up and it is likely he will sign then.

General Manager Weiss combined business with pleasure in his stopover at Arizona, according to Patterson. The Yankee executive, visiting co-owner Del Webb, inspected the site for a Yankee yearling training camp which will be in operation at Phoenix Jan. 23 to Feb. 12. At this camp it is proposed to school Yankee minor league prospects under the teaching of Manager Stengel and a staff of coaches which will include Frankie Crosetti, Bill Dickey, Jim Turner, Johnny Neun, Bill Skiff, Joe Devine, Eddie Leishman and Chief Scout Paul Krichell. The pre-minor training idea will cash dividends if it gets a player to the Yankees a year ahead of the customary schedule, Patterson said.

Arrangements also are being made for the opening of the spring training campaign for the Yankee varsity at St. Petersburg, Fla., looking to the launching of the 1950 baseball season, when the Yanks will resume where they left off last year against the Red Sox. The schedule makers have fashioned a four-game Yankee-Red Sox series to open the season in Boston for the first time in many years. A single game is scheduled for April 18, with a morning–afternoon double-header April 19, Patriots' Day, and a single game April 20.

Most of Champions Regard DiMaggio as Player They Most Admire

Bombers Vote for Jolting Joe as Mr. Yankee

Reveal Their Preferences and Big Thrills in Game in Questionnaire

WALLY HOOD, JR.   BOBBY BROWN   YOGI BERRA   GENE WOODLING

WALLY HOOD, SR.   FRANK CROSETTI   JOE MEDWICK   EARL AVERILL

YANKEES AND THEIR MODELS   **OLD HEROES OF BOMBER STARS**

By DAN DANIEL
NEW YORK, N. Y.

Early in the new year, it is the custom of the Yankee front office to send out questionnaires to all the players on the club's reserve list. The answers never fail to intrigue. In the past, these questionnaires were regarded as somewhat confidential. But this time they have been opened to the press, and they certainly are revealing.

The players are asked to tell about their families. Married? If so, how many children? What is your war record, if any? What is your baseball genealogy? What was your biggest baseball thrill? Which player do you most admire?

Naturally, there is a strong majority in favor of Joe DiMaggio as the model of the Yankees. But here and there surprises cropped up. As, for example, Yogi Berra's written preference for Joe Medwick.

This is understandable, because Medwick and Berra are a couple of look-alikes at the plate. "I always admired the way Medwick hit the ball," says the Yogi, who as a kid studied Ducky Wucky with the Cardinals. Berra is from the Hill in St. Louis.

* * * *

Wakefield's Big Thrill—$51,000 Bonus

Three Yankees failed to fill out the line about their diamond models. They are Vic Raschi, Allie Reynolds and the newcomer, Dick Wakefield.

Wakefield said that he got the biggest thrill of his baseball life when he signed with Detroit. He got a bonus of $51,000, plus a $4,000 Cadillac.

One player went to bat for his dad. Wally Hood, Jr., the pitcher, voted for Wally, Sr., who used to play in the outfield for Brooklyn. Junior wrote that his dad's coaching had landed him with the Yankees.

Jackie Jensen, the new $100,000 outfielder from Oakland, writes that he hopes to be like DiMaggio, but he plans to be Joe's successor, that he some day wants to be a college coach, and that his big thrill was hitting a homer with the bases loaded off Guy Fletcher when that worthy was the top pitcher of the Pacific Coast League last season.

Tommy Henrich's answer to that question about the biggest thrill is, "Being a Yankee is quite an experience." Thomas names Joe DiMaggio as his model in the game and adds, "He comes closer to perfection, doing anything in baseball, than anybody else."

Billy Martin, the $80,000 second baseman who will report

JOE DIMAGGIO

with Jensen at St. Petersburg, reveals his model as Cookie Lavagetto, "who helped me so much at Oakland." Martin says he is of Italian extraction, but his parents are listed as James and Mrs. Downey.

Gerald Coleman lists quite a war record. Two DFCs, seven Air Medals and two Naval Citations.

"DiMaggio is better than anybody else, no matter what he does on the field. Effortless greatness," exuberates Gerry.

Billy Johnson says, "More than any other ball player does DiMaggio put his heart and soul into every game. My big

Ruth Fails to Receive Mention

Curiously enough, none of the present-day Yankees listed Babe Ruth as the player they most admired although the late home run king was the greatest of all the Bombers. In fact, Yankee Stadium is known as the "House That Ruth Built."

thrill? Hitting that triple with the bases loaded in the third game of the 1943 World's Series."

Johnny Lindell praises DiMaggio's spirit and leadership, and exults over his own .500 batting average in the 1947 Series.

Hank Bauer writes that he is doing well as a steam fitter, adds to the praise for DiMaggio, and reveals two Purple Hearts and a Bronze Star in his war record with the Marines. He is of Austro-Hungarian extraction, he says.

John Mize's hero is Dizzy Dean. "A great pitcher, great hitter, great fielder, great base runner," says John of his one-time Cardinal teammate.

* * *

'38 Homer Spree Stands Out for Mize

Mize did some interesting pinch-hitting for the Yankees in the 1949 World's Series, but his thrills go back to 1938. He hit three homers in one game against Boston, and a week later repeated against the Giants.

Bobby Brown writes the accolade of Frankie Crosetti. "I admire him because he was a great clutch player, and because he did things I cannot do," the third baseman adds.

Golden Boy batted .500 in the 1949 World's Series, with six blows in 12 tries. However, the thrill of his baseball career, he says, traces to the 1947 classic. "My third straight pinch hit of that Series, in the last game."

There are several votes for Lou Gehrig, from unexpected sources—Clarence Marshall and Jimmy Delsing, among them.

Gene Woodling, brought up on Cleveland baseball, as a native of nearby Akron, modeled himself after Earl Averill, the old Indian outfielder, and gives his vote to that worthy.

Bob Porterfield, one of the Gehrig boosters, says he is working as a plumber. "Lou had a great love for his fellow player," the pitcher writes.

Marshall says, "Lou was just a grand guy. My big thrill was being told to pitch the Yankees' first night game in the Stadium, in 1946."

What does Joseph Paul DiMaggio himself say about all this? His questionnaire has yet to come back.

Joe Makes 'Em Click, Even in Off-Season

NEWSREEL AND PRESS CAMERAMAN train a big battery of range finders on Jolting Joe DiMaggio, shown in the background with General Manager George M. Weiss of the Yankees, after the Clipper had inked another contract with the Bombers for a reported salary of $100,000.

Jolter's $100,000 Tops Richest Club Payroll in Game's History

DiMag Signs for Duplicate of '49 Salary; 'I Feel Great,' He Tells Press

By DAN DANIEL
NEW YORK, N. Y.

Lavish is the word for it. The way that dough is being tossed around the Yankee offices, it makes your bank balance water.

Joe DiMaggio, $100,000, no strings attached. Tommy Henrich, $40,000. Phil Rizzuto, $40,000. Allie Reynolds, $25,000. Joe Page sure to get $35,000. It all will come to the richest payroll in the history of baseball, and it traces to our federal income tax setup.

Time was when a player landing a $10,000 increase and signing a contract for 40 grand came out with exultation. Now he emerges from the George Weiss sanctum with the look of a big business man who just had made a fair-to-middling deal. He says, "I got what I wanted, but the club could have given me more and lost nothing by it. Instead of the Yankees handing it to Uncle Sam, I get the chance to do so."

The first successful Yankee to encounter Weiss in a salary discussion was Reynolds. He visited George on the morning of January 20. Wahoo got nowhere and left, registering discouragement.

Weiss apparently had decided to hold firm. The dope was that he had set himself to begin whittling DiMaggio's base pay by 25 per cent and to offer the Clipper a bonus contract under which he still could get a hundred grand if he played 130 games. The idea was to look ahead with an eye to the rule which prevents cutting a player more than 25 per cent any year.

Dan and Del soften George.

However, on the evening of January 20, Weiss talked with Dan Topping and Del Webb, owners of the Yankees, over the telephone.

George also had a long distance conversation with DiMaggio, who was in San Francisco.

"Don't be tough on the boys," said Topping. Webb must have made some reference of the tax setup. Then the fat contracts began to pour out of George's office like spring flood waters over a dam.

When Rizzuto came out of Weiss' office, he said, "George has been softened up. I am going to tip off all the unsigned boys to dash in here and grab while Weiss is in this mood."

DiMaggio came into town, January 23, and attended the Charlie Keller dinner held that night. Joe was happy and carefree and tipped the fact that he already had made his deal with the club.

The following afternoon, with the newsreels grinding, Joe signed a one-year contract for $100,000.

Weiss refused to talk about the salary, but Red Patterson's dope sheet on Joe, listing all his salaries, had a $100,000 figure for 1949, which meant a hundred grand for 1950.

DiMaggio said, "I feel great. No pains, no twinges, no spurs in the heels. Maybe I can go through an entire training season and even play the pennant-opener. I sure have had rotten luck in the past. Now I look forward to some compensating breaks.

"We will have to knock down the Red Sox again. They will be rougher. The Tigers could be tougher. The Athletics? I can't see them better than fifth.

"I will return to San Francisco on February 3 and go back to golf.

"I have become quite a golf addict," related Joe. "I used to joke about those links nuts. Now they can kid me, because I have it pretty badly. I hope to break 100 for the first time before I leave San Francisco for St. Petersburg, Fla.

"Once I start training, I will drop golf. I am sure that the baseball and golf swings do not get on together very well.

"Some day, when I am through as a ball player, I will give golf a real go-

Other Yanks Get Luscious Pacts; Team's Liberality Laid to Income Tax Setup

ing over. It is exercise. It is a stimulus."

Joe was more sunburned than he ever is during the summer.

"I plan to be on two more championship teams. After that? Well, why don't you write the ticket for me?" Joe laughed.

Just what will the ticket read? There are a lot of folks around here who believe Joe will be the next pilot of the Bombers.

But there also are a lot who tell you that Tommy Henrich holds a priority.

Rating Joe With the Babe— $545,000 Toward $840,000

NEW YORK, N.Y.—With a $100,000 contract for 1950, Joe DiMaggio will have collected $545,750 from the Yankees in salary when October rolls around.

Joe started with $7,500 in 1936. Here are comparative DiMaggio and Babe Ruth figures:

DiMaggio		Ruth	
1936	$ 7,500	1920	$ 20,000
1937	15,000	1921	30,000
1938	25,000	1922	52,000
1939	27,500	1923	52,000
1940	32,000	1924	52,000
1941	37,500	1925	52,000
1942	43,750	1926	52,000
1943 ⎫	In	1927	70,000
1944 ⎬	Serv-	1928	70,000
1945 ⎭	ice	1929	70,000
1946	43,750	1930	80,000
1947	43,750	1931	80,000
1948	70,000	1932	75,000
1949	100,000	1933	50,000
1950	100,000	1934	35,000
Total	$545,750	Total	$840,000

'Howdy, Fans, This Is Joe' Jolter Jolts Radio World

DiMaggio Already Thinking of Post-Diamond Security

By WILL CONNOLLY
Of the San Francisco Chronicle
SAN FRANCISCO, Calif.

When Joe DiMaggio comes to the end of his days in baseball, he'd like to pursue a new career in radio.

Big Joe is already in radio and doing all right. Late last month, he went to New York, where he cut seven records in five days for his weekly program on CBS called the "Joe DiMaggio Show."

"That's quite a chore—transcribing seven 30-minute shows in five days," Joe said before his departure. "But I like it. It's a lot of fun. My friends tell me I can earn a living in radio after I'm too old for baseball. The deal sounds good to me."

DiMag, at the moment, has no ambition of becoming a sportscaster of games. He prefers the entertainment end, which he is doing now. Broadcasting games requires special training, he says. His show embraces small boys in the studio audience, and, having a son of his own, he dotes on this kind of stuff.

No Thought of Managing

But what about graduating to manager of a big league club, say, the Yankees? Wouldn't that be down his alley, more so than radio work?

"I haven't given a thought yet to managing," Joe said. "After all, I'm not decrepit at 35. But even if I do become a manager I could follow radio in the off-season, I think."

Recently, while spinning the dial, we accidentally tuned in on Di-Maggio's program. The guy is good. We were pleasantly surprised, for most ball players are not exactly Arthur Godfreys on the wireless.

DiMag's voice and manner were just as appealing as those of the professional CBS announcer in New York. In fact, it was hard to tell them apart.

Somewhere along the line, the shy, anti-social DiMaggio of the Seal days has picked up an enormous amount of polish and front. He is a man of limited formal education and never was famous as a book scholar in North Beach.

But lo and behold, he rattles on in a rich, deep voice on a national broadcast without stumbling over a syllable. You'd think he had been born contemporaneously with Marconi.

Of course, the script is written for him, as it is for 99 percent of radio artists—especially comedians—but even so, he handles the language in crisp, sure fashion.

Not all the program is rehearsed. Kids in the studio are invited to shoot questions at him. Joe handles the impromptu material with equal aplomb.

Such culture in his voice and such poise in his microphone manner. The Basil Rathbone touch.

This inspired us to ask a rude question:

"Hey Joe, have you been taking one of those Dale Carnegie charm courses? Or voice training?"

"Nope. Never took a lesson in my life," DiMag lapsed into San Franciscoese. "I guess my voice became heavier as I grew older.

"I was encouraged to try radio by broadcasters around the American League circuit. They were nice enough to say that I sounded good on those 'spot' interviews in the dugout and clubhouse. Gosh, I had no idea I had a mike voice until they pushed me into it."

* * *

Kids Stump Joe

Kids in the studio gallery give him a bad time, DiMag owns up. For expediency's sake, six or eight boys are selected beforehand by the producer. They are supposed to submit their questions in writing.

"They cross me up," DiMag laughs. "I am all set to answer what do I think of Ted Williams, for example, but the kid who wrote that on a slip of paper only ten minutes before changes his mind. He gets up before a live mike and blurts: 'Joe, were you the teacher's pet in grammar school?'

"They catch me unprepared. You have got to be fast on the trigger to keep up with the ten- and 12-year olds. The things they ask!"

Our evaluation of the new Joe is supported by Stanley McCaffrey, editor of the California alumni monthly and before that first baseman on Clint Evans' varsity nine a decade ago.

McCaffrey happened to be in New York on October 1, the day DiMag was lionized in Yankee Stadium. Being a horsehide nut, McCaffrey went to the ball game.

The Cal man told us later: "Darnedest thing I ever saw or heard. DiMaggio stole the show from nationally-known radio men. His address was more articulate and his voice came over the public address system better. The mike was at home plate.

"DiMaggio was sharp enough to begin his short talk with an apology to fans in the cheap seats. He explained that he had to turn his back on them in order to face the mike. They roared approval."

* * *

Dom Wider in Shoulders!

What we didn't know before is that Dominic, the infanta or dauphin of the DiMaggio dynasty, has the widest shoulders of all. This was brought out in one of Joe's broadcasts. A small boy raised the issue. A little monster would.

Big Joe had to confess that Brother Dom is two inches broader across the shoulders, though you'd never guess it to look at him. Dominic wears glasses and has a scrawny neck. He gives the appearance of frailness. A strong wind would blow him away. That's what you think.

"Dom is a compact package," Brother Joe diagnoses. "It's true his shoulders are broader than mine. I have sloping shoulders. I

Has Right Voice

Joe at the Mike

get my power to smack the ball and give it a ride from my chest muscles. Across the chest I am thick."

J. DiMag has tried his hand at golf this winter for the first time. Heretofore he hibernated in bed or in cinemas.

"I'm not playing golf as a game," he specifies. "I'm lousy at it. I'm simply using golf as an excuse to get out in the open and stretch my legs. I recognize that walking over the hills is good for my legs, now that I'm in the middle 30s."

DiMag is frank to confess that he felt pretty good at carding a 104 in the first time out. This is a pushover. Big Joe discovered that a round of golf makes him as hungry as a she wolf.

"I didn't have much of an appetite before this," he says. "Also, I couldn't sleep eight hours at a stretch. But after hacking away at what I call golf, I gobble up everything my mother puts on my plate.

"I'm trying to put on weight. In the World's Series I was down to 179 pounds. I'd like to fatten up to 212 pounds as a cushion. I'll lose some in spring camp. I reckon I'll be at my best at 204."

The man says 204. We ribbon clerks think we're as fat as a Christmas goose at 155 pounds.

DiMag is a big guy and on him 204 pounds look good. Not an ounce to spare.

DiMag Says He's Fit to Play 154

By the United Press.

SAN FRANCISCO, Feb. 15.—Joe DiMaggio, tanned and in the pink of condition after a winter of golfing, predicted today he would be ready to start the season and play a full 154 games.

"I'm in better all-around condition than at any time since I started in the major leagues," said the big Yankee outfielder.

"My legs are as strong and in as good shape as any youngster just coming up to the majors. My heel is in perfect condition. In fact, it feels as though nothing ever had happened to it."

DiMaggio said he would leave by plane late in the month for the Florida training camp.

"I still have a bit of dental work that must be done," he said, "but I'm planning on playing golf as often as possible.

"I weigh 202 pounds now and would like to weigh 208 when the season opens. The only way I can put on weight is to get lots of exercise—and golf is the thing to do it."

In all his years in the majors, DiMaggio has only started two seasons at his regular post. Always an injury or illness of some kind kept him on the bench. Joe said he had played only one full season—in 1942 when he played in 153 games.

DiMag credits golf with his fine condition now and says he plans to spend all his winters in San Francisco in the future.

"After my baseball ability starts to dwindle," said the $100,000-a-year star, "then I'll take up golf seriously."

He hasn't been able to break 100 on the tough Sharp Park oceanside course. His best round has been 103.

DiMag predicted a five-way race for the pennant among New York, Boston, Philadelphia, Cleveland and Detroit. He expected Joe Page would have another great season. "He has a rubber arm that always is good."

He refused to predict how long he would continue as a major leaguer.

"I don't know, and neither does anyone else," he said. "I might be good for two or three years—or five or six.

"Anyway, the way I feel right now—and your baseball ability depends upon the way you feel —I'm good for quite a few years yet."

Joe DiMaggio and a variety of friends. Top, left to right: the Clipper and his manager, Casey Stengel; with Charlie Keller and Tommy Henrich at a dinner given in honor of the three ''Greatest Ever'' ballplayers by the New York Writers' Association; and with Ethel Barrymore, an enthusiastic baseball fan, at the Stork Club. Below, left to right: with his New York attorney, Julian Rosenthal; eating dinner with Toots Shor at the latter's restaurant; with the great W. C. Fields.

Setting the Pace

By GRANTLAND RICE

Where are the champions I once knew?
Lost in the Land where dreams came true?
Dempsey, Ruth and the Slashing Cobb,
Jones and Thorpe on the winning job—
Matty and Johnson—Alex and Cy,
Rainbows gone from a golden sky?
"Over the hills"—the gray winds say,
"Over the hills and far away."

———

LOS ANGELES, Feb. 20.—Joe DiMaggio arrived from San Francisco a few days ago to call on some of his southern California pals. While in this vicinity Joe admitted he was harboring or nursing a very pleasant dream. "That dream," DiMag said, "is to start the season in first class condition and play in more than 140 games. I'm tired of being sick or hurt at the start of too many seasons."

Joe never looked better. He has recovered his lost weight, his color is good and he is evidently a physically fit man.

"I didn't come into baseball yesterday," he said. "I've been around a long time—about 18 years at San Francisco and New York. There are very few now around who were on hand when I went East some 15 years ago. But I still don't feel old. My throwing arm never felt better."

Grantland Rice.

"How about the heel?" we asked, giving Joe his chance to answer this query for the 200th time.

"This time I expect to be all set," he said. "I won't be in quite as big a rush in my training and I have a special shoe that helps protect the heel."

One factor that has kept Joe young so long is his effortless style. He makes every play look easy. There is never any sign of straining. He is a drifting, shifting ghost with perfect timing.

An outfield that carries DiMaggio in center is on its way to being a very good one. Certainly from Gene Woodling, Hank Bauer, Cliff Mapes and others, Casey Stengel should have little trouble in setting up a high-grade outfield.

DiMaggio recognizes the all-round strength of the Red Sox.

"They'll get much better pitching this year," Joe said, "and we'll have to keep moving. The Red Sox won't be any 12 or 13 games back around July Fourth this year. But we are not due to get so many rough bumps again. I don't believe that could happen twice. All we need is for Rizzuto and Page to have the same sort of season they had in 1949. If they do. I don't think anything can stop us."

DiMaggio thinks, with many others, that the Tigers will be the most improved team this season. "They have a lot of pitchers who can bother you and that's where a flock of ball games are won," Joe admitted. "More than most people know about."

———

IS JOE GOING SOFT ?

any more like these, and joe is through

SPRAINED ANKLE and sun lamp burns delayed Joe's start with Yanks in 1936.

TORN MUSCLES in calf of his right leg kept DiMaggio out of the lineup for several weeks early in the 1939 season.

Joe isn't getting any younger . . .

and further injuries might

ring down the curtain

on the greatest career since Babe Ruth

BONE SPUR in his foot caused outfielder to miss 1947 spring training, and at end of 1948, he developed one on other foot.

■ Plagued by the memories of a vast assortment of physical ailments, Joe DiMaggio stands at the cross roads in one of the most distinguished careers in the history of the major leagues. The great center fielder of the Yankees reached his 35th birthday last November 25th, and is now at what ball players call the dangerous age. Athletically speaking, only a freak of nature would be expected to show improvement as he moves toward the shady side of 40. In the case of DiMaggio, there's no room for improvement. The Yankee Clipper came to New York from the San Francisco Seals 14 years ago and he has been on top all the way, exclusive of his three years in the army. He played only half of the 1949 season, and for those 76 games, his batting average of .346 was four points better than that of the American League's leader, George Kell of Detroit. But as he prepares to open another campaign, he must wonder when he can expect to slide off the pedestal, and the descent is sometimes swift. How long can he maintain the batting form that has carved deep furrows in the brows of opposing pitchers? And the speed afoot that has evoked moans of anguish from the batsmen who have watched him catch mighty clouts to distant pastures? DiMaggio insists he's physically fit to play a full season in 1950. He's deeply tanned after a winter of relaxation in California, but his black thatch has turned gray around the temples, and only in the wear and tear of the rigorous day-by-day campaign will he be able to prove he's as good as he looks and says he feels.

No other ball player who reached DiMaggio's stature, and they have been exceedingly few, was forced to go through the physical tortures endured by the tall, slim San Franciscan ever since the day he dug his spikes into a baseball diamond. Ty Cobb remained in the major leagues for 24 years because, as Cobb himself has pointed out, he was fortunate enough to escape serious injury and illness. DiMaggio's troubles have been in varying degrees of severity, but they have been almost uninterrupted. Stories of his brittleness preceded him to New York. As a minor leaguer on the Pacific Coast, he compiled a fabulous record, but in the second of his three seasons with the San Francisco club, he was benched for a third of the time by a troublesome knee. Most of the big league scouts who were on his trail looked askance at this lame-legged fellow, but the Yankees decided to risk it, and because of the question about his physical fitness, they negotiated one of the greatest bargains ever. DiMaggio was purchased for $25,000 and five minor league players, none of whom ever amounted to very much. The Yankees had reason to be concerned about their deal before Joe played a single American League game for them.

He reported at their training camp in St. Petersburg, Fla., in 1936, promptly sprained his ankle, and in taking heat treatments, his foot was burned by a sun-ray lamp. That was the beginning of a well-filled medical chart. The following year a tonsillectomy was just a minor matter, in 1939 he tore the muscles in his right leg sliding into a base, and in 1940 a similar maneuver in a Brooklyn exhibition game resulted in a twisted knee on the eve of the season's inaugural.

During his army service, in 1944 and 1945, Joe was frequently hospitalized by a bad case of ulcers, and in the postwar period his difficulties have become more serious. Before the end of the first season after his return, 1946, his left heel began to pain him and during the winter he underwent an operation for the removal of a bone spur. He went to spring training in 1947 on a crutch and before long was back in the hospital for further treatment to the slow-healing heel. Before the 1948 campaign closed, Joe was hobbling again. Now it was the right heel and more surgery during the off-season. This time he missed the first 65 games, and in late September, a bout with pneumonia sidelined him for two more weeks. Altogether, DiMaggio has been out of the opening day lineup for seven of his eleven seasons of big league competition. Of course while he was in there, and except for 1949 his troubles were mainly of the pre-season variety, he was superb. Only once has his average fallen below .300, he has won two batting championships, a couple of home run titles, has thrice been called the American League's most valuable player, and has played in eight world series.

Normally affable, but inherently shy, DiMaggio is inclined to brood when troubles weigh heavily upon him. Only once has he been irascible, and that was when interviewers who besieged him in Johns Hopkins Hospital, Baltimore, last spring, insisted upon asking him if he thought he'd ever play again.

Ruminating over his future, the Yankee outfielder can glance at the records if he'd like to determine whether 35 is old. Players who reached the big leagues early in the century apparently were of a hardier race, or perhaps the game, without arc lights, didn't take as heavy a physical toll. The immortal Babe Ruth played until he was 40, and in his final season, with the Boston Braves, was good enough to bash three home runs in one game. Cobb and Honus Wagner went to 42, Eddie Collins and Nap Lajoie to 41, Walter Johnson and Tris Speaker to 40, Willie Keeler, George Sisler and Max Carey to 39, Harry Hooper to 38, Frank Chance and Sam Crawford to 37. Harry Heilmann, three times American League batting champion, was through at 36, and at the same age, Rogers Hornsby, a .400 hitter in the National League, played 100 games for the last time, then eased off for a few subsequent seasons. On the other side of the ledger, one finds Pie Traynor and Mickey Cochrane, who had their last big years at 34 and 32, respectively. Christy Mathewson, Duffy Lewis, Johnny Evers, Charley Grimm and Chick Hafey, all of whom were at the end of the string before they reached 35. Oddly enough, the great Yankee teams of the mid-1920s, except for Ruth, were notable for stars who were dimmed too early. Joe Dugan and Bob Meusel were on the way out at 32, Everett Scott left the majors at 33 and Wallie Pipp departed when he was a year older. That crew was inclined to sneer at training regulations, and Miller Huggins, who managed the club to six American League championships, was in the habit of warning his athletes, "You fellows are doing all right now, but you're cutting five or six years from your baseball careers."

Huggins proved to be a wise prophet, although he didn't live to see his prediction come true. DiMaggio, the ideal ball player on and off the field, never required that type of admonition, and if he can evade the doctors in the immediate future, he may be able to go along for a few more years. "I'd like to play with two more championship teams," he says. With the proper supporting cast that desire may be fulfilled.

Mama DiMaggio's home cooking, enjoyed by the Yankee Clipper throughout the Winter, has restored the weight Joe lost during the late season bout with virus. As he limped off the field in Brooklyn after the World Series, he was down to 178 pounds. When he came into New York to sign his 1950 contract he was up to 205, the closest he has been to his normal playing poundage in several years. A healthy DiMaggio is bound to be a menace at the plate. Older players can always hit. It's their legs that invariably undermine them.

how old is 35?
for these supermen, not so old...

BABE RUTH slowed down in later years but continued heavy slugging until he was 40.

WALTER JOHNSON'S trusty right arm went on winning ball games for the Senators after usual retirement age.

TRIS SPEAKER, considered one of the game's greatest outfielders, successfully chased fly balls until he was 40.

CARL HUBBELL baffled batters with screwball long after the lefty passed his 35th birthday.

for these, quite old...

MICKEY COCHRANE, heavily overburdened with problems of managing and playing, retired at 34.

PIE TRAYNOR legendary infielder, found going to rough at 3rd base, he took refuge in dugout at 32.

for joe...

BOB MEUSEL faded swiftly along with other big Yankee stars of the early 20's.

WALLY PIPP was somewhat short of 35 when Lou Gehrig replaced him on first base for the Bronx Bombers during the 1925 campaign.

JOE DI MAGGIO plans to keep smiling through the 1950 season. At 35, Joe says he would like to play with two more championship teams and contribute his share to victories.

Stengel Has Word For DiMaggio's Training-Caution

Special to World-Telegram and Sun.

ST. PETERSBURG, March 4. —Casey Stengel today began to pay closer attention to Joe DiMaggio.... "The Clipper runs well, without favoring that heel, and looks great at the plate," Casey said. "I would like him to take it easy right through the training season, but he may have different ideas.

"I want DiMaggio to play only a few innings each exhibition game," Casey went on. "But if Joe prefers to stick around, that will be his privilege.... I said I would let him train himself, and that still goes."

Stengel is giving more time to bunting than any other manager in the business is likely to be devoting to the art of using the bastinado.... The pitching machine has been moved to a softball diamond out in right at Miller Huggins Field, and there Johnny Neun feeds Iron Mike, and the boys keep bunting and bunting.

Stengel said to one of the kids, "Now drag one," and the boy did not know what was meant.... The fact is, there is not a single able drag bunter in the major league.... Jackie Jensen, right-handed hitter, proved surprisingly adept in bunting down the first-base line.

HOPES TO KEEP BUSY - - - By Alan Maver

JOE DIMAGGIO, THE YANKEES' ACTIVE IMMORTAL, HOPES HIS 12TH WILL BE ONE OF HIS BETTER AND BUSIER SEASONS — SO DOES STENGEL!

ACHILLES SHOULD COMPLAIN

A POPOUT LEFT ARM IS THE NEWEST ADDITION TO THE ROSTER OF DiMAGGIO INFIRMITIES WHICH IN THE PAST HAVE MADE HIM MISS AN AVERAGE OF 20 GAMES PER SEASON— ONLY ONCE HAS JOE PLAYED A FULL 154-GAME SCHEDULE!

ALAN MAVER

Distributed by King Features Syndicate

Joe Blistering Again—but With Hot Bat

By DANIEL,
Staff Writer.

MIAMI, March 17.—Joe DiMaggio charged into town with the Yankees today, and found much of the classic atmosphere of last October re-created.

A March exhibition, even between the Bombers and the Dodgers on so gala an occasion as St. Patrick's night, hardly could be rated of devastating import. But for tonight's meeting Miami picked up where New York left off last October.

It was a grand fiesta particularly for DiMaggio, who never before had appeared in this area. In fact, it was only the second showing of the Yankees in Miami in the club's history. They came here from Jacksonville in 1920 to engage the world champion Reds.

DiMaggio arrived in spectacular form. He had contributed a homer and two singles, and driven in five runs, in a brief, three-inning participation in the Bombers' 13–2 victory over Washington, in St. Petersburg.

Giuseppe had achieved the distinction of producing tallies in his seven most recent trips to the plate, and already his runs-driven-in total came to nine. With six blows in nine efforts, he was batting .667.

There were many indications that the Yankee Clipper was moving into one of his most successful post-war seasons. His four-bagger off left-hander Lloyd Hittle of the Senators, came with two on in the second inning, and rifled over the left field fence at the 440-foot mark.

**Stengel Has Mound Plans
Set for Miami Tilts.**

On arrival here for the arc light battle with Brooklyn, and afternoon engagements with the Red Sox tomorrow and Sunday, Casey Stengel announced that he would send rookie Dick Carr and the veteran Allie Reynolds against Barney Shotton's pennant favorites.

It is conceivable that the Dodgers were not too greatly pleased with Casey's selection of Reynolds. Allie's name brought back for Brooklyn unpleasant memories of the things Wahoo did to that outfit last October, when he beat Don Newcombe in the series

opener, 1 to 0, and saved Ed Lopat's victory in the fourth contest by stopping the Superbas cold in the sixth inning.

"I will pitch Frank Shea and Bob Porterfield in tomorrow's game with Boston, and Fred Sanford and Wally Hood on Sunday," Stengel said.

Ready for relief calls was Joe Page. The left-hander, unveiled in yesterday's affair with Washington, pitched the last two innings without allowing a run. Irving Noren, Bucky Harris' $60,000 rookie from Brooklyn's Hollywood farm, got to Joe for a single.

Phil Rizzuto and Yogi Berra made their debuts in the mauling of the Senators. The Scooter drew a couple of passes, and Yogi matched that little trick, plus a single.

DiMag Starts Regular Play Tomorrow

By DANIEL.
Staff Writer.

ST. PETERSBURG, March 23. —"Joe DiMaggio returns to center field against the Tigers at Lakeland tomorrow and will play against Brooklyn in Miami on Saturday and Sunday," Casey Stengel announced today just before the Yankees took the field against the Cardinals.

"I am ready to play today," said DiMaggio.

"Joe is all set to go," added Dr Sidney Gaynor, orthopedic specialist with the New York club. "He no longer is bothered by that Charley horse."

Continuing to discuss his condition, DiMaggio made light of his old shoulder ailment.

"It is true that from time to time my left arm, not the throwing one, does jump out of position, but don't write that I am washed up as a ball player," DiMaggio laughed.

"The popping usually happens when I am relaxed. It does not affect my baseball playing."

Stengel said, "DiMaggio's left arm popped last season, in our last series in Cleveland, when he tumbled in stealing second. However, if this trouble has recurred recently, I do not know about it."

**'Popping No Secret,'
DiMaggio Insists.**

DiMaggio went on, "That I have had that popping trouble has been no secret, has it? At any rate, it was not my intention to keep it quiet.

"The last time it popped was in

November. I played golf since, I have been hitting well here, and again assure you that I am not handicapped seriously.

"Sure, the greatest years of my baseball career are not in front of me, but watch me this season, anyway."

Di Maggio has made eight hits in 13 trips for an average of .615. One of his blows was a 440-foot homer, one of the longest he has blasted here since he came to the Yankees in 1936.

"I could play Joe today," said Stengel when the conversation shifted back to the Yankee manager.

"But I want to take every precaution, and not because of any arm-popping either.

"I am sorry that we have run into alarmist stories. Dr. Gaynor says Tommy Henrich is ready, but I am not going to play him for just a while. Johnny Mize still can't throw, so he is out, too.

"That scare about Rizzuto is founded on nothing serious. Phil plays here today. Because of his wife's condition, I will permit him to pass up the trip to Miami. But he will play with our B team against the Tigers Saturday and Sunday."

The Yankees do not look good. They have won only six out of 12 even 1st to Washington, 11 to 9 in yesterday's eight-inning affair at Orlando.

But before long Casey will have a regular lineup in action, and Joe will be out there regularly even with the trick shoulder.

All Boston Eyes DiMaggio, But Yanks Wait on Tommy

Special to World-Telegram and Sun.

BOSTON, April 18.—All eyes were on Joe DiMaggio here today, as the Yankees faced a series of four games with the Red Sox. There will be morning and afternoon contests, with the annual Boston marathon sandwiched in tomorrow, Patriot's Day, a legal holiday in Massachusetts.

DiMaggio ruined the Sox last season, and the way he has been going he very well could do it again. Joe finished training with a batting average of .403.

Boston fans hated to hark back to June 28, 29 and 30, 1949. It was on the 28th that the Yankee Clipper made his season's debut after having missed the first 65 games.

In those three contests here, DiMaggio hit four homers and a single in 11 efforts, and drove in nine runs.

In the last two games of the season, in the Stadium, DiMaggio, weak from a pneumonia attack, helped inspire the Bombers in their pennant-clinching achievement.

To be able to play in the opener was quite an experience for DiMaggio. He did it in 1948, missed the inaugural in 1947, played in it in 1946, and was out of most of the first battles before the war. He missed the opening game in his first season with the Yankees in 1936.

Henrich's Work
In Boston Vital.

Whereas the Red Sox and local fans will be watching DiMaggio, the eyes of the Yankees will be fastened on Tommy Henrich. What Old Reliable does in the Fens will be of ultraimportance to the New York club, and of vital significance in the race.

If Henrich finds it impossible to play now, it is difficult to see when he would be able to take care of first base.

One thing may be set down as definite. Tommy Henrich, the outfielder, has ended his career.

Henrich the first baseman, on the other hand, may go on for several years more if he can weather the next fortnight without mishap.

With Henrich at first base, the Yankees may be counted on as strong contenders.

With Tommy out of action, the Bombers will face a most rugged adventure.

Stengel Cites DiMaggio For Success in Hub

By DANIEL.

"Joe DiMaggio's all-around form was the most important feature of our two-out-of-three visit to Boston," said Casey Stengel today, as the Yankees moved into the Stadium to open the local American League campaign.

"I am not ignoring the important fact that Tommy Henrich, whose left knee had appeared a serious problem, played through with skill in the field, and hit a homer, two triples and a single, and drove in seven runs.

"However, DiMaggio was a tremendous factor in every possible way. His six hits, for a .375 average, his spectacular fielding, and the way he stood up there, defying that Boston pitcher, made Joe the standout, in my opinion.

"Our number three man up there was Yogi Berra. His half dozen hits gave him a .400 record. But he was not successful at the plate alone."

Henrich Confident
He Will Make It.

"Berra has made himself a really fine catcher. He is more mobile than ever, and the pitchers will tell you he has a certain intuition which is so important in the handling of hurlers.

"I believe that Berra can make himself still more useful if he will run bases. He is much faster than he is given credit for being.

"I don't mind telling you that I was not too unhappy over having been rained out in Boston yesterday.

"However, I am sure that Joe McCarthy welcomed the layoff more than I did.

"As a matter of fact, the schedule makers should have given us the day off after the two games on Wednesday, which kept us in Fenway Park from 9 in the morning until long after 6 in the evening."

Henrich came into the Stadium with high confidence in his ability to remain in the New York lineup. That he had been eliminated as a possibility in right field hardly disturbed Old Reliable.

"I think it is safe for you to dismiss me as a convalescent, and to expect me to go right on playing," said Henrich. "That is, unless I run into another bat rack, or some other such nonsense. I certainly discovered a lot of odd ways to get hurt last season."

Stengel landed in the Bronx with no jubilation over the way his starting pitchers had reacted to their Fenway opportunities. Allie Reynolds, Vic Raschi and Ed Lopat all had failed to last through, and Casey had got a total of only 13 innings out of his star trio. However, there was Engine Company No. 11, Joe Page.

It developed that Lopat, who had been having slight trouble with his arm, tightened up in the cold Wednesday afternoon. "I should have taken Ed out in the sixth," Stengel admitted. "When he walked Dominic, Johnny Pesky and Ted in succession in the seventh, I didn't feel so well."

Bob Porterfield no longer shows a limp from that bang on the left shin he suffered from a Dr. Brown liner on Tuesday, and is scheduled to pitch against the Senators tomorrow.

Plain Dealer Photo by Norbert Yassanye

NO. 2,000 FOR YANKEE CLIPPER. Joe Di-Maggio, the New York Yankees' brilliant center fielder, lashes the 2,000 hit of his major league career in the seventh inning of last night's game at the stadium. It was a single to left off Chick Pieretti that scored Gene Woodling, who had doubled. The catcher is Jim Hegan and the umpire, Ed Hurley. The Yanks triumphed, 8-2.

DI MAGGIO FORGETS PAINS AS HE CRASHES 2,000 CLASS

By Charles Heaton

"It's been a long time coming this season and it brought a feeling of relief."

That was Joltin' Joe DiMaggio's reaction to his second single last night at the stadium—the 2,000th hit in the American League for the famed Yankee Clipper.

It was a looper into centerfield in the seventh inning that turned the trick and moved him into the select company of Luke Appling of the Chicago White Sox and Philadelphia's Wally Moses as the only active players to reach that figure.

A broad grin split the usual poker-face of the great center-fielder as he posed for the photographers kissing the ball that he had belted over Pitcher Marino Pieretti's head a half hour before.

After Larry Doby returned the ball to the infield, the tiny hurler walked over to first base and handed the baseball to DiMaggio as a souvenir.

"The hits have been so few and far between this season that it almost seemed I never was going to get there," said Joe who is in his 13th season with the Yankees. "I feel great about getting into such an exclusive club though. It's a long grind and there haven't been many that went all the way to 2,000."

Cobb Holds Record

The brilliant Ty Cobb holds the major league record for the most base hits with 4,191 but his came over a span of 24 years with Detroit and Philadelphia.

DiMag started this season with 1,947 hits and last night's game with 1,998. His single off Bob Lemon, the hit that sent the Cleveland starter to the showers in the third inning, was his other safety.

There was some doubt about the Clipper playing when the Yankees hit town on Monday as he had to withdraw from action Sunday with leg cramps.

However, the Big Bomber was not feeling any pain after the Yankees' 8-2 victory over the tribe.

"Everything's okay tonight," declared DiMaggio. "No leg cramps, no sore arm, no aching heel. Just feel great."

Two admirers ran out on the playing field and up to DiMaggio in the eighth inning and Joe's half swing on what would have been a third strike in the third got Plate Umpire Ed Hurley into an imbroglio with Lemon and Manager Lou Boudreau.

"It probably seemed as though those kids wanted autographs but that wasn't it," Joe explained. "The first one handed me a letter, which I haven't read yet, and the second one just said he wanted to shake hands."

About the controversial swing, DiMaggio himself was in some doubt.

"I honestly don't believe I broke my wrists but I might have slipped some as I tried to hold back. At any rate, I figure Hurley was in a better position to observe it than I was."

Ed Lopat, who hiked his jinx over the redskins to a lifetime record of 25 victories and six defeats, was at a loss to explain his ability to beat the tribe.

"I didn't pitch a particularly good game," the wily southpaw declared. "My control was poor and the heat had me tired in the late innings. I just throw the same pitches up there and if any complex it's on their part, not mine."

In 1950, a happy Joe DiMaggio holds the ball that he belted for his 2,000th major league hit.

The two greatest hitters of their time: Joe DiMaggio of the New York Yankees and Ted Williams of the Boston Red Sox.

This oil portrait, which captures the quintessential Joe DiMaggio, was painted in 1950 by Victor Freudeman.

Yankees Riding High Again As DiMag Goes on Hit Spree

By MILTON GROSS

Cleveland, May 22—Roaring through the west like a team possessed, the Yankees have picked up three and a half lengths at the mid-point of a two-week tour and show promise of making their 2½-game league lead a mere jumping off point to another championship binge.

At no point this season have the Bombers been so hot. They've won six straight and 13 of their past 15 games as their hitting, fielding, running, throwing and competitive spirit appear finally to have blended into something that is a fair imitation of an unbeatable combination if, in fact, it isn't so.

When the Stengels left home last Monday a game out of the lead after blowing a 7—1 margin to bow to the lowly Athletics, their pitching staff appeared shot, Joe DiMaggio was dragging a fading bat to the plate and the future looked wretched indeed, with Tommy Henrich's left knee weaker than it had been since spring training opened.

79,570 Attendance

Henrich has been on the bench since the first six innings of this tour, but the Yankees appear not to have missed him, just as they struggled through the first half of last season without DiMaggio.

That last game they blew to the Athletics after winning five straight is all but forgotten. Equally lost in the past is the fear that DiMag would continue being a drag to the offense. The western air has braced the Clipper. The sight of his happy hunting grounds here in the Indians' tepee has made him a menacing scalp hunter.

Before 79,570 paid fans, the fourth largest attendance in all of baseball's history, DiMag yesterday gave one of the best exhibitions of his career and so did the Yankees as a whole. They whipped the Indians, who had won 9 of their past 11, by 14—5 in the opener as DiMag drove in six

runs with two homers, one clearing full bases, and walloped the Tribe, 12—4, in a nightcap that saw the Yankees reach a new 19-hit high for the season. Joe collected two of the hits in this one and banged home another pair of tallies.

Raschi Goes Tonight

When the Yankees are playing in form, their games invariably resolve themselves into statistical surveys. That is what happened on this trip. With the exception of Vic Raschi, who comes off the sick list tonight to battle the Tribe's Mike Garcia, himself a refugee from the trainer's bay, every starter on this tour has hurled a complete game. Five victories have been route-going jobs.

Allie Reynolds has paced the pitchers with two wins, opening the trip with a nine-strikeout shutout performance in St. Louis

and fanning another nine yesterday as he outgamed the Indians in the nightcap for his fourth triumph of the season. Ed Lopat also gained his fourth in the opener.

Thus with two shutouts and one one-run game being hurled against the opposition, Reynolds, Tommy Byrne, Lopat and Fred Sanford yielded only 19 runs while the Yankees have pounded out 53 in six games. Besides enabling Henrich to rest to the fullest, this overpowering attack and forceful hurling necessitated Joe Page being beckoned from the bullpen but once since leaving home. Page needs rest, too for the day must come when he'll be called on for concentrated relief hurling.

POST PITCHING FORM

Jerry Mitchell (11-11) picks the Dodgers.
Milton Gross (14-10) picks the Indians.

Club	Pitchers	1949 Record	1949 vs Club	Lifetime vs Club
Reds	Ramsdell (1—3)	0— 0	0—0	0— 0
DODGERS	Newcombe (2—1)	17— 8	3—1	3— 1
Yankees	Raschi (3—2)	21—10	4—2	9— 4
INDIANS	Garcia (1—1)	14— 5	1—0	1— 0
Senators	Scarborough (3—3)	13—11	1—3	3— 9
Tigers	Newhouser (0—1)	18—11	3—0	28—18
Red Sox	McDermott (3—1)	5— 4	2—0	2— 0
White Sox	Kuzava (0—3)	10— 6	1—2	1— 2

TODAY'S LINE

Tigers 9½-10½ over Senators.

TONIGHT'S LINE

Dodgers 11-13 over Reds; Yanks 5½-6½ over Indians; Red Sox 9-11 over White Sox.

The home run Joe DiMaggio has just hit in this June 1950 game against the Chicago White Sox at Yankee Stadium traveled 425 feet before dropping into the left field seats. It was a three-run homer and provided the margin of victory in the 6–3 win. The Yankees waiting to greet him are Yogi Berra (8), Hank Bauer (25), and Gene Woodling (14). The White Sox catcher is Ed Malone and the umpire is Ed Rommel.

DiMaggio's Switch To 1st Base Is Aimed At Prolonging Career

By ARCH MURRAY
New York Post Correspondent

Washington, July 3—The one basic thought behind the stunning but carefully premeditated move that today saw Joe DiMaggio, the greatest centerfielder of his time, moving in to plug the old Yankee trouble spot at first base was to prolong a great career. Born neither of desperation nor of panic over the recent Yankee skid, it was calculated simply with the hope of adding a couple of years to the baseball lifetime of one of the game's super-stars.

The idea that led to yesterday's startling announcement in Boston came as no overnight hunch. Recent Yankee failures were a contributing factor, but actually they were of minor consideration. The big thing is that the Yanks don't want to lose DiMaggio's services any sooner than is absolutely necessary. The Bomber brain trust firmly believes this will provide him with a reprieve.

An Unknown Quantity at First

Whether it will or not remains for the future to reveal. There is no evidence that the Clipper can even play the bag. He has played exactly three games in the infield during his years in organized ball. That was in the fall of 1932 when, as a kid of 17, he broke in as a shortstop with San Francisco. It wasn't until the next spring that he became an outfielder.

But Joe is willing to go along with the idea. It didn't take Dan Topping, the Yankee president, long to convince him that it was worth a shot. It was Topping who sold Joe the bill of goods after broaching it to him Saturday night in Boston. DiMag, who doesn't want to reach the sunset any quicker than his bosses want him to, will go along with anything that may stave off the encroaching years.

Joe worked out around the bag briefly at Fenway Park yesterday before the game but he was in his accustomed spot in centerfield during the course of the 15—9 demolition of the Red Sox.

Tommy Henrich, scheduled to play first for possibly the last time yesterday, couldn't make it and Big Jawn Mize took over, contributing a homer and a single to the 13-hit barrage that gave the Yanks a split of the four-game series.

DiMag was a bit self-conscious with photographers snapping him from all angles as he took over his new post in infield practice. But he handled himself with all his natural ease and instinct and there was no indication that he wouldn't be able to do a good job. But time and game-pressure alone can provide the real answer.

Worth the Gamble

If he can make it, it will prove a two-fold miracle for the Yanks. And that is what Stengel is hoping. It would eliminate the worst trouble spot in the Yankee lineup and also enable Stengel to get more use out of his young, strong-armed outfielders who seem ripe for every-day duty. It would put youth, speed and a strong arm in centerfield in the person of Cliff Mapes and give Hank Bauer, who becomes the new regular right-fielder, the chance to play every day he has been asking.

It could be the making of the Yankees in their faltering stand in defense of their world championship. It has been evident for quite a spell that they couldn't make it as they have been constituted. As Stengel said, "I just can't wait for Henrich any more. I've been doing it all season and now it's almost half-gone."

Old Reliable made what was probably his last regular stand the first two days in Boston and the effort was tragic to watch. His knee just won't stand up. Even his straightaway speed has gone and he can't make the quick turns and stops at all.

Still another factor in Stengel's final resolution to put an idea which has been long germinating in his mind into bold action was the Yankees' recent failures against southpaw pitching. They have an overall record of 20 and 12 against left-handers but they have dropped seven out of their last 10 to southpaws. With DiMag at first, Stengel can get another starboard bat in the lineup against the wrongsided breed, the one wielded by Jackie Jensen who will henceforth share left-field with Gene Woodling.

The Washington Post Sports

10   Tuesday, July 4, 1950   ***

This Morning

With Shirley Povich

JOE DI MAGGIO sat by his locker, diligently pounding a pocket to his liking in the first baseman's mitt Johnny Mize provided for the Yankees' newest experiment. "Now if somebody will just show me where first base is, I'm ready," said DiMag.

It was typical Di Mag reaction to a situation. If he was feeling any pressure at being shoved into a new position after 15 years as the league's finest center fielder, it wasn't apparent.

His total experience as a first baseman had been as a kid on the San Francisco sandlots, 19 years ago, but he wasn't letting that throw him. He was as composed as if he were up at the plate with the bases full and 70,000 fans screaming in his ears—you know, the kind of a situation in which Di Maggio is the calmest person in the park.

Out on the field during infield practice, Di Mag drew a swarm of cameramen eager to record his debut as a first baseman. "Shoot your head off, boys" he grinned. "I don't know what kind of a first baseman I am yet, but I can put on an act for you."

POVICH

———

TOMMY HENRICH, who had made a go of it at first base after ten years in the outfield, opined that DiMaggio would "do all right." Henrich said, "He's all ball player. There are a couple of things he'll have to learn about the job, but I don't know anybody who could learn quicker."

There were things like finding the bag with his feet, said Henrich. "Unless you're brought up on first base, you're apt to be groping for the bag with your feet," said Henrich. "Later on, you get the habit, and it's a breeze."

There will be the item, too, about learning how the infielders throw, said Tommy. "Some of 'em throw you balls that sink, others shoot you throws that take off. And Joe may be troubled about when to get off the bag and haul in a wild throw, but his instincts will take care of that after a while.

"And where do you find a ball player with better instincts?" said Henrich. "He won't make us or himself look bad, that I know."

———

THE MAJESTY OF Di Maggio and all the respect he commands in the baseball business is nevertheless no insulation against the barbs from opposing benches. Up in Fenway Park, where he worked out with a first baseman's mitt for the first time on Sunday, Joe became aware of that.

"Hey, Di Mag, better get some shinguards," yelled Birdie Tebbetts.

And at Griffith Stadium yesterday in the pre-game drill, Coach Joe Fitzgerald of the Nats couldn't resist the temptation to prod him. "Hey, Di Mag, you're just a fill-in," hollered Fritz. "They'll have Yogi Berra on first base next week."

The shift of Di Maggio to the infield was Casey Stengel's idea. He squared it with Joe first, in a hotel-room session at Boston Saturday, when he told his troubles to Di Mag. Stengel moaned that the Yankees couldn't use all their good-hitting outfielders; with the rest of the club in a batting slump, better hitters were riding the beach.

First Baseman Joe Collins wasn't hitting, and he couldn't ask pain-wracked Tommy Henrich to fill in, Stengel said, and would Joe try it? "Anyway you can help the club," was the answer he got.

———

IN STENGEL'S VIEW, Di Maggio at first base will be a double blessing to the Yanks. It will enable them to use such hitting outfielders as Bauer, Mapes and Woodling regularly, and bring out the full potential of Rookie Jackie Jensen. But Stengel had something else in mind.

"It will add a couple of years to Di Maggio's playing life," he declared. "Other outfielders stand out there and day-dream, but Di Mag is racing all over the place, backing up everybody's play when he isn't going for the ball himself. At his age, he's getting little rest. As a first baseman, he won't have to go so far."

Stengel broke Di Mag's travels down to a finer point by pointing out, "Joe won't have to take that long trip from the bench into center field and back 16 times a game, either. That's a long way, coming and going. To play first base, he'll just have to cross the diamond from the bench. And when we're in Yankee Stadium, he's not 20 feet from his job."

Shift to Infield Found Joe Ready, Willing, But Unable

'All Set,' Said DiMag, 'If Someone Will Show Me Where First Is in This Park'

By SHIRLEY POVICH

NEW YORK, N. Y.

When the New York Yankees asked Outfielder Joe DiMaggio to try his gloved hand at first base in the nation's most widely-heralded noble experiment since prohibition, they found him ready, willing—and quite unable.

The bright idea lasted only one day, with DiMaggio and the Yankees extricating themselves somewhat gracefully from an embarrassment that threatened appalling proportions.

The coincidence of an injury to Hank Bauer that left the Yankee outfield shorthanded was the official excuse for the return of First Baseman DiMaggio to the center field job he knows best. One nine-inning experience with a first baseman's mitt left DiMaggio quite disenchanted.

"The time for me to learn how to play first base is in spring training, not when we're trying to win a pennant," DiMaggio muttered after the game, with his initial enthusiasm for the change having worn off quickly.

DiMaggio speedily realized he was a green hand at first base despite the 1,000 fielding average he showed at the end of the day for the 13 chances he accepted. The old master of the outfield couldn't conceal his awkwardness at his new job.

Typifying the guy, though, was the alacrity with which he consented to take a whirl at the job. Casey Stengel didn't have to ask him twice. At Stengel's first suggestion, in a hotel room in Boston two days before, that DiMag might give the team a lift if he could move into first base, Joe quickly agreed.

"He told me if I thought it would help the team, he'd pitch, catch or play third base," said Stengel. "Watta man."

* * *

At Least He Knows the Motions

When DiMag's well-advertised debut as first baseman in Washington rolled around, camera men swarmed into the Yankee's dressing room and found him pounding a pocket to his liking into the first baseman's mitt he had borrowed from Johnny Mize.

He was the least excited fellow in the place at that moment, and was ribbing his teammates about his new career. "I'm all set," he grinned. "Now, if somebody will just lead me to that bag and show me where first base is in this park."

During infield practice, Joe submitted to every known pose for the camera men, simulating leaping catches, out-of-the-dirt pickups and all of the hackneyed postures of the first-base picture-taking art. "I don't know yet what kind of a first baseman I am, but I can put on an act for you guys, anyway," he said.

Quickly-Ended Role

JOE DI MAGGIO ... at first

There was the occasion when Joe showed his greenness and unfamiliarity with the quick start-stops of the journeyman first baseman, and fell on his face after starting for a ball that properly belonged to Second Baseman Gerry Coleman. He lay there sprawled for all to see and his expression wasn't a happy one.

But a couple of innings later, DiMag got his first hard chance, a fiery drive over the bag by Irv Noren, and he handled it like an artist. The ball player in DiMaggio came out on that one, and in the eighth inning he made a really difficult play, taking a high throw that pulled him off the bag and into the path of Base-Runner Sherry Robertson. Deftly, DiMag made the tag and the out as if to the manner born.

Summed up, though, DiMag didn't look like a first baseman in his one shot at the job. That's not saying, however, that his first base career is over. A lot of the Yankees think it isn't. Tommy Henrich is one.

"Joe will give you a good job anywhere they play him," declared Henrich. "He has all that natural ability going for him, and he could convert into a first baseman quicker than anybody I know, if they give him a shot at the job."

Henrich declared that the chief problem of the new first baseman was finding the bag with his feet. "Even when I was playing first base and switching in from the outfield, I'd grope for the bag with my feet for a few innings. After that, it became habit to know where the bag was."

Stengel is still visioning the conversion of DiMag into a first baseman as a double blessing — for the Yankees and DiMaggio himself. "It'll take care of our first base problem, I hope. It will give us a chance to see what our young outfielders can do, and it will add a couple of years to Joe's playing career."

Before another season sets in, DiMag will be 36, and Stengel was thinking about that. "Playing first base would save wear and tear on Joe's legs. He won't have to take that long trip from center field to the bench, 16 times a day. If he's playing first, he'll just have to walk across the diamond, and when we're playing in Yankee Stadium, it's only 20 feet from the dugout to his job."

in first on Independence Day were almost certain to meet in the World Series. That is only a half-truth. Data for the past 15 years show that 13 of

over second ... but the front-run... St. Louis Cardinals, stand almost as good a chance of winning the pennant.

to
...tter than ...shed to sign

the place up and ...ut of the bonus for

Bauer Injury Gives Casey Excuse to Get DiMag Off 1st

By ARCH MURRAY

This is the day Big Jim Mize was scheduled to pack his bags and move on again ... baseball port of call. But... the Yanks came home to open a 17-gan... ...n was their re... ...n and ... ...in had mov...

THE NEW YORK POST headlined the return of Joe DiMaggio to the outfield after a brief trial at first base in the above fashion.

DiMaggio and his weapon—"He is the most generally admired personage in his profession today."

Why They Cheer Joe DiMaggio

The fans admire the Yankee outfielder as much for his personal qualities as for his tremendous authority on the ball field.

By GILBERT MILLSTEIN

JOSEPH PAUL DiMAGGIO, one of the two highest-salaried practitioners in baseball and a man who has, without visible strain, acquired the rich patina of an institution, is currently afflicted with the most spectacular batting slump of his twelve years in the major leagues. Because of his institutional status, DiMaggio has made more news with his slump than he would have if he had been leading both leagues in hitting. He also has become the object of widespread solicitude and of a sort of kindly evasion on the part of sportswriters, who like to point out that anyway he has hit more home runs and batted in more runs so far this season than any other *Yankee.* His value to the Yankee organization was pointedly reaffirmed last week when the team, in desperate case for a first baseman, shifted DiMaggio, an outfielder, to that position. He last played first base when he was a boy.

Earlier in the season in the course of a business engagement at the Yankee Stadium—a double-header with the Cleveland Indians—he came to bat eight times but was unable, as the trade says, to buy a hit. Despite this painful consistency, the center fielder for the New York Yankees was applauded with more vigor and greater warmth the last time he took his turn than he had been the first.

THE effect was much as though the stockholders of United States Steel had got up at an annual meeting and cheered Benjamin F. Fairless for reporting that the corporation was about to omit a dividend. The expectation, in both instances, is that such aberrations are, at worst, temporary. Like United States Steel, DiMaggio is called "Big," and is known to be an awesome producer. He enjoys the further advantage of not being a corporate abstraction and is, as well, the most generally admired personage in his profession today. This, of course, has not prevented him from being booed at irregular intervals, but the cash customers appear to boo him only half-heartedly and mostly for the sake of keeping the franchise.

In DiMaggio's case, the public faith in his ultimate productivity was rewarded almost at once. The following day, against Detroit, although he got only one hit, he made nine putouts in the field, only two short of the Ameri-

GILBERT MILLSTEIN, a member of The Times Sunday staff, for this article spent hours in the dugout with DiMaggio and talked with his intimates outside the game.

can League record. Two weeks later, in Cleveland, he hit two home runs, one of which scored four runs, and a double in the first game of a double-header. He got two more hits in what the sportswriters term the "afterpiece," or second game. Toward the end of last month, although his batting average was still a poor thing, DiMaggio had, nevertheless, achieved another intimation of immortality: he became the eighty-eighth among roughly 30,000 major-league baseball players since 1876 to make 2,000 hits, whereupon the photographers posed him kissing the historic baseball with which he made his 2,000th hit. Next Tuesday, at Chicago, he will appear in his eleventh All-Star game.

At one time or another, every baseball player becomes the victim, inexplicably and miserably, of a slump. This is a condition which can be remedied, neither by clean living nor right thinking, two things which DiMaggio, like other members of a notoriously upright baseball team, practices both professionally and privately. "I know a lot of players," he said, somberly at the time of his last falling-off, "who get to bed every night at 10 and don't get to hit just the same."

THE phenomenon is one that has also bemused Tommy Henrich, the Yankees' right fielder and first baseman, who is another proficient hitter. "The idea," he said, in discussing DiMaggio, "is to go out and relax. Forget the doggone game. I don't mean get tight. Just go away from it, like a business man does at the end of the day. Joe's a very serious guy, though. He has a bad day and gets mad at himself. I think a slump hurts him more than it does most. He's not the type that can relax."

Many players, when they are not hitting, become peevish, eat little and lose weight. They are avoided elaborately by their teammates at such times and are offered neither advice nor condolences. In DiMaggio, the symptoms of a slump are manifested by an almost monastic silence. Normally a friendly, if not overly talkative, man, he maintains an air of stricken quiet and takes on the sorrowful dignity of a flawed masterpiece.

The only instance in which he has had any difficulty in his public relations came at a time when he wasn't even playing, and under considerable provocation. That was last year when his right heel—very likely the most exhaustively discussed heel outside of mythology—was operated on. He was being wheeled up to the operating

room in a Baltimore hospital when a photographer took his picture, using a flash-bulb. DiMaggio lost his temper. The photographer apologized, destroyed the negative and was permitted to photograph DiMaggio after the operation was over.

ALWAYS one of the last players to leave the Yankee dressing room at the end of a game, since he believes in a precise course of drying out, showering and dressing, DiMaggio is usually the very last when he is not hitting. Once, at the end of a particularly trying night game, he left the Stadium in a mood of quiet distaste for himself, at 2:30 o'clock the following morning. A pitcher who used to room with DiMaggio recalls how, one night, he awoke to find a bed light on. DiMaggio's bed was empty. He was standing in front of a mirror, taking cuts at non-existent pitches with an imaginary bat. "Joe," said the pitcher admiringly, "is the kind of guy he's got to be—that's all—he's just got to be."

DiMaggio is aware that none of these expedients does him much good. "Hitting's all timing," he observed recently. "Your timing goes off and you're in a slump. Nobody likes to be in a slump, but it's got to come out naturally. You start pressing and you get in a rut. You lose your snap, your whip. So you get up to the ball park earlier and take more turns at batting practice. Nothing works. And then you come out of it without knowing it. You think you're doing the same things wrong and suddenly you're hitting." Even when he is hitting, DiMaggio is nagged by certain misgivings. "A man is never satisfied," he has said. "You go up there and get four hits and you want five so bad you can taste it."

THERE is little question in the minds of most people that DiMaggio is the finest player of his era, a judgment which some are inclined to dispute on a niggling statistical basis, but not in the round. Casey Stengel, the manager of the Yankees, watched DiMaggio working out in the batting cage one morning recently, and then said to an acquaintance: "He tends to business. He knows where the ball park is and he knows when to get there. He comes out and goes

The DiMaggio swing—Many pitchers regard him as most dangerous when there are men on the bases.

to work. You never see him gassing. There isn't a point he is lacking in and he does everything easy. He makes big-league baseball look simple. It isn't that simple. He would make any manager look good. That's about the best thing you can say about any ball player."

Others, not necessarily Yankee fans, sometimes go further. In the opinion of Hank Greenberg, the general manager of the Cleveland Indians, who used to be outstanding himself, DiMaggio is the greatest ball player he has ever seen. "He can hit, throw and run," says Greenberg, "and do a lot of other things you wouldn't normally expect from a long-distance hitter—things only the tradespeople appreciate. Ted Williams may have the percentage on Joe at the bat, but Joe is the better all-around player. He'll go from first to third, for example, on the kind of ball nobody would expect a guy of his size to run on. And he does all these things automatically."

A number of pitchers are of the belief also that DiMaggio,

whether he is in a slump or not, is the most dangerous man in either league to have at bat when there are men on base. Unlike some other baseball stars, he is primarily a team player and is prepared to sacrifice percentage points on his batting average if a bunt will advance a man. A couple of days after DiMaggio made one of his infrequent errors in the field—the result of a confusion in signals with another outfielder—a sports columnist wrote that he "doesn't have to apologize when he boots one, his fielding is so superb. But his reaction * * * was that of a kid who feels he has let the team down." This was a reaction confined solely to DiMaggio and the sort of thing that made almost the entire Yankee squad answer "DiMaggio" when asked by the Yankee front office, "Who is your baseball model, and which player do you admire most?"

AMONG the things DiMaggio does automatically, or at least with such consummate ease that they appear to be automatic, is play his position.

He catches fly balls, retrieves ground balls and throws to the proper bases with such tremendous authority that his artistry in these matters is frequently lost on the lay spectator, who has come to expect it, but not on base runners, who not only expect it but rarely try for extra bases on a hit to DiMaggio's field.

His natural ability is reinforced by a great many minutiae he has picked up over the years. He knows roughly where each of his 175 American League opponents (and his potential 200 opponents in the National League) is likely to hit; that a right-handed power hitter, to take just one type, will pull a ball toward left field, but that there are other factors to be considered. He has studied the vagaries of every ball park in which he plays. In the Yankee Stadium, if the wind is blowing south overhead, it is certain to be blowing north along the ground because of the backwash created by the right-field stands.

THUS DiMaggio must

equate the tendency of the hitter; head in one direction for a high fly; in another for a lower line drive; figure just when to flip down the lenses of his sunglasses (he does this when the ball is three-quarters out of the sun) and precede all of these moves and calibrations by getting the jump on the ball, or starting in the proper direction the instant the batter hits it.

DiMaggio has performed with unflagging zeal and great distinction ever since he came to the Yankees in 1936 from the San Francisco Seals, who were paid $25,000 and five minor workmen for his services. He was one of baseball's most inexpensive purchases and came that way because he had injured a knee getting out of a jitney and the Yankees were not too sure of his future. Although he has been afflicted with ulcers, an ankle that was burned by a diathermy lamp; tooth, tonsil and adenoid troubles; charley horses; a trick right shoulder and a bad elbow; bone spurs in both heels which required painful operations and threatened to end his baseball career; virus pneumonia and a pulled muscle in his back, DiMaggio has risen above all infirmities.

Last summer, after his right heel had undergone surgery, and he had missed the first sixty-five games of the season, DiMaggio went back to work in Boston, hit a home run the first night, two the following day and one the third. At the end of the season, after a bout with virus pneumonia, he dragged himself, sick and fifteen pounds underweight, out of a sickbed, and helped the Yankees to win the American League pennant in the last two games of the schedule.

HOW much longer he can do this is a matter of speculation among the sportswriters. He will be 36 in November; there is some gray in his black hair, and some authorities claim they have detected the signs of baseball senescence in him. Before the season began, one writer thought it was a "sound guess" that DiMaggio would last another two years. "With the breaks," he added, "Joe could make it four."

Undoubtedly the most dazzling accomplishment of DiMaggio's baseball career occurred between May 15 and July 16, 1941, when he hit safely in fifty-six consecutive games or twelve more than any other major league player had ever done. This produced considerable tension in the United States and caused DiMaggio to do something he had never before done in his life, as he says in his autobiography, "Lucky to Be a Yankee." An umpire called a strike on him. DiMaggio, a singularly unargumentative man, turned and looked at him in reproach. The umpire fidgeted for a moment and then murmured unhappily. "Honest to God, Joe, it was right down the middle."

SOME time later, in a game with Chicago at the Stadium, DiMaggio hit a ground ball that struck a stone and ricocheted over the shortstop's head. This was in the days before the Stadium scoreboard registered hits and errors, and the entire Yankee team poured anxiously out of the dugout to see whether the scorer up in the pressbox would register a hit for DiMaggio or an error for the shortstop. After some reflection, the scorer held up a finger to indicate a hit. The team applauded wildly. The next time he was up, however, DiMaggio hit a home run.

In recognition of his talents, DiMaggio has been named the most valuable player in the American League three times by an official committee of the Baseball Writers' Association of America, or once more than his closest rival, Ted Williams. He has played in eight World Series, all but one of which were won by the Yankees. At the end of the 1949 season he had hit 317 home runs, batted in 1,344 runs and accumulated a lifetime batting average of .331. He also held the distinction of having been hit more times by a pitcher in one season than any other American League player, or eight.

For all of these things, DiMaggio has been suitably rewarded. This year he is being paid $100,000. This is some $25,000 less than Ted Williams. But in his years with the Yankees, DiMaggio has earned, altogether, $592,585.67.

In addition, he is currently getting paid at the rate of $50,000 a year for performing on a recorded radio program, and he endorses a cigarette (which he smokes in moderation), a line of toiletries (which he uses with discretion), a boy's T-shirt, a sport shirt, a sweater, a rubber ball with his signature stamped on it, and a baseball glove. He has made an album of children's records known as "Little Johnny Strikeout." These fringe emoluments bring him in about $25,000 a year, according to his lawyer, Julian Rosenthal, who says DiMaggio could make a lot more that way if he cared to. "Joe," says Rosenthal, "just isn't very commercial."

LAST October, in the Stadium, DiMaggio was accorded a "Day." A baseball player's "Day" is an occasion of great sentiment, during which he receives a large number of gifts and suitable speeches are made. DiMaggio received gifts and cash, the value of which was estimated at $50,000, and included an automobile, a boat, a bicycle for his son, 300 quarts of ice cream and a plaque from the opposing team of the day, the Boston Red Sox. He made a brief, moving speech, which he concluded by saying, "I want to thank the good Lord for making me a Yankee." Upon conclusion of the ceremonies, DiMaggio went to work. He got two hits and the Yankees beat Boston. They beat Boston again the next day and won the American League pennant.

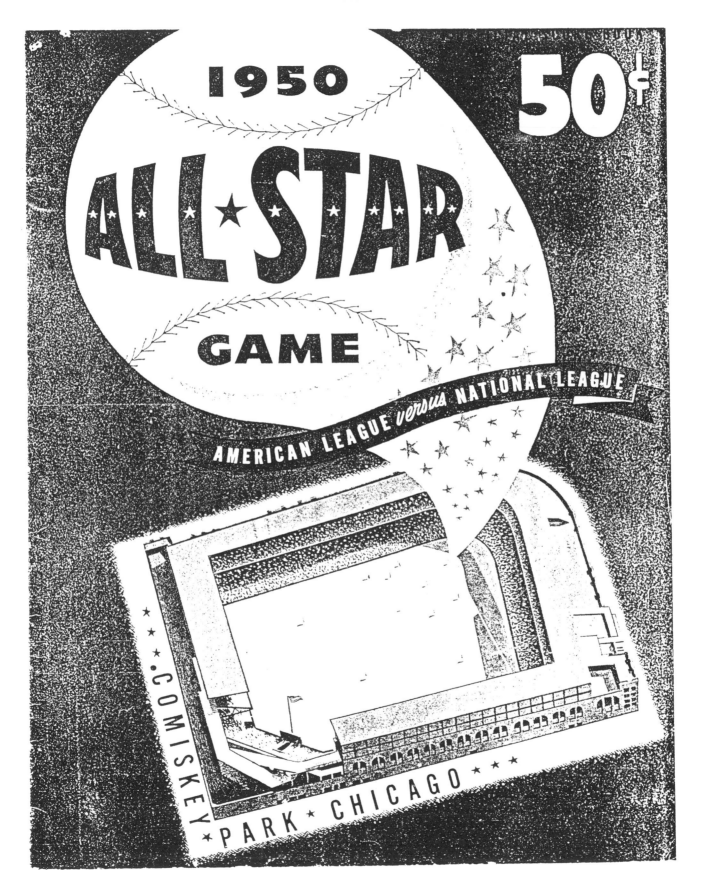

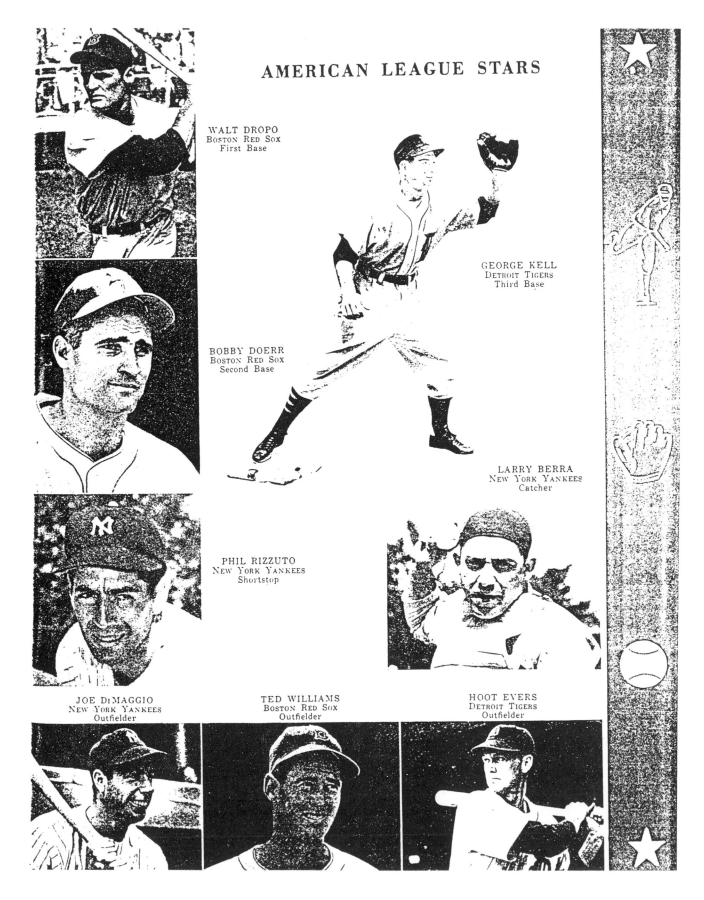

AMERICAN LEAGUE STARS

WALT DROPO
BOSTON RED SOX
First Base

GEORGE KELL
DETROIT TIGERS
Third Base

BOBBY DOERR
BOSTON RED SOX
Second Base

LARRY BERRA
NEW YORK YANKEES
Catcher

PHIL RIZZUTO
NEW YORK YANKEES
Shortstop

JOE DiMAGGIO
NEW YORK YANKEES
Outfielder

TED WILLIAMS
BOSTON RED SOX
Outfielder

HOOT EVERS
DETROIT TIGERS
Outfielder

Pitchers Dominated Greatest All-Star Thriller

Shining Moments for Nationals at 17th Glitter Game

RALPH KINER crossing the plate after smashing his ninth-inning home run to tie up the All-Star Game, 3 to 3, at Chicago, July 11. Stan Musial of the Cardinals congratulates Kiner.

THE HAPPIEST MAN in Comiskey Park after the National League's 4 to 3 victory—Manager Burt Shotton—with his two home run clouters, Kiner (left), in the ninth, and Red Schoendienst (right), in the fourteenth.

Hurlers Spike 'Juiced-Up Ball' Charge; Receipts of $126,179 Set New High

Americans' Favorite Homer Weapon Turned Against Them by Victorious N. L.

By DAN DANIEL

CHICAGO, Ill.

Analysis of the seventeenth All-Star Game, in which the National League defeated the American League in the fourteenth inning, 4 to 3, at Comiskey Park, July 11, proves conclusively that the contest achieved every goal for which it aimed, and quite a few other peaks it had not hoped to attain.

'Pitch, Didn't Have Much On it,' Says The Redhead

CHICAGO, Ill.—Ted Gray's pitch that Red Schoendienst hit into the upper tier of the left field stands to win the All-Star Game was described as a "double knuckleball" by the grinning redhead. "The pitch didn't have much on it," Red explained, "because I pulled it." Gray said it was a low, fast one.

To begin with, the battle was the most thrilling and fascinating in the long series of inter-league games inaugurated at Comiskey Park in 1933. Never before had an All-Star Game gone into extra innings. Never before had the

Jansen and Schoendienst Share Heroes' Laurels; Many Defensive Gems

National League been able to win an All-Star contest held under American League auspices.

With the pension fund as the beneficiary, the two major organizations were eager for a sellout and something beyond $100,000 as the take. The game drew 46,127 persons, who paid $126,179.51, a new high in receipts for this extravaganza.

The money total went $20,864.61 over the best previous record, set in Chicago at Wrigley Field in 1947, with $105,314.90.

Only the Windy City has been able to lift the All-Star take over the $100,-000 level.

* * *

"Rabbit" Ball Tamed

In the opinion of qualified experts, the 14-inning struggle killed the charge that the Spalding people, perhaps at the behest of the majors, had juiced-up the 1950 ball.

The insistence of the manufacturers that poor pitching, and not a change in ingredients and method of manufacture of the ball, had produced the 1950 epizootic of home runs and other extra-base slugging was supported by what happened at Comiskey Park.

In the All-Star Game, only the mound elect performed. The American League could not produce a single homer. The National League did get two four-baggers—the ninth-inning blow of Ralph Kiner, which tied the score at 3 to 3, and Red Schoendienst's fourteenth-round drive into the left field stands which won for the old circuit after four consecutive defeats in the interleague interlude.

However, these two home runs stood out with intaglio-perfection against a background of stirring competition in which spectacular pitching held the day's entire batting production to 18 hits in three hours and 19 minutes of vehement effort.

* * *

More Whiffs Than Hits

Let it be noted that as against the 18 hits there were no fewer than 19 strikeouts.

It was demonstrated beyond all possibility of debate that in the hands of capable pitchers, the 1950 horsehide is no livelier than the 1949 and 1948 baseballs had been.

The American League, which had won 12 of the 16 previous All-Star games, found itself frustrated by the very weapon with which it had been so successful against the National League.

In other years, American League sluggers whipped their National rivals with homers, but this time the old league, desperate, determined, called on the four-bagger to achieve what it had not been able to do in the All-Star engagement since the night of July 11, 1944, in Pittsburgh, when it put over an easy triumph, 7 to 1.

Various heroes have been nominated in the aftermath of the 14-inning struggle. Some experts hold that Larry Jansen, righthander of the Giants, with his five innings of gorgeous shutout hurling blemished only slightly by just one hit, must go down in baseball history as the star of the day.

However, the man who won the game was Schoendienst. No home run hero had he been in pennant competition this season. Red had not even been named by the fans as a starter. He was thrown into the fight no earlier than the eleventh inning. Johnny Wyrostek batted for Jackie Robinson in that round, and Red then dashed into the fray as the new second baseman for Barney Shotton's brilliant argosy.

"I am going to surprise all you birds by hitting a homer, if I ever get into

this fight," Schoendienst kept telling his teammates on the bench.

Perhaps Shotton heard this and was assailed by a hunch.

In any event, Barney made what some of the critics called a boner when he let Wyrostek bat for Robinson, leading hitter of the National League. But since the removal of Robinson led to the entry of Schoendienst, and to the eventual conquering homer of the Cardinal infielder, Shotton must be credited with an inspired move dictated by none less powerful than the very gods of the diamond.

Not to be ignored in the allotment of laurels is Kiner, whose ninth-inning homer saved the National League from a 3 to 2 defeat. In the eleventh, Ralph got a double, but this went to waste.

Then there was Enos (Country) Slaughter, who played center field as if to the manor born, and got a triple and a single, walked, and reached base on an error by Gerald Coleman. Slaughter's three-base drive, following Robinson's single in the second inning, staggered the American leaguers. When the much-discussed Hank Sauer followed with a long fly to Hoot Evers, the National League had a two-run lead. And a sense of impending doom struck the rival camp.

* * *

Blackwell a Star, Too

Still another National League hero, who appears to have been overlooked by most of the star pickers, is Ewell Blackwell, the Whip of the Reds, who received official credit for the victory. Blackwell pitched the last three innings, faced just 12 batters, and allowed only one hit, Ferris Fain's single with one out in the fourteenth. This was erased by the double play into which Joe DiMaggio proceeded to jam. Blackwell was especially spectacular in the twelfth, in which he fanned Jim Hegan and Coleman, and got rid of Pinch-Hitter Tommy Henrich, who flied to Andy Pafko.

Disposing of Henrich was not exactly easy. As a matter of fact, Tom's drive looked like a homer all the way. Then, as Pafko was prepared to see the ball go into the stands for the game, it sank, and Andy made one of the great catches of the battle.

Of the eight hits made by the American League, six came before the sixth inning, only two in the last nine rounds.

After Ted Williams had singled to right with two gone in the fifth to drive in the American League's last run, that side did not hit safely again until, with two out in the tenth, Larry Doby whacked a one-bagger to center.

Certainly not the least brilliant of the many interesting hurlers for the National League was Jim Konstanty, relief marvel of the Phillies, who in his one inning of work faced just three men and fanned two of them. The American leaguers never before had seen anything like the ball thrown by Jim. Some guessed it was a knuckler. As a matter of fact, it was Konstanty's famous "palm ball."

{ **AFTER KINER** tied up the game with a homer, Schoendienst of the Cardinals won it with a four-bagger in the fourteenth. Here Schoendienst is being greeted by the Cubs' Andy Pafko.

All-Star Game

For the American League, offensive heroes being so utterly scarce in a defeat, the day's laurels must be shared by Pitchers Bob Lemon and Allie Reynolds. In his three innings, Lemon blanked the Nationals with one hit, Dick Sisler's pinch single. In Reynolds' three-round stint, the Nationals were held to Kiner's wasted two-bagger.

The Americans got their first run in the third inning on Cass Michaels' pinch double, Phil Rizzuto's bunt single and a long fly to Slaughter by George Kell. The batting leader and 1949 champion of the American League played the entire game, but in six efforts failed to get a hit. He drove in a second run with another fly ball.

In the fifth inning, Lemon walked, Rizzuto fanned, Doby caromed a double off Robinson into center to advance Lemon to third, Kell hoisted to Slaughter for the third consecutive time, to score Bob, and Williams singled to right, scoring Doby, to complete the A. L. run production for the day.

Williams' catch on Kiner, which resulted in Ted's left elbow fracture in the first inning, Ted's catch of Kiner's liner in the third, Rizzuto's job on Willie Jones' slow grounder in the eighth and Dom DiMaggio's catch on Pafko in the eleventh were American League defensive gems.

Slaughter's catch on Walt Dropo in the second, Kiner's job on Williams in the third, and Pafko's game-saving catch on Henrich in the twelfth were thrillers in National League defense.

Both Winner Shotton and Loser Casey Stengel ran their teams well. Captious critics have picked a couple of spots in which they have held each leader remiss. But the managers did the best they could with the wealth of material on hand, tried to give every man a shot at the game, and helped to produce the greatest All-Star struggle yet witnessed.

The 1950 game, to be played at Shibe Park under the auspices of the Phillies, will have a terrific mark at which to shoot.

ALL-STAR RUNDOWN

FIRST INNING

NATIONALS—Jones flied to Doby. Kiner flied to Williams. Musial popped to Doby. No runs, no hits, no errors.

AMERICANS—Rizzuto singled to left. Doby grounded out, Robinson to Musial, Rizzuto taking second. Kell flied to Slaughter, Robinson threw out Williams. No runs, one hit, no errors.

SECOND INNING

NATIONALS—Robinson singled to right. Slaughter tripled off the scoreboard in right-center, scoring Robinson. Sauer flied to Evers, Slaughter scoring. Doerr threw out Campanella. Marion fouled to Berra. Two runs, two hits, no errors.

AMERICANS—Slaughter made a brilliant gloved-hand catch of Dropo's 415-foot drive. Evers walked. Berra forced Evers, Jones to Robinson. Doerr lined to Sauer. No runs, no hits, no errors.

Longest and Best of Summer Classics

NATIONAL LEAGUE

	AB.	R.	H.	O.	A.	E.
Jones (Phillies), 3b......	7	0	1	2	3	0
Kiner, (Pirates), lf......	6	1	2	1	0	0
Musial (Cardinals), 1b...	5	0	0	11	1	0
Robinson, (D'gers), 2b...	4	1	1	3	2	0
fWyrostek (Reds), rf...	2	0	0	0	0	0
Sl'ghter (Cards), cf-rf..	4	1	2	3	0	0
Sch'dienst (Cards), 2b...	1	1	1	1	1	0
Sauer (Cubs), rf......	2	0	0	1	0	0
Pafko, (Cubs), cf......	4	0	2	4	0	0
Ca'panella (D'gers), c...	6	0	0	13	2	0
Marion (Cardinals), ss...	2	0	0	0	2	0
Konstanty (Phils), p...	0	0	0	0	0	0
Jansen (Giants), p......	2	0	0	1	0	0
gSnider (Dodgers)......	1	0	0	0	0	0
Blackwell (Reds), p......	1	0	0	1	0	0
Roberts (Phillies), p...	1	0	0	0	0	0
Ne'combe (D'gers), p...	0	0	0	0	1	0
cSisler (Phillies)......	1	0	1	0	0	0
dReese (Dodgers), ss...	3	0	0	2	4	0
Total	52	4	10	42	17	0

AMERICAN LEAGUE

	AB.	R.	H.	O.	A.	E.
Rizzuto (Yankees), ss......	6	0	2	2	2	0
Doby (Indians), cf......	6	1	2	9	0	0
Kell (Tigers), 3b......	6	0	0	2	4	0
Williams (Red Sox), lf..	4	0	1	2	0	0
D. DiM'gio (R. Sox), lf..	2	0	0	1	0	0
Dropo (Red Sox), 1b...	3	0	1	8	1	0
eFain (Athletics), 1b...	3	0	1	2	1	0
Evers (Tigers), rf......	2	0	0	1	0	0
J. DiM'gio (Yanks), rf...	3	0	0	3	0	0
Berra (Yankees), c......	2	0	0	2	0	0
bHegan (Indians), c......	3	0	0	7	1	0
Doerr, (Red Sox), 2b...	3	0	0	1	4	0
Coleman (Yanks), 2b...	2	0	0	0	0	1
Raschi (Yankees), p...	0	0	0	0	0	0
aMichaels (Senators)...	1	1	1	0	0	0
Lemon (Indians), p...	0	1	0	0	0	0
Houtteman (Tigers) p..	1	0	1	0	0	0
Reynolds (Yanks), p...	1	0	0	0	0	0
hHenrich (Yankees)...	1	0	0	0	0	0
Gray (Tigers), p......	0	0	0	0	0	0
Feller (Indians), p......	0	0	0	0	0	0
Totals	49	3	8	42	13	1

aDoubled for Raschi in third.
bRan for Berra in fourth.
cSingled for Newcombe in sixth.
dRan for Sisler in sixth.
ePopped out for Dropo in eighth.
fFlied out for Robinson in eleventh.
gFlied out for Jansen in twelfth.
hFlied out for Reynolds in twelfth.

National League	0 2 0	0 0 0	0 0 1	0 0 0	0 1—4
American League	0 0 1	0 2 0	0 0 0	0 0 0	0 0—3

Earned runs—National League 4, American League 3.

Runs batted in—Slaughter, Sauer, Kell 2, Williams, Kiner, Schoendienst. Two-base hits—Michaels, Doby, Kiner. Three-base hits—Slaughter, Dropo. Home runs—Kiner, Schoendienst. Grounded into double plays—Jones, J. DiMaggio. Double plays—Rizzuto, Doerr and Dropo; Jones, Schoendienst and Musial. Left on bases—National League 9, American League 6. Bases on balls—Off Roberts 1 (Evers), Newcombe 1 (Lemon), Houtteman 1 (Slaughter), Reynolds 1 (Musial), Feller 1 (Reese). Struck out—By Raschi 1 (Roberts), Roberts 1 (Doby), Lemon 2 (Campanella, Kiner), Newcombe 1 (Rizzuto), Konstanty 2 (Evers, Hegan), Jansen 6 (Houtteman, Doby, Kell, Williams, Hegan, Coleman), Reynolds 2 (Jansen, Reese), Blackwell 2 (Hegan, Coleman), Gray 1 (Campanella), Feller 1 (Blackwell). Hits and runs—Off Raschi 2 and 1 in 3; Roberts 3 and 1 in 3; Lemon 1 and 0 in 3; Newcombe 3 and 2 in 2; Konstanty 0 and 0 in 1; Houtteman 3 and 1 in 3; Jansen 1 and 0 in 5; Reynolds 1 and 0 in 3; Blackwell 1 and 0 in 3. Gray 3 and 1 in 1⅓; Feller 0 and 0 in ⅔. Wild pitch—Roberts. Passed ball—Hegan. Winning pitcher—Blackwell. Losing pitcher—Gray. Umpires—McGowan (A. L.), plate, Pinelli (N. L.), first base, Rommel (A. L.), second base, Conlan (N. L.), third base, Stevens (A. L.), right field, Robb (N. L.), left field, first 4½ innings; Pinelli, plate, Rommel, first base, Conlan, second base, McGowan, third base, Robb, left field, Stevens, right field, 9½ innings. Time of game—3:19. Attendance—46,127. Receipts $126,179.51. Official Scorers: Chester Smith, Irving Vaughn, Howard Roberts, Jim Enright.

THIRD INNING

NATIONALS — Roberts struck out. Jones fouled to Kell. Kiner lined to Williams. No runs, no hits, no errors.

AMERICANS—Michaels batting for Raschi, bounced double into the center field bullpen. Rizzuto beat out a bunt down the third base line, Michaels reaching third. Rizzuto took second on a wild pitch. Doby fanned, Campanella throwing to Musial for the putout. Kell flied to Slaughter, Michaels scoring and Rizzuto going to third. Kiner made a leaping catch of Williams' smash. One run, two hits, no errors.

FOURTH INNING

NATIONALS—Lemon pitching for the Americans. Musial and Robinson flied to Doby. Slaughter was out, Dropo to Lemon, who covered first. No runs, no hits, no errors.

AMERICANS—Newcombe pitching for the Nationals. Dropo tripled off the center field wall. Dropo held third as Marion threw out Evers. Berra tapped to Newcombe and Dropo was trapped and retired, Newcombe to Campanella to Jones. Hegan ran for Berra and was forced by Doerr, Conlan to Robinson. No runs, one hit, no errors.

FIFTH INNING

NATIONALS—Hegan went behind the plate for the Americans. Kell threw out Sauer. Campanella struck out, Hegan throwing to Dropo for the putout. Kell tossed out Marion. No runs, no hits, no errors.

AMERICANS—Pafko went to center and Slaughter shifted to right for the Nationals. Lemon walked. Rizzuto fanned. Doby got a double on a sharp grounder behind second which Robinson knocked down. Kell flied to Pafko, Lemon scoring and Doby going to third. Williams singled, Doby scoring. Dropo fouled to Jones. Two runs, two hits, no errors.

SIXTH INNING

NATIONALS—Sisler batting for Newcombe, singled to right. Reese ran for Sisler. Jones hit into a double play, Rizzuto to Doerr to Dropo. Kiner fanned. No runs, one hit, no errors.

AMERICANS—Reese went to short and Konstanty replaced Newcombe in the box for the Nationals. Evers and Hegan struck out. Doerr grounded to Reese. No runs, no hits, no errors.

SEVENTH INNING

NATIONALS — Houtteman was the new hurler for the Americans. Musial bounced to Doerr. Doby took Robinson's pop. Slaughter walked. Pafko singled off Rizzuto's glove into left, Slaughter stopping at second. Campanella flied deep to Doby. No runs, one hit, no errors.

AMERICANS—Jansen went to the hill for the Nationals. Houtteman struck out,

Rizzuto fouled to Campanella. Doby struck out. No runs, no hits, no errors.

EIGHTH INNING

NATIONALS—Jansen rolled to Doerr. Reese fouled to Hegan. Rizzuto threw out Jones. No runs, no hits, no errors.

AMERICANS—Kell and Williams fanned. Fain, batting for Dropo, popped to Reese. No runs, no hits, no errors.

NINTH INNING

NATIONALS—Joe DiMaggio went to right, Dom DiMaggio to left, Coleman to second and Fain to first for the Americans. K i n e r slammed Houtteman's first pitch into the upper left field stands. Musial went out, Fain to Houtteman, who covered first. Robinson popped to Rizzuto. Slaughter singled to center. Kell threw out Pafko. One run, two hits, no errors.

AMERICANS — J. DiMaggio flied to Pafko. Hegan and Coleman fanned. No runs, no hits, no errors.

TENTH INNING

NATIONALS — Reynolds t o o k the mound for the Americans. Campanella popped to Rizzuto. Jansen fanned. Reese fouled to Kell. No runs, no hits, no errors.

AMERICANS—Jones threw out Reynolds. Rizzuto popped to Reese. Doby singled to center. Kell forced Doby, Reese to Robinson. No runs, one hit, no errors.

ELEVENTH INNING

NATIONALS—Kell threw out Jones. Kiner doubled to right-center. Musial drew an intentional pass. Wyrostek, batting for Robinson, flied to Doby. Coleman fumbled Slaughter's grounder, filling the bases. Dom DiMaggio made a leaping catch of Pafko's drive with his back against the left field wall. No runs, one hit, one error.

AMERICANS—Schoendienst went to second and Wyrostek to right for the Nationals. Reese threw out D. DiMaggio. Fain was out, Musial to Jansen. J. DiMaggio popped to Campanella. No runs, no hits, no errors.

TWELFTH INNING

NATIONALS — Campanella fouled to Hegan. Snider, batting for Jansen, flied to J. DiMaggio. Reese was called out on strikes. No runs, no hits, no errors.

AMERICANS—Blackwell was the Nationals' fifth pitcher. Hegan struck out for the third straight time. Coleman also fanned. Henrich, batting for Reynolds, sent Pafko back to the right-cen-

ter scoreboard for his drive. No runs, no hits, no errors.

THIRTEENTH INNING

NATIONALS—Gray went to the box for the Americans. Jones singled to left. Kiner flied to J. DiMaggio. Musial flied to Doby. Wyrostek flied to J. DiMaggio. No runs, one hit, no errors.

AMERICANS — Rizzuto flied to Pafko. Doby grounded to Musial. Reese threw out Kell. No runs, no hits, no errors.

FOURTEENTH INNING

NATIONALS—Schoendienst hit a home run into the upper deck of the left field stands. Pafko singled to left. Campanella struck out and when Hegan let the ball get away for a passed ball, Pafko took second. Feller replaced Gray. Blackwell fanned. Reese walked. Jones flied to Doby. One run, two hits, no errors.

AMERICANS—D. DiMaggio bunted and was out, Blackwell to Musial. Fain singled to left. J. DiMaggio hit into a double play, Jones to Schoendienst to Musial. No runs, one hit, no errors.

Chicago Packs the Park for All-Stars

AERIAL SHOT of Comiskey Park showing the crowd of 46,127 which witnessed the 17th annual All-Star Game.

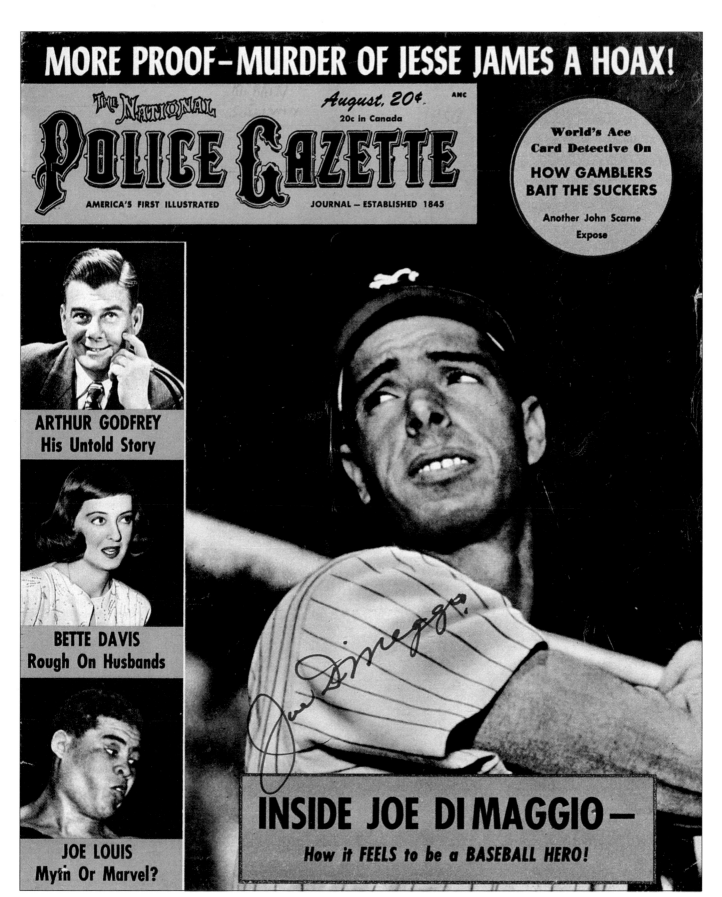

Joe DiMaggio makes the cover of *Police Gazette* in August 1950.

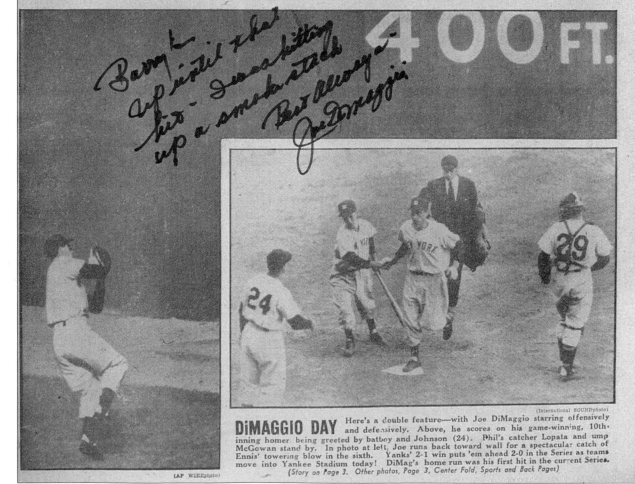

3¢

U. S. Weather Forecast
MOSTLY SUNNY
(Details on Page 2.

Daily Mirror

4c In Suburbs
5c Elsewhere

3¢

Vol. 27. No. 90.   NEW YORK 17, N. Y., FRIDAY, OCTOBER 6, 1950   C   COMPLETE SPORTS

YANKEES WIN ON JOE'S HOMER

Take Second Game of Series 2-1 in 10

400 FT.

DiMAGGIO DAY Here's a double feature—with Joe DiMaggio starring offensively and defensively. Above, he scores on his game-winning, 10th-inning homer being greeted by batboy and Johnson (24). Phil's catcher Lopata and ump McGowan stand by. In photo at left, Joe runs back toward wall for a spectacular catch of Ennis' towering blow in the sixth.   Yanks' 2-1 win puts 'em ahead 2-0 in the Series as teams move into Yankee Stadium today! DiMag's home run was his first hit in the current Series.
(Story on Page 3. Other photos, Page 3, Center Fold, Sports and Back Pages)

(AP WIREphoto)

(International SOUNDphoto)

The headline of October 6, 1950 says it all.

A pair of Hall of Famers, Joe DiMaggio and Rogers Hornsby, discuss the techniques of gripping a bat during the 1950 season. Hornsby, then manager of the Beaumont, Texas team in the minor leagues, had a lifetime batting average of .358 during his 23-year major league career and batted over .400 three times (.401 in 1922, .424 in 1924, and .403 in 1925).

VIEWS OF SPORT

By RED SMITH

It Never Happened Before

FOURTEEN years, three months, one week and two days ago, a slender, dark haired kid played in the outfield for the Yankees against the St. Louis Browns and made three hits in six times at bat, including a triple off Elon Hogsett. The Yankees won, 14 to 5.

Since that date, May 3, 1936, the Yankees have won nine American League pennants and eight world championships. Since his first game in the major leagues he wasn't able to play during the first two weeks of that season because of his ankle had been burned under a sun lamp in the training room Joe DiMaggio has walked alone, comparably and indisputably the finest baseball player of his time.

Night before last, with the Yankees playing the frowzy Athletics, DiMaggio was benched. Nothing like that ever happened before. Over the years, DiMaggio has missed many Yankee games, because of injuries or illness or military service. This was the first time a manager ever looked down a bench, looked past a hale Joe DiMaggio, and said, "Mapes, you play centerfield."

In the seventh inning Cliff Mapes hit a home run with a playmate on base and the score tied at 5-all. DiMaggio's substitute won the game, 7 to 6.

Red Smith

DiMaggio was taken out of the line-up so he could rest. This wasn't the end. He will be back and he will win a great many more games for the Yankees. Nevertheless, it was something that never happened before. Casey Stengel benched him.

The Things a Guy Remembers

THE rest of this space could be filled, easily, by the statistical record of DiMaggio's contributions to the Yankees—his 1,552 American League and World Series games, his 2,090 hits, his 344 home runs, his unexampled feat of hitting safely in fifty-six consecutive championship games.

But that would make dull writing and duller reading and it's an old story, anyway. The little things which a fellow remembers furnish a clearer idea of what he has meant to the Yankees than the record books ever could. A fellow remembers, for instance, a remark Bill Terry made fourteen years ago.

The Yanks had run second three times in a row before DiMaggio joined them, but in 1936 they won the pennant by nineteen and a half games. The rookie hit .323 that season and batted in 125 runs. In the World Series with the Giants he batted .346 and in the sixth and deciding game he made an unbelievable catch, racing back past the Eddie Grant monument in the Polo Grounds to the foot of the clubhouse stairs to grab a fly by Hank Leiber.

It was the last putout of the series. Joe kept on running as he caught the ball, mounted a step or so up the clubhouse stairs, then remembered and stood at attention until President Roosevelt left the park. As his car rolled through the centerfield gate, the President lifted a hand in salute to the ball player there on the steps.

A little later in the Giants' clubhouse, when the newspaper men had run out of questions, Terry volunteered a statement.

"I'd like to add one thing," said the manager of the defeated team. "I've heard about how one player made the difference in the Yankees this year, made a championship club out of a loser. I never understood how that could happen, until today. Now I know."

It was not, you see, a coincidence that the Yankees, who won four pennants in the eleven years before DiMaggio joined them, won eight in his eleven active seasons with the team.

The Way the Guys Acted

ONCE a newspaper man did pennance for his great sins by ghost writing a magazine series called "My Greatest Thrill," as told by assorted athletic heroes. He started, naturally, with DiMaggio. "Champ," he asked, "what was your greatest thrill?"

Joe started talking. He told about how, when he was a kid in high school in San Francisco, they had a teacher who would bring a radio to class during a World Series and tune in the game, and how he had sat there listening and dreaming of playing in a World Series and hitting a home run. At that time, Joe explained, he was just a sandlotter, but after a while he got into organized ball and finally he was in the Coast League and, he felt, coming closer to realization of his dream.

As he talked, he kept filling in the background with small details, a better newspaper man than the guy who was interviewing him. He told about coming to the Yankees and getting into a World Series in his first year. He had a great series, but he didn't hit a home run. He waited another year and got into another World Series, and he had to wait until the very last game of that one before he hit the big one.

That was it, he said. "That was my biggest thrill." He paused a moment, and then he said, "hitting in fifty-six straight games, that was no slouch, either. What I remember, when I broke George Sisler's record of forty-one games in Washington, our whole club ran out of the dugout to congratulate me. And when I broke Willie Keeler's National League record of forty-four in a game against Boston, they all came running out again. That's what I remember, the way the guys on the club acted."

Feeling Don't Matter

THIS was a shy and lonely guy talking. He is still, after all these years, a shy and lonely guy. They have been saying lately that he wasn't taking his decline gracefully. There have been pieces written criticizing him, and pieces defending him. He needs no defense and there'll be nothing like that here. Just one last item:

He came downtown the other evening, after a game when he'd got no hits and the Yankees lost, to cut a record for his weekly radio show. The program began with Joe answering questions mailed in by fans, and one of the questions concerned the popular practice of switching right-handed and left-handed hitters against left-handed and right-handed pitching. How did the guy who was taken out of the batting order feel about that?

"As far as his feelings are concerned," Joe said without hesitation, "it doesn't matter. His job is to help the club win." Anybody got a better answer?

DiMaggio's 22d Homer in 9th Gains 15th Victory for Raschi

Jolter's Blast Is Only Hit Off Brissie in Last 5 Innings; Berra's 2 Doubles Aid New York

By Ed Sinclair AUG 19 1950

PHILADELPHIA, Aug. 18.—Joe DiMaggio, the king of them all in his prime, tonight showed his critics he is far from the washed-up ball player they say he is. Back in the line-up after a week's rest and appearing in his old familiar role as clean-up hitter, the mighty Clipper slammed a ninth-inning home run to bring Casey Stengel's embattled Yankees a 3-to-2 decision over the Athletics.

A powerful wallop high into the upper deck deep in left center field, DiMag's blow—his twenty-second of the ___ nd his first since July 30 ___ -balanced three previous an ___ less times at bat and lifted the Yankees a half game closer to the league-leading Detroit Tigers and the second-place Cleveland Indians.

The homer was the only hit off Lou Brissie in the last five innings.

A's Lose Sixth in Row

It also overshadowed a strong six-hit pitching performance by Vic Raschi, the big right-hander who demonstrated once again that with four days' rest he is as tough a competitor as any manager could want. Achieved at the expense of Lou Brissie, Philadelphia's fine left-hander, and the sixth straight loss for the A's, Raschi's victory was his fifteenth of the season and his fourth of the year over the local club.

Broad-shouldered Vic had to work diligently to get it. Successive doubles by Phil Rizzuto and Yogi Berra, who was upped to the No. 3 slot in the order, gave him a one-run edge in the first inning, but Eddie Joost, tied it up in the third with his fifteenth homer of the campaign.

Then Berra doubled again in the fourth, advanced to third base on DiMaggio's infield out and scored on Billy Johnson's line single into center field. Raschi proceeded to shut out the A's through the sixth. In the seventh, however, his control deserted him and the home forces tied the score again.

Berra Waxes Poetic Over DiMaggio Slump

RICHMOND, Va., Aug. 18 (AP). —A Richmond youngster beamed over the autograph of New York Yankee catcher Yogi Berra today. He got the Yankee star's signature yesterday when 700 Richmond youngsters were in Washington to watch the Senators down the Yankees, 2 to 1.

Berra wrote jokingly:

"To Joe DiMaggio:

"Roses are red. Violets are blue.

"Ted Williams can bit. Why can't you?   YOGI BERRA."

Slips 3d Strike by Joost

Between two outs Mike Guerra doubled down the leftfield line and Raschi issued three consecutive bases on balls to Joost, Barney McCosky and Paul Lehner. These forced in the tying run and brought Sam Chapman, a slugger, to bat. Raschi thwarted him by getting him to pop up to Rizzuto and from that point the New York pitcher was invulnerable.

Aided by DiMaggio's fine running catch of a short fly ball in the eighth, big Vic retired the next three men in order. After DiMaggio's homer with one out in the ninth, he repeated the performance and completed the assignment by slipping a third strike past Joost.

Hank Bauer rejoined the Yankees today after spending twenty-four hours at Georgetown Hospital in Washington . . . He sported one stitch in his left ear where Al Evan's throw hit him yesterday afternoon, but other than that he said he felt fine . . . although he was not in uniform tonight he will be tomorrow.

DiMag Resurgence Buoys Yankees for Tribal Series

By JERRY MITCHELL

The Yankees expect Joe DiMaggio to take charge again. This series with the Cleveland Indians at the Stadium can mean the American League pennant and they look for the big guy to show them the way as he did so many times in the past.

Thus far in his comeback from what you might call a rest cure, DiMaggio has been a true leader with his hitting, fielding and baserunning. He hit a hearty .442 in the 11 games since his return to good working order and before this four-game series with the Indians.

DiMaggio's comeback may have had nothing to do with Hank Bauer's rise as a hitting authority, the recent flow of home runs and other extra base blows from Yogi Berra's bat, the contribution made by Johnny Mize and Tommy Henrich, when able, and the quality pitching of Allie Reynolds, Eddie Ford, Vic Raschi and Tom Ferrick. Maybe not, but the way the Big Guy took Stengel's orders could not help but affect the rest of the club.

Rest Boon to DiMag

That week of rest benefitted DiMaggio physically and his return was a tremendous hypo to club morale. They are still up, as the saying goes, as a result of it all and despite the loss of a game to the Chicago White Sox yesterday, 6—4, that could easily have been won.

They lost because Stengel gambled with Fred Sanford and the latter wasn't up to it. The Yanks got him four runs, a lot in competition with tough Ray Scarborough, a cagy pitcher who does not hurt himself. But Sanford, with Gus Zernial about the only slugger who could damage him in the Chicago lineup, beat himself with base on balls.

There won't be any gambling in this series because the men who figured to be most effective against the Clevelands were readied for it. Ed Lopat, always effective against the Indians, is to work tomorrow's game and will be followed by young Ford, who is just as left-handed. Reynolds will be in the bullpen.

On the whole, the Yank pitching has been good, the men delivering six complete jobs in the last 11 games. The Indians got four full games from starters in the same stretch. Lou Boudreau has, moreover, had to employ Bob Lemon and Bobby Feller in relief as well as starting roles.

The Indians, overcome by a late Boston rally again yesterday, are also having trouble with their all-rookie infield. Six infield errors in the last four games gave their opponents a lot of extra outs. In Boston it meant two games.

Aside from Henrich, the Yanks were in top shape for the Cleveland series. Henrich, who won Sunday's game with a pinch-blow, got two of the six hits permitted by Scarborough yesterday, but his bad leg bothered him noticeably as the game wore on.

Stengel would like to rest the old pro as much as possible, saving him for the big spots or, possibly, withdrawing him in mid-games hereafter if the Yanks take an early lead. That was his idea yesterday, but they never did get that early lead.

Yankees Fear DiMag Loss May Slow Pennant Drive

By Hugh Bradley

Our Yankees are sitting pretty today but they are mindful that they also may be perching on a keg of dynamite. Leading the league by two full games over the Tigers, with the Red Sox trailing by 2½ and the Indians by five, they are far from counting the pennant as in the bag.

Joe DiMaggio   Casey Stengel

Causing them more than a modicum of worry is the condition of Joe DiMaggio's knees. The wear and tear of playing has strained both of them so badly that the Clipper was unable to get into action while a clean sweep of the four game Cleveland series was made with a 7 to 5 triumph yesterday.

RETURN INDEFINITE.

"When I'll be able to get back into action is something I can't even guess," he said while waiting for the start of the four-game series with the Senators tonight. "When I tried to bend over in practice esterday the blamed things were so stiff that I almost fell smack on my face."

Because DiMaggio had been moving at his fastest pace of the season during the recent spell in which the Yankees have taken over the league lead by winning 13 of their last 15, his absence for more than a day or two could be serious. He continues pretty much the sparkplug of the club, as well as the guy who causes the opposition the most worry.

Seeking to offset his possible loss somewhat, however, the head gees have called up Hank Workman from the Kansas City farm. He's the husky 24-year-old graduate of Southern California, who can play either first base or the outfield and has been frequently touted in this space.

Performing with the Blues this season he has been getting special mileage from a .280 batting average, slamming 23 homers and driving in 90 runs.

"Maybe I won't play him tonight because he'll be tired from a long train ride, but you can expect to see him in action over the week-end," Stengel said.

WEEKEND REAL TEST.

Actually the week-end is regarded by the league leaders as one of their toughest tests of the year, albeit it merely causes them to play six games with second division teams. One reason for that is the fact the Senators, who arrive for four games, including a doubleheader Sunday, are regarded as the circuit's wrecking crew.

During the past few days they slapped down the Tigers three out of four, just to prove they don't play any favorites. But their main enemies are the Yankees. They've won seven out of 13 from our side this season and it's a cinch Bucky Harris will have them bearing down again.

Scurvily treated by the Yankee bosses after he failed to win the pennant in 1948, during just such a dog fight as the current one, the Buckeroo wouldn't be human if he failed to try to get hunk.

Another aspect of the week end is that it calls for a pair of double bills. Meeting the Senators in the Bronx ballyard on Sunday the Stengeleers also have to take on the Athletics in a twin attraction Monday. That calls for a considerable manipulation of pitchers, particularly with a series with the red hot Red Sox coming up in Boston next week.

OSTROWSKI IS WORRY.

Stengel figures to use Allie Reynolds tonight in the last Stadium arc-lighter of the season, Joe Ostrowski tomorrow, Vic Raschi and Ed Ford Sunday and Tommy Byrne and Ed Lopat Monday.

Ostrowski is the lad who provides the main worry. He hasn't started since June 29 and on that occasion he was racked by the Senators during a 1 1-3 inning stay on the hill. It's figured, however, that the Nats may be loaded with lefthand hitters this time and his southpaw curving can be used to advantage.

DiMaggio Wallops 3 Homers

BOMBERS TRIUMPH AT WASHINGTON, 8-1

Raschi, Aided by Tom Ferrick, Chalks Up No. 19—Second Contest Is Washed Out

DIMAGGIO SETS A RECORD

First Player to Hit 3 Homers in One Game at Griffith Stadium—Also Doubles

By JOHN DREBINGER
Special to The New York Times.

WASHINGTON, Sept. 10—In a bizarre "day" of almost seven hours, which saw Joe DiMaggio crash three tremendous home runs for the first time this feat has ever been achieved in spacious Griffith Stadium, while repeated showers wore a ground crew almost down to exhaustion, the Yankees today managed to make off with one game in their twin bill with the Senators.

The second one was washed down the drain and will be played off as part of a double-header starting at noon tomorrow. The early starting time was deemed necessary because both clubs must catch trains later in the day for the west.

The opener, during which DiMaggio drove his three circuit clouts into the distant left field bleachers, went to Casey Stengel's Bombers, 8 to 1. It marked the third time in his career that the Clipper had clubbed three in one game and the first time any batter, left or right-handed, had ever been able to gain this distinction in the 30-year-history of the present arena. All three clouts traveled well over 400 feet.

Then luck gave the Yankees a helping hand. Since the first game, interrupted three times by rain, was not completed until 5:50 P. M., the second encounter did not get under way until 6:12 under floodlights and black clouds threatening to crack down again at any moment. Three and a half innings later they cracked.

Senators Ahead, 6—2

With the Senators leading, 6 to 2, and just going to bat in the last half of the fourth a final deluge broke loose and when the rain continued for more than an hour, the umpires, with the clock now showing 8:15, decided to call it off.

For the Yanks, of course, this proved a timely intervention, for their Tommy Byrne had gotten off to a bad start in the first inning when the Nats scored four runs, three riding in on a homer by Sam Mele which also is now washed out of the records.

In the end, therefore, the Yanks came out all right. For by winning their one game while the front-running Tigers split even with the White Sox, the Bombers moved up to within half a length of the leaders, while the Red Sox remained a half game behind the Yanks.

In addition to his three homers, which sent his total to 27, DiMaggio also doubled and drew a pass for a perfect game at the plate. And behind the Clipper's heavy cannonading Vic Raschi had no trouble whatever in posting his nineteenth mound victory although the big righthander went only seven innings.

Big Vic doubtless would have made the distance easily enough under normal conditions. But when the third interruption by rain delayed matters an hour and fifteen minutes, Stengel decided to take no further chances of putting an unnecessary strain on Raschi's arm.

Holds Nats in 2 Innings

So, with the Bombers leading, 5 to 1, at the time, Tom Ferrick came on as play was resumed in the last half of the eighth to blank the Nats in their final two rounds.

In all, the Bombers plastered Sid Hudson and Mickey Harris for an even dozen blows, with Tommy Henrich getting two of these. Making one of his infrequent appearances at first base, Old Reliable warmed up on a single and in the eighth smacked one off the wall in deep right center which he outgalloped, game leg and all, for a triple.

DiMaggio's first two homers, each with the bases empty, were struck off Hudson, the first in the second inning, the other in the sixth. The third one came off Harris in the ninth after Bauer had singled. Thus the Clipper picked up four RBI's for the game.

The first time DiMaggio hit three in one encounter was on June 13, 1937, his second season with the Bombers. He then had to wait eleven years before he was able to turn the trick again on May 23, 1948.

The record for having hit three in a game the most number of times is held by another present day Yankee, Mize, but Big Jawn did it all in his years as a National Leaguer.

Another odd feature of the DiMaggio homers is that of the five circuit blows the Yanks have hit here this year, the Clipper made four. Bauer hit the other . . . the Jolter's 4 RBI's sent him over the century mark for the ninth time as a Yankee.

The box score:

NEW YORK (A.)	ab.	r.	h.	po.	a.	e.
Rizzuto, ss.	5	2	1	1	4	0
Hopp, lf.	4	1	1	2	0	0
Bauer, rf.	5	1	2	1	0	0
DiMaggio, cf.	4	4	4	1	0	0
Berra, c.	5	0	1	6	1	0
Henrich, 1b.	4	0	2	8	0	0
Collins, 1b.	0	0	0	4	0	0
Johnson, 3b.	4	0	0	1	0	0
Coleman, 2b.	4	0	1	2	5	0
Raschi, p.	1	0	0	1	0	0
Ferrick, p.	1	0	0	0	1	0
Total	37	8	12	27	11	0

WASHINGTON (A.)	ab.	r.	h.	po.	a.	e.
Yost, 3b.	1	0	0	1	2	0
Stewart, lf.	4	0	1	2	0	0
Noren, cf.	4	0	0	3	0	0
Vernon, 1b.	4	0	0	11	1	0
Mele, rf.	4	0	0	2	0	0
Michaels, 2b.	3	0	0	4	2	0
Dente, ss.	4	0	1	1	8	0
Grasso, c.	2	0	1	3	1	0
Hudson, p.	2	1	1	0	2	1
aCoan	1	0	0	0	0	0
Harris, p.	0	0	0	0	0	0
Total	29	1	4	27	16	1

aStruck out for Hudson in seventh.

New York ....0 1 2 0 0 1 0 1 3—8
Washington ....0 0 0 0 0 1 0 0 0—1

Runs batted in—DiMaggio 4, Bauer 2, Stewart, Henrich.

Two-base hit—DiMaggio. Three-base hit—Henrich. Home runs—DiMaggio 3. Sacrifice—Raschi. Double plays—Hudson, Dente and Vernon; Collins (unassisted). Left on bases—New York 6, Washington 6. Bases on balls—Off Raschi 5, Hudson 3. Struck out—By Raschi 6, Hudson 1, Harris 1. Hits—Off Hudson 7 in 7 innings, Harris 5 in 2, Raschi 4 in 7, Ferrick 0 in 2. Winning pitcher—Raschi (19—8). Losing pitcher—Hudson (12—13). Umpires—Berry, Passarella and Honochick. Time of game—2:23. Attendance—23,350.

DiMag's Feat Makes History

Washington, Sept. 11—Old inhabitants can't remember any other righthanded hitter belting as many as three home runs into the distant (405 feet) leftfield bleachers at Griffith Stadium here, a feat accomplished by Joe DiMaggio yesterday. Al Rosen of the Indians did it twice earlier in the season.

DiMaggio had three in a game on two previous occasions—June 13, 1937 and May 23, 1948. His last yesterday was his 28th of the season. In the seventh he doubled down the line and scored his fourth run when Tommy Henrich tripled off the rightfield wall.

All box and reserved seats for the Sunday, Sept. 24th game at Yankee Stadium with the Red Sox are sold out, but some still remain, the club announced, for Saturday, Sept. 23d . . . Sunday will, of course, also be Johnny Mize's special day . . . Wally Hood, reporting from Kansas City, will rejoin the club in Cleveland after a medical exam in New York today . . . Joe Page reports his arm somewhat better as a result of his Johns Hopkins Hospital visit. MITCHELL.

EASTER'S 2D HOMER STOPS BOMBERS, 8-7

Indians Win With 2 Out in 9th on 3-Run Blow Off Ferrick —Doby Connects in 3d

DIMAGGIO BLOW SCORES 3

Rizzuto and Berra Also Clout 4-Baggers, but Yanks Fall Half Game Behind Tigers

By JOHN DREBINGER
Special to The New York Times.

CLEVELAND, Sept. 12—For more than four and a half hours the Yankees fought a heroic battle to retain their half-game lead in the sizzling American League flag race tonight.

They outrode a thunderstorm that interrupted play midway in the first inning for an hour and a half and they piled up a six-run lead in the first two rounds with the aid of a trio of homers by Joe DiMaggio, Phil Rizzuto and Yogi Berra.

But, in the last of the ninth, with Allie Reynolds still clinging to a three-run advantage, disaster overtook the Bombers as Lou Boudreau's Indians rushed four tallies over the plate, the final three riding in on Luke Easter's second circuit smash of the night.

Half Game Above Third

That clout, stroked off Relief Pitcher Tom Ferrick, sank the Stengeleers, 8 to 7, and as a result the New Yorkers skidded back into second place, a half a length behind the leading Tigers, and only a half game in front of the third-place Red Sox.

As the struggle moved into the ninth, Reynolds had allowed only four hits, though two of these were circuit shots, one by Larry Doby in the third, and the other, Easter's first of the evening, in the fifth. But with one down in the closing round Reynolds walked Pinch-Hitter Joe Gordon and Thurman Tucker.

Casey Stengel here called on Ferrick, but the Indians, out to square a score with the Bombers for their recent four-straight thrashings in New York, refused to be denied. Bob Kennedy lashed a double into left center and Gordon counted.

Ferrick then fanned Doby and with big Easter ambling to the plate, Stengel went into a huddle with his men on the mound. They elected to pitch to the giant Negro only to regret it a moment later as Luke larruped the ball over the right-field barrier for his twenty-fourth homer of the year while 29,454 onlookers went into a wild frenzy.

The victory, of course, still left the hopelessly outdistanced Tribe seven lengths behind the leaders, but it still was something to have spilled the proud Bombers in such dramatic fashion.

28th Homer for DiMaggio

Up to the finish, it had been all in the Yanks' favor. In fact, the Bombers' biggest concern at the outset was the weather when rain threatened to wash out the entire evening after the Stengeleers had made off with a three-run splurge in the opening round, all three the result of DiMaggio's No. 28 blast into the left-field stand off Early Wynn.

For more than an hour it poured and as intermittent showers had soaked the field earlier in the day it didn't look as though further play would ever be possible. However, swift work by the ground crew had protected the infield and when the rain ceased the umpires decided to continue the game, although numerous puddles glistened in the outfield.

When play was resumed, Reynolds quickly snuffed out three Indians in their half of the first inning and in the second the Bombers routed Wynn, rushing off with three more runs, the first on Rizzuto's sixth and the next two on Berra's twenty-first four-bagger with Johnny Hopp on base.

But here their attack stalled as Dick Weik blanked them for the next four innings while the Indians kept picking away at the long lead. A hit batsman and three walks pushed one tally over in the second. Doby's No. 23, with Kennedy aboard, accounted for two more in the third and Easter's wallop in the fifth added one more to the mounting Cleveland total.

At that, matters still looked safe, especially after the top half of the eighth, which saw the Yanks grab another run off Steve Gromek on a single by Berra, a wild pitch, an infield hit by Joe Collins and a force play at second.

But in the end it was Gromek who emerged the winner. The defeat was charged to Ferrick, his sixth of the year.

Gene Woodling rejoined the Yanks, apparently recovered from his recent groin injury.

RASCHI WINS NO. 20 AT DETROIT, 7 TO 5

Yankee Hurler Settles Down After Yielding 4 Runs in First on 3 Hits, 3 Walks

DIMAGGIO BLASTS NO. 29

Mize, Mapes Also Connect as Newhouser Loses—Byrne Will Face Tigers Today

By JOHN DREBINGER
Special to THE NEW YORK TIMES.

DETROIT, Sept. 14—Vic Raschi became the second pitcher in the American League today to post his twentieth mound victory as the Yankees tripped the Tigers, 7 to 5, to move back into first place by half a length. But there is no getting away from the fact that both Big Vic and the Bombers made it the hard way.

For as the opener of this crucial three-game series got under way under an ominously gray sky that had dripped rain most of the morning to hold the attendance down to 20,853, it looked for a time as though Red Rolfe's Bengals would rush the Stengeleers right out of the arena.

Taking advantage of an extraordinary streak of wildness on the part of the New York righthander, the Detroiters lashed out for four runs in the first inning and with Hal Newhouser, the talented southpaw on the mound for the Tigers, even the most conservative in the gathering were ready to place their World Series orders.

But picking themselves off the floor has long been an established custom with our Bombers and beginning with the second round they started rolling. Joe DiMaggio hit a homer. So did Johnny Mize. With the end of the fourth, Newhouser had vanished from the scene and two innings later Cliff Mapes belted one into the seats.

A Miraculous Recovery

In the meantime, Raschi, staging an almost miraculous recovery, never gave the Bengals another look-in. Even a misjudged line drive that helped the Tigers to a tally in the seventh failed to disturb the strapping upstate New Yorker as he held the opposition to four hits in the last eight innings.

It marked the second successive year Vic has come home a 20-game winner—he bagged 21 last year. It was also his sixth triumph in a row and his sixteenth complete game. In three years he has won exactly 60 games for the Yanks.

However, in those first few harrowing minutes, which saw Casey Stengel probably die a thousand horrible deaths, it didn't look as though Vic would survive the opening round as the entire Tiger batting order came to the plate.

Don Kolloway grounded out, but Johnny Lipon and George Kell singled. Then came three successive passes, to Vic Wertz, Hoot Evers and Johnny Groth, forcing two runs over. Next Gerry Priddy singled and another scored and when Aaron Robinson lifted a fly to Mapes in right, Evers streaked home with the fourth tally of the inning. Not until Newhouser fanned for the third out did Stengel breathe easily again.

Then, in almost record time, Casey was his old smiling self. For as the second opened DiMaggio, first up, drove his No. 29 into the left-field stand. Hank Bauer walked and a moment later Mize rocketed his No. 20 into the right-field seats. In almost no time at all the Tiger lead had been cut down to one.

Forge Ahead in Fourth

In the third that margin disappeared as Yogi Berra singled, DiMaggio walked and Bauer singled, driving in Yogi. And in the fourth, the last for Newhouser, the Yanks forged head by two on singles by Jerry Coleman, Mapes and Phil Rizzuto and a fly by Berra.

Hal White took over the Detroit pitching with the fifth and thereafter kept the Bombers pretty well bottled up, except for Mapes' No. 11 high in the upper deck of the right-field stand in the sixth. But Raschi by now needed no more help.

The only Yankee flaw after the first came in the seventh when Kolloway led off with a sharp drive to left which Bauer momentarily lost sight of, the ball going over his head for a double. Don presently scored on two outs. But there were no more Tiger hits the rest of the way.

Coleman was 26 years old today and the Yanks' slick second sacker celebrated the occasion by extending his current hitting streak to eight games.

Setting the Pace

By GRANTLAND RICE

In 1946 Joe DiMaggio came out of the Army to bat .290. This was the first time in his career that Joe fell below the measurement of class— the .300 mark.

Grantland Rice

Since reporting to the Yankees in 1936, Joe's hitting marks have been .323, .346, .324, .381, .352, .357, .305, .290, .315, .320 and .346. His lifetime average going into 1950 was .331.

In 1946 Dominic DiMaggio left the Navy to bat .316, 26 points above the Yankee Clipper. The slender studious-looking Dom arrived with the Red Sox in 1940 where he proceeded to hit as follows: .301, .283, .286, .316, .285 and .307. Dom's lifetime average up through 1949 has been .294.

But unless big brother Joe has a sensational finish or little brother Dom takes a big dive, the younger DiMaggio will soon lead Joe for the second time.

At last reading, Dom DiMaggio was hitting .330. Joe was at .298 after a long, desperate climb. Joe had to hammer his way from .240 up the steepest hill he ever faced.

This, however, doesn't mean Dom has been the more effective hitter in spite of the Boston war cry:

He's better than his brother Joe—
Dominic DiMaggio

For Dom has had seven home runs to date and has batted in 65 runs. Against this, Joe has had 31 home runs and has batted in 113 runs. There has never been argument between the two when it comes to power.

Over the years the big brother is far ahead of the kid who has had a fine career, but well below the power-slashing of the bigger and older man.

The two DiMaggios have contributed as much to baseball as any family one can recall. Joe is three years older and five inches taller. That extra leverage counts.

What Part Does Luck Play in Sport?

I once asked Connie Mack what part he figured luck played in baseball. After some consideration his answer was around 3 per cent. There are times when it seems higher.

For example, there was Sal Maglie and his bid for the shutout record. The ball that Gus Bell hit after 45 scoreless frames was only an easy outfield fly, little better than a pop-up. At 257 feet most outfielders would have had to come in for it. And it landed just one inch or less from the foul line.

The odds against this sort of a ball being a home run were at least 200 to 1. And yet except for that, Maglie might easily have passed the brilliant Carl Hubbell's record and set sail for Walter Johnson's famous 56.

Then there was Jake LaMotta's finish against Laurent Dauthuille.

For 44 minutes and 40 seconds Dauthuille had piled up a winding margin that could only be wiped away by a knockout.

LaMotta had less than 20 seconds left.

He drew good breaks. One was facing a fighter too dumb to use those few seconds strictly on defense. Another was in landing one of his swings at the right spot after missing most of the night.

It will be interesting to see what part luck plays in this next world series. In short the fickle Dame can put on quite an act.

DiMag Saves Hit Skein

The Yankees returned here today from Chicago, with an 8-and-6 record for their six-city tour which opened with two straight defeats in Boston. ... They won 5 and lost 4 in the West.

Joe DiMaggio came back with a batting streak which had run through 13 consecutive contests. He saved his streak in the Comiskey Park final with a seventh-inning single off Howie Judson. ... The Clipper has 113 runs driven in, Yogi Berra boasts 114.

Phil Rizzuto finished the Western tour in a batting slump.

He came up 18 times for one hit, an infield safety.

Berra caught his 138th game of the season, and unless Ed Sweeney, away back in the Russ Ford days on the Hilltop, did better, the Yogi has a Yankee record.

The Yankees brought with them the 18-year-old Mickey Mantle Joplin shortstop.... His first visit to New York. ... Mantle is regarded as the boy wonder of the minors.... Also here is shortstop Bill Skowron, Purdue football player to whom George Weiss recently paid a bonus of $30,000.

Joe's Streak Reaches 15

With 66,924 paid for the second game with the Red Sox, and 130,922 for the two contests, Yankee Stadium attendance today had gone over the two million mark for the fifth consecutive year. ... The exact today was 2,041,527. ... With two double-headers with Washington to come.

Joe DiMaggio's batting streak stretched to 15 games with a single in five trips.

Yogi Berra drove in two runs and reached the 116 level, as against 114 for DiMaggio. ... Yogi belted a triple and three singles and was retired only once, on a liner to Dom Di-Maggio.

It was Johnny Mize Day. ... He got a car and many other gifts while Mrs. Mize received a set of furs. ... Horace Stoneham of the Giants brought a set of silver mugs for his former first sacker.

Tommy Henrich got a rifle from Meriden, Conn., friends, and Scranton pals of Steve O'Neill presented a purse to him.

Fairbanks, Alaska, got the game play by play ... Phil Rizzuto's homer was No. 25 off Ellis Kinder this season....

Ted Williams belted Vic Raschi for two homers, and Babby Doerr for a third, bringing the total of gopher balls pitched by the Yankee star this season to 17 ... It was only the second homer Doerr had hit in the Stadium in a career started in 1937....

When Williams dropped Dr. Brown's easy fly ball in the sixth, a lot of harsh customers waved their handkerchiefs at Ted....

The Yankees have 152 homers, club tops for the decade, and show 41 for their most recent 25 contest....

Clipper at Helm as Yanks Near Flag Harbor

By DANIEL,
Staff Writer.

PHILADELPHIA, Sept. 27.— After a split double-header with the Senators, which ended the season in the Stadium, the Yankees today faced the golden opportunity of clinching their pennant before leaving Shibe Park tomorrow afternoon.

A victory over the Athletics today would assure the Bombers of nothing worse than a tie.

A second triumph over the Mackmen tomorrow would leave the New York club with 98 won and 54 lost, and official entry into the World Series with the Phillies here next Wednesday.

Yankees Sign Nevel,
Use Him Twice.

Joe DiMaggio arrived here in a batting streak which had run through 19 consecutive contests. A triple in one game, and a single in another, had kept his string going in the double-header with Washington.

Joe had driven in four runs during the long and fantastic day, and had lifted his total for the season to 123, moving five beyond Yogi

The Stretch Runaway

	W.	L.	Pct.	G.B.	To Play
Yankees	96	54	.640	—	4
Tigers	92	57	.617	3½	5
Red Sox	91	57	.615	4	6

Remaining schedule:

	YANKEES	TIGERS	RED SOX.
Wed., Sept. 27	At Philadelphia	With St. Louis	With Washington (2)
Thurs., Sept. 28	At Philadelphia	With St. Louis	With Washington
Fri., Sept. 29	OPEN	OPEN	With Washington
Sat., Sept. 30	At Boston	With Cleveland (2)	With New York
Sun., Oct. 1	At Boston	With Cleveland	With New York

Berra who had lorded it over him virtually the entire season.

With 32 home runs, an average of .302, and his zest for baseball never at a higher pitch, Giuseppe looked forward to still another opportunity to flout those who had begun to toss him among the baseball washups.

"I told you when things looked darkest for me that I still would finish with better than .300, that I might even hit 35 homers," DiMaggio exuberated on the trip from New York. "Who knows? I might even belt three in our remaining four games."

Stengel gave a certificate for effort and high promise to righthander Ernie Nevel, who won 21 and lost 12 for Beaumont's Texas League pennant winners this season, and appeared in both games with Washington.

Yesterday morning, the Yankees acquired Nevel from Kansas City, to which he already had been assigned.

In the first contest, Ernie pitched the ninth inning and retired the side in order, with two strikeouts.

In the afterpiece, Nevel replaced starter Joe Ostrowski in the fifth, and worked nearly three innings. Things got a trifle too torrid for the newcomer in the seventh, and with two out he was lifted for Tom Ferrick.

The official scorer could have awarded the victory to Nevel if he had been so disposed. But he gave it to Ferrick, who needed the tonic badly after a lacklustre western trip.

Nevel is big and strong, and looks like a pitcher. "He has a good fast ball, his curve is not at all bad, and everything considered he made an interesting showing." Casey said.

What he hinted about Tommy Byrne, who in the first game suffered his ninth consecutive retirement, was not too elegant. Byrne has not gone through a game since he blanketed the Indians with three hits on Aug. 6. Tommy lost his father shortly thereafter.

That Old Yankee Spirit Keeps Burning

To You . . . the Flaming Torch   *By Burris Jenkins, Jr.*

JOE DIMAGGIO — HENRICH — RIZZUTO —

COLEMAN — BROWN — COLLINS — BAUER — MAPES — JOHNSON — BERRA — WOODLING —

'N. Y.' on Blouse Boosts Players' Desire to Win

Makes Skilled Performers Better and Lifts Mediocre Athletes to Greater Peaks

By DAN DANIEL

NEW YORK, N. Y.

Tommy Henrich had been sidelined with that aching left knee, and Joe Collins had gone to first base. The replacement was batting well over .300 and doing a splendid job in the field, too.

"How do they do it?" exclaimed a visiting manager in the Stadium. "I saw Collins down in Florida and was confident that by now he would be back with Kansas City.

"They put a Yankee uniform on a player who appears to be bread-and-butter class and the next thing you know he is beating your brains out."

Well put, that was. And that's exactly how it works out. There is something intangible, but nonetheless powerful, in merely being a Yankee. It makes the strong, and usually turns the weak, into factors of strength. Now and then the formula fails. But such experiences serve all the more to stress the strength of the psychology of the New York uniform, the New York clubhouse, the New York atmosphere.

* * *

Team Comes First

The Yankees have had stars innumerable since they began to win pennants in 1921. They have had Babe Ruth, Lou Gehrig, Tony Lazzeri, Waite Hoyt, Herb Pennock, Wilcy Moore, Wally Pipp, Earle Combs, Bob Meusel, Lefty Gomez, Spud Chandler, Joe Di-Maggio, Red Ruffing, Tommy Henrich,

Stengel's Crew Again Displays Its Gameness

Not Even Great '27 Champs Showed Greater Fight Than Casey's Battlers

Joe Page, Frankie Crosetti, Red Rolfe —oh, just scads of them.

But, no matter how outstanding a hero might be on the New York club, he never allows himself to forget that the team comes first.

In analyzing the factors which enter into the making of the Yankees, it would be well to examine, first, the Stadium atmosphere.

New York is called too cosmopolitan, too cold, by those who come in from other places. As a matter of fact, it is a warm, sympathetic city.

Being the largest city in America,

New York has diverse interests, myriad attractions and distractions.

It is large enough to swallow up even a World's Series. You will see stories on the first pages of its newspapers when a classic is in town, especially if it should happen to throw the Yankees against the Dodgers. You will see more strangers around the hotels, and night club business picks up a bit. But Pop Knickerbocker can take his World's Series, his big football game, his world's championship fight, in stride.

As a consequence, New York fans are not subject to the violent ups and downs which mark devotion to baseball in so many other cities in the major leagues.

• • •

Kindly Attitude at Game

New York newspapers do not shout, "Go Get Them, Indians!" across Page 1 one week, and berate the home team as a bunch of bums a fortnight later.

This does not mean that New York is blase. Far from it. The old town can get itself into quite a boil with 70,000 watching a hot Sunday double-header, or a dramatic nocturne, in the big Stadium.

However, New York has a kindly attitude at the ball game. Mind, I am speaking of New York, and in baseball, that emphatically does not take in Brooklyn. That faubourg is as distant from Gotham, in a baseball sense, as is St. Louis, geographically.

Nowhere else in the big leagues will the visiting club get the support, the cheers, it receives in New York.

Nowhere else is there so large a daily percentage of outlanders among the spectators. There will be 50,000 excursionists among 80,000 onlookers when the Yankees come to Cleveland. But, day after day, no city will have so many visitors as New York at its ball games.

Not only the out-of-town fans, but the home-grown type, as well, will give the visiting team a treatment it cannot possibly receive, as a regular practice, in any other locale.

Yes, they did hoot Babe Ruth in the sunset of his career. But those were not native fans. Occasionally, when Joe DiMaggio is not going so well, you will hear some boos as he comes to bat. But those are strangers from Brooklyn, who wish they had Joe over in Flatbush.

Major leaguers tell me that they like New York best of all cities, that the fans in the Stadium and at the Polo Grounds are the fairest and the most appreciative in the country. They are kind to visitors, they are utterly fair to their own players.

This attitude doubtless stems from the sports pages. There rarely are diatribes against erring players, against managers, in the newspapers of the big city.

Nowhere else is your umpire treated with such kindness. In fact, his name scarcely ever is printed.

First Place—or Season Is Failure for New York

NEW YORK, N. Y.—Playing for a New York club has its obvious advantages. But it also has some very important disadvantages. To be a Yankee is not what the English call all beer and skittles.

In some other cities, finishing in the first division is regarded by the fans as satisfactory.

In New York, if you cannot win, you might as well be last, for all the recognition a second, third or fourth place will get from the customers.

Yankee fans, especially, have got into the habit of climaxing their season's attendance with a World's Series. If they cannot achieve this fillip, the season is a total loss, even if the Bombers should finish second.

Yes, we recall that rhubarb in September last year, when Umpire Bill Grieve called Johnny Pesky safe, and Catcher Ralph Houk of the Yankees, assisted by a packed Stadium, insisted that the Boston player had been tagged out. But even that incident was treated with New York suavity and calm. Nobody was shot.

In no other city is there so keen an appreciation of the fact that the player is doing his best, that the umpire is a trained honest official who calls them as he sees them.

For all this, Pop Knickerbocker does not arrogate unto himself any special distinctions, nor does he ask for special accolades. It's just the way he was brought up.

The position of the "foreign" player in a New York park is a somewhat complex one.

He will admit that when he plays in the Stadium, he will give out something special, expand everything he has. But he also will admit that the Yankee uniforms do something to a lot of those visiting technicians.

• • •

Rivals Play Harder, Too

We who write about baseball in New York very often get false ratings on players of other clubs. They play harder against our teams than they do in battle with others.

This is nothing new. It has been true for 50 years, anyway.

Years ago, landing on a New York team meant getting the maximum in salary. Now, other clubs vie with the Yankees in the lavishness of their financial treatment of players. But New York still is the big magnet.

"It costs 20 per cent more to live in New York than it does in any other city, but I would rather play for the Yankees for 15 grand than for some other outfit for 20," a Bomber told me not so long ago. "Don't go quoting me.

George Weiss might get ideas," he laughed.

The club which represents the Yankees today is not what we would call a really spectacular one, measured by Yankee standards. It is not a great outfit if we throw it against the background of, let us say, the 1927 team, for which Babe Ruth hit 60 homers, and which compiled a club average of .308.

However, this 1950 Bomber crew, substantially the one with which Casey Stengel won the world's championship in 1949, boasts one quality which not even the 1927 club had to a greater degree. That is fight.

Our current Yankees are a game, aggressive, never-say-die, unquenchable bunch of battlers as they proved in the flag race this year. If the rival club makes a mistake during a game, these Bombers will go tearing through to victory.

Let me cite an example. On the night of June 8, 62,264 paying guests turned out to see the world's champions go against the youthful Art Houtteman of the Tigers.

As the Yanks came up in the sixth, they had no runs and just one flukey hit.

Houtteman retired Gerald Coleman, and then Tommy Byrne also grounded out. Art got two strikes on Phil Rizzuto. One strike more and the side would be out, with Detroit leading by 2 to 0. But Houtteman hit Phil in the back with a sidearm curve. Then Cliff Mapes rifled a single to center.

• • •

Art Sensed His Doom

Houtteman had made the fatal error, and he sensed it. At once his stuff deserted him. The Yankees got seven runs with two out, and drove Art to cover.

It is true that other clubs do that, too. It is not cited as an exclusive Yankee specialty. But it is a steady Yankee trait.

I have mentioned the 1950 Yankees in comparison with the 1927 club. That was hitting below the belt, and I apologize. We do not have the type of players we had in 1927. There was a war, a whole generation of young players was lost, another generation was hampered, if not killed off, in its cradle. Now we are waiting for the old standards to be achieved again. But it will take much longer than we had expected.

The bellwethers of this New York club are its liaisons with the glories of the past—Joe DiMaggio, who came up from San Francisco in 1936, and Tommy Henrich, who became a Yankee the following year.

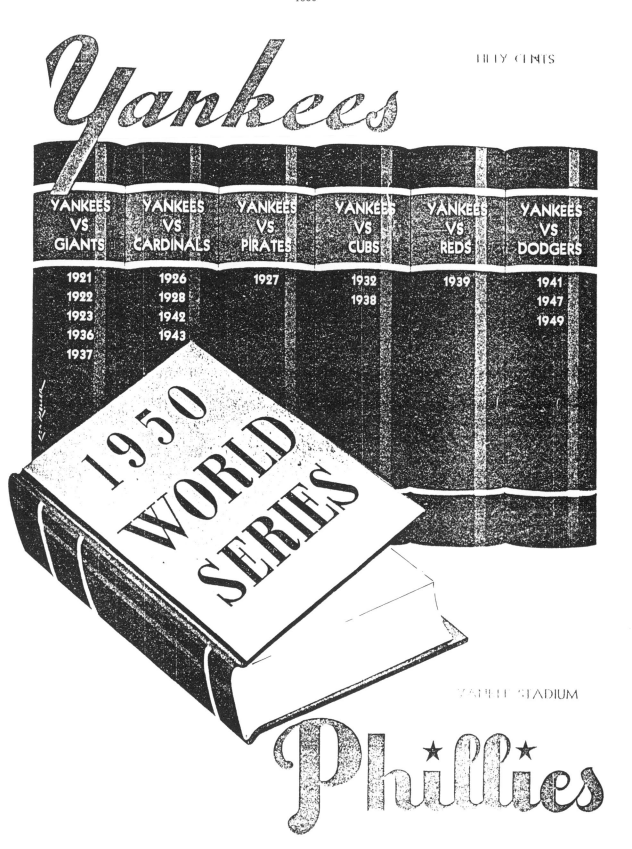

FIFTY CENTS

Yankees

YANKEES VS GIANTS	YANKEES VS CARDINALS	YANKEES VS PIRATES	YANKEES VS CUBS	YANKEES VS REDS	YANKEES VS DODGERS
1921	1926	1927	1932	1939	1941
1922	1928		1938		1947
1923	1942				1949
1936	1943				
1937					

1950 WORLD SERIES

YANKEE STADIUM

Phillies

Game 1 October 4 at Philadelphia

New York	Pos	AB	R	H	RBI	PO	A	E
Woodling	lf	3	0	1	0	1	0	0
Rizzuto	ss	3	0	1	0	0	2	0
Berra	c	4	0	0	0	7	0	0
DiMaggio	cf	2	0	0	0	2	0	0
Mize	1b	4	0	0	0	7	0	0
Hopp	1b	0	0	0	0	3	0	0
Brown	3b	4	1	1	0	1	0	0
Johnson	3b	0	0	0	0	0	0	0
Bauer	rf	4	0	1	0	5	0	0
Coleman	2b	4	0	0	1	1	2	0
Raschi	p	3	0	1	0	0	3	0
Totals		31	1	5	1	27	7	0

Pitching	IP	H	R	ER	BB	SO
New York						
Raschi (W)	9	2	0	0	1	5
Philadelphia						
Konstanty (L)	8	4	1	1	4	0
Meyer	1	1	0	0	0	0

N Y	000	100	000					1
Phi	000	000	000					0

Philadelphia	Pos	AB	R	H	RBI	PO	A	E
Waitkus	1b	3	0	0	0	9	2	0
Ashburn	cf	4	0	0	0	2	0	0
Sisler	lf	4	0	0	0	3	0	0
Ennis	rf	3	0	0	0	4	0	0
Jones	3b	3	0	1	0	4	3	1
Hamner	ss	3	0	0	0	0	1	0
Seminick	c	3	0	1	0	1	1	0
Goliat	2b	3	0	0	0	3	2	0
Konstanty	p	2	0	0	0	1	0	0
a Whitman		1	0	0	0	0	0	0
Meyer	p	0	0	0	0	0	1	0
Totals		29	0	2	0	27	10	1

a Flied out for Konstanty in 8th

Double—Brown. Sacrifice Hits—Raschi, Rizzuto. Left on Bases—New York 9, Philadelphia 3. Umpires—Conlan (N), McGowan (A), Boggess (N), Berry (A), Barlick (N), McKinley (A). Attendance—30,746. Time of Game—2:17.

1st Inning
New York
Woodling walked
Rizzuto singled between short and third, Woodling stopping at second
1 Berra flied to deep right, Woodling going to third after the catch
2 DiMaggio flied to Waitkus
3 Mize flied to right
Philadelphia
1 Waitkus fouled to Berra (previously he fouled to left where Woodling was stunned after crashing into the wall)
2 Ashburn bunted back to the mound
3 Sisler bounced to the pitcher

2nd Inning
New York
1 Brown flied to right
2 Bauer grounded to short
3 Coleman fouled to Sisler
Philadelphia
1 Ennis grounded to second
2 Jones popped (fair) to Berra
3 Hamner grounded to short

3rd Inning
New York
Raschi singled to left
Woodling walked
* Rizzuto sacrificed both runners, Waitkus to Goliat covering first
2 Berra flied to short left
DiMaggio got an intentional walk
3 Mize popped to third
Philadelphia
1 Seminick struck out
2 Goliat flied to left
3 Konstanty grounded back to the mound

4th Inning
New York
* Brown got a double inside the third base line
* Bauer flied to deep center with Brown going to third after the catch
2 Coleman flied to deep left, Brown scoring after the catch
3 Raschi grounded to third
Philadelphia
1 Waitkus grounded to second
2 Ashburn flied to center
3 Sisler struck out

5th Inning
New York
1 Woodling grounded out, Waitkus to Konstanty covering first
2 Rizzuto fouled to Seminick
3 Berra fouled to Waitkus
Philadelphia
1 Ennis flied to right
Jones singled through the box
2 Hamner flied to right
Seminick singled to left, Jones stopping at second
3 Goliat struck out

6th Inning
New York
DiMaggio walked
1 Mize popped to third
2 Brown lined to right
3 Bauer forced DiMaggio at second, Jones to Goliat
Philadelphia
1 Konstanty struck out
Waitkus walked
2 Ashburn flied to center
3 Sisler popped to first

7th Inning
New York
1 Coleman grounded to third
Raschi safe at first on Jones low throw
Woodling singled to left with Raschi stopping at second
2 Rizzuto popped to third
3 Berra grounded to first
Philadelphia
1 Ennis flied to right
2 Jones flied to center
3 Hamner flied to deep right

8th Inning
New York
1 DiMaggio popped to third
2 Mize grounded to second
3 Brown grounded to second
Philadelphia
For New York—Hopp at first, Johnson at third
1 Seminick fouled to Hopp
2 Goliat lined to second
3 Whitman, pinch-hitting for Konstanty, flied to right

9th Inning
New York
For Philadelphia—Meyer pitching
Bauer singled off Jones' hand
1 Coleman flied to center
2 Raschi sacrificed Bauer to second, Meyer to Goliat covering first
3 Woodling out on a bouncer, Seminick to Waitkus
Philadelphia
1 Waitkus grounded to short
2 Ashburn bounced to first
3 Sisler struck out

Hurlers Give Yanks
Fast Start in Series

Raschi and Reynolds Win Hill Duels, Hold
Phils to Total of Nine Hits in First Two Games

By STAN BAUMGARTNER

PHILADELPHIA, Pa.

Vic Raschi

Yankee pitching sent the American League champions off to a two-to-nothing World's Series lead over the National League Phillies in the first two games at Shibe Park, October 4 and 5.

Vic Raschi and Allie Reynolds held the Phils to nine hits in the first 19 innings. Raschi allowed only two safeties as he blanked the National League champions, 1 to 0, in the first tilt for the second World's Series victory of his career. Reynolds permitted only seven safeties in ten innings as he won, 2 to 1, and ran his string of consecutive scoreless innings in the classic to 16 and two-thirds innings.

The big surprise in the first two tilts was the failure of the power hitters of the Yankees (except for Joe DiMaggio's game-winning home run) to hit Jim Konstanty and Robin Roberts.

Konstanty, who appeared in a record 74 games in relief during the regular season, was a surprise starter in the first game and did an excellent job. Roberts was equally as effective in the second. Bill Dickey called Roberts the best young righthanded pitcher in either league.

In the first two games, Yogi Berra and Johnny Mize each went to bat nine times with one hit. DiMag had one safety in seven trips.

--------- FIRST GAME ---------

Raschi Shades Konstanty
on Two-Hit Gem in Opener

PHILADELPHIA, Pa.

Pupil turned on his teacher as the Yankees defeated the Phillies, 1 to 0, in the first game of the forty-seventh World's Series before 30,746, who paid $160,130.20.

Vic Raschi, who learned his baseball under the Phillies' manager, Eddie Sawyer, when the latter piloted Amsterdam in the Canadian-American League for the Yankees, held the Whiz Kids to two hits, walked only one and retired the National leaguers in order in seven of the nine innings.

Willie Jones, who made the first hit in the fifth inning, was the only Phil to reach second base. He went to the keystone sack when Andy Seminick also hit safely.

Jim Konstanty, veteran relief pitcher who established a modern record of 74 appearances during the season—all in rescue roles—made his first start since 1948, when he was with Toronto, and held the New Yorkers to five safeties.

The Yankees won the game in the fourth frame, when Bobby Brown doubled along the third base line with none out, went to third on Hank Bauer's fly to Richie Ashburn and scored on Gerald Coleman's hoist to Dick Sisler.

Bobby Brown

It was the Yankees' ninth consecutive opening game triumph in Series competition. Carl Hubbell of the Giants was the last twirler to defeat them in an opening game in 1936.

Using a crackling fast ball, an occasional slider, a change of pace and a curve now and then with excellent control, Raschi was complete master of the Phillies.

Konstanty Tight in Pinches

Konstanty pitched almost as well as Raschi and was tight in the pinches. The bespectacled righthander was in trouble in three innings, besides the fatal fourth. The Yankees had men on first and third and one out in the first; second and third and one down in the third; first and second and one out in the seventh, but each time Konstanty shut the door.

Yogi Berra, Joe DiMaggio and Johnny Mize, the power of the Gotham attack, failed to make a hit in ten trips.

It was the third successive 1 to 0 opening Series game, and almost a replica of the initial tilt last year when Allie Reynolds gave the Dodgers two safeties and Don Newcombe yielded only five to the Yanks. Tommy Henrich won that game with a home run.

Bob Feller allowed the Braves only two safeties in 1948, but lost, 1 to 0.

Outfielder Gene Woodling and Umpire Jocko Conlan suffered slight injuries, but remained in action. Woodling bruised his knee, head and arm when he fell into the concrete retaining wall

One Big Run That Won Game No. 1

BOBBY BROWN, who scored the only run in the Yankees' 1 to 0 first-game victory in the 1950 World's Series, crossing the plate on Gerald Coleman's long fly. The umpire is Jocko Conlan and the catcher Andy Seminick.

surrounding the left field seats chasing Eddie Waitkus' foul. Conlan was hit on the right arm by a foul tip off Mike Goliat's bat in the fifth inning.

Opening Breezes

LONG PERIOD OF SILENCE IN PHILLY

STARTING with a 30-second silent prayer for peace before the first game opened, rooters for the Phillies went through two hours and 17 minutes of virtual silence as their favorites were shut out. Except for the fifth inning, when Willie Jones and Andy Seminick singled for the only hits off Vic Raschi, the Philadelphia fans, who had little to cheer about, remained unusually quiet throughout the afternoon. . . . Only three Phils got on base—Seminick and Jones on hits, and Eddie Waitkus on a pass in the sixth inning. . . . In the very first inning, Jim Konstanty almost ran into serious trouble when, after Gene Woodling walked, Scooter Rizzuto dropped a bunt down the third base line. Jones allowed it to roll and it looked like an infield single until the ball hopped over the foul line at the last minute. . . . Rizzuto then singled, but Yogi Berra, Joe DiMaggio and Johnny Mize were retired in order and the fans let up their

first whoop of the day. . . . The first protest came in the second inning when Hank Bauer hit a grounder to Gran Hamner and thought he beat the Philly shortstop's throw to first. Umpire McGowan, however, saw it otherwise and called the Yankee out. . . . DiMaggio threw a scare into the Philly rooters when he opened the sixth with a screaming liner into the left field stands. However, the ball was foul. Then the Yankee Clipper drew a base on balls. . . . Play was halted as Konstanty fanned to open the Phils' sixth. For at that instant, the sun broke through the clouds and outfielders began yelling for their dark glasses. . . . Jones was charged with the first error of the Series when he fielded Raschi's seventh-inning grounder but followed with a low throw to first, giving the pitcher a life.

Catcher Yogi Berra disagreed when Vic said this was the best game he had ever pitched. "Naw," protested Yogi. "That game he pitched in Cleveland was much better." Vic was wise-cracking when photogs asked him to pose for pictures with Berra. After they flashed several shots, Raschi said: "Hurry up and get your pictures; how long do you think I can stand here looking at Yogi?"

PHIL TRIBUTE TO RASCHI

EVEN the Phils agreed that Vic Raschi pitched a great game. As they entered their dressing room after the game, Dick Sisler remarked: "No use making excuses when you lose a well-played game like that; that Raschi certainly had it." Dick said he never had a chance to duplicate his feat of hitting a homer as he had against the Dodgers three days before. "Raschi never gave me anything good to hit; he had my number." Del Ennis, too, thought Raschi outsmarted him. "All afternoon," remarked Del, "he kept me hitting to right field." . . . Jim Konstanty said the Yanks scored their run off his best pitch, the slider. Brown hit a double off a slider and Hank Bauer and Gerry Coleman raised their flies which produced the run off the same pitch. . . . The Phil hurler didn't think he got his biggest baseball thrill out of his first World's Series start. "I got a greater kick out of the All-Star Game—just talking to some of those stars," he admitted. . . . Gran Hamner probably took the loss hardest of all. For a long time, the Phils' shortstop simply sat in front of his locker with his face buried in his hands, refusing to talk to anyone. . . . Manager Sawyer told newsmen why he ordered Joe DiMaggio, a righthander, passed so Konstanty, a righthander, could pitch to

Mize, a lefthander. "That might defy the percentages," he admitted, "but not in this case, because Konstanty is more effective against lefthanded batters than against righthanders."

When Johnny Mize was asked if Jim Konstanty threw much breaking stuff, he replied, "The only time his ball doesn't break is when he is warming up between innings."

SCALPERS REALLY SCALPED

WORLD'S SERIES scalpers took a real licking for the initial game. They were offering box seats for $4 as the game got under way . . . The last word in requests for tickets was reached in Stan (Philadelphia Inquirer) Baumgartner's house the morning the Series opened. Bonnie, his eight-year-old daughter, was called to the phone. "Guess who?" said the voice. "These are my initials, J. V." "Oh, you're the little girl who sat next to me in school last year," said Bonnie. "Yes," replied the voice on the other end of the wire. "My daddy wants to know if your daddy can get him two tickets for the game today." . . . Manager Eddie Sawyer of the Phillies had 19 persons staying at his house in Wayne the first two days of the Series. He slept on a rug in the living room. . . . Before the game, Del Ennis taped a small gold horseshoe on the lining of his hat for luck . . . and then popped out three times. . . . Babe Alexander and Frank Powell, public relations director and traveling secretary, respectively, of the Phillies, issued stringent regulations not to allow anyone to move around without a proper badge. Then they forgot to keep tickets themselves and were refused entrance to the park until they called from outside and got proper credentials. After that, they walked around with deputy sheriff badges.

STENGEL'S STRATEGY PAYS OFF

HANK BAUER made a fine catch on Gran Hamner's drive with two out in the seventh. For a time, it looked like an extra-base hit, but Bauer, with his back to the wall, plucked off the liner and avoided a Phil scoring threat. . . . Manager Casey Stengel, as a defensive move, sent Johnny Hopp to first and Bill Johnson to third for his Yankees in the ninth inning. . . . Hopp justified Manager Stengel's faith in his defensive ability by making a great stop of Richie Ashburn's hot ninth-inning smash and beating him to the bag. The blow looked like a triple into the right-field corner as it left Ashburn's bat. . . . Russ Meyer, who hurled the ninth for the Phils, gave up just one safety, a scratch hit by Bauer. . . . Dick Sisler, whose home run whipped the Dodgers, October 1, and clinched the National League pennant, brought the World's Series opener to an inglorious finish (for the Phils) by striking out. . . . Johnny Mize, on his first two times up, stranded five base runners. In the third, Manager Sawyer ordered DiMaggio purposely passed with two out, filling the bases. Jim Konstanty got Mize on a pop fly to Jones.

Two of a Kind

WILLIE JONES, Phillies' third baseman, greeting his boyhood idol, Pie Traynor, all-time great of the Pirates. Jones had missed meeting Traynor in Pittsburgh this summer, but they got together before the first game of the Series.

■———————————■

Yankees' No. 1 Win Third 1-0 Opener in Three Years

PHILADELPHIA, Pa.—The Yankees' 1 to 0 victory over the Phillies, October 4, marked the third straight year that the World's Series opener had been decided by that score. Johnny Sain of the Braves inaugurated the 1948 Series with a 1 to 0 triumph over the Indians, and Allie Reynolds of the Yankees posted a victory by the same score over the Dodgers in the first game of last year's fall classic.

Vic Raschi's decision in the battle with Jim Konstanty was the eleventh 1 to 0 game in World's Series competition and was the fourth in three consecutive years. After Reynolds beat the Dodgers in the opener last fall, Preacher Roe came back to shade the Yankees, 1 to 0, in the second game of the Series.

■———————————■

Old Tommy Disappointed, But Approves Pick of Hopp

PHILADELPHIA, Pa.—Though he could scarcely hold back his feeling of disappointment, Tommy Henrich, the Old Pro, when told that he had been taken off the Yanks' World's Series eligibility list and replaced by Johnny Hopp, said: "I want my team to be at its best for this World's Series. And if the powers-that-be want me to sit out this one in order to allow Hopp to play, that's okay with me. Johnny's been a valuable man to this club. He's in fine shape and his hitting might help us win some games."

Henrich admitted he was disappointed when George Weiss, Yankee general manager, notified him of the move.

■———————————■

Special Guest

PHIL RIZZUTO, Yankee shortstop, meets Mrs. Grace Coolidge, widow of the former President, who is an ardent fan. She was the guest of Will Harridge, president of the American League, during the Series.

Game 2 October 5 at Philadelphia

New York	Pos	AB	R	H	RBI	PO	A	E
Woodling	lf	5	0	2	1	2	0	0
Rizzuto	ss	4	0	0	0	2	1	0
Berra	c	5	0	1	0	7	0	0
DiMaggio	cf	5	1	1	1	3	0	0
Mize	1b	4	0	1	0	6	0	0
Johnson	3b	1	0	0	0	0	2	0
Brown	3b	4	0	2	0	0	0	0
b Hopp	1b	1	0	0	0	3	0	0
Bauer	rf	5	0	1	0	1	0	0
Coleman	2b	3	1	1	0	5	6	0
Reynolds	p	3	0	1	0	1	2	0
Totals		40	2	10	2	30	11	0

Pitching	IP	H	R	ER	BB	SO
New York						
Reynolds (W)	10	7	1	1	4	6
Philadelphia						
Roberts (L)	10	10	2	2	3	5

N Y	0 1 0	0 0 0	0 0 0	1		2
Phi	0 0 0	0 1 0	0 0 0	0		1

Philadelphia	Pos	AB	R	H	RBI	PO	A	E
Waitkus	1b	4	0	2	0	8	0	0
Ashburn	cf	5	0	2	1	4	0	0
Sisler	lf	5	0	0	0	3	0	0
Ennis	rf	4	0	0	0	1	0	0
Jones	3b	4	0	0	0	3	0	0
Hamner	ss	3	0	2	0	2	2	0
Seminick	c	2	0	0	0	5	0	0
a Caballero		0	0	0	0	0	0	0
Silvestri	c	0	0	0	0	1	0	0
c Whitman		0	0	0	0	0	0	0
Lopata	c	0	0	0	0	1	0	0
Goliat	2b	4	1	1	0	2	2	0
Roberts	p	2	0	0	0	0	0	0
d Mayo		0	0	0	0	0	0	0
Totals		33	1	7	1	30	4	0

a Ran for Seminick in 7th.
b Ran for Brown in 8th.
c Intentionally walked for Silvestri in 9th.
d Walked for Roberts in 10th.

Doubles—Ashburn, Coleman, Hamner, Waitkus.
Triple—Hamner. Home Run—DiMaggio.
Stolen Base—Hamner.
Sacrifice Hits—Roberts, Waitkus.
Double Plays—Johnson to Coleman to Hopp.
Rizzuto to Coleman to Hopp
Left on Bases—New York 11, Philadelphia 8
Umpires—McGowan, Boggess, Berry, Conlan,
McKinley, Barlick. Attendance—32,660
Time of Game—3:06

1st Inning
New York
Woodling beat out a slow roller to
short.
1 Rizzuto fouled to Seminick.
Berra singled to left, Woodling going
to third
2 DiMaggio popped to second
3 Mize fouled to Seminick
Philadelphia
1 Waitkus grounded to second
Ashburn doubled to right as Bauer
missed a shoestring catch
2 Sisler struck out
3 Ennis grounded to second

2nd Inning
New York
1 Brown lined to center
2 Bauer fouled to Jones
Coleman walked
Reynolds singled to right, sending
Coleman to third
Woodling got another hit on a roller
to short, Coleman scoring and Reynolds
stopping at second
3 Rizzuto flied to center
Philadelphia
1 Jones called out on strikes
Hamner tripled to right-center
2 Seminick grounded to second, Hamner
holding third
3 Goliat flied to center

3rd Inning
New York
1 Berra struck out
2 DiMaggio popped to second
Mize singled to right
3 Brown flied to center
Philadelphia
1 Roberts struck out
Waitkus doubled down the right field
line
2 Ashburn fouled to Berra
3 Sisler grounded to second

4th Inning
New York
1 Bauer popped to short
Coleman doubled into center
Reynolds walked
2 Woodling fouled to Sisler
3 Rizzuto lined to right
Philadelphia
1 Ennis struck out
2 Jones popped to first
Hamner walked
Hamner stole second
3 Seminick struck out

5th Inning
New York
1 Berra popped to short
2 DiMaggio popped to third
3 Mize struck out
Philadelphia
Goliat singled between first and second
1 Roberts popped to the pitcher on an
attempted sacrifice
Waitkus singled over Coleman's head,
Goliat moving to third
2 Ashburn flied to left, Goliat scoring
after the catch
3 Sisler fouled to Mize

6th Inning
New York
Brown singled to left-center
1 Bauer fouled to Waitkus
2 Coleman popped to first
3 Reynolds struck out
Philadelphia
1 Ennis flied out to DiMaggio in very deep
right-center. A spectacular running
catch
2 Jones lined to short
3 Hamner popped to second

7th Inning
New York
1 Woodling flied to Sisler
Rizzuto walked
2 Berra flied to center
3 DiMaggio fouled to Waitkus
Philadelphia
Seminick walked
Caballero ran for Seminick
1 Goliat flied to left
2 Roberts sacrificed Caballero to second,
Reynolds to Coleman
3 Waitkus lined to center

8th Inning
New York
For Philadelphia—Silvestri catching
1 Mize fouled to Waitkus
Brown singled over third
Bauer singled between short and third
Brown stopping at second
Hopp ran for Brown
2 Coleman grounded to short, advancing
both runners
3 Reynolds took a called third strike
Philadelphia
For New York—Hopp at first (batting 6th)
and Johnson playing third (batting 5th)
Ashburn singled on a bunt toward third
1 Sisler forced Ashburn at second, on a
bunt, Reynolds to Rizzuto
2,3 Ennis hit into a double play, Johnson
to Coleman to Hopp

9th Inning
New York
1 Woodling grounded to second
2 Rizzuto grounded to second
3 Berra fouled to Jones
Philadelphia
1 Jones flied to right
Hamner doubled to right-center
Whitman, batting for Silvestri, was
given an intentional walk
2,3 Goliat grounded into a double play,
Rizzuto to Coleman to Hopp

10th Inning
New York
For Philadelphia—Lopata catching
DiMaggio homered into the upper left
field stands
1 Johnson struck out
2 Hopp flied to left
3 Bauer grounded to short
Philadelphia
Mayo, batting for Roberts, walked
1 Waitkus sacrificed Mayo to second,
Johnson to Coleman
2 Ashburn fouled to Hopp
3 Sisler looked at a called third strike.

Joe DiMaggio pulls in a long drive to center field off the bat of Del Ennis of the Philadelphia Phillies, in Game 2 of the 1950 World Series. The Yankees won the game, 2–1, on DiMaggio's 10th-inning home run.

Chandlers Hail Hero of Phillies' Flag-Clincher

COMMISSIONER A. B. CHANDLER meets Dick Sisler, of the World's Series. Left to right, Phil Pilot Eddie Sawyer, Chandhero of the Phillies' pennant-clincher, before the opening game ler, Mrs. Chandler, the Chandlers' daughter Mimi, and Sisler.

—— SECOND GAME ——

DiMaggio's Homer Wins 10-Rounder

PHILADELPHIA, Pa.

Joe DiMaggio

A man named Joe DiMaggio gave the Yankees a 2 to 1 victory over the Phillies in the second contest of the World's Series at Shibe Park, October 5, before 32,660 to put the New Yorkers two games up on the National League pennant winners. DiMaggio, coming to bat in the first half of the tenth inning with none out and the score tied at 1 to 1, blasted Robin Roberts' fourth pitch into the upper tier of the left field stands for his seventh World's Series home run.

The mighty wallop broke up a brilliant pitching duel between Allie Reynolds and young Robin Roberts and gave Reynolds his third Series triumph without a defeat.

The count was two balls and one strike when Roberts threw a fast ball over the center of the plate. DiMaggio, who had gone to the plate six official times in the two games without even hitting the ball out of the infield, met the pitch on the fat of his bat.

DiMaggio not only won the game with his hitting, but also saved it with spectacular fielding. In the sixth inning, he robbed Del Ennis of a potential triple with a catch near the 400-foot light standard in deep right center, and in the ninth he held Gran Hamner's bid for a triple with one out to a two-bagger.

The Yankees scored their first run in the second inning after two out. Gerald Coleman walked and Reynolds, a .185 hitter during the regular season, poked a single to right, sending Coleman to third. Gene Woodling followed with a high bounder out of Willie Jones' reach. Hamner fielded the ball, but could not throw to second in time to get Reynolds and Coleman scored.

The Phillies tied it at 1 to 1 in the fifth with the aid of an infield hit and a lucky bounce. Mike Goliat opened with a grounder between first and second on which Coleman made a great stop but could not throw him out. Roberts popped out, trying to sacrifice. Waitkus hit a routine grounder to second, but it hit a spike indentation in the clay, bounced over Coleman's head and Goliat went to third. He scored when Waitkus flied to Woodling.

Second Game Sidelights

SISLER ENDS GAME WITH WHIFF

THE PHILLIES had only three assists in the first nine innings of the second game, tying a World's Series mark held by many clubs. The Whiz Kids came up with another assist in the tenth. . . . Johnny Mize explained his failure to hit Robin Roberts with the simple admission "he has too much stuff. His fast ball rises and we hit under it all day." . . . The Yankee scouts picked up Dick Sisler's weakness and the Yankee pitchers certainly worked on it — a high inside pitch. Sisler ended the first two games with strikeouts. . . . Gran Hamner's wide-awake base running caught the Yankees on their heels. He stretched a two-bagger into a triple in the second inning with one out, but failed to score. In the fourth inning, Hamner walked and stole second on the astonished Reynolds. Allie paid him little attention and he started running as Reynolds started to throw. Yogi Berra did not even make a peg to second.

For the second straight day, Gene Woodling opened for the Yanks by getting on base. In the opener, he walked; this time he singled.

HENRICH LEARNS ABOUT FAME

THE attendance at the second game was 32,600, nearly 2,000 larger than the throng that viewed the opener. . . . At last year's Series, special policemen had to clear the way for Tommy Henrich of the Yankees. This year, however, police blocked Henrich's entry into the Yanks' clubhouse after the game when Tommy, in civvies, tried to get through the door. "Who are you?" asked a cop. "I'm a ball player," said Henrich, who was taken off the eligible list of the Series. While the clubhouse guardians were continuing to question Old Reliable, another player came along and confirmed the fact that Tommy was a real ball player. . . . Allie Reynolds confessed he pulled a boner while pitching to Richie Ashburn in the fifth inning. "I wanted to throw him a fast one, but not fast and away from him where he could hit it," the Yankee pitcher said as he discussed the ball the Phil outfielder hit to score the losers' only run. . . . Phil Rizzuto thought Robin Roberts was tougher to hit than Jim Konstanty. "Roberts' fast ball overpowers you," the Scooter said. "His fast one hops; Konstanty's sinks."

Mayor Bernard Samuel of Philadelphia ordered the American flag flown from all Municipal buildings throughout the World's Series. He also asked the citizens of Philadelphia to fly Old Glory from their homes as a tribute to the Phillies' victory in the pennant race for the first time in 35 years.

PHILS LACK CLUTCH PUNCH

IN SIX of the nine innings, the Phils got runners to second base. In another, they stranded a runner on third. Then there was the frame in which they scored. Thus, in eight of the ten frames, the Phils had men in scoring position. . . . In only one inning, the sixth, did the Phils fail to put a man on base. It was a fine catch by Joe DiMaggio in this stanza that stopped them, the Clipper pulling down a terrific smash off Del Ennis' bat. . . . This overtime game was the first extra-inning contest in Series play since 1946 between the Cardinals and Red Sox. It was the twenty-fourth extra-inning affair in World's Series history. . . . Ashburn got the Phils' first extra-base blow, an arching double to right-center in the first inning, which Hank Bauer missed in attempting a diving catch. . . . In the fifth, Johnny Mize, Yanks' first sacker, registered a mild beef when he thought a ball he fielded off the bat of Eddie Waitkus was fair. The Phils' first baseman then got a single on a bad hopper over Coleman's head. . . . Repeating his move in the first game, Manager Stengel sent Johnny Hopp to first base in the eighth inning while Billy Johnson took over at third. . . . In this frame, the Yanks turned the first double play of the Series when, with one out after Ashburn beat out a bunt, Ennis tapped to Johnson, who started the twin-killing.

AWARD FOR DIMAGGIO

Columbia Civic Club of Newark To Honor Him on Thursday

NEWARK, N. J., Oct. 5 (AP)— The Columbia Civic Club announced today that it will honor Yankee outfielder Joe DiMaggio at its annual meeting next Thursday.

He will receive the club's award for his outstanding contribution to the development of fair play, sportsmanship and his inspirational effect on the youth of America.

DiMaggio, whose home run won today's world series game for the New York Yankees, is scheduled to share the rostrum at the dinner with Governor Driscoll and Newark Mayor Ralph Villani.

World Series Schedule

Today—At Yankee Stadium.

Tomorrow—At Yankee Stadium.

Sunday—At Yankee Stadium (if necessary).

Monday—At Shibe Park (if necessary).

Tuesday—At Shibe Park (if necessary).

In event of postponement, game will be held over until played on field where originally scheduled.

By Joe Williams

DiMaggio Spanks Sassy Small Fry With Big Stick

Trouble with precocious kids—and they can be as cute, cunning and cuddly as all get out—is that sooner or later the brat in them shows. Like this Robin Roberts and the shocking lack of respect he had for the old Yankees over in Philly yesterday.

It had been sickening enough the afternoon before when Jim Konstanty had DiMag and Mize falling on their kissers trying to get a piece of his custard pudding pitch but at least he was mannerly and matured about it. An old guy himself, he was properly sympathetic.

Besides the Yankees had got one run in the fourth and behind the strong-arm pitching of Vic Raschi were making it look like a million, so the Whiz Kids, as the fuzz-cheeked members of Bob Carpenter's scout troop are heroically called, had small chance to get fresh with their elderly visitors.

It was somewhat different in the second game of the World Series. The children were getting on bases more often and some of them were making real grown-up noises with their bats. In the second inning Granny Hamner, the shortstop who didn't start playing pro baseball until he was 17—just wouldn't eat his spinach!—hit one of Allie Reynolds' pitches all the way to the fence in left and didn't stop running until he pulled up at third.

Those of us in the TV audience could only imagine the great wave of boyish joy which must have swept over the Philly bench and the happy shrieks of "Oh, you Superman!" . . . "Just like Capt Marvel." . . . "Wait till Hopalong hears about this." All against a staccato background of bubble gum explosions and a shower of torn comic books.

* * *

No Respect for Gray Hairs.

After nine innings the score was tied and the children had not only held the old people even on the board but were becoming increasingly brash and assertive. Once Master Hamner, who must be no less than an Eagle Scout, and who was particularly obnoxious all afternoon, stole second so easily and with such gay abandon it was impossible to make a play on him.

But this was simply a manifestation of animal energy and youthful spirit, a quality to be admired and encouraged, though as Mr. Shaw has observed—or was it Connie Mack?—'tis a pity to waste it on the young. There was not, however, in this incident any suggestion of impudence or disrespect for gray hairs.

Unfortunately it appears that Master Roberts has not been as well disciplined as most of Prof. Carpenter's eager little beavers. Possibly he is just naturally incorrigible, a confirmed problem child. It has been clinically established that most children have a curious capacity for cruelty. Very likely a psychologist would find Master Roberts' background a revealing and perhaps a horrifying study.

It was significant that he made no effort to torture the younger Yankees. Woodling got two hits. So did Brown. And Coleman's pass with two down in the second became the Yankees' first run. It was against the venerable antiques that Master Roberts threw the full force of his disdain. There was something fiendish, even fanatical about the way he slashed at the royal robes of greatness and mocked the enduring tablets of time.

The TV voice which helps us understand the pictures became a monotone of misery. . . . "DiMaggio pops to Goliat . . . Mize goes down swinging . . . DiMaggio pops to Jones . . . Waitkus camps under Mize's infield fly . . . DiMaggio is easy." . . . etc., etc., etc.

* * *

They Learn the Hard Way.

Rizzuto, who is getting along, too, hadn't got a hit all day either. Mize was taken out in the eighth, his record for the series showing one demure single. Coming up to the tenth, DiMag hadn't got the ball past the infield in two full games. By now the malevolent moppets in the Philly nursery pen no doubt were laughing like crazy at the big bad man's feeble efforts to solve Master Roberts' magic. It was funnier than Howdy Doody or Lucky Pup.

To others it was more like tragedy. None of us could remember a series in which the Clipper had started so poorly or looked more pathetic at the plate. Time, of course, was catching up with him. Conceivably, he could be making his bow out as a series stalwart. It was no sure bet he'd be strong enough to play regularly another year. Was this then to be his role at the finish, one of dismal fumbling frustration?

. . . "It's going, it's going and it's in there for a home run and the Yankees are back in front, 2 to 1!"

That's how the voice with rapturous suddenness told us DiMag had snapped out of it in the tenth with a thunderous wallop which was not only to win the ball game but teach Master Roberts and the rest of the small fry a lesson most of us old-fashioned people learned years ago. Never laugh at an old man. Might be your own pop.

Game 3 October 6 at New York

Philadelphia	Pos	AB	R	H	RBI	PO	A	E
Waitkus	1b	5	0	1	0	8	0	0
Ashburn	cf	4	0	1	0	0	0	0
Jones	3b	3	0	1	0	1	2	0
Ennis	rf	4	1	1	0	3	0	0
Sisler	lf	4	0	1	1	2	0	0
Mayo	lf	0	0	0	0	1	0	0
Hamner	ss	4	1	3	0	2	2	1
Seminick	c	2	0	1	0	5	0	1
Goliat	2b	3	0	1	1	4	1	0
d Caballero		0	0	0	0	0	0	0
Bloodworth	2b	0	0	0	0	0	0	0
Heintzelman	p	2	0	0	0	0	2	0
Konstanty	p	0	0	0	0	0	0	0
e Whitman		1	0	0	0	0	0	0
Meyer	p	0	0	0	0	0	0	0
Totals		32	2	10	2	*26	7	2

* Two out when winning run scored.
a Popped out for Lopat in 8th.
b Safe on error for Bauer in 8th.
c Ran for Brown in 8th.
d Ran for Goliat in 9th.
e Hit into fielder's choice for Konstanty in 9th.

Doubles—Ennis, Hamner. Stolen Base—Rizzuto. Sacrifice Hits—Heintzelman, Jones, Seminick 2. Double Play—Hamner to Waitkus. Left on Bases—Philadelphia 8, New York 9. Umpires—Boggess, Berry, Conlan, McGowan, Barlick, McKinley. Attendance—64,505. Time of Game—2:35.

Phi.	000	001	100	2
N.Y.	001	000	011	3

New York	Pos	AB	R	H	RBI	PO	A	E
Rizzuto	ss	3	1	1	0	1	1	0
Coleman	2b	4	1	3	2	3	1	0
Berra	c	2	0	0	0	6	1	0
DiMaggio	cf	3	0	1	0	1	0	0
Bauer	lf	3	0	0	0	1	0	0
b Brown		1	0	0	0	0	0	0
c Jensen		0	0	0	0	0	0	0
Ferrick	p	0	0	0	0	0	0	0
Mize	1b	4	0	0	0	9	2	0
Collins	1b	0	0	0	0	1	1	0
Johnson	3b	4	0	0	0	1	3	0
Mapes	rf	4	0	0	0	3	0	0
Lopat	p	2	0	1	0	1	4	0
a Woodling	lf	2	1	1	0	0	0	0
Totals		32	3	7	2	27	13	0

Pitching	IP	H	R	ER	BB	SO
Philadelphia						
Heintzelman	7⅔	4	2	1	6	3
Konstanty	⅓	0	0	0	0	0
Meyer (L)	⅔	3	1	1	0	1
New York						
Lopat	8	9	2	2	0	5
Ferrick (W)	1	1	0	0	1	0

1st Inning
Philadelphia
Waitkus singled between first and second into right
1 Ashburn struck out.
2 Jones rolled back to the mound, Waitkus moving to second
3 Ennis grounded to third
New York
Rizzuto walked
1,2 Coleman blooped to Hamner who easily doubled Rizzuto at first
Berra walked
3 DiMaggio flied to right.

2nd Inning
Philadelphia
1 Sisler grounded to second
Hamner singled off Johnson's glove
Seminick singled to center, Hamner going to third
2 Goliat grounded to the pitcher. Seminick to second while Hamner held third.
3 Heintzelman grounded to third
New York
1 Bauer bounced back to the mound.
2 Mize popped to second
3 Johnson struck out

3rd Inning
Philadelphia
1 Waitkus flied to right
2 Ashburn called out on strikes
Jones singled to left
3 Ennis popped to short
New York
1 Mapes popped to first
2 Lopat took a called third strike
Rizzuto walked
Rizzuto stole second and went to third when Seminick's throw went into center field
Coleman singled to right, Rizzuto
3 scoring, but was out trying for a double Sisler to Hamner to Goliat.

4th Inning
Philadelphia
1 Sisler grounded to first
2 Hamner flied to right.
3 Seminick struck out.
New York
1 Berra grounded to the pitcher.
DiMaggio singled to left
2 Bauer flied to Ennis in deep right-center.
3 Mize grounded to first.

5th Inning
Philadelphia
1 Goliat grounded to short.
2 Heintzelman grounded out, Mize to Lopat.
3 Waitkus fouled to Johnson
New York
1 Johnson grounded to third.
2 Mapes flied to left.
Lopat singled to center.
3 Rizzuto popped to second.

6th Inning
Philadelphia
1 Ashburn struck out
2 Jones struck out
Ennis doubled into the left field corner
Sisler singled over Rizzuto's head, Ennis scoring
3 Hamner missed an attempted surprise bunt and Sisler was picked off of first, Berra to Mize
New York
Coleman singled to left
1 Berra fouled to Seminick
2 DiMaggio flied to deep left
3 Bauer popped to second

7th Inning
Philadelphia
Hamner singled into center
1 Seminick sacrificed Hamner to second, Lopat to Coleman
Goliat singled to center, Hamner scoring
2 Heintzelman sacrificed Goliat to second, Lopat to Coleman
3 Waitkus flied to left
New York
1 Mize flied to right
2 Johnson struck out
3 Mapes grounded to second

8th Inning
Philadelphia
Ashburn singled past first
1 Jones sacrificed Ashburn to second, Mize to Coleman
2 Ennis flied to center
3 Sisler popped to first
New York
For Philadelphia—Mayo in left
1 Woodling, pinch-hitting for Lopat popped to short
2 Rizzuto bounced to third
Coleman walked
Berra walked
DiMaggio walked loading the bases
For Philadelphia—Konstanty pitching
Brown, batting for Bauer, was safe at first on Hamner's fumble, Coleman scoring.
Jensen ran for Brown.
3 Mize fouled to third.

9th Inning
Philadelphia
For New York—Woodling in left, Collins at first, Ferrick pitching
Hamner doubled to left-center
1 Seminick sacrificed Hamner to third Johnson to Collins
Goliat intentionally walked.
2 Whitman, pinch-hitting for Konstanty, hit into a fielder's choice, Collins throwing to Berra to get Hamner at the plate.
Caballera ran for Goliat.
3 Waitkus flied to right.
New York
For Philadelphia—Meyer pitching. Bloodworth at second.
1 Johnson lined to left.
2 Mapes struck out
Woodling singled to second
Rizzuto lined a single beyond second, Woodling stopping at second
Coleman singled to left-center, Woodling scoring the winning run

Game 4 October 7 at New York

Philadelphia	Pos	AB	R	H	RBI	PO	A	E
Waitkus	1b	3	0	1	0	9	1	0
Ashburn	cf	4	0	0	0	3	0	0
Jones	3b	4	1	2	0	0	4	0
Ennis	rf	3	0	1	0	1	0	0
Sisler	lf	4	0	0	0	2	0	0
b K. Johnson		0	1	0	0	0	0	0
Hamner	ss	4	0	1	0	2	2	0
Seminick	c	4	0	0	0	3	1	0
c Mayo		0	0	0	0	0	0	0
Goliat	2b	4	0	1	0	4	4	1
Miller	p	0	0	0	0	0	0	0
Konstanty	p	2	0	1	0	0	1	0
a Caballero		1	0	0	0	0	0	0
Roberts	p	0	0	0	0	0	0	0
d Lopata		1	0	0	0	0	0	0
Totals		34	2	7	0	24	13	1

a Struck out for Konstanty in 8th.
b Ran for Sisler in 9th.
c Ran for Seminick in 9th.
d Struck out for Roberts in 9th.

Doubles—DiMaggio, Jones. Triple—Brown. Home Run—Berra. Double plays—Mize to Berra, Coleman to Rizzuto to Mize. Hit by Pitchers—DiMaggio (by Konstanty), Ennis (by Ford). Wild Pitch—Miller. Left on Bases—Philadelphia 7, New York 4. Umpires—Berry, Conlan, McGowan, Boggess, McKinley, Barlick. Attendance—68,098. Time of Game—2:05.

Phi.	000	000	002	2
N.Y.	200	003	00x	5

New York	Pos	AB	R	H	RBI	PO	A	E
Woodling	lf	4	1	2	0	4	0	1
Rizzuto	ss	4	0	0	0	2	4	0
Berra	c	4	2	2	2	10	0	0
DiMaggio	cf	3	1	2	1	1	0	0
Mize	1b	3	0	1	0	5	1	0
Hopp	1b	1	0	0	0	1	1	0
Brown	3b	3	1	1	1	0	1	1
B. Johnson	3b	1	0	0	0	0	0	0
Bauer	rf	3	0	0	1	1	0	0
Coleman	2b	3	0	0	0	2	3	0
Ford	p	3	0	0	0	1	0	0
Reynolds	p	0	0	0	0	0	0	0
Totals		32	5	8	5	27	10	2

Pitching	IP	H	R	ER	BB	SO
Philadelphia						
Miller (L)	⅓	2	2	1	0	0
Konstanty	7⅔	5	3	3	0	3
Roberts	1	1	0	0	0	0
New York						
Ford (W)	8⅔	7	2	0	1	7
Reynolds (SV)	⅓	0	0	0	0	1

1st Inning
Philadelphia
Waitkus walked
1 Ashburn flied to left
Jones hit a ground-rule double into the right field stands, Waitkus moving to third
2 Ennis hit into a fielder's choice as Brown threw to Berra nipping Waitkus at the plate with Jones holding second
3 Sisler called out on strikes
New York
Woodling safe at first on Goliat's fumble
1 Rizzuto grounded to third, moving Woodling to second
Berra singled to right, Woodling scoring
Berra went all the way to third on a wild pitch
DiMaggio doubled to right, scoring Berra
For Philadelphia—Konstanty pitching
2 Mize grounded to second, moving DiMaggio to third
3 Brown grounded to second

2nd Inning
Philadelphia
1 Hamner grounded to short
2 Seminick grounded to short
3 Goliat flied to left
New York
1 Bauer popped to short
2 Coleman flied to left
3 Ford took a called third strike

3rd Inning
Philadelphia
1 Konstanty grounded to second
Waitkus singled to center
2 Ashburn struck out
3 Jones forced Waitkus at second, Rizzuto to Coleman
New York
1 Woodling flied to center
2 Rizzuto grounded to third
3 Berra grounded to second

4th Inning
Philadelphia
Ennis beat out a roller down the third base line.
1 Sisler flied to right.
Hamner singled to right, sending Ennis to third.
2,3 Seminick bounced into a double play. Mize stepping on first to Berra getting Ennis at the plate
New York
1 DiMaggio struck out.
Mize singled to right.
2 Brown singled to center.
3 Bauer forced Mize at second, Jones to Goliat.

5th Inning
Philadelphia
1 Goliat struck out
Konstanty singled to right
2 Waitkus flied to left
3 Ashburn popped to second
New York
1 Coleman grounded to third
2 Ford grounded to the pitcher
Woodling singled to right
3 Rizzuto grounded to first

6th Inning
Philadelphia
1 Jones called out on strikes
Ennis safe at first when Brown booted his grounder
2,3 Sisler grounded into a double play Coleman to Rizzuto to Mize
New York
Berra homered into the right field lower deck
DiMaggio hit by a pitched ball
1 Mize out as his grounder went off of Waitkus' glove to Goliat who threw back to Waitkus for the out. DiMaggio moved to second
Brown tripled to deep center, DiMaggio scored
2 Bauer lined to left, scoring Brown after the catch
3 Coleman popped to short

7th Inning
Philadelphia
For New York—B. Johnson at third, Hopp at first
1 Hamner took a called third strike
2 Seminick flied to left
3 Goliat fouled to Hopp
New York
1 Ford struck out
Woodling singled to center
2 Woodling caught stealing, Seminick to Goliat
3 Rizzuto flied to center

8th Inning
Philadelphia
1 Caballero, pinch-hitting for Konstanty, struck out.
2 Waitkus grounded out, Hopp to Ford
3 Ashburn flied to center.
New York
For Philadelphia—Roberts pitching
1 Berra flied to right.
DiMaggio singled off Goliat's glove
2 Hopp forced DiMaggio at second, Hamner to Goliat.
3 Johnson forced Hopp at second, Hamner to Goliat

9th Inning
Philadelphia
Jones singled to left-center.
Ennis hit by a pitched ball.
1 Sisler forced Ennis at second, Coleman to Rizzuto. Jones moved to third.
K. Johnson ran for Sisler.
2 Hamner struck out.
Seminick was safe at first when Woodling dropped his deep fly to score Jones and K. Johnson.
Mayo ran for Seminick.
Goliat singled to left, Mayo to second.
For New York—Reynolds pitching
3 Lopata, pinch-hitting for Roberts, fanned

BOMBERS OPEN FAST

Get Two Runs in First and Add Three in 6th for 5-0 Lead

BERRA CLOUTS A HOME RUN

Ford, Relieved in 9th When Phils Get Their Tallies, Is Victor—68,098 at Stadium

---

By JOHN DREBINGER

Closing in on a helpless and totally outclassed foe with one final devastating flourish, the Yankees, to the thunderous cheers of 68,098 at the Stadium yesterday, crushed Eddie Sawyer's bewildered Whiz Kids from Philadelphia, 5 to 2, to bring the 1950 world series to a swift ending with a four-game sweep.

It gave to this most amazingly successful organization in all baseball history its thirteenth world series title in addition to marking the sixth time the Bombers achieved their triumph in par four figures without a defeat.

And for Charles Dillon (Casey) Stengel it brought to this 60-year-old grizzled campaigner his second successive world title in as many years of managing in the American League.

It could have been accomplished even more decisively, for as this final encounter moved into the ninth, the Bombers, behind their own astonishing Whiz Kid, the 21-year-old left-handed Eddie Ford, held an overwhelming lead of 5 to 0.

Open Game With Rush

They had opened with a rush in the first inning, routing the Phils'

youthful Bob Miller with a two-run splurge. Then, stalled for a time by Jim Konstanty, they finally got around to ripping into this ace relief specialist, and three runs came hurtling over the plate in the sixth with the aid of a home run by Yogi Berra and a triple by Bobby Brown.

However, in the top of the ninth the Stengeleers suddenly must have given way to a charitable mood. With two out and two forlorn Phils on the base paths, Gene Woodling, Yankee left fielder, made a most astonishing "final out" muff of a high fly ball and the error allowed two runs to score.

But when, a few minutes later, it looked as though these Phils meant to take some more liberties, Stengel hastily came out of his dugout and waved to the bullpen. Up came Allie Reynolds, who had hurled the Yanks to victory in the second game of the series in Philadelphia, and the Chief was in no mood to delay matters any longer.

He blazed three strikes over on pinch-hitter Stan Lopata and with a triumphant shout the Yanks raced off the field, leaving in their wake another sadly disillusioned array of National Leaguers.

For the thirtieth time in world series history the American League emerged on top. Only seventeen times in the past has the National loop ever won it, the senior circuit's last victory coming in 1946, when the Cardinals toppled the Red Sox in a seven-game struggle.

With the attendance slightly higher than on Friday, the receipts for the day were $313,355.04, making a grand total of $953,-669.03. To this figure must also be added the $175,000 for radio and $800,00 for television rights, thus making this the eleventh straight series to top the million-dollar mark.

Ford, though he lacked one out of going the distance, nevertheless received credit for the victory and as he left the field the fans showered him with a great ovation.

The astonishingly cool youngster from the sandlots of Long Island City who came to the Yanks in

mid-season from the Kansas City farm club to reel off nine victories in a row before suffering his first and only setback in the regular campaign, had the Phils helpless all the way.

In all he allowed only seven hits, fanned seven, walked only one and hit one other batsman. But for Woodling's almost incredible muff it would have been a simple shutout.

Miss Lucy Monroe, who, they say, has sung the Star - Spangled Banner more times than the Yanks have won world series games, had barely finished the national anthem when Ford found himself in difficulties in the top half of the first inning only to find the Phils still in a strikingly obliging mood.

Move in Wrong Direction

In fact, just how the Whiz Kids contrived not to score in this round probably is still mystifying their National League sympathizers. One moment they had runners on second and third. The next they seemed to be moving in retreat with runners on first and second while a third strike ended the inning.

Eddie Waitkus led off by working Ford for a pass after running the count up to three and two. Richie Ashburn flied out, but Willie Jones sliced a drive close to the right-field line that bounced into the stand on one hop for an automatic double. Waitkus held up at third.

It proved just another tough break for the Phils, for had the Jones hit caromed off the stands as they frequently do in that sector, Waitkus most likely would have completed the circuit.

But the ground rule on this type of two-bagger held Eddie on third and when he finally did make a break for home it was to crash into a certain out as Brown fielded Del Ennis' sharp grounder and fired the ball to the plate in ample time.

To complicate matters still further for the Phils, Jones for some reason made no effort to move up to third on the play at the plate, so there were Sawyer's bright young men further from a score than they had been a few minutes earlier, and when Ford calmly slipped over a third strike on Dick Sisler the threat collapsed completely.

Faces Only Four Batters

Contrasting sharply with this was the deadly manner in which

the Yanks polished off Miller for two runs and had him out of there before he had faced more than four batters.

The troubles of the tall right-hander from Detroit, making his first start, began when Mike Goliat fumbled Gene Woodling's grounder close to second base for an error. Advancing to second on Phil Rizzuto's infield out, Woodling skipped over for the first run on Berra's sharp single to right.

On the heels of that came a wild pitch which took Andy Seminick so long to retrieve, Berra tore all the way around to third. A moment later Yogi was thumping over the plate on Joe DiMaggio's two-bagger into right.

That was all for Miller, and Konstanty, who had pitched so well in defeat as the Phils' surprise starter in the opener and had turned in a brief relief chore in Friday's third game, made another one of his familiar marches from the bull pen. Seventy-four times had he made that trudge for the Phils during the regular season.

The appearance of the scholarly, bespectacled right-hander also was to bring the Yanks' early splurge to an abrupt halt. Johnny Mize, after fouling off a couple of lusty shots into the stands, grounded sharply to Goliat, Big Jawn getting tossed out at first while Di-Maggio moved into third and Brown ended it with another grounder to Goliat.

Keeps the Bombers Shackled

Konstanty, in fact, kept the Bombers shackled for quite a spell, a single by Mize in the fourth and another one-base blow by Woodling in the fifth being the only times a Yank got on base for the next four innings after that damaging first.

But in the last of the sixth the Bombers erupted again. This time they piled up enough runs to make it unanimous and even take care of some of the shenanigans in the ninth.

Berra, doubtless noting that quite a few of the customers by now were really experiencing difficulty in keeping awake, brought the fans up with a start when, first up in this New York round, he rifled his homer into the right-field stand. It was the second world series homer of Yogi's career and also only the second of this series, DiMaggio having hit the only other

one when he won the second game in Philadelphia last Thursday.

For a moment it looked as though the Bombers would weigh in with a few more circuit clouts as DiMaggio unfurled a couple of shots that just curved foul in left.

Konstanty finally ended his duel by hitting the Clipper with a pitched ball. Mize grounded out, but Brown crashed into the ball for a long triple into right center and DiMag counted.

Presently came the third and last tally of the inning. Hank Bauer lifted a fly to Sisler in left and Brown galloped home after the catch and on this the Bombers elected to stand pat.

Collapse Again in Fourth

The Phils, after their futile first, gave another demonstration of utter frustration in the fourth when Ennis singled and with one out dashed to third on Granny Hamner's single to right.

But Andy Seminick followed with a grounder down the first base line which Mize scooped up. Stepping on the bag for one out, Big Jawn then tossed it home and Ennis became just another Philly expiring at the plate.

For a moment, oddly, nobody seemed to realize a double play had been completed and both the Yanks and Phils started tearing around in bewildering fashion. But Jocko Conlan, first-base umpire, finally got it home to one and all the inning had ended with a twin killing and the one-sided contest staggered on.

A single by Willie Jones started the Phils' last-ditch gasp in the ninth. Ennis got hit by a pitched ball, but the rally seemed to fade out then and there as Sisler slapped into a force play at second and Hamner struck out.

But then came a long fly to left by Seminick. Woodling seemed troubled sighting the ball in the slanting rays of the autumn sun and though he finally got both hands on it he dropped it.

Both Jones and Ken Johnson, running for Sisler, scored and when Goliat followed with a single to left the Phils actually had the tying run at the plate. But they might just as well have had it posted at the North Philadelphia station.

For Reynolds here came on. Lopata, batting for Robin Roberts, the Phils' hurler in the eighth, had the count at two strikes and one ball. Then he swung with tremendous fervor only to connect with

nothing at all and another world series had gone to history.

Lost Only Four Times

Only four times in their seventeen world series appearances since 1921 have the Yanks ever tasted defeat, twice by John McGraw's Giants in 1921 and 1922, once by Rogers Hornsby's Cardinals in 1926 and by Billy Southworth's Redbirds in 1942.

Their clean-sweep victims in the past include the Pirates in 1927, Cardinals in 1928, Cubs in 1932, Cubs again in 1938 and Reds in 1939.

As for the Phils, they have been in only two world series and have blown both. What is more, their total of five runs for the four games is the lowest ever posted by a club in a four-game series.

Also the total for the two teams, sixteen runs in all, is the lowest on record for a world series of any length.

In victory the Yanks once again proved themselves admirably equipped in all departments. Their right-handed ace Vic Raschi had started them off with a two-hit shutout in the opener. Then Allie Reynolds blazed through to win the second with the help of Di-Maggio's tenth-inning homer.

Tom Ferrick, a relief veteran picked up from the Browns early in the season, bagged the third which the southpaw Eddie Lopat had started, and yesterday the white-haired Ford, one of the youngest hurlers to appear in a world series, tossed the clincher.

68,098 Pay $313,355 To Watch Fourth Game

By The Associated Press.

Final Standing of Clubs

	W.	L.	Pc.
New York (A)	4	0	1.000
Philadelphia (N)	0	4	.000

Fourth Game Statistics

Attendance—68,098.
Receipts—$313,355.04.
Commissioner's share-$47,003.26.
Players' share—$159,811.07.
Clubs' and leagues' share—$106,540.71.

Four-Game Statistics

Attendance—196,009.
Receipts—$953,669.03.
Commissioner's share — $143,050.35.
Players' share—$486,371.21.
Clubs' and leagues' share—$324,247.47.

Highlights

- The Yankees won their thirteenth world title and recorded their sixth Series sweep.
- The Phillies scored just five runs in the four games and batted only .203.
- Vic Raschi pitched a two-hit shutout for the Yanks in Game 1.
- Joe DiMaggio hit a home run in the top of the tenth in Game 2 to give the Yanks a win.
- With the score tied, 2–2, in Game 3, Jerry Coleman rapped a single to score Gene Woodling with the winning run in the bóttom of the ninth inning. Coleman had three hits and two RBIs in the game.
- Yogi Berra homered and drove in two runs to pace the Yankees in Game 4.
- Whitey Ford got the victory in Game 4, the first of ten he would get during his Series career, the most ever compiled.

Best Efforts

Batting

Average	Gene Woodling	.429
	Granny Hamner	.429
Home Runs	Joe DiMaggio	1
	Yogi Berra	1
Triples	Bobby Brown	1
	Granny Hamner	1
Doubles	Granny Hamner	2
Hits	Gene Woodling	6
	Granny Hamner	6
Runs	(five players)	2
RBIs	Jerry Coleman	3

Pitching

Wins	(four players)	1
ERA	Vic Raschi	0.00
	Whitey Ford	0.00
Strikeouts	Allie Reynolds	7
Innings Pitched	Jim Konstanty	15

NEW YORK YANKEES —— 1950
PHILADELPHIA PHILLIES

Reprinted, with permission, from
The World Series, A Complete
Pictorial History, by John Devaney
and Burt Goldblatt (Rand McNally
and Company, Chicago, © 1972).

Casey Finds a Ford in His Future

Winning over the Phils in four straight, the Yankees picked up their sixth sweep of a Series. (The only other team to sweep in four games up to then was the 1914 Braves.) It was the Yankees' 13th championship in 17 Series. The Philadelphia Whiz Kids almost folded in the pennant stretch, losing 8 of their last 11 and winning the pennant on the last day, when Dick Sisler hit a 10th-inning homer against the Dodgers. However, the Phils' strong pitching performed well in the Series but was weakened by several costly fielding lapses.

The Phillies' manager Eddie Sawyer surprised fans by starting his relief ace, Jim Konstanty, in the first game. It was the first start of the season for Konstanty, who was also seeing his first Series game. Konstanty allowed only four hits, but the Yanks' Vic Raschi gave up only two and won, 1-0.

Robin Roberts, a 20-game winner, was the second starter for the Phillies and lost, 2-1, to Allie Reynolds, Joe DiMaggio winning the game in the tenth inning with a home run. The Phils were winning the third game, 2-1, in the eighth inning when an error by shortstop Granny Hamner let in the tying run. In the ninth, second baseman Jimmy Bloodworth couldn't handle two infield hits, and the Yankees got another run to win, 3-2.

Stengel started a rookie, 21-year-old Ed (Whitey) Ford, in the fourth game. The cocky kid from Long Island told reporters, "I never get butterflies." He shut out the Phillies for eight innings and won, 5-2, missing a shutout when Gene Woodling dropped a flyball. It was the first of 10 Series victories for Ford.

"I never dreamed I'd be the manager of a team that won a Series in four straight," Stengel said. For Joe DiMaggio the championship was his ninth —a record to then.

Andy Seminick: I remember DiMaggio

Andy Seminick, the Phil catcher in the '50 Series, said: *I can still see that ball that Granny Hamner booted. He took his eyes off the ball for an instant and that's all you have to do. If he had made that play, we would still have been alive. It was a pitchers' Series. We didn't hit to our potential, but neither did the Yankees. Still, we felt embarrassed. I think most players do when they lose a Series in four straight. We told ourselves we would come back and win a Series because we were a young ball club, but then we had injuries, and it didn't happen. When I think of the Yankees, I can see DiMaggio hitting a perfect pitch from Bob Miller—it was low and outside, just where we wanted it—but DiMaggio hit it to rightfield for a single. He could handle Miller's stuff even when Bob put the ball exactly where we wanted to put it. Robin Roberts could handle DiMaggio —he could get him out with a pitch inside—but Roberts had to get the pitch in the exact spot inside. If it was a speck off, DiMaggio could put it into the seats on you.*

Bombers Wing to 13th World Title on Pitching

Yank Staff Shows Flashy Earned-Run Mark of 0.73

DiMaggio, Coleman and Woodling Shine on Attack; Hamner in Hero and Goat Roles for Beaten Phillies

By STAN BAUMGARTNER

NEW YORK, N. Y.

Sparked by great pitching and splendid defense, the New York Yankees, American League champions, swept the National League Philadelphia Phillies to defeat in four straight games, 1 to 0, 2 to 1 in ten innings, 3 to 2 and 5 to 2, in the forty-seventh World's Series. The first two games were played in Shibe Park, Philadelphia, the final pair at Yankee Stadium.

It was the American League's thirtieth victory in the fall classic, the Yankees' thirteenth triumph in 17 tries and the sixth time they had won in four straight games. The National League has not won a championship since the St. Louis Cardinals defeated the Boston Red Sox in 1946.

The Phillies' four defeats were their eighth straight in Series competition, as the 1915 club, the only other Philadelphia National League flag winner, lost the final four encounters with the Boston Red Sox.

The hurling of the Yankees was little short of phenomenal. Vic Raschi, Allie Reynolds, Ed Lopat, Tom Ferrick (who pitched one inning) and Ed Ford had a combined earned-run average of only 0.73, permitting the Phils only three untainted tallies. The total of five runs scored by the Phils was the lowest ever made in a four-game Series, but was two above the all-time low of three made by the Philadelphia Athletics in the 1905 Series against the Giants.

Joe DiMaggio was the hitting and fielding ace of the Series. His home run in the tenth inning won the second game and he made three great defensive plays that helped the Yanks win. In the sixth inning of the second game, Joe caught Del Ennis' drive two feet from the right-center field light standard and in the ninth inning he held Gran Hamner's drive to a two-base hit. In the ninth inning of the third game, with the score tied, DiMag again held Hamner, leadoff hitter, to a double when a triple might have given the Phils the game.

Joe DiMaggio

* * *

Coleman Struts Stuff at Bat, Fancy Dan in Field

Gerald Coleman was equally brilliant. The Yankee second baseman figured in five of the first six Yankee runs scored in the first three games. He drove in the only run in the first game, scored the first one in the second, batted in the first tally in the third game, scored the second and drove in the winning counter in the ninth. In the field, Coleman was equally efficient. He robbed Ennis of a hit in the first inning of the second game with Ashburn on second and made the most spectacular stop of the Series on Mike Goliat in the fifth inning of the same contest, although Gerry was unable to throw out the batter.

Gene Woodling was a close second to DiMaggio and Coleman. He led the Yanks in hitting with .429, drove in the initial run in the second game, scored the winning tally in the third game and the first run in the fourth contest.

Gran Hamner was a hero and goat for the Phillies. He led the Phils in hit-ting with .429 and made the most extra-base hits of the Series, three. However, his fumble allowed the Yanks to tie the score at 2 to 2 in the eighth inning of the third game.

'Kids Should Be Home Early'

Clubs Refund $600,000

NEW YORK, N. Y.—Right after the Yankees had achieved their world's championship in four straight games, the New York and Philadelphia clubs began the job of refunding some $600,000 which they had received for tickets for fifth, sixth and seventh games.

The Yankees announced that they were returning $354,700 for fifth game tickets. The Phillies were giving back more than $240,000 for sixth and seventh game ducats.

Admiring a portrait of the Yankee Clipper, painted by artist Victor Freudeman, besides the subject himself, are restaurateur Toots Shor (center) and Frank Sinatra. The painting, commissioned by Avon Products, was presented to DiMaggio at a dinner at Toots Shor's restaurant in 1950. (See color plate opposite page 641.)

WHAT ABOUT DiMAGGIO *Now?*

Harassed by physical difficulties and batting slumps, the Yankee Clipper was having

a tough season. The experts started to write him off. But they buried him too soon

By The Editors of Sport

FOURTEEN months ago, SPORT Magazine published a full-length SPECIAL entitled, "Joe DiMaggio—The Man Behind the Poker Face," written by Jack Sher. We haven't published a DiMaggio story since.

There are two good reasons why the Yankee Clipper has been so long absent from our pages. First, there are many other important stories and personalities in the sports world which clamor for space each month. Second, no self-respecting editor likes to do repeat stories on any one individual unless he has something new to say about him.

Along with a number of gently sarcastic letters congratulating us for putting out a string of issues with no articles on DiMaggio, we have also received a steady stream of demands for additional material about him. Meanwhile, the ballplayer himself—considered by a vast number of people to be the greatest of his generation—continued to make news. He was in and out of the headlines from March through October. He was in good shape, he was in bad shape, he was hitting, he wasn't hitting, he was happy, he was unhappy—but always, he was news. From California to Maine, from Texas to Florida, the people wanted to know about

him. Was he through? Was he feuding with Casey Stengel? Was he going to play next year? Would he soon be the manager of the Yankees?

Most of these questions were old stuff. When a ballplayer gets to be DiMaggio's age (he will be 36 on November 25), they are always saying that he is washed up—and sooner or later they are right. But a great slugger like DiMaggio causes as much excitement when he isn't hitting as when he is. And whenever a perennial pennant contender like the Yankees runs into trouble, there is talk of internal dissension, of jealousy, of feuding.

It is equally inevitable that, as the close ones are won instead of lost, as the storm center begins to hit home runs instead of pop-ups, the mournful post-mortems turn into paeans of praise. That is the DiMaggio story for 1950. As the Jolter sparked the Yankees' pennant push, as he passed the 30-homer mark, everybody forgot to gossip about whether or not he was sulking, brooding, drawing away from the rest of the ball club, acting like a spoiled kid.

But before Joe began to hit, bales of newsprint were expended on the controversy. And it was a controversy,

make no mistake about that. For every reporter who questioned DiMag's conduct, there were six who hotly defended it. For every fan who booed the big fellow with the No. 5 on his back, there were dozens who cheered him to the skies.

What's the story behind the unprecedented duel between DiMaggio and the press that, for so long, threatened to overshadow the pennant race as far as the Yankees were concerned? The Editors of SPORT, who deliberately left Joe off their September cover this year for the first time in the magazine's five-year history, solely because they didn't want to talk about DiMaggio unless there was something new to discuss, have no intention of ducking one of the biggest stories in sport today.

What about DiMaggio now?

* * *

YOU walk past the bar in Toots Shor's famous New York restaurant and turn sharply to the right just as you enter the dining room on the main floor. There, snug against the wall, overlooking the entire room but out of the view of neck-craners, is Joe DiMaggio's favorite table in Joe DiMaggio's favorite meeting and eating place.

Here, one night not so long ago, two close friends of the Yankee outfielder sat and discussed the twilight days of this modern immortal.

"It's been rough for him the last few years," one of them said. "Especially this year. Maybe this will be his last one. Who knows? He might have another, and I hope if he does it's a good one. But if he does, I hope the fellows who write about him will stop trying to deify him and start trying to humanize him. After all, he's only a man, not a superman. He never was anything else."

The other sat and listened in astonishment. "I never expected to hear you putting the slug on the guy," he said.

"What are you talking about?" the first shot back. "You know Joe. Why don't you admit he's just a man like all the rest of us? It's guys like you who are making it tough on him. When he looks bad out there, when he gets upset and moody because he can't do the things he used to do, you go off half-cocked and start reading all kinds of crazy reasons into his attitude. If you ask me, the windup would be a lot easier for Joe if the writers would just try to stress that the guy is only human—just like you and me."

It is a strange twist that the first real effort to understand Joe DiMaggio had to wait until he started down his personal homestretch as an active ballplayer. But, belated though the effort is, it is nonetheless important. In the end, its effect will be beneficial to DiMaggio. Babe Ruth went through the same experience and came out of it no worse off for the public awareness that he favored the high life, that he lived harder and played harder than most men. When the story is told of the ungovernable tempers and fiery dispositions Ty Cobb and Lefty Grove brought to baseball, it is told proudly. One can appreciate a Cobb who wept in rage when he was unable to hit a pitcher the way he thought he should.

So it should be with DiMaggio. But up to now, it has not been. Partly by accident and partly by design, a virtual conspiracy has existed to avoid writing about DiMag as you would about others. Ted Williams, for instance, has taken his beatings in the press regularly. So has Bob Feller, the third of our generation's trio of baseball immortals. But DiMaggio has rarely been forced to read harsh words about himself.

Only Joe DiMaggio could escape scot-free from an encounter with the press such as the one he had outside Johns Hopkins Hospital in Baltimore before the start of the season in 1949. That was the time when Joe, undergoing treatment for his famous injured heel bone, refused to pose for photographers or talk to reporters, growling, "Leave me alone. You guys are driving me crazy!"

If Williams had said that, angry editorials would have been written from coast to coast. But DiMaggio said it, and his viewpoint was quickly defended by the ardent DiMaggiophiles who dominate not only the powerful New York City press but also much of the copy sent out over the nation's great wire services, not to mention radio networks, newsreels, and other important communication media.

Only Joe DiMaggio could afford to be as indifferent to the wishes and opinions of his front office as Joe frequently has been. The Yankees cannot "deliver" DiMaggio for public appearances the way they can their lesser stars. He is above that. If a friend asks him, he will generally do his best to help out. But his relations with the Yankee office are strictly formal.

The little matter of autograph-hunters is also enlightening. If Ted Williams dodges a gang of signature-grabbers, he is condemned as arrogant, selfish, and inconsiderate. If DiMaggio does it, it's only because he is so harassed that he can't do anything else.

Or take the question of off-field activities. If Bob Feller signs a contract to do a little good-will work for a confection corporation, or goes on a barnstorming tour, he is roundly assailed for taking his mind off his pitching. Jackie Robinson has had the same experience. But not DiMaggio. When he gets a chance to pick up a few dollars on the side, everybody applauds.

In his relations with the very men who are responsible for the protective curtain that has been thrown around his real personality and habits, Joe gets away with more than any other contemporary star. He has never been the easiest subject in the world to interview, but there are times when he is downright uncooperative with the press. For example, when the Yankees were heading North from Spring training last Spring, DiMag suddenly began avoiding the reporters as though they carried the plague. He exhibited indignation whenever any of the boys delicately suggested that he might be nearing the end of the road. Later, he got off the spot by telling the writers that he had been upset by a lot of private troubles.

THERE'S nothing wrong with that. Everybody has private troubles and we all know how galling they can be. The only thing is, nobody but DiMaggio got such protective treatment, and when the reaction set in, it was just as unusual.

It was inevitable that a good part of the press conspiracy in behalf of the Clipper should boomerang—and that's what happened last Summer. Conditioned for years, by this tacit conspiracy on the part of the boys with the typewriters, to regard DiMaggio as a demi-god who could do no wrong, the fans were astonished to read conflicting reports about the great ballplayer's personal behavior.

In early August, the New York *Daily News* carried a story to the effect that DiMaggio had become so moody and out of sorts that he was giving a sophomoric snub to manager Casey Stengel. Writer Joe Trimble speculated that DiMag might be acting in such fashion because his pride had been hurt by the lineup shift that saw him dropped to fifth place in the batting order while Johnny Mize took over his old cleanup spot.

Naturally, the story excited attention. If DiMaggio were in truth feuding with Stengel and grumpily refusing to talk to his teammates, the Yankees were unlikely to make a successful defense of their American League championship.

The pot boiled still more noisily when a second article was tossed into the controversy. This was written by Ben Epstein of the New York *Daily Mirror*, long considered a friend and confidant of DiMaggio. Epstein ridiculed the theory that Joe was letting his ballplaying go to pot for the sake of a feud with Stengel. "He swings, fields, and runs to win," said the reporter.

"On the other hand," Epstein went on, "the Clipper today sulks in the midst of probably his longest temperamental outburst as a standout athlete . . . It's quite possible that DiMag has fallen victim of incredible national worship from old and young alike and, if you'll excuse the expression, has 'grown too big for his breeches.' Like Babe Ruth, Joe's appearance on any scene attracts the imbecilic as well as the rational. All in all, it slowly but surely creates the deadly 'I' and Joe could be suffering from a 'tech' of it."

Epstein hid nothing from his readers. "It's understood," he went on, "that DiMag bitterly resented a story by the writer about the possibility of his eventually becoming a pinch-hitter. After all, the 35-year-old Clipper's reflexes aren't what they used to be.

"'What's he want to do, get me killed?' DiMag was reported to have snarled over what we thought was a helpful service. It hurt, but let's keep personalities out of it. His childish indifference to all newsmen and broadcasters traveling with the club is beside the point. Our racket is to write it objectively."

The only trouble with Epstein's remarkably honest and analytical story was that it pointed up one ancient failing of the New York press with respect to DiMaggio. This was simply that because the DiMaggio story had not always been written objectively, it was difficult to do so at this late date without creating hard feelings all around.

The reaction to the Epstein article was in itself revealing. Instead of using the *Mirror* reporter's facts and opinions as a springboard for an all-out airing of the problem, most of the writers—from force of habit, perhaps— sprung to Joe's defense so vigorously that they spent more time attacking Epstein than they did writing about DiMaggio.

THROUGH the 14 years his name has been on the Yankee roster, Joe has not only benefited from an extraordinarily friendly press but has also been able to conceal his true feelings behind an unfailing poker face. Good days and bad, he took them all in stride. When the mask was lowered, Joe's fans couldn't help an exaggerated reaction to the disclosure that their hero not only owned a perfectly normal temper —but temperament, as well. When he went into a short-term pout, his sulking was construed as mutiny against his manager. This was ridiculous.

The fact is, Stengel, like Joe McCarthy, Bill Dickey, Johnny Neun, and Bucky Harris, the Yankee managers under whom DiMaggio had played previously, doesn't care whether DiMaggio speaks to him or not. Home runs in bunches, great catches, speed on the bases, and a throwing arm of the first magnitude were items far more important than polite chit-chat.

If DiMag had any feeling at all in relation to Stengel which roughly coincided with annoyance or anger, it arose not because he had been replaced temporarily as cleanup hitter in the Yankee lineup, but rather because he was bothered by the abortive attempt the Yanks made to switch him to first base. The one game he played at that position in Griffith Stadium, Washington, early in July, was torture for Joe —mental and physical. It made a lasting, bitter impression on him. Owner Dan Topping was the one who originally suggested the shift to him. DiMag wondered why Stengel, rather than the boss, hadn't come to him with the idea.

ONCE you accept the fact that DiMaggio is as human as the next person, despite his rare athletic gift, you find it easy to rationalize his occasional lapses.

When you recall the sight of him struggling painfully through the end of the 1949 season, you know how richly he has earned the rewards of his spectacular career. You know that Joe has never asked out of the lineup unless he was in dire trouble.

Take the time the Yankees were in the process of sweeping a late August series with the Indians at Yankee Stadium, and DiMag walked up to Stengel in the dugout and said, "You'll have to make a change."

"The knee again?" Stengel asked, with concern.

"Both," Joe replied, turning and moving painfully along the dugout duckboards and down the steps to the dressing room. There, he sat in front of his locker and said, "If I tried to bend over right now, I'd fall flat on my face. The left knee's worse than the right. I've been favoring both. That's why I'm not hitting. I can't get the upper part of my body into the swing. It looks as if I'm swinging late. I am. A thing like this affects your timing. I don't know what to think except that this is one hell of a time to be out of the lineup."

Out of the lineup when he was needed, in pain, and alibiing even as all the rest of us do on occasion, DiMag at that moment was lovable, human, decent, and worthy. You couldn't help but sympathize with him.

Remember, the next time you see or hear or read of an instance in which the Yankee Clipper doesn't appear to best advantage, that it's easy to grin and be a good fellow when you're hitting the ball hard, but it's tough to be everybody's pal when the pitchers are fooling you and your legs won't take you where you want to go. Affability and success go hand in hand.

So do criticism and failure. Once Joe began to lay the wood to the ball and the Yanks began to eat up ground in the race, there were no more columns about DiMaggio being "through." Joe still had very little to say, but his bat spoke eloquently. Maybe he has only a few seasons left, but it's on the record that it never pays to count DiMaggio out too soon. And even if he does decide to go into radio or television full time, you can be sure his fans will follow him.

Whatever he does, he'll be good at it. To borrow a phrase from The Old Arbitrator, Bill Klem, he's a champion.
— ■ —

By Joe Williams

Should DiMaggio Get More Than Casey Stengel?

Apropos of the constant shifts in baseball managers there is a communication at hand from one of the customers who introduces a point which is seldom considered when the problem comes up for scholarly discussion.

Stated briefly, if not simply, it is this: How can you expect a manager to be a manager in reality when he gets less than some players he is paid to manage? "There is the example of Ted Williams," writes Michael E. Bash, 30 Church St., N.Y.C., "who has announced he will be his own boss in the Red Sox camp next spring. Williams is paid at least $50,000 more than Steve O'Neill, his manager of record."

Mr. Bash proceeds to amplify: "It is only natural that a manager in such circumstances cannot hope to receive the full respect of his high-salaried star who is, in most cases, the player who must come through for him if he is to maintain his prestige as a manager."

Williams is not the only player who, in Mr. Bash's reasoning, represents this economic absurdity. There is Ralph Kiner who gets $65,000, which is substantially more than Pittsburgh has been paying Billy Meyer, its manager, and there is the Yankees' Joe DiMaggio whose $100,000 is close to double Casey Stengel's take. But doesn't the implication here dispute the accepted tenet that the laborer is worthy of his hire?

The Stars Don't Draw.

Mr. Bash dissents: "I do not subscribe to the insistence these fellows are gate attractions and therefore should be paid accordingly. Babe Ruth, admittedly, was the best but he's gone and the Yankees have set new attendance records. Popular and talented as Mel Ott was, the Giants did not miss him at the gate. And when Brooklyn sold Dixie Walker, 'the peepul's choice', down the river, the crowds did not dwindle. Next year figures to be DiMaggio's last as a Yankee. Even now Tommy Henrich appears to be through. It sounds harsh, but if the Yankees continue to win they won't even be missed."

It is Mr. Bash's notion that the late Jake Ruppert was responsible for the secondary position the manager holds on a team where there is an outstanding star, contending that the normal relationship between employer and employee became dislocated when Ruth was consistently paid more than Yankee managers, of whom there were several. The gentleman agrees, of course, the Old Slambino was extra special but wonders if the long-range effect of the Ruppert precedent hasn't served to lower the dignity and weaken the position of all managers. "And would not this help to explain," he asks, "why they come and go like so many messenger boys?"

In this connection, Mr. Bash applauds the economic philosophy of Branch Rickey who "has never allowed the player to get the upper hand." Rickey's marked distaste for the high-salaried player is well known. PeeWee Reese and Jackie Robinson, each listed at $35,000, topped the Brooklyn pay roll last season. Burt Shotton, the departing manager, I'd guess, got about the same.

They Manage Themselves.

I'm assuming my correspondent is correct when he writes that such all-time greats as Christy Mathewson and Walter Johnson never got as much as their managers. But when he includes Ty Cobb I'm rather certain he errs. In the beginning, yes, but not in Cobb's later years. This would make Frank Navin, not Ruppert, the first to low-rate the manager. But even that would be wrong. Cleveland's owner, Jim Dunn, was surely paying Tris Speaker more than Lee Fohl, his manager—and that was some time before Ruppert even had Ruth on his ball club.

I can imagine that privately the manager must resent a situation of this sort, and that it does affect his relations with the player whose pay check is sufficient testimony of his superior importance. It is significant that these players are generally permitted to manage themselves. When Williams states he'll play in the spring games, or not, depending on his mood of the moment, he is merely reading from a page out of an old Ty Cobb book. Ruth did as he pleased under Joe McCarthy, Stengel gives DiMaggio wide latitude—though you can bet it was not DiMaggio's idea to go to first base, or surrender the No. 4 spot in the batting order last season.

Mr. Bash thinks the manager should demand a clause in his contract guaranteeing he'll always be paid more than any of the hired hands. "How long do you think industry would survive if the employee was paid more than the president?" the gentleman asks, by way of conclusion. I pass. This one's too complex for me. You wanna play with it, Mac?

DiMaggio Korea-Bound

By the Associated Press.

TOKYO, Nov. 9.—Joe DiMaggio, New York Yankee outfielder, and Frank (Lefty) O'Doul, manager of the San Francisco Seals, will leave for Korea tomorrow to visit Armed Forces hospitals.

After the 1950 World Series was banked by the Yankees, Joe DiMaggio visited Korea to help entertain the American troops there. In that country, he and Lefty O'Doul (left), his friend and then manager of the San Francisco Seals, met with General Douglas MacArthur (center), supreme commander of the United Nations forces fighting in that nation.

While in Japan on his Far East junket of 1950, the Yankee Clipper took some time to give a little batting instruction to some young Japanese ballplayers.

Massacre Survivor Gets Thrill Meeting DiMaggio

By The Associated Press.

SEOUL, Korea, Nov. 10 — Baseball stars Joe DiMaggio and Lefty O'Doul, putting in a 20-hour day visiting American wounded, have met Pvt. Eugene Jones of Herrin Ill.

Jones, a survivor of the Sunchon Tunnel massacre of Oct. 20, gripped the Yankee player's hand and said, "I never dreamed I'd get to meet Joe DiMaggio."

"And Joe never thought he'd meet a guy who had to go through what the Jones kid did," said O'Doul, San Francisco Seals manager.

The two baseball men took a brief break tonight by dining with Lieut. Robert G. Ferguson of Carmel, Calif., Eighth Army Intelligence officer and an old friend of O'Doul. Then they made a theater and also radio appearance, ending a day that had begun at 4 A. M.

DiMag Lights Hot Stove For North Korean Winter

By WILLIAM CHAPMAN.
United Press Staff Correspondent.

PUKCHONG, Korea, Nov. 13.— Joe DiMaggio and Lefty O'Doul— two hitters who always had a quick cure for a slump—pulled a little front line hospital out of the dumps in jig-time yesterday.

Leaving a trail of smiles and laughter in their wake, the Yankee outfielder and the San Francisco manager conducted a whirlwind visit with veterans who were wounded on the farthest north U.N. front in Korea.

DiMaggio's off-hand anecdotes and O'Doul's humor touched off the first laughter heard in the First Mobile Surgical Hospital since it was set up here a week ago.

Pfc. Frank Shymer, 21, of Wilkes-Barre, Pa., smiled selfconsciously as O'Doul shook his hand.

"You say you live near Pottsville, boy," boomed O'Doul. "The brewer in Pottsville is a great friend of mine."

Shyner laughed for the first time since he was hospitalized.

DiMaggio paused a few minutes at the bed of Pvt. Donald Sutton, 18, of Macon, Ga., when DiMag got set to move on, Sutton yelled after him:

"That's my boy!"

Later, the veteran Yankee slugger stopped to give a cigarette to Pfc. Donald Edie of Port Huron, Mich., who was hit in the knee by sniper fire here in Pukchong.

"It was wonderful of you to come," Maj. Maurice Powers, senior chaplain of the Seventh Division, told the visitors. "It means a lot to the morale of these men that you would take time out to come all the way up here just for them."

DiMaggio and O'Doul flew to the hospital despite murky weather and landed in a small L-17 observation plane on an improvised airstrip.

They spent an hour with the soldier patients here and wanted to stay longer but said they had to return to 10th Corps Headquarters at Hamhung to keep other hospital appointments.

"There go a couple of good guys," said Pfc. Ernest Rodrigas, 20, of Baltimore.

Rodrigas was wounded by rifle fire on the Ungi River front north of Pungsan where the 17th Regiment dug in for a week.

DiMaggio, O'Doul Receive Medals

By the Associated Press.

TOKYO, Nov. 24.—Joe DiMaggio and Frank (Lefty) O'Doul have been awarded medals of appreciation for their morale-bolstering work among U.S. fighting men in Korea and Japan.

They are similar to the medal presented the late Al Jolson after he made a tour of the fighting front shortly before his death. The name of the recipient is on one side. On the other are the names of the fronts visited and the dates.

DiMaggio and O'Doul, Back Home, Laud Troops in Bitter Korean War

Deeply Moved by Hardships of Soldiers; Jolter Lost Seven Pounds on Tour

By JACK McDONALD
SAN FRANCISCO, Calif.

Bogged down with pottery, Satsuma ware, parasols, dolls, swords and even baby blue silk kimonos, the gifts of admiring Japanese fans, Joe DiMaggio and Lefty O'Doul are back home after a 25-day trip which took them within hearing distance of mortars on the North Korean front.

It was with a feeling of humbleness that they returned, deeply impressed and moved by the grimness and hardships of American troops in the bitter North Korean weather at the front and by their visits to 18 service hospitals in 17 days which, at times, kept them on the go 20 hours out of 24.

DiMaggio lost seven pounds during the trip.

It was no junket. Sure, it had its pleasant aspects. It was nice getting adulation from Toyko fans and attending receptions in their honor in Kobe, Osaka, Nagoya and Hiroshima. Everywhere he went, Joe was practically mobbed, O'Doul reports, with Japanese boys, six or seven of them at a time, climbing on DiMag's back.

Impressed in Korea

But it was Korea which made the deepest impression on them. Joe has never kicked about paying taxes on his $100,000-a-year salary with the Yankees and you can be certain he won't after four days and nights in Korea. Most Americans need not be told it's no picnic in Korea, but DiMag says the one gripe that U. S. troops there have, though their morale is good, is that they think the prevailing impression in this country is that they're only on a policing job.

"It looked like an all-out war to me," said Joe. "And the boys want the people in this country to know they're not just a police force. They want credit for what they are doing, and I don't blame them."

Maj. Gen. Edward Almond, commanding the Tenth Corps, wanted Lefty and Joe to visit combat units of the Seventh Division just behind the lines, so the two were given fur-lined coats, caps and boots and climbed into a little buglike Army L-17 plane with a single motor. The plane landed in a school yard and, needing a longer runway when it took off, used the street of a little town. A siren blew just before the takeoff to warn the townspeople to stay off the street.

"We were less than 12 miles from the front," said DiMag, "and could hear guns booming to the north. Let me tell you, it's no country club life up there. Troops can't even brush their teeth in the contaminated water without first boiling it. And they bathe out of their helmets."

The most touching incident on the trip occurred in a Tokyo hospital. They greeted a Texas boy, Sherman Jones, who had one side of his jaw shot away in the tunnel massacre.

"His jaw was all wired up," said Joe. "But he shook hands with us bravely and tried to talk. He didn't want me to leave. He made motions that he would like my autograph."

DiMag had a baseball in his back pocket which he signed and gave to the young soldier. Joe promised to return the next day. The boy had the nurse hang the baseball down from a string in front of his bed where he could look at it. The next day a sergeant in the next bed said the young Texan had hardly taken his eyes off the baseball.

O'Doul reported seeing virtually miles of Russian equipment alongside Korean roads, including trucks and jeeps abandoned by North Koreans in flight. South Koreans were stripping the trucks of tires and accessories.

O'Doul says DiMag was plied with questions about the 1950 American League race, the boys asking: "What was the matter with the Red Sox? Why did the Tigers fold? What happened to the Indians?"

DiMag patiently answered all questions in his visits to rest camps of recuperating combat troops, at the bedsides of Army hospital patients or talking to ambulatory cases in base hos-

'A Swing and a Miss' as Joe Opens Jap World's Series

TOKYO, Japan—Joe DiMaggio, New York Yankee slugger, opened the Japanese "World's Series" here, November 22, with a swing and a miss.

DiMag deliberately swung and missed a pitch thrown by his traveling partner, Lefty O'Doul, San Francisco manager, with Major General William Marquat behind the plate.

pitals or recreation halls.

Joe and Lefty saw the first two games of the Japanese "World's Series" between Mainichi Orions, pennant winners of the Pacific League, and the Shochiku Robins, Central League champs. The Orions won both games.

The Japanese series is played on a four-out-of-seven basis, and the teams move from one league city to another in playing.

Military authorities in Japan were loud in their praise of the morale-boosting effect of the visit of DiMaggio and O'Doul.

In the hospitals, they visited every bed and every patient, chatting informally about baseball or any other sport in which the patient was interested. Said Maj. Gen. William Marquat, commissioner in Japan for the National Baseball Congress: "O'Doul supplied the comic relief with ad lib wisecracks that kept the men laughing. DiMaggio's approach was more serious, but his interest in the game and in the welfare of American soldiers wounded in action deeply impressed everyone.

"They used no 'act,' no script and no 'props,' yet they contributed a service that will long be remembered by those with whom they came in contact in the Orient. They signed autographs on baseballs, bats and every type of material that would record ink."

General and Mrs. MacArthur honored the two with a luncheon and other Occupation officials and prominent Japanese paid their respects to them.

The trip was sponsored by the Hawaiian Travel Service, of which Cappy Harada is the director. The U. S. Army Special Service, under Brig. Gen. Paul Kelly, arranged for their visits to military personnel and establishments.

1951
THE FINAL YEAR

Joe DiMaggio takes a few swings during the last spring training of his Yankee career. He would retire at the end of the 1951 season.

TWO TEAMS

During my thirteen years of active play with the Yankees, I really played on two different teams. Both had a roster of great players, and proved to be two separate dynasties. The team I joined in 1936 already had four future Hall of Famers in it — Lou Gehrig, Bill Dickey, Red Ruffing, and Lefty Gomez — and a manager, Joe McCarthy, another destined for enshrinement in Cooperstown. We also had the likes of Tony Lazzeri, Frankie Crosetti, Red Rolfe, Johnny Murphy and, a few years later, Joe Gordon, Tommy Henrich, and Charlie Keller. In seven years, we won six World Series.

By 1951, all were gone from the Yankees. In place of them was another raft of outstanding players equally dedicated to winning pennants and World Series; such as Yogi Berra, Phil Rizzuto, Hank Bauer, Billy Martin, and pitchers like Vic Raschi, Allie Reynolds, Ed Lopat, and Whitey Ford. Casey Stengel, on his own road to the Hall of Fame at Cooperstown, was our manager. And in 1951 there was a nineteen-year-old rookie most anxious to take over my spot in center field, Mickey Mantle. In the six years I played after the war, we won four more World Series.

Joe DiMaggio

1951

JOE DiMAGGIO STATISTICS

Games	116
At Bats	415
Hits	109
Doubles	22
Triples	4
Home Runs	12
Runs Scored	72
Runs Batted In	71
Bases on Balls	61
Strike Outs	36
Stolen Bases	0
Slugging Average	.422
Batting Average	.263

STANDINGS

	Won	Lost	Percentage	Games Behind
New York Yankees	98	56	.636	
Cleveland Indians	93	61	.604	5
Boston Red Sox	87	67	.565	11
Chicago White Sox	81	73	.526	17
Detroit Tigers	73	81	.474	25
Philadelphia A's	70	84	.455	28
Washington Senators	62	92	.403	36
St. Louis Browns	52	102	.338	46

DiMag Still Top Man On Base Pay List

The Yankee announcement that Joe DiMaggio would be offered the same salary he drew last year maintains the Clipper as the player with the highest base pay in baseball, $100,000. Ted Williams may have received more, but did not touch the hundred grand in base pay, on which cuts are computed. DiMag has the comforting knowledge he cannot be offered less than $75,000 for 1952, because a 25 per cent drop is the limit under the management-player agreement.

Williams will have to dicker soon, and the third big shot of the sport, Stan Musial, is now working on Fred Saigh, Cardinal prexy, for a boost from his $50,000 plus bonuses. Musial is asking for $100,000. He is worth it if Saigh can afford to pay it.

As for Williams, rumors continue he will be traded. The latest is a Boston Post yarn that Ted will go to the A's. Tom Yawkey, Williams' boss, has said he is not "considering" dealing off his super slugger. But he hasn't said he wouldn't consider it.

H. I. Miranda of Lexington, Ky., doesn't figure to get far with his plan to unionize players. The fact is the players need no outside help, because they have an ideal working structure in their committee for dealing with management. The magnates, eager to retain this "company union" setup, have granted benefits professional organizers might not have been able to obtain. The pension deal is surely the biggest steal of all time in labor relations.

DiMaggio's Third $100,000 Pact Lifts His Yank Take to $700,000

Feels Wonderful

Reports He Weighs 200, Shoulder Still Pops Out, Knee Injury Appears Gone

By DAN DANIEL

NEW YORK, N. Y.

Joseph Paul DiMaggio has signed his third straight $100,000 contract with the Yankees. Dan Topping and George Weiss were especially enthusiastic in their announcement, because they felt that Giuseppe's signing would break the big holdout jam.

DiMaggio was only the fourth regular to sign, on a date as late as February 7, with batterymen slated to start training on February 22.

Joe's acceptance of terms came in the course of a telephone talk with Topping and Weiss.

They called him at his mother's home in San Francisco, and he said that he just had signed his contract, which he had had for three weeks, and was putting it right into the mails.

The writer was delegated to speak to DiMaggio over the telephone.

Joe said he felt fine, had been playing a lot of golf, and even had broken 100.

"I am shooting 102 and 103 regularly, with an occasional bigger day," he explained. "I beat Dom fairly often for a quarter.

"I weigh 200, which is great for me at this time of the year, and if I can pick up five more pounds at Phoenix, fine. If not, fine.

"I will report for training March 1.

I may come into Phoenix a few days in advance to play a little golf and get acclimatized.

"The pop-out shoulder? Oh, it still pops now and then but does not bother me.

"The bad left knee I had during the 1950 World's Series? No reminder of it still exists.

"Am I satisfied with my contract? Sure, what's the use of squawking?"

With revenue from radio, testimonials, etc., DiMaggio's total baseball earnings are well over $1,000,000.

Although DiMaggio has signed and many of the younger players have hopped aboard George Weiss' bandwagon, some of the first-liners have not been accepting George's salary offers. Yogi Berra made the mistake of discussing his situation with the press in St. Louis. This is regarded as a violation of the Yankee code.

At times, there is a belief in Yankee headquarters that some of the players have got into a combine. However, the athletes never have entered into a pact and it is safe to predict that they never will.

One of the New York stars said recently, "Now and then you hear about suspicions that certain players have entered into an agreement not to sign unless their terms are met.

"The fact is, we do not know what each of us gets. I have some faint idea of what half a dozen of our players might have received in 1950 but I have no definite information. It is one thing we do not discuss with each other."

Joe DiMaggio

Thinks Red Sox May Again Bother Yanks to Finish, With Help of Boudreau

"Each player has his own ideas of his value. Each player has his special label for the club, and to attempt to form a combine of let us say a dozen players, to force their demands on the front office, would result in failure and defeat. For one thing, they never would stick together."

Holdout jams used to be broken by trades. The general practice was to ship one of the recalcitrants down the river to a second-division club and consequently scare the holdouts into action.

This stunt has fallen into disuse. But it is certain that Weiss has been considering its revival.

Ruth Had His Gehrig, Di Maggio's Got His Berra

By DANIEL,
Staff Writer.

PHOENIX, March 1.—It used to be said that if Babe Ruth and that homely, smiling pan of his appeared on the field in action, the spring training season of the Yankees was pronounced officially under way.

In later years, Joe DiMaggio gained recognition as the March bellwether in Bomber drives toward fresh pennant achievements.

As Casey Stengel's regulars today reinforced the batterymen who had been working here since Feb. 22, Giuseppe discovered that, although he still was very much the biggest attraction in the leagues, he was hooked up with an interesting associate feature listed as Lawrence Peter Berra, better known as Yogi.

Berra's new salary, acquired within the last 24 hours, was only $30,000, as compared with DiMaggio's $100,000.

But for an allegedly dumb guy who started with $5000 in 1947, Berra was doing exceedingly well.

For an adjective wrestler supposed to be slow of thought, and even grotesque in his mental reactions, the Yogi was making some clever baseball people look sheepish. The Yankees suddenly realized that, just as Ruth had had his Lou Gehrig, DiMaggio now has his Berra.

Barely 24 hours after George Weiss had announced that Yogi's financial demands were so out of line as to preclude further negotiations, the box car-like catcher got the $30,000 contract for which he had been angling for months, with the able coaching of a lady named Carmen, who is Mrs. Berra.

Weiss realized that, after all, Berra had batted .322, as against DiMaggio's .301 last season, that Yogi had driven in 124 runs, in comparison with Joe's 122, and the pride of The Hill in St. Louis had unfurled 28 homers, while Giuseppe had blasted 32.

Berra had a beautiful case, and the whole world, Weiss included, knew it.

"There goes my record," said Bill Dickey today. His $28,000 contract for 1938 had been bettered by his pupil. Now Berra was the highest paid catcher in the history of the New York club. He had matched the $30,000 paid by the Giants to Walker Cooper after they had purchased him from the Cardinals for $175,000 on Jan. 5, 1946. The Yogi had passed the highest salary Mickey Cochrane had received before he became manager in Detroit. Others had slipped on reaching their peaks, Berra was going higher. That was certain.

Back with Yankees as a coach, with the retirement of Bucky Harris and the hiring of Casey Stengel, Dickey said, "In two seasons, Berra will be an accomplished receiver. By the spring of 1951, he will be the No. 1 catcher of the major leagues."

The dopesters looked dubious. But Dickey became a true seer. In fact, he was guilty of an underprophecy. Berra already was the standout last March. He merely clinched the title during the 1950 season.

Take Mr. Berra's bag and golf sticks and see that he gets the suite right next to DiMaggio's. And stock it up with plenty of comic books.

Aches Gone, DiMag Set To Show 'Em

Special to World-Telegram and Sun.

PHOENIX, March 2.—Joe DiMaggio today had started on his 13th training season with the Yankees minus a physical handicap, an ache or a fear.

For one, the opening of the regular training campaign had found Joe signed to a satisfactory contract, calling for $100,-000, and recovering from no operation on foot or heel or arm.

"I feel great," exuberated the Clipper. He looked it too. "I am out to surprise those who believe I am finishing up my career," Giuseppe continued.

Casey Stengel said that once more he would permit DiMaggio and Phil Rizzuto to train themselves.

"Everything was fine this winter, except my mother is very bad," Joe concluded in batting practice. He rapped a few off the fence.

Joltin' Joe and The Mick. Joe DiMaggio has a few words of advice for the nineteen-year-old rookie named Mickey Mantle, who was being groomed to replace him in center field at Yankee Stadium in 1951.

DiMaggio's 'Decision' to Quit In '52 Stuns Stengel and Weiss

$100,000 Centerfielder's Talk Takes Front Office by Surprise; Nothing Definite, He Says

By Harold Rosenthal

PHOENIX, Ariz., March 3.—A jittery Joe DiMaggio, obviously having slept poorly on his own announcement that 1951 might be his last year in baseball, wanted to know today what all the fuss was about.

"I said this year might be my last," he said, "and I think I made it plain enough that this is the way I feel now."

Had he changed his mind since he spoke to a group of newspaper men the night before?

"No," answered DiMaggio, "I still say the same thing I did then. It's nothing definite."

In that interview, one which set the world championship ball club going off like a battery of Roman candles, DiMaggio stated that he hoped he would have a good year at the end of which he would hang up his spikes. He said he didn't want to go on after he was past his peak and that he had no managerial aspirations.

"I have enough headaches running myself," he said wryly, "without trying to run a bunch of other men."

Front Office Flabbergasted

DiMaggio denied that his physical condition had anything to do with the way he felt. "I'm not a brittle ball player like a lot of writers would have you believe. I'm a good strong fellow and always have been."

DiMaggio's decision to make this thirteenth year with the Yankees possibly his last flabbergasted the front office.

In a terse statement issued this morning, George M. Weiss, vice-president and general manager, indicated that this was a complete surprise and that he hoped his $100,000 centerfielder would have a change of heart.

Wiss's statement read: "Joe DiMaggio hasn't discussed this angle with any club official. We regret to hear anything like this. We hope he will have the sort of season which will cause him to change his mind."

DiMaggio had left himself a possible loop-hole with the statement that he would have an announcement at the end of the year.

It really stunned his manager, Casey Stengel. Stengel didn't hear about it until breakfast and his response was "Well, what can you do; you can't stop a man from doing what he wants. What am I supposed to do, get a gun and make him play?"

DiMag's Move Recalls Babe's

Special to World-Telegram and Sun.

PHOENIX, March 3.—Joe DiMaggio's "this might be my last year" created quite a stir in the camp of the Yankees today. His statement brought back memories of the opening of the 1934 season, when Babe Ruth, dissatisfied with playing for Joe McCarthy, talked about retirement. The Babe asked for, and received, his unconditional release the following January, and made a brief and ill-fated connection with the Braves.

DiMaggio came to the Yankees in 1936, having been purchased from San Francsico for $25,000 and five players. He was born on Nov. 25, 1914, at Martinez, Calif., and broke into baseball in 1932 with the San Francisco Seals.

The Yankee Clipper went into the 1950 campaign with a career average of .331. Last season he hit .301 and, in 139 games, drove in 122 runs and blasted 32 homers.

Joe won the American League most valuable player citation in 1939, 1941 and 1947. He has been in nine World Series and 11 All-Star games. For three years, from 1943 through 1945, he was in the Army.

How Come That .111 Doesn't Worry DiMaggio?

By DANIEL,
Staff Writer.

LOS ANGELES, March 21.— Joe DiMaggio is not hitting. That is nothing about which the Yankees and Casey Stengel are disposed to become alarmed. But his lack of success has been about as emphatic as it ever was in past training seasons in which Giuseppe suffered a slow start.

DiMaggio was charged with three more futile efforts at the plate in the 5-0 loss to the White Sox in Glendale. It was Casey Stengel Day, and the town turned out strong for its leading citizen and outstanding financier. But once the game had got under way, it was anything but a gala for Ole Case, or anybody else connected with the Bombers.

Jolting Joe has achieved just two blows, both homers, in 18 trips to the plate, and is struggling at a .111 clip. Ordinarily he would react to that state of affairs with glum silence. Now he jokes with his team mates, and appears oblivious of his temporary failure. The former Mrs. DiMaggio has been a spectator at every game in which Joe has appeared around here.

DiMaggio's timing is not too bad. He is meeting the ball, but cutting under, or topping it.

Stengel hopes that DiMaggio will be over his trouble by Friday night, when the Yankees open in San Francisco. They play in Oakland on Saturday afternoon and Sunday morning, and in San Francisco again on Sunday afternoon.

"I'd like to see Joe have a big weekend on his old stomping ground," said Stengel, who could not have helped contrasting the lackluster start of his $100,000 a season hero with the .571 average of Mickey Mantle, Joe's 18-year-old replacement.

DiMaggio certainly is not the only Yankee who has been experiencing serious trouble at the plate. On Monday night, in Hollywood, the Bombers gathered only six blows, three of which did not show up until the ninth, in a 6-3 defeat.

At Glendale yesterday, the champions looked particularly bad as they were blanked with a mere four scattered hits.

Hector Brown, from Seattle, held the Yankees to three hits in four innings, and left-hander Marvin Rotblatt did a really outstanding job on them in the last five heats.

After Hank Bauer got an infield single, Rotblatt did not yield another safety. Phil Rizzuto reached first on an error in the sixth, and Gerald Coleman walked in the ninth.

New York's pitching was nothing to write home about, either. In the first five innings, Bob Porterfield did a fair job, after having allowed four blows and three runs in the opener.

In the last four heats, Tom Ferrick was cuffed for six hits and a couple of tallies.

With the exception of Vic Raschi's brilliant five innings of shutout pitching against Los Angeles on Sunday, the work of Stengel's hurlers in this area has been disappointing.

Considering that the pitchers started training on February 22, a week earlier than had been customary since before the war, and that they have been working for almost a month, they hardly have been devastating.

Fred Sanford's poor showing on Monday night did not further endear him to Casey and you might say that the man from Utah definitely is on the block.

IT PROBABLY ISN'T SERIOUS AND CERTAINLY IT IS NOTHING NEW... BUT THE OTHER DAY IN A SPRING PRACTICE GAME, JOE DIMAGGIO SPRAINED HIS LEFT KNEE...

...AND THE YANKEE FANS HAVE GONE INTO THEIR WORRYING ACT.

DiMag's Bat Stirs Hope He's on Way

By DANIEL,
Staff Writer.

PHOENIX, March 30.—Joe DiMaggio's worst succession of batting experiences in 13 training seasons with the Yankees today finally took precedence over the Mickey Mantle saga.

Giuseppe's double with the bases loaded in the seven-run fourth inning, which beat the Cubs, 7–5, stirred the hope that he finally had recovered the magic formula which had made him so spectacular in other years.

Those three runs which DiMaggio drove in off the left-handed Johnny Schmitz constituted his most important contributions to the Bomber offensive this spring. The two pinch homers which Joe achieved in early games came with nobody on base.

In 38 efforts, the Yankee Clipper has contrived only eight blows for an average of .215. This is in striking contrast with Mantle's .429, Yogi Berra's .400 and Hank Bauer's .444.

DiMaggio's lacklustre training season could be the result of a combination of factors. First may be a confessed lack of zest for training. Then there is Joe's

Vic Raschi   **John Mize**

statement that this may be his final year, which psychologists say traces to a deep appreciation of dwindling abilities at 36. There is Joe's strained left knee, which he was supposed to rest for a few days.

In Los Angeles the other day a prominent figure of the race tracks watched Joe for a few innings and said, "What kind of odds do you suppose I could get on the proposition that Mantle plays more innings this year than DiMaggio, for the Yankees?"

The press box laughed this off. But that evening, on the trip back to Phoenix, some of the writers began to wonder if the horseman hadn't had something very interesting.

———

Raschi Rocked Again, But Joe and Yogi Hit

By DANIEL,
Staff Writer.

EL PASO, Tex., April 4.—Although the Yankees were none too happy over a 6–3 trouncing by the Indians in the sixth and final game of their training series, chiefly because Vic Raschi turned in another lackluster performance in his seven inning chore, there were compensating factors.

First, there was Joe DiMaggio's budding batting streak, which had run through eleven innings in three starts. He had come up with four hits in as many official trips to the plate, and had lifted his average to a respectable .283. In the trouncing at Tucson by the Tribe, Giuseppe got a single and a walk, and scored twice.

Secondly, there was Yogi Berra's second homer in two games, with a .408 average which was moving the catcher in to a position to challenge Mickey Mantle and his .443.

Despite DiMaggio's improvement, he still has quite a way to go. He is not bringing that bat around against fast ball pitching in the old style. But his timing is coming back.

Since Casey Stengel has decided not to play DiMaggio nine innings until the Bombers reach Kansas City, Joe faces six more outings at a reduced pace.

Berra singled and put the Yankees' first run in scoring position, and later homered with DiMaggio on base, in the Arizona finale.

This was against the right-handed Mike Garcia. Last Sunday, against Pittsburgh, he got his first four-bagger of the year off southpaw Cliff Chambers.

"Berra, you are away over your head with that .408 average," the interviewer needled. "If you start pulling for the right field wall, your average will be whittled down."

The Yogi chuckled, "They tell me Joe McCarthy used to tell you writers 'let me worry about that.'"

———

**Raschi Keeps Working
To Perfect Control.**

In seven innings punctuated by 11 Cleveland hits for 17 bases and six runs, Raschi hardly looked like a 21-game winner who had had 40 days of training. He is said to have a bad knee.

Luscious Easter rocked Victor with three blows, one a 410-foot triple, another a double. Bobby Avila exploded a triple, and Lou Klein a two-bagger.

Raschi did not have any more than he had shown against the Cubs last Thursday, when they got five runs and a dozen blows in eight innings.

However, Vic is not as bad as he has looked. He is working hard on his control. He has found that too often, in the spring, he is off the plate.

"I can pitch nine innings," Raschi explained. "I could have gone the distance in any of my three recent starts. I am in fine shape, and I believe that you soon will see me look lots better."

"Raschi does not worry me," Stengel explained. "But Allie Reynolds and Joe Page are giving me bad nights.

"Reynolds should come around before long. There are times when he throws hard.

"Page, however, has got nowhere. He is now in fine condition. He is running more than ever before.

"But, pitching in batting practice yesterday, Page showed me nothing."

Ole Case turned to Bill Dickey and asked, "How did he look to you?"

Bill was a reluctant witness. Stengel insisted.

"He did not throw the ball," Dickey finally replied.

———

Situation Is Normal

As Always: DiMag Wears the Mantle

By DANIEL,
Staff Writer.

DALLAS. April 9.—Joe DiMaggio today was on his way, at last. In the Yankee 15-9 victory, Giuseppe, playing nine innings for the second time this spring, belted his fourth homer, with a runner on base, and two singles, lifting his average to .378. He had hit safely in his eighth consecutive contest.

"Casey Stengel had me scheduled to start playing through in Kansas City tomorrow, but I decided to beat that plan by a couple of days," Joe explained. "I would have played the nine in Beaumont on Saturday if the outfield hadn't been so poor.

"I am getting into great shape. I used to rush my conditioning because I wanted to have a reserve if I got hurt. This time I decided to take it easy. The new scheme has worked to perfection. I have one regret. I weigh only 191, I wish it were at least 198."

DiMaggio picked up a sports page which carried a story picking Cleveland to win the pennant, and stressing the allegation that "Joe is tired and irritable."

'I never was on an unfriendly footing with my teammates," he protested. "I am not tired, and I am not irritable. Some guy is taking pot shots at me."

DiMaggio referred to the interview he had given at the outset of the training season, in which he had said that this might be his last year in baseball.

THE CLIPPER

"What do you think about it now that you have seen me work for 40 days, and play in every one of our 29 games?" the Yankee Clipper asked.

"You will not quit this year," the interviewer replied. "You look good enough for two more years, anyway."

"Right you are," DiMaggio laughed. "But will I want to go on?"

"You will unless training becomes too tough, and you have reached the point at which putting on the uniform every day is a chore," was the reply.

"Well, it hasn't reached that stage," was Giuseppe's rejoinder. "I don't hate training, or playing."

DiMaggio eulogized Mickey Mantle as "the greatest young player of my experience. He can do everything. Don't worry about his unfamiliarity with certain outfield essentials."

Talking about the pennant race, DiMaggio said, "There will be four clubs in the fight. New York, Boston, Cleveland and Detroit.

"I note that many of the experts are writing the Tigers out of the race. That is a mistake, even with Art Houtteman in the service. Red Rolfe's club has a tremendous potential.

"We will win again because of our reserve strength. We will have some of it on the field all the way, and some in our minor league chain, where it will be available for our September drive, or for service in an emergency before then. The other clubs will have all their strength already in action.

"Don't think I am underrating the Red Sox. If Steve O'Neill rearranges his infield, it will be a tougher club, defensively. Lou Boudreau will help them and it is likely Steve will pick up pitching strength through Ray Scarborough and Will Wight.

"If everything breaks right for the Boston club, it might rip this league apart with its power.

"I am not inclined to overrate the Cleveland threat, because Al Lopez's infield may not turn out quite as strong as it appears to be right now."

DiMaggio went no further. But among the Yankees there is a belief that Roberto Avila will not develop into a first-class double-play man because he is gun shy.

"One thing I would like to impress on the fans up in New York," Joe concluded. "I will do my part. They need not worry about me."

Di Mag Still Out— Pain in Neck Moved to Shoulder

Although the pain in Joe Di-Maggio's neck has left, it has shifted to his shoulder. ... "I don't know how soon I'll get back," Joe says today. ... The Clipper takes batting practice now but is supposed to be kept on the bench because it still pains him to throw.

With Jackie Jensen having gone 0 for six yesterday and slipped to .276, this would seem the right time to put DiMag back in center.

New York is glad to be back in the Stadium, where it has won all seven starts this campaign. ... On the road the Yanks went 9–8. ... Ed Lopat and Vic Raschi better not slump. ... The Bomber mound situation could get serious quite suddenly.

DIAMOND DUST—
DiMag Out With Leg Injury

YANKEES (Chicago, June 9): Joe DiMaggio out for the third time with the season not a third over. The Clipper pulled a muscle in his left leg while chasing a fly during last night's 4-2 win here. He took himself out of the game and may be missing for a week.

Berra's left eye still inflamed. He may catch one game tomorrow. . . . Comiskey Park record of 53,940 which saw Friday night's game will be challenged by crowds trying to see tomorrow's twin bill. . . . Frank Lane, Sox' aggressive manager, says Yankees have best chance to snatch Garver from Browns because Bombers have young players St. Louis wants in return. Roy Hamey, aide to George Weiss, is offering such as Sanford, Ferrick and Ostrowski. St. Louis wants Tom Morgan, the pitcher at Kansas City, and Bob Cerv, the Blues slugging outfielder, as well as Jack Jensen and Billy Martin. The latter pair cost $125,000 two years ago.

Hose management has swiped Cleveland idea of riding relief pitchers in from bullpen. Tribe uses a red jeep, Sox a cream-gray station wagon. When he takes over Browns, Veeck is going to try a new twist. He's buying a hearse to carry out the starting pitcher.

J. T.

Mother of DiMaggios Dies at 72 in Frisco

San Francisco, June 18 (AP).—Mrs. Rose DiMaggio, baseball's number one mother, died today. She was 72. Her encouragement and support helped her famous sons—Joe and Dominic—to rise to major league stardom.

Both rushed by plane to her bedside, Joe from the Yankees, Dom from the Red Sox, but she saw neither of them before she died.

MRS. JOE DIMAGGIO was in a coma when Joe arrived three hours before her death this morning. Dominic, unable to make connections from Boston, arrived half an hour after her death.

Dom, quiet, bespectacled "Professor" of the Red Sox, was the only one of the nine DiMaggio children who was unable to reach his mother's bedside before she died.

THE OTHERS ARE Vince, who preceded Joe and Dom in the major league and for the past two years has managed the Pittsburg Diamonds of the Far West League; Tom and Mike, who never played baseball, and four sisters—Mrs. Nellie Helquist, Mrs. Mamie Scrivani, Mrs. Marie Convery and Mrs. Frances Petromilli. Joseph DiMaggio, Sr., their father, died in 1949.

Papa DiMaggio was a fisherman in his native Italy, where he and Mrs. DiMaggio were wed. He remained a fisherman when they came to San Francisco.

The DiMaggio brothers, Dom, of the Boston Red Sox, and Joe, board an airplane to take them back to the east coast to resume their baseball seasons after attending the funeral of their mother in San Francisco in June 1951.

The DiMaggio brothers, outfielders all, remember their baseball roots in this painting by S. Rini. Vince (upper left) played for the Boston Braves, Cincinnati Reds, Pittsburgh Pirates, and Philadelphia Phillies during a period from 1937 through 1946. Dom was with the Boston Red Sox from 1940 through 1953. And Joe, of course, covered center field for the Yankees from 1936 to 1951.

Joe DiMaggio, painted late in his career by artist Doug West.

Yank Staff Holds Cipher Monopoly

Special to World-Telegram and Sun.

WASHINGTON, June 28.— The Yankee pitching staff has 11 shutouts . . . The seven other clubs in the American League have only 17 among them.

Joe DiMaggio had a strange experience in the sixth inning of last night's battle . . . His two bagger struck his own glove in short left center . . . Gene Woodling's infant batting streak reached the eight game stage with his first round single . . . He is pulling himself up to the .300 level by slow stages . . . Gene is at .291.

Irv Noren escaped a shutout by Allie Reynolds with a single in the ninth . . . He is 11 for 27 against New York pitching, for .407.

Bobby Brown's revised batting stance, with feet closer together, got him a single . . . The ball which DiMaggio belted to Gil Coan in the third would have been a homer in the Stadium.

The Yankees close here today, and tomorrow play at 1:30 and again at 8:30 in the Stadium, against the Red Sox, with Bob Kuzava and Raschi their pitchers.

DiMag Writes Off White Sox

By DANIEL.

"It will be a finish fight between the Red Sox and us," said Joe DiMaggio today, donning the regalia of the seer while the New York and Boston contenders went into a day and night double bill in the Stadium.

The Bombers had taken two out of three in Washington, finishing with a second straight shutout, 3–0, in which Tom Morgan and Cliff Mapes, with a pinch double with the bases loaded, were the heroes.

As the White Sox and Red Sox were idle yesterday, the Yankees came into town only half a game out of the lead, with a golden opportunity to grab first place before this day was out.

"The White Sox will make trouble right to the end, but they are not going to win because, when Paul Richards will need his pitching most, it will sag," DiMag declared.

"Some of those Chicago hurling records just do not add up for me. But the fact remains that Richards has made his club hustle, and has brought in some fighting ball players to spice his batting order.

"The Sox will finish in the first division. Detroit is slow, and if it had any chance to overcome the loss of Art Houtteman, lost it when Ray Herbert went, too.

**Declines Comment
On Dropo Situation.**

"Cleveland has not been quite the factor we expected from the form it showed us in Arizona. Al Lopez has pitching, but there seems to be trouble in other spots."

Not until this season is finished will Joe be asked to make up his mind on the question of coming back for a 14th year with the Bombers. He joined them in 1936, but had three years out in the Army.

Back in February, at Phoenix, Joe said that this might be his last season. But indications are that he will return.

On the trip from Washington, DiMaggio evidenced an unusually keen interest in the 1952 spring training plans of the Yankees, for a man with retirement ideas.

"We are not going to make the usual long tour," Red Patterson revealed. "First stop, Atlanta, then only four more, and a hop into Brooklyn."

"Well, that's interesting," was DiMaggio's stamp of satisfaction.

Joe has always been loath to comment on the Boston situation, perhaps because brother Dominic is on that club.

When the Dropo matter came up, Giuseppe just listened. He refused to be drawn in.

"The Red Sox still are the power club and they must be beaten," said Joe.

It was recalled that the Yankees had 15 more meetings with the Fenway fusileers, six of them in the Hub, where Casey Stengel's defenders have dropped five in a row.

DiMaggio predicted a rugged time for Bill Veeck in St. Louis, but felt that the miracle man of Cleveland would perk up the long moribund Browns, and make the old river town a more interesting baseball stop.

"Poor Garver," exclaimed Giuseppe, and there he stopped.

Major League Standings

AMERICAN LEAGUE.

									W	L	Pct.	GB
Chicago	—	4	7	6	4	10	5	6	42	23	.646	—
N.Y.	7	—	2	8	5	5	7	7	41	23	.641	½
Boston	4	5	—	5	5	6	7	7	39	26	.600	3
Cleve.	2	3	7	—	6	4	6	6	34	30	.531	7½
Detroit	3	3	5	.0	—	8	7	5	31	30	.508	9
Wash.	1	3	2	5	3	—	5	6	25	37	.403	15½
Phila.	5	3	1	3	3	1	—	8	24	41	.369	18
St. L.	1	2	2	3	4	3	4	—	19	45	.297	22½
Lost	23	23	26	30	30	37	41	45	—	—		

NATIONAL LEAGUE.

									W	L	Pct.	GB
Bklyn.	—	6	8	7	5	3	7	5	41	24	.631	—
N.Y.	3	—	6	7	5	3	7	7	38	31	.531	5
St. L.	2	6	—	5	7	5	4	4	33	32	.508	8
Cincin.	3	3	5	—	6	9	2	4	32	33	.492	9
Phila.	3	4	4	2	—	4	7	8	32	33	.492	9
Boston	3	6	4	4	4	—	3	6	30	34	.469	10½
Chicago	4	2	4	3	3	7	—	5	28	33	.459	11
Pitts.	6	4	1	5	3	3	3	—	25	39	.391	15½
Lost	24	31	32	33	33	34	33	39	—	—		

Yanks Top Red Sox and Lead League

LOPAT WINS NO. 11 FOR BOMBERS, 5-2

He Limits Red Sox to 6 Blows as Yanks Take League Lead by 4 Percentage Points

---

COLEMAN, PESKY CONNECT

Doerr Gets His 2,000th Hit of Major Career at Stadium—Parnell Loses in Box

By JOHN DREBINGER

The Red Sox, it seems, cannot nail down the one they must win. Inversely, on such occasions, the Yankees seldom miss.

Certain it is the Bombers never even came close to missing at the Stadium yesterday when, before a cheering crowd of 58,815, they toppled Steve O'Neill's Bosox, 5 to 2, in the deciding encounter of the three-game series.

With the victory, the Yankees rose to first place by four percentage points over the White Sox. The teams are tied in games, however.

Slick pitching by Southpaw Eddie Lopat, a robust nine-hit attack that included a Jerry Coleman homer off Mel Parnell and the usual mystifying managerial moves by Prof. Casey Stengel combined to trip the Sox in this encounter which meant so much to the Boston entry. For had they won it, the Sox would have pulled themselves right up on the necks of the Bombers. Instead, they now trail the Yanks by three and a half lengths.

Pesky Connects in Sixth

Lopat, in ringing up his eleventh victory against only three defeats, allowed only six hits. One of these was a sixth-inning homer by Johnny Pesky, while another, a ninth-inning single by Bobby Doerr, not only paved the way for Boston's second and concluding tally, but gave the veteran second sacker the 2000th hit of his major league career.

Perhaps most baffling of all, however, were the mystic maneuverings of Prof. Casey. In open defiance of one of baseball's funda-mental precepts, Stengel started three of his alternating left-handed hitters—Gene Woodling, Cliff Mapes and Bobby Brown—even though the opposition was tossing its ace southpaw.

To be sure, the three batsmen didn't contribute much. Mapes got a single, Woodling a pass, and both got themselves picked off first. But it's a cinch it did puzzle the Bosox and by the time they thought they had it all solved Casey had a few more left in the eighth that helped fetch home the final pair of Yankee tallies.

Luck rode with the Yanks in the first when, with Phil Rizzuto on third and Yogi Berra on first, the result of a pair of singles, Joe DiMaggio slapped the ball back to Parnell for a simple double play to end the inning. But Doerr's throw from second to first went wide and Rizzuto scored the first Yankee run.

Ball Skids Off Mapes' Glove

The second came in the fifth when Coleman larruped his No. 3 of the year into the left field seats, an admirable piece of foresight since in the top of the sixth the Sox broke in with their first run on Pesky's homer which skidded off Mapes' glove in right as Cliff's arm crashed into the front railing.

In the same round the Yanks picked up another on Rizzuto's second single, a pass to DiMaggio and a single by Johnny Mize. That inning ended Parnell and Bill Wight came on to get cuffed for two more in the eighth which Ellis Kinder had to finish. With two out and two on, the result of a pass to Rizzuto and an intentional walk to DiMaggio, Casey now made another notable shift.

He called upon Hank Bauer to bat for Joe Collins who had gone in to run for Mize in the sixth and the ex-Marine blasted a single to right to score Li'l Phil. On came Kinder only to be greeted by a single by Gil McDougald who by now had replaced Brown at third and that produced the second marker and fifth for the day.

All this reduced the Sox ninth inning demonstration to a mere flurry when they counted their final tally with the help of a pinch double by Lou Boudreau.

The big stickers of the Boston battlefront, Ted Williams, Dom DiMaggio and Vern Stephens were all held hitless.

Stengel weakened a bit on his hunch of shooting left-handed swingers against southpaw pitching when he called on McDougald to bat for Bobby Brown in the sixth, but that one didn't pan out so well. Neither did the move that sent Collins in to run for Mize after Big Jawn singled in this inning. For McDougald's grounder to Stephens got DiMaggio trapped between third and home and Collins got doubled up rounding second too far.

Major League Baseball

Monday, July 2, 1951

American League

YESTERDAY'S GAMES

New York 5, Boston 2.
  Chicago 2, St. Louis 1
    (1st, 11 innings).
  St. Louis 3, Chicago 1 (2d).
  Cleveland 2, Detroit 1 (1st).
  Cleveland 2, Detroit 0 (2d).
  Philadelphia 10, Washington 7
    (1st).
  Philadelphia 3, Washington 2
    (2d).

STANDING OF THE CLUBS

	New York	Chicago	Boston	Cleveland	Detroit	Philadel.	Wash'n'n	St. Louis	Won	Lost	Perc'tage	Games Behind
N. Y.	—	7	4	8	5	7	5	7	43	24	.642	—
Chic.	4	—	7	6	4	5	10	8	44	25	.638	—
Bost.	6	4	—	5	5	7	6	7	40	28	.588	3½
Cleve.	3	2	7	—	10	6	4	6	38	30	.559	5½
Det.	3	5	6	—		7	8	5	31	34	.477	11
Phila.	3	5	1	3	3	—	5	8	28	41	.406	16
Wash.	3	1	2	5	3	5	—	6	25	41	.379	17½
St. L.	2	3	2	3	4	4	3	—	21	47	.309	22½
Lost..	24	25	28	30	34	41	41	47	—	—		

National League

YESTERDAY'S GAMES

New York 4, Boston 1.
  Brooklyn 2, Philadelphia 0.
  Chicago 7, Cincinnati 0 (1st).
  Chicago 7, Cincinnati 5
    (2d, 11 innings).
  St. Louis 5, Pittsburgh 4
    (12 innings).

STANDING OF THE CLUBS

	Brooklyn	New York	St. Louis	Philadel.	Cincinnati	Chicago	Boston	Pittsb'gh	Won	Lost	Perc'tage	Games Behind
Bklyn..	—	6	8	7	7	3	5	43	25	.632	—	
N. Y.	3	—	6	5	7	7	4	7	39	32	.549	5½
St. L.	2	6	—	7	5	4	5	6	35	32	.522	7½
Phila.	4	4	4	—	2	7	4	8	33	35	.485	10
Cinc.	3	3	5	6	—	2	9	4	32	35	.478	10½
Chic.	4	2	4	3	5	—	7	5	30	33	.476	10½
Bost.	3	7	4	4	3	—		6	31	35	.470	11
Pitts..	6	4	1	3	5	3	3	—	25	41	.379	17
Lost....	25	32	32	35	35	33	35	41	—	—		

The box score:

BOSTON (A.)	ab.	r.	h.	po.	a.
D. DiM'g'io. cf.	4	0	0	4	0
Pesky. ss.	3	1	1	0	1
Williams. lf.	3	0	0	0	0
Stephens. ss.	3	0	0	1	2
Doerr. 2b.	4	0	1	3	2
Goodman. 1b.	4	1	1	8	1
Olson. rf.	3	0	0	2	0
cBoudreau.	1	0	1	0	0
dMcDermott.	0	0	0	0	0
Rosar. c.	3	0	1	4	2
aHatfield.	0	0	0	0	0
Moss. c.	1	0	0	2	0
Parnell. p.	2	0	1	0	3
bVollmer.	1	0	0	0	0
Wight. p.	0	0	0	0	2
Kinder. p.	0	0	0	0	0
eEvans	1	0	0	0	0
Total	32	2	6	24	13

NEW YORK (A.)	ab.	r.	h.	po.	a.
Woodling. lf.	3	0	0	1	0
Rizzuto. ss.	3	3	2	2	4
Berra. c.	4	0	1	4	0
J. DiM'g'io. cf.	2	1	1	3	0
Mize. 1b.	3	0	1	5	1
Collins. 1b.	0	0	0	1	0
fBauer.	1	0	1	0	0
Hopp. 1b.	0	0	0	0	0
Brown. 3b.	2	0	0	1	1
McD'gald. 3b.	2	0	1	1	1
Mapes. rf.	4	0	1	5	0
Coleman. 2b.	3	1	1	4	3
Lopat. p.	3	0	0	1	1
Total	30	5	9	27	11

Total ...30 5 9 27 11

aRan for Rosar in seventh.
bHit into double play for Parnell in seventh.
cDoubled for Olson in ninth.
dRan for Boudreau in ninth.
eHit into force play for Kinder in ninth.
fSingled for Collins in eighth.

Boston ....0 0 0 0 0 1 0 0 1—2
New York ....1 0 0 0 1 1 0 2 .—5

Runs batted in—Pesky, Moss, J. DiMaggio, Coleman, Mize, Bauer, McDougald. Two-base hit—Boudreau. Home runs—Coleman, Pesky. Stolen base—Rizzuto. Double plays—Stephens, Rosar, Pesky, Rosar and Doerr; McDougald, Coleman and Collins. Left on bases—Boston 7, New York 5. Bases on balls—Off Parnell 1, Wight 3, Lopat 4. Struck out—By Parnell 1, Wight 2, Lopat 1. Hits—Off Parnell 7 in 6 innings, Wight 1 in 1 2-3, Kinder 1 in 1-3. Winning pitcher—Lopat (11-3). Losing pitcher—Parnell (8-5). Umpires—Stevens, Paparella, Hubbard and Rommel. Time of game—2:14. Attendance—58,815.

Jimmy Cannon Says:

There has been only one truly great baseball player in this generation. Some one should remind Casey Stengel the man's name is Joe DiMaggio who could do it all. Since '36, the season DiMaggio came to the Yankees, there hasn't been any one like him in the big leagues. The guys on his ball clubs knew what he meant to them. They decided his value. It doesn't show in the averages but DiMaggio belongs with Cobb and Ruth. What DiMaggio did can't be broken up into fractions. There was no place for decimal points in the way DiMaggio took the Yankees and picked them up. They, who know him better than any one, wanted him in centerfield in '49 when he was still blurry and sore after pneumonia. They want him out there now.

DiMaggio has been my friend since he broke in. It has been more than the relationship of a reporter covering a famous athlete. We are as close as our businesses will allow. We have gone on vacations together, sat around the same restaurants, killed a lot of time together and know the same Broadway people. It hasn't impaired my job of writing about him. He is one of the few baseball players who remembers a column of praise. He has never complained about anything I've ever written.

*   *   *

Only Joe Louis matches him for genuine dignity. This is no chew-tobacco ballplayer. It would be unfair to him to describe him as a $100,000 a year athlete, although that is what he earns. It is not enough to call him the greatest of his time. I believe DiMaggio to be a model for ballplayers. It goes for all of them, past or present. I don't make Ruth or Cobb exceptions.

Baseball is still a game played nine men to a side. As one of nine DiMaggio has never had a superior. No one ever contributed more to the whole. It is the most unselfish skill possessed by any man who ever played the game for a living. It is an accidental gift, I believe.

It comes out that way when he plays. There has never been a more unique talent. The idea is not original with me. Connie Mack instigated it after watching DiMaggio play a couple of seasons in the big leagues. I knew what he thought about Cobb. I asked him to compare them.

"DiMaggio is the greatest team player that ever lived," Mack told me.

*   *   *

DiMaggio may be in his last season. Time has warped the great gifts. You must take such as his brother, Dom, over him. But Stengel seemed to humiliate him deliberately last Saturday up in Boston. The manager allowed DiMaggio to trot out to centerfield. Then he chased Johnny Hopp out to inform him that he was out of the game. Jackie Jensen, who had hit a home run batting for the pitcher, took his place.

It was a mean little decision. It was a thoughtless act of panic and insensitivity. It was nasty and petty and follows the pattern of cheapness which has assumed shape since Lonesome George Weiss, the friendless general manager, took charge. The prestige of the Yankees diminishes rapidly.

It is Stengel's right to bench any one. That's the manager's privilege. DiMaggio hasn't been hitting. He needed a rest. But why didn't Stengel sit him down before the game? If Stengel had gone that far with him he should have continued to stick for seven innings more. It's a tough game when a fellow who has won so many games for the Yankees isn't granted seven innings to save him from a public reprimand for being 37 years old. Not in modern times has a great ballplayer been so ferociously handled.

The abrupt substitution exposed Stengel as a guy who will allow desperation to set ambushes for him. There have been crises in the two years that Stengel has been with the Yankees. But this time the ball club is coming apart on him and he is behaving like a man who doesn't know what to do. It astonishes me, because I defended Casey when most of the baseball journalists in this town were denouncing him as a comedian. I thought that he has a deep knowledge of ball players. But after Saturday I'm positive he doesn't understand the team that has won him two pennants. Proof of Stengel's insecurity was that he reinstated DiMaggio as a regular yesterday. But an aggravated muscle staked DiMaggio to the afternoon off.

There is no similarity between Stengel resting DiMaggio last season and jerking him out of Saturday's game. This is a hostile act, no matter what explanation Stengel gives. The ball club wants DiMaggio to lead them. They are not what they used to be. They are a club that has slipped. But if they have a chance it would be arranged only because DiMaggio led them.

Stengel may have dismantled the DiMaggio myth. The other clubs, especially the Red Sox, didn't look at the averages. They didn't like to see DiMaggio against them. They regarded him with awe. Sick or well, going good or bad, they believed DiMaggio was a special man. So did the Yankees. Stengel lost the ball game Saturday. He could have also lost the ball club.

1951 ALL STAR GAME

AMERICAN - NATIONAL LEAGUES

BRIGGS STADIUM

For the 13th time in his 13 active years in the major leagues, Joe DiMaggio was selected to play for the American League in the All-Star game, but a torn muscle in his left leg kept him on the bench in 1951.

AMERICAN LEAGUE STARS

JIM HEGAN
Cleveland Indians

JOE DiMAGGIO
New York Yankees

CONNIE MARRERO
Washington Senators

NED GARVER
St. Louis Browns

LARRY DOBY
Cleveland Indians

JIM BUSBY
Chicago White Sox

"MINNIE" MINOSO
Chicago White Sox

Casey in Middle on Use of DiMag

Whenever Stengel Gives Jolter a Needed Rest, He Faces Accusation of Slighting Aging Star

By ROBERT L. BURNES
Of the St. Louis Globe-Democrat

ST. LOUIS, Mo.

Joe DiMaggio

The oft-reported feud between Casey Stengel and Joe DiMaggio of the Yankees has cropped up again and the more denials there are concerning it, the more suspicion grows that there is something to it.

Casey's the guy in the middle of the thing and we feel sorta sorry for him if it's possible to feel sorry for a guy who has won two pennants and as many World's Series in two whacks at it and is earning the money befitting somebody in that position.

To paraphrase an old expression for the sake of politeness, Casey is doomed if he does and doomed if he doesn't in his use of DiMaggio.

To get back to the reported feud, perhaps it is dignifying it to say that it exists at all. Actually, according to people who have been close to the scene the whole time that Stengel has been with the Yankees, the word is that they just don't hit it off.

"So what?" the fellow who told u about it exclaimed. "They don't have too much in common except they both work for the Yankees and both are famous. They respect each other. Casey thinks DiMag is tremendous although he knows he's slipping. If that's a feud then there are a thousand of them in the major leagues today."

Stengel is a gregarious, garrulous character who enjoys being with people, who still cuts a few capers on the bench but masks a deadly seriousness about the game behind that air of geniality.

By contrast, DiMaggio is all business. He seldom smiles on the field, takes the game of baseball seriously at all times and, while he isn't aloof, does manage to keep to himself as much as possible.

A Johnny-Come-Lately With Yanks

As mentioned, though, Stengel is in a peculiar position concerning DiMag, primarily because Joe got there first. Joe was an established great with the Yankees while Stengel was still trying to get out of the second division in the National League.

So Ole Case was in the position, even at his advanced age, of being a Johnny-Come-Lately with the Yankees when he joined the club. By the nature of his job, though, he has to give orders.

That he has done an excellent job in this respect has to be admitted. You can't laugh off two championships in two years.

This is just one angle to a situation which has many complications.

For instance, Stengel took the job under difficult circumstances. He replaced a popular manager, Bucky Harris. The latter won a pennant and World's Series in 1947 and then missed the next flag by two and one-half games. For that miss he was fired. At least, ostensibly for that reason. It's

been generally accepted for a long time that a clash of personalities between Harris and General Manager George Weiss was the real reason for the hatcheting.

Yankee players burned over this, which made Stengel's arrival doubly difficult.

Finally there is the obvious problem arising from the fact that Stengel's debut was at a time when DiMag was starting to slide. Joe is now 36 years old and it's apparent that he can't do the things today that he did at 25—at least, as consistently.

Picked Joe on All-Star Squad

So Stengel had to prepare for that. Marty Marion has encountered much the same problem with Enos Slaughter on the Cardinals. Enos needs an occasional rest, so does Joe. Yet there will always be the feeling that the manager is slighting his player.

There could be fuel heaped on the flames over the All-Star Game.

Stengel by-passed several candidates to name Joe as one of his outfielders. DiMag was fairly far down the list, yet Stengel reached down to get him—and then didn't use him.

The obvious answer should be the right one. The oldest player in point of All-Star service, DiMag belonged on the ball club. More important, Stengel probably had him there for a clutch emergency.

Wouldn't you do the same thing? Even if such a situation never arose, as it didn't here, it's worth the risk.

We're not taking sides in this so-called feud because we don't believe sides exist. Joe McCarthy and Babe Ruth had the same problem 20 years ago. But we think it worthy of mention that Stengel's position throughout is unhappy, no matter which way he has turned, is turning or will turn.

DiMaggio Benches Self as Casey Raps Reports About Rift
By DAN DANIEL

CLEVELAND, O.

When the Yankees resumed play here, after the All-Star interlude, Joe DiMaggio was on the bench. He had placed himself there, because of a torn muscle in his left calf, and had announced that he believed he would be out for ten or 11 days.

This development came right on top of stories in a New York newspaper, the Post, that DiMaggio and Casey Stengel were not talking to each other. Since the report came at the time of the All-Star Game, it got a lot of attention from baseball men in general, in Detroit.

DiMaggio and Stengel never had any long talks. However, neither did Babe Ruth and Joe McCarthy have any conferences.

Ruth resented McCarthy's having come in to become manager. DiMaggio harbors no such feeling toward Stengel. It is just that DiMaggio is a reticent man. He never has been voluble. He is not a man who invites conversations.

Joe Is Sore, but at Father Time

If Casey and Joe are not holding any tete-a-tetes, it is nothing new and it is no prima facie evidence of a feud.

The idea that there is dissension on the New York club is unworthy of discussion.

DiMaggio hasn't too far to go as a player, and being a prideful man, resents the situation—ergo, he is sore—but mostly at himself and Father Time.

Ruth felt he should have been named manager. Joe has no such feeling insofar as Stengel's presence on the club is concerned.

No Ambition for Job as Pilot

Last March, in Phoenix, Joe said, "This may be my last year as a player. When I go, I want no other job in baseball. I do not want to be a manager."

The rumor that all is not well between DiMaggio and Stengel started when Joe appeared resentful when he was taken out of the lineup in the second inning of the game at Boston, July 7.

"I was taken out, and if you want to know more about it, see Casey Stengel," Joe barked to reporters in the clubhouse after the game.

DiMaggio went into the field in the second inning, apparently ignorant of the fact that he had been removed from the lineup.

Casey sent Johnny Hopp into center to notify DiMaggio that he no longer was a participant. At the time the score was 6 to 1 against New York.

Stengel said he had removed DiMag to rest him.

Reports that the pair are not on speaking terms drew a sharp blast from Stengel.

"They're nonsense—those stories that DiMag and I don't speak to each other," roared the Yankee manager. "If I weren't talking to him, would I have picked him for the All-Star team, despite the fact the popular poll had not placed him in a leading spot?

"Joe, at 36, isn't as great a player as he used to be. Still, he's better than a lot of guys I have now.

Speaking Out

By Milton Gross

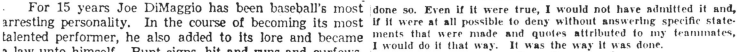

For 15 years Joe DiMaggio has been baseball's most arresting personality. In the course of becoming its most talented performer, he also added to its lore and became a law unto himself. Bunt signs, hit and runs and curfews, which circumscribed lesser players, never applied to DiMag. Which is as it should have been, because he showed almost at once that in his hands, feet, body and head were the elements that reduced his game to the simplest essentials and would be limited by managerial over-direction.

On the field he never disobeyed an order, and most managers, including Casey Stengel, were wise enough to recognize his over-abundance of talent could make them respected as bench geniuses in their strange business.

Because of this DiMaggio had the courage to do what others would not. When, for instance, Larry MacPhail, in his explosive Yankee regime, was feuding with Toots Shor, he laid down the law against his players being seen in the 51st street eatery. Yet one afternoon MacPhail asked Joe to have dinner with him that night and DiMag replied, "I'm sorry. I have a previous engagement. I'm having dinner at Toots'."

* * *

On another occasion Joe refused to cooperate with front office promotion plans and MacPhail slapped a fine on him. Yet last year when DiMag was ordered to play first base in a short-lived experiment, which was extreme in its cruelty since it reflected the management's unwillingness to allow their meal ticket to grow old gracefully, DiMag played the base without a whimper.

He did not like it, but he did it awkwardly and uncertainly. The heat of the day was not the only reason for his uniform becoming black with sweat that afternoon at Griffith Stadium.

One of the Yankee players, who had regarded Joe with the deities, remarked to me that evening, "The big guy was scared. Imagine Joe being scared," he said, his voice brimming with the astonishment that DiMag, like all others, possessed the normal complement of fear, anxiety, depression and other emotion which ties a man's insides into tight little knots.

I mention this now because of Joe DiMaggio's answer in The Post yesterday to my Monday column which reviewed his increasing moodiness and introversion that have made him a stranger to his teammates. If I were DiMaggio or Manager Casey Stengel of the Yankees, I would have defended myself too. I cannot blame them for having

DIMAGGIO

done so. Even if it were true, I would not have admitted it and, if it were at all possible to deny without answering specific statements that were made and quotes attributed to my teammates, I would do it that way. It was the way it was done.

* * *

DiMaggio made the point that I joined the Yankees Sunday. He does not know what I am talking about and he doesn't think I do. As one of the DiMaggio army of idolaters for the past 15 years, I must wonder what good purpose I had served covering them as world champions so many times during the decade.

Actually I had picked up the team last Friday for this road trip; but in effect I had never been away. Like Joe I broke in the big leagues with the Yankees. They've always been my team and always will be. We don't stick press cards in the upturned brims of our fedoras in fantastic Hollywood fashion, but we writers do pretend indifference to the teams and athletes with whom we travel. Yet beneath it there is always a loyalty to the team with which we started, because even after a dozen years, that first team and first season mark a milestone in our lives.

Therefore on Friday I did recognize a profound difference in the personal climate which surrounds DiMaggio and the Yankees this season. It is a frigid one, all because Joe, who always was a strange man, difficult to understand, is now living in a shell that is virtually impenetrable. I grew up with these players, DiMag, Henrich, Rizzuto and the others, and, like an old friend or relative who has been away a short time I could recognize the Yankees' feeling over DiMag's increasing non-talkativeness, when I came back.

* * *

It was not necessary to have players tell it to me, although they did, nor was it news to me that Joe and his manager do not embrace when they meet. DiMag rarely spoke to McCarthy, Dickey, Neun or Harris, who preceded Stengel on the Yankee bench but that did not mean he ever did less than his best for any of them. Unfortunately the flesh decomposes faster than the spirit. Joe also said he never had a difference of opinion with Stengel, who concurs. So do I.

But several questions still confuse me. Why didn't Joe tell Casey he was hurt on Saturday? Why didn't he tell Trainer Gus Mauch? Why is it that only Johnny Mize knew and was he the player who told Stengel he thought Joe limped? Why did Stengel announce after Joe's strange removal from the game on Saturday that DiMag was not injured, but being rested? Either he knew Joe was hurt or he didn't; why doesn't somebody, especially the one most vitally concerned, tell him? Like I say, I don't blame Joe or old Casey for waving their arms about and shouting, "I'm innocent." I'm just curious, that's all. The Yankees pride themselves on the efficiency of their organization. They should unsnarl their communication line.

'I'll Lick It,'
DiMag Says of Hit Famine

By JOE REICHLER
Associated Press Sports Writer

Joe DiMaggio sat in front of his locker, stripped of his baseball gear, puffing absent-mindedly on a cigaret. He was alone except for a close friend.

All around him teammates were still talking about Wednesday's dramatic 2—1 victory over the Indians. Prospects of three straight over the Tribe appeared very bright as Allie Reynolds, who had conquered Cleveland four times this season, was due to pitch.

DiMaggio watched silently for a while, then spoke for the first time.

"Notice the way we've been winning them lately? 1—0, 2—1, 3—2. The pitchers have been carrying nearly all the load. The boys have been in a hitting slump.

"Maybe I should talk about myself only," he said with a rueful grin.

"I haven't been dong anything to help the club. I just can't seem to buy a base hit."

He went hitless in yesterday's game, getting on base only once and that via a walk.

Since DiMaggio himself broached the subject about his non-hitting, you asked:

"What's the matter, Joe? Can you account for your failure to hit the way you used to?"

DiMaggio didn't answer for a minute. He got up, blew a cloud of smoke out through his nostrils and flipped the cigaret away.

"Yes," he answered. "I know what's the matter with me. I'm not getting the old snap into my swing."

DiMaggio cocked his wrists and went through an imaginary swing. "Right here," he said, looking down at his doubled fists as he finished the swing. "I just

JOE DIMAGGIO

don't seem to give it that old follow through."

"Up around here, too," he continued, drawing his right hand across his chest from one shoulder to the other. "I just haven't been able to make the bat came around as quick as I used to."

You suggested politely that maybe he was swinging late and hitting at bad balls.

"Yes, I am swinging late," Joe said. "But it's not because I'm biting at bad balls. Oh, of course, I'll go for a bad one now and then. But most of the time, they're right down the middle. I see them coming and set myself. But when I swing, the ball shoots right up at me."

DiMaggio bent down and you couldn't help but notice the streaks of grey in his hair. Even his beard of one day's growth

was sprinkled with white hairs giving unmistaken evidence that age was creeping up on the great star.

"It's not that I don't know what's the matter with me," he said. "I know what Im doing wrong. It's just that I can't seem to do anything about it."

You asked whether he was worrying too much about it—if it affected his eating, sleeping, etc.

"No," he shook his head emphatically. "I don't allow it to get me down too much. Naturally, I'm concerned, but not to a point where it's got me down in the dumps."

Could it be that his long layoff due to an injury might have dimmed his batting eye and all he needed was a little more actual competition?

"No," he answered honestly. "That's the way it has been all season. Right from the start."

What did he intend to do about it?

"Beat it," Joe answered without hesitation. "I'm going to beat it. I'm going to keep swinging until I get the old snap back. It will come back to me. I know it.

"I know I haven't been of much help. But I'm going to hang on there. I'm going to battle it till I lick it."

"Remember what I said," he repeated. "I'm going to lick it."

DiMaggio said it very quietly, through tight lips. Seeing the serious, determined look on his face when he said it, and hearing the quiet, calm and confident way in which he said it, you left with the feeling—and hope—that Joe will "lick it."

Stengel Hedges on Shifting DiMag From Cleanup Spot

By LOU MILLER.

Historians who follow the daily heroics of the Yankee baseball club were in a slight dither after yesterday's 4–1 setback by sixth-place Washington. Their boys just had been dropped out of first in the frenzied American League race. Something drastic had to be done to regain the lead from Cleveland, now half a game in front.

"Are you thinking of moving Joe DiMaggio out of the cleanup spot?" one queried Casey Stengel in the press hideout in the Yankee Stadium catacombs after the game. "He hasn't been hitting much since the Chicago series. Didn't do much cleaning up today."

"I never know until just before a game what my lineup is gonna be," the startled New York manager came back with his favorite stall. "But I don't think I'll change, just because we lost one. Besides, who could do better? Nobody hit today. That and Mickey Vernon's two home runs, both with a man on, is what beat us. And I will say Bob Porterfield pitched well for them."

Over in the visiting team section of the underground, Bucky Harris, Senator manager, paused before leaving. Bucky is supposed to take special delight in walloping the New York club, which he managed before being fired in 1948 by Lonesome George Weiss, Yankee general manager. Washington has beaten the Bronx entry six times in 13 meetings, a very noteworthy achievement for a second-division club.

"Porterfield must've had a great kick out of beating the Yanks," chuckled Bucky. "They gave him to me for Bob Kuzawa this season. Porterfield is going to be a good pitcher. He never had a real chance with the Yanks, mostly because of injuries, I guess.

"Funny about Vernon, too," continued Harris. Cleveland traded him to us and he puts them into first place today with his hitting."

Vernon still was in the dressing room and the big first sacker didn't mind talking. "I always seem to have good luck in New York," he agreed. "Even when I used to come in with Cleveland.

"First I whacked today was a slider. Vic Raschi had two strikes on me and I had to protect the plate. Second was a fast ball. He only had one strike on me then."

Raschi, now 16–7, didn't pitch badly. He gave up only seven safeties to Porterfield's nine allowances. The major league strikeout leader fanned five to boost his total to 119. But oh, those gophers. That's one department he leads the team in that he isn't bragging about. He has given up 18 circuit smashes. Ed Lopat and Frank Shea, with 10 each, are closest on the Yankee staff.

Yank Flag Hopes Rest On DiMag and Mize

By Hugh Bradley

Two older Yankees today are being closely eyed by Casey Stengel. He's not blaming Joe DiMaggio and Johnny Mize for the fact the club has dropped out of the lead for the first time since July 22, but he's wondering just how he must handle them for the pennant fight that lies ahead.

Definitely the 37-year-old Clipper and the 38-year-old Big Jawn are the men Stengel is depending upon to provide the power at the plate. If they can sock throughout the rest of 1951 with the same vigor they displayed at a similar period last year, he is confident he can beat out the Indians who yesterday moved into the lead by four percentage points.

What perturbs him is the recent evidence that neither of the two big gees are quite on the beam.

Although he is hitting .264, a three-point gain since he returned to the lineup at the start of the current home stand, DiMaggio has been in trouble during the last four games. In that time he has made only three hits in 17 trips to the plate and —as happened while the Senators were beating our side, 4 to 1, yesterday — he's leaving men on the bases in the clutch.

Mize also has failed to blast with customary diligence. During the home stand when he's played almost daily while 1 2have been won and five lost, he's made only eleven hits in 45 trips to the plate, driving in seven runs and compiling a .244 average for the period.

Obviously such falling off by the power houses indicates one of two measures is necessary.

Either the gents, who apparently are a trifle tired, should be rested for a few days, or they should be dropped in the batting order, so that they will not almost constantly be coming to the dish with victory depending upon their swings.

That Stengel may decide to rest one or both of them during the eight games with the Athletics. and Senators, which makes up the Eastern tour upon which the club embarks tomorrow, seems possible. While shying away from forthright statements on the subject, he admits it's been on his mind for several days.

DiMag's Voice Booms Over Bat in Slapback at Critical Writers

'Silly Stuff'

'Just Because I Have a Bad Day, You Guys Want to Fire Me,' Joe's Reply to Strikeout Stories

By DAN DANIEL

Joe DiMaggio

NEW YORK, N. Y.

That all was not honey and sugar plums between some of the baseball writers covering the Yankees and Joseph Paul DiMaggio long had been suspected on the outside. Now the situation is a matter of public knowledge, and Joe is the man who has made it so.

In a defeat by Washington in the Stadium, by former Yankee Bob Porterfield, which temporarily dropped the Bombers behind the Indians, DiMaggio was struck out.

The following day, after the Yankees had whipped the Senators, with the help of a tremendous outburst by Joe, with his tenth homer and a triple, the Clipper let go at the scribes.

"What's the idea of writing that Porterfield purposely threw me three bad ones, then two straight strikes, then a curve to strike me out?" said Joe, with a lot of asperity, to one of the reporters.

"Casey Stengel told you that? Then I will have to ask him. I am certainly going to ask him.

"The plate is only so wide. If the pitcher could put the ball exactly where he wanted to, the batters would just have to go home.

"You guys call that good reporting, I call it silly stuff."

Before Joe crashed his homer and triple, there had been journalistic questions as to when Casey would take the Clipper out of the cleanup spot in the batting order.

Some had hinted that it might be a good idea to give Giuseppe another rest.

"You are darn right that I wanted to make you writers look bad," DiMaggio vehemed.

"I'll always try to make you look bad. Just because I have a bad day, you guys want to fire me. Some of you guys are the ones who washed me up in 1946. But here I am, five years later. How are you going to explain the hits I made today? Are they going to fire me every time I have a bad day?

"Did anyone ever see me give up on a fly ball in the outfield? Bet your life, no. The only thing I am interested in is to win the pennant again this season."

The situation between some of the writers and Joe is quite understandable. Every time at bat now is ultra-important. The Yankees have a tough job in front of them, and the men in the press box are rooting for that third straight pennant.

There are times when Joe does not look like a No. 4 batter, and in their keen disappointment, some of the reporters lay considerable stress on this passing condition. The writers cannot see why Casey should be forced to keep Joe in the cleanup spot, even when he is in a slump.

However, there isn't a really competent No. 4 hitter on the New York club. Yogi Berra comes closest.

Joe Resentful of Father Time

Even when he is under .270, DiMaggio inspires a lot of fear in enemy pitchers, a lot of confidence in his teammates, and certainly the loyalty and encomium of the fans.

Much as the position of the writers is understandable, so is that of DiMaggio himself no puzzle.

Here he is, nearing his thirty-seventh birthday, fading out, considering retiring. If not in 1952, then in 1953. He has a tremendous pride, and is resentful at Nature, at Time, at Circumstance, at the men who, doing their job, have to record Joe's failures as well as his triumphs.

Certainly those writers are more than eager to play up his triumphs. But, if he fans at a critical point of a game, they cannot bypass the fact.

The writers are not trying to fire Joe. They know it will be the blackest day since Lou Gehrig was forced to leave the New York lineup when Joe asks for his release, and quits the Stadium.

There have been times, in the past, when unmerited and at times poison-tipped darts were blown at Joe.

Sweet Days and Sour Ones

But this season there has been considerable tendency to sympathize with the outfielder.

That there is a very bad situation between DiMaggio and some of the writers certainly is apparent to anyone who might visit the Yankee clubhouse.

There are days on which Joe is affable, there are days on which he invites no approach.

Some of the scribes have tired of guessing which kind of day it might be around Joe's locker, and have stopped dropping by.

While Joe was in his late July slump, only one interview with him got into the papers and it was not obtained by a writer covering the Yankees. Joe Reichler of the Associated Press happened to drop into the clubhouse, and Joe asked him to chin a while.

There isn't a writer attached to the New York club who would not be delighted to talk things over with Joe every day.

If DiMaggio is going to break out with a homer and triple every time he gets sore at the writers, the writers will be content to let Joe get sore, and keep socking.

Nobody is trying to fire Joe. Nobody except Father Time, a terrible, soulless, vindictive old guy.

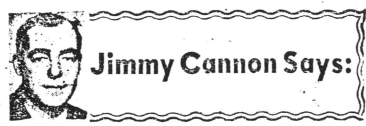

Jimmy Cannon Says:

It was a glorious day, gleaming and serene, a summer afternoon lost from its season. I imagined there was a sweet defiance in its splendor as though it were proud of its triumph over the winds of autumn. There appeared to be an affinity between the shining afternoon and Joe Di-Maggio. Yesterday was a rebuke to the calendar. It was the summer-time refusing to be evicted from the world and lingering obstinately and without malice to be enjoyed by all within its horizons.

There is no valid association between the vagrant summer's day and the great ball player except each contradicted the way by which time is measured. The clocks were wrong yesterday.

The cynical will find this column ludicrous because DiMaggio is well paid to play baseball. The young men will doubt it because they seldom comprehend how the years nag a man who earns a living with his body. It is written then for the middle-aged and the wonderfully naive who still have faith in the trivial justice of sports. I consider myself both.

You do not have to be an old man to realize what happened to DiMaggio yesterday. But if you are made sad because Joe Louis continues to fight you qualify. It was, of course, only one ball game in a tournament of a hundred and fifty-four but it put the Yankees in first place, three points ahead of the Indians, whom they beat, 5—1.

It was a triple which didn't decide the ball game but it was struck by the greatest ball player of his generation who was hitting .266 at the end of the nine innings. It was a hit I shall remember long after I have forgotten the importance of the contest.

*   *   *

There were 70,040 in the Stadium when the line-ups came from the horns of the public address system with a harsh bellow. There was no ceremony when the iron voice related that Yogi Berra was batting fourth. But it stirred up an inconsequential murmur among the true devotees present. They understood that DiMaggio had been dropped down to fifth place. It was not unexpected and had the approval of the unsentimental.

It seemed like a sensible alteration be-cause Berra struck a triple in the first inning and the Yankees led, 1—0. Up fifth, DiMaggio hit a ball back to Bob Feller who flapped it down with his glove and threw him out. In the second DiMaggio, going with unimpaired grace, caught Jim Hegan's fly in left center. It was a spectacular play, made simply by DiMaggio's poise, which creates the impression he is unhurried.

"He can still field," a guy said in the press box.

What he meant was he doubted him as a hitter. So did Al Lopez, who manages the Cleveland team.

*   *   *

It was a remark that seemed to be founded in logic because in the next inning DiMaggio hit into a double play. We talked among ourselves in the reporters' gallery and wondered what he was thinking about as he trotted back to the center field, trotting with that high-legged, bent-necked lope. But this is a quiet man of internal rages, living inside of himself and never soliciting pity with the dramatized angers some ball players use.

There was a man on second and two were out when Berra came up to hit in the fifth. They decided to walk the catcher purposely and throw to DiMaggio. It must have infuriated him because, until this season, DiMaggio hit Feller with destructive consistency. In the circle where the next hitter kneels, DiMaggio leaned on his bat. At no other time has this posture of genuflec-tion been significant for me. Before this multitude, a reputation unmatched in baseball was being defaced with contempt.

It had happened twice before this year but never in the Stadium. Washington succeeded because they forced DiMaggio to hit into a double play. But against Cleveland he had crossed them before by getting home a run with a single.

*   *   *

The seasons have changed Feller's style, too. He has invested in deceit and located control. The slider takes a crooked little jump. The change-up wabbles with a tantalizing indolence. Instead of trying to blow the ball by, Feller now gambles with the tricky stuff.

The first pitch was a strike, the second a ball. The third was a strike which nicked DiMaggio's bat as he hesitated in broken swing. The next one was a slider.

The sound identified it as a base hit. It fled on a true line and the cries of the crowd billowed out from the stands, thick as the cigarette smoke. The ball bounced in deep left center field. It rolled by Larry Doby and reached the fence. Two runs scored and DiMaggio, running with that round-shouldered, long-gaited stride, pulled up at third. The hit journeyed 457 feet from the bat to the base of the bleacher wall. There were a stack of telegrams on the stool of DiMaggio's locker after the game.

"When I get a hit now," he said, "they send me wires."

70,972 SEE BOMBERS TRIUMPH BY 8-3, 2-0

DiMaggio Wallops 2 Homers, Raschi Hurls 15th Victory for Yanks in Opener

KUZAVA BLANKS WHITE SOX

Limits Fading Chicagoans to Five Hits in Afterpiece—Kretlow, Rogovin Bow

By JOHN DREBINGER

The White Sox' pennant bubble, which sprung a slow leak about ten days ago, suffered a blowout at the Stadium yesterday as the Yankees blasted Paul Richards' Chicagoans in both games of a double-header before a crowd of 70,972.

The opener went to Casey Stengel's Bombers, 8 to 3, with Joe DiMaggio exploding two home runs that accounted for five of the tallies. Vic Raschi did the pitching and did it so well that even though he had to retire in the ninth after getting smashed on the bare hand by a drive off Chico Carrasquel's bat, the big righthander left twelve strikeout victims in his wake.

That, in addition to giving Raschi his fifteenth triumph, gave him the lead league in strikeouts with 108, topping the 102 figure the Red Sox' Maurice McDermott had reached on Saturday.

In the afterpiece, Bob Kuzava stepped in to toss a five-hit shutout while the Stengeleers toppled Saul Rogovin, 2 to 0.

The triumphs enabled the Bombers to sweep the three-game series, score their ninth victory in their last ten encounters and move two full lengths in front of the Red Sox and Indians, now tied once again for second place.

The Fading Pale Hose

As for the hapless Pale Hose, beaten in nine of their last ten, the double defeat sent them staggering back to a distance of six and a half games from the top.

After the exciting thrills of the opener, the afterpiece was more or less a cut-and-dried affair. The Yanks made off with a tally in the first inning on a double by Gene Woodling and a single by Bobby Brown.

To this they added another in the fourth when DiMaggio and Johnny Mize weighed in with a pair of singles. Here Gil McDougald came through with a beautifully timed delayed squeeze bunt which saw DiMaggio slide over the plate a flash ahead of Eddie Robinson's throw.

Fortified behind that margin, Kuzava put on his best mound effort of the year in ringing up his sixth victory, third as a Yank. The former Senator and White Sox southpaw fanned nine, allowed only three runners to reach third and the five base hits he gave up were all singles. It marked the sixteenth shut-out by a Yankee hurler this year.

The combination of Raschi's strong arm pitching and DiMaggio's power hitting proved more than the Chicagoans were able to cope with in the opener.

The Clipper's first homer off Lou Kretlow came in the first inning with Joe Collins aboard and wiped out a two-run lead which the Sox had stored up for themselves in the top half of the round on Nelson Fox' double, Minnie Minoso's single and steal of second, and Ed Stewart's one-base clout to right that drove in both runners.

Stewart Connects in Ninth

After the brief scoring outburst the Sox remained dormant until Stewart homered in the ninth, but by that time the Yanks had put the game well beyond reach. The Bombers broke the 2-all deadlock in the fifth when they counted three times with a varied assortment of offensive moves.

Woodling drew a pass, and Collins, Stengel's right fielder for the day, banged a triple off the right field bleacher wall. That scored one and another followed as Stewart and Carrasquel collided on Brown's pop fly in short left that fell for a double. Then, as Brown broke for third on a wind-up, inducing Minoso to hustle toward the bag, Yogi Berra slammed a single through the spot just vacated by the Sox third sacker and Robert, counted.

There was nothing so involved in the sixth. This time Collins walked, Brown singled and DiMaggio drove his second clout of the afternoon and ninth of the season into the left field stand. That three-run shot scuttled Kretlow on the spot and virtually finished the rest of the Sox as well.

Following Stewart's ninth inning homer, Jim Busby walked and, after Bud Sheely flied out, Carrasquel came up with his third single, this being the blow that caromed off Raschi's bare hand and sent him into the pits for repairs. Joe Ostrowski came on to collect the final two outs. Later it was reported that Raschi had suffered nothing worse than a pair of bruised fingers.

Raschi Twice Fans Side

In piling up his twelve strike-outs, Raschi twice fanned the side, although his three in the second were interspersed by a pair of singles. In the eighth, however, Vic fanned three in a row.

When Rizzuto singled in the second inning of the opener it gave Li'l Phil the distinction of becoming the first Yankee to reach the century mark in base hits. . . . Berra is next in line with a present total of 98. . . . Saturday's rained-out game with the White Sox will be played off as a single encounter at the Stadium on Sept. 19, originally an open date. . . . The Bombers need only four more homers to gain the 100 figure for the twenty-eighth season. The Yanks have missed only four times since 1920, the lean years being 1922, '24, '44 and '45.

Joe DiMaggio crosses the plate after one of the last of the 361 home runs he hit as a Yankee. The site was Fenway Park in Boston in a 1951 game against the Red Sox. Number 8 is Yankee catcher, Yogi Berra.

World Series Gives DiMag Tie With Babe Ruth at 10

By DANIEL.

Joe DiMaggio today was preparing for his 10th World Series, and a tie with Babe Ruth for the all-time record for classic participation. Frankie Frisch and Bill Dickey took part in eight series.

DiMaggio had been on a loser only once. That was in 1942 when the Cardinals surprised and ran over the Bombers, four games to one. Joe hit .333 against the Redbirds. He was in the Army in 1943, when the Yankees took sweet revenge on St. Louis.

Having played 45 World Series games for the Bombers, the Clipper had one record all to himself. Frisch competed in 50 contests, but only 25 were with the Giants, the other 24 for the Cardinals.

Giuseppe enjoys still another record. He was on a world championship winner in his first four years in the major leagues from 1936 to 1939, the four seasons in which the Yankees matched the mark of the four pennant-winning Giant clubs from 1921 through 1924.

With 176 World Series at-bats, DiMaggio ran second to Frisch's 197 but Frankie was finished, and it was conceivable that Joe was not yet ready to offer himself as a candidate, in retirement, for the Hall of Fame.

In four series DiMaggio had come up with .300 averages, as against six for the Babe. Ruth was on seven classic winners, but only four of these represented the New York club. In the other three he was with the Red Sox.

DiMaggio has appeared in three series against Brooklyn, and two with the Giants.

His showing against the Polo Grounders has been much the more impressive one. He batted .346 against them in his freshman year of 1936, and .273 in 1937, for a mean average of .309.

Showing in Series
May Sway Decision.

Giuseppe's hitting against the Dodgers has not been up to his standard. He batted only .263 in the 1941 classic, .231 in 1947 and a mere .111 in 1949 when he was convalescent from virus pneumonia. His average against Flatbush hurling is an undistinguished .202.

In the American League of 1951, DiMaggio played in 122 games with 415 times at bat, 71 runs, 109 hits, 22 doubles, four triples, 12 homers, 171 total bases, 72 runs driven in, and an average of .263.

This did not betoken the brilliant, powerful DiMaggio of other years, of his .381 in 1939, his 46 homers and 167 runs accounted for, in 1937. But for a guy who will be 37 on Nov. 25, he did well enough. His fielding still was brilliant, his arm at times amazingly strong and accurate.

Last March at Phoenix, Joe said, "This might be my last year."

At the time he did not seem to believe he would play in more than 100 games this season. His taste for baseball appeared to be jaded.

It may be that DiMaggio's showing in the world series starting on Thursday will sway his decision.

He had talked of waiting until spring training to make up his mind on the question of retiring after 13 years of hard play for the Yankees. But now he believes that Casey Stengel is entitled to know after the classic.

It is believed that DiMaggio will come back in 1952. Should the New York club decide that it has to take a crack at Joe's $100,000 salary it would be able to cut him only 25 per cent to $75,000 after income taxes the difference would come to not more than 15 per cent.

Stay? Retire? It soon will be up to Joe to decide. New York and baseball join in saying "Stick around yet a while, Giuseppe."

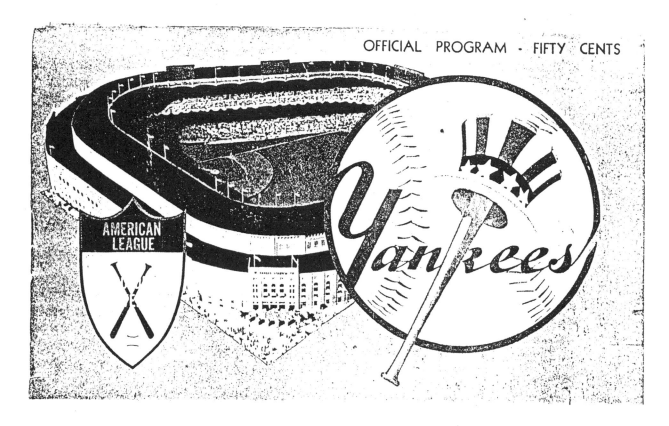

OFFICIAL PROGRAM · FIFTY CENTS

AMERICAN LEAGUE

Yankees

1951 WORLD SERIES

Giants

1876

NATIONAL LEAGUE

75th Anniversary

1951

1951

PHIL RIZZUTO

JOE DiMAGGIO

Once again Phil Rizzuto has been a spark plug in a pennant-winning Yankee team. Just a few years back when Phil, in his first post-War season, batted a mere .257, there was talk of replacing him at shortstop in the Yankee infield. How hasty was that judgement! In the last five years Phil has played brilliantly for four pennant winners and in 1949 and 1950 enjoyed his peak seasons. Runner-up to Ted Williams for the American League's Most Valuable Player award in '49 the little Scooter off the sidewalks of New York, who played his first major league ball for the champions of 1941, took that high honor by a wide margin in '50.

There's a spot waiting for Joe DiMaggio in Baseball's Hall of Fame. He is the outstanding player of our day—a star in the same mold as Ruth and Gehrig and Cobb and Wagner. Only player in the history of the game to play on four World Championship teams his first four years in the major leagues (1936 to 1939), Joe established his greatest of many records in the season of 1941 when he hit safely in fifty-six consecutive games from May 15 through July 16. Three times Joe has been picked for the MVP award in the American League—1939, 1941 and 1947. Each year, of course, he paced the Yankees to a pennant. Picked on All-Star teams annually since he came to the Yankees.

★

LARRY BERRA

VIC RASCHI

Strongest bid for the Most Valuable Player award by a Yankee this season was made by Yogi Berra, the most active catcher in either league and the most robust slugger among the pennant-winning Bronx Bombers. This will be Yogi's fourth World Series and his third against the Brooklyn Dodgers. Returning to competition with the Flatbush crew gives Berra an added thrill for it was against them in 1947 when, while still suffering from a late-season illness, Berra was pictured as the near-goat of the series. As a matter of fact the October Classic of 1947 sent Yogi from behind the plate to right field for most of 1949. Bill Dickey, the Yankee coach, put the mask and pads back on Berra in '49 and he has become the best in his league under Dickey's careful tutelage.

A 21-game winner in 1949 and 1950, Vic Raschi once again in 1951, took over the Ace's chores on Casey Stengel's pitching staff. A Yankee farm product all the way, having started with Amsterdam in 1941, Vic is one of the leading percentage winners in American League history. Vic came up to the Yankees late in '46, after serving with Newark and Binghamton, dropped back to the minors for a spell in '47 but returned to the Yankees that year to hurl two victories (including the last) in New York's pennant-clinching, record-tying 19-game winning streak. He has been the staff's sturdiest ever since.

ALLIE REYNOLDS

ED LOPAT

On July 12 of the 1951 season Allie Reynolds realized the dream of a lifetime. He pitched a no-hit, no-run game. How vital was that victory only later events proved. It was scored over Bob Feller and over the Cleveland Indians by the narrowest of margins, 1 to 0. A home run by Gene Woodling was the only tally of the game. Both Reynolds and Woodling were playing against the club with which they broke into major league ball. Allie, now known as "Superchief", has been one of the Yankees' finest World Series pitchers. He has scored one victory in each of the Yankees' last three World Championships.

Steady Eddie Lopat has been the Yankees' best earned-run average mound artist every year since George Weiss obtained him from the Chicago White Sox in his first deal as General Manager of the Yankees. And Eddie gets better with each added year. He pitched more complete games than any Yankee this season and had his top year in victories.

Star of tomorrow

Star of Tomorrow is the title of this oil painting by the artist Mayo, which features Joe DiMaggio in the role of a batting coach. The original painting was done for the National Baseball Hall of Fame calendar of 1957.

A retired Joe DiMaggio still dons the uniform at the Yankees' spring training camp in Florida in the 1950s.

Game 1 October 4 at New York (A)

New York-N	Pos	AB	R	H	RBI	PO	A	E
Stanky	2b	4	1	0	0	4	2	0
Dark	ss	5	1	2	3	1	2	0
Thompson	rf	3	1	0	0	3	0	1
Irvin	lf	5	1	4	0	4	0	0
Lockman	1b	4	0	1	1	4	1	0
Thomson	3b	3	0	1	0	2	2	0
Mays	cf	5	0	0	0	4	0	0
Westrum	c	3	1	2	0	5	0	0
Koslo	p	3	0	0	0	2	0	0
Totals		35	5	10	4	27	7	1

Pitching	IP	H	R	ER	BB	SO
New York-N						
Koslo (W)	9	7	1	1	3	3
New York-A						
Reynolds (L)	6	8	5	5	7	1
Hogue	1	0	0	0	0	0
Morgan	2	2	0	0	1	3

NY-N	200	003	000	5
NY-A	010	000	000	1

New York-A	Pos	AB	R	H	RBI	PO	A	E
Mantle	rf	3	0	0	0	4	0	0
Rizzuto	ss	4	0	2	0	1	2	0
Bauer	lf	4	0	0	0	0	0	0
DiMaggio	cf	4	0	0	0	3	0	0
Berra	c	4	0	1	0	5	1	0
McDougald	3b	4	1	1	0	0	2	1
Coleman	2b	3	0	1	0	3	3	0
Collins	1b	3	0	1	0	11	0	0
b Mize		1	0	0	0	0	0	0
Reynolds	p	2	0	1	0	0	3	0
Hogue	p	0	0	0	0	0	1	0
a Brown		1	0	0	0	0	0	0
Morgan	p	0	0	0	0	0	1	0
c Woodling		1	0	0	0	0	0	0
Totals		34	1	7	0	27	13	1

a Struck out for Hogue in 8th
b Popped out for Collins in 9th
c Struck out for Morgan in 9th.

Doubles—Lockman, McDougald.
Triple—Irvin. Home Run—Dark.
Stolen Base—Irvin. Sacrifice
Hits—Koslo 2. Double Play—McDougald
to Coleman to Collins. Left on
Bases—Giants 13, Yankees 9.
Umpires—Summers (A), Ballantant (N),
Paparella (A), Barlick (N), Stevens (A),
Gore (N). Attendance—65,673.
Time of Game—2:58.

1st Inning
Giants
1 Stanky grounded to short.
2 Dark flied to right.
  Thompson walked.
  Irvin singled to right-center, moving
  Thompson to third.
  Lockman bounced a ground-rule double
  into the left field stands, Thompson
  scoring and Irvin stopping at third.
  Irvin stole home, sliding in
  under a high pitch.
  Thomson walked.
3 Mays flied to right.
Yankees
1 Mantle flied to right.
  Rizzuto singled to left.
2 Bauer flied to Irvin in left, who made
  a leaping one-handed catch at the
  400-foot mark.
3 DiMaggio flied to right.

2nd Inning
Giants
  Westrum walked.
1 Koslo forced Westrum at second on a
  bunt, Reynolds to Rizzuto.
2,3 Stanky hit into a double play,
  McDougald to Coleman to Collins.
Yankees
1 Berra grounded to first.
  McDougald doubled into the left
  field corner.
  Coleman singled to right, McDougald
  going to third, but Thompson fumbled
  the hit allowing McDougald to score.
2 Collins forced Coleman at second,
  Thomson to Stanky.
  Reynolds singled to right, Coleman
  stopping at second.
  Mantle walked, loading the bases.
3 Rizzuto grounded out, Lockman to Koslo.

3rd Inning
Giants
1 Dark struck out.
2 Thompson grounded back to the mound.
  Irvin singled to right.
  Lockman walked.
  Thomson singled to left, loading
  the bases.
3 Mays lined to second.
Yankees
1 Bauer popped to third.
2 DiMaggio flied to left.
3 Berra fouled to Thomson.

4th Inning
Giants
  Westrum walked.
1 Koslo sacrificed Westrum to second,
  Reynolds to Collins.
2 Stanky grounded to third, Westrum
  holding at second.
3 Dark flied to center.
Yankees
1 McDougald fouled to Westrum.
2 Coleman grounded to short.
  Collins singled to right.
3 Reynolds grounded out, Stanky to Koslo.

5th Inning
Giants
1 Thompson flied to center.
  Irvin tripled over DiMaggio's head.
2 Lockman grounded to second, Irvin
  holding third.
3 Thomson grounded to short.
Yankees
  Mantle walked.
1 Rizzuto struck out.
2 Bauer lined to center.
3 DiMaggio flied to deep right.

6th Inning
Giants
1 Mays flied to right.
  Westrum singled to left.
2 Koslo again sacrificed Westrum to
  second, Berra to Coleman.
  Stanky walked.
  Dark hit a three-run homer into
  the lower left field stands.
  Thompson walked.
  Irvin singled to center, Thompson
  going to third (Irvin's 4th hit).
3 Lockman grounded to second.
Yankees
1 Berra popped to second.
2 McDougald flied to left.
3 Coleman grounded to third.

7th Inning
Giants
  For the Yankees—Hogue now pitching.
1 Thomson bounced back to the mound.
2 Mays flied to center.
3 Westrum fouled to Berra.
Yankees
1 Collins bunted out to second.
2 Brown, pinch-hitting for Hogue,
  struck out.
3 Mantle flied to Westrum.

8th Inning
Giants
  For the Yankees—Morgan pitching.
1 Koslo called out on strikes.
  Stanky safe at first on McDougald's
  wild throw of his grounder.
  Dark singled to right, Stanky
  stopping at second.
2 Thompson flied to deep right, Stanky
  going to third after the catch.
3 Irvin was finally retired, lining out
  to first.
Yankees
  Rizzuto singled to right-center.
1 Bauer forced Rizzuto at second, Dark
  to Stanky.
2 DiMaggio flied to left.
  Berra singled to right, Bauer
  stopping at second.
3 McDougald popped to second.

9th Inning
Giants
1 Lockman grounded back to the mound.
  Thomson walked.
2 Mays struck out.
  Westrum singled to left, Thomson
  stopping at second.
3 Koslo struck out.
Yankees
  Coleman walked.
1 Mize, pinch-hitting for Collins,
  popped to short.
2 Woodling, pinch-hitting for Morgan,
  took a called third strike.
3 Mantle flied to center.

Game 2 October 5 at New York-A

New York-N	Pos	AB	R	H	RBI	PO	A	E
Stanky	2b	3	0	0	0	1	4	0
Dark	ss	4	0	1	0	0	4	0
Thomson	3b	4	0	0	0	2	3	0
Irvin	lf	4	1	3	0	3	0	0
Lockman	1b	4	0	1	0	11	0	1
Mays	cf	4	0	0	0	2	0	0
Westrum	c	2	0	0	0	5	0	0
b Schenz		0	0	0	0	0	0	0
Hartung	rf	1	0	0	0	0	0	0
Thompson	rf	2	0	0	0	0	0	0
a Rigney		1	0	1	0	0	0	0
Spencer	p	0	0	0	0	0	0	0
Jansen	p	2	0	0	0	0	0	0
c Noble	c	1	0	0	0	0	0	0
Totals		32	1	5	1	24	11	1

a Flied out for Thompson in 7th.
b Ran for Westrum in 7th.
c Fouled out for Jansen in 7th.

Home Run—Collins. Stolen Base—Irvin.
Double Play—Dark to Stanky to Lockman.
Left on Bases—Giants 6, Yankees 2.
Umpires—Ballantant, Paparella, Barlick,
Summers, Gore, Stevens.
Attendance—66,018. Time of Game—2:05.

1st Inning
Giants
1 Stanky grounded to second.
2 Dark grounded to short.
3 Thomson flied to left.
Yankees
  Mantle beat out a bunt past the mound.
  Rizzuto also beat out a bunt past
  Jansen, but Lockman fielding the ball
  threw wildly past Stanky at first and
  Mantle raced to third with Rizzuto
  holding first.
  McDougald singled to right, scoring Mantle as
  Rizzuto going to third.
1,2 DiMaggio grounded into a double play,
  Dark to Stanky to Lockman with
  Rizzuto going to third.
3 Berra struck out.

2nd Inning
Giants
  Irvin singled to left-center.
  Irvin stole second.
1 Lockman bounced back to the mound,
  Irvin holding second.
2 Mays grounded to third, Irvin
  still holding at second.
3 Westrum grounded to third.
Yankees
1 Woodling flied to left.
2 Brown grounded to second.
  Collins hit a home run into the
  right field stands.
3 Lopat grounded to first.

3rd Inning
Giants
1 Thompson grounded out, Collins to
  Lopat.
2 Jansen flied to center.
  Stanky walked.
3 Dark flied to left.
Yankees
1 Mantle struck out.
2 Rizzuto flied to left.
3 McDougald lined to third.

4th Inning
Giants
1 Thomson flied to center.
2 Irvin popped to second.
3 Lockman grounded to short.
Yankees
1 DiMaggio struck out.
2 Berra grounded to short.
3 Woodling flied to center.

5th Inning
Giants
1 Mays flied to DiMaggio in right-center.
  For the Yankees—Bauer replaced Mantle in
  right after he wrenched his knee on the
  previous play.
2 Westrum flied to left.
3 Thompson was called out on strikes.
Yankees
1 Brown grounded to short.
2 Collins fouled to Thomson.
3 Lopat took a called third strike.

6th Inning
Giants
1 Jansen popped to second.
2 Stanky bounced back to the mound.
  Dark singled to left.
3 Thomson flied to DiMaggio in deep
  left-center.
Yankees
1 Bauer grounded to short.
2 Rizzuto grounded to third.
3 McDougald struck out.

7th Inning
Giants
  Irvin singled to center.
  Lockman singled to center, Irvin
  stopping at second.
1 Mays forced Lockman at second on a
  bunt, Brown to Rizzuto as Irvin
  went to third.
  Westrum walked loading the bases.
  Rigney, up batting for Thompson.
  Schenz ran for Westrum.
2 Rigney flied to right, Irvin scoring
  and Mays going to third after the catch.
3 Noble, batting for Jansen, fouled
  to Berra.
Yankees
  For the Giants—Noble stays in as catcher.
  Spencer pitching (batting 8th), and
  Hartung in right (batting 7th).
1 DiMaggio grounded to third.
2 Berra grounded to second.
3 Woodling grounded to short.

8th Inning
Giants
1 Stanky popped to first.
2 Dark flied to left.
3 Thomson grounded to third.
Yankees
  Brown singled over second, the first
  Yankee base runner since the second.
  Martin ran for Brown.
1 Collins grounded to third, Martin
  moving to second.
  Lopat singled to center, scoring Martin.
2 Bauer flied to deep left.
3 Rizzuto flied to center.

9th Inning
Giants
  For the Yankees—McDougald moved to third,
  as Coleman went to second.
  Irvin singled to center.
1 Lockman forced Irvin at second,
  McDougald to Rizzuto.
2 Mays forced Lockman at second,
  McDougald to Coleman.
3 Hartung grounded out, Collins to Lopat.

NY-N	000 000 100							1
NY-A	110 000 01x							3

New York-A	Pos	AB	R	H	RBI	PO	A	E
Mantle	rf	2	1	1	0	0	0	0
Bauer	rf	2	0	0	0	1	0	0
Rizzuto	ss	4	0	1	0	2	2	0
McDougald	2b-3b	3	0	1	1	2	3	0
DiMaggio	cf	3	0	0	0	4	0	0
Berra	c	3	0	0	0	2	0	0
Woodling	lf	3	0	0	0	4	0	0
Brown	3b	3	0	1	0	0	4	0
d Martin		0	1	0	0	1	0	0
Coleman	2b	0	0	0	0	1	0	0
Collins	1b	3	1	1	1	9	2	0
Lopat	p	3	0	1	1	2	2	0
Totals		29	3	6	3	27	13	0

Pitching	IP	H	R	ER	BB	SO
New York-N						
Jansen (L)	6	4	2	2	0	5
Spencer	2	2	1	1	0	0
New York-A						
Lopat (W)	9	5	1	1	2	1

d Martin ran for Brown in 8th.

Game 3 October 6 at New York-N

New York-A	Pos	AB	R	H	RBI	PO	A	E
Woodling	lf	4	1	1	1	3	0	0
Rizzuto	ss	4	1	1	0	2	4	1
McDougald	2b	3	0	2	0	2	4	0
DiMaggio	cf	4	0	0	0	4	0	0
Berra	c	3	0	1	0	5	1	1
Brown	3b	3	0	1	0	0	1	0
Collins	1b	3	0	0	1	6	0	0
Bauer	rf	4	0	0	0	2	0	0
Raschi	p	3	0	1	0	0	0	0
Hogue	p	0	0	0	0	0	0	0
a Hopp		0	0	0	0	0	0	0
Ostrowski	p	0	0	0	0	0	0	0
b Mize		1	0	0	0	0	0	0
Totals		30	2	5	2	24	8	2

a Walked for Hogue in 7th.
b Flied out for Ostrowski in 9th.

Double—Thomson. Home Runs—Lockman,
Woodling. Double Plays—Stanky to Dark
to Lockman, Hearn to Lockman to Dark
to Lockman, Rizzuto to McDougald to
Collins. Hit by Pitchers—Stanky
(by Raschi), Rizzuto (by Hearn).
Left on Bases—Yankees 10, Giants 5.
Umpires—Paparella, Barlick, Summers,
Ballantant, Stevens, Gore.
Attendance—52,035. Time of Game—2:42.

1st Inning
Yankees
1 Woodling fouled to Thomson.
  Rizzuto singled to left.
2 Rizzuto was caught trying to steal
  second, Westrum to Dark.
  McDougald singled off the left
  field wall.
3 DiMaggio flied to left.
Giants
  Stanky was hit by a pitch.
1 Dark flied to center.
2 Thompson struck out.
  Irvin walked.
3 Lockman grounded to second.

2nd Inning
Yankees
  Berra beat out a roller to first.
1 Brown forced Berra at second, Dark
  to Stanky.
2,3 Collins grounded into a double play,
  Stanky to Dark to Lockman.
Giants
  Thomson doubled down the left field
  line.
  Mays singled to right, scoring Thomson.
1 Westrum popped to short.
2 Hearn popped to second.
3 Stanky took a called third strike.

3rd Inning
Yankees
  Bauer safe at first when Lockman
  dropped Dark's throw.
1,2 Raschi on a bunt forced Bauer at
  second. Hearn to Dark but Dark's throw
  to first was wild and Raschi tried
  for second. He was out, Lockman to
  Dark for a weird double play.
  Woodling walked.
3 Rizzuto grounded to first.
Giants
1 Dark flied to right.
  Thompson walked.
2 Irvin lined to center.
3 Lockman flied to left.

4th Inning
Yankees
  McDougald walked.
1 DiMaggio forced McDougald at second,
  Thomson to Stanky.
2 Berra fouled to Thomson.
3 Brown flied to left.
Giants
1 Thompson flied to left.
2 Mays grounded to short.
3 Westrum flied to center.

5th Inning
Yankees
1 Collins grounded to first.
2 Bauer grounded to third.
  Raschi walked.
3 Woodling flied to deep center.

NY-A	000 000 011							2
NY-N	010 050 00x							6

New York-N	Pos	AB	R	H	RBI	PO	A	E
Stanky	2b	2	1	1	0	2	2	0
Dark	ss	4	1	1	1	4	4	0
Thompson	rf	3	1	1	1	1	0	0
Irvin	lf	3	1	0	0	2	0	0
Lockman	1b	4	1	3	3	10	1	1
Thomson	3b	4	1	1	0	3	4	0
Mays	cf	4	0	2	1	3	0	0
Westrum	c	4	0	0	0	2	1	1
Hearn	p	3	0	0	0	0	2	0
Jones	p	0	0	0	0	0	1	0
Totals		31	6	7	5	27	15	2

Pitching	IP	H	R	ER	BB	SO
New York-A						
Raschi (L)	4⅓	5	6	1	3	3
Hogue	2⅔	1	0	0	0	0
Ostrowski	2	1	0	0	0	1
New York-N						
Hearn (W)	7⅓	4	1	1	8	1
Jones (SV)	1⅔	1	1	1	0	0

5th Inning (continued)
Giants
1 Hearn struck out.
  Stanky walked.
    Stanky went all the way to third
    when Stanky kicked the ball thrown
    by Berra out of Rizzuto's hands.
  Dark singled to left, scoring Stanky.
  Thompson singled to right, Dark
    going to third.
  Irvin safe when Berra dropped Brown's
    throw getting Dark at the plate as
    Thompson stopped at second.
  Lockman lined a three-run homer into
    the lower right field stands.
  For the Yankees—Hogue took Raschi's
    place on the mound.
2 Thomson fouled to Berra.
3 Mays flied to center.

6th Inning
Yankees
1 Rizzuto grounded to third.
  McDougald walked.
2 DiMaggio struck out.
  McDougald went to second on
  Westrum's error, dropping a pitch.
  Berra walked.
3 Brown grounded to second.
Giants
1 Westrum fouled to Collins.
2 Hearn flied to right.
  Stanky singled to left.
3 Dark flied to left.

7th Inning
Yankees
1 Collins flied to deep center.
2 Bauer fouled to Westrum.
  Hopp, batting for Hogue, walked.
3 Woodling grounded to third.
Giants
  For the Yankees—Ostrowski pitching.
1 Thompson grounded to short.
2 Irvin grounded to short.
3 Lockman struck out.

8th Inning
Yankees
  Rizzuto was hit by a pitch.
  McDougald singled to center, Rizzuto
  stopping at second.
1 DiMaggio popped to third.
2 Berra grounded back to the mound,
  advancing both runners.
  Brown walked, loading the bases.
  Collins walked, forcing Rizzuto over
  the plate.
  For the Giants—Jones came in to pitch.
3 Bauer bounced back to the mound.
Giants
1 Thomson popped to short.
  Mays singled to left.
2,3 Westrum hit into a double play,
  Rizzuto to McDougald to Collins.

9th Inning
Yankees
1 Mize, batting for Ostrowski, flied
  to right.
  Woodling homered into the lower
  right field stands.
2 Rizzuto flied to deep center.
3 McDougald fouled to Lockman.

Hitless Joe Hears O'Doul

Joe DiMaggio, whose failure to hit safely the first three World Series games, has the entire baseball world feeling sorry for him, revealed today he had asked Lefty O'Doul, his old manager, for help.

The Yankee outfielder, probably the best ballplayer of our time, is fully aware he has gone 11-for-0 during the series, and has left 10 runners stranded on the bases while the Yankees were losing two out of three to the Giants.

"I've just been lousy," Joe admitted frankly. "That's all. I'm not looking for sympathy. I don't want any."

It was while O'Doul had called for discussion of the post-season baseball tour to the Orient which Lefty is conducting, that DiMaggio asked him:

"What am I doing wrong up there? I think I've lost the strike zone."

O'Doul, who twice led the National League in batting 20 some odd years ago, asked DiMag what kind of a bat he was using.

"Thirty-four ounces," Joe answered. "I used it yesterday for the first time. Before that, 35, and earlier in the season, 37."

"Thirty-four is light enough," commented the man who managed DiMaggio when Joe was with San Francisco in 1935. "It seems to me, from what I've seen, that you're getting your body too far out in front of your arms, and, therefore, you're pushing the ball. You're swinging too hard."

DiMaggio, who believes the Yankees will still win the series, called the Giants a good club and praised their pitching staff.

"I knew it was going to be tough," he said, "go maybe seven games. But I think we can win it—if I start hitting."

Game 4 October 8 at New York-N

New York-A	Pos	AB	R	H	RBI	PO	A	E
Bauer	rf	4	0	2	0	0	0	0
Rizzuto	ss	5	1	1	0	5	5	0
Berra	c	5	1	1	0	8	1	0
DiMaggio	cf	5	1	2	2	2	0	0
Woodling	lf	4	2	1	0	1	0	0
McDougald	2b-3b	4	0	1	1	3	2	0
Brown	3b	4	1	2	0	0	0	0
Coleman	2b	0	0	0	0	1	1	0
Collins	1b	3	0	1	1	7	0	0
Reynolds	p	4	0	1	1	0	2	0
Totals		38	6	12	5	27	11	0

Pitching	IP	H	R	ER	BB	SO
New York-A						
Reynolds (W)	9	8	2	2	4	7
New York-N						
Maglie (L)	5	8	4	4	2	3
Jones	3	4	2	0	1	2
Kennedy	1	0	0	0	0	2

		NY-A	0 1 0	1 2 0	2 0 0		6
		NY-N	1 0 0	0 0 0	0 0 1		2

New York-N	Pos	AB	R	H	RBI	PO	A	E
Stanky	2b	4	0	1	0	3	0	1
Dark	ss	4	1	3	0	2	1	0
Thompson	rf	3	1	0	0	1	0	0
Irvin	lf	4	0	2	1	3	0	0
Lockman	1b	4	0	0	0	4	0	0
Thomson	3b	4	0	2	1	2	3	1
Mays	cf	4	0	0	0	5	1	0
Westrum	c	2	0	0	0	7	1	0
Maglie	p	1	0	0	0	0	0	0
a Lohrke		1	0	0	0	0	0	0
Jones	p	0	0	0	0	0	0	0
b Rigney		1	0	0	0	0	0	0
Kennedy	p	0	0	0	0	0	0	0
Totals		30	2	8	2	27	6	2

a Popped out for Maglie in 5th.
b Struck out for Jones in 8th.

Doubles—Brown, Dark 3, Woodling. Home Run—DiMaggio. Double Plays—Rizzuto to McDougald to Collins, Reynolds to Rizzuto to Collins 2, Rizzuto to Coleman to Collins. Left on Bases—Yankees 8, Giants 5. Umpires—Barlick, Summers, Ballanfant, Paparella, Gore, Stevens. Attendance—49,010. Time of Game—2:57.

1st Inning
Yankees
  Bauer walked
1 Rizzuto struck out
2 Berra lined to center
3 DiMaggio called out on strikes
Giants
1 Stanky lined to short
  Dark doubled off the left field wall
2 Thompson grounded to second, Dark going to third
  Irvin singled to left, scoring Dark
3 Irvin caught trying to steal second, Berra to Rizzuto.

2nd Inning
Yankees
  Woodling doubled down the left field foul line
  McDougald safe at first on Thomson's fumble as Woodling held second
1 Brown flied to deep center. Woodling moving to third after the catch
  Collins singled to right, Woodling scoring with McDougald stopping at second
2 Reynolds flied to left
3 Bauer's grounder hit McDougald giving Bauer an automatic single with an automatic out on McDougald with Dark getting credit for the putout
Giants
1 Lockman struck out
  Thomson walked
2,3 Mays hit into a double play, Rizzuto to McDougald to Collins

3rd Inning
Yankees
1 Rizzuto grounded to third
2 Berra lined to third
  DiMaggio singled to left
3 Woodling flied to left
Giants
1 Westrum struck out
2 Maglie called out on strikes
3 Stanky fouled to Berra

4th Inning
Yankees
1 McDougald flied to center
  Brown beat out a hit to deep short
  Collins walked
  Reynolds singled to center, Brown scoring and Collins going to third
2 but Reynolds was trapped after rounding first and was out Mays to Dark to Lockman.
3 Bauer grounded to third
Giants
  Dark again doubled off the left field wall
1 Thompson popped to second
2 Irvin struck out
3 Lockman flied to deep center

5th Inning
Yankees
1 Rizzuto popped to second
  Berra singled to right
  DiMaggio blasted a two-run homer into the upper deck of the left field stands
2 Woodling popped to short
3 McDougald struck out
Giants
  Thomson walked
1,2 Mays again hit into a double play, Reynolds to Rizzuto to Collins
  Westrum walked
3 Lohrke, batting for Maglie, popped to second

6th Inning
Yankees
  For the Giants—Jones pitching
  Brown doubled to left-center
1 Collins flied to left
2 Reynolds grounded to third, Brown holding at third
3 Bauer popped to second
Giants
1 Stanky struck out
  Dark got his third consecutive double this one down the left field line
2 Thompson popped to short
3 Irvin fouled to Collins

7th Inning
Yankees
  Rizzuto singled to right
1 Berra flied to center
2 DiMaggio popped to second
  Woodling walked
    Westrum trapped Rizzuto off second throwing to Stanky but Rizzuto was racing for third and Stanky's throw hit Rizzuto in the back for an error enabling Rizzuto to score and Woodling to get to second
  McDougald singled to left, scoring Woodling and took second on the throw to the plate
3 Brown flied to center
Giants
  For the Yankees—Coleman came in to play second as McDougald moved to third
1 Lockman grounded to short
  Thomson singled to left
2 Mays flied to center
3 Westrum struck out

8th Inning
Yankees
1 Collins popped to third
2 Reynolds struck out
  Bauer singled to left
3 Rizzuto called out on strikes
Giants
1 Rigney, pinch-hitting for Jones, struck out
  Stanky singled to left
2,3 Dark bounced into a double play, Reynolds to Rizzuto to Collins

9th Inning
Yankees
  For the Giants—Kennedy pitching
1 Berra popped to third
2 DiMaggio called out on strikes
3 Woodling struck out
Giants
  Thompson walked
  Irvin singled to center, Thompson stopping at second
1 Lockman flied to left
  Thomson singled to left, scoring Thompson with Irvin going to third
2,3 For the third time in the game, Mays hit into a double play, Rizzuto to Coleman to Collins

DiMaggine!

By Robert C. Ruark

The Big man belted the fat three-zero pitch. He swung from his old sore heels and he hit it the way he al-ways used to hit it and it shoulda g o n e for a triple but it was a beaut double, anyhow. It didn't make any difference t h a t he got thrown out on a s a c r i f i c i a l bunt that day.

Robert C. Ruark

He had been walked twice on purpose, so's the Giant pitcher could get at a guy who had merely won the semiclincher the day before with a base-crammed homer. And the walk was the win, it turned out.

* * *

And he had more or less taken the tough one Monday with the only homer that looked and sounded like a real one, this beat-up old boy who is just about through. And I hope he is through. I hope this was the last time he ever swings a bat in anger, because Mr. Joseph Paul DiMaggio, festooned in broken records, wound up what might well be his last season with pride, as he always worked with pride. All the pride of the man was seen in the eighth inning when he went for the fat pitch, sure and haughty, when he just as easy could have waited out the third walk.

DiMaggio was weary of walks

the last day that put the finish on the series and could be said to have also put the finish on DiMaggio. Twice they passed him to get to Gil McDougald, the Yankees' best hitter—the man who set up the kill with a four-run homer which is so rare in a series that the honor is shared by only two others. That is respect, in spades, to a tired old fellow with a slow swing, who is generally conceded to be all done. I expect that it is the greatest compliment I have ever seen paid a true competitor.

* * *

The tragedy of age in sports—DiMag is just on 37, and with his bad legs and bad feet and bad elbows this is old—is that yesterday's hero always goes out in a wave of boos and tsks, tsks, and ain't-it-a-shame kind of talk.

Already they were suffering for DiMaggio. The most rabid Giant fan, and by far the noisiest, that I know, a Miss Aileen Wilson, completed the wreckage of her vocal cords when Joe hit the homer the other day. Miss Wilson sells some sort of cigaret by singing, when she is not annoying me and the world with shrill screams in favor of the Giants, and she is intolerant of Yankee fans to the point of physical combat. But she turned to my one undeafened ear just before Joe hit the homer and said, quite honestly: "Please, God, let DiMaggio hit just one good one."

I told this misdirected thrush

that she need not waste her sympathy, her possibly spurious pity, on a good man. So Joe hit one, about that time, and I swear she hollered louder than when Stanky kicked the throw out of Rizzuto's fist.

Point is that DiMaggio, on a very so-so season, and a from-hunger series in the first three games, finally delivered in the face of compassion tinged with contempt, and he quit it with a high head and all the honor that any athlete may accrue. For him no anticlimax, no pathos, as happened to Babe Ruth, when he left it too late. Joe, if he quits, quit real loud.

* * *

You can always be wrong, but I think he wouldn't quit strong if he attempts to play regularly next year. Maybe they take him out of the cleanup spot. Maybe he is benched for a newer and fresher candidate. Maybe he begins to reap the boos, which had started already this year—and what's worse, the pity, so that the opposition is even considering the idea of a cheap pitch, a fat, juicy pumpkin ball, to salve his aching pride. This I do not want to see.

My boy Joe wound up right, with the big swing on the ball he didn't have to hit, and when he hit it I knew where it was headed. I can't think of a better epitaph for a guy who always handled himself with fierce pride. When he strode off the field he was still dangerous. He was still the Big man.

The Yankee Clipper drives a shot to left for a single in the fourth game of the 1951 World Series against the New York Giants. It was his first hit in thirteen at bats in the Series, but he would collect five more hits before the Series ended and post a .261 average. The Giant catcher is Wes Westrum, and the umpire is Al Barlick.

This panoramic shot captures Joe DiMaggio's 5th-inning home run blast into the upper deck at the Polo Grounds in Game 4 of the 1951 World Series against the New York Giants. It was the Clipper's eighth and last home run in ten World Series. The Yanks won the game 6-2.

Waiting at home plate to greet DiMaggio after his last World Series home run are teammates Yogi Berra (8) and Gene Woodling (14). When Joe DiMaggio retired after the 1951 series, the 8 home runs he hit in World Series play were the third most in major league baseball annals, following Babe Ruth's 15 and Lou Gehrig's 10.

Bombers Whack Sal Maglie; The Jolter Shakes His Slump

AT THE POLO GROUNDS.

Following the Sunday postponement due to rain, the Yankees again drew on even terms by winning the fourth game from the Giants, 6 to 2, at the Polo Grounds, October 8, deadlocking the Series at two victories each. A crowd of 49,010 saw Joe DiMaggio snap out of his slump with his eighth World's Series homer, and the entire Bomber team showed some of its erstwhile power.

Discussing his team before the fourth game, Stengel remarked, "In my three years as Yankee manager, I've never seen the club play as listless ball as we have shown so far. But that's about to change." Casey was correct. He made some helpful changes in his lineup, and his club changed its demeanor. The Yanks whacked Sal Maglie, Durocher's 23-6 ace; played alert, inspired ball and backed Reynolds with perfect support. Four snappy double plays—three on ground balls hit by the fleet-footed Willie Mays—helped the Oklahoma Creek out of much of his trouble.

Reynolds won his fourth World's Series game against one defeat. The chunky righthander wasn't as sharp as when he nosed out big Don Newcombe of the Dodgers, 1 to 0, in the 1949 Series opener, or when he shaded Robin Roberts of the Phillies, 2 to 1, in ten innings last year. But Allie pitched what unquestionably was his most courageous Series game. He was constantly in hot water; ten times during the game he had a count of three balls and two strikes on the batter, but when he had to get the ball over, he came in hard with his fast one.

The Giants had him tottering in the ninth, but with one run in, runners on third and first, only one out, and the count three and two on Mays, he fed Willie his third double-play ball. Allie yielded eight hits, walked three and struck out seven.

While Reynolds held six regular Giants and two of Durocher's pinch-hitters in check, he encountered three toughies in Alvin Dark, Bobby Thomson and Monte Irvin. Captain Alvin reeled off three straight doubles before slapping into a double play in the eighth; Bobby, the fighting Scot of Glasgow and Staten Island, batted 1.000 with two singles and two walks, and the amazing Monte collected two more singles to bring his total hits to nine.

Maglie Proves Soft Touch

The Giant starter, Maglie, present-day meal ticket for the Stoneham forces, proved a disappointment in his first Series start, giving up eight hits and four runs in five innings. Per- haps the first inning showed he wasn't quite right, even though he fanned Phil Rizzuto and DiMaggio. Hank Bauer walked on four straight balls, and little Phil fouled off four pitches after Sal got two strikes on him. And it took the Niagara Falls barber ten pitches to subdue DiMaggio.

The Giants spotted Maglie to a 1 to 0 lead in the opening frame on Dark's first double and Irvin's single. The Yankees cancelled it in the second on Gene Woodling's Texas League double to left, Thomson's fumble of Gil McDougald's grounder and Joe Collins' single. Reynolds broke the 1 to 1 tie in the fourth by singling Bobby Brown home from second. DiMaggio gave Reynolds a bigger cushion when, after Berra's single, Jolting Joe reached the upper left field stands with a homer.

After five innings, Sheldon Jones relieved Maglie. Two runs scored on Jones in the seventh were tainted. With two out, Rizzuto on second and Woodling on first, Wes Westrum caught the Scooter off second. Phil tried to make third, and in the rundown Eddie Stanky hit Phil with the ball. Rizzuto scooted home, as the ball rolled into left field, and McDougald's single scored Woodling.

The Giants threatened in the ninth when Hank Thompson led off with a walk and Irvin singled. Whitey Lockman flied out to Woodling, but Thomson kept the rally going with a single, scoring Thompson. Then Willie Mays silenced the Giant fans by grounding into a double play.

DiMaggio Day

10-YEAR-OLD IN BLEACHER LINE

WHILE his parents stood close by with a late-night snack and to see that he was comfortable in two blankets, Johnny Crawford, a 10- year-old Giant fan, was one of the first bleacherites in line for the fourth game. "I think he's a little crazy to do this," Johnny's dad admitted, "but promised him he could do it if he kept up his good marks at school." Johnny's mother, a Yankee rooter, said only, "The two will be sorry males when the Yanks romp in, but I can't tell them that."

Press box occupants were slightly bewildered at the start when they overheard a broadcaster chattering in a foreign language. It was the Voice of America broadcast being transcribed for short wave transmission to Japan. The Nipponese radio men scored the game with Jap symbols.

JOE HIT ONE FOR ALLIE IN '50

WHEN Joe DiMaggio clouted his fifth-inning homer to account for the deciding runs, it marked the second time in two classics that a circuit clout by The Clipper had enabled Allie Reynolds to win. In the second game of the 1950 classic, Joe belted a tenth-inning round-tripper that provided the winning margin in Allie's

Tables Turned

Yankees	AB.	R.	H.	O.	A.	E.
Bauer, rf	4	0	2	0	0	0
Rizzuto, ss	5	1	1	5	5	0
Berra, c	5	1	1	8	1	0
DiMaggio, cf	5	1	2	2	0	0
Woodling, lf	4	2	1	1	0	0
McDou ld, 2b-3b	4	0	1	3	2	0
Brown, 3b	4	1	2	0	0	0
Coleman, 2b	0	0	0	1	1	0
Collins, 1b	3	0	1	7	0	0
Reynolds, p	4	0	1	0	2	0
Totals	38	6	12	27	11	0
Giants	AB.	R.	H.	O.	A.	E.
Stanky, 2b	4	0	1	3	0	1
Dark, ss	4	1	3	2	1	0
Thompson, rf	3	1	0	1	0	0
Irvin, lf	4	0	2	3	0	0
Lockman, 1b	4	0	0	4	0	0
Thomson, 3b	4	0	2	2	3	1
Mays, cf	4	0	0	5	1	0
Westrum, c	2	0	0	7	1	0
Maglie, p	1	0	0	0	0	0
*Lohrke	1	0	0	0	0	0
Jones, p	0	0	0	0	0	0
†Rigney	1	0	0	0	0	0
Kennedy, p	0	0	0	0	0	0
Totals	30	2	8	27	6	2

*Popped out for Maglie in fifth.
†Struck out for Jones in eighth.

Yankees	0 1 0	1 2 0	2 0 0—6
Giants	1 0 0	0 0 0	0 0 1—2

Runs batted in—Irvin, Collins, Reynolds, DiMaggio 2, McDougald, Thomson. Two-base hits—Dark 3, Woodling, Brown. Home run—DiMaggio. Double plays—Rizzuto, McDougald and Collins; Reynolds, Rizzuto and Collins 2; Rizzuto, Coleman and Collins. Bases on balls—Off Maglie 2 (Bauer, Collins), off Jones 1 (Woodling), off Reynolds 4 (Thomson 2, Westrum, Thompson). Struck out—By Maglie 3 (Rizzuto, DiMaggio, McDougald), by Jones 2 (Reynolds, Rizzuto), by Kennedy 2 (DiMaggio, Woodling), by Reynolds 7 (Lockman, Westrum 2, Maglie, Irvin, Stanky, Rigney). Pitching record—Maglie 8 hits, 4 runs in 5 innings; Jones 4 hits, 2 runs in 3 innings; Kennedy 0 hits, 0 runs in 1 inning. Earned runs—Yankees 4, Giants 2. Left on bases—Yankees 8, Giants 5. Winning pitcher—Reynolds. Losing pitcher—Maglie. Umpires—Barlick (N. L.) at plate; Summers (A. L.) first base; Ballanfant (N. L.) second base; Paparella (A. L.) third base; Gore (N. L.) left field foul line; Stevens (A. L.) right field foul line. Time of game —2:57. Attendance—49,010.

The Old Champ Gets Back in Stride

"THE DiMAG OF OLD" took the place of "Old DiMag" in the fourth game when The Clipper broke out with a single and a two-run homer to lead the Yankees to a 6 to 2 victory. Here Joe receives congratulations from his teammates in the dugout.

2 to 1 decision over Robin Roberts of the Phillies.

A barber shop next to the Polo Grounds announced an increase in its rates for a shave after the game, offering the excuse that "Faces Are Longer."

Casey Stengel made no attempt to arouse the Yanks with a stirring pep talk before the game. "All I told them," said Case, "was that none of us had been doing anything worth a darn, including me, so let's go."

CASEY GIVES DYKES THE NEEDLE

ONE OF the best cracks of the Series was credited to Casey Stengel, who spotted Jimmie Dykes wandering around the field wearing a press badge on his lapel before the game. "Come here, Jimmie," the Yank skipper beckoned to the Athletics' manager. "I'll give you an exclusive for your shoe ad column." Dykes has endorsed a popular brand of footwear which is widely advertised.

Workmen dismantling a band-stand in center field caused a four-minute delay in the start of the game.

Joe DiMaggio's first hit of the Series, a single to left field in the third inning, brought a roar from spectators, who had applauded the Yankee Clipper politely even when he drew the collar in 12 previous trips to the plate.

The second-guessers hopped on Leo Durocher for not ordering Hank Thompson to bunt following Alvin Dark's leadoff double in the third, thereby moving the potential tying run to third, but the strategy made no difference as Monte Irvin whiffed and Whitey Lockman flied out after Thompson had popped out.

SEVENTEEN SCALPERS ARRESTED

SEVENTEEN alleged ticket scalpers were arrested in the vicinity of the Polo Grounds before and during the game. Ten, including a lieutenant-commander in the Navy, were charged with violating the general business law and the others were booked for disorderly conduct.

Jim Farley, former Postmaster General, who had been mentioned prominently as a candidate for the commissionership before Ford Frick was elected to the post, presented a striking figure in the press room before the game in his black suit and black homberg.

In addition to the six umpires working the game, eight other major league arbiters watched the contest from the stands. They included Larry Goetz,

Bill Stewart, Frank Dascoli and Jocko Conlan of the National League and Bill McKinley, Jim Duffy, Bill Grieve and Charley Berry of the American.

Alvin Dark, with a chance to tie Frank Isbell's mark of four doubles in a game for the 1906 White Sox, tapped into a double play in the eighth inning after the Giant captain had connected for two-baggers on his first three trips.

Informed after the game that he was within one of tying the record for doubles in a Series tilt, Alvin Dark replied, "Suppose I had hit the fourth double, what would we have got? Two runs and the Yanks already had six. If we can win the game, that's fine. If we lose, records don't mean a thing."

JOE HIT FOUL BETTER THAN HOMER

JOE DI MAGGIO'S homer was clouted with a Babe Ruth model bat, The Clipper revealed. Joe said the bat weighed 34 ounces compared to the 35-ounce model he had been using. Although the round-tripper was the big blow of the day, DiMag said his foul drive off the left field roof in the first inning was hit better. "That one was really tagged," smiled Jolting Joe. "It was an inside curve and I hit it as good as I've hit all year." DiMaggio's home run was his eighth in Series competition. The Yankee Clipper has failed to connect for the circuit in only three of his ten classics—in 1936, '41 and '42.

Casey Stengel, who had accused the Giants of winning the third game with "Stanky's five-point field goal," used another football phrase in commenting on the Yankee victory, saying, "Reynolds did okay with a single wing from the right."

Leo Durocher and Whitey Lockman disagreed on the pitch on which Whitey lined to Gene Woodling with two runners aboard and none out in the ninth inning. "The pitch was up around Lockman's eyes," The Lip fumed. "If he takes it, he walks with none out and the bases are loaded for Bobby Thomson's single." Lockman took another view. "The pitch may have been a little high, but I couldn't afford to let it go," Whitey said.

GRABBED BALL AFTER DROPPING IT

WILLIE MAYS, whose spectacular back-to-the-plate catch of Bobby Brown's liner in the second inning prevented the Yanks from scoring more than one run, admitted after the game that he dropped the ball as he fell, but managed to grab it before it touched the ground.

After collecting four singles and a triple in his first five appearances against Allie Reynolds, Monte Irvin was stopped by the Yankee righthander in the fourth inning when he struck out with Alvin Dark on second base.

Phil Rizzuto, goat of the third game when Eddie Stanky kicked the ball out of the Yankee shortstop's glove to touch off a five-run inning, laughed back at The Brat in the seventh inning when Stanky's error enabled The Scooter to score after being trapped off base. A throw from Catcher Wes Westrum to Stanky caught Rizzuto off second, but in the rundown the Giant keystoner's toss to Third Baseman Bob Thomson struck Phil on the shoulder and bounced to the stands, permitting Rizzuto to score.

PARK EMPLOYES MOP UP EARLY

SIXTEEN groundskeepers, armed with sponges, mops and buckets, went to work at the Polo Grounds early in the morning to get the field ready for the game following the heavy rain which caused the postponement the previous day. The workmen used the sponges to lift the water from the grass, into buckets, which were then emptied into drains.

More than half a million calls were made to the New York Telephone Company's time bureau, which also gave World's Series scores, from October 4 to 7.

Mrs. Clara Durocher, 74-year-old mother of the Giants' manager, accommodated photographers before the game by embracing her son several times.

Postponement of the fourth game from October 7 to the next day caused some confusion among ticket holders. Many expected that ducats marked No. 5 would be honored, October 8. However, tickets were issued by game number rather than date, and the pasteboards marked No. 4 were honored for the October 8 tilt.

If Somebody Had to Homer, Sal Glad It Was The Jolter

NEW YORK, N. Y.—"If somebody had to hit a homer off me, I'm sure glad it was Joe DiMaggio," was Sal Maglie's reaction to The Clipper's round-tripper that proved to be the deciding wallop in the Yankees' 6 to 2 victory in the fourth World's Series game.

"Joe's a great guy and has taken a lot of abuse," continued the Giant ace. "He means a lot to that ball club."

Sal said that Joe had hit a low, inside curve for his homer. "It might have been only a fly in another park," said Sal, "but it was a homer today."

Despite Monte Irvin's lusty hitting, which produced seven hits in the first two games, the National League's RBI king of '51 did not drive in his first Series tally until he singled in the first inning, scoring Alvin Dark, who had doubled.

COLD WEATHER AFFECTED SAL

SAL MAGLIE, asked what had accounted for his ineffectiveness, replied, "I couldn't get loose. Maybe it was too cold. I was behind the hitters, couldn't get my curve over. It was just one of those bad days—and of all times to have it." Sal's batterymate, Wes Westrum, added, "It's the worst I've ever seen him. He threw very few good pitches." Sal used 24 pitches to retire the Yanks in the first inning.

Gil McDougald was the only Yankee casualty, suffering a slight bruise on his right thigh as a result of being struck by Hank Bauer's line drive in the second inning.

At the request of Rud Rennie of the New York Herald Tribune, radios were installed in front of the clubhouse entrances so that reporters assigned to cover post-game clubhouse activities would know what happened in the late innings while waiting for the players to come off the field.

"I'LL GET 'EM," ALLIE TOLD CASEY

ALLIE REYNOLDS showed his customary calmness when the Giants threatened to pull the game out of the fire in the ninth inning. "My stuff was working good," said the Chief. "When Casey came out I told him I'd take care of them. I was dealing them mostly fast balls and sliders and I wasn't particularly worried even when they got a run and had two men on base."

When Joe Collins singled home Gene Woodling in the second inning,

'Relax, Ease Up,' O'Doul's Tip to Slumping DiMaggio

SAN FRANCISCO, Calif.—Lefty O'Doul, former manager of the San Francisco Seals, on his return from the World's Series, said the advice he gave the slumping Joe DiMaggio during the Series, was "to relax, ease up."

"Specifically," said O'Doul, "I told Joe to try to hit the ball just over the shortstop's head.

"He looked terrible, really," said Lefty. "He was doing all the things he used to tell his brother Vince not to do, lunging, finishing up off balance, swinging too hard."

O'Doul spoke to DiMaggio over the phone for an hour after The Clipper couldn't buy a base hit after 12 trips to the plate in the first three games of the classic.

"Joe was discouraged and wasn't even going to take batting practice the next day he hit that homer," said Lefty. "But I told him that was what he needed."

DiMaggio said that Lew Fonseca, motion picture director of the major leagues and who led the A. L. hitters in 1929, batting .369, supported O'Doul's analysis.

DiMag also said that he had received a message at Toots Shor's via phone from Ty Cobb, the former Detroit star who had watched the games on the Coast over television. "Tell him to get his right foot closer to the plate," Cobb advised Joe.

The homer which DiMaggio hit against Sal Maglie was his eighth in Series play. WALTER ADDIEGO.

making the score, 1 to 1, it marked the first time in the Series that the score was deadlocked.

Whitey Lockman was given five strikes on his first official trip to the plate. The count was two strikes against the Giants' first baseman in the opening stanza when Monte Irvin was thrown out trying to steal. When Whitey came up to open the second frame, he was quickly struck out by Allie Reynolds.

FIRST BAUER HIT A FREAK

AFTER going hitless on his first ten trips to the plate, Hank Bauer needed an assist from Gil McDougald to get credit for his initial safety. In the second inning, Bauer's hopper toward shortstop struck McDougald, running between second and third. Under the scoring rules, Alvin Dark, who was nearest to the play, was credited with the putout on McDougald.

Game 5 October 9 at New York-N

New York-A	Pos	AB	R	H	RBI	PO	A	E
Woodling	lf	3	3	1	0	5	0	1
Rizzuto	ss	4	3	2	3	0	6	0
Berra	c	4	2	1	0	3	0	0
DiMaggio	cf	5	1	3	3	3	0	0
Mize	1b	3	1	1	1	6	0	0
Bauer	rf	1	0	0	0	0	0	0
McDougald	2b-3b	5	1	1	4	2	2	0
Brown	3b	3	0	2	0	1	3	0
c Coleman	2b	1	1	0	0	0	1	0
Collins	rf-1b	5	1	1	0	7	0	0
Lopat	p	5	0	0	0	0	2	0
Totals		39	13	12	11	27	14	1

Pitching	IP	H	R	ER	BB	SO
New York-A						
Lopat (W)	9	5	1	0	1	3
New York-N						
Jansen (L)	3	3	5	5	4	1
Kennedy	2	3	2	2	1	2
Spencer	1⅓	4	6	6	3	0
Corwin	1⅔	1	0	0	0	1
Konikowski	1	1	0	0	0	0

NY-A	0 0 5	2 0 2	4 0 0					13
NY-N	1 0 0	0 0 0	0 0 0					1

New York-N	Pos	AB	R	H	RBI	PO	A	E
Stanky	2b	4	0	0	0	1	4	0
Dark	ss	4	1	2	0	2	3	0
Thomson	3b	4	0	0	0	1	3	1
Irvin	lf	4	0	2	0	2	0	1
Lockman	1b	4	0	0	0	9	3	0
Mays	cf	2	0	0	0	2	0	0
Hartung	rf	3	0	0	0	1	1	1
Westrum	c	3	0	1	0	7	0	0
Jansen	p	0	0	0	0	1	1	0
a Lohrke		1	0	0	0	0	0	0
Kennedy	p	0	0	0	0	0	1	0
b Rigney		1	0	0	0	0	0	0
Spencer	p	0	0	0	0	0	1	0
Corwin	p	0	0	0	0	1	0	0
d Williams		1	0	0	0	0	0	0
Konikowski	p	0	0	0	0	0	0	0
Totals		31	1	5	0	27	17	3

a Struck out for Jansen in 3rd.
b Flied out for Kennedy in 5th.
c Ran for Brown in 7th.
d Grounded out for Corwin in 8th.

Doubles—DiMaggio, Mize, Westrum.
Triple—Woodling. Home Runs—McDouglad,
Rizzuto. Double Play—Lopat to
McDougald to Mize. Wild Pitch—Corwin.
Left on Bases—Yankees 7, Giants 4.
Umpires—Summers, Ballanfant, Paparella,
Barlick, Stevens, Gore.
Attendance—47,530. Time of Game—2:31

1st Inning
Yankees
1 Woodling struck out
2 Rizzuto grounded to second.
  Berra walked
3 DiMaggio forced Berra, Dark to Stanky.
Giants
1 Stanky grounded to third.
  Dark singled to left.
2 Thomson flied to center.
  Irvin singled to left, Dark going to
  third but when Woodling fumbled the
  ball, Dark scored and Irvin went to
  second.
3 Lockman flied to center.

2nd Inning
Yankees
1 Mize flied to center.
  McDougald got safely to second when
  Thomson threw wildly to first.
2 Brown flied to left.
3 Collins grounded out, Lockman to Jansen.
Giants
  Mays walked
1,2 Hartung bounced into a double play,
  Lopat to McDougald to Mize
3 Westrum grounded to third

3rd Inning
Yankees
1 Lopat bounced back to the mound
  Woodling walked
  Rizzuto walked.
2 Berra forced Rizzuto at second, Lockman
  to Dark, Woodling moving to third
  DiMaggio singled to left, scoring
  Woodling and when Irvin kicked the
  ball, Berra went to third and
  DiMaggio to second
  Mize got an intentional walk,
  loading the bases
  **McDougald hit a grand slam home run
  into the left field stands.**
  Brown singled to center
3 Collins flied to center.
Giants
1 Lohrke, pinch-hitting for Jansen,
  struck out
2 Stanky bounced back to the pitcher
  Dark singled to center.
3 Thomson flied to left.

4th Inning
Yankees
  For the Giants—Kennedy pitching.
1 Lopat called out on strikes.
  Woodling walked.
  Rizzuto hit a two-run homer into
  the right field stands.
2 Berra popped to short.
  DiMaggio singled to left.
3 Mize fouled to Westrum.
Giants
1 Irvin grounded to third.
2 Lockman grounded to short.
3 Mays flied to left.

5th Inning
Yankees
1 McDougald grounded to third.
  Brown singled to left.
2 Collins struck out.
3 Lopat's grounder was deflected by
  Kennedy to Stanky who threw to
  first for the out.
Giants
1 Hartung flied to deep center.
  Westrum doubled to left-center.
2 Rigney, pinch-hitting for Kennedy,
  flied to left.
3 Stanky flied to left.

6th Inning
Yankees
  For the Giants—Spencer pitching.
1 Woodling grounded to second.
  Rizzuto singled to left.
  Berra singled to right, Rizzuto going
  to third, and as Hartung was
  fumbling the ball, Rizzuto scored
  and Berra got to second.
2 DiMaggio flied to right.
  Mize doubled to center, scoring Berra
3 McDougald grounded to third.
Giants
  For the Yankees—Bauer came in to play
  right field as Collins moved to first
  replacing Mize.
1 Dark grounded to short.
2 Thomson lined to third.
  Irvin singled to center (**his 11th hit
  of the Series**)
3 Lockman grounded to short

7th Inning
Yankees
1 Brown walked.
  Collins beat out a bunt, Brown going
  to second.
  Coleman ran for Brown
1 Lopat bounced back to the pitcher,
  advancing both runners
  Woodling walked, his third of the
  game, loading the bases
  Rizzuto walked, forcing Coleman in
  with a run
  For the Giants—Corwin pitching.
  On a wild pitch, Collins scored and
  the other runners each advanced
2 Berra flied to left
  DiMaggio doubled to left, scoring
  Woodling and Rizzuto.
3 Bauer hit into a fielder's choice,
  DiMaggio being out at third, Dark
  to Thomson.
Giants
  For the Yankees—Coleman stays in
  playing second as McDougald moves to
  third.
1 Mays struck out.
2 Hartung grounded to second.
3 Westrum struck out.

8th Inning
Yankees
1 McDougald grounded to short.
2 Coleman struck out.
3 Collins grounded out, Lockman to
  Corwin.
Giants
1 Williams, batting for Corwin,
  grounded to short.
2 Stanky grounded to short.
3 Dark lined to third.

9th Inning
Yankees
  For the Giants—Konikowski pitching.
1 Lopat fouled to Westrum.
  Woodling tripled to right-center.
2 was out trying for a home run,
  Hartung to Stanky to Westrum.
3 Rizzuto grounded to second.
Giants
1 Thomson grounded to third.
2 Irvin flied to deep left.
3 Lockman grounded to short.

Game 6 October 10 at New York-A

| | | | | | | NY-N | 0 0 0 | 0 1 0 | 0 0 2 | | 3 |
| | | | | | | NY-A | 1 0 0 | 0 0 3 | 0 0 x | | 4 |

New York-N	Pos	AB	R	H	RBI	PO	A	E
Stanky	2b	5	1	1	1	3	4	0
Dark	ss	3	1	1	0	1	2	0
Lockman	1b	5	0	3	0	10	0	0
Irvin	lf	4	0	0	1	3	0	0
Thomson	3b	4	0	1	1	2	0	0
Thompson	rf	3	0	1	0	0	0	1
d Yvars		1	0	0	0	0	0	0
Westrum	c	3	0	1	0	3	0	0
b Williams		0	0	0	0	0	0	0
Jansen	p	0	0	0	0	0	1	0
Mays	cf	3	1	2	0	2	0	0
Koslo	p	2	0	0	0	0	1	0
a Rigney		1	0	1	0	0	0	0
Hearn	p	0	0	0	0	0	0	0
c Noble	c	1	0	0	0	0	1	0
Totals		35	3	11	3	24	9	1

a Singled for Koslo in 7th.
b Ran for Westrum in 8th.
c Struck out for Hearn in 8th.
d Lined out for Thompson in 9th.

Doubles—Berra, DiMaggio, Lockman.
Triple—Bauer. Double Plays—Rizzuto to
Mize 2, Rizzuto to Coleman to Mize,
Dark to Stanky to Lockman. Passed
Ball—Berra. Wild Pitch—Koslo. Left
on Bases—Giants 12, Yankees 5.
Umpires—Ballanfant, Paparella, Barlick,
Summers, Gore, Stevens
Attendance—61,711. Time of Game—2:59.

New York-A	Pos	AB	R	H	RBI	PO	A	E
Rizzuto	ss	4	0	1	0	4	4	0
Coleman	2b	4	1	1	0	2	1	0
Berra	c	4	1	2	0	4	0	0
DiMaggio	cf	2	1	1	0	1	0	0
McDougald	3b	4	0	0	1	1	3	0
Mize	1b	2	1	1	0	6	0	0
Collins	1b	1	0	0	0	0	0	0
Bauer	rf	3	0	1	3	4	0	0
Woodling	lf	3	0	0	0	5	0	0
Raschi	p	1	0	0	0	0	0	0
Sain	p	1	0	0	0	0	0	0
Kuzava	p	0	0	0	0	0	0	0
Totals		29	4	7	4	27	8	0

Pitching	IP	H	R	ER	BB	SO
New York-N						
Koslo (L)	6	5	4	4	4	3
Hearn	1	1	0	0	0	0
Jansen	1	1	0	0	0	0
New York-A						
Raschi (W)	*6	7	1	0	5	0
Sain	**2	4	2	2	2	0
Kuzava (SV)	1	0	0	0	0	0

*Pitched to two batters in 7th.
**Pitched to three batters in 9th.

1st Inning
Giants
1 Stanky grounded to third.
2 Dark took a called third strike.
Lockman bounced a ground-rule double
into the right field stands.
3 Irvin grounded to short.
Yankees
1 Rizzuto flied to left.
Coleman singled to center.
Berra doubled off the right field
wall, Coleman stopping at third.
DiMaggio intentionally walked,
loading the bases.
2 McDougald flied to center, Coleman
scoring after the catch.
3 Mize lined to second.

2nd Inning
Giants
Thomson beat out a hit to deep short.
1 Thompson popped to short.
Westrum walked.
2 Mays lined to right.
3 Koslo popped to short.
Yankees
1 Bauer popped to short.
2 Woodling grounded to second.
3 Raschi struck out.

3rd Inning
Giants
1 Stanky flied to deep left.
Dark walked.
2,3 Lockman hit into a double play,
Rizzuto to Mize.
Yankees
1 Rizzuto fouled to Lockman.
2 Coleman flied to left.
3 Berra fouled to Lockman.

4th Inning
Giants
Irvin walked.
1 Thomson forced Irvin at second,
McDougald to Coleman.
Thompson singled to right, Thomson
going to third.
2,3 Westrum grounded into a double
play, Rizzuto to Coleman to Mize.
Yankees
1 DiMaggio flied to center.
2 McDougald popped to first.
Mize singled to right.
3 Bauer struck out.

5th Inning
Giants
Mays singled to center.
Mays took second on Berra's
passed ball.
1 Koslo flied to right, Mays going to
third after the catch.
2 Stanky flied to left, Mays scoring
after the catch.
Dark walked.
Lockman beat out a hit down the third
base line, Dark stopping at second.
3 Irvin grounded to third.
Yankees
1 Woodling bunted out to the mound.
Raschi walked.
2,3 Rizzuto bounced into a double play,
Dark to Stanky to Lockman.

6th Inning
Giants
Thomson walked.
1,2 Thompson bounced into a double play,
Rizzuto to Mize.
3 Westrum popped to Berra.
Yankees
1 Coleman called out on strikes.
Berra singled to right and went to
second on Thompson's fumble.
DiMaggio got an intentional pass,
Berra went to third and DiMaggio to
second on a wild pitch.
2 McDougald lined to third.
Mize walked, loading the bases.
Bauer tripled to deep left, scoring
Berra, DiMaggio and Mize.
3 Woodling grounded to second.

7th Inning
Giants
For the Yankees—Collins playing first.
Mays singled to right.
Rigney, pinch-hitting for Koslo, singled
to right, Mays stopping at second.
For the Yankees—Sain now pitching
1 Stanky flied to right.
2 Dark struck out.
3 Lockman flied to center.
Yankees
For the Giants—Hearn pitching.
1 Sain grounded to short.
Rizzuto singled to deep short.
2 Coleman fouled to Lockman.
3 Berra grounded to second.

8th Inning
Giants
1 Irvin flied to left.
2 Thomson fouled to McDougald.
Thompson walked.
Westrum singled over second, Thompson
stopping at second.
Williams ran for Westrum.
Mays walked, loading the bases.
3 Noble, pinch-hitting for Hearn, was
called out on strikes.
Yankees
For the Giants—Noble stays in to catch
with Jansen pitching.
DiMaggio doubled to right.
1 McDougald bunted into a fielder's
choice as DiMaggio was out at third,
Jansen to Thomson.
2 Collins flied to left.
3 McDougald was caught attempting to
steal second, Noble to Stanky.

9th Inning
Giants
Stanky singled to left.
Dark beat out a bunt down the third
base line, for his 10th hit of the
Series, Stanky stopping at second.
Lockman singled to center, loading
the bases.
For the Yankees—Kuzava replaced Sain
on the mound.
1 Irvin flied to left, Stanky scoring
and both other runners advancing
after the catch.
2 Thomson flied to left, Dark scoring
after the catch.
3 Yvars, batting for Thompson, lined to
right.

The final blow. Joe DiMaggio smashes a double in the final game of the 1951 World Series off New York Giant pitcher, Larry Jansen.
It was his last hit in his last at bat as a major league baseball player. The Giant catcher is Ray Noble.

Highlights

- Casey Stengel became only the second manager to win three consecutive world championships (Joe McCarthy won four for the Yankees, 1936–39).
- Monte Irvin's ten singles tied the record for a six-game Series.
- Irvin got a triple, three singles, and stole home for the Giants in Game 1.
- Alvin Dark provided the Giants with their margin of victory in Game 1 by cracking a three-run homer.
- Joe Collins slugged a homer to give the Yankees a lead in Game 2 which they would not relinquish.
- Whitey Lockman hit a three-run homer for the Giants to provide the winning runs in Game 3.
- The big hit in the Yankee win of Game 4 was Joe DiMaggio's two-run homer in the fifth inning.
- Gil McDougald of the Yankees became only the third player to hit a grand slam homer in a Series when he belted one in the third inning of Game 5. Joe DiMaggio and Phil Rizzuto drove in three runs apiece in the same game.
- Hank Bauer tripled with the bases loaded to provide the game-winning runs in Game 6 for the Yanks.

Best Efforts

Batting

Average	Monte Irvin	.458
Home Runs	(seven players)	1
Triples	Hank Bauer	1
	Gene Woodling	1
	Monte Irvin	1
Doubles	Alvin Dark	3
Hits	Monte Irvin	11
Runs	Gene Woodling	6
RBIs	Gil McDougald	7

Pitching

Wins	Eddie Lopat	2-0
ERA	Eddie Lopat	0.50
Strikeouts	Allie Reynolds	8
Innings Pitched	Eddie Lopat	18

1951

NEW YORK YANKEES

NEW YORK GIANTS **1951**

Reprinted, with permission, from
The World Series, A Complete
Pictorial History, by John Devaney
and Burt Goldblatt (Rand McNally
and Company, Chicago, © 1972).

Hello To Willie and Mickey . . .
and Where Have You Gone, Joe DiMaggio?

Shouting "Let 'er rip," their season-long battle cry, the Giants rode into this Subway Series still exuberant over Bobby Thomson's climactic play-off home run against the Dodgers. Two rookie outfielders played against each other in this, their first World Series: Willie Mays for the Giants and Mickey Mantle for the Yankees.

In the second game Mantle was chasing a fly-ball when he suddenly crumpled to the grass and lay motionless. He was taken to a hospital where doctors diagnosed the injury as a weakened knee and Mantle played no more in the Series. It was the first of many knee injuries that would hobble Mantle throughout his career. Mays, who had been hitting poorly in the Giants' stretch run for the pennant, hit only .182 in the Series.

The Giants won two of the first three games without the help of their two aces, Sal Maglie and Larry Jansen, both of whom were arm-weary after the Giants' exhausting dash from 13½ games behind to catch the Dodgers. Neither won a game in the Series. The Yankees, with Phil Rizzuto and Joe DiMaggio doing most of the hitting, won the next two games to pull ahead, three games to two, Allie Reynolds and Eddie Lopat the victors.

In the sixth inning of the sixth game Hank Bauer drove a bases-loaded triple over Monte Irvin's head in leftfield, and the Yankees went into the ninth ahead, 4-1. But these Giants tried to stage one more miracle finish. They scored twice and had the tying run on base with two out. Stengel relieved with lefty Bob Kuzava, who would become a Stengel favorite in getting the last outs in hairy World Series situations. Kuzava threw to pinch-hitter Sal Yvars, who hit a twisting liner to rightfield. Hank Bauer lost the ball, then saw it, and grabbed it with a skidding catch inches off the ground, ending the Series.

In the bottom of the eighth of that game Joe DiMaggio had smacked a double and a little later was retired at third base. He trotted off the field, a crescendo of applause rising in Yankee Stadium, the crowd sensing this would be Joe DiMaggio's last game. It was his 51st Series game, a record. A few weeks later he announced his retirement, his No. 5 never to be worn again by a Yankee.

Eddie Lopat:
What Branca threw to Thomson

Eddie Lopat, the former Yankee pitcher, now lives in New Jersey. He said: *A lot of the Yankees, we went to the three games of the playoffs between the Dodgers and the Giants that year. Most of us were rooting for the Giants because we had played the Dodgers before and the Giants played in a bigger park* [so there would be a bigger player pool]. *Also it was closer to home than Ebbets Field. I saw Bobby Thomson hit that home run off* [Ralph] *Branca. I thought Branca pitched to Thomson just the way he should have, from everything our scouts had told us about Thomson. Branca pitched the fastball in, he kept it tight. I pitched Thomson tight all during that Series and I don't think he got a hit off me. . . . It was a sad affair for us, that Series, because we knew DiMaggio was retiring. It's always sad; you hate to lose a big guy like that.*

FOUR NEW MARKS SET BY DIMAGGIO

Clipper Runs Series Contests
Total to 51, Most at Bats,
199—With 9 Winners

Joe DiMaggio of the Yankees set four records during the world series which ended yesterday.

DiMaggio played in all six games to increase his total series games to 51, one more than Frank Frisch performed in. Joe also has played the most series games for one club, 51. The Clipper has stepped to the plate more than any other series performer, 199, and has played on the most winning teams, nine.

Outstanding records tied included Monte Irvin's steal of home in the opener for the Giants and Gil McDougald's grand-slam homer for the Yanks in the third inning of the fifth game.

The records broken and tied include:

BATTING

INDIVIDUAL RECORDS SET

Most Games Played Total Series—Joe DiMaggio, Yankees, 51.

Most Games Played With One Club—DiMaggio, 51.

Most Times at Bat Total Series—DiMaggio, 199.

Most Times on Winning Club—DiMaggio, 9.

INDIVIDUAL RECORDS TIED

Most Series Played—DiMaggio, 10.

Most Runs Batted in One Inning—Gil McDougald, Yankees, 4.

Most Base Hits Six-game Series—Monte Irvin, Giants, 11.

One or More Hits in Each Game of Series—Phil Rizzuto, Yankees, 8, and Al Dark, Giants, 10.

Most Base Hits One Game—Irvin, first game, 4.

Home Run with Bases Loaded—McDougald.

Stealing Home in Series Game—Irvin.

FIELDING

INDIVIDUAL RECORDS SET

Shortstop Chances Accepted Six-game Series—Rizzuto, 40.

INDIVIDUAL RECORDS TIED

Participating in Most Double Plays One Game—Rizzuto, 4.

PITCHING

INDIVIDUAL RECORDS TIED

Most Games Lost Six-game Series—Larry Jansen, Giants, 2.

Most Bases on Balls Six-Game Series—Allie Reynolds, Yankees, 11.

CLUB BATTING RECORDS SET

Most Times at Bat, One Club, Total Series—Yankees, 3,130.

Most Bases on Balls Both Clubs Six-game Series—51 (Yankees 26, Giants 25).

CLUB FIELDING RECORDS TIED

Most Double Plays, One Club, One Series—Yankees, 10.

Most Double Plays, One Club, Game—Yankees, 4.

GENERAL SERIES RECORDS

Club Playing Most Series—Yankees, 18.

Club Winning Most Series Games—Yankees, 63.

Club Losing Most Games—Giants, 41.

Most Winning Series—Yankees, 14.

Most Losing Series—Giants, 9.

Most Series Won—American League, 31.

Most Series Lost—National League, 17.

Most Players Participating, One Club, Six-Game Series—Giants, 24.

Most Players Participating, Both Clubs, Six-Game Series—45 (Yankees 21, Giants 24).

Largest Receipts Players' Pool Six-Game Series—$560,562.37.

At an Old-Timers game, Joe DiMaggio asks for a resin bag, just as he did in the those golden days when the Yankees ruled the American League.

Joe DiMaggio and the world's foremost collector of baseball memorabilia, Barry Halper, pose beside a license plate honoring the Yankees' famous number 5. Halper has in his collection more memorabilia associated with Joe DiMaggio than any other person or institution in the world.

The graceful swing, the raw power came to an end after the 1951 season. In his thirteen years as a Yankee, Joe DiMaggio had a career batting average of .325, a slugging average of .579, hit 361 home runs, scored 1,390 runs, and batted in another 1,537.

Journal NEW YORK American
AN AMERICAN PAPER FOR THE AMERICAN PEOPLE

Sports
by Bill Corum

| A Great Ball Player, And an All Right Joe | April's a Long Way Off, So Why Get Excited? |

IF HE'S GONE, THERE WENT ONE OF BEST.

JOE DIMAGGIO

NEW YORK, N. Y.

The Associated Press carried a story the other day that Joe DiMaggio said just before he boarded a plane for California that he had played his last game of big league baseball. This could be true and may well prove to be.

If Joe Reichler of the A. P., who wrote the story, says that DiMaggio told him that, you may be sure that the great Yankee star did. Reichler is a first rate and conscientious reporter, which settles that part of the story permanently as far as this column is concerned.

Whether DiMaggio's announced decision will be as permanent is something else again. Apparently Joe went to Dan Topping, president of the Yankees, to tell him that he had decided to quit.

It would seem that Topping was unable to talk him out of the decision, but did get the player to agree either to reconsider, or, at least, to refrain from making the decision public at this time. It's possible that Joe's tongue slipped at the last moment at the airport. Or that he just got fed up and said, "Aw, to hell with it."

He's a moody and temperamental fellow and it's easy enough to imagine him doing that. And the better you know him, the easier to imagine, I should say.

• • •

It's a Long Time Until April

There are, however, a few verities about the situation. The most obvious one is that if Joe's really gone from the Yankees and baseball for good, that there goes the best since Ruth.

There have been times when I thought that DiMag was about the most confused young man I'd ever seen. None of those times ever was when he was going for a fly ball.

If we have seen the last of him, we saw him doing that with a skill that seldom has been paralleled in the history of the game right to the final fly that he caught with such graceful, smooth-as-silk skimming ease.

If, perchance, on a few occasions and notably during the past season, he fell to hitting like a Monday morning washerwoman who'd had a rough Sunday night, it wasn't, of course, really DiMaggio, or the real DiMaggio up there swinging the bat.

Still, he always snapped out of it at the opportune time, as in the last World's Series. And in the Series, incidentally, he was as physically okay as it would be possible for an athlete of his age to be.

If he really has, therefore, hung up the Yankee uniform that he graced for so long, the reason will have been more mental—or temperamental—than physical.

However, it's a long time until another season starts in April and it's traditionally true that the baseball grass looks greener in the spring.

• • •

Topping and Webb Will Take the 100 G's

I've said that this is a story of many verities. Another of them is that if DiMag goes through with his plan to retire at this late stage of his career—and if it is painted plain that he and not they made the decision—that Owners Topping and Webb will take the hundred grand in 1952 salary that he so kindly endorsed back to them.

Rich men can always use the money. The Yankees want Ted Williams badly for next year and it is my information that the also somewhat temperamental Theodore locks with pleasure on their efforts to suit him up in a N. Y. uniform.

Williams has given out with a soulful interview in which he pulled out all the stops to prove that his heart belongs to Boston. But there are some who have heard him sing a different tune, or so they have told me.

And there is yet another verity. It's been a good many years since the writer traveled with a baseball team and a longer time since he traveled with the Yankees. DiMag was just arriving with the gentlemen of the Bronx, when I took my portable elsewhere.

But the kids in the streets must have known these past three years that any expressed feeling of cordiality between Manager Casey Stengel and DiMaggio was purely for professional purposes.

Stengel paid Joe many a public tribute and there isn't any question that, professionally, he was sincere. When any manager has the greatest player in the game on his side, he can't exactly hate the situation.

I can't recall ever hearing DiMaggio return these compliments in print. Nor can you. Joe didn't. Dig me up just one interview, one clipping, to prove that I'm wrong and I'll not only be glad to print it, I'll also be glad to read it.

• • •

The Yanks Didn't Know—Don't Know Now

The facts are that the Yankee management hasn't known in recent weeks where it stood for 1952 with either Stengel or DiMaggio. I don't believe that it does now.

But why belabor something to which only time will give the final answer? Again, it's a long time until spring training. That drastic changes loom is obvious. And that they better had for the Yanks is even more obvious.

If Joe DiMaggio really said his farewell to N. Y. C. at LaGuardia, it would be one of the strangest departures of a tremendous sports hero from the city that made him, ever recorded. Yet, I can't truthfully say that it wouldn't be quite typical of DiMaggio.

Still, if you missed him, you missed one of the all-time best and, like the rest of us, Joe is what he is.

And now, if you'll excuse me, I think I'll go down to Florida and lie in the sun for about a week, leaving others to wrestle with all these "grave problems."

DIMAGGIO OFF FOR JAPAN

Brother Dom, 14 Others, to Play Series of Exhibition Games

SAN FRANCISCO, Oct. 15 (AP)— Joe DiMaggio of the Yankees, his brother Dom from the Boston Red Sox and fourteen other baseball stars were in the Lefty O'Doul party which departed by plane this afternoon, bound for Japan, to play a series of exhibition games in the island Empire.

The take-off was delayed for hours. The plane finally got away an hour and ten minutes late. Half an hour later it returned to the mainland and after some mechanical tinkering got away again at 2 P. M.

Besides the DiMaggios, the party included Ferris Fain, American League batting champion; Ed Lopat, winner of two world series games; Bill Werle, Bob Shantz, Mel Parnell, George Strickland, Billy Martin, Joe Tipton, Al Lyons, Lou Stringer, Dino Restelli, Chuck Stevens, Ed Cereghino and Nini Tournay.

They will be gone a month and play games with various Japanese teams, as O'Doul's stars did when they made a similar tour last year.

Million Japs Shout Banzai For Touring DiMag Nine

By LESLIE NAKASHIMA,
United Press Sports Writer.

TOKYO, Oct. 17.—World Series Stars Joe DiMaggio and Ed Lopat of the Yankees and other members of an American all-star team were welcomed to Japan today by more than 1,000,000 fans, who stopped traffic for more than an hour in Tokyo's busiest downtown district.

Although the Pan American plane from Honolulu did not touch ground at Haneda Airport until 4.30 p.m. and it was dark by the time the cavalcade of open cars arrived in the city, thousands upon thousands of people jammed the Ginza, Tokyo's Broadway, to cheer Frank (Lefty) O'Doul and his 20-man squad which arrived for a goodwill series of at least 15 games.

As magnesium flares signalled the arrival of the baseball stars, pandemonium broke loose. Young people, old people, girl high school students, male university students, office workers swarmed into the street and the lead car bearing O'Doul and DiMaggio could move only at a snail's pace.

And that was managed only because American military police in a jeep, aided by Japanese policemen, cleared the way.

Shouts of "Banzai O'Doul and Banzai DiMaggio" gave the occasion a greater atmosphere of celebration than any victory registered in the last war and twice as great as the recent signing in San Francisco of the long-awaited peace treaty, according to Japanese observers.

Other thousands looked down from windows of department stores and office buildings lining the route of the cavalcade.

More thousands stood in front of the newspaper, Yomiuri Shimbun, t h r e e blocks away from the Ginza street, and awaited the arrival of the baseball stars. The players had been expected to make a brief courtesy call there to their sponsors of the series before going to their hotel.

But Japanese police feared another tough time there to control the crowds and the players' visit to the newspaper was abandoned, the players going direct to their hotel after the procession on the Ginza.

A loudspeaker from the newspaper building bellowed, "We thank you for this enthusiastic turnout to welcome the baseball stars but the authorities concerned thought it was better for the players to go direct to their hotel, so they are not coming here. Please break up and go home."

A large crowd of baseball officials and fans, including Maj. Gen. William F. Marquat, American Baseball Congress commissioner for Japan, greeted the team at Haneda Airport.

DiMaggio said he was glad to be back in Japan. Asked whether he intended to retire, he replied, "I haven't made up my mind yet."

Besides the Yankee Clipper and Lopat, players on the s q u a d included American League batting champion Ferris Fain of the Athletics: Dominic DiMaggio, of Red Sox; pitchers Mel Parnell of the Red Sox; Bob Shantz of the Athletics and Bill Werle of the Pirates; infielder Billy Martin of the Yankees, and catcher Joe Tipton of the Athletics.

The other players who arrived were infielders George Strickland of the Pirates, Lou Stringer and Chuck Stevens of Hollywood, catchers Nini Tornay and Ray Perry of the San Francisco Seals, and outfielders Dino Restelli of the Seals and Al Lyons of Seattle.

Trainer Leo Hugher of the Seals and baseball comedian Johnnie Price accompanied the team.

The Americans play their first game in Tokyo Saturday against the Yomiuri Giants, who today won the second annual Japan "World Series" by defeating the Mankai Hawks, 8-2, for a four games-to-one victory in a best-of-seven series.

In 1951, Joe DiMaggio returned to Japan and was feted with a parade in Tokyo. Thousands of Japanese baseball fans filled the streets to welcome him, shouting "Banzai, DiMaggio!"

U.S. Baseball Stars Score, 3–2, On Joe DiMaggio Homer at Tokyo

Yankee Clipper Belts 400-Footer in the Eighth Inning—He Plans to Fly Home Today for 'Business' Conferences

TOKYO, Nov. 10 (UP)—Fifty thousand Japanese baseball fans gave Yankee Clipper Joe DiMaggio a rousing ovation when he belted a 400-foot homer in the eighth inning today and helped the visiting American All-Stars to a 3–2 victory over Japan's Central League All-Stars at Meiji Park.

The fans were clamoring for what they hoped would be the first Japanese victory over an American visiting team of major leaguers since 1931 but they had come to see DiMaggio hit and were pulling for him to come through as he led off in the eighth.

Joe fouled a long fly and then connected for one high into the left-field stands off righthander Shigeru Sugishita. DiMaggio was cheered enthusiastically as he ran around the bases.

Brother Dom Triples

Then, it was Joe's brother, Dominic of the Boston Red Sox, who tripled down the rightfield line to score Al Lyons, Seattle Rainiers' pitcher, in the ninth to put the Americans ahead, 2–1. Yankee infielder Billy Martin followed with a long fly to center and Dominic scored what proved to be the winning run.

Fifty wounded veterans of the Korean war, hospitalized in Tokyo, were cheered as they entered the field just before the game began. They sat on special benches below the first-base bleachers.

It was a cold day but the fans, including about 5,000 soldiers and occupation personnel, remained to witness the entire game. The floodlights were turned on in the seventh inning.

A walk, a wild throw to first by Lou Stringer of the Hollywood Stars and a long fly to center gave the Japanese their first run in the fourth.

Kenny Lehman, 40th Division moundsman who is the property of the Brooklyn Dodgers, pitched two-hit ball for six innings, but had to be lifted for a pinch-hitter in the top half of the seventh.

The Japanese scored a run off Lyons, who had relieved Lehman, and had the tying run on second and winning run on first in the last half of the ninth. But Lyons struck out Catcher Akira Noguchi on three straight pitches for the final out.

It was the visitors' twelfth game on their current tour. Aside from the 2–2 tie game called by darkness against the Pacific League-All Stars in Osaka on Thursday, they have won all games.

```
                      R. H. E.
U. S. All-Stars......0 0 0  0 0 0  0 1 2—3 9 2
Central All-Stars...0 0 0  1 0 0  0 0 1—2 4 0
```
Batteries-Lehman, Lyons (7) and Tipton, Tornay (7); Matsuda. Bessho (3), Kaneda (6), Sugishita (6) and Kusunocki, Noguchi (6). Winning pitcher—Lyons. Losing pitcher—Sugishita.

DiMaggio Flies Home Today

TOKYO, Nov. 10 (AP)—Joe DiMaggio said today he will fly back to the United States Sunday for business reasons which "have nothing to do with my contract" with the New York Yankees.

He declined to discuss the business affairs that will cause him to leave the American All-Star baseball team now touring Japan.

"I've certainly enjoyed Japan—it's my second visit here in two years—but I simply have to get back to the States," he said.

He is scheduled to leave Tokyo at 11:30 P. M., Sunday (11:30 P. M., Saturday, E. S. T.) The rest of the team will stay on in Japan until about Nov. 20.

Beans Not all That Boston Bakes, There's Also DiMag to Sox Story

"It looks as if we are going to spend considerable time this winter denying stories originating in Boston," said Red Patterson in Yankee headquarters today.

"We have not approached the Red Sox about Ted Williams. We have not discussed sending Joe DiMaggio and other players for Williams or any other member of the Boston club.

"We have not given permission to the Boston club to talk with Joe, nor have we told the Clipper he could discuss a deal with Joe Cronin.

"That DiMaggio expressed a willingness to go to Boston, if he decided to remain in baseball, is all news to us.

"That we have offered Jackie Jensen, Gerald Coleman, Hank Bauer, Charley Silvera and Billy Martin, as well as the Clipper, for Williams, is one of Aesop's fables."

Patterson admitted that George Weiss was working on something new, but would not confirm the story from Philadelphia about an offer for Ferris Fain.

It is reported that Weiss has been in touch with DiMaggio, who is in Los Angeles, and may have something definite on Giuseppe's plans within the fortnight.

White Sox, Browns Finally Spill Deal.

After a wait of nearly three months, the White Sox and Browns finally have announced the trade they made last September, revealed then in the World-Telegram and Sun.

The Chicago club has obtained catcher Sherman Lollar, pitcher Al Widmar and infielder Tommy Upton, in exchange for outfielder Jim Rivera, lefthanded hurler Dick Littlefield, infielder Joe De Maestri, catcher Gus Niarhos, and first baseman Gordon Goldsberry.

The Sox then sent Upton to the Senators in exchange for utility infielder Sam Dente.

Rivera is the Bronx citizen who started with Atlanta, dropped into a lower classification in 1950, and this past season played remarkable ball for Rogers Hornsby at Seattle.

Just as soon as Hornsby had made his deal with Bill Veeck, to manage the Browns, he advised William to lose no time in bidding for Rivera.

The trade is very lopsided in favor of St. Louis, especially if Hornsby's extravagant praise of Rivera is founded on even 50 per cent of fact.

Chicago was eager to get a hitting catcher, and grabbed Lollar, former Yankee, before the Red Sox could move in with a new offer.

It is believed around the American League that St. Louis will ship two more players to the White Sox in this deal.

Pride of Yankees Too Proud to Linger for Full Fadeout

DiMag Bows Out After 16 Years as Bomber

Hired at Once By Club as TV Commentator

Says Night Ball Took Two Years Off His Career; Mantle Will Play Center

By DAN DANIEL
NEW YORK, N. Y.

At 2 p. m., Tuesday, December 11, in the 745 Fifth Avenue offices of the Yankees, Mickey Mantle was installed as the new center fielder of the Bombers by Casey Stengel.

Joseph Paul DiMaggio, for 13 of his 16 years on the New York roster, with three out for Army service, just had announced retirement, and no sooner had he made his move than Casey Stengel came along with his ring out the old, ring in the new.

In a press conference during the minor league meeting in Columbus, Stengel had said, "If DiMaggio retires, it will be Mantle or Jackie Jensen in center field."

In the immediate wake of the DiMaggio announcement, Casey said, "My center field plans start with Mantle. In Columbus, I had to bracket him with Jensen because I was doubtful about Mickey's right knee, injured in the second game of the World's Series.

"Now I have no such uncertainty. I have been assured by Dr. Sidney Gaynor, as well as Dr. George Bennett of Johns Hopkins, that Mantle will be in fine condition when we summon him to our St. Petersburg (Fla.) training camp.

"I do not, at this time, expect to have Mantle work out in the preliminary camp at Lake Wales, Fla., which will open February 12. I plan to have Mickey report with the first squad at St. Petersburg on February 22. However, all this will be worked out later.

'All the Fun Had Gone'

HE KNEW '51 WOULD BE HIS LAST YEAR

"Mantle has youth, only 21, the age at which DiMaggio reported to Joe McCarthy in 1936.

"Mantle has speed. He is a hitter. He learns fast. He is eager. But, unlike DiMaggio in 1936, Mickey is green. He has been an outfielder for only one season. Joe came to the Yankees from tremendous successes with San Francisco."

* * *

Doubtful About Trade

Asked if it were likely that the Yankees would make a deal for an experienced center fielder, Stengel replied:

"I do not believe we will make a trade before the opening of training. In fact, right now all trades are off insofar as I am concerned."

With Mantle moving over to center field, and Jensen his understudy, Stengel will start training with Hank Bauer, Gene Woodling, Bob Cerv and Archie Wilson as availables for the other positions.

Alone With His Memories

AFTER ANNOUNCING RETIREMENT

Three Hits in Debut

NEW YORK, N. Y. — From the very first day that Joe DiMaggio stepped into a major league batter's box in 1936, there was no doubt that he was headed for all-time greatness.

Because of injuries, Joe was delayed in his Big Time bow until May 3. The delay, however, had no effect on his batting eye. Facing Elon (Chief) Hogsett of the Browns, The Jolter rapped a triple and two singles.

'It Had to End Some Time,' Joe Said After Bat Streak

NEW YORK, N. Y.—Regardless of whether Joe DiMaggio was on a hitting streak or had just gone "0 for 4," he rarely displayed his emotions. On July 18, 1941, for example, the Yankee Clipper had gone hitless before Jim Bagby and Al Smith of the Indians, to snap his record-breaking 56-game hitting streak. Instead of kicking waterbuckets, or crying "robber" at Ken Keltner, whose spectacular fielding had deprived him of a couple of bingles, Joe took it all philosophically, saying only, "The streak had to end some time."

'I Felt Myself Slip After '48,' Jolter Reveals

Cerv, whose arm is not too highly regarded, may be thrown into the first base scramble.

The retirement of DiMaggio surprised many. To others it was no surprise at all.

The Clipper hit .263 last season, with 12 homers and 71 runs driven in, a record good enough to encourage him to play another year with the Bombers.

However, the prideful Joe did not like the idea of lingering for a complete fadeout. Besides, as he revealed in the December 11 press conference, "Old injuries caught up with me, and brought on new ones. I found that it was a chore for me to straighten up after I had retrieved a ground ball. In short, I was not pleased with myself any longer, and all the fun had gone out of playing the game."

Joe was out of work exactly 24 hours. When DiMag told the world he had played his last game, Dan Topping said Joe would be retained "in some capacity" by the club. And the next day Topping announced that the Yankees had hired the former center fielder as the Stadium television narrator. The contract calls for a before-and-after game job, the stint formerly filled by Dizzy Dean.

After DiMaggio told the press and radio men of his decision, December 11, Topping said: "Del (Webb) and I worked on Joe until 10 o'clock last night, trying to talk him into remaining as a player, but he was firm.

"Then we talked television with him." Joe admitted that he had received many TV and radio propositions and was interested in the Stadium job. He said he'd "like to loaf for a year, but I can't afford it," with a chuckle.

On December 12, Topping announced Joe had been signed for the video work. It is believed that with outside commitments, and possibly a play-by-play program added to his before-and-after-game stuff, The Clipper will better the $100,000 a year he got as the champions' center fielder. And the club still will be cashing in on Joe's popularity.

The press conference in which Joe announced his retirement was without precedent in size and confusion.

The writers were far out-numbered by the newsreel, radio and TV specialists. The sandwiches, coffee and cheese cake had to be replenished thrice.

DiMaggio first issued a formal, typed statement, and then sat down and answered questions.

* * *

Recalls Spring Prediction

The statement referred to the interview which Joe gave to three evening newspaper writers in his quarters in the Adams Hotel in Phoenix, Ariz., last February. That was the interview in which he said, "This could be my last year." Joe explained that he knew then it would be his last season. The statement follows:

"I told you fellows last spring I thought this would be my last year.

Clipper's Record in 'The Game's 400'

Year.	Club.	League.	G.	AB.	R.	H.	2B.	3B.	HR.	RBI.	B.A.	F.A.
1932—San Francisco		P. C.	3	9	2	2	1	1	0	2	.222	.917
1933—San Francisco		P. C.	187	762	129	259	45	13	28	*169	.340	.963
1934—San Francisco		P. C.	101	375	58	128	18	6	12	69	.341	.989
1935—San Francisco		P. C.	172	679	173	270	58	18	34	154	.398	.957
1936—New York		Amer.	138	637	132	206	44	†15	20	125	.323	.978
1937—New York		Amer.	151	621	*151	215	35	15	*46	167	.346	.962
1938—New York		Amer.	145	599	129	194	32	13	32	140	.324	.963
1939—New York		Amer.	120	462	108	176	32	6	30	126	*.381	.986
1940—New York		Amer.	132	508	93	179	28	9	31	133	*.352	.978
1941—New York		Amer.	139	541	122	193	43	11	30	*125	.357	.978
1942—New York		Amer.	154	610	123	186	29	13	21	114	.305	.981
1943-44-45—N. Y.		Amer.				(In Military Service)						
1946—New York		Amer.	132	503	81	146	20	8	25	95	.290	.982
1947—New York		Amer.	141	534	97	168	31	10	20	97	.315	*.997
1948—New York		Amer.	153	594	110	190	26	11	*39	*155	.320	.972
1949—New York		Amer.	76	272	58	94	14	6	14	67	.346	.985
1950—New York		Amer.	139	525	114	158	33	10	32	122	.301	.977
1951—New York		Amer.	116	415	72	109	22	4	12	71	.263	.990
Major League Totals			1736	6821	1390	2214	389	131	361	1537	.323	.978

WORLD'S SERIES RECORD

Year.	Club.	League.	G.	AB.	R.	H.	2B.	3B.	HR.	RBI.	B.A.	F.A.
1936—New York		Amer.	6	26	3	9	3	0	0	3	.346	.947
1937—New York		Amer.	5	22	2	6	0	0	1	4	.273	1.000
1938—New York		Amer.	4	15	4	4	0	0	1	2	.267	1.000
1939—New York		Amer.	4	16	3	5	0	0	1	3	.313	1.000
1941—New York		Amer.	5	19	1	5	0	0	0	1	.263	1.000
1942—New York		Amer.	5	21	3	7	0	0	0	3	.333	1.000
1947—New York		Amer.	7	26	4	6	0	0	2	5	.231	1.000
1949—New York		Amer.	5	18	2	2	0	0	1	2	.111	1.000
1950—New York		Amer.	4	13	2	4	1	0	1	2	.308	1.000
1951—New York		Amer.	6	23	3	6	2	0	1	5	.261	1.000
World's Series Totals			51	199	27	54	6	0	8	30	.271	.993

ALL-STAR GAME RECORDS

Year.	League.		AB.	R.	H.	2B.	3B.	HR.	RBI.	B.A.	F.A.
1936—American			5	0	0	0	0	0	0	.000	.500
1937—American			4	1	1	0	0	0	0	.250	1.000
1938—American			4	1	1	0	0	0	0	.250	.667
1939—American			4	1	1	0	0	1	1	.250	1.000
1940—American			4	0	0	0	0	0	0	.000	1.000
1941—American			4	3	1	1	0	0	0	.250	1.000
1942—American			4	0	2	0	0	0	0	.500	1.000
1947—American			3	0	1	0	0	0	0	.000	1.000
1948—American			1	0	0	0	0	0	1	.000	.000
1949—American			4	1	2	1	0	0	3	.500	.000
1950—American			3	0	0	0	0	0	0	.000	1.000
All-Star Game Totals			40	7	9	2	0	1	6	.225	.875

* Led league. † Tied for leadership.

I only wish I could have had a better year. But even if I had hit .350, this would have been the last year for me.

"You all know I have had more than my share of physical injuries and setbacks during my career. In recent years these have been much too frequent to laugh off. When baseball is no longer fun it's no longer a game.

"And so, I've played my last game of ball.

"Since coming to New York I've made a lot of friends and picked up a lot of advisers, but I would like to make one point clear—no one has influenced me in making this decision. It has been my problem and my decision to make.

"I feel that I have reached the stage where I can no longer produce for my ball club, my manager, my teammates and my fans the sort of baseball their loyalty to me deserves.

"In closing, I would like to say that I feel I have been unusually privileged to play all my major league baseball for the New York Yankees.

"But it has been an even greater privilege to be able to play baseball at all. It has added much to my life. What I will remember most in days to come will be the great loyalty of the fans. They have been very good to me."

In discussing reasons for his retirement while yet rated a fine ball player, The Clipper charged night ball with cutting two years off his career.

* * *

It's the Next Afternoon

"Playing after dark is not, in itself, tough," Joe revealed. "But the next afternoon you need four or five innings to get back on the beam.

"Night ball presents a lot of problems. If it were all night ball except on Sundays, it would not be so rugged."

DiMaggio insisted that he had made up his mind to retire after the 1951 season as early as last February, when he told the World-Telegram and Sun that "this could be my last year."

That DiMaggio would not play in 1952 was predicted last April by a specialist in Dallas, Tex., to whom Joe had been sent by Del Webb.

"DiMaggio has spurs in both shoulders, and I believe he has other arthritic involvements which will force him to quit after this season," the medico told Del.

Only One Losers' Cut

NEW YORK, N. Y.—In his 13 active seasons with the Yankees, the retired Joe DiMaggio missed only three World's Series. In addition, The Clipper appeared in only one losing Series. That was in 1942, when the Cardinals defeated the Yankees. The Yankees' World's Series record with DiMaggio follows:

Year.	Pos.	World's Series
1936—First		Beat Giants, 4-2.
1937—First		Beat Giants, 4-1
1938—First		Beat Cubs, 4-0
1939—First		Beat Reds, 4-0
1940—Third		
1941—First		Beat Dodgers, 4-1
1942—First		Lost to Cardinals, 4-1
1943-44-45		In Service
1946—Third		
1947—First		Beat Dodgers, 4-3
1948—Third		
1949—First		Beat Dodgers, 4-1
1950—First		Beat Phils, 4-0
1951—First		Beat Giants, 4-2

DiMaggio Labels Williams Best Hitter He Ever Saw

NEW YORK, N. Y. — Take it from the now retired Joe DiMaggio, Ted Williams, left fielder of the Red Sox, is the greatest hitter he has seen, and Dominic DiMaggio, also of Boston, is the outfielder who has made the greatest catches against Joe, and who did his career batting average the most damage.

DiMaggio said that his greatest feat as a fielder made Hank Greenberg the victim in Yankee Stadium in 1939.

"Hank hit one toward the flagpole in center, and I figured I had a chance to cut it down to three bases," Giuseppe related. "I got behind the pole, stuck out my glove, and got the ball. Earl Averill was on first, with one out. I got so excited, I thought the side had been retired, and ran half way down the field before I realized my error.

"My biggest thrills came with the 56-game batting streak in 1941, and my comeback in Boston in 1949, after I had missed 65 games because of heel trouble." Joe beat the Red Sox three straight in that series.

"The injuries forced me to quit," DiMaggio explained.

"I reached my peak in 1948. And then I felt myself slide. I discovered that base-runners were moving on me, and that straightening for the throw after bending for a ground ball was a difficult operation."

DiMaggio said he was not interested in a chance to manage a big league club.

"The fact is, I do not want to put on a baseball uniform again, and I do not want to worry about 25 other men," he concluded.

The Clipper's Record Clippings

American League batting champion 1939 (.381) and 1940 (.352).

American League leader in runs batted in 1941 (125) and 1948 (155).

American League leader in home runs 1937 (46) and 1948 (39).

Tied with 15 others by making 200 or more hits in his first full season in the majors: 206 hits in 138 games in 1936.

Most consecutive games batted safely in one season (a record for both leagues): 56 games, May 15 to July 16, 1941.

Tied with 11 others for most extra bases on long hits in one inning (two home runs): June 24, 1936.

Tied with 12 others for most total bases in one inning (same as above).

Tied with nine others for most triples in one game: Three on August 27, 1938.

Tied with 11 others for most home runs in one inning: Two, June 24, 1936.

Hit three home runs in one game on three occasions: June 13, 1937, May 23, 1948, and September 10, 1950.

Had a fielding mark of .9968 for 139 games in 1947.

Won the most valuable player award for the American League (THE SPORTING NEWS) in 1939 and 1941 and of the Baseball Writers' Association of America in 1939, 1941 and 1947.

Tied with George Herman Ruth for playing in most World's Series—10.

Holds record for playing most times in a World's Series with winning club—9.

Holds record for most games played in total World's Series—51.

Holds record for most Series games with one club—51.

Holds record of most times at bat in total Series—199.

Tied with 12 others for most times at bat in one nine-inning Series game: 6, on October 6, 1936.

Tied record held by numerous players of most times at bat in one inning in World's Series: 2, on October 6, 1936.

Tied with five others for most base hits in one inning of a World's Series game: 2, October 6, 1936.

Made one or more base hits in each game of a World's Series in 1939.

DiMaggio hit home runs in the following World's Series: 1937, 1938, 1939, 1947, 1949, 1950 and 1951.

Holds the record of most chances accepted as an outfielder in a five-game World's Series: 20, in 1942.

Holds record for most putouts by an outfielder in five-game World's Series: 20, in 1942.

Tied for record with five others for most putouts by an outfielder in one inning of a World's Series game: 3 on October 2, 1936, and October 7, 1937.

Lights Out

NEW YORK, N. Y.—Joe DiMaggio's retirement announcement was a four-way event, with newsreels and television cameras in one room, newspapermen in a second, radio recordings in another and still cameramen in a fourth. Joe flitted in and out of the various gatherings.

Red Patterson also was kept busy, handing out scripts to DiMaggio, Co-Owners Dan Topping and Del Webb and Manager Casey Stengel. The Jolter autographed his script, "To Cecil De-Mille Patterson."

The special lighting effects for the television and still cameras put such a heavy load on the circuit that a fuse was blown, throwing the Yankee offices into darkness about the time the press conference was being completed.

Uniform, Bat, Glove to Go to Hall of Fame

Suit Retired, Like Those of Bambino and Gehrig

By DAN DANIEL
NEW YORK, N. Y.

The famous No. 5 that adorned Joe DiMaggio's uniform has been retired by the Yankees. President Dan Topping announced the club's action the day after the Clipper told the world he was through as a player.

Since Babe Ruth's No. 3 and Lou Gehrig's No. 4 already had been taken out of circulation, no future Bombers will find these three numbers available.

DiMaggio's home uniform, worn in the World's Series, the bat with which he hit his last homer, in the fourth

Good Luck, Joe!

By BILL CORUM
Of the N. Y. Journal-American

You can take the boy out of the outfield but you can't take the outfield out of the Stadium. This is one way of saying that the world's champion Yankees face a bigger problem because of Joe DiMaggio's retirement than does DiMag.

For the first time since Babe Ruth was bought from the Boston Red Sox, the fabulous Yanks find themselves without a great star and the biggest name attraction at the gate in baseball. As long as they had Babe, it was the Old Guy Who Stood Alone by himself. Since then DiMag has been almost equally outstanding as the game's top star.

Joe D. probably will become the Dizzy Dean of 1952. Without the hillbilly songs, one presumes. Unless, that is, Joe is going to take singing lessons from his theatrical pal, "Gentleman George" Soltaire, over the winter.

It likely will be easy enough on the ears listening to DiMag. But it will never be as easy as it was on the eyes watching him play the outfield. Even last summer when he was doing it somewhat from memory.

That was the reason he quit, of course. He didn't have it any more and knew it and, knowing it, he didn't want to be out where all could see that he didn't have it. I used to turn my eyes away from the TV screen at times late last season when he came to bat.

There appeared to be times when it was impossible for him to get his bat around to pull the ball to left field, which was his natural way of hitting.

Mel Allen covered up for him at times by saying, "Joe is intentionally hitting to right field," or words to that effect. He was, too. But only because, I feel sure, that was the only way he could hit at all at that time.

Good luck, Joe. You were a big man in our town and always will be.

game of the classic with the Giants, and his glove will be presented to the Hall of Fame before the first game in the stadium next April.

With Charlie Keller released after the 1949 season, Tommy Henrich taken off the player roster in 1950 and DiMaggio gone now, the Yankees have lost one of the greatest outfields of all time within a space of three years.

* * *

Goodbye, JOE...

'I'll Never Forget My First Impression of You That March Morning at St. Pete'

By DAN DANIEL

NEW YORK, N. Y.

Goodbye, Joe! It scarcely appears possible that 16 years have rolled by since we said "Hello" to each other at Miller Huggins Field in St. Petersburg, Fla., in March, 1936.

You walked up to me and said: "My name is Joe DiMaggio. Tom Laird of the San Francisco News told me to see you as soon as I arrived here, and to be guided by your advice."

Sixteen years, three of which you spent in the Army, and now you have said "Farewell" to the diamond, and retirement has claimed you, even as it had claimed Babe Ruth, Lou Gehrig, Bill Dickey, Tony Lazzeri, Charlie Keller, Tommy Henrich and Earle Combs before you.

Within a space of three years, one of the greatest outfields of all time—Keller in 1949, Henrich in 1950 and now yourself—has gone from the Yankees. Before this trio, Bob Meusel, Ruth and Combs. Star-spangled dynasties, trios of marvelous achievement. Their feats will live long in the memories of those who witnessed them, and in the record books of the game forever.

Goodbye, Joe! It is not quite as final as it sounds. Unlike other heroes of the past, in Yankee history, you will continue to live in the Stadium, though your playing career is closed. Day after day, you will be the television narrator, replacing Dizzy Dean.

"Lucky to be a Yankee," you have said so often. But you did not appreciate how lucky. It seems likely that your financial returns from television work both during and out of the baseball season will net you something more than the $100,000 a year you received as a center fielder for the past three seasons.

Just how lucky you are is driven home for me as I compare your joyous retirement fiesta with the passing of Ruth and Gehrig from the Yankees.

When, on the afternoon of December 11, in the 745 Fifth avenue offices of the New York club, you announced that you never again would put on a uniform, there was cheese cake. There were turkey sandwiches. There was coffee.

The place swarmed with newsreel men, photographers from newspapers, television directors and technicians. It looked like opening night at the Metropolitan Opera, except there was no bediamonded dowagers. Your going off the Yankee roster occasioned more excitement than a Ruth signing. That used to mark the annual zenith of Bomber furor.

• • •

Contrast to Ruth Valedictory

How different your valedictory from that of Ruth. How different the reasons. You walked out of the ranks of the Yankees at a time when, at 37, still able to play ball, you could have continued at $100,000 a year. You walked out minus managerial ambitions. You said, "So long, Casey.

It was fun to play for you, and I'll be seeing you in the Stadium."

Ruth left the Yankees because Col. Jacob Ruppert, supporting Joe Mc-Carthy's regime staunchly, refused to fire Marse Joe and hire the Babe.

"Go to Newark and prove your ability to lead," Jake told the Babe.

"I should not be forced to undergo any such apprenticeship, considering the things I have done for your club," the Bam retorted.

Some years later, Ruth was to beg Col. Larry MacPhail for a chance to manage in Newark—to beg, and to be turned down.

"Colonel, I have no hard feelings toward you, but the time has come for

An Idol to Former Roomie, Page

PITTSBURGH, Pa.—Joe Page, former star relief pitcher of the Yankees who lives in Springdale, Pa., on the outskirts of Pittsburgh, knows Joe Di-Maggio as well as any Yankee because they roomed together on the road. And even to Page, the Clipper was an idol.

"There's something about DiMag that commands respect and indicates leadership," said Page.

"As long as I can remember, when the Yankees took the field, they all waited for Joe to make the first break. Nothing was said about this ritual, but everybody held back and waited for Joe to lead us out."

Although DiMaggio often has been called the "deadpan" type, Page said: "Don't think for a moment he didn't show emotion. I remember a game in Detroit one day when I was on third base. Snuffy Stirnweiss tripled between the outfielders and I jogged home, turning to watch the fielders chase the ball.

"After I crossed home plate, DiMaggio grabbed me and chewed me out or not running. 'You're a Yankee,' he said, 'and Yankees always hustle.'"

Hail and . . .

At Yankee Stadium, May 3, 1936

St. Louis	AB.	R.	H.	O.	A.	E.
Lary, ss	5	1	1	1	2	0
Pepper, cf	5	1	3	5	1	0
Solters, lf	5	1	2	3	0	0
Bottomley, 1b	3	1	1	4	0	0
Bell, rf	4	1	1	2	0	0
Clift, 3b	3	0	2	0	2	0
Hemsley, c	1	0	0	1	1	0
Giuliani, c	3	0	0	6	1	0
Carey, 2b	4	0	3	2	1	0
Knott, p	0	0	0	0	0	1
Caldwell, p	2	0	0	0	1	0
*Coleman	1	0	0	0	0	0
Hogsett, p	0	0	0	0	0	0
†West	1	0	0	0	0	0
Van Atta, p	0	0	0	0	0	0
Totals	37	5	13	24	9	1
New York	AB.	R.	H.	O.	A.	E.
Crosetti, ss	5	1	1	2	4	0
Rolfe, 3b	5	3	2	0	0	1
DiMAGGIO, lf	6	3	3	0	0	0
Gehrig, 1b	5	5	4	7	0	0
Dickey, c	3	1	0	8	1	0
Chapman, cf	4	0	4	1	0	0
Hoag, cf	0	1	0	2	0	0
Selkirk, rf	3	0	1	4	1	0
Lazzeri, 2b	5	0	1	2	2	0
Gomez, p	2	0	0	0	1	0
Murphy, p	3	0	1	0	1	0
Totals	41	14	17	27	9	1

*Batted for Caldwell in sixth.
†Batted for Hogsett in eighth.

St. Louis .... 3 0 1 0 1 0 0 0 0— 5
New York .... 4 3 0 2 0 4 1 0 *—14

Runs batted in—Pepper 2, Bell, Clift 2, Chapman 5, Lazzeri 2, Gehrig 2, Dickey, Lary, DiMAGGIO, Selkirk. Two-base hits—Clift, Chapman, Pepper, Rolfe. Three-base hits—Crosetti, Chapman 2, DiMAGGIO. Home run—Pepper. Double plays—Selkirk and Gehrig; Crosetti and Gehrig; Lazzeri, Murphy and Gehrig. Base on balls—Off Knott 3, off Caldwell 1, off Hogsett 3, off Gomez 1, off Murphy 1. Struck out—by Gomez 3, by Murphy 4, by Caldwell 1, by Van Atta 1. Hits—Off Knott 2 in ⅓ inning, off Caldwell 7 in 4 innings, off Hogsett 7 in 2⅔ innings, off Gomez 9 in 4 innings. Hit by pitcher—By Hogsett 1. Wild pitch—Hogsett 1. Winner—Murphy. Loser—Knott.

. . . Farewell

At Yankee Stadium, October 10, 1951

Giants	AB.	R.	H.	O.	A.	E.
Stanky, 2b	3	1	1	3	4	0
Dark, ss	3	1	1	1	2	0
Lockman, 1b	4	0	0	10	0	0
Irvin, lf	4	0	3	0	0	0
Thomson, 3b	4	0	1	2	0	0
Thompson, rf	3	0	1	0	0	0
§Yvars	1	0	0	0	0	0
Westrum, c	3	0	1	3	0	0
†Williams	0	0	0	0	0	0
Jansen, p	2	0	0	0	1	0
Mays, cf	3	1	2	2	0	0
Koslo, p	2	0	0	0	1	0
*Rigney	1	0	1	0	0	0
Hearn, p	0	0	0	0	0	0
‡Noble, c	1	0	0	0	1	0
Totals	35	3	11	24	9	1
Yankees	AB.	R.	H.	O.	A.	E.
Rizzuto, ss	4	0	1	4	4	0
Coleman, 2b	4	1	1	2	1	0
Berra, c	4	0	0	6	1	0
DiMAGGIO, cf	2	1	1	1	0	0
McDougald, 3b	4	0	1	0	3	0
Mize, 1b	2	1	1	6	0	0
Collins, 1b	1	0	0	0	0	0
Bauer, rf	3	0	1	4	0	0
Woodling, lf	3	0	0	5	0	0
Raschi, p	1	0	0	0	1	0
Sain, p	1	0	0	0	0	0
Kuzava, p	0	0	0	0	0	0
Totals	29	4	7	27	8	0

*Singled for Koslo in seventh.
†Ran for Westrum in eighth.
‡Called out on strikes for Hearn in eighth.
§Flied out for Thompson in ninth.

Giants ...... 0 0 0 0 1 0 0 0 2—3
Yankees ..... 1 0 0 0 0 3 0 0 *—4

Runs batted in—McDougald, Stanky, Bauer 3, Irvin, Thomson. Two-base hits—Lockman, Berra, DiMAGGIO. Three-base hit—Bauer. Double plays—Rizzuto and Mize 2; Rizzuto, Coleman and Mize; Dark, Stanky and Lockman. Bases on balls—Off Koslo 4 (DiMAGGIO 2), Raschi, Mize), off Raschi 5 (Westrum, Dark 2, Irvin, Thomson), off Sain 2 (Thompson, Mays). Struck out—By Raschi 1 (Dark), by Sain 2 (Dark, Noble), by Koslo 3 (Raschi, Bauer, Coleman). Pitching record—Koslo 5 hits, 4 runs in 6 innings; Hearn 1 hit, 0 runs in 1 inning; Jansen 1 hit, 0 runs in 1 inning; Raschi 7 hits, 1 run in 6 innings (pitched to two batters in seventh); Sain 4 hits, 2 runs in 2 innings (pitched to three batters in ninth); Kuzava 0 hits, 0 runs in 1 inning. Wild pitch—Koslo. Passed ball—Berra. Earned runs—Yankees 4, Giants 3. Left on bases—Giants 12, Yankees 5. Winning pitcher—Raschi. Losing pitcher—Koslo.

the Yankees and me to part company," Ruth had told Ruppert in February, 1935.

"I have a chance to go to the Braves, as player, vice-president and assistant manager. I hate to leave New York, but, as you know, Boston was my first baseball stop in the majors. I would like you to give me my unconditional release."

The following day, we straggled into the offices of the New York club, on West 42nd street. Ed Barrow handed out slips of paper not more than two inches long. On them was typed one of the most poignant messages a big league club has given to the press.

"George H. Ruth this day has been given his unconditional release by the New York Yankees."

Joe, you have had a lot of advice in your time. Good advice, and bad. Most of it, apparently, good. Ruth got a lot of poor advice that February 16 years ago. He should have investigated the financial condition of the Braves. It was low. He should have been warned that he could be neither vice-president nor assistant manager. On June 2, the Babe quit the Boston club, his playing career ended. He had hit .181 in the few games he had played for the Braves.

* * *

Lou's Fadeout in '39

Had Ruth chosen to remain with the Yankees, he could have gone on to his last day a coach.

You, Joe, found utterly no appeal in continuing in any capacity with the Yankees, even if Stengel had wanted to quit and let you take his place.

The day Gehrig retired, you were present, Joe. You had been with the Yankees since 1936, and Lou passed out of the picture as a player on May 2, 1939.

You were as affected by this sad happening as were any of us. Gehrig had played in 2,130 consecutive games. He had set an iron man record without possible approach in the years to come of our national pastime.

Joe McCarthy had asked us newspapermen to meet him in the lobby of the Book-Cadillac at noon. We were told, "Lou Gehrig will not be in the lineup today. Babe Dahlgren will take his place. I do not know when Lou will be able to play again."

There was a lump in Joe's throat, there was a catch in his voice, and within a couple of minutes, he was on his way to Briggs Stadium, and we were dashing for our typewriters, and one of the saddest stories I yet have written. One of the saddest? Well, the saddest. For all of us knew that Gehrig would not play again, and that any day the rare form of paralysis which had attacked him would snuff out his life.

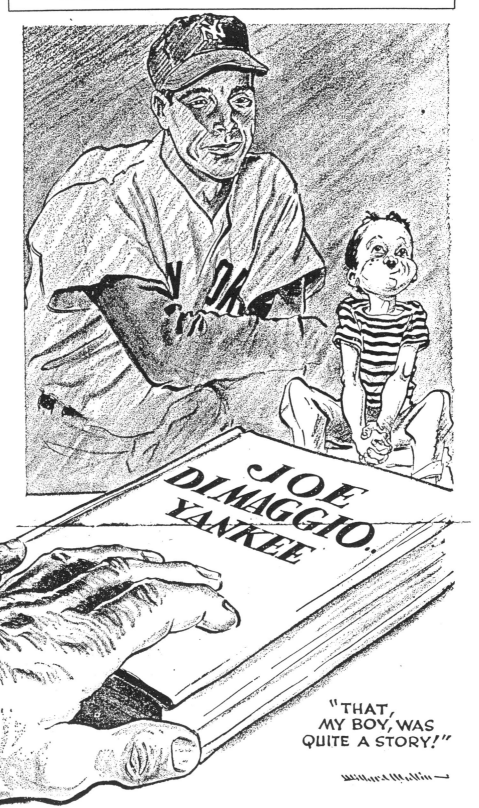

A Tale That Time Will Never Dim

JOE DIMAGGIO. YANKEE.

"THAT, MY BOY, WAS QUITE A STORY!"

Willard Mullin

No One Can Ever Fill Their Niches

Ruth was finished. Gehrig was through. But you, Joe, you could have gone on into 1952, "still as good as any center fielder in the American League," take it from Hank Greenberg, who has Larry Doby on his Indians, and who knows about your own "kid" brother Dominic, on the Red Sox.

For the Babe, a small slip of paper, "Gone from the Yankees." For Lou, a lobby conference, "Out of the lineup." For you, Joe, cheese cake. Then a rich contract in TV. Do you know how lucky you are?

When asked to list your biggest thrills, you said, the other day, that your great batting streak of 56 consecutive games, in 1941, came first.

Then your 1949 belated debut in Boston, after you had missed the first 65 games because of heel trouble.

Finally, your best fielding feat—your catch of Hank Greenberg's bid for a homer behind the centerfield flagpole in the Stadium, in 1939.

* * *

That Batting Streak of '41

I never will forget that batting streak because, for a good part of it, I was the official scorer in the Stadium.

I don't know how you felt as, day after day, you kept adding to your collection of hitting contests; as you passed the records of Willie Keeler, Rogers Hornsby and George Sisler.

But I was under tremendous pressure up in the press box. Usually I resent going on the road. But that season I welcomed the shift from the Stadium as a relief from the participation in your batting streak.

Yet, I was chagrined when, in a night game in Cleveland in July, Pitchers Al Smith and Jim Bagby, with the flashy assistance of Ken Keltner and Lou Boudreau, stopped you.

Your 1949 gala in Fenway Park also will linger long in my memory. You took charge at a time when the Yankees needed taking charge of, and beat the Red Sox three straight times. Boston club never recovered from your blows, and the Yankees won the pennant.

I remember, too, very vividly, the catch you made on Greenberg. Earl Averill was on first base. He had moved from the Indians to the Tigers that season. One out.

Greenberg drove a terrific fly which appeared to be destined for the centerfield bleachers. Nobody had hit one into that locale. Nobody yet has done it.

You legged it hard, hoping, as you later explained, to cut the hit down to three bases, if it landed on the grass.

Well, Joe, the ball did not go into the bleachers and it did not hit the turf. You got behind the flagpole, and somehow, you caught it.

You made so brilliant a catch that you got excited over it. You figured it was three out and began to run in. Halfway to the infield, it suddenly struck you that there were only two out, with a runner on base, and you threw the ball in.

I have a vivid recollection, too, of your DiMaggio Day in the Stadium after your recovery from virus pneumonia late in the 1950 season.

I remember how proud your mother was of her Joe, how your brother Dom was moved to tears, how you, the usually placid Giuseppe, were affected.

I never will forget my first impression of you, that March morning at Miller Huggins Field in St. Petersburg.

I said to myself, "This kid is the greatest rookie it has been my good fortune to view in action." You were only 21, and had had three big years in San Francisco.

After I had seen you work the second day, I was more enthusiastic than ever. On the third day I said, "Here is the replacement for Babe Ruth."

As you know, when the Babe left the Bombers, the fans and the press box united in the feeling that the New York club never would recover from the loss. But with you in their lineup the Yankees went on to bigger things than ever before. Bigger things which included five consecutive years, through 1950, which saw the Stadium paid attendance pass the two million mark.

In that first season with the Yankees, you made 206 hits. In your second year you batted .346 and unfurled 46 homers.

THE LOCKERS of Babe Ruth and Lou Gehrig were retired during Ruth Day ceremonies at Yankee Stadium, April 27, 1947.

Joe's No. 5 Joins Babe's 3, Lou's 4 on Retired List

NEW YORK, N. Y.

Joe DiMaggio's famous No. 5 has followed Babe Ruth's No. 3 and Lou Gehrig's No. 4 into retirement.

Never again will a Yankee wear No. 5 on the back of his uniform shirt, never again will a No. 5 designate a Bomber on the scorecard, never again will a Yankee clubhouse locker bear the numeral 5.

"Having honored the achievements and the memory of Ruth and Gehrig by taking their numbers out of competition, we felt that we should do no less for Joe," Dan Topping, club president, explained.

"DiMaggio's home uniform, last worn in the World's Series, his glove and the bat with which he hit his last homer, in the fourth game with the Giants, will be presented to the Cooperstown Hall of Fame before our opening game next spring in the Stadium.

"No other club has had so glorious a trio—Ruth, Gehrig and DiMaggio."

Ruth's No. 3 was not retired immediately after his departure from the New York roster in 1935 to join the Braves as player, vice-president and assistant manager. George Selkirk, who inherited the Babe's post in right field, also took over his number. However, after Gehrig's No. 4 was taken out of circulation, Ruth's No. 3 also was retired.

Now, No. 5 joins Nos. 3 and 4 as Yankee numerals that always will remain dedicated to the memory and achievements of an immortal trio of players.

Goodbye Joe

Great Team Man, Says Marse Joe

BUFFALO, N. Y.—No one is more keenly aware of Joe DiMaggio's value to the Yankees than Joe McCarthy, who managed the Bombers during much of The Jolter's career with the club.

"I don't think you could put into words the nice things I'd like to say about Joe DiMaggio," said Marse Joe, who now resides on a farm near Buffalo.

"I didn't think he'd have to call it quits so soon. But I guess I didn't realize how much his injuries had been troubling him.

"I do know that he has played a lot of times when he shouldn't have, because he's that kind of fellow. He has been a great ball player and a great team man, and he is a fine man now and always will be. He'll be just as big a credit to whatever new field he goes into as he has been to baseball."

Thrice, in 1939, 1941 and 1947, you were named the most valuable player of the American League. Year after year, you made the All-Star team. In 1939, THE SPORTING NEWS called you the greatest ball player in the entire country.

You played in ten World's Series. You set record after record. You always gave everything you had, and then some. You left an indelible imprint

∴ *in Yankee History*   New Stance   ∴ By Darvas

JOE DiMAGGIO'S locker in the Yankee clubhouse, showing his No. 5 uniform, which also will be retired.

Goodbye, JOE

on baseball history, you made a spot sui generis for yourself in the brilliant annals of the great Yankees. you won the heart of Little Old New York.

We are going to miss you a lot out there in center, and at the plate. Even when you were batting .263 last season, you still inspired the highest respect of the opposition pitchers.

As you watch Mickey Mantle fight to establish himself in your old spot, I know you will offer him your help and advice, even though you no longer will be wearing the uniform of the Yankees.

Goodbye, Joe! And Good Luck!

Yankees Retire DiMaggio's '5' To Hall of Fame

Bat and Glove Also Going to Baseball Shrine; Only 7 of 1947 Team Remain

By Harold Rosenthal

The Yankees retired Joe DiMaggio's uniform number yesterday, putting the Yankee Clipper's No. 5 into mothballs along with the late Babe Ruth's No. 3 and Lou Gehrig's No. 4. DiMaggio's uniform will be retired to the Hall of Fame in Cooperstown, N. Y., in opening-day ceremonies at the Yankee Stadium next spring.

At the same time his favorite glove, along with the bat with which he hit the final homer of his career in the fourth game of the last World Series off Sal Maglie, will also be sent to the baseball shrine. If DiMaggio takes the Yankee television job he will be in the unique position of being required to describe the proceedings.

Yesterday Arthur Patterson, Yankee publicity director, unearthed the information that DiMaggio's departure left only seven men who had played with the 1947 Yankees. They are Phil Rizzuto, Yogi Berra, Vic Raschi, Allie Reynolds, Frank Shea, Bobby Brown and Ralph Houk. In each of the last three seasons a big outfielding name has stepped down. In 1949 it was Charley Keller, in 1950 it was Henrich and now it is DiMaggio.

The numbers 1 and 2 in the Yankee system are in no immediate danger of following 3, 4 and 5 into retirement. Billy Martin, the young utility infielder wore No. 1 last season, after returning from his hitch in the Army. His name is often mentioned in trade rumors.

However, No. 2 is an esteemed number which Frankie Crosetti has worn for years as an active player and now as a coach.

AFTER THE GAME

The famous number 5, formally retired by the Yankees, and DiMaggio's glove, are turned over for display to the National Baseball Hall of Fame in Cooperstown, New York, in a ceremony at Yankee Stadium in 1952. Accepting them is Hall of Fame vice president, Rowan D. Spracker.

ON BATTING

After I retired from the game, Yankee owner, Dan Topping, asked me to come down to Florida to help coach batting at spring training, which I did voluntarily. I gave some serious thought as to just why a ballplayer is a good hitter and realized that a good part of anyone's hitting talent is there from birth.

The first requirement is good vision. I remember sportswriter John Kieran once was asked what made Babe Ruth such a great home run hitter.

"His eyes," Kieran said. "He could read license plate numbers so far away that I couldn't even tell the color of the plate."

The good hitter also needs to have quick reflexes, coordination, good timing, and strength in his arms, wrists and shoulders. Basically, a good hitter inherits those things. There are some elements besides these natural attributes, however, over which a batter does have control. He has to build confidence, be comfortable with the type of bat he uses and in his stance, and, of course, he has to work to develop the natural attributes.

Then you have to combine all those things to hit a ball less than three inches in diameter that is traveling over a 60-foot, 6-inch distance at about 95 miles an hour. You have about two-fifths of a second to decide whether it is a good pitch or a bad one, whether to swing or not, and then to get the bat around and hit the ball.

Joe DiMaggio

Ruth, DiMaggio and Dickey Only Unanimous All-Time Yankees

By DANIEL,
Staff Writer.

ST. PETERSBURG, March 12.—Babe Ruth, Joe DiMaggio and Bill Dickey were the only unanimous choices on the All-Time Yankee team selected in a poll of 48 baseball experts marking the 50th anniversary of the New York club.

The chief objection in this writer's opinion, to the team as chosen was the omission of Jack Chesbro, right-hand pitcher, who won 41 games, with one tie, for the club in 1904.

George M. Weiss' official designation of the All-Time heroes celebrated New York's admission to the American League on March 12, 1903, in a meeting in the old Fifth Avenue Hotel. Two months later, as the Highlanders, the club made its debut at the Hilltop grounds on Broadway at 165th St.

There will be a toast to Chesbro and his spitball legerdemain at the dinner given by Dan Topping, Del Webb and Weiss in Tampa tonight before the Bombers entrain for West Palm Beach and Miami. But in the Stadium Hall of Fame which will be set up this summer, the name of Charley (Red) Ruffing, and not that of Happy Jack, will be emblazoned in bronze. For it is Ruffing whom the electors have honored as No. 1 right-hander of Yankee history,

with 28 votes, as against 11 for Waite Hoyt and only four for Chesbro.

The balloting for southpaw laurels produced a tie at 24 votes between Vernon (Lefty) Gomez and Herb Pennock. Here again there appeared to be a miscarriage of justice. Pennock's career record is more brilliant than Lefty's. But Gomez did all of his great pitching for New York, while Pennock came to the Yankees after he had achieved his peak with the Athletics and had begun to slide with the Red Sox.

The voters named the proper candidate when it came to picking the greatest relief hurler. They gave 25 votes to Johnny Murphy, the Fireman, with 11 for Wilcy Moore, who won 19 games in 1927, and 10 for Joe Page.

2 Voters Pick Chase Over Gehrig.

Here is how the 48 voters picked the all-time lineup:

First base, Lou Gehrig; second base, Tony Lazzeri; third base, Red Rolfe; shortstop, Phil Rizzuto; right field, Babe Ruth; left field, Bob Meusel; center field, Joe DiMaggio; catcher, Bill Dickey; right-handed pitcher, Charley Ruffing; left-handed pitcher, tie between Vernon Gomez and Herb Pennock; relief pitcher, Johnny

Murphy; utility infielder, Frankie Crosetti.

The team of 1927, which set an American League record with 110 victories and won the pennant by a margin of 19 games over the Athletics, was voted the Yankees' greatest. It got 45 votes, with two going to the 1937 outfit and one to the 1928 club.

For reasons known only to a couple of the pollsters, who named Hal Chase, Gehrig failed to achieve a sweep.

That Hal was a superlative fielder nobody will dispute. That he matched Gehrig in power and in all-around value cannot be maintained. Then there is the fact that Chase left baseball under a cloud.

Lazzeri, with 36 votes against 12 for Joe Gordon, the only contender, made an expectedly strong showing at second.

Rizzuto, with 42 votes, achieved a surprisingly big triumph, since Crosetti polled only three and Roger Peckinpaugh was remembered by just one voter.

At third base Rolfe ran off with top honors by 38 to 10 over Joe Dugan.

Every one of the all-timers named, except Meusel, played under Marse Joe McCarthy.

Meusel beat Earle Combs by 24 to 14 for the third outfield job.

Out of uniform, but bat in hand, Joe DiMaggio is never far from the national pastime.

The classic image of Joe DiMaggio has been used to promote a variety of products, from Mr. Coffee coffeemakers to the Bowery Bank of New York.

It All Depends on the Point of View

Jolter Learning How to Play
New Field as TV Commentator

By DAN DANIEL
NEW YORK, N. Y.

Adjacent to the big clubhouse of the Yankees, under the grandstand in the Stadium, is a new set-up. It is the television studio of Commentator Joseph Paul DiMaggio, the old Yankee Clipper, who at 37 retired as a ball player this past winter.

The DiMaggio studio makes Casey Stengel's office look like a subway ticket seller's booth.

DiMaggio's desk makes Casey's roll-top look like a banged-up antique. However, all the equipment in the studio is for TV. Casey doesn't have to appear on anybody's 21-inch screen.

"How do the Yankees look?" DiMaggio asked. We had entered the studio with the intention of interviewing The Clipper on his impression of the DiMaggio-less Bombers.

"This television commentator job is all new to me, and it will take me a while to get accustomed to it. Once

Casey, DiMag's TV Guest, Hands Him a Dictionary

NEW YORK, N. Y.—Admitting he was "as jittery as a scared hen" in going through his first 15-minute television program preceding and following the Yankees' game of April 11, Joe DiMaggio was amused when his old boss, Manager Casey Stengel of the Bombers, presented him with a 140,000-word dictionary. Besides Stengel, Joe also had Manager Charley Dressen of the Dodgers as a special guest.

Stengel, when told by DiMag that he should have given him a bat instead of a dictionary, came back with the announcement that he was only lending Joe the book as he hadn't finished reading it.

I get a little experience, I know I will do a good job with it.

"I have been concentrating on the TV job to the point at which I walk it and sleep it, and eat it."

DiMaggio gets $50,000 a year from the Yankees for two 15-minute jobs, before and after games.

He has a lucrative contract with the Buitoni spaghetti people, and he will pick up enough other work on TV to bring his annual salary well over the $100,000 he used to collect for playing center field for the New York club.

Asked to discuss the American League race, DiMaggio said, "Those Indians now worry me. The stories you hear about their hitting are terrific. Their pitching we know about from 1951.

"Well, if Luke Easter does the things he may do, if Ray Boone decides to be the shortstop he can be, if Al Rosen controls his throws and Larry Doby comes back strong—well, if all those things happen and Al Lopez' pitching matches that of 1951, it won't be so good for Casey.

"Do I miss getting into uniform every day?" Joe walked into his office and laughed, "Man, are you kidding?"

Joe DiMaggio, the broadcaster, interviews his former manager, Casey Stengel, in 1952.

Joe DiMaggio, Lyons, Vance and Hartnett
Elected to Baseball's Hall of Fame

FORMER YANKEE HEADS BALLOTING

DiMaggio Obtains 223 Votes —Lyons Gets 217, Vance 205 and Hartnett 195

By JOHN DREBINGER

Joseph Paul DiMaggio, son of a humble San Francisco fisherman, swept into baseball's Hall of Fame yesterday.

With the renowned Yankee Clipper, who retired as an active player after the 1951 season, went three others. They were Ted Lyons, pitching star of the Chicago White Sox between the years 1923 and 1946; Dazzy Vance, fireballing right-hander of the Dodgers and strike-out king of the National League in the Twenties, and Gabby Hartnett, slugging catcher of the Chicago Cubs between 1923 and 1941.

The announcement of the result of the election, conducted by the members of the Baseball Writers Association of America, came after a day-long counting of the ballots in Commissioner Ford C. Frick's office. With only writers of ten or more years of service eligible to vote, a total of 251 ballots was cast. A three-fourths vote, or 189, was necessary for election.

DiMaggio, a brilliant outfielder for the Bombers starting in 1936, had fallen short in two previous elections since his retirement. He made it this time with a decisive count of 223 votes. Lyons was next with 217, followed by Vance with 205 and Hartnett with 195.

Four Named in 1947

This was the first time since 1947 that a cluster of four made it in one election. That year Carl Hubbell, Frankie Frisch, Mickey Cochrane and Bob Grove were chosen.

Only once were there as many as five. That was in 1936, the first year of the Hall of Fame. Then Ty Cobb, Honus Wagner, Babe Ruth, Christy Mathewson

Four Named to Cooperstown Shrine

Joe DiMaggio

Ted Lyons

Dazzy Vance

The New York Times
Gabby Hartnett

and Walter Johnson were picked.

The names of DiMaggio, Lyons, Vance and Hartnett will become enshrined at Cooperstown, N. Y., and swell to 77 the number of diamond immortals in the Hall of Fame.

However, only thirty-five of these have been elected by the writers. The others were chosen by a special old-timers committee that passes on stars of long ago, as well as others who have made notable contributions to baseball.

The scribes vote only on players active within the last twenty-five years. Also ineligible were players who were active within the last five years or in that time had served as managers or coaches. However, when this rule was adopted in 1953, exceptions were made for those who in the last previous election had received 100 or more votes.

But for this neither DiMaggio, who played through 1951, nor Lyons, who coached with the Dodgers last year, would have been eligible. They were the last on the list to receive this special dispensation.

157 Votes For Greenberg

Heading the list of also rans yesterday was Hank Greenberg, former Tiger slugger and now general manager of the Indians. Hank polled 157 votes.

Only three others topped the 100 mark. They were Joe Cronin, a former star shortstop and now general manager of the Red Sox; Max Carey, brilliant outfielder a quarter of a century ago, and Ray Schalk, long a catcher with the White Sox.

Although general interest doubtless ran highest in DiMaggio's third bid to make it, the news that Vance had been elected struck a responsive chord in Brooklyn. The Old Dazzler became the first Dodger to be elected by the writers.

Walter F. O'Malley, Dodger president, immediately sought to communicate with Vance, who lives in Homosassa, Fla. As it later developed, Vance was flagged down by a motorcycle police officer on a highway near his home.

The Daz thought he was about to get a ticket. But the officer said, "I don't know what it's all about, but your house is full of photographers and they are looking for you."

Meanwhile things were moving in Flatbush. Vance was invited

by O'Malley to attend the New York baseball writers' dinner at the Hotel Waldorf-Astoria, while Borough President John Cashmore proclaimed next Monday as Dazzy Vance Day in Brooklyn. At 11:45 Monday morning Vance will receive special honors on Brooklyn's Borough Hall steps.

Hears News En Route Here

DiMaggio likewise received the news "en route." After spending the week-end in Boston, Joe was driving to New York when, stopping for a traffic light, he was recognized by a truck driver, who called to him "congratulations, Joe." DiMaggio then turned on his car radio and got the news in detail.

On arriving here the Clipper exclaimed, "I'm thrilled to death. I played in Cooperstown once in an exhibition game. But this time when I go there it will be something special and you can bet I won't miss it."

DiMaggio was referring to the annual Hall of Fame day held in July when the newly chosen are officially inducted and their plaques hung alongside those of the other immortals.

Curiously, Lyons also was traveling at the moment the announcement was made of his election. He had just left his home in Vinton, La., and was heading for New York and the baseball meetings over the week-end where he hoped to land a job.

Oddly, all four of the latest Hall of Fame entrants curently have no employment in baseball. DiMaggio, who retired as one of the game's highest salaried performers—he drew more than $100,000 in each of his last three seasons—has occupied himself since 1951 chiefly in television and radio.

Vance has been living in Florida, where, since his retirement, he has spent most of his time operating a hotel. Hartnett, who in his last year as a player put in a season with the Giants in 1941, has spent most of his time since then conducting a bowling alley in Chicago.

In the matter of ages, DiMaggio is the youngest of the four. The Clipper turned 40 on last Nov. 14. Lyons and Hartnett are only a few days apart. Ted was 54 on Dec. 28. Gabby hit that figure on Dec. 20. Vance is the oldest. He will be 62 March 4 next.

Although Vance is the first Dodger player to make it—his manager, the late Wilbert Robinson, was chosen by the old-timers' committee in 1945—DiMaggio became the fifth Yankee elected.

The Bombers already enshrined in Cooperstown are Babe Ruth, Lou Gehrig and Herb Pennock, all deceased, and Bill Dickey, who made it with the Giants' Bill Terry and Rabbit Maranville last year. The late Ed Barrow, founder of the Yankee dynasty, was a committee choice in 1953.

In all, the writers voted for sixty-five players yesterday. Among those to draw at least fifty but fewer than 100 votes were such former stars as Eddie Roush, Hank Gowdy, Hack Wilson, Lefty Gomez, Tony Lazzeri, Red Ruffing and Zach Wheat.

The leading players in the Hall of Fame voting:

	Votes		Votes
Joe DiMaggio	223	Hank Gowdy	90
Ted Lyons	217	Hack Wilson	81
Dazzy Vance	205	Lefty Gomez	71
Gabby Hartnett	195	Tony Lazzeri	68
Hank Greenberg	157	Red Ruffing	60
Joe Cronin	135	Zach Wheat	51
Max Carey	119	Ross Youngs	48
Ray Schalk	113	Kiki Cuyler	35
Eddie Roush	97	Rube Marquard	35

Following are sketches of the four players elected to the Hall of Fame:

Joseph Paul DiMaggio

Joseph Paul DiMaggio, a native of San Francisco, appeared headed for stardom virtually from his first game with the Yankees. That was on May 3, 1936. He hit a triple and two singles that day.

From then until he retired at the close of the 1951 campaign Joe was the "big guy" of the Bombers. He put in thirteen seasons with the Yanks, exclusive of three years of military service in World War II.

Joe appeared in ten world series, only one of which the Yankees lost, and he played in eleven All-Star games for the American League. His fifty-one world series games stand as a record.

He compiled a lifetime batting mark of .325 and poled 361 home runs. He was voted the American League's most valuable player three times — 1939, 1941 and 1947. Twice he carried off the league batting crown, in 1939 with a mark of .389 and in 1940 with .352. He also led twice in homers, 1937 with forty-six, and 1948 with thirty-nine.

But perhaps his greatest achievement came in 1941, when he set a major league record of hitting safely in fifty-six consecutive games. The streak began on May 15 and did not end until July 17 in a night game in Cleveland.

Although plagued with injuries throughout his career, the Clipper nevertheless rose to defensive heights that matched his batting prowess. A perfectionist in the field, his flawless style gave him rank as one of the game's greatest center fielders.

Joe was 37 when he retired. Injuries hastened his decision.

Theodore A. (Ted) Lyons

Theodore Amar (Ted) Lyons is one of those rare athletes who stepped off a college campus into a major league uniform.

He signed with the White Sox in 1923, on his graduation from Baylor, and, with time out for three years of World War II service, was a fixture at Comiskey Park until 1948, when he ended a three-year term as manager of the Chicago Southsiders.

In twenty-one seasons of active pitching, Lyons won 260 games while losing 230, a remarkable record considering that the White Sox were a second-division team during most of that period. He won more than twenty games a season three times.

Ted was noted for his pinpoint control, his ability to go the route, his fielding and his hitting. He has record-book listings in all these phases of performance. He pitched a no-hitter against the Red Sox on Aug. 21, 1926. Perhaps his most remarkable achievement was that of 1942. Then 42 years old and working once a week as a "Sunday pitcher," Ted completed all twenty of his starts, compiled a 14-6 record and led the American League with an earned-run average of 2.10.

Born Dec. 28, 1900, at Lake Charles, La., Lyons now makes his home in Vinton, La.

Arthur C. (Dazzy) Vance

Arthur Charles (Dazzy) Vance closed out his career in 1935, but his name still is bright in Brooklyn.

A late-blooming star who did not win a major league game until he was 29 years old, Vance scored all but seven of his eventual 197 victories in the livery of the Dodgers.

He arrived at Ebbets Field in 1922, after unsuccessful trials with the Pirates and Yankees and much kicking around in the minors. Almost at once he became a Flatbush favorite.

One of baseball's greatest fastball pitchers, Dazzy led the National League in strike-outs seven straight years, from 1922 through 1928. He also won the circuit's earned-run title three times, in 1924, 1928 and 1930.

Vance reached his peak in 1924, when he won twenty-eight games while losing only six, fanned 262 batters and had an earned-run average of 2.16. He won twenty-two games each season in 1925 and 1928. He pitched a no-hit game against the Phillies on Sept. 13, 1925.

With much of the fire gone from his high, hard one, the Dazzler was traded to the Cardinals in 1933. He moved on to the Redlegs in 1934 and returned to his beloved Brooklyn the following year to play out his string.

Born in Orient, Iowa, on March 4, 1893, Vance now resides in Homosassa, Fla.

Charles L. (Gabby) Hartnett

Charles Leo (Gabby) Hartnett was a fiery competitor who liked baseball so much that he often wondered out loud why players were paid.

As the National League's top catcher over much of his 1922-1941 career span, Gabby was well-rewarded for his services. He gave value received, with something extra, by catching 100 or more games in twelve seasons, eight of them consecutive.

Besides being an outstanding receiver and handler of pitchers, Hartnett was a formidable slugger. He had a lifetime batting average of .297 and hit 236 home runs.

Gabby's most dramatic four-base wallop was delivered in the twilight of his career. In the final game of the 1938 season, he blasted the ball out of Forbes Field to give the Cubs a pennant-clinching victory over the Pirates.

At the time, Gabby was the manager of the Cubs as well as their catcher. He had succeeded Charley Grimm on July 20, 1938. He continued as pilot the next two seasons, then was released and passed out of the majors as a part-time performer with the Giants in 1941.

Born in Woonsocket, R. I., on Dec. 20, 1900, Hartnett now resides in Chicago.

JOSEPH PAUL DI MAGGIO
NEW YORK A.L. 1936 TO 1951

HIT SAFELY IN 56 CONSECUTIVE GAMES
FOR MAJOR LEAGUE RECORD 1941. HIT 2
HOME-RUNS IN ONE INNING 1936. HIT 3
HOME-RUNS IN ONE GAME (3 TIMES). HOLDS
NUMEROUS BATTING RECORDS. PLAYED IN
10 WORLD SERIES (51 GAMES) AND 11 ALL
STAR GAMES. MOST VALUABLE PLAYER
A.L. 1939, 1941, 1947.

Joe DiMaggio was officially inducted into the National Baseball Hall of Fame in 1955, where this plaque was hung, along with other illustrious Yankees like Babe Ruth, Lou Gehrig, and Bill Dickey.

The National Baseball Hall of Fame at Cooperstown, New York, where memorabilia of Joe DiMaggio's baseball career and his fabled 56-game hitting streak are exhibited along with his plaque of enshrinement.

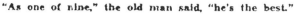

JIMMY CANNON

The long-boned grace was there from the beginning and that shaped his style but the purity was Joe DiMaggio's marvelous talent. The game of baseball was simple for him and he never attempted to make it complicated. He had greatness but he didn't stress it as so many of them do. He never pressed when he didn't have to and this was a beautiful skill.

It was this that made him exceptional, this stately reserve, as though the desperation of the competition should remain a private matter. Never forfeit the natural grace to make a catch appear difficult or was a posture that would encourage applause. He was solemn on a ball field and that was right, too, because baseball was never a humorous matter to DiMaggio.

It stayed pure and so did he and they couldn't bribe him with $100,000 for another season because he was being pulled out of that grace by the time of his life. He held the rages inside, too, and concealed his pride which was immense.

He was running toward Cooperstown the first day he ever chased a baseball because this was a boy formed early to be what he became. It appeared to be a serene talent and untouched by emotion but it wasn't and he was made despondent by temporary failure and was elated by success. He took it out on himself and was cruel about it.

The loneliness was always in him and the shyness and the circus of his fame depressed him. But no one ever had more dignity on a ball field and remember this

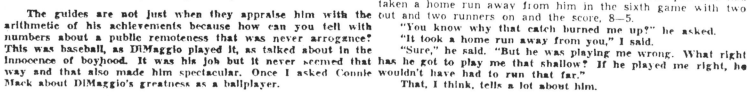

DIMAGGIO

is a place where a lot of them use the sneaky little tricks they call showmanship. There was none of it in DiMaggio and he came to the big leagues that way and that's the way he left.

*   *   *

The guides are not just when they appraise him with the arithmetic of his achievements because how can you tell with numbers about a public remoteness that was never arrogance? This was baseball, as DiMaggio played it, as talked about in the innocence of boyhood. It was his job but it never seemed that way and that also made him spectacular. Once I asked Connie Mack about DiMaggio's greatness as a ballplayer.

"As one of nine," the old man said, "he's the best."

There were guys who played with him for years and considered him a stranger but on the field he was the closest any one ever came to them. He was a ballplayer and this is a game played nine men to a side and that's the way it worked for him. His greatness was part of the whole of the team and the loneliness was defeated because this is where he belonged with eight other guys.

The money was his reward but that purity couldn't be bought. He once turned down a theatrical tour because it would have embarrassed him and I asked him why and he explained he was a ballplayer and not an actor. The game for him was center field and hitting and running the bases and that was all there was to it.

There was a manager's spot open a couple of years ago and I asked the general manager of the club why he didn't hire DiMaggio. The general manager said he didn't think DiMaggio was available and asked me if I could contact him and feel him out.

"You interested?" I asked DiMaggio.

"No," he said, "see if you can send in Lefty O'Doul."

Now he would like to work for a franchise, if the big leagues settled in California, as a front office help. He knows a lot about baseball and I think he could help ballplayers more than any one I know. He never got big-mouthed about it but his feeling for his sport approaches reverence. He loathed the show-boats and the malingerer's because they demeaned baseball.

He enjoyed it but that was also hidden. Sometimes he was cranky and sharp and often he was happy after a game. But that was not part of his performance. He argued with baseball reporters and some he disliked but that was in his last years and he resented going and in those seasons all the interviews concerned his departure.

*   *   *

There were instances when despair seized him and he grieved about his vanishing gifts. One afternoon I watched him in batting practice and he hit flabby pop flies that just fell beyond the infield. He came out of the cage, his face clenched with a sad anger and then he turned to me.

"The old boy can't be that bad," he said but he knew it was going but he still made it pure.

There were pieces in the papers that said he was deliberately hitting the ball to right field. He was a left field hitter and he couldn't get around on the ball and this he knew and the articles amused him.

"I'm hitting to right field," he said, "because I can't hit to left."

*   *   *

I went on a fishing trip with him after the Series of '47. Al Gionfriddo had gone back to the fence of the bull pen and had taken a home run away from him in the sixth game with two out and two runners on and the score, 8—5.

"You know why that catch burned me up?" he asked.

"It took a home run away from you," I said.

"Sure," he said. "But he was playing me wrong. What right has he got to play me that shallow? If he played me right, he wouldn't have had to run that far."

That, I think, tells a lot about him.

In Rome in 1955, Joe DiMaggio poses for a youthful sculptor at Boys' Town, a home for orphans, for which he was helping raise funds.

Joe DiMaggio's second sport — golf.

This is where the classic number 5 hung, from 1936 through 1951. Joe DiMaggio's locker, once a fixture in Yankee Stadium, now stands on display in the National Baseball Hall of Fame in Cooperstown, New York.

A quiet moment in the locker room after an Old-Timers game. Joe DiMaggio regularly took part in these games and still appears at them as one of the game's most honored guests.

Out of baseball, perhaps, but Joe DiMaggio is never out of sight.

At a 1956 exhibition game between Old-Timers from the San Francisco Seals and the Los Angeles Angels of the Pacific Coast League, the three DiMaggio brothers were teamed to handle the outfield chores.

DiMag's No. 5 Brightens St. Pete Scene

Joltin' Joe Returns on 25th Anniversary of Dazzling Debut

From Out of the Past ∴ Famed Yankee ∴ Cuts Up Old Touches

IT WAS LIKE old times when Joe DiMaggio reported at Miller Huggins Field in St. Petersburg, to serve as batting instructor for the Yankees. At left the Yankee Clipper is interviewed by Fred Lieb, former New York baseball scribe and author of the accompanying article. At right, the Hall of Famer holds a reunion with three teammates on the last Yankee team of which he was a member, the 1951 club which won the world's championship in a six-game Series with the Giants. Left to right, they are Yogi Berra, Mickey Mantle and Ralph Houk, now manager of the Yankees.

Graying Ex-Clipper Grabs Spotlight at Bomber Camp

Old-Timers Recall Glory Days as Famed Rapper Steps to Dish and Wallops Drives to Far Reaches of Arena

By FREDERICK G. LIEB

ST. PETERSBURG, Fla.

Old No. 5 is back in Yankee uniform! It is only for a fortnight, but it surely is a pleasant sight seeing Joe DiMaggio, one of the Yankees' all-time greats, take a cut at a ball during batting practice and watch what Dizzy Dean calls a "blue-darter" streak to the outfield.

Yes, Joseph Paul still has the knack that made him one of the game's top hitters. What's more, he still weighs the same 195 pounds that he did when he was in his prime and gets around with the same rhythmic, graceful motion that always characterized his play.

Except for a little more gray hair around the temples, he looks little different from the DiMaggio of 1951, who closed his playing career that year by helping the Yankees win their eighteenth American League pennant and fourteenth World's Series.

The ten years that Joe has been away from baseball, other than an annual appearance in an Old-Timers' game at Yankee Stadium, have taken nothing from his stature as one of the game's foremost stars. Not only is he a Hall of Famer, but one of the upper echelon boys of the Hall. As Pete Sheehy, the Yankees' clubhouse man, put it, "Joe is a real pro; not only in baseball, but in every other way.

"Yes, he's a real pro!"

Joe DiMaggio doffs his cap to the crowd at an Old-Timers game at Yankee Stadium in 1962. There was good reason to cheer him
— he had just hit an inside-the-park home run.

Pips of Tips From Yankee Clipper

'Little Guys Should Carry Big Sticks'--DiMag

Joe Bemoans Shortage of .300 Hitters

Says Clete Boyer Could Add 40 Points to Average If He Forgot About Homers

By TIL FERDENZI
FORT LAUDERDALE, Fla.

Joe DiMaggio, professor-at-large at the Yankee advance training camp, says little men might do well to carry big sticks. The Yankee Clipper isn't knocking home runs and the home-run swing. He just thinks one man's meat is another man's poison.

Joe, one of the gifted few who hit home runs without loss of prestige in the batting average department, says the light bats now in vogue are, "in a lot of cases," knocking points off batting averages.

"A kid comes up and hits two homers one year, so the next season he's whipping those light bats around trying for five," DiMaggio said. "The result usually is the same in these cases. The boy gets to over-swinging and pulling his head off the ball. That throws his timing off-kilter. The home-run swing and the light bats will put balls into the seats now and then, but that's not the formula for a respectable batting average. Not for the average hitter, anyway."

DiMaggio said he didn't want to be cataloged as a professional old-timer.

* * *

McNair Swung Heavy Bat

"The facts are there," he said.

"Back when I was playing ball, which wasn't too long ago, I remember a lot of little guys who swung the bat good enough to hit .300," DiMag said. "Remember Eric McNair? He used to swing around the .300

level. And do you know why he hit for average? He swung a heavy bat, not these light things they use now. He was meeting the ball and going for base-hits.

"McNair was a good example of a line-drive hitter who realized the value of thinking," DiMaggio said. "He knew his capabilities. That's the secret.

"I say leave the home runs to guys who are capable of hitting 25 or more a season—and there are darned few of them.

"After all," the former outfield great added, "you've got to have somebody to get on base so the big guys can knock them around. The way it's getting to be now, though, everybody seems to be swinging with one eye on the seats."

* * *

Tabs Dom as Good Example

It was suggested that a fellow named Dom DiMaggio wasn't such a bad hitter.

"He certainly wasn't," Joe said. "Do you realize Dom's lifetime batting average was .299? And don't forget. It took Dom a couple of years to get himself untracked."

Joe smiled, then pushed his cap back.

"Pardon me if I keep this subject sort of in the family," he said. "But my brother Dom is a good example of what I'm driving at.

"Dom made himself a good hitter," Joe said. "You know why? I'll tell you why. He studied the opposition's weaknesses and then made the most of them.

"He'd see the third baseman playing back and he'd push one down there for a base-hit. Then he learned to hit behind the runner. He played in Fenway Park, yet he never permitted the left field wall to govern his swing.

"In other words," Joe said, "he was thinking. And thinking ball players are rare nowadays. You know what? If a player is the kind of hitter who hits to one field exclusively, he's not a genuine hitter. That proves he's not trying to improve himself."

Joe wanted it made "very clear" that he didn't mean everybody ought to be a .300 hitter.

* * *

Yankees' Winning Tradition 'Seeps Into You,' Says DiMag

FORT LAUDERDALE, Fla. — Joe DiMaggio, a most successful Yankee from 1936 to '51, says it's a little different playing for the Yankees.

"The Yankees have made a tradition out of winning, and when you're on the club, it kind of seeps into you," the Yankee coach said. "It's almost as though you have got to be a winner. It never occurs to you that it's going to be otherwise.

"I guess you would say this team is used to winning," he added. "It's no place for individuals."

More Homers, More Whiffs

FORT LAUDERDALE, Fla. — As Joe DiMaggio pointed out, the rise in home runs has been accompanied by an increase in strikeouts in the major leagues.

Last season, for example, the American League set a record for most players with 100 or more strikeouts, 8. A total of 56 players whiffed on 50 or more occasions during the year.

Too Many .250 Hitters

"It's impossible to think that much," he laughed. "What I do mean is that there shouldn't be so many .250 hitters around as there are now.

"Some of the averages in the majors today are awful," he said. "I can't help but think of a guy like Earle Combs. There was a good hitter. Imagine, he'd lead off and hit around .340."

Joe said the home-run swing was responsible for many strikeouts.

"You've got to protect that plate with two strikes," he said. "Nowadays, too many hitters forget that. They're still going for the home run with two strikes. If they don't get the pitch they're looking for, chances are they'll take it, and there you are, another strikeout."

DiMaggio says the game has "really changed in the last ten or 15 years."

"It's a matter of record that there were more .300 hitters around then," he said. "There were fewer little guys taking that big riffle.

"Where's it all going to end?" Di-Mag exclaimed. "Unless I miss my guess, the cycle will switch the other way.

"This is a definite cycle. Baseball has been like that. I can predict one thing," he said. "Some of these little hitters with home-run ideas will get back to average hitting when enough of them hit under .250. You can bet on that."

• • •

Clipper Used 39-Ounce Bat

DiMaggio recalled he used a 39-ounce bat up to his last few years as a Yankee. Then, when age was beginning to sap some of his strength, he dropped down to a 36-ounce bat. The last home run he hit—in the 1951 World's Series against the Giants—was stroked with a 35-ouncer. Many big home-run hitters today use 32 and 33-ouncers.

DiMaggio was asked if it was possible to make a fair hitter into a good hitter.

"Maybe," he said. "Maybe you can improve him some. The important improvement comes from the hitter himself. He's got to work at it. He's got to work at keeping his head on the ball.

"He's got to work at not over-swinging. He's got to work—period. There is no substitute for work."

Then, as though to emphasize a point.

"What did Cletis Boyer hit last year?" Joe asked.

"He hit .224."

"Now there's a young man who ought to hit more," DiMaggio said. "He's got good, natural ability. He's capable of adding another 40 points or so on that average.

"But there you go again," he said with a grin. "He's got to forget that big, home-run swing."

The Jolter ∴ Takes Swing ∴ at HR Craze

"...AND WHAT AN INSPIRATION HE IS TO THE YOUNGSTERS!"

THE MOST POPULAR FELLOW AT THE YANKEE ADVANCE CAMP IN FT. LAUDERDALE IS JOE DI MAGGIO, THE BATTING IN-STRUCTOR, WHO LOOKS AS IF HE COULD STEP RIGHT BACK INTO THE LINEUP.

MANAGER RALPH HOUK

THAT'S JOE DI MAGGIO!

NO KIDDING! GOSH!

WHERE DO YOU THINK YOU'RE GOING?

HOME!

Joe Used Heavy Bat to Check Swing

FORT LAUDERDALE, Fla.—"It has always been my contention that too many modern big league players swing too hard," Joe DiMaggio said. "You're a patsy for a pitcher if you do that.

"It's hard not to swing from the heels," the Yankee Clipper added, "but whenever I found myself doing that too much, I'd reach for a heavier bat. The heavy bat and the wide stance I used helped me cut down on my swing. When I first broke in, I used a bat that weighed 39 ounces and was 36 inches long. In any big league rack today, you'll find a lot of bats weighing 32 and 33 ounces."

JOE DIMAGGIO receives the Sultan of Swat crown from his old Yankee teammate, Hank Bauer, now Oriole manager.

Foxx, DiMaggio Spur Ticket Sale for Yank Old-Timer Day

Joe DiMaggio

NEW YORK, N. Y.—The Yankees report a brisk advance sale for their annual Old-Timers' Day scheduled for Yankee Stadium, Saturday, July 27.

"We could go around 55,000 for this one," reported Bob Fishel, the Yankees' energetic public relations man.

It is a matter of record that the Yankees have never put on anything but a smash hit on Old-Timers' Day. This one should be no exception.

The motif this year will feature former stars of the game who distinguished themselves by establishing major league records. The list includes folks who need no introduction. For example, Jimmie Foxx, Johnny Vander Meer, Carl Hubbell, Joe DiMaggio and Lefty O'Doul, to name a few.

Foxx will be honored for having hit the most home runs by any righthanded hitter in the history of the game. He socked 534. Vander Meer, of course, will be there because of his consecutive no-hitters. DiMaggio is to be remembered for his 56-game hitting streak and O'Doul for having the highest lifetime batting average of any living former player.

The Yankees and Twins will play following the pre-game ceremonies.   FERDENZI.

★   ★

Jolting Joe Saluted as '39 Swat Sultan

By DOUG BROWN

BALTIMORE, Md.

Even ten inches of snow didn't discourage baseball fans from turning out to see Joe DiMaggio receive a retroactive salute as the 1939 Sultan of Swat at the Tops in Sports banquet here, January 13.

There was a near-capacity crowd in the Lord Baltimore Hotel ballroom when the former Yankee great rose to accept the crown from Hank Bauer, his old teammate and current Oriole manager.

After the people gave him a standing ovation, the band swung into a rendition of "Joltin' Joe DiMaggio." Wearing a smile that flickered between shyness and amusement, DiMag waited until the band finished and prefaced his remarks with:

"Played by Les Brown and written by Les Brown."

Although other stars, including Steve Barber and Hank Aaron, were honored at the affair sponsored by the Maryland Professional Baseball Players' Association, DiMaggio was clearly the hit of the evening.

Jolter Impressed Crowd

But the most impressive thing about the Yankee Clipper's visit here was not so much his mere presence, his great reputation or tremendous crowd appeal.

It was his attitude. True, he was well paid for his trip from the West Coast, but lesser stars have come here and made poor impressions with their ho-hum conduct.

Here was a man who has been through the banquet routine hundreds of times the last 25 years, yet he was attentive, articulate and interested in what other people had to say.

Bauer also received a standing ovation when it was pointed out he was making his first major public appearance as Oriole manager.

"I'm not going to predict a pennant," he said, "but I'm going to say that I hope we can battle Yogi Berra right down to the wire this year."

Barber was honored as the Most Valuable Oriole of 1963 and the Yankees' Johnny Neun received the Scout of the Year award.

Tom Phoebus, a pitcher in the Oriole farm system, was acclaimed as a Star of the Future. The Yanks' Elston Howard was to be honored as the American League's Most Valuable Player, but he was stranded in New York by the snow.

Frisco Opens Its Heart to Favorite Son, DiMag

'Happier Than Any Man Has Right To Be,' Joe Tells 1,100 at 50th Birthday Party

By JACK McDONALD

SAN FRANCISCO, Calif.

Joe DiMaggio, the famed Yankee Clipper of yesteryear, had his 50th birthday party here, November 16, and it was a whopper. Greying, but still trim, erect and dapper, the man who brought great renown to San Francisco and who became baseball's first $100,000 player really packed 'em in.

The Garden Court of the Sheraton Palace Hotel was jammed to its 1,100 capacity and from the moment an opening wire from President Lyndon B. Johnson was read by toastmaster Mel Allen until Joe, with a lump in his throat, climaxed the night with a talk, all in attendance listened with rapt attention.

Joe's closing words were, "I'm proud to have been a Yankee, but I have found more happiness and contentment since I came back home to San Francisco than any man has a right to deserve. This is the friendliest city in the world."

In his earlier remarks he said he felt honored to belong to the rich baseball heritage that is San Francisco's. "No other city can match it. For half a century it has sent legions of diamond greats to the majors and their names became synonymous with pennants, World Series and batting and pitching titles.

* * *

Clipper Deeply Touched

"This night I shall always remember. I feel humble at the sight of this tremendous turnout and am also deeply grateful to those who traveled great distances to share this night with me. It's wonderful. It's heartwarming. How can I ever thank you?"

Together for the first time at a speakers' table were the four DiMaggio brothers—Joe, Tom, Dominic and Vince. All but Tom, the oldest, were major league stars. Tom was a semi-pro infielder on local sandlots but he had to stay home and help his father man the fishing boat to feed the nine hungry mouths in the growing DiMaggio family.

Hundreds converged on the dais to get the DiMag quartet's autographs, but even a bigger target in their

Nerve in Eyelid Kept Joe From .400 Society in 1939

SAN FRANCISCO, Calif. — Joe DiMaggio told the story to friends before the ceremonies began at his fiftieth birthday party. In 1939 he was hitting .412 with three weeks of the season left. Then a nerve in his eyelid started giving him trouble. It made him blink at the plate.

The pennant was all but clinched, but Manager Joe McCarthy said, "If I take you out of the the lineup, they'll say I did it to make you a .400 hitter and they'll call you a cheese champion."

So Joe stayed in. His average dropped 31 points. But he still led the league with .381.

sights were four of the greatest center fielders of the modern era, sitting together—Joe, Dominic, Willie Mays and Mickey Mantle, who succeeded Joe as center fielder with the Yankees.

"It is one of the big experiences of my life, to be sitting next to Joe at his birthday party," Mays told the audience. "He was the greatest. I've tried to do things like him on the field, but there was only one Joe.

"He almost ruined my career when I came to San Francisco to play, because he had set such a high standard for a center fielder in his home town that nobody could match it."

A ten-foot birthday cake, inscribed with Joe's old Yankee number "5," was cut and served to the guests. DiMag received, among other gifts, the keys to a new car, a life membership in the private Presidio Golf Club here, and a "life-sized" gold-plated bat, presented to him by Mantle.

Dom Recalls Joe's Feats

There was much good-natured banter and ribbing. Dom told the crowd, "Joe's bat beat our Red Sox out of half a dozen pennants and World Series, but since some individual did it, I can't begrudge my own brother."

During his talk, Joe told of the year he was battling Hank Greenberg for the league RBI title. "We had al-

ready clinched the pennant and I trailed Hank by only two RBIs, so I decided to try and beat him out," the Clipper said. "We were playing the Red Sox and my own brother made two great catches of hard line drives, as hard as I ever hit any. They cost me six RBIs that day, enough to lose the title.

"Before the game, I had invited Dom to my apartment for dinner. When he came in, he looked a little sheepish. Trying to think of something consoling that would smooth things over, Dom told me, 'Joe, if you had hit those two smashes just one inch farther, I never could have caught either of them.' "

Just before Joe got up to talk, a short film of his great moments at bat and in the field were shown with a series of sequences on his batting form. They had been spliced together by Lew Fonseca in Chicago for the occasion.

The day the films were shot, Joe explained, Fonseca had him at Comiskey Park for two hours before a game so they'd catch "the great DiMaggio" in a perfect swing.

Blanked by White Sox

"I may have looked like the cover boy on The Sporting News Guide in those movies you just saw," said Joe, "but it may interest you to know that right after they were taken, I was horsecollared 0 for 6 by the White Sox."

But Joe wasn't horsecollared at his birthday party. He took his cuts against some of the most talented talkers in the game and he wasn't out-hit in this orators' league.

If he was ribbed, he was also eulogized. His many baseball feats were recalled, as well as some big things he did off the field. One speaker told of the day he walked into a Philadelphia hospital to visit a dying boy, whose idol he was. In his haste, Joe had forgotten to bring along an autographed ball, or some other memento. So he pulled an expensive watch off his wrist, handed it to the boy and said, "This is for you."

Another told of the time Joe flew all the way from San Francisco to Miami to spend a few hours with

FOUR OF THE game's greatest center fielders and four brothers of one of the game's most famous ball-playing families were photographed during Joe DiMaggio's birthday party, November 16. At left, Dominic DiMaggio, Willie Mays, The Jolter himself and Mickey Mantle engage in a round-robin hand- clasp. At right, the DiMaggio brothers, in an infrequent public appearance, line up from left with Tom, Vince, Joe and Dom.

cardiac children at Mending Heart Village. "I'll go, but no publicity," Joe had said. He raised thousands of charity dollars at a dinner that night and a ball game in which he appeared the next day.

Gomez in Top Form

Lefty Gomez, Joe's Yankee roomie, had the audience in an uproar with his many tales about the Clipper.

"As you know, Joe came from a family of great fishermen," Lefty related, "but when I took him out in a boat one day in Florida, I had to bait his hook for him. His first cast boomeranged and the hook caught in the back of his coat."

Recalling an incident that occurred the day Joe's memorable hitting streak of 56 consecutive games was halted in Cleveland on July 16, 1941, Lefty said:

"The two of us took a cab for the park and when we got in, the driver looked at Joe and said, 'You're Joe DiMaggio, aintcha? Well, I got a feelin' you're gonna be stopped cold today.'"

Gomez said he was so mad he ordered the cab stopped and called the cabbie about every name under the sun. "Joe and I got out and walked the rest of the way."

Turned out the cab driver was right. Pitchers Al Smith and Jim Bagby held Joe hitless. "Two balls down the third base line were among the hardest I had hit all during my streak," DiMag recalled. "But Ken Keltner was playing me way back on the grass. He backhanded both drives and threw me out by half a step each time."

Joe, incidentally, after being stopped that day, launched another streak which went 16 games.

Joe recalled another incident when his streak had run to 47 straight games. Johnny Babich of the Athletics obviously wanted the honor of being the first pitcher to stop him. He walked Joe on four straight pitches the first two times at bat.

"The third time he threw three balls, but Joe McCarthy gave me the hit sign anyway. Babich threw one high and away, but I reached out and slammed a shot right between Johnny's legs for a single. I can still see him flat on his face and looking up white as a ghost."

Lefty O'Doul, who got a big hand when introduced, called DiMag a maker of managers. "My first year as manager of the San Francisco Seals (1935), Joe hit .397 and won the pennant for us. So we sent him up to the Yankees for $25,000 and six players, one of the biggest bargains in baseball history.

Just What McCarthy Needed

"Joe McCarthy was known as 'Second-Place Joe' until DiMag arrived. He made a winner of McCarthy."

Del Webb, part-owner of the Yankess, said he had never seen DiMag throw to a wrong base in 13 years with the club.

"I have never revealed this before but doctors told us two years before Joe retired that it would be a miracle if his heel spur injury permitted him to finish out the season. We didn't tell Joe," said Webb.

"The heel would often be as red as a tomato, but he stuck it out for two more seasons. There was never any doubt he was our inspirational leader throughout his 13 years with us."

Gene Autry saluted the Clipper, reminding that at the age of 25 Joe

Series of Wires Hailed Joe, But LBJ's Topped Them All

SAN FRANCISCO, Calif. — Joe DiMaggio received scores of telegrams at his fiftieth birthday party here, including one from his fellow Hall of Famer, Joe Cronin. But the one he prized the most was from President Lyndon B. Johnson.

It read, "Your achievements in baseball have been an inspiration to young people throughout our land. Mrs. Johnson and I am happy to say Happy Birthday to an American sports hero."

poled 46 homers, drove in 167 runs and scored 151.

Besides those already mentioned as guests at the speakers' table were baseballers Horace Stoneham, Ernie Nevers, Herman Franks and Carl Hubbell. Also Lou Spadia, president of the 49er football team; Ken Venturi, the pro golf ace; Freddie Apostoli, former middleweight champion; Bud Poile, coach of the Seals hockey team, and Wilt Chamberlain and Coach Alex Hannum of the NBA basketball Warriors.

Joe's 18-year-old son, Joe, Jr., was unable to attend. He was recuperating from a leg injury in Los Angeles.

Others present included Willie McCovey, Dolph Camilli, Tom Haller, Charlie Silvera, Frank Luchesi, Charlie Walgren, Chub Feeney, Garry Schumacher and Jack Schwarz.

Joe and Dom DiMaggio at an Old-Timers game.

Joe DiMaggio helps to break ground with city officials of Clearwater, Florida, for a park that has been named in his honor.

The Yankee Clipper, the famed number 5, turns 50 in 1964 and is honored at a party in his hometown of San Francisco.

The DiMaggio brothers, Joe and Dom, give some double-barreled batting instruction to a youngster in San Francisco in 1966. Joe batted .325 over his thirteen active years with the New York Yankees, while Dom posted a career average of .298 in his eleven years with the Boston Red Sox.

Joe DiMaggio drives a double to center field in a 1966 Old-Timers game. The catcher is Mickey Owen, infamous for letting a would-be game-winning third strike get away from him in the fourth game of the 1941 World Series. As a result, the Dodgers did not win on that pitch and the Yankees came back to win the game. The umpire is Al Schacht, known as the "Clown Prince of Baseball" for his wacky antics on the baseball field.

Mrs. Robinson

Words and Music by Paul Simon

A song from the film score of *The Graduate*, composed by Paul Simon in 1968, which mentions "Joltin' Joe DiMaggio".

DiMaggio, A's Vice President, Will Be Full-Time Coach, Too

53-Year-Old Yankee Clipper Says Oakland Players Are Eager to Learn

BIRMINGHAM, Ala., April 5 (AP)—Joe DiMaggio, citing a bunch of eager young players, added full-time coaching duties today to his job as vice president of the Oakland Athletics.

"I have become attached to these kids. I have never been around a group so eager to learn," said DiMaggio, who has spent the last five weeks helping the A's with their hitting.

The 53-year-old Hall of Fame member previously had gone to spring training as a batting instructor with the New York Yankees. Until this year he hadn't done anything beyond that in baseball since retiring as a player 17 years ago.

Close to Home

But when the Athletics moved from Kansas City to Oakland, near DiMaggio's San Francisco home, Charles O. Finley, the owner, asked DiMaggio if he would be a vice president.

Then, while here for an exhibition game against Cincinnati, Finley announced the great Yankee Clipper also would serve as a full-time coach.

"The players and I and the other coaches are very happy about this, and I know that Joe is, too," said Manager Bob Kennedy, adding that DiMaggio would sit with him on the bench and not be on the coaching lines.

DiMaggio said he saw no conflict between his front-office duties and his job on the field.

"Bob Kennedy is my boss," he said. "Whatever he wants me to be, I'll be."

Many baseball people were surprised when DiMaggio agreed to go with Finley in the first place. They thought if he ever

Associated Press
Joe DiMaggio

got back into the game more actively than just as a part-time batting instructor, it would be with the Yankees.

But DiMaggio said the Yankees never had offered a job to him and the Yankees countered that Joe never had indicated he was willing to return to an active status.

Possibly the biggest factor in his return was the proximity of the A's to his home. "It's only 25 minutes away," he said.

Suited up again, this time as a coach for the Oakland A's in 1968, Joe DiMaggio talks baseball with onetime sportscaster and then California governor, Ronald Reagan.

DiMag to Hang 'Em Up as Coach After This Season

By RON BERGMAN

OAKLAND, Calif.—Joe DiMaggio says this definitely will be his last year as a coach for the Athletics.

"Despite the enjoyment I've had, the deal was only for one year," DiMag said. "Of course, I've got a two-year contract. I expect to go to spring training with the club."

The old Yankee Clipper was hired originally as an executive vice-president, but was asked by Manager Bob Kennedy to travel with the A's as a coach this season.

What DiMag will do next year for the A's is unclear. Although he has an impressive title, he doesn't have a desk or a secretary.

"I'll play it by ear," DiMaggio said when asked about his 1969 plans with the A's organization.

Finley Vague on Subject

"We'll cross that bridge when we come to it," said Owner Charlie Finley.

In any case, being a coach in uniform this year has enabled DiMaggio to escape a desk job with vague responsibilities and ill-defined duties and make a real contribution to the team.

It may sound a trifle corny, but his mere presence has inspired the young A's players, who hold him in high esteem, but not the overwhelming awe they showed him when he first appeared in spring training.

"It was a feeling-out process," DiMag said about those first days. "They didn't know what to expect. But this is what happens when you join a new organization."

During the spring, DiMag worked mainly with the outfielders on all phases of the game. Other players got hitting tips.

"Now, I talk to the players, give them little helpful hints," said Joe. "Hitting is something they'll have to learn themselves. They've just got to see more pitching.

Big Uplift From DiMag

"I just try to give them some little hints so they can start thinking with the pitchers, so they won't be so anxious with men on base."

Kennedy, an excellent teacher of young players, of course deserves the largest amount of credit for the surprise showing of the A's so far. But DiMag has been a definite factor.

"Improvement has shown in so many ways in everything, since the spring," said DiMag. "It's hard to believe that this team has improved so much."

DiMag actually is the biggest star on the A's. He has been the subject of numerous magazine articles since the season began.

He is the main object of attention in the nine other American League parks. He gets standing ovations when he is introduced, television and radio men line up to interview him and he signs hundreds of autographs.

"I enjoy the travel," he said. "I haven't made some of these cities, like Anaheim and Minneapolis. Of course, going back to New York gives me a chance to see my old friends, although I do travel on my own, too."

Perhaps the biggest thrill was hitting one out of County Stadium in Milwaukee in batting practice before a White Sox game.

Still Likes to Hit 'Em!

"That would have been a home run in Yankee Stadium," said Jolting Joe, obviously pleased with the belt.

Even at the age of 53, it still feels good to put one in the seats.

A's Acorns: Although only a rookie, A's relief pitcher Ed Sprague was given a "day" at the Oakland Coliseum July 28 and received a new car. He's from Hayward, a community nearly adjacent to Oakland. . . . Trainer Billy Jones has quit after eight years, effective at the end of the season. . . . Charlie Finley's latest gim-

Joe DiMaggio

mick involved a retired railroad engineer in left-center field who rings a railroad bell for rallies, home runs and the like. . . . Out-of-town sports writers will be interested to know that Col. Sanders, himself, visited the Coliseum July 26 and ate in the pressroom where his fried chicken is served every night. He had meat loaf.

Campy Campaneris raised his average 19 points with 15 hits in 33 at-bats on a seven-game trip and also added five stolen bases to his major league high total. . . . Sal Bando also began to raise his average by going 15 for 31 in one stretch. . . . The A's players really enjoyed their one-night stand in Milwaukee, perhaps because of the excellent food in the clubhouse after the game against the White Sox. . . . Catcher Jim Pagliaroni, who suffered a broken bone in his right wrist June 9 when hit by a pitch from Baltimore's Eddie Watt, was re-activated July 28 and first baseman Ramon Webster was optioned to Vancouver.

Autographing a ball at one of the numerous Old-Timers games which Joe DiMaggio has attended since retiring from the game in 1951.

50,945 JAM STADIUM
Oldtimers Thrill Fans; Yankees Win

A Couple of Fair-Haired Boys. Uncovered for the National Anthem, Joe DiMaggio shows a silvery pate and Mickey Mantle shows the same old blond thatch at Yankee Stadium's Oldtimers' Day game yesterday. Among highlights: Bob Feller struck out Mantle. Oldtimers played scoreless tie. —*Stories on page 34*

NEWS photo by Frank Hurley

DiMaggio at 59 still a hero

By Pat Harmon

SPORTS EDITOR

JOE DiMAGGIO

MARCO ISLAND, FLA.: Joe Di-Maggio's hair is white, and he rides a golf cart. Otherwise, there are no concessions to age. He is 59 but he weighs only three pounds more than he did when he set the incredible record.

In 1941 DiMaggio made at least one base hit in 56 consecutive baseball games. A poll of sports editors in 1970 deemed this the most remarkable athletic achievement of the 20th century, so far. It is the least attainable of any record in any sport.

They talk now of Henry Aaron and his pursuit of Babe Ruth's home run total, but Ruth had many homerless games between his big hits, and Aaron has them, too. DiMaggio had to deliver something every day. He could not stop. When he did, the record was ended.

The man did more than set a record. He batted .325, lifetime. He was a great base runner and a certain fielder. The Yankees have been in business 71 years, but this is the only man who earned the name Yankee Clipper. He got it because he sailed so smooth, they said.

He played from 1936 through 1951, with three years out for war, and he was the nation's hero. People wrote songs about him. In 1941, Les Brown recorded "Joltin' Joe DiMaggio," and it was a smash. As recently as 1965, in the movie, "The Graduate," his name comes alive again as Simon and Garfunkle sing, "Where have you gone, Joe DiMaggio? . . . Joltin' Joe has left and gone away."

JOLTIN' JOE was not left and gone away when they teed up here this week for the Tony Lema Memorial Golf Tournament. The Tony Lema is the best one-day pro-amateur show in the country, an 18-hole event that brings in the top pro golfers plus celebrities. The field at Marco Island included the coaches of the No. 1 pro and No. 1 college football teams—Don Shula of the Miami Dolphins and Ara Parseghian of Notre Dame. From thoroughbred racing came Eddie Arcaro and Walter Blum, from harness racing Del Miller. Baseball alumni included Joe Garagiola, Ralph Kiner, John Mize, and Roger Maris. Current football stars included Bob Griese, Ed Podolak, and Terry Bradshaw.

DiMaggio had the biggest gallery at the first tee. It may have been because the spectators seem-ed to be of the age who would have remembered DiMaggio's best years. He was on 10 championship teams.

In his day Joe was a shy guy who would sit in the locker room an hour after the game so he wouldn't have to face the fans who massed outside. He never could understand why strangers wanted to walk up to Joe DiMaggio and tell him what a hero he was.

At 59 the shyness is not so apparent. DiMaggio's gentleness stood out as he signed autographs at all 18 holes. He talked with strangers at every tee.

JOE SHOOTS a fair game of golf. A score of 85 pleases him. He is in demand for all the pro-ams, the ones put on by Bing Crosby, Bob Hope, Jackie Gleason, and—as here at Marco—Frank, Bob and Elliott Mackle.

"But I'm getting tired," he said. "I think I'll cut down on my golf."

He has been in Florida for a month, playing in one pro-am after another. Next week he will be home in San Francisco. He may go out in his boat named the Yankee Clipper. "It's a 36-footer," he said, "and I let my brother Tom handle it. He knows where the best fishing is."

There were five brothers—Tom, Mike, Vince, Joe and Dom, in that order. The three youngest made the major leagues. Joe was the best, and he's remembered for class. He never got into a clubhouse argument with teammates, and he played 1700 games without being chased by an umpire.

The nearest he came to getting into a fight with an ump was when one of them called a third strike on Joe during his 56-game streak. Joe looked back at the ump. And the ump blurted, "I swear, Joe, that ball was right over the middle." The ump grinned at Joe. Joe nodded, grinned back and walked away.

JOE NEVER COULD understand the questions put to him by the press. He had such a smooth style, no one knew how he could jolt so many home runs. "They keep asking me where my power comes from, and I'm worried because I can't explain it," Joe told Lefty Gomez.

"That's no worry," replied Gomez. "If they ever ask you where your power went, then you can worry about it."

Joe savors the life of a part-time golfer and boatman. He has turned down chances to be a manager, to work for the commissioner's office, to be someone's employe. He wants no pressure, no aggravation. He takes no orders. He reports to no one.

Joe has been married twice. His first wife was Dorothy Arnold, a Broadway celebrity. The marriage lasted from 1939 to 1944. (Their son, Joe Jr., is 32.) The second marriage was to Marilyn Monroe. It also ended in divorce.

Joe is handsome, quiet, and modest. He is everything a hero should be at 59. He does TV commercials for a New York bank. Last month he was in New York and a man and woman passed him on the street.

He heard the woman say, "That face is familiar. I think that is . . ."

Joe turned to hear what she might say. He thought she would finish the sentence, ". . . Joe DiMaggio."

All she said was, ". . . the man in the bank commercials."

The Tony Lema Tournament lasted 18 holes here. When all the scores were put together, the winning team was headed by that old, familiar name—Joe DiMaggio. It was a foursome, and their best-ball score with handicaps was 56. It was a nice figure, just like his record.

Five Yankee Hall of Famers queue up in the dugout at Yankee Stadium during a 1974 Old-Timers game: from the left, Mickey Mantle, Yogi Berra, Whitey Ford, Joe DiMaggio, and Casey Stengel.

The Yankee Clipper demonstrates that he still has the swing of a champion as he connects with one at an Old-Timers game in the 1970s.

Joltin' Joe pays a visit to Yankee Stadium during a massive renovation of the edifice in the mid-1970s.

DiMag, at 60, Still a Beloved Living Legend

By MAURY ALLEN

NEW YORK—That glistening black hair, combed straight back, is styled neatly in a $10 razor cut now all silver and gray. There is some fleshiness around the neck and chin, some slight paunch around the middle. The nose is prominent, as always, the voice, deep and thick, the walk, graceful, the manner, commanding, the presence, overwhelming.

Joe DiMaggio, 60 years old on November 25, is more strikingly handsome now than he was 30 years ago.

"Even now when he comes back for Old-Timers' Day and he walks into the clubhouse," said Yankee clubhouse man Pete Sheehy, a Yankee since 1927, "he makes the room light up."

At 60, his face on television often for the Bowery Savings Bank in New York, for Mr. Coffee, at this charity event or that, playing golf here or appearing there, DiMaggio is more famous, more recognized, certainly more loved, than he ever was as one of the game's greatest players.

HE LAST PLAYED in 1951 and, unlike the bitter retirement of Babe Ruth or the reclusive retirement of Ted Williams, except for his unhappy managerial tour, DiMaggio has become a giant figure on the American landscape, a legend that seems to span the past and the future, a true, untarnished, unspoiled American hero. Maybe the last American hero.

For more than a year now in researching a book on DiMaggio, appropriately enough entitled "Where Have You Gone, Joe DiMaggio?" to be published by E. P. Dutton next spring, I have interviewed some 200 people from Sicily to San Francisco, from Los Angeles to New York, from Westwood to the West Bronx. The measure seems the same. Incredibly private, slightly mysterious, he is universally loved by friends and tenderly loved by fans.

"Joe hasn't changed much over the years," said his pal, Lefty Gomez. "He's still a man of mystery. I played golf with him at the Ladies Pro-Am in Las Vegas last year and I was going to meet him for a drink after the round. I asked the bartender if he had seen Joe in the last hour. 'No, but I've seen Howard Hughes four times.' "

GOLF IS HIS passion now, an 18-handicap golfer, who enjoys the game, does well, but hasn't the dedication on the golf course he had on the baseball field.

"I once asked Joe what made him great," said Edward Bennett Williams, the famed Washington attorney and president of the Washington Redskins. "He said he burned in his belly to excel. He once told me he played as hard before 5,000 people at old Sportsman's Park against the Browns as he did before 70,000 in Yankee Stadium. 'I have to, Ed. There might be a kid out there who will see me only this one time. I owe it to him.' "

In his retirement, unlike so many other baseball greats, DiMaggio has protected his image, his obligation to the public, his heroic station.

Tom DiMaggio is Joe's older brother, a 70-year-old smaller picture of the Yankee Clipper. He runs the family restaurant on Fisherman's Wharf in San Francisco, a tourist landmark since 1937.

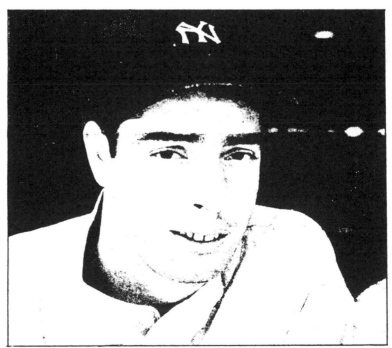

Joe DiMaggio in 1940 Pinstripes . . .

"I don't know why I keep the place going," he said. "I probably should close it. We don't need it any more. I guess we just feel an obligation. We feel people come out here, they want to see the place, remember what it was, maybe see Joe if he's in town."

A sense of obligation, a sense of loyalty, a sense of owing something to the legend seems to drive DiMaggio. It becomes clearer perhaps when one thinks back to the fall of 1951, when DiMaggio had played his last game as a Yankee, and Dan Topping and Del Webb asked him to reconsider his plans and play another year for another $100,000. DiMaggio had a bad back and bad knees, but he still could squeeze another season out of the body that had given baseball so much. Instead, he quit.

"WHY?" I ASKED his brother Tom, as he sipped coffee and looked out at the small fishing boats across the wharf. "Why didn't he play another year?"

Tom DiMaggio paused and looked away. Then he turned back and said softly, "He quit because he wasn't Joe DiMaggio anymore."

This fierce pride, this dedication to excellence, this burning passion to be the best, dominated his playing career and commands his retirement.

"I remember when he played," said Toots Shor, the famed New York restaurateur. "If he had a good day, he would come into the joint, have a belt and relax. If he was oh-for-four and the Yankees lost, he would stay outside and send the doorman in. 'Joe's out there.' I'd go out and we'd walk for blocks without a word. He couldn't stand losing. If the Yankees lost and he didn't hit, he always figured it was his fault."

DiMaggio left the Yankees in 1951, worked as a television broadcaster for them for a while, spent some years in spring training as a batting instructor, signed on with Charlie Finley to increase his pen-

. . . And as He Neared 60th Birthday

sion take-home pay in 1968 and lost his last chance at a return to baseball in 1973 when an ownership situation with the Yankees foundered.

"I'm through with baseball," said DiMaggio, one day last spring as he sat at a table during a break at the Doral in Miami. "I talked to the commissioner about a position and when it came to finalizing it, the deal was embarrassing. I don't like to be embarrassed. Then the ownership thing with the Yankees came up. They said they would get back to me. They never did."

AT 60, HEALTHY, handsome and financially independent, Di-Maggio can pick and choose his spots, play golf to his heart's content, relax with old friends in San Francisco and New York, stay aloof and removed from some of the swirling gossip about his past

It was not unlike DiMaggio that he would refuse to talk to Norman

Mailer about Marilyn Monroe or that we both understood the ground rules of a DiMaggio interview: no mention of Marilyn.

In a way, the loyalty, dedication and martyred bereavement he has shown for the past 12 years for his late wife is typical of the man. Suffering is a private matter. Denial of gossip about her would be tasteless.

DiMaggio, at 60, off the field, is what he was at 30, on the field, stylish, graceful, in complete command, a man for all seasons.

His career was brilliant. His retirement has been dignified. The legend is intact.

"I remember once we went to a fight with Ernest Hemingway," said Edward Bennett Williams. "The kids swarmed all over Joe. 'Sign this, Joe, sign here, please Joe.' Everybody ignored poor Papa. Joe DiMaggio was America's greatest hero."

Joe DiMaggio still is.

Joe DiMaggio poses with former cowboy movie star and present-day owner of the California Angels, Gene Autry.

Joe DiMaggio displays the baseball signed for him by U.S. President Ronald Reagan and Soviet leader Mikhail Gorbachev at the historic summit meeting in 1988 at the White House.

Another Hall of Fame center fielder, Willie Mays, cannot find a paunch on Joe DiMaggio at an Old-Timers game at Shea Stadium in New York in 1975. Mays hit 660 home runs in his 20-year career with the Giants in New York and later San Francisco, the third most in baseball history after Hank Aaron and Babe Ruth.

'Cooperstown South': DiMaggio 5th Hall of Famer in Oldtimers

By JACK ELLISON
St. Petersburg Times Staff Writer

Never far from a baseball.

The annual Oldtimers Baseball Game at Al Lang Stadium is also "Cooperstown South" because of the many Hall of Famers who have participated in the March of Dimes benefit.

In the previous 23 games, a total of 18.

This year's 24th game happily will be no exception.

Five members enshrined at the Cooperstown Hall will either play or take a bow Saturday at the 1:30 p.m. baseball funtime.

They are Edd Roush, Al Lopez, Ralph Kiner, Early Wynn and

Joe DiMaggio.

The inimitable Yankee Clipper is in the area on an annual appearance at a Clearwater youth benefit and Oldtimers' co-chairman Frank Schnorrbusch said Thursday night the renowned Yankee Clipper, also known to younger generations as "Mr. Coffee", will interrupt his schedule to throw out the first ball. It will repeat an appearance he made here three years ago — one, you might expect, which was greeted by a standing ovation.

Roger Maris also is scheduled to be introduced — for the second straight year — and, as Mel Allen, the renowned former Yankee broadcaster, would say if on hand, "How ABOUT that . . . two of the greatest names in a great Yankee history."

Joe DiMaggio is scheduled to throw out the first ball for the Hall-of-Fame hallowed Oldtimers Game at Al Lang Stadium Saturday.

And with three other noted sluggers — Kiner, Ted Kluszewski and Frank Howard — set to play, the waterfront stadium should take on a homey atmosphere for lovers of the home run.

Tickets ($3 box seat, $2 grandstand) for the game, which features former stars living in the area as well as coaches here for spring training, are on sale today at March of Dimes, 3144 34th St. N; Chamber of Commerce, 225 4th St. S; Egerton & Moore, 300 Central Ave.; Bill Hulse Sporting Goods, 7100 5th Ave. N.

With some Los Angeles Dodgers: from DiMaggio's left, manager, Tommy Lasorda; Hall of Fame pitcher, Sandy Koufax; and scout, Ed Liberatore.

DiMaggio: Still a Marquee Moniker

Joe D. Is Remembered Fondly—36 Years Following His Last At-Bat

By DWIGHT CHAPIN

SAN FRANCISCO—It's hard to believe, since he has aged so gracefully, but Joe DiMaggio turned 72 last November. Even harder to believe, he now has a pacemaker, which was installed in February to correct a balky heartbeat.

"I was down in the Florida Keys, fishing, for a few days after the Super Bowl," DiMaggio was saying. "I felt a little shortness of breath one night, and the next day I was tired and had to sit down after walking up some flights of stairs. The surgery was easy. The doctor went in with a laser, and everything is OK now. I feel fine.

"I can do pretty much what I want. I have arthritis all over—arms, legs, back—but I like to stay active. I still play golf and walk to exercise, and I pick up and take off whenever I want."

DiMaggio was at Bay Meadows Race Track, where he is often a visitor when he is in San Francisco, and where people are ever so respectful of him and the privacy he has always sought.

But they notice him, the bettors and the waiters and the elevator operators. While he nursed a second cup of weak, decaffeinated coffee—one-third coffee, two-thirds water—a guy in the men's room was saying:

"Joe looks good, doesn't he? You'd sure never know he'd had surgery."

DiMaggio had a fat sack of autograph requests he had brought to the track to answer, but he is a man of his word. He had agreed to an interview and he settled into an extended afternoon of reminiscing. Race after race passed without him placing a bet, and only occasionally did he look out to see which horse was going across the finish line first.

It is 1987, but Joe DiMaggio was temporarily lost in the '30s, and beyond.

He apologized for his recall, saying he's terrible with names. But, in truth, he seems to have forgotten nothing.

He thinks back to the North Beach playground, not far from where he grew up, and playing baseball or basketball or tennis with the kids from around the block. Those kids included Freddie Apostoli, world middleweight boxing champion-to-be, and budding basketball star Hank Luisetti.

"There was no grass," DiMaggio said. "We played on asphalt, with a big ball—a softball—but we threw it overhand and played regular baseball rules. Later on, when I was 11 or 12, I started playing with older fellas, guys in their 20s. I guess they saw something in me."

From 14 to 16, he didn't even play baseball, because he wasn't particularly interested. Then Rossi Olive Oil, a Class B semipro team, was looking for a shortstop, and somebody said, "Hey, why not get Joe DiMaggio?"

In the playoffs that year, he hit two home runs against Maytag Washing Machines, and his team won the league championship.

"They gave us little hollow gold baseballs—for watch fobs or belt trinkets," he said. "It was the first award I ever got in baseball."

The next year—1932—DiMaggio moved up to the "A" league "with the real big boys" on Funston Field, and was given his first pair of new spikes for having the highest season batting average. "Six hundred and something," he said.

When his Sunset Produce team finished the season, the San Francisco Seals of the Pacific Coast League were still playing.

"Augie Galan got permission to go to Hawaii with Henry Oana to play in a couple of exhibition games, and the Seals were left without a shortstop," DiMaggio said. "A bird dog named Spike Hennessy used to watch the sandlot kids play, and he asked my brother Vince, who was already with the Seals, if I would mind coming out and playing the last three games of the season with them."

DiMaggio smiled. "Like I was going to turn it down," he said.

He had no doubts about his ability as a hitter.

"I used to watch the PCL fellas play at Recreation Park. I saw Howard Craighead of Oakland, who was supposed to be one of the best in the league, throw and I knew I could hit his stuff. But I didn't run around telling people so."

His first at-bat was against veteran Ted Pillette.

"Frankly, I wasn't nervous," he said. "A little tense just being in the ball game, maybe, but not nervous."

DiMaggio tripled to right center. His fielding was not as unqualified a success, however. He might have killed somebody if he had remained at shortstop.

"I've still yet to throw anybody out from there," he said. "My arm was very, very strong—strong enough to break the seats back of first base—but not at all accurate. As the series went on, no fans would sit over there. I wound up the season 2 for 9 batting, but I never did count the errors.

The next year, after training camp, the Seals offered him a contract. "My brother Tom had to put it together for me," DiMaggio says. "I wasn't yet 18."

The package included a bonus. "Two suits," DiMaggio said. "And Tom got both of them. I wound up with nothing. I wasn't even reimbursed the 30 cents I spent in streetcar fare to get to the park to sign. I remember how much it was

because nickels were very hard to come by then."

DiMaggio got $225 a month, and a contract stipulation that the Seals couldn't send him to a lower league.

He had never traveled much before. "I think the longest distance I'd ever gone was when my family moved from Martinez to San Francisco when I was 11 months old," he says. "I was very lonesome at first on the road. I missed the old gang."

And he'd undergone some changes that startled Seals Owner Charley Graham.

"I'd grown several inches—too fast," DiMaggio said. "Graham said I looked like a young fawn chasing the ball, legs going every which way."

But once he got into the starting outfield early that season, he was

there to stay. He hit .340 in 1933, .341 in 1934 and .398 in 1935. In 1933, he set a PCL record with a 61-game hitting streak.

He was oblivious to pressure during that streak—unlike the pressure of 1941, when the Yankee Clipper set the lasting major league mark of 56 straight.

"I didn't know what pressure was in '33," DiMaggio said. "I just went about my work every day. But I do remember in one key game there were a lot of people on the field, including about 15 flash photographers, and after I swung and missed on the first pitch, Charley Graham came running onto the field, hollering at the photographers, 'Get out of here! You're blinding him.' I guess maybe they were. When they left, I got a hit."

On the final day of the 1935 season, DiMaggio went 8 for 10 in a doubleheader, losing the PCL championship by a single point to Ox Eckhardt of the San Diego Missions.

Joe certainly looked ready for the major leagues as the New York Yankees purchased his contract from the Seals.

"My first time up in training camp at Miller Huggins Field in 1936," DiMaggio said, "Bump Hadley threw me a pitch right on the fists, and I hit a ticky-ticker to shortstop. The next day the writers said, 'So this is the great phenom.' "

Memory is suddenly sweet, and DiMaggio smiled at what happened after that inauspicious beginning.

"I caught on," he said.

It has been 36 years since Joe DiMaggio's last time up in the major leagues, but his name is still right at the top of the marquee wherever he goes. And he goes plenty of places.

He lives in Florida and is in the Bay Area once in a while but, he said, "I think I spend six months a year on an airplane. One day I may say, 'That's enough,' but I've traveled all my life."

He no longer represents Mr. Coffee but he still works for the Bowery Bank in New York, and he frequently attends black-tie dinners and youth fund-raisers.

"I don't do as much for pay as I used to," he said. "Actually, I could have stopped working 20 years ago. I didn't make a whole lot of money playing baseball or doing commercials, but I made some good investments. I turn down an awful lot of things. I've never overexposed myself. I work to maintain my privacy.

"Take my years with the Yankees. We had our fun, believe me—

but we did it discreetly. I remember one night I went to the International Club to see the late show and when I tried to duck out the back when it was over, I ran smack into Walter Winchell. Of course, he wanted to know what I was doing out so late when I had a doubleheader tomorrow, and I thought I was dead. But I tied a record with three triples the next day and all Walter wrote was, 'Saw Joe DiMaggio on Broadway and he told me three triples are harder to hit than one home run. . . .' "

During his recent health crisis, DiMaggio said, "I was in the hospital in Florida five days before people realized I was there. The only reason they knew at all is because the hospital announced it the day I was getting out."

That need to shield, to protect DiMaggio, still extends into subjects like his marriage to Marilyn Monroe. "I've never thought that anybody's business but my own," he said.

Clearly, he is not happy that author Roger Kahn has made it public business in his book, "Joe and Marilyn."

"It's pretty bad," DiMaggio said. "I haven't read it, but a friend has read parts of it to me, and 90 percent of what I've heard is untrue. I don't think I've ever even talked to Roger Kahn. He probably wrote it because he needed a buck. I can take a knock when I have to, but when things are said that are untrue, I don't like it at all. I'd have to be an idiot to say I do."

He was into his third cup of decaff now, his mood softening. Many of the people who have been close to him—people like his brother Vince, San Francisco restaurateur Reno Barsocchini and other childhood pals—have died. There is no one to confirm a lot of things about Joe DiMaggio but himself.

After all these years, he says he still doesn't know why people sense a unique aura about him.

"I don't have a coherent answer for that," he said. "I don't try to knock people, hurt their feelings or beat them out of money, but I also haven't tried to create or maintain an image."

There is, he concedes, a burden in being Joe DiMaggio, an enduring American icon.

In his fashion, he has tried to remain accessible, and that accessibility has increased as he has aged. He is less shy now, mellower, more consistently personable.

When fans ask for autographs, for example, he almost always accommodates them.

"I must have signed hundreds of thousands of times," he said. "I have six bags of letters that have accumulated now, and I'll sign everything that comes with a stamped return envelope."

After all these years and all those signatures, he is still concerned about what people will think of him if he refuses a request.

"If I don't sign," he said, "I know they're going to call me a fathead."

Which, for Joe DiMaggio, would be even harder to handle than being called a hero.

Joe DiMaggio still gets headlines wherever he goes, more than three decades after he left the major leagues.

The Yankee Clipper, Joe DiMaggio.

ACKNOWLEDGMENTS

The contents of *The DiMaggio Albums*, which include such material as articles, excerpts, news items, photographs, cartoons, program covers, statistics and tables, and memorabilia, have been elicited from a variety of sources, both public and private. The publisher and compiler gratefully appreciate the assistance and cooperation rendered by the many collectors, institutions, newspapers, magazines, book publishers, and others who are represented in these albums.

Every attempt has been made to identify and obtain permission from the various copyright holders, but in certain cases this has proven impossible. The publisher would be pleased to hear from anyone who has claim to acknowledgment in regard to the materials used in these albums.

The publisher and all others concerned express their appreciation to the following and hereby acknowledge them as sources of the materials used in *The DiMaggio Albums*.

Printed Matter
Associated Press: 31, 48, 114, 123, 124, 125, 186, 191, 196, 197, 213, 231, 239, 240, 296, 317, 327, 351, 389, 400, 451, 453, 455, 460, 465, 469, 489, 490, 496, 515, 619, 681, 692, 703, 712, 739, 774
Baseball Digest: 356–7, 360–1, 462–3, 570–1, 606–7
Cleveland Plain-Dealer: 182, 352, 639
Contemporary Books: 115, 175, 233, 281, 390, 444, 523, 620, 682, 734. *The World Series Illustrated Almanac*, copyright © 1984 by Richard Whittingham. Published in arrangement with Contemporary Books Inc.
Estate of Grantland Rice: 410, 632, 665
NEA Inc.: 40
New York Daily News: 66. © 1936 New York News Inc. Article by Stuart Rogers, reprinted with permission
New York Herald Tribune: 367, 535, 658
New York Journal-American: 61, 67, 68, 262, 474, 738
New York Post: 555, 579, 641, 643, 646, 707, 711, 715, 759. Reprinted by permission of *New York Post*
New York Times: 29, 45, 86, 110, 114, 126, 137, 153, 170, 174, 189, 191, 192, 195, 197, 202, 214–5, 227, 228, 231, 232, 240, 244, 247, 250, 261, 265, 266, 268, 275, 277, 279, 280, 291, 294, 295, 297, 299, 310, 311, 331–2, 339–40, 350–1, 365, 384, 388–9, 399, 439, 441, 475–6, 515, 521, 526, 532, 533, 537–8, 545, 562, 568–9, 572, 580, 585, 595, 599, 600–1, 615, 616, 619, 625, 647–50, 662, 663, 664, 680–1, 706, 716, 755–6. Copyright © 1934/36/37/38/39/40/41/42/46/47/48/49/50/51/55 by The New York Times Company. Reprinted by permission
New York World-Telegram: 18, 31, 33, 34, 35, 41, 44, 46, 50, 51, 52, 55, 56, 58, 60, 62, 63, 64–5, 69, 70, 71, 73, 74, 75, 76, 79, 81, 83, 84, 87, 96, 100, 101, 119, 131, 132, 134, 135, 138, 142, 143, 155, 158, 164, 187, 190, 193, 199, 204, 213, 239, 245, 246, 257, 263, 284, 288, 290, 291, 293, 294, 298, 312, 316, 318, 319, 321, 323, 334, 362, 368, 369, 370, 371, 392, 396, 397, 410, 415, 416, 421, 423, 425, 433, 450, 464, 467, 490, 491, 492, 495, 496, 534, 543, 636, 637, 638, 666, 678, 689, 696, 697, 699, 700, 701, 702, 705, 710, 718, 752
Rand McNally & Co.: 116, 176, 234, 282, 391, 445, 524, 621, 683, 735. *The World Series* by John Devaney and Burt Goldblatt, copyright 1972
Random House Inc.: 511. *The Red Smith Reader*, copyright 1982
San Francisco Examiner: 15, 788
Sport Magazine: 553–4, 596–8, 633–5, 686–8
Sports Products Inc.: 108–9, 111–3, 170–3, 227–9, 231, 275–6, 278, 380–3, 385, 438, 440–3, 508, 510, 512, 514, 517, 521, 612–3, 617–8, 670, 674, 679, 721–3, 731–2. *The World Series* by Richard M. Cohen, David S. Neft, Gordon A. Deutsch (St. Martin's Press), copyright 1979
St. Petersburg Times: 786

INDEX

Pages 1–400 are in Volume 1, 401–800 are in Volume 2. Numbers in italics refer to illustrations. Where a color plate is referred to, the entry reads, for example: *facing* 193, or *between* 376–77.

A

Abbaticchio, Ed, 87
Advertisements, *facing* 193, *facing* 225, 295, *facing* 345, *facing* 753
Alexander, Babe, 673
All-American baseball team (1941), 392
Allen, Johnny, 75, 206, 209, 214, 216, 305, 311
Allen, Mel, 515, 538, 602, 745, 786
All-star games, *146*
  1933, 343
  1936, 85, *90, 91,* 92–94
  1937, 141, *144,* 145, *145,* 147, *148,* 149–51
  1938, 205–6, *207,* 208–9, *208, 210–11*
  1939, 206, *251–52,* 254–56
  1940, 206, 293, *302,* 303–7
  1941, *336,* 339–43, *344*
  1942, *427,* 428–29, *429–31,* 431, 432
  1946, *483*
  1947, 496, *497–99,* 499–500
  1948, *546, 547,* 548–50, *549*
  1949, *586,* 587–91, *588, 589, 591, 592*
  1950, *651,* 653–56, *653, 654, 656*
  1951, *708, 709*
  DiMaggio's statistics in (1936–50), 744
All-star teams
  1939, 238, *283*
  1942, 446
  1943 (Army-Navy), 453
  The Army Times, 455
  Babe Ruth's selections for (1940), 312
All-Time Yankee team, 752
American Association, 167
Anderson, Clary, 44
Andres, Ernie, 428, 429
Andrews, Ivy Paul, 99, *166,* 168, *168,* 215, *221*
Anton, Leroy, 37
Apartment in New York, DiMaggio's, 320
Appling, Luke, 92, 93, 94, 266, 305, 312, 339, 361, *498,* 500, 639
Army Air Force, U.S., DiMaggio in, *448, 452, 453,* 455, 457, *457–59,* 460, 463, 464, 465, *466,* 468, 560
  release from (1945), 469
Army-Navy all-star team (1943), 453
Army Times, The, 455
Arnovich, Morrie, 255
Ashburn, Richie, *547,* 548, 673, 677, 680
Assessment of career of DiMaggio, 597–98, 648–50, 658, 686–88, 707

statistics, 744
Association of Professional Ball Players of America, 209
Attendance at ball games, 58
  1936, 84, 97, 119, 123
    world series, 114
  1937 world series, 173
  1938 all-star games, 209
  1939, 270
  1941, 334, 367
  1949, 595
  all-star games (1933–40), 305
Auker, Eldon, 328, 359, 362, 365, 533
Autographs, 788
Autry, Gene, 768, *facing* 784
Averill, Earl, *626,* 627
  1936, 85, *91,* 92
  1937, 145, *145*
  1938, 206, 213–16, 219
  1939, 256
Avila, Bobby, 701
Awards. *See also* Joe DiMaggio Day; Most valuable player award
  1938, 192, *facing* 224, 235
  1940, 296, 297, *297*
  1941, 399
  1942, 412
  1949, 602
  1950, 677, 692
  Pacific Coast League's most valuable player (1935), 96
  "player of the year" award (1937), 122

B

Babe Ruth All-America award (1938), *facing* 224
Babich, Johnny, 356, 365, 533, 768
Bacon, J. W. (Gee), 209
Bagby, Jim, 315, 350, *350,* 351, 355, 357, 358, 361, *363,* 364, 428, 429
Baker, Bill, 55
Baker, Del, 93–94, 339, 340, 341
Baker, Tom, 44, *166*
Ball, liveliness of, 209
Bankhead, Tallulah, 564
Banta, Jack, 607, 615, 616
Barber, Red, *210*
Barber, Steve, 766
Barnes, Don, 196
Barney, Rex, 515
Barrett, Richard, 37, *37*
Barrow, Ed, 541, 746
  1935, 29, 35
  1936, 44–46, 68, 82, 84, 119
  1937, 126, 136, 182
  1938, 189–91, 195, 197, 213, 219
  1939, 239, 250, 263, 275,
  1940, *289,* 291, 295
  1941, 316, *316,* 317
  1942, 412, 413, 415, 467

Bartell, Dick
  1936, *105*
  1937, 149, 150, *166*
  1938, 188
Baseball cards, *facing* 576
Baseball Magazine, 89
Baseball Writers' Association of America, 256
  1938 all-star team selected by, 188
  1942 all-star team selected by, 446
  most valuable player award. *See* Most valuable player award
  "player of the year" award (1937), 122
Base running, 451. *See also* Running
  1939, 280
Basketball, denial of permission to play, 182
Bates, Ray, 87
Bats, *facing* 113
  oiling, 262
Bat size and weight, 476, 764, 765
  1936, 51, 55, 65
  1937, 131, 155
  1938, 201
  1939, 262
  1941, 347
  1947, 496
  1951, 729
Batter's box, 479
Batting, DiMaggio on, 751
Batting averages, 764. *See also* Batting championship; Statistics, DiMaggio's
  1940 leaders, 307
  DiMaggio's
    1933–1939, 266
    1936, 99
    1939, 265
    1940 prospects, 291
Batting championship
  1938, 216
  1939, 242, 245
  1939 prospects, 260
  1940, 312
  1940 prospects, 293
  1942 prospects, 416
Batting instructor, DiMaggio as, *facing* 720, 762. *See also* Coach, DiMaggio as
Batting order, N.Y. Yankees
  1936, 52
  1951, 713, 715
Batting practice, 474
Batting stance and swing, 51, *facing* 96, 764. *See also* Grip
  1937, 142, 155
  1941, 329, 347
  1948, 559
  DiMaggio on (1942), 478–80, *479–80*

Batting title. *See* Batting championship
Bauer, Hank, 572, 575, *578,* 580, 595, *610,* 627, 643, 645, 646, 659, 662, 664, 677, 700, 706, 728, 730, 734, 735, 741, 742, 766, *766*
Beazley, Johnny, 409, 444, 445
Beck, Clyde, 37
Beggs, Joe, 202
Behrman, Hank, 504
Bell, Beau, 84, 99, 150, 158
Bennett, George E., 33, 489, 525, 564, 572, 575, 742
Benton, Al, 369, 429, 432
Berardino, Johnny, 310, 328, 366
Berger, Walter (Wallie), *91, 167, 271,* 280
Berra, Yogi
  1947, 491, 492, 494, 523, 524, 526
  1948, 545, *551*
  1949, 585, *589,* 600, 611, *611,* 615, 621
  1950, *626,* 637, 638, *652,* 659, 664, 665, 671, 680, 681, 682
  1951, 696, 697, 701, 703, 706, 715, 716, *717,* 720, *720*
  1961, *762*
Berry, Charlie, *477,* 545
Bertig, Joe, 209
Bevens, Floyd (Bill), 504, *504,* 523, 524
Bickford, Vern, *589,* 589
Bildilli, Emil, 310
Biscan, Frank, 545
Blackburne, Russell (Lena), 256
Blackwell, Ewell, *facing* 225, 500, *589,* 589, 590, 654
Blaeholder, George, 76
Blair, Lou (Buddy), 291
Blanton, Cy, 149
Bloodworth, Jimmy, 683
Bodie, Ping, 28, 87
Bongiovanni, Anthony, *271*
Bonham, Ernest (Ernie, Tiny), *140,* 323, 331, 332, 366, *376,* 388, 446
Bonura, Zeke, 87, 202, 270
Bordagaray, Stanley (Frenchy), *271,* 376, 377, *379*
Borowy, Hank, 379
Boston baseball writers, 412
Boston Braves, 746
Boston Browns, 79
Boston Red Sox
  1935 offer to San Francisco Seals, 35, 49
  1936, 47
  1937, 123
  1938, 70, 185
  1939, 260
  1940, 303
  1950 prospects, 632
  1951 prospects, 702

games against
  1936, 79, 81
  1937, 142
  1939, 261
  1940, 300
  1941, 331
  1948, 537–38, 558
  1949, 580, 584, 585, 599, 600,
    606–7
  1951, 706
trade talks with (1939), 244
Bottarini, John, 37
Bottomley, Jim, 158
Boudreau, Lou, 311, 342, 357,
  358, 361, 364, 428, 432, 433,
  498, 499, 500, 526, 548, 558,
  639, 660, 702
Boyer, Cletis, 765
Braddock, James J. (Jimmy),
  188, 295
Bradley, Alva, 362, 430
Bramham, William G., 151, 209
Branca, Ralph, 503, 504, 504,
  515, 548, 589, 615, 735
Brancato, Al, 460
Branch, Norman, 320, 376, 378
Brawl (1936), 75
Breadon, Sam, 64
Brecheen, Cat, 500
Brennan, Don, 166
Breslin, Jimmy, 360
Breuer, Marvin, 321, 376, 377,
  384, 441
Bridges, Thomas (Tommy), 149,
  156, 245, 254, 255, 266, 283,
  294, 306
Briggs, Spike, 256
Brissie, Lou, 589, 590, 595, 659
Broaca, Johnny, 74, 81, 105
Brooklyn Dodgers
  1936, 44, 45, 46, 62, 63, 78
  1939, 270
  1940, 299
  1941 world series, 372–90, 373
  1947 world series, 503–4,
    505–7, 508, 509, 510, 512, 513,
    514–15, 516, 517, 518–19,
    520–25, 522
  1949 pennant race, 606, 607
  1949 world series, 609, 612–13,
    614, 615–21
Brougham, Royal, 37
Brown, Bobby, 489, 491, 492,
  521, 576, 595, 615, 620, 626,
  627, 671, 672, 682, 706, 730
Brown, Clint, 266
Brown, Hector, 700
Brown, Jimmy, 432, 435, 439
Brown, Les, 361, 766
Brown, Mace, 206
Brown, Walter, 105
Brown, Warren, 548
Brush, John T., 167
Bryant, Clay, 220, 227
Budge, Don, 296
Bukeforth, Clyde, 615
Bunting, 34, 35, 636
Burk, Joe, 296
Busby, Jim, 709, 716
Busch, Noel F., 246
Bush, Bullet Joe, 325
Byrne, Tommy, 496, 579, 584,
  595, 616, 661, 662, 666

C

Caldwell, Earl, 76, 559
Camilli, Dolf, 87, 392, 392
Camilli, Dolph, 379, 397
Campanella, Roy, 588, 589, 591,
  615, 620, 621
Campaneris, Campy, 776
Campbell, Bruce, 214
Campbell, Soup, 351
Caps, 288
Carey, Max, 634, 755
Carleton, Tex, 232
Carpenter, Bob, 678
Carr, Dick, 637
Carrasquel, Alex, 368
Carrasquel, Chico, 716
Cascarella, Joe, 87
Case, George, 266, 312
Casey, Hugh, 384, 386, 391,
  504, 512, 523, 595,
Cashman, Joe, 17
Castleman, Clydell, 105, 114,
  149, 166
Cavarretta, Phil, 87
Caveney, James (Jim; Jimmy;
  Ike), 15, 17, 18, 19, 27, 28, 30,
  37, 65
Cereghino, Ed, 739
Ceres, Jimmy, 564
Cerv, Bob, 703, 742, 743
Chambers, Cliff, 701
Chance, Frank, 634
Chandler, A. B., 527, 538, 549,
  619, 676
Chandler, Mrs., 676
Chandler, Spurgeon (Spud),
  202, 203, 213, 221, 257, 272,
  298, 320, 331, 370, 429, 432,
  441, 491, 492, 494
Chapman, Ben
  1935, 33
  1936, 49, 52, 58, 66, 69, 72, 95,
    100
  1937, 147
Chapman, Sam, 285, 321, 659
Charity exhibition games
  1939, 285
  1943, 447
Chase, Hal, 752
Chase, Kendall, 202
Chelini, Italo, 87
Chesbro, Jack, 752
Chicago Cubs, 70
  1936 prospects, 70
  world series (1938), 220–34,
    222–26, 230
Chicago White Sox
  1919 scandal, 268
  1951 prospects, 705
  games against
    1936, 86, 87
    1939, 245, 245, 246, 247
    1941, 370
    1942, 433
    1951, 716
Children's Aid Society, 159
Children's Cardiac Clinic, 565
Chiozza, Louis (Lou), 87, 166,
  290
Ciaffone, Frank, 433
Cincinnati Reds, 1939 world
  series against, 268–82, 273, 272
  attendance and money
    statistics, 278

evaluation of teams, 268, 270
facts on, 269
highlights, 281
Cissell, Bill, 37
Cleveland Indians, 560
  games against
    1936, 75
    1937, 156
    1938, 214–16
    1939, 245, 257
    1940, 298, 299, 311
    1941, 350–51, 355, 362
    1950, 641, 660, 663
Cleveland Municipal Stadium,
  124
Clift, Harlond, 84, 139, 188, 310,
  425
Coach, DiMaggio as, 774, 774,
  776, 776
Cobb, Ty, 34, 87, 131, 325, 334,
  479, 559, 634, 639, 689
  advice from, 262
Cochrane, Mickey, 78, 85, 95,
  96, 164, 343, 428, 429, 430, 634,
  635
Coffman, Dick, 105, 114, 166
Coffman, George, 155, 310
Cohen, Sid, 96
Coleman, Jerry, 580, 607, 615,
  616, 620, 621, 627, 654, 664,
  678, 682, 684, 706, 741
Coleman, Joe, 595
Collins, Eddie, 35, 64, 151, 412,
  542, 634
Collins, Jimmy, 91, 92, 148
Collins, Joe, 575, 644, 730, 734
Collins, Ripper, 102, 149
Columbia Civic Club, 677
Combs, Earle, 51, 52, 75, 221,
  280, 299, 328, 752, 764
Comiskey Park, 656
Conlan, Jocko, 671, 672, 672,
  681
Connolly, John, 37
Connolly, Tommy, 151
Contracts (contract
  negotiations, salary talks),
  facing 240, 450
  1934, 28
  1936, 44, 45
  1937, 122, 124, 126, 128, 129
  1938, 185, 187, 188–91, 195,
    196, 197
  1939, 239, 284
  1940, 289, 291
  1941, 316, 316, 317
  1942, 367, 412, 413, 415
  1950, 624, 625, 628–29
Coolidge, Grace, 673
Cooper, Harry, 219
Cooper, Morton, 432, 439, 446
Cooper, Walker, 435, 439, 445,
  548, 589
Coppolla, Harry, 87
Corriden, Red, 256
Corum, Bill, 176, 589
Coscarart, Joe, 60, 66, 71, 87
Coscarart, Pete, 299, 305,
  384
Coughlin, Gene, 40
Cox, Billy, 310, 489
Crab fishing, 124, 125
Craft, Harry, 271, 277
Craighead, Howard, 37, 788

Cramer, Roger (Doc), 145, 145,
  206, 219, 312
Crawford, Sam, 634
Crespi, Creepy, 435
Crespi, Frank, 439
Cronin, Bob, 40
Cronin, Joe, 488, 499, 755
  1936, 48, 65, 81, 94
  1937, 123, 146, 148, 148, 149,
    150
  1938, 188, 206, 209, 219
  1939, 238, 254–56, 266, 285
  1940, 304–6
  1941, 331, 340, 343
  on DiMaggio, 451
Crosetti, Frank, 752
  1936, 28, 43, 49, 52, 56, 61, 67,
    69, 75, 86, 87, 102, 104, 110,
    115, 119
  1937, 130, 166, 169, 169
  1938, 202, 221, 226, 227, 228,
    232–34, 265
  1939, 240, 250, 261, 271, 277,
    279, 283
  1940, 299, 311
  1941, 316, 369, 371, 398
  1942, 433, 435
  1950, 625, 626
  operation (1935), 33
Crosley, Paul, Jr., 275
Crosley Field, 208, 208
Cuccinello, Tony, 87
Cullenbine, Roy J., 338, 366,
  435, 435, 439
Curtiss, Julian W., 297, 297

D

Daglia, Pete, 87
Dahlen, Bill, 325, 328
Dahlgren, Ellsworth (Babe),
  221, 226, 240, 245, 250, 261,
  270, 271, 281, 290, 292, 311
Daley, Arthur, 192
Damon Runyon Cancer Fund,
  602
Daniel, Dan, 333, 361, 464, 603
Danning, Harry, 105, 166, 177,
  178, 305, 340
Danning, Ike, 209
Dark, Alvin, 728, 729, 730, 734
Daughton, Ralph, 209
Davis, Curt, 92, 94, 384
Davis, George, 105
Davis, Harry, 37
"Deadpan Joe" nickname, 22,
  23, 28, 40
Dean, Chubby, 433
Dean, Dizzy, 305, 410, 627
  1936, 61, 90, 92, 93
  1937, 132, 141, 149, 151, 152
  1938, 220, 227, 228, 232, 234
Defense Bond campaign, 396
Delahanty, Ed, 82
Delsing, Jimmy, 627
De Maestri, Joe, 741
Demaree, Frank, 37, 92, 148
Dempsey, Jack, 429, 431
Densmore, James, 34
Dente, Sam, 741
Derringer, Paul, 254, 255, 268,
  271, 279–81, 305, 339
DeShong, Jimmy, 56
Detroit Tigers
  1935, 33

1936 prospects, 70
1950 prospects, 632
1951 prospects, 702
games against
  1936, 76, 96
  1938, 213
  1939, 245, 257
  1950, 664
Devine, Joe, 34, 118, 625
Dewey, Thomas E., *527*, 537
Dickey, Bill
  1936, 52, 56, 73, 79, 86, 87, 92,
    96, 103, *105*, 106, 110, 115, 206
  1937, 132, 142, *146, 148,* 149,
    154, 166
  1938, 188, 195, 202, 209, 215,
    219, *221, 226,* 233
  1939, 240, 242, 245, 250, 260,
    264, 265, 266, *269,* 270, *271,*
    277, 279, 280, *283*
  1940, 299, 312
  1941, *316,* 316, 327, *339,* 340,
    343, 351, 368, 371, 374, *374,*
    392
  1942, 421, 435, 439
  1944, 465
  1948, *536*
  1950, 625
  1951, 701
  on All-Time Yankee team, 752
  Berra and, 697
Dickman, Emerson, 294
Dietrich, Bill, 214
DiMaggio, Dom, *26, facing* 97,
  131, 191, 285, 396, *447, 502,*
  511, 559–60, 696, 703, *704,*
  facing 704, *761, facing* 768, *768*
  with Boston Red Sox, 300, *300,*
    301, 331, *338,* 365, 398, *537,*
    538, 559, 580, 585, *599,* 602,
    706, 744
  compared to Joe, 665
  in Japanese tour, 739, 741
  physical build, *630*
DiMaggio, Joe. *See also specific
  topics*
  in 1932, 15–17
  in 1933, 18–28, 48
  in 1934, 29–31
  in 1935, 33–41
  in 1936, 42–119
  in 1937, 120–83
  in 1938, 184–235
  in 1939, 237–85
  in 1940, 286–313
  in 1941, 314–400
  in 1942, 408–47
  in 1943–1945, 448–69
  in 1946, 470–87
  in 1947, 489–529
  in 1948, 530–65
  in 1949, 566–621
  in 1950, 622–93
  in 1951, 694–749
  from 1952 to the present,
    750–89
  assessment of career of,
    597–98
  background of, 64–65
  boyhood, 347, 788
  50th birthday party, 767–68
  first game in the major
    leagues, 72

off-field activities. *See also*
  Restaurant, DiMaggio's
  1938, 188, 188, 190, 192, *194*
  1939, 240
  1941, 334
  1950, 650, 687
  golf, 630, 696, *facing* 760,
    779
  radio career, 629–30
  television commentator, 743,
    753, *753, 754*
origin of name, 71
photographs and drawings of.
  See Photographs and
  drawings of Joe DiMaggio
prospects as major leaguer
  (1933), 28
rapid rise of, 219
retirement, 699, 738, 742–49
  announcement of, 742, 745
  uniform retired, 745, 748,
    749
with San Francisco Seals. *See*
  San Francisco Seals
spelling of name, 23
surprise party (1941), 371
2000th hit (1950), 639, *639, 640*
DiMaggio, Joe, Jr. (son), 542,
  564, *599,* 619, 768
DiMaggio (father), 173, 559,
  703
DiMaggio, Tom, 15, *599, 768*
DiMaggio, Vincent (Vince),
  facing 97, 101, 347, *447,* 559,
  facing 704, *761, 768*
  1933, 23
  1934, 30, 31
  1935, *36*
  1936, 48, 65
  1937, 131
  1938, *184,* 191
  with Hollywood team, 18
  with San Francisco Seals, 17,
    18, 67
DiMaggio Day
  1936, 96
  1940, 298
  1947, *501*
  1949, 599, *601,* 602, 603, *603–5,*
    650
DiMaggio restaurant (San
  Francisco), 188, 190, 240, 396,
  559
Dinneen, Bill, 82
Doby, Larry, 589, *591,* 639, *709*
Doerr, Bobby, *337,* 500, 538,
  562, 580, 584, 585, 607, *652,*
  665, 706
Donald, Atley, 199, 245, 247,
  257, 270, *271,* 366, 384, 433
Doyle, Charley, 256
Drebinger, John, 298, *311*
Dressen, Chuck, 512, 515
Dropo, Walt, *652,* 655, 705
Duffy, Hugh, 412
Dugan, Joe, 634
Duncan, C. William, 38
Dunn, Jim, 689
Durocher, Clara, 730
Durocher, Leo, 92, 142, 206,
  305, 340, 378, 384, 389, 525,
  615, 730
Durst, Cedric, 37

Dyer, Bill, *210*
Dyer, Eddie, 500, 535
Dykes, Jimmy, 85, 96, 479–80,
  729

E

Early, Jake, *326,* 543
Earnshaw, George, 45, 429
Easter, Luke, 663, 701
Eatalano, Joseph, *facing* 177
Eckhardt, Oscar, 37, 41, 63
Edwards, Bruce, *513,* 515, 521,
  523
Eisenstat, Harry, 44, 299
Elliott, Bob, *facing* 225, 340, 548
Embree, Red, 538, 545
Emslie, Bob, 209
Engel, Joe, 150
English, Gilbert, 37
Ennis, Del, *675,* 676, 680
Epstein, Ben, 688
Equipment bag, DiMaggio's,
  facing 577
Essick, Bill, 15, 29, 30, 31, 31,
  450, 542
European vacation plans
  (1948), 565
Evans, Al, 659
Evans, Bill, 151
Evans, Russell, 86
Evers, Johnny, 634
Evers, Walter (Hoot), *547,* 548,
  652, 664
Exercise, 624
  DiMaggio on, 559
Exhibition games, *456. See also*
  Spring training
  charity
    1939, 285
    1943, *447*
  in Japan, 739, *740,* 741

F

Faber, Red, 468
Fabian, Henry, 106, 110
Fain, Ferris, 739, 741
Fan mail, 571
Farley, James A. (postmaster
  general), 110, 149, 171, *249,*
  729
Farley, Jim (player), 585
Farrell, Edward (Eddie, Doc),
  34, 534, 542
Farrell, Jackie, 571
Feller, Bob
  1937, 156, 164
  1938, 204, *207,* 213, 216, *217*
  1939, 254–56, 266, *283*
  1940, 305, 311
  1941, 323, 334, *340,* 342, 366,
    392, 400
  1942, 428, 429
  1946, 474, *476,* 476, *481,* 486,
    488
  1947, *498*
  1948, 532, 543
  1950, 660, 687
  1951, 715
Felsch, Oscar, 256
Fenway Park, 258
Ferdenzi, Til, 29
Ferguson, Lieut. Robert G., 692
Ferrazzi, Bill, 87

Ferrell, Rick, *200*
Ferrell, Wesley Cheek (Wes),
  145, *145, 226*
Ferrick, Tom, 662, 663, 681
Fette, Lou, 188, 254, 255
Fielding, DiMaggio's, 598. *See
  also* Positions played by
  DiMaggio; Throwing arm,
  DiMaggio's
  1933, 28
  1934, 31
  1936, *77,* 80, 84, 92, 97, 118
  1937, 149, 158
  1938, 213
  1939, 242, 247, 256, 258, 744
  1940, *313*
  1941, 329, 389
  1947, 525
  1948, 559
  1950, 649, 676, 684, 684
  greatest feat as fielder, 744
Finley, Charles O., 774
First baseman, DiMaggio as,
  643–46, *645*
Fitzgerald, Joe, 644
Fitzsimmons, Freddy (Fat
  Freddie), *105,* 109, 208, 391
Fletcher, Art, 55, 208, *221,* 256,
  280, 291, 371, *375,* 439
Flores, Jess, 494
Flynn, Art, *417, 464*
Fohl, Lee, 689
Fonseca, Lew, 209, 730
Ford, Eddie, 660, 661
Ford, Whitey, 682, 683
Foster, John B., 151
Fothergill, Fat, 76
Fox, Nelson, 716
Fox, Pete, 73, 219, 256
Foxx, Jimmy, 471, 766
  1936, 92, *95*
  1937, 145, *145, 146,* 150
  1938, 185, 188, 206, *207,* 216
  1939, 242, 256, *259,* 260, 263,
    265, 266
  1940, 298, 300, 306, 312
  1941, *337,* 341, 398
Frasier, Chick, 33
Frederick, John, 37
French, Larry, 227, 232, 305
French, Ray, 25
Freudeman, Victor, *685*
Frey, Linus R. (Lonny), 254, 256,
  271, 277, 280, 340
Frick, Ford C., 106, 206, 209,
  256, 275, 429
Frisch, Frankie, 56, 64, 132, 479
Fritzsimmons, Freddy, 114
Froelich, Ed, 494
Furillo, Carl, 515, 520, 523, 615

G

Gabler, Frank, *105*
Galan, Augie, 15, 17, 18, 65, *91,*
  92–94, *93,* 347
Galehouse, Dennis (Denny,
  Dinty), 215
Gallagher, Joe, 299
Gamble, Lee, *272*
Gandil, Chick, 87
Garcia, Mike, 641, 701
Garver, Ned, 578, 703, *709*
Gaynor, Sidney (Sid), 572, 578,
  579, 637, 742

Gehrig, Lou, *facing* 48, 256, 627
  1934 triple crown, 263
  1936, 51, 52, 55, 56, 62, 72, 73,
    75, 76, 84, 86, 87, 91–93, *95,*
    96, 104, 106, 115
  1937, *128,* 132, 141, 142, *146,*
    149, 150, *154,* 156, 159, *166,*
    174, 175, 176, 182
    contract negotiations, 126,
    128, 129
  1938, 188, 189, 195, 199, 202,
    206, 213, *221, 226,* 233, 234
  1939, 237, 240, 256, 270, 280,
    284
    illness and retirement, 248,
    282, *289,* 747
    Lou Gehrig Appreciation
    Day, 250
  DiMaggio compared to, 59
  locker, *748*
  photographs of, *53*
  uniform retired, 748
Gehringer, Charlie, 303
  1935, 40
  1936, 76, 92, 94
  1937, 122, 145, *145, 146,* 148,
    149, 164, 182
  1938, 188, 219
  1939, 238, 255, 260, 266
Geisel, Harry, 62, 67, 209
George, Steve, 25, 37
Giles, Warren, 280
Gionfriddo, Al, 515, *518, 519,*
  520, 523, 524, 535
Girard, P. M., 572, 575
Giuliani, Angelo, 87
Glenn, Joe, *105, 167,* 169, *169,*
  215, *221, 226*
Glove, DiMaggio's, *facing* 49,
  facing 577
Golden Laurel Award (1940),
  296, 297, *297*
Goldsberry, Gordon, 741
Golf, 630, 696, *facing* 760, 779
Goliat, Mike, 676, 681, 684
Gomez, Vernon (Lefty), 238,
  facing 240, 488, 752, 768
  1936, 69, 73, 74, 96, *105,* 106,
    110, 114, 115, 119
  1937, 124, 128, 132, 141, 149,
    164, *167,* 170, 171, 174, 182
  1938, 188, 188, 199, 204, 206,
    206, 209, *221,* 227, 228
  1939, 245, 246, 247, 250, 264,
    268, 268, *271,* 277, 280, *283*
  1940, 304, *308*
  1941, 318, *318,* 329, 351, 371,
    396
    apartment in New York, 320
  1943, *451*
  1948, 535
  1949, 571
  DiMaggio on, 449
Goodman, Ival R., 206, *207,* 209,
  254, 256, 268, *271,* 277, 279,
  280, 282
Gordon, Joe, 460, 752
  1938, 185, 190, 199, 202, *221,*
    226, 228, 233
  1939, 240, 247, 250, 255, 257,
    266, 270, *271,* 279, 280, *283*
  1940, 293, 306, 310, 311

1941, 319, *339,* 340, 351, 355,
  368, 370, 374, *374,* 379, 390,
  392, 400
1942, 421, 423, 425, *425,* 429,
  435, 445
1943, 446
1947, *498, 499,* 500
1949, 589
Gordon, Jules, 572
Gordon, Sid, *589*
Gordon, Tommy, 214
Gorman, John, 45
Goslin, Goose, *91,* 92
Gould, Joe, 189, 295, 450, *450*
Gowdy, Hank, 429, 468
Grace, Joe, 428, 429
Graham, Charley, 15, 17, *19,*
  23, 28–30, 31, 34, 65, 347, 450,
  542, 788
Gray, Ted, 653
Grayson, Harry, 40
Greenberg, Hank, 410, 532,
  598, 649, 744, 748, 755, 767
  1937, *146,* 155, 164
  1938, 187, 213, 219
  1939, 254, 255, 256, 260, 263,
    265, 266, *283*
  1940, 294, 312
  1941 salary, 316, 317
  1946, 471, *476*
Gregg, Hal, 504, *504,* 523
Gregory, L. H., 37
Gregory, Paul, 37
Griffith, Clark, 80, 93, 150, 209,
  255, 343
Griffith, Mrs. Clark, 209
Grimes, 366
Grimm, Charley, 70, 92, 93, 634
Grip, DiMaggio's, *476,* 479
Grissom, Lee, 149, *272, 277, 285
Gromek, Steve, 663
Groth, Johnny, 664
Grove, Robert (Lefty), 73, 81,
  92, 206, *207,* 209, 266, 332
Guerra, Mike, 494, 659
Gumbert, Harry, *105,* 110, 114,
  166, 439
Gyselman, Dick, 83

H

Hack, Stanley (Stan), 206, 209,
  233, 234, 254–56, 340, 342, 446
Hadley, Irving (Bump), 310
  1936, 56, 81, *105,* 109, 115
  1937, *166*
  1938, 215, *221*
  1939, 245, *271,* 277
Hafey, Chick, 634
Hafey, Tom, 290
Haines, Jose, 441
Hale, Odell, 75
Hallahan, Bill, 56
Hall of Fame, *facing* 377, *758*
  DiMaggio's uniform, bat, and
  glove given to, 745, 749, *750*
  induction of DiMaggio into,
  365, 755–56, *757*
Halloran, Wild Bill, 512
Hamey, Roy, 703
Hamner, Granny, 673, 676, 678,
  682–84, 684
Hanrahan, Edward M., 489

Harder, Mel, 92, 124, 131, 145,
  145, 149, 190, 216, 264, 328,
  347, 366, 474, 486
Harridge, William, 94, 106, 199,
  209, 256, 275, 280, 334, 468, 538
Harris, Bob, 359, 366
Harris, Bucky, 80, *facing* 225,
  489, 490, 491, 504, 520, 521,
  524, 525, 526, *530,* 533, 561,
  571, 713
Harris, Charlie, 595
Harris, Luman, 423
Harris, Mickey, 331, 333, 340,
  428, 537, 662
Harrison, Cliff, 40
Harrison, Pat, 150
Hartman, Harry, *210*
Hartnett, Charles (Gabby), 92,
  94, 149, 182, 188, 190, 219, 220,
  227, 232–34, 255, 256, *283,* 755,
  755, 756
Hash, Herb, 299
Hassett, Buddy, 421, 433, 435,
  439, *451*
Hatten, Joe, 504, 520
Hawaii, DiMaggio in (1944),
  458–59
Hawaii League, 460
Hayes, Frank, 266, 398
Heath, John G. (Jeff, Jeffrey,
  Geoffrey), 216, 266, 311, *338,*
  340, 398
Heffner, Don, 62, 106, *166,* 169,
  169, 310
Hegan, Jim, *498, 551,* 654, *709*
Heilmann, Harry, 78, 395, 634
Heintzelman, Ken, 607
Hemsley, Rollie, 306
Hennessy, Spike, 15, 788
Henrich, Tommy, *facing* 240,
  507, *507,* 611, *611,* 620
  1937, 138, *140,* 158, *167,* 169,
    169
  1938, 204, *212,* 214, 215, *221,*
    225, 232, 233
  1939, 244, 247, 250, 256, 270,
    271
  1940, 291, 298, 300
  1941, 321, 328, 332, 365, 366,
    368, 371, 372, 374, *375,*
    384, *387,* 388, 390, 391
  1942, *419,* 421, 428, 432, 432
  1947, 492, 492, 494, *494,* 496,
    503, 512, 520, 521, 523, 526,
    526
  1948, 545, 548, *556,* 562
  1949, 572, 575, 578, 584, 600,
    620, 621
  1950, 625, 626, 628, 637, 638,
    641, 643–46, 648, 654, 662,
    665, 667, 673, 677
Herbert, Ray, 705
Herman, Babe, 410
Herman, Billy, *91,* 92, *95,* 149,
  206, 255, 304, 305, 342
Herrmann, LeRoy, *19*
Hershberger, Willard, *271*
Herzog, Buck, 288
Hewsome, Heber, 365
Heydler, John, 151, 256, 343
Hickey, Rudy, 40
Hickey, Thomas Jefferson, 208
Higbe, Kirby, 379, 384
Higgins, Pinkie, 94, 294, 312

Hildebrand, Oral, 139, 158, 213,
  245, 261, 270, *271,* 279
Hill, Jess, 52
Hillerich & Bradsby Company,
  209
Hinrichs, Paul, 575
Hitting slump(s)
  1941, 319, 320
  1942, 421
  1950, 648, 659
  1951, 700, 701, 712, 728, 730
  DiMaggio on, 559
Hitting streak
  1933, 15, 18, 22, 23, *24,* 25, 29,
    328, 364, 788
  1937, 155
  1941 (56-game streak), *314,*
    322, 323, facing 344, *346,*
    facing 376, *between* 376–77,
    facing 377, 650, 743, 744, 748
    41-game AL record broken,
    325, *326,* 327–29
    44-game major league
    record tied, 331, *331,* 333,
    335
    56th consecutive game, *349*
    day-by-day record of, 348,
    350
    DiMaggio's recollections in
    1969, 356–57
    end of, 350–53, *353, 354,*
    355–58, *358,* 361, 362, *363*
    looking back on, 360–61,
    364–65, *facing* 377
    pledge to dying boy, 327
    statistics, 359
  1950, 665
Hitting title. *See* Batting
  championship
Hitting weaknesses (1936), 74,
  76
Hittle, Lloyd, 637
Hoag, Myril, 255, 266, *283,* 468,
  541
  1936, 49, 106
  1937, 138, *167*
  1938, 199, 202, *212, 221, 225,*
    234
Hodge, Sam, 69
Hodges, Gil, *589,* 590, 620, 621
Hogsett, Elon (Chief), 72, 248
Hollywood team (Pacific Coast
  League), 453, 455
Holmes, Burton, 209
Home-run hitter, DiMaggio as
  1936, 86, 87
  1937, 139, 159
  1938, 204
  1939, 242, 256
  1940, 310
  1941, 321, 323, 371
  1948, 462–63
  1949, 583
  1950, 662, 663
Home run hitters, DiMaggio on,
  764–65
Hood, Wally, Jr., 626, *626*
Hood, Wally, Sr., 626, *626*
Hooper, Harry, 634
Hoover, Herbert, 152, 171
Hopp, Johnny, 435, 439, 673,
  677, 707, 710
Hornsby, Rogers, 74, 99, 119,
  142, 158, 328, 356, 634, *657,* 741

Houk, Ralph, 668, *762, 765*
Houtteman, 474, 668
Howard, Elston, 766
Hoyt, Waite, 752
Hubbell, Carl, 549, *635* 1936,
  92, *105,* 109, 110, 114, 115, 116
  1937, 131, 147, 149, 164, *167,*
  170, 171, 174, 176, 182
  1938, 188, 197, 206
  1940, 305
  1941, 339, 341, 342
Hudson, Sid, 340, 341, 342, 428,
  662
Huggins, Miller, 61, 280, 634
Hugher, Leo, 739
Hughes, Ed R., 37
Hughes, Roy, 75
Hughson, Tex, 428, 446, 474,
  607
Humphries, Johnny, 214
Hunt, Mike, 37
Hurley, Ed, 639
Hutson, Don, 399

I

Injuries and ailments,
  DiMaggio's, 598, 649–50
  1934, 29, 30, 34, 49, 542
  1936, 60, 62, 66–68, 71, *633*
  1937, 136–39
  1938, 202
  1939, 237, 244, *244,* 245, *289,*
    633
  1940, 294, 298
  1941, 318, 369, 370
  1944, 460, 464, 465
  1946, 541–42
  1947, 489, 490, 525, *540, 633*
  1948, 540, 547, 563–65, *633*
  1949, 567, 572, *573,* 575, 576,
    577, 578–79, 625, 688
  1950, *636,* 637, 661
  1951, 696, 702, 703, 708, 743,
    744
  1987, 788
  general history of, 634
  operations
    1947, 489, 490
    1950, 676
Irvin, Monte, 728, 730, 734
Italian-American players, 87

J

Jackson, Joe, 28, 100, 119
Jackson, Travis, *105*
Jansen, Larry, 654, 735
Japan, *691,* 693
  exhibition games in, 739, *740,*
    741
Jenkins, Burris, 297
Jensen, Jack, 703
Jensen, Jackie, 626, 636, 643,
  644, 702, 703, 707, 741, 742
Joe DiMaggio Day
  1936, 96
  1940, 298
  1947, *501*
  1949, 599, *601,* 602, 603, *603–5,*
    650
Joe DiMaggio Park
  (Clearwater, Florida), *facing*
  769
Joe DiMaggio Show, 629–30
Johnny Mize Day, 665

Johnson, Billy, 489, 491, 492,
  496, 523, 526, 538, 555, 572,
  575, 576, 584, 585, 595, 600,
  627, 659, 673
Johnson, Bob, 266, 321
Johnson, Earl, 585
Johnson, Henry W., *272*
Johnson, Lyndon B., 767, 768
Johnson, Roy, 49, 51, 52, 55, 58,
  69, 96, 99, *104,* 138
Johnson, Walter, 151, 219, 255,
  343, 634, *635,* 689
Johnston, James A., 284
Jolley, Smead, 37
"Joltin' Joe DiMaggio" (song),
  between 344–45, 766
Jones, Billy, 776
Jones, Jesse, 150
Jones, Sheldon, 728
Jones, Willie, 655, 672, *673,* 680,
  680, 681
Joost, Eddie, 83, *271,* 492, 526,
  590, 659
Jordan, Jimmy, 45
Jorgens, Arndt, *105, 167,* 169,
  169, 221, 226, 271
Judnich, Walter, 240, 457
Judson, Howie, 665
Jurges, Bill, 234, 299, 304

K

Kahn, Roger, 788
Kann, James, 54
Kase, Max, 201
Kaval, William, 352–53
Kazak, Eddie, 588
Keeler, Wee Willie, 18, 325,
  328, 331, 333, 634
Kell, George, *499,* 500, 526, 590,
  652, 655, 664
Keller, Charlie, *203,* 266
  1939, 258, 264, 266, *269,* 270,
    271, 274, 277, 279–82
  1940, *292, 293, 309,* 310
  1941, 318, 319, 321, 323, *338,*
    339, 351, 355, 368, 371, 372,
    374, *375,* 384, 390, 392, 400,
    398
  1942, 413, *414,* 415, 421, 425,
    433, 435, *435,* 439, 444
  1947, 496, *498,* 503, 520
  1948, *551*
  1949, 575, *610,* 611, *611,* 619
Kellogg's All-American
  baseball popularity contest
  (1938), 219
Keltner, Ken, *265,* 266, *303,* 315,
  350, 355, 357, 361, *363,* 364,
  365, 428, 429, 533, 548, 549, 768
Kennedy, Bill, 578
Kennedy, Bob, 663, 774, 776
Kennedy, Vernon, 93, 208
Kieran, John, 751
Kilgallen, Dorothy, 201, *201*
Killen, Frank, 332
Kinder, Ellis, 585, 599, 601, 607,
  665, 706
Kiner, Ralph, 520, *547,* 588, *589,*
  653, 654, 655, 689
King, Joe, *527,* 538
Klein, Lou, 701
Kleinhans, Ted, 106
Klem, Bill, 209

Knickerbocker, William (Billy),
  75, 158, *221,, 225,* 240, *272,* 299
Knott, Jack, 84
Koenecke, Len, 38
Koenig, Mark, 61, *104,* 106
Kofoed, Jack, 28
Kolloway, Don, 664
Konstanty, Jim, 654, 672, 673,
  680, 681, 682, 683
Kopf, Herb, 213
Korean War, 689, *690,* 692, 693
Koupal, 139
Koy, Ernie, 299
Kozar, Al, 540
Kreevich, Mike, 206, 266
Kretlow, Lou, 716
Krichell, Paul, *137,* 625
Kryhoski, Dick, 576
Kuhel, Joe, 147, 266
Kuk, Steve, 44
Kurowski, Whitey, 435, 439,
  444, 445
Kuzava, Bob, 716, 735
Kuzuru, Makoto, 623

L

LaGuardia, Fiorello H., *facing*
  48, 96, 171, *181,* 275, 298, 299,
  311, 432
Laird, Tom, 31, 40, 83, 463, 541,
  561
Lajoie, Nap, 634
Landis, Kenesaw M., 295, 339,
  430, 489
  1937, 150–52, 174, *181, 183*
  1938, 192, *192,* 208
  1939, 256, 275
Lane, Frank, 703
Lanier, Max, 439
Larkin, Edward, 202
La Rocca, Jack, 126
Lary, Lyn, 29, 31, 49, 214, 541
Laux, France, *210*
Lavagetto, Cookie (Harry), 255,
  304, 391, *477,* 515, 520, 523,
  524, 627
Lawing, Gene, 209
Lawson, Roxie, 155
Lazzeri, Tony, 752
  1933, 28
  1934, 31
  1936, 43, 52, 54, 61, 75, 86, 96,
    102, 103, *104,* 106, 110, 115,
    119
  1937, *130,* 139, *166,* 168, *168,*
    170, 174, 175
Lee, Bill, 206, 220, 232, 254, 255
Lee, Thornton, 246, 247, 298,
  340, 342, 362, 370, 400
Lefebvre, Wilfrid, 261
Lehman, Kenny, 741
Leiber, Hank, *304*
  1936, 86, 87, *105,* 110, 116, 118
  1937, *167*
Leishman, Eddie, 625
Lemon, Bob, 474, 589, 639, 655,
  660
Leonard, Dutch, 325, 339
Leonard, Emil, 266, 294
Leonard, Lank, *36*
Leslie, Sam, *104, 166*
Lewis, Buddy, 100, *243, 499*
Lewis, Duffy, 634
Lewis, Johnny, *265*

Liberty (magazine), *198*
Lieb, Fred, 147
Life (magazine), *236,* 246, *594*
Lillard, Gene, 34, 37
Lindell, Johnny, 379, 421, 491,
  513, 523, 538, 575, 580, 585,
  610, 627, 699, *600*
Lindstrom, Freddy, 245
Lipon, Johnny, 664
Lipton, Art, 602
Littlefield, Dick, 741
Litwhiler, Daniel, 432
Locker, DiMaggio's, *576, 749,*
  between 760–61
Lockman, Whitey, 730, 734
Lodigiani, Dario, 457
Lollar, Sherman, 741
Lombardi, Ernie, 87, 206, *207,*
  209, *211,* 218, 254, *271,* 277,
  279, 282, 306, 479, 511
Lombardi, Vic, 504
Lopat, Ed (Eddie), 578, 620, 621,
  638, 639, 641, 660, 661, 681,
  706, 720, *720,* 734, 735, 739
Lopata, Stan, 680, 681
Lopez, Al, 343, 705
Los Angeles Angels, *456*
Louis, Joe, 296, 399, 465
Louisville Sluggers, *95*
Loy, Ernest, 126
Lucadello, Johnny, 428
Luck, 665
Lucky to Be a Yankee, facing
  480
Luque, Adolfo (Dolf), 106, 126
Lyons, Al, 491, 739, 741
Lyons, Ted, 76, 266, 370, 496,
  755, *755,* 756

M

MacArthur, Gen. Douglas, *690*
McCaffrey, Stanley, *630*
McCarthy, Joe, 31, 34, 43, *105,*
  131, 488, 748, 768
  1936, *42,* 49, 50, *56,* 66, 69, 74,
    75, 92, 93, 114, 119
  1937, 147, 150
  1938, 195, 199, *207, 221,* 227,
    232, 233
  1939, 242, *249,* 254, 256, 257,
    280, *283*
  1940, 291, 293, 296
  1941, 315, 318, *332,* 351, 369,
    377, 378, *378,* 389
  1942, *417,* 421, 429, *436,* 437
  1945, 467
  1946, 486
  1948, 537
  1949, 601, 602, *605,* 606, 607
McCarthy, John, *166*
McCormick, Frank, 206, 254,
  256, 263, 268, *272,* 277, 303
McCormick, Mike, 457
McCosky, Barney, 263, 266,
  312, 460
McCoy, Benny, 428
McCrabb, Lester, 319
McDermott, Maurice, 580, 716
McDougald, Gil, 706, 716, 724,
  728, 730, 734
McGowan, Bill, 150, 389, 538
McGraw, John, 232, 341
Mack, Connie, 38, 80, 151, 158,
  160, 232, 256, 396, 488, *536,* 707

Mack, Ray, 355, 366
McKechnie, Bill, 209, 256, 268, *272,* 305, 339, 340, 341, 342, *589*
McNair, Eric, 266, 764
MacPhail, Larry, 467, 469
  1946, 475, 476
  1947, 521, 525
  1948, 533, 542
  1949, 597
McQuinn, George, 266, 425, 494, 496, *498, 499,* 500, 503, 507, *507, 513,* 526, 545, 548
Madjeski, Ed, *166*
Maglie, Sal, 728, 730, 735
Mailho, Emil, 37
Mails, Walter, *19*
Makosky, Frank, 139, 158, *166, 169, 169*
Mallory, Pete, 455
Malone, Pat, 51, 69, 73, 74, 79, 96, *105,* 106, *166*
Mancuso, Gus, 87, *105,* 161, *166*
Manes, Cliff, 615
Manhattan Merry-Go-round (film), *162, facing* 176
Manning, Tom, *210*
Mantle, Mickey, *facing* 560, 665, 695, *698,* 700, *701,* 702, 735, 742, *762, 767, 768*
Manush, Heinie, 31
Mapes, Cliff, 585, *610,* 616, 620, 621, 643, 658, 706
Marble, Alice, 296
Marchildon, Phil, 371, 468
Marion, Marty, 435, 444, 710
Maris, Roger, 786
Marrero, Connie, *709*
Marshall, Clarence (Cuddles), 535, 627
Marshall, Willard, 500, 588
Martin, Billy, 703, 739, 741, *741*
Martin, Hershel, 467
Martin, Stu, 91
Marty, Joe, 31, 228, 233
Marun, Billy, 626–27
Masi, Phil, 548
Masterson, Walt, 325, 460, 548, 585
Matheson, William, 240, 291
Mathewson, Christy, 634, 689
Mauch, Gus, 491, 579
May, Merrill, *304*
Mayo (painter), *facing* 720
Mayo, Eddie, *104*
Mays, Willie, *facing* 560, 730, 735, 767, *768*
Meany, Tom, 33, 192, *192*
Medwick, Joe, 238, 255, 304, 390, *626,* 626
  1937, 122, 142, 143, 147, 148, 149, 150, 164, 182
  1938, 190, 206, 209, 219
Medwick, Mickey, *95*
Meehan, Chick, *565*
Mele, Sam, 662
Melillio, Oscar, 87
Melton, Cliff, 164, *166,* 176
Melton, Rube, 489
Meola, Emile, 87
Mercer, Sid, 192, 298, 511
Merman, Ethel, 602
Metheny, Bud, 467
Meusel, Bob, 51, 634, *635,* 752
Meyer, Billy, 689

Meyer, Russ, 673
Michaels, Cass, 655
Miksis, Eddie, 520, 521, 524
Miller, Bob, 680, 681
Miller, Eddie, 255, 340
Millies, Walter, 147
Mills, Howard, 310
Milnar, Al, 215, 299, *303,* 366
Minoso, Minnie, *709,* 716
Miranda, H. I., 696
Mitchell, Dale, 588
Mize, Johnny, 148, 149, 256, 316, 340, 446, 460, *476,* 496, 500, 548, *589,* 615, 616, 620, 621, 627, 637, 643, 662, 664, 665, 672, 673, 676, 678, 681, *701,* 716
Molesworth, Keith, 37
Monroe, Lucy, 680
Moore, Joe, *95, 105, 167, 175*
Moore, Lloyd A., *272*
Moore, Randy, 44
Moore, Terry, 305, 435, 441, 445, 520
Moore, Whitey, 277
Moore, Wiley, 752
Morgan, Tom, 703
Moriarty, George, 100
Mose, Robert, 73
Moses, Wally, 639
Mostil, Johnny, 256
Most valuable player award
  1935 (San Francisco Seals), 37
  1938, 285
  1939, 266, 298, 311, *311*
  1939 prospects, 260
  1941, 364, 400, 395, 410
  1947, *facing* 496, 511, 526, 538
"Mrs. Robinson" (song), 772–73
Mullin, Pat, *547,* 548
Muncrief, Bob, 361, 365, 543
Munger, George (Red), 589, *589,* 590
Mungo, Van Lingle, 85, 149, 156
Murphy, Johnny, 294, 425, 449, 752
  1936, 73, 74, 96, *105,* 114
  1937, 139, *166*
  1938, 215, *221,* 228
  1939, 245, 247, 257, *271,* 279
  1941, 316, 321, 351, 368, 371, 384, 390
Murphy, Sam, 27
Murray, Jack, 158
Musial, Stan, *facing* 225, 435, 439, 444, 445, *476, 547,* 548, 549, 588, *589,* 590, 696
Myatt, George, 290
Myer, Charles (Buddy), 31, 145, *145,* 147
Myers, Billy, *271,* 277, 279, 280, 281

N
Nallin, Dick, 151
Nano, Fray, *549*
National Association, 437
National Baseball Hall of Fame. *See* Hall of Fame
Navin, Frank, 689
Ness, Jack, 22, 23
Neun, Johnny, 625, 636, 766
Nevel, Ernie, 666
Newark Bears, 34

Newcombe, Don, 588–90, *589, 591,* 620, 621
Newhouser, Hal, 369, 474, 495, *499,* 526, 548, 559, 664
Newkirk, Floyd, 34
Newsom, Bobo (Buck), 18, 65, 80, 204, 245, 257, 264, 266, 305, 316, 319, 364, *419,* 504, *504, 522*
Newsome, Dick, 412
New York, New Haven and Hartford railroad, 602
New York Chapter of the Baseball Writers Association
  1938 Player of the Year award, 192, 235
  1942 Player of the Year award, 410
New York City, 667–68
New York Daily Mirror, facing 657
New York Giants, 44, 45, 78, 220
  1939, 270
  1940, 299
  scorecard (1942), *426*
  in world series
    1936, 103, 106, *107,* 108–16
    1937, 164, 165, *166–67,* 167, *168,* 171–76, *177–81*
    1951, 718, *719,* 721–4, *725–27,* 728–32, *729, 733,* 734–36
New York Heart Association, 602
New York Nationals, 167
New York World's Fair (1940), 296
New York Yankees. *See also* Spring training; Standings (end of season); World Series; Yankee Stadium; *and specific players, managers, and owners*
  1940 statistics, 312
  1942 fielding averages, 435
  1948 pennant race, 560
  1949 pennant race, 606–7
  deal with San Francisco Seals, 30, 31, 34, 35, 450
  farm system, 29
  grooming of DiMaggio (1935), 33
  as home run-hitting team
    1938, 213
    1939, 250
    1941, 333, 334
  Italian-American players in, 87
  pennants, *facing* 192
  pride of players, 667
  scorecard (1942), *422*
  winning tradition of, 764
Niarhos, Gus, *556,* 741
Niggeling, Johnny, *272,* 310, 366
Night games, *482,* 744
Noble, Ray, *733*
Norbert, Ted, 34
Norelia, Tony, 327
Noren, Irving, 637, 705

O
Oakland Athletics, DiMaggio as coach for, 774, *774,* 776, *776*
O'Connell, Jimmy, 31, 38, 49
O'Dea, June, 206, 329

O'Dea, Kenneth, 232, 435, 439
O'Doul, Frank (Lefty), 15, 18, 31, *35,* 48, 65, 67, 131, 285, *536,* 602, 623, 689, *690,* 692, 693, 723, 730, 739, 766, 768
O'Dwyer, William, 602
Off-field activities. *See also* Restaurant, DiMaggio's
  1938, 188, 190, 192, *194*
  1939, 240
  1941, 334 1950, 650, 687
  golf, 630, 696, *facing* 760, 779
  radio career, 629–30
  television commentator, 743, 753, *753, 754*
Oglesby, Jim, 25, 37
Old-Timers Day (or game), *facing* 768
  1956, *761*
  1962, *763*
  1966, *771*
  1969, 365, *778*
  1982, 786
Olmo, Luis, 607, 615, 620, 621
O'Malley, Walter F., 755
O'Neill, Buck, 150
O'Neill, Steve, 565, 665, 702
Opening games missed, 634
  1940, 294, 295
  1949, 572
Operations
  1947, 489, 490
  1950, 676
Orsatti, Ernie, 87
Ostermueller, Fritz, 81, 261
Ostrowski, Joe, 661, 716
Ott, Mel, 689
  1936, 45, *91, 95, 104,* 114
  1937, *166,* 174
  1938, 206, *207,* 219
  1939, 238, 254–56
  1941, 340, 341, 343
  1942, 429, 432
Outen, William, 37
Owen, Marvin, 76
Owen, Mickey, 340, 384, 388, 390, 391, 446, 615, *771*

P
Pacific Coast League, 34
  most valuable player award (1935), 37, 96
Padgett, Don, 428
Pafko, Andy, 548, 589, 654, *654,* 655
Page, Joe
  1947, *498,* 500, 504, 512, 521, *522,* 526
  1948, 538, 542, 548, 561, 564
  1949, 575, 580, 595, 599, 600, 601, 611, *611,* 616
  1950, 625, 628, 630, 637, 638, 641
  1951, 701
  1952, 752
  DiMaggio as idol to, 746
Page, Vance, 232
Pagliaroni, Jim, 776
Painter, Doc, 202, 541
Painter, Earl, 60, *221*
Parnell, Mel, 585, 588, 589, 599, 607, 706, 739
Passarella, Art, *551*
Passeau, Claude, 339, 341, 432

Patterson, Arthur, 569, 625
Patterson, Red, 525, 741, 745
Patterson, Reese, 136
Pearson, Monte
  1936, 75, 99, *105*, 106
  1937, 147, *167*
  1938, 202, 214, *221*, 227, 233
  1939, 245, 250, 257, 261, 262,
    271, *274*, 281, 282
  1940, 310
Peck, Steve, 321
Peckinpaugh, Roger, 328, 351,
  752
Peek, Steve, 320, *376*, 376
Pennock, Herb, 410, 752
Pesky, Johnny, 446, 538, 580,
  706
Pezzullo, John, 87
Phelps, Babe, 86
Phelps, Ray, 85
Philadelphia Athletics, 158, 220
  games against
    1936, 73, 99
    1939, 250
    1949, 595
Philadelphia Phillies, 607
Phoebus, Tom, 766
Phoenix training camp, 625
Photographs and drawings of
  Joe Di Maggio, *15, facing* 48,
  facing 97, *facing* 177, *facing*
  225, *facing* 240, *facing* 241,
  facing 289, *facing* 560, *facing*
  561, *facing* 640, *facing* 721,
  facing 752, *facing* 753, *facing*
  760, *facing* 761, *facing* 768,
  facing 769
  1933, *19, 22, 24, 26, facing* 32
  1934, *12, 30, 32*
  1935, *17, 35, 41*
  1936, *42, 48, 53, 56, 61, 64–66,
    77, 86, 88, 90, 95, 96, 98, 102,
    104, 117, 118*
  1937, *120, 127, 129, 133, 136,
    140, 154, 157, 161–63, 168,
    177–81, 183*
  1938, *184, 188, 189, 191, 192,
    194, 198, 200, 201, 203, 210,
    212, 213, 217, 218, facing* 224,
    225, 229, 230, 235
  1939, *236, 241, 243, 249, 252,
    259, 265, 269, 271, facing* 272,
    facing 273, *274, 294, 331*
  1940, *286, 289, 290, 292, 297,
    299, 300, 301, 303, 308, 309,
    311, 312*
  1941, *314, 318, 322, 324, 329,
    330, 332, 335, 337, 339, 344,
    facing* 344, *345, 354, 357, 358,
    360, 363, 369, 370, 374, 387,
    facing* 376, *facing* 377, *393,
    397, 400*
  1942, *408, 411–14, 417, 419, 420,
    424, 435*
  1943, *447, 448, 451, 452, 453,
    454*
  1944, *457, 464, 466*
  1946, *470, 473, 476, 477, 479–80,
    facing* 481, *484, 485*
  1947, *489, 490, 493, facing* 496,
    *501, 502, 507, 509, 513, 516,
    518, 522, 526–29*
  1948, *530, 536, 539, 540, 543,
    544, 547, 551, 556, 557, 558–60,
    564, 565*
  1949, *574, 577, 578, 578, 581,
    582, 583, 589, 592, 593, 594,
    596, 599, 601, 603–5, 608, 610,
    614*
  1950, *622, 624, 627, 630, 635,
    636, 639, 642, 645, 647, 649,
    652, facing* 656, *657, 661, 675,
    685, 686, 690, 691*
  1951, *694, 696, 698, 700, 702,
    702, 704, 709, 711, 712, 714,
    717, 720, 725, 726, 727, 729,
    733, 737, 739, 740, 742, 743,
    747, 749*
  1952, *750, 753–55*
  1956, *761*
  1960s, *356, 763, 765, 766, 768,
    769, 771, 777, 778*
  1980s, *facing* 785, *786–89*
  advertisements, *facing* 193,
    facing 225, *facing* 345
  portraits and paintings
    by Victor Freudeman, *facing*
      641
    by Mayo, *facing* 720
    by S. Rini, *facing* 704
    by Norman Rockwell, *facing*
      288
    by Doug West, *facing* 705
Physical condition, DiMaggio's.
  See also
  Exercise;
  Injuries and ailments,
    DiMaggio's; Spring training
  1950, 630, 632
  1951, 699
Pieretti, Marino, 639
Pilette, Herman, 17
Pillette, Ted, 15, 788
Pinelli, Babe, 67, 87, 343
Pipp, Wally, 343, 634, *635*
Pitchers
  1940 statistics, 307
  DiMaggio on, 474, 486, 496
  left-handed, 643
Player of the Year award. *See*
  New York Chapter of the
  Baseball Writers Association
Police Gazette, facing 656
Pollet, Howie, 589
Polo Grounds, *726*
Porterfield, Bob, 627, 638, 713
Positions played by DiMaggio.
  See also Fielding, DiMaggio's
  center field (1935), 33
  first base (1950), 643–46, *645*
  left field (1936), 67
  right field (1935), 33, 33
  shortstop (1932–33), 15–18, 22
  Yankee plans (1936), 48, 49
Potter, Nelson, 332
Powell, Alvin J., *271*
Powell, Frank, 673
Powell, Jake, 244, 261
  1936, 80, 86, 87, 103, *104*, 115
  1937, 128, 138, 147, 155, 156,
    167, 169, *169*, 182
  1938, *212*, 221, *225*
Powers, Leslie, 34
Price, Johnny, 739

Priddy, Gerald (Gerry), 369,
  370, 376, 377, *377*, 379, 457,
  460, 545, 664
Publicity, 152, 182
Puccinelli, George, 87
Pytlak, Frankie, 75, 214, 428

Q

Quante, Marvin, 56
Queen, Mel, 491, 496
Quinn, Johnny, 325

R

Radcliff, Rip, ·93, 247, 312
Radio, career in, 629–30
Raimondi, Bill, 34
Raschi, Vic, 545, 548, 585, 588,
  588, 589, 590, 595, 599, 600,
  606, 607, 620, 638, 641, 659,
  661, 662, 664, 671–73, *671*, 700,
  701, *701*, 716, 720, *720*
Rasmussen, M. W., *431*
Records set by DiMaggio, 745
Reese, Jimmy, 29, 31, 49, 541
Reese, Pee Wee, 432, *457*, 460,
  476, 500, 503, *503*, 515, 523, 689
  1949, 588, *589*, 607, 616, 620
Regan, Bill, 86, 87
Reiser, Pete, 340, 341, 343, 376,
  379, 384, 390, 392, *476*, 503,
  511, 524
Restaurant, DiMaggio's (San
  Francisco), 188, 190, 240, 396,
  559
Restelli, Dino, 739
Retirement, DiMaggio's, 699,
  738, 742–49
  announcement of, 742, 745
  uniform retired, 745, 748, 749
Reynolds, Allie
  1947, 491, 503, 504, *504*, 520,
    526
  1948, 542
  1949, 578, 580, *589*, 600, 620,
    621
  1950, 628, 637, 638, 641, 655,
    660, 661, 663, 671, 676–77,
    680, 682
  1951, 701, 705, 720, *720*,
    728–30, 734, 735
Reynolds, Carl, 147
Richards, Vinnie, 219
Richardson, Nolen, 45, 106
Richardson, Tommy, 209
Richardson, Tony, *102*
Rickey, Branch, 61, 451, 488,
  689
Riggs, Lewis, *272*
Rigney, Johnny, 266, 362, 425,
  428
Rini, S., *facing* 704
Ripple, Jim, *105, 167*
Risberg, Swede, 28
Rivera, Jim, 741
Rizzuto, Phil, 752
  1941, *316*, 321, 366, 369, 374,
    374, 376–77, *377*, 379, 391
  1942, 425, 428, 435, 439, 444
  1944, 465
  1947, 491, 492, 507, *507*, 520,
    521
  1948, 538, 545, 564
  1949, 580, 584, 585, 595, 600,
    611, *611*, 615

1950, 625, 628, 637, *652*, 655,
  659, 664, 665, *673*, 677, 678
1951, 697, 700, 706, 716, 720,
  720, 728, 730, 734
Roberts, Robin, 671, 676, 677,
  678
Robinson, Aaron, *522*
Robinson, Bill, 361
Robinson, Jackie, 503, *503, 509*,
  523, 524, *589*, 589, *591*, 607,
  620, 621, 687, 689
Rockwell, Norman, *facing* 288
Roe, Preacher, *589*, 589, 590,
  620, 621, 673
Rogers, Will, 410
Rogovin, Saul, 716
Rolfe, Robert (Red), 238, 240,
  247, 752
  1936, 52, 56, 69, 72, 87, 103,
    104, 115
  1937, *140*, 141, 149, *166*, 169,
    169
  1938, 188, 202, *203, 221, facing*
    224, *225*
  1939, 263, 265, 266, 266, *271*,
    277, 279, *283*
  1940, 291, 299, *303*, 310, 312
  1941, 316, 351, 371, 374, *375*
  1942, 415, 416, 421, 433, 435,
    439, 444
Rommel, Eddie, 255, *513, 642*
Roosevelt, Franklin D., 110,
  116, *144*, 147
Root, Charlie, 232
Rosar, Warren (Buddy), *271*,
  428, 435, *499*
Rose, Pete, 361
Rosenberg, Harry, 37
Rosenthal, Julian, 650
Rosenthal, Larry, 351
Rossi, Angelo, *24*, 364
Rotblatt, Marvin, 700
Roth, Mark, 231
Rowe, Schoolboy, 76, 81, 92, 94,
  96, 264
Rowland, Clarence, *549*
Ruel, Muddy, *589*
Ruether, Dutch, 67, 256
Ruffing, Charles (Red), 752
  1936, 58, 69, 73, 74, 76, 96, 99,
    105, 106, 115
  1937, 128, 129, 142, 149, 156,
    164, *167*, 175
  1938, 188, 202, *221*, 232, 233
  1939, 238, 240, 244, 245, 254,
    256, 261, 266, 270, *271, 283*
  1940, 291, 293, 294, *294*, 305,
    306
  1941, *316*, 316, 323, *339*, 366,
    370, 390, 390, 391
  1942, 415, 439, 444
  1944, 460
Running (speed). *See also* Base
  running
  1936, 80, 100
Ruppert, Col. Jacob (Jake), 38,
  41, 42, 119, *130, facing* 240,
  689, 746
  1937, 122, *128, 181*
  contract negotiations with
    players, 126, 128, 129
  1938, *188*, 191, 195, 196, 197,
    199
  1939, 237, 239

deal for DiMaggio (1934), 31,
  81
first look at DiMaggio playing
  (1935), 40
Ruppert, George, 275
Russell, Jack, 155
Russo, Marius, 270, *271,* 328,
  331, 339–40, 366, 368, 369, 388,
  391, 489
Russo, Rusty, 299
Ruth, Babe, 256, 488, 538, *539,*
  627, 634, *635*
  1923 most valuable player
    award, 395
  1925 stomachache, 575
  1933, 28
  1936, 59, 73, 78, 94
  1937, 150–51
  all star team selected by
    (1940), 312
  on All-Time Yankee team, 752
  DiMaggio compared to, 147,
    158, 160–61, 598
  locker, *748*
  personal characteristics of,
    152
  radio appearance, 101
  retirement of, 699, 746–47
  salary, 187, 367
  uniform retired, 748
Ryan, John, *166*
Ryan, Ray, 209
Ryba, Mike, 55, 332, 333

S

Sain, Johnny, 499, 500, 549
St. Louis Browns
  1938 offer made to Yankees
    for DiMaggio, 196
  games against
    1936, 72, 74, 99
    1937, 158
    1938, 204, 213
    1939, 245
    1940, 310
    1941, 323, 366
    1948, 545
St. Louis Cardinals, 55, 606
  1936 prospects, 70
  1937 spring training game
    against, 132
  1942 fielding averages, 435
  1942 world series against, *434,*
    437–45
Salary, DiMaggio's. *See also*
  contracts (contract
  negotiations, salary talks)
    1933, 15, 18
    1935, 44
    1936, 44, 45, 122, 126
    1936–1942, 413
    1936–1948, 569
    1937, 129, 285
    1938, 197, 201, 219, 285
    1940, 291, 295
    1941, 316, 317
    1942, 413, 415
    1948, 532–34, 541
    1949, 568–69, 570
    1950, 628, 650, 689
    1951, 696
Saltzgaver, John (Jack), 54, *104,*
  106, *166,* 169, *169*
Samford, Fred, 421

Samuel, Bernard, 677
Sanders, Ray, 435
San Diego Padres, 67
Sanford, Fred, 578, 585, 660,
  700
San Francisco
  50th birthday party in, 767–68
  restaurant in, 188, 190, 240,
    396, 559
  San Francisco Seals, 13–41,
    facing 33, 131, 191, 347, 788
    1932, 15–17
    1933, 18–28, *18, 19, 20, 21, 22,
      24, 26, facing* 32, 48
    1934, 29–31, *30, 32*
    1935, 33–41, *35, 36, 39, 41*
    deal with Yankees, 30, 31
    first game with, (1932), 16, 17
    price paid by Yankees for
      DiMaggio, 30, 31, 49
    score book, 20
    scorecard, *21*
    shortstop, DiMaggio as, 15–18,
      22
Santa Ana (Calif.) Army Air
  Base, 457
Sarno, Capt. Dick, *464*
Saturday Evening Post, 205
Sauer, Hank, 654
Sawyer, Eddie, 672, 673, 680
Scarborough, Ray, 660
Scarsella, Leslie, *271*
Schacht, Al, 93, 171, 208–9, *208,
  241, 771*
Schalk, Ray, 755
Scheib, Carl, 595
Schmitz, Johnny, 548, 701
Schoendienst, Red, 653, *653,
  654, 654*
Schott, Gene, 59
Schreiber, Paul, *221*
Schulte, John, 169, *169, 221,* 329
Schulte, Johnny, 280
Schumacher, Hal, *105,* 114, 115,
  147, *167*
Scott, Everett, 634
Sears, Ziggy, 240
Seats, Tom, 294
Seeds, Bob, *104*
Segar, Charley, 150
Selkirk, George, 748
  1936, 49, 51, 52, 55, 56, 58, 76,
    103, *104,* 114, 115
  1937, 126, 132, 147, *154, 167,
    168, 168,* 171, 175
  1938, 202, *212,* 213, *221, 225,*
    234
  1939, 247, 250, 254, *269, 271,
    283*
  1940, 294, 298, *298,* 299, 311
  1941, 316, 321, 368, 369, 371,
    374, *375*
  1942, 435, *435*
Seminick, Andy, 588, *589,* 681,
  683
Seventh Regiment Band, 538
Sewell, Luke, 299, 361
Seys, John O., 56, 64
Shannon, Paul, 412
Shantz, Bob, 739
Shaughnessy, Frank J., 209
Shea, Frank (Spec), 495, 496,
  499, 500, 504, *504,* 515, *516,*

521, 523, 526, 537, *556,* 575,
  579, 595
Shea, Marv, *344*
Sheehan, Jimmy, 126
Sheehan, Ken, 285
Sheehy, Pete, 762
Shellenback, Frank, 37, 300
Shoffner, Milburn, *272*
Shor, Toots, *464, 484, 685*
Shortstop, DiMaggio as, 450,
  788
  1932–33, 15–18, 22
Shotton, Burt (Barney), 504, 515,
  520, 524, *549, 589, 653,* 654
Siebert, Dick, 321
Silvera, Charley, 741
Silvestri, Ken, 332, 369, 376,
  377, *377*
Simmons, Al, 38, 55, 70, 87, 99,
  272, 279, 280
Sisler, Dick, 673, *676,* 676
Sisler, George, 18, 325, 328,
  330, 634
Skiff, Bill, 625
Skowron, Bill, 665
Slaughter, Enos (Country), 263,
  392, 432, 435, 439, 441, 445,
  446, 496, 500, 520, 548, 548,
  589, 654, 710
Slocum, Bill, 208
Smith, Al, *105, 166,* 298, 315,
  350, *350,* 351, 355, 357, 362,
  363, 364
Smith, Bruce, 399
Smith, Edgar (Ed), 245, 328,
  341, 342, 355
Smith, Kate, 101
Smith, Lefty, 321
Smith, Mac, 219
Smith, Peoli, 87
Smith, Red, 29
Smith, Vincent, 429
Snider, Duke, *facing* 560, 607
Snyder, Frank, 106
Solters, Julius, 214, 215
Sorrell, Vic, 96
Souchock, Steve, 538
Southworth, Billy, 435, 589
Spahn, Warren, *588, 589,* 589,
  590
Speaker, Tris, 51, 97, 213, 343,
  597, 634, *635,* 689
Spence, Stan, 365, *499,* 500,
  526
Spencer, Doc, 15
Spencer, Roy, *105*
Spink, J. G. Taylor, *549*
Sport (magazine), *487, 502,
  552–54*
Sporting News, The,
  questionnaire, *285*
Spracker, Rowan D., *750*
Sprague, Ed, 776
Spring training
  1933, 31
  1936, 46, 50–52, 54–56, 58–69, *61*
  1937, 121, 124, 131, 132
  1938, 195, 199
  1939, 239, 240, 262
  1940, 291, 293
  1942, 416
  1946, *470,* 475
  1947, 491
  1949, 575

1950, 625, 636, 637
1951, 696, 700–1
Stainback, Tucker, 467
Stallings, George, 548
Stanceu, Charley, 320, 369, 376,
  377, *378*
Standings (end of season)
  1937, 121
  1938, 185
  1939, 237
  1940, 287
  1941, 315
  1942, 409
  1946, 472, 503
  1947, 472, 503
  1948, 532
  1949, 567, 623
  1951, 695
Stanky, Eddie, 515, 523, 728
Statistics, Joe DiMaggio's. *See
  also* Batting average,
  DiMaggio's
    1932–1941, 397
    1932–35, 13
    1933–1939, 266
    1936, 43
    1937, 121
    1938, 185
    1939, 237, 264, 265
    1940, 287
    1941, 315
    1942, 409
    1946, 472
    1947, 472
    1948, 532
    1949, 567, 623
    1951, 695
  career, 744
Statz, Arnold, 37
Stengel, Casey, 15, 256, 445
  1948, 565
  1949, 572, *574,* 575, *577,* 578,
    578, 580, 584, 600, 615, 616,
    619, 620, 621
  1950, 636, 638, 643–46, 648–49,
    660–64, *661,* 666, 673, 677,
    680, 688, 689
  benching of DiMaggio, 658
  1951, 697, 701, 706, 710, 711,
    713, 714, 728, 729, 730, 734,
    742
  benching of DiMaggio, 707,
    710, 711
  1952, *754*
Stephens, Bryan, 545
Stephens, Vern, 562, 580, 585,
  589, 706
Stepp, Billy, 40
Stevens, Chuck, 739
Stevens, Mal, 489, 491, *565*
Stewart, Bill, 94
Stewart, Ed, 716
Stewart, Gabby, 290
Stewart, James G., *275*
Stine, Lee, 199
Stirnweiss, George, 491, 507,
  507, 522, 545, *551,* 625
Stockton, J. Roy, 205
Stone, Johnny, 80
Stoneham, Horace, 290, 429,
  597, 665
Strand, Paul, 38
Strickland, George, 739
Strickland, John H., 60

Strikeouts, 76, 764
Stringer, Lou, 739, 741
Sturm, Johnny, 332, 351, 355, 366, 368, 370, 376, *378,* 379, 384, 428
Suder, Pete, 398
Sukeforth, Clyde, 515
Sullivan, Billy, 294
Sullivan, Tim, *221*
Sundra, Stephen R., *221,* 245, 270, *271,* 293, 298, 299, 311
Superstitions, 262
Surprise party (1941), 371
Susce, George, 366
Swope, Tom, 209

T

Tabor, Jim, 320, 333
Taylor, Harry, 504
Tazzeri, Tony, 58
Tebbetts, Birdie, 538, *582,* 585, *589,* 600, 601, 644
Television commentator, DiMaggio as, 743, 753, *753, 754*
Temple Cup series, 167
Terry, Bill, 256, 270, 410, 429
1934, 29
1936, 45, *95, 105,* 114, 115, 119
1937, 147, 149, 150, 174, 176
1938, 192, *207*
Testimonial (1939), *267*
Thompson, Bobby, *589,* 728, 730
Thompson, Eugene, *272*
Thompson, Gene, 268, 277
Thompson, Kay, *162*
Throwing arm, DiMaggio's, 65, *facing* 561
1936, 73, 83
1937, 124, 149
1939, 242
1941, 329
1942, 416
1948, 540, 541
Time (magazine), *117, 557*
Tipton, Joe, 739
Tobin, James, 45
Tonsilectomy (1937), 136–39
Topping, Dan, *530,* 532, *568,* 628, 643, 688, 696, 743, 745, 751, 752
Tournay, Nini, 739
Trade rumors, 525
1938, 219
1951, 741, 742
Training camp, Phoenix, 625
Trautman, George M., 209
Travis, Cecil, 216, *337,* 340, 342, 359, 428
Traynor, Pie, 634, *635, 673*
Trevisone, Pat, 602
Trimble, Joe, 688
Triple crown, 318
1939 prospects, 263
Triplett, Coaker, 435
Trosky, Hal, 216, 263, 266, 351
Trotter, Bill, 310
Trout, Paul, 369

Troyanovsky (Soviet ambassador), 150
Trucks, Virgil (Fire), 468, 474, 588, 589
Tunney, Gene, *430*
Turbeville, George, 73, 76
Turner, Jim, 625
2000th hit, 639, *639, 640*

U

Uhalt, Bernie, 34, 37, 45, 55
Umpires and umpiring, 62, 67
Unionization of players, 696
United Service Organization, 339, 341, 357
Upton, Tommy, 741

V

Van Atta, Russ, 72
Vance, Dazzy, 755, *755,* 756
Vandenberg, Hi, 147
Vander Meer, Johnny, 206, *207,* 209, 214, 238, *272,* 282, 432, 766
Vaughan, Arky, *91, 95,* 149, 150, 254, 255, 256, 305, 340, 341
Veeck, Bill, 558, 565, 703, 741
Venezia, Frank, 193
Vermeer, Al, 37, 38, 40
Vernon, Mickey, 548, 713
Villani, Ralph, 677
Vision, 476, 751
Vitt, Oscar (Ossie), 190, 299
Vosmik, Joe, 139, 158, 299, *299*

W

Wagner, Honus, 192, 479, 598, 634
Wagner, Robert F., 110
Waitkus, Eddie, 548, 677, 680
Wakefield, Dick, 468, *476,* 626
Walberg, Rube, 142
Walker, Dixie, 62, 390, 515, 689
Walker, Gerald, 247, 266, 351
Walker, Harry, 435
Walker, Willie, 55
Walkup, Jim, 139
Walsh, Christy, 297, *297*
Walsh, Ed, 18, 25, 27, 65, 325
Walsh, Robert Emmet, 294, 295
Walters, William H. (Bucky), 15, *252,* 268, *271,* 279, 280, 296, 305, 339, 343, 343, 432, *589*
Waner, Lloyd, 219
Waner, Paul, 149, 150, 188
Ward, Arch, 151, 208, 343
Warmerdam, Cornelius, 399
Warneke, Hal, 92
Warneke, Lon, 94, 339, 341, 341
Wasdell, Jimmy, 384
Washington Senators, 147
games against
1938, 202
1950, 661–63
1951, 713
Watt, Eddie, 776
Weatherly, Roy, 100, 311, 351
Webb, Del, 628, 743, 752, 768

Weight, DiMaggio's, 131, 542, 624
1951, 696
Weik, Dick, 663
Weiland, Bob, 132
Weiss, George M., 29, 40, 290, 450, *450,* 532, *530, 568,* 572, 625, 628, *628,* 629, 696, 697, 707, 713, 741, 752
Werber, William M., 100, *271,* 277, 282
Werle, Bill, 739
Wertz, Vic, 589, 664
Wesley Ferrell, 150
West, Doug, *facing* 705
West, Max, 305, 305, 548
West, Sammy, 150
Westrum, Wes, 730
White, Ernie, 409, 441, 444
White, Hal, 495, 496, 664
White, Herman, 209
Whitehead, Burgess, *105, 148,* 149, *166,* 175, 270
Whitehill, Earl, 96
Whitney, Art, 188
Whitney, Pinky, 92
Who's Who in Baseball, 411
Wicker, Kemp, *105,* 106, 138, *166*
Widmar, Al, 545, 741
Wight, Bill, 706
Wignall, Trevor, 83
Wilhoit, Joe, 27, 328–29, 351
Williams, Joe, 541
Williams, Ken, 86, 87
Williams, Ted, *facing* 225, 465, *476, facing* 640
1939, *259,* 261, 263, 264, 265, 266
1940, 298, *301,* 312
1941, 334, *337,* 340–43, *344, 345,* 359, 364, 392, *393,* 400, 395, 398, 399, 410
1942, 412, 416, 428, 433
1943, 446, 451
1946, *485*
1947, 496, *499,* 500, 511, 525, 526
1948, 537–38, 558, 562, 570–71
1949, 580, 588–90, *592*
1950, 650, *652,* 654, 655, 665, 687
1951, 696, 706
trade rumors, 738, 741
DiMaggio on, 471, 744
Wilshere, Whitey, 73
Wilshire, Vernon, 76
Wilson, Aileen, 724
Wilson, Archie, 742
Wilson, Hack, 86, 245
Wilson, Jack, 331, 333
Winsett, Tom, 460
Witek, Nick, 290
Wood, Craig, 399
Woodall, Larry, *19*
Woodling, Gene, 572, *610,* 616, 620, 621, 625, *626,* 627, 643, 663, 671–72, 676–78, 680–82, 684, 705, 706, 728, 734, 742

Workman, Hank, 661
World series
1903–1938 winners and losers, 268
1936, *102,* 103, 106, *107,* 108–16, 131, 280, 658
ring, *facing* 112
1937, 164, 165, *166–67,* 167, *168,* 171–76, *177–81,* 164, 280
1938, 220–34, *222–26, 230*
1939, 268–82, *273, 272*
attendance and money statistics, 278
evaluation of teams, 268, 270
facts on, 269
highlights, 281
1941, 372–90, *373*
new Yankee players, 376–77, *376–77, 387*
1942, *434,* 437–45
1947, 503–4, *505–7,* 508, *509,* 510, 512, *513,* 514–15, *516,* 517, *518–19,* 520–25, *522*
homerless series, possibility of, 503
1949, *609,* 612–13, *614,* 615–21
1950, *669,* 670–74, *672, 675,* 676–84
1951, 718, *719,* 721–4, *725–27,* 728–32, *729, 733,* 734–36
DiMaggio's participation in, 718
DiMaggio's statistics (1936–51), 744
history of, 167
records tied or broken by DiMaggio, 598, 736
Wray, John Edward, 364
Wright, Al, 34
Wright, Harry, 437
Wright, Taft, 202
Writers, baseball, 714. *See also* Baseball Writers' Association of America
Wyatt, Whitlow, 254, *304,* 305, 339, *340,* 342, 379, 388, 390, 392
Wyrostek, Johnny, 654

Y

Yankee Stadium
1939, *253*
1946, *482*
alterations to, 123, *782*
Yawkey, Tom, 696
York, Rudy, *207,* 266, 312, 323, 343, 428, 432, 432
Young, Babe, 270, 290, 575
Young, Cy, 565
Yvars, Sal, 735

Z

Zernial, Gus, 660
Zinn, Jimmy, *19*
Zuber, Bill, 299

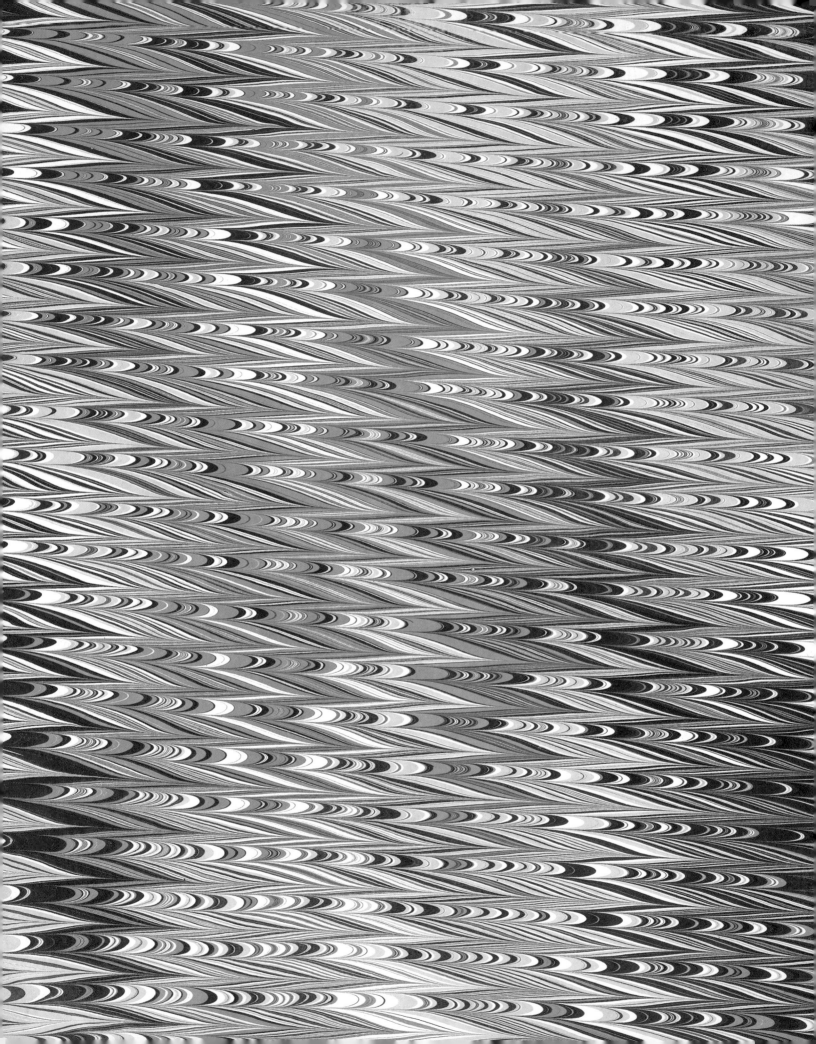